Christianity's Dangerous Idea

Christianity's Dangerous Idea

The Protestant Revolution—A History
from the Sixteenth Century
to the Twenty-First

Alister E. McGrath

HarperOne
A Division of HarperCollins*Publishers*

HarperOne

Scripture references are from the NRSV unless otherwise noted.

CHRISTIANITY'S DANGEROUS IDEA: *The Protestant Revolution—A History from the Sixteenth Century to the Twenty-First.* Copyright © 2007 by Alister E. McGrath. All rights reserved. Printed in the United States of America. No part of this book may be used or reproduced in any manner whatsoever without written permission except in the case of brief quotations embodied in critical articles and reviews. For information address HarperCollins Publishers, 10 East 53rd Street, New York, NY 10022.

HarperCollins books may be purchased for educational, business, or sales promotional use. For information please write: Special Markets Department, HarperCollins Publishers, 10 East 53rd Street, New York, NY 10022.

HarperCollins Web site: http://www.harpercollins.com
HarperCollins®, ☐®, and HarperOne™ are
trademarks of HarperCollins Publishers.

FIRST EDITION
Designed by Joseph Rutt

Library of Congress Cataloging-in-Publication Data is available.

ISBN: 978–0–06–082213–2
ISBN-10: 0–06–082213–9

07 08 09 10 11 RRD (H) 10 9 8 7 6 5 4 3 2 1

In memory of
Stephen Charles Neill (1900–1984)

Contents

Introduction

In July 1998, the bishops of the Anglican Communion met in the historic English cathedral city of Canterbury for their traditional Lambeth Conference, held every ten years. The intention was to address the many challenges and opportunities that Anglicanism faced worldwide—such as the burgeoning growth of the church in Africa and Asia, its slow decline in the West, and the new debates on sexuality. The bishops gathered every day for prayer and Bible study, a powerful affirmation of the role of the Bible in sustaining Christian unity, guiding the church in turbulent times, and nourishing personal spirituality.

But how was the Bible to be interpreted—for example, on the contentious issue of homosexuality, a major cause of friction within Anglicanism at that moment? Despite the best efforts of the conference organizers, a tempestuous debate erupted over precisely this thorny question in the public sessions of the Conference, reflecting multiple tensions between religious liberals and conservatives, modern and postmodern worldviews, and the very different cultural contexts of the West and the emerging world. To paraphrase Hugh Latimer, Bishop of Worcester (executed in 1555), everyone meant well—but they certainly did not mean the same thing.[1]

In the view of many observers, the Anglican Communion came dangerously close to breaking apart at that point over the interpretation of the text that was meant to bind them together. How, many Anglicans wondered, could the Bible be the basis for their identity and unity when there was such obvious disunity on how it was to be understood? How could a text-based movement have a coherent inner identity when there was such clear and fundamental disagreement on how that text was to be interpreted and applied on an issue of critical importance?

The idea that lay at the heart of the sixteenth-century Reformation, which brought Anglicanism and the other Protestant churches into being, was that the Bible is capable of being understood by all Christian believers—and that they all have the right to interpret it and to insist upon their perspectives being taken seriously. Yet this powerful affirmation of spiritual democracy ended up unleashing forces that threatened to destabilize the church, eventually leading to fissure and the formation of breakaway groups. Anglicanism may yet follow the pattern of other Protestant groups and become a "family" of denominations, each with its own way of reading and applying the Bible.

The dangerous new idea, firmly embodied at the heart of the Protestant revolution, was that all Christians have the right to interpret the Bible for themselves.[2] However, it ultimately proved uncontrollable, spawning developments that few at the time could have envisaged or predicted. The great convulsions of the early sixteenth century that historians now call "the Reformation" introduced into the history of Christianity a dangerous new idea that gave rise to an unparalleled degree of creativity and growth, on the one hand, while on the other causing new tensions and debates that, by their very nature, probably lie beyond resolution. The development of Protestantism as a major religious force in the world has been shaped decisively by the creative tensions emerging from this principle.

THE DANGEROUS IDEA

To its supporters, the Protestant Reformation represented a necessary correction and long-overdue renewal of the Christian faith, liberating it from its imprisonment to the transient medieval intellectual and social order and preparing it for new challenges as western Europe emerged from the feudalism of the Middle Ages. Christianity was being born all over again, with a new potency and capacity to engage with an emerging new world order.

Yet from its outset, the movement was seen by its opponents as a menacing development, opening the way to religious mayhem, social disintegration, and political chaos. It was not simply that Protestantism seemed to revise, corrupt, or abandon some of the traditional beliefs and practices of the Christian faith. Something far more significant—and ultimately much more dangerous—lay beneath the surface of the Protestant criticisms of the medieval church. At its heart, the emergence and growth of Protestantism concerned one of the most fundamental questions that can confront any religion: Who has the authority to define its faith? Institutions or individuals? Who has the right to interpret its foundational document, the Bible?[3]

Protestantism took its stand on the right of individuals to interpret the Bible for themselves rather than be forced to submit to "official" interpretations handed down by popes or other centralized religious authorities. For Martin Luther, perhaps the most significant of the first generation of Protestant leaders, the traditional authority of clerical institutions had led to the degradation and distortion of the Christian faith. Renewal and reformation were urgently needed. And if the medieval church would not put its own house in order, reform would have to come from its grass roots—from the laity. Luther's radical doctrine of the "priesthood of all believers" empowered individual believers. It was a radical, dangerous idea that bypassed the idea that a centralized authority had the right to interpret the Bible. There was no centralized authority, no clerical monopoly on biblical interpretation. A radical reshaping of Christianity was inevitable, precisely because the restraints on change had suddenly—seemingly irreversibly—been removed.

The outbreak of the Peasants' War in 1525 brought home to Luther that this new approach was dangerous and ultimately uncontrollable. If every individual was able to interpret the Bible as he pleased, the outcome could only be anarchy and radical religious individualism. Too late, Luther tried to rein in the movement by emphasizing the importance of authorized religious leaders, such as himself, and institutions in the interpretation of the Bible. But who, his critics asked, had "authorized" these so-called authorities? Was not the essence of Luther's dangerous new idea that there was no such centralized authority? That all Christians had the right to interpret the Bible as they saw fit?

In the end, not even the personal authority of Luther could redirect this religious revolution, which anxious governments sought to tame and domesticate. By its very nature, Protestantism had created space for entrepreneurial individuals to redirect and redefine Christianity. It was a dangerous idea, yet it was an understanding of the essence of the Christian faith that possessed an unprecedented capacity to adapt to local circumstances. From the outset, Protestantism was a religion designed for global adaptation and transplantation.

This book sets out to tell the story of the origins and development of this radical form of Christianity, not to record the past but to understand the present and anticipate the future. It is a subject of immense historical, intellectual, and social importance. The English Civil War of the seventeenth century was ultimately a battle for the soul of Protestantism, as rival visions of what it meant to be Protestant collided, with disastrous results. Yet not only has Protestantism survived the first five hundred years of its existence, but it seems poised for further growth and adaptation in the twenty-first century. As religion once again comes to play a significant role in world affairs, an understanding of the complexities of this great religious power becomes progressively more important.

Although this book makes use of the best historical scholarship, it is not yet another chronicle of the development of Protestantism. Rather, it is an interpretative history of the movement that sets out to clarify the identity and inner dynamics of Protestantism through its historical manifestations. Whereas many older studies thought of Protestantism as being analogous to a seed, capable of development and growth along predetermined lines, the evidence presented in this analysis suggests that this model is inadequate and misleading. To use an alternative biological imagery, Protestantism turns out to be more like a micro-organism: capable of rapid mutation and adaptation in response to changing environments, while still maintaining continuity with its earlier forms. This insight gives a new importance to critical historical analysis: what does the historical development and transformation of the movement tell us about its genetic makeup—and hence its possible future forms?

This study is written at a highly significant time in the history of Protestantism. Throughout its existence, the United States of America has been a predominantly Protestant nation. Many of the developments that have shaped the modern religious world can be traced back to American influence. Yet a series of recent studies have suggested that the era of the Protestant majority in the United States is coming to an end, possibly within the next few years.[4] With such a seismic development now imminent, the time is clearly right to explore the past, present, and future of this movement and to ask where its epicenters will lie in the twenty-first century and what forms it will take.

THE INVENTION OF A WORD: *PROTESTANTISM*

This book sets out to tell the story of the emergence of Protestantism against the turbulent backdrop of the waning of the Middle Ages and the birth pangs of early modern Europe. Although popular accounts of the origins of Protestantism often identify Martin Luther's posting of the Ninety-five Theses against indulgences on October 31, 1517, as marking the origins of the Reformation, the truth is much more complex and interesting.[5] Although undoubtedly influenced and catalyzed by significant individuals—such as Martin Luther and John Calvin—the origins of Protestantism lie in the greater intellectual and social upheavals of that era, which both created a crisis for existing forms of Christianity and offered means by which it might be resolved.

The use of the term "Protestantism" to refer—somewhat vaguely, it must be said—to this new form of Christianity appears to have been a happenstance of history. Its origins can be traced back to the Diet of Worms (1521), which issued an edict declaring Martin Luther to be a dangerous heretic and a threat to the safety of the Holy Roman Empire. Any who supported him were threatened with severe punishment. It was an unpopular move with many German princes, a growing number of whom were sympathetic to Luther's demands for reform. One of them, Frederick the Wise, Elector of Saxony, arranged for Luther to be abducted and given safety in Wartburg Castle, where he began his great German translation of the Bible. This hostility on the part of many German rulers toward his policies led Emperor Charles V to dilute the Edict of Worms. In 1526 the Diet of Speyer decreed that it was up to individual princes to enforce its draconian anti-Lutheran measures. The outcome—though clearly not the intention—of this measure was to allow Luther's reforming vision and program to gain strength in many regions of Germany.

Emperor Charles V was seriously preoccupied with other matters at this time and therefore was distracted from dealing with the rise of this unpredictable new form of religious faith within Germany. His empire was under immediate and serious threat. One worrying challenge came from a perhaps unexpected source: Rome itself had challenged his authority. Exasperated, in 1527 Charles V sent a task force of twenty thousand mercenaries to sack Rome and place Pope Clement VII under house arrest. The episode undoubtedly dampened any slight enthusiasm Charles might have had for dealing with the pope's enemies in Germany.

Yet a far greater danger lay to the east, where decidedly ominous storm clouds were gathering. Following their capture of the great Byzantine city of Constantinople in 1453, Islamic armies were pressing westward, making deep inroads into hitherto Christian areas of eastern Europe as they pursued their *jihad*. These armies had occupied much of the Balkans, where Islamic spheres of influence were well established (a development that has resounded throughout the subsequent history of the area, especially in the Bosnian civil war of 1992–95). Following their defeat of the Hungarians in 1526, Turkish armies headed north. By 1529 they had laid siege to Vienna. The Islamic conquest of western Europe suddenly became a real possibility. Urgent action was required to deal with this clear and present danger to western Christendom.

The second Diet of Speyer was hurriedly convened in March 1529. Its primary objective was to secure, as quickly as possible, a united front against the new threat from the east. Hard-liners, however, saw this as a convenient opportunity to deal with another, lesser threat in their own backyards. It was easy to argue that the reforming movements that were gaining influence throughout the region threatened to bring about destabilization and religious anarchy. The presence of a larger number of Catholic representatives than in 1526 presented conservatives with an opportunity they simply could not ignore. They forced through a resolution that demanded the rigorous enforcement of the Edict of Worms throughout the empire. It was a shrewd tactical move, with immense strategic ramifications. Both enemies of the Catholic church—Islam and the Reformation—would be stopped dead in their tracks.

Outraged, yet ultimately powerless to change anything, six German princes and fourteen representatives of imperial cities entered a formal protest against this unexpected radical curtailment of religious liberty. The Latin term *protestantes* ("protesters") was immediately applied to them and the movement they represented. Although its origins lay in the religious situation in Germany, the movement rapidly came to be applied to related reforming movements, such as those then associated with Huldrych Zwingli in Switzerland, the more radical reforming movements often referred to at the time as "Anabaptism" (though now more generally known as "the Radical Reformation"), and the later movement linked with John Calvin in the city of Geneva. Older reforming movements—such as the Waldensians in northern Italy and the Bohemian reforming movements tracing their origins back to Jan Hus—gradually became assimilated within this new larger entity.

Although a word had been invented, its connotations remained vague, subject to the whims and agendas of propagandists on both sides of the Reformation controversies. Faced with a significant political and theological threat, the Catholic church used the term to lump together a series of threats arising from a group of loosely interconnected but ultimately distinct movements. The tense and dangerous situation demanded unity within the Catholic church; presenting the various evangelical groupings as a coordinated anti-Catholic movement proved instrumental in catalyzing unity within that church and galvanizing its members into action.

Protestants, for their part, saw a revitalized Catholic church as posing a serious threat to their continuing existence. Anglican and Lutheran, Reformed and Anabaptist—the four main evangelical strands present by the 1560s—saw their antagonisms, divisions, and mutual distaste eclipsed as the need for collaboration against a coordinated and dangerous opponent became clear. Whatever their differences, they reasoned, they were all "Protestants"—even though there was a conspicuous lack of clarity over what that actually meant.

THE NEED FOR A NEW STUDY

So why is there a need for another study of the origins and shaping of Protestantism? While there are a number of commendable older studies of the origins and nature of Protestantism, the rapid pace of change

in the field makes a new investigation of its origins, distinctive characteristics, and future potential necessary.[6] Those changes relate both to
significant revisions of the scholarly understanding of the origins of
Protestantism and to highly important recent developments within the
movement that have yet to find their way into more general works of
this nature. Five points are of particular importance in this respect.

First, recent scholarship has moved decisively away from the older
tendency—evident in such a distinguished work as Geoffrey Elton's
Reformation Europe (1963)—to underplay the social and economic aspects of the emergence of Protestantism in order to emphasize its religious and political elements.[7] A new interest in social history has cast
new light on the origins of the Reformation—especially in relation to
its impact on how the broad mass of the population lived and
thought—and has rightly cast doubt on any attempt to define the
movement solely or chiefly in terms of the theological agendas of its
leading figures. At times, this new approach has led to ridiculous overstatements, such as some frankly embarrassing attempts to eliminate
Martin Luther altogether from accounts of the Reformation or to rel-
egate him to the sidelines as a bit player. While such nonsense can now
be safely disregarded, it is now beyond dispute that any attempt to
make sense of the origins, the popular appeal, and the transmission of
Protestantism demands careful study of the structures and institutions
of contemporary society.[8]

In the second place, the tidal wave of studies of local archives and
private correspondence has confirmed the suspicions of an early generation of scholars—that it is unacceptable to determine the state of the
pre-Reformation European church through the eyes of its leading critics, such as Luther and Calvin. It is increasingly clear that attempts to
depict the late medieval church as morally and theologically corrupt,
unpopular, and in near-terminal decline cannot be sustained on the
basis of the evidence available. As in every period, the church possessed
strengths and weaknesses and sought to consolidate the former and address the latter. It is now clear that Catholic reforming movements
were not a response to the criticisms of the Protestant reformers but
were deeply enmeshed within the pre-Reformation church—where,
paradoxically, they created an appetite for reform that laid the ground
for Protestantism in some respects.[9]

A third concern is perhaps of theological rather than historical importance. Although an earlier generation of Protestant writers tended to assume that "the Reformation" and "Protestantism" were essentially synonymous terms, there is a growing appreciation that the relationship between them is more complex than has hitherto been realized.[10] Protestantism emerged from the Reformation through a complex and as yet not fully understood process that involved reception and interpretation, which led to a series of local reforming movements that developed a broader, yet far from total, sense of shared identity. The historical origins and intellectual foundations of Protestantism are such that diversity and tension have been essential aspects of its identity from the beginning. Protestantism is best thought of as a "movement of movements" that share common aspirations while differing on how these are, in the first place, to be articulated and, in the second, to be attained.

A fourth factor pointing to the need for a new study is the realization that many existing analyses have been unduly influenced by popular stereotypes of Protestant leaders and ideas, which have distorted perceptions of the nature and development of the movement. The most glaring example of such a misrepresentation is John Calvin, who is regularly presented as an "icon of intolerance" in school history textbooks, in contrast to Luther, who is regularly portrayed as a pioneer of individual freedom.[11] Such parodies of Calvin and Geneva still linger, along with other unexorcised ghosts, within earlier treatments of Protestantism—even including Elton's *Reformation Europe*. Where modern scholarship tends to see Calvinism as an "effective proto-modern insurgency movement," studies of the 1960s, perhaps viewing its emergence through the prism of the cold war of that era, found it natural to see "Geneva as 'Moscow on the Leman,' spreading its tentacles through Catholic France."[12]

Finally, a new study is essential precisely because Protestantism itself has changed, decisively and possibly irreversibly, in the last fifty years, in ways that would have astonished an earlier generation of scholars and historians. Much scholarship has yet to catch up with the astonishingly rapid growth of Pentecostalism and offer a critical analysis of its significance for the future of Protestantism in particular and of Christianity in general.[13] According to the standard account of its origins, Pentecostalism came into being in the first decade of the twentieth century. Although estimates of its present numerical strength are difficult to verify, the movement today is the largest constituency within Protestantism and is widely believed to have more than 500 million adherents, mostly in Asia, Africa, and Latin America. Its potential to transform Protestantism is undeniable, as is the need for an evaluation of its impact and its future.

THE SHAPE OF THIS STUDY

This book tells a story, in the belief that the past not only shapes and illuminates the present but anticipates the future. The book avoids an essentialist reading of history, as if any single controlling narrative were adequate to account for the messy and complex realities of history. History can illuminate the multivalent and often extraordinarily fluid ideas and forms taken by Protestantism in response to a series of historical contingencies—but it cannot tell us what Protestantism actually *is*, still less what it *should be*.[14] Historical meta-analysis allows us to discern trends and developments and to identify which proved to be important and productive in the shaping of modern Protestantism.

I first began to study the origins and development of Protestantism under the direction of Professor Gordon Rupp at Cambridge University back in the late 1970s. My initial work focused on the origins of the reforming ideas of Martin Luther,[15] then rapidly expanded into a study of the historical development of the notion of "justification of faith" (so central to the Reformation debates),[16] followed by a detailed study of the intellectual currents that shaped the emergence of the ideas of the movement.[17] In undertaking these analytical works, which often focused on fine points of detail, I became increasingly aware of the need for a work of synthesis that would weave the burgeoning scholarly literature on the origins and development of Protestantism together into a single, organized narrative. This work, though based on the best detailed scholarly studies, tries to discern the bigger picture underlying them and to assess its significance for understanding the past and present and illuminating future trends. Above all, it tries to identify the big idea that lies at the heart of Protestantism and to trace its impact on the unfolding of the movement in the past and its development in years to come.

Like Julius Caesar's Gaul, the work is divided into three parts, dealing with the origination, consolidation, and transformation of Protestantism. It opens by considering how Protestantism came into existence, exploring its historical development during its first great period of expansion. To provide a thorough survey of this vast subject is not only unrealistic but also not the intention of the approach adopted. A principle of selective attention is used: those aspects of the narrative of emergence are accentuated that its subsequent development show to have been of the greatest significance. What is offered is an interpretative history, a highly focused reading, a broad-brush approach that aims to identify and interpret what turns out to have been significant rather than to chronicle everything that happened. An understanding of the origins of Protestantism is essential to any attempt to make sense of its subsequent development. From the outset, the movement was indelibly stamped with hallmarks that would shape its evolution.

The second part of the book deals with the basic ideas of Protestantism and its impact on culture. This section brings together historical, cultural, and conceptual analysis, offering a description of basic Protestant attitudes and the manner in which they have shaped values and actions during the last five hundred years. The strongly entrepreneurial mind-set characteristic of many (but by no means all) Protestants had a great impact on the shaping of Western culture, particularly in the economic sphere, but a surprisingly small impact in other areas. Once more, those who long for simplicities can only be frustrated by the way in which the diversity of Protestantism has led to a significant variety of cultural outcomes.

The final part of the work considers the history of Protestantism during the twentieth century, which has seen the movement undergo radical change and development, especially through its expansion in Latin America, Asia, and Africa and the emergence of Pentecostalism as a new form of Protestantism that is unusually well adapted to meeting the needs and aspirations of the urban poor in the global South. Protestantism now has a strong presence in regions of the world in which it was a total stranger at the beginning of the twentieth century and manifests itself in forms that were unknown at that time. It is no exaggeration to say that the second half of the twentieth century witnessed the transformation of global Protestantism in ways that raise new questions about its future shape and impact. Many of these are addressed in the final chapter of the work, which considers how Protestantism is likely to mutate in the future, as well as how these patterns of mutation illuminate recent developments in Islam.

In writing this book over many years, I have accumulated debts far too great and numerous to list in detail. Scholarship is always a corporate undertaking in which the individual depends on the work of others at every point. I acknowledge with the greatest appreciation the assistance so generously given by many, primarily at universities, libraries, and seminaries in the United States, Canada, Great Britain, Australia, New Zealand, Switzerland, Germany, France, Italy, the Netherlands, Singapore, Hong Kong, Japan, and the Philippines. I also acknowledge helpful conversations with scholars and leading church figures from Argentina, Brazil, Chile, Kenya, Mexico, Nigeria, and South Africa. While I take full responsibility for the ideas developed in this work, I could not have reached them without extensive discussion and debate with others over the last twenty years. I also owe many thanks to Roger Freet, my editor at HarperOne, for a highly productive and stimulating dialogue that led to the emergence of this book in its present form.

Finally, I need to say that this book has not been written for scholars, although it tries to bring together the best scholarship presently available in a coherent synthesis, weaving a grand narrative out of many complex and significant smaller strands and stories. As many will recognize, I have at times had to make adjudications over complex debates in the vast research literature dealing with the subjects covered by this book. While I believe those judgments to be defensible, they are most certainly open to challenge and criticism. I have tried to indicate which scholarly studies have led me to draw certain conclusions, without cluttering the work with the conventions of academic annotation. The conclusions of this book are rather like scholarship itself—fallible and provisional. Understanding the past and predicting the future are both precarious undertakings, the latter more so than the former, even though both are attempted on the basis of the best authorities available.

But whether readers agree with my conclusions or not, it is my hope that they will enjoy the ride as we explore the contours of one of the world's most fascinating and important religious movements. It has had its moments in the past. It will unquestionably have them in the future as well.

Alister E. McGrath
November 2006

PART I

Origination

Pope Leo X with cardinals Giulio de Medici (later Pope Clement VII) and Luigi de Rossi, 1517, by Raphael (Rafaello Sanzio) (1483–1520).

I

The Gathering Storm

The ability to see beyond the horizon of one's own location in history is given to few. Who could have imagined, in the gently sunlit heyday of Edwardian England, that the grimmest and most devastating war ever to afflict the human race lay less than a decade away? There was little sense at the time of a gathering storm, of standing close to the edge of a cataclysmic precipice. Hindsight is invariably infallible, allowing later observers to discern the fault lines, the tensions, the shifting in the tectonic plates of history that presaged the tidal waves that would engulf nations and cultures. Yet at the time these often passed unnoticed, their significance not appreciated until after the deluge.

Could the turmoil of the Reformation have been predicted? Could it have been deferred, perhaps even deflected, by some skillful footwork on the part of the church hierarchy? What would have happened if the son of Hans and Margarette Luther had died shortly after his birth on November 10, 1483? These questions, though illuminating and not a little provocative, cannot be answered with any confidence. The historian, however, can hope to achieve at least some degree of understanding and appreciation of what actually happened, and above all to discern why a seemingly trivial protest by an unknown German academic at one of Europe's most insignificant universities proved to be the spark that ignited a conflagration that engulfed much of the Western church.

THE CHURCH AND THE SOCIAL FABRIC OF WESTERN EUROPE

The social, cultural, and intellectual impact of the Protestant Reformation can be fully grasped only through an appreciation of the place of the church in late medieval Europe. The church was a major player in international politics and the internal affairs of regions, and it fostered a sense of identity at the level of local communities and gave individuals a sense of location and purpose within a greater scheme of things.[1]

The church had always played an important international role in European society. Medieval Europe bore little relation to its modern counterpart composed of individual, well-defined nation-states.[2] In the Middle Ages, Europe consisted of an aggregate of generally small principalities, city-states, and regions, often defined and given a shared sense of identity more by language and historical factors than by any sense of common political identity. At the start of the fourteenth century, for example, Italy was little more than a patchwork of independent city-states and petty principalities. These were consolidated into six major political units during the fifteenth century: the kingdoms of Naples and Sicily, the Papal States, and the three major city-states of Florence, Venice, and Milan. The modern nation-state of Italy was a nineteenth-century invention. In much the same way, Germany, destined to play a particularly significant role in the events of the age, consisted of a myriad of tiny territories.[3] Even as late as the nineteenth century, there were still thirty-two German states and territories, which were only finally united into the German empire under Otto von Bismarck (1815–98).

The church was the only international agency to possess any significant credibility or influence throughout the Middle Ages, and into the era of the Renaissance. It played a decisive role in the settling of international disputes.[4] Under Innocent III (pope from 1198 to 1216), the medieval papacy reached a hitherto unprecedented level of political authority in western Europe.[5] This was given theological justification in the decree *Sicut universitatis conditor*, issued in October 1198, in which Innocent III set out the principle of the subordination of the state to the church. His argument? Just as God established "greater" and "lesser" lights in the heavens to rule the day and night—a reference to the sun and moon—so God ordained that the power of the pope exceeded that of any monarch. "Just as the moon derives her light from the sun, and is inferior to the sun in terms of its size and its quality, so the power of the king derives from the authority of the pope." That authority was often recognized with great reluctance; there was, however, no other institution in western Europe with anything remotely approaching its influence.

Power tends to corrupt, as Lord Acton remarked. There were many within the church at the time who were troubled by the soaring power and influence of the papacy and who sought to prevent it getting out of control. The Conciliarist movement argued that ecclesiastical power should be decentralized: instead of being concentrated in the hands of a single individual, it should be dispersed within the body of the church as a whole and entrusted to a more representative and accountable group—namely, "general Councils."[6] This movement reached the height of its influence in the fourteenth and fifteenth centuries. Its moment seemed to have arrived when a crisis emerged in the papacy during the fourteenth century.

Those who believed that the identity of the church was safeguarded by the authority of the pope found themselves in a dilemma toward the end of the fourteenth century. Irritated by the tensions arising from the factionalism and infighting between some of the great Roman families, Clement V decided to move the papal court away from Rome to the southern French city of Avignon. From 1309 to 1378, the papacy endured this self-imposed exile from Rome—a period the great poet Petrarch referred to as the "Babylonian Captivity" of the papacy.[7] Yet a number of factors—including growing French political interference in papal affairs and tensions within Italy as a result of the papal absence—led Gregory XI to decide to return to Rome in 1377.

Yet Gregory died shortly afterward. His successor, Urban VI (1378–89), was unpopular with the French cardinals, who returned to Avignon and elected a rival pope, Clement VII. For a period of more than forty years, there were two claimants to the title of the papacy in Europe, a state of affairs that caused confusion and seriously weakened the authority of the church. England, Germany, Hungary, most of Italy, Poland, and the Scandinavian countries supported Urban VI at Rome; France, Scotland, Spain, and southern Italy supported the "anti-pope," Clement VII, at Avignon.

Many senior church figures quietly came to the conclusion that these tensions could not be sustained without doing permanent damage to the church. The schism was finally resolved by the Councils of Pisa (1409) and Constance (1414–18). Given that there were three serious candidates for the papacy and no obvious alternative means of resolving the issue, the Council of Constance elected Martin V as pope in 1417. The "Great Schism" was ended. From that point onward, there would be only one pope in Rome. Yet the Council's role in electing the new pope and ending the schism introduced new uncertainties into the medieval Catholic understanding of authority within the church. Did not this imply that Councils had authority over popes? It seemed as if the rules of the game had changed.

Yet within decades the balance of power had shifted once more toward the papacy. Conciliarism may have remained an aspiration for many in the early sixteenth century, but it was no longer seen as a serious political option.[8] Although the Conciliarist debate can be interpreted as evidence of a crisis of authority—and hence a weakness—within the late medieval church, it can equally be regarded as an exploration of reforming options that tended to strengthen the church as it emerged through a difficult transitional period following the Great Schism.

At the local level, the church provided a focus of social identity and an agency for pastoral care. The local priest was often the only person of any learning in the neighborhood. Many churches were adorned with wall paintings, illustrating key episodes in the life of Christ or offering visions of heaven or judgment to remind the faithful of their ultimate accountability. The local church provided social stability, while at the same time enabling individuals to locate themselves in terms of the great narrative of creation, fall, redemption, and final judgment that lay at the heart of the Christian faith. Baptism, marriage, and funeral rites were all markers along the journey of life at which the church connected with the lives, hopes, and fears of its members.

Throughout medieval Europe, serious attention was given to ensuring that the core ideas and rites of the church connected with ordinary people. The famous York cycle of mystery plays can be seen as a deliberate instrument of religious education on the part of a proactive clerical establishment during the period 1360 to 1420.[9] Sociologists of knowledge argue that in every human society there is what Peter Berger terms "a plausibility structure," that is, a structure of assumptions and practices, reinforced by institutions and their actions, that determines what beliefs are persuasive. This must not be confused with the pure idealism of a "worldview." What Berger is referring to is a socially constructed framework that is mediated and supported by social structures.[10] In the Middle Ages, the most important such social reality was the church and its rites, from baptism through marriage through funerals; the church mediated and affirmed a view of reality.

The church was no abstract theological notion, no peripheral social institution; it stood at the heart of the social, spiritual, and intellectual life of western Europe throughout the Middle Ages, and into the era of the Renaissance. The older view, which saw the Renaissance as a secular interlude between the medieval "age of faith" and the unruly religious passions unleashed by the Reformation, never really made much sense and is painfully difficult to sustain on the basis of the evidence.[11] An individual's hope of salvation rested on her being part of the community of saints, whose visible expression was the institution of the church. The church could not be bypassed or marginalized in any account of redemption; there was, as Cyprian of Carthage had so cogently argued in the third century, no salvation outside the church. It was a point tangibly expressed and reinforced in the architecture of churches.

An excellent illustration of this point can be see in the French Benedictine priory church of St. Marcel les Sauzes, which was founded in 985 and extensively developed during the twelfth century.[12] An inscription over the main door to the church reads: "You who are passing through, you who are coming to weep for your sins, pass through me, since I am the gate of life." Those who were searching for the consolation of heaven or the forgiveness of sins could not secure these benefits without the intervention and interposition of the institution of the church, and its authorized ministers.[13] Salvation had been institutionalized.

TENSIONS AND ANXIETIES WITHIN WESTERN CHRISTIANITY

By the end of the fifteenth century, the position of the church within Western society seemed to many to be a permanent fixture of a stable world. Yet this entire way of thinking about the world was about to undergo radical change. New social and intellectual forces began to destabilize its foundations and to offer alternatives. Growing pressure for reform developed. In part, this reflected abuse and corruption within the church; in part it also reflected an increased confidence on the part of clergy—and increasingly laity—to voice their complaints and expect to be heard.

It is not difficult to list the many abuses and corruptions that clouded the history of the late medieval church. There was much to criticize, from the pope down to the most menial of the clergy. The Renaissance papacy was widely criticized for its financial excesses and preoccupation with social status and political power. Pope Alexander VI, a member of the Borgia family (perhaps chiefly remembered for its lethal dinner parties), managed to bribe his way to victory in the election to the papacy in 1492 despite the awkwardness of having several mistresses and at least seven known illegitimate children.[14] Niccolò Machiavelli, the great theorist of naked power, put the immorality of his age down to the appalling example set by the papacy.

It is easy to find much to criticize among the senior clergy of the age, whose appointments often rested on the influence of family, fortune, and power rather than any merit on their own part. In 1451, Duke Amadeus VIII of Savoy secured the appointment of his son to the senior position of bishop of the city of Geneva, later to be noted for its association with John Calvin. The appointment was not a great success. But what could you expect from an eight-year-old? In many parts of France, the senior clergy were generally outsiders, often nobility imposed upon the diocese by royal patronage. Rarely resident within their diocese, these clergy regarded their spiritual and temporal charges as little more than sources of unearned income, useful for furthering their political ambitions elsewhere. In France, Antoine du Prat (1463–1535), Archbishop of Sens, was so preoccupied with state duties that he found time to attend only one service at his cathedral. Appropriately enough, it was his funeral.

Lower clergy were often the butt of crude criticism.[15] Monasteries were regularly depicted as lice-infested dens of homosexual activity. The poor quality of the parish clergy basically reflected their low social status: in early sixteenth-century Milan, chaplains had incomes lower than those of unskilled laborers. Many resorted to horse and cattle trading to make ends meet. Illiteracy was rife among the clergy. Because many of them had learned the Latin words of the mass by heart from older colleagues, they were known to make mistakes as time passed and memories failed. As levels of lay literacy soared in the late fifteenth century, the laity became increasingly critical of their clergy. One English squire of the early sixteenth century grumbled that he had distinctly heard his local priest use the accusative case when the ablative was clearly called for. Many educated laity resented the distinction between the "sacred" and "secular" orders, which implied that the clergy enjoyed a closer relationship with God than they did.

Unsurprisingly, the hostility toward the clergy partly reflected their incompetence and partly the privileges they enjoyed. The tax breaks enjoyed by clergy were a source of particular irritation, especially in times of economic difficulty. In the French diocese of Meaux, which would become a center for reforming activists in the period 1521 to 1546, the clergy were exempted from all forms of taxation, provoking considerable local resentment. In the diocese of Rouen, there was popular outcry over the church's windfall profits made by selling grain at a period of severe shortage.

Yet it is important not to exaggerate the extent of such anticlericalism. While there were undoubtedly areas in which such hostility was particularly pronounced—in cities, for example—the clergy were often valued and respected. In rural areas, where levels of lay literacy were low, the clergy remained the most highly educated members of the local community. More importantly, many of the great monasteries of Europe were respected on account of their social outreach and their significant contributions to the local economy. Yet when all this is taken into account, a rumbling discontent remained, often expressed in what is known as "grievance literature."

Underlying such criticisms was a significant change taking place within the laity. Although the fifteenth century was regarded as a period of religious degeneration by an earlier generation of historians, more recent research has decisively overturned this verdict.[16] Toward the end of this period, on the eve of the Reformation, religion was perhaps more firmly rooted in the experience and lives of ordinary people than at any time in the past. Earlier medieval Christianity had been primarily monastic, focused on the life, worship, and writings of Europe's monasteries and convents. Church building programs flourished in the later fifteenth century, as did pilgrimages and the vogue for collecting relics. The fifteenth century has been referred to as "the inflation-period of mystic literature," reflecting the growing popular interest in religion. The fifteenth century witnessed a widespread popular appropriation of religious beliefs and practices, not always in orthodox forms.

The phenomenon of "folk religion" often bore a tangential relationship to the more precise yet abstract statements of Christian doctrine that the church preferred—but that many found unintelligible or unattractive. In parts of Europe, something close to "fertility cults" emerged, connected and enmeshed with the patterns and concerns of everyday life.[17] The agrarian activities of rural communities—such as haymaking and harvesting—were firmly associated with popular religion. Thus, in the French diocese of Meaux in the early sixteenth century, the saints were regularly invoked in order to ward off animal and infant diseases, the plague, and eye trouble, as well as to ensure that young women found appropriate husbands. The direct connection between religion and everyday life was taken for granted. The spiritual and the material were interconnected at every level.

This growing popular interest in religion led to lay criticism of the institutional church where it was felt to be falling short of its obligations. Yet this criticism reflected a new interest in religion that was reflective, whereas in the past the laity might have been somewhat uncritical. Christians became dissatisfied with approaches to their faith that stressed its purely external aspects—such as just attending church. They demanded a form of Christianity that was relevant to their personal experience and private worlds and capable of being adapted or mastered to meet their personal needs. If anything, it was adaptation, rather than reformation, that seemed to be the primary concern of the articulate laity. Not only were people more interested in their faith, but levels of lay literacy had soared, enabling laypeople to be more critical and informed about what they believed and what they expected of their clergy. Studies of inventories of personal libraries of the age show a growing appetite for spiritual reading. With the advent of printing, books became more widely available and now lay well within the reach of an economically empowered middle class. Devotional books, collections of sermons, traditional "books of hours," and New Testaments are featured prominently in these inventories.[18] Laypeople were beginning to think for themselves and no longer regarded themselves as cravenly subservient to the clergy in matters of Christian education.

The importance of this point can be seen from the publishing history of one of the most important works of the early sixteenth century—Erasmus of Rotterdam's *Handbook of the Christian Soldier*, which first appeared in 1503.[19] The work made a powerful appeal to educated lay men and women, whom Erasmus regarded as the church's most important resource. The future of the church, Erasmus argued, rested on the emergence of a biblically literate laity, whom the clergy were to respect and go to as a resource. The soaring popularity of the work, especially in the late 1510s, suggests that a radical alteration in lay self-perception was taking place. The work was translated into English in 1520 by William Tyndale during his time as tutor to the children of Sir John Walsh at Little Sodbury, Gloucestershire.[20]

Erasmus's success also highlighted the importance of printing as a means of disseminating radical new ideas, a point that Martin Luther could hardly fail to overlook when his turn came to propagate such ideas. Recent scholarship has stressed the critical role of the new technology of reusable type in the dissemination of new ideas across Europe, whether those ideas were Protestant or humanist.[21] Without the advent of printing, there would have been no Reformation, and there might well have been no Protestantism either.

Important though these developments were, in and of themselves they do not adequately explain, still less necessarily entail, the rise of Protestantism. The root and branch "reformation" demanded by so many at that time could easily have taken the form of an internal review of the church's teachings and practices, not unlike the great Gregorian reforms of the eleventh centuries.[22] The key question is why and how this group of movements working for renewal and reform within the church came to crystallize as an entity *outside* the church structures of the day, and how it managed to survive.

Every single one of the points of difficulty noted here could have been addressed, and possibly resolved, by a gradual process of reappraisal and reform within the church similar to the program introduced in Castille, Spain, in the 1480s by the Franciscan provincial of the kingdom, Francisco Ximénez de Cisneros (1436–1517), which so radically transformed the Spanish church during this era of transition. He is widely regarded as having laid the foundations for the predominant role of the Spanish church in the Spanish Golden Age of the sixteenth and early seventeenth centuries.[23]

Most of Cisneros's reforming measures were put in place after he became archbishop of Toledo in 1495. Although nearly sixty years of age at that time, he spent the remainder of his life reforming the church, encouraging learning and a revival of religious vocations, and maintaining Spanish political unity at a time of rapid change and potential instability. The University of Alcalá and the Complutensian Polyglot (a multilingual version of the Bible) were perhaps the most tangible results of Cisneros's educational reforms. These reforms were not entirely successful and took a long time to take root. Nevertheless, they point to the capacity of the church to transform itself in response to the great challenges facing Spain at that time—most notably after the final re-Christianization of Spain following the military defeat of Islamic invaders from North Africa.[24]

A similar pattern can be identified elsewhere in Europe. A significant reform movement emerged in southern France about the year 1170 as a result of the activity of a wealthy Lyonnais merchant by the name of Valdes.[25] Valdes embarked on a reforming ministry based upon a literal reading of the Bible, particularly injunctions to poverty and biblically based preaching in the vernacular. This ethos contrasted sharply with the somewhat loose morality of the clergy at that time and attracted considerable support in southern France and Lombardy. Though persecuted during the Middle Ages, the movement survived and allied itself with the Protestant Reformation in 1532. The Waldensian movement represents an important historical link between early medieval reforming movements, which were predominantly moral in their agendas and biblical in their foundations, and the Reformation. Yet the fact remains that, until 1532, this movement saw itself as firmly embedded *within* the Catholic church, despite that church's official hostility toward its values and agendas.

In Italy the movement often known as "catholic evangelicalism," or "evangelism," with its stress on personally assimilated faith, became firmly established within the church, even penetrating deeply within its hierarchy, without being regarded as in any way heretical, schismatic, or even problematic.[26] Local initiatives for reform and renewal were springing up throughout the Western church, even if they lacked the central coordination and encouragement that might have transformed the western European church.

In this section, we have noted some of the failures, shortcomings, and abuses associated with the medieval church. Others could be added without the slightest difficulty. The enterprise would be at times amusing, at others depressing, and occasionally even enlightening. Yet such failings do not amount to a portrait of an institution in crisis, meltdown, or even serious difficulty. Such shortcomings, it has to be said with sadness, are the routine headaches of most occasionally dysfunctional institutions, whether they be the medieval church, modern multinational corporations, or the presidency of the United States of America.

While the whole enterprise of seeking "causes" of Protestantism is in itself almost as problematic as defining what "Protestantism" actually was, it is clear that, to understand its emergence at this time, we need to go much deeper than cataloging the shortcomings of the church. Such a list cannot offer an adequate account of why Protestantism emerged, still less why this development took place at this specific moment in history and not some other. The roots of the new movement must lie deeper than the moral shortcomings that are arguably a perennial characteristic of any institution over an extended period of time.

While no explanation is ultimately entirely satisfactory, perhaps the most persuasive account of the origins of Protestantism points to a double shift within Western culture at this time concerning values and ideas, on the one hand, and personal and social aspirations, on the other. Hitherto static and stable tectonic plates were shifting in both academy and society, opening up faults and fissures that threatened the old ecclesiastical order at a much deeper level than anything in the previous half-millennium. The advent of printing allowed both discontentment with existing paradigms and enthusiasm for an alternative to spread with unprecedented rapidity.

In the first place, we must consider the intellectual tumult that was taking place at this time and raising fundamental difficulties for traditional Catholic beliefs. It was one thing to suggest that the church had got itself into something of a mess; it was quite another to suggest that some of its fundamental ideas might rest on misunderstandings of the

Bible and thus might need to be reviewed, and possibly rejected. To understand this velvet revolution in the world of ideas, we must consider the rise of humanism at the time of the Renaissance and its implications for the transformation of Christianity. Ideas have the power to change society; the Renaissance set in motion a change in the world of ideas that was soon to be mirrored in the greater world of social reality.

We need to consider a second factor as well: the deeper cultural changes taking place around the dawn of the sixteenth century, which led many to yearn to break with the tradition of the past and to see the medieval church as hindering such a change. Change was in the air: individuals sensed that alternative means of self-actualization might lie to hand, and communities longed for increasing autonomy and less interference from traditional sources of authority—such as the church. The paradoxes and apparent contradictions of late medieval attitudes to the church can be resolved to some extent by noting that the church and its agents were valued when they protected, encouraged, or affirmed personal and communal fulfillment, and they were disliked when they sought to impose the church's own authority or supported the authority of unpopular clients.

We may turn immediately to consider the first of these factors—the rise of the "new learning," which proved to be so formidable a catalyst for change at this time.

RENAISSANCE HUMANISM AND THE "NEW LEARNING"

Christianity is a complex, multilayered reality. As we have seen, particular criticisms were leveled at the institutional level during the late medieval period, including the questionable morals of the papacy, the absence of senior bishops from their dioceses, and the poor quality of local parish clergy. All of these could be remedied without undue difficulty by appropriate measures. Yet what if criticism was directed at a more fundamental level—that of the *ideas* on which the institutions of the church were ultimately based?

In the case of Christianity, the ideas in question derive from the Bible. As with any classic religious text, three fundamental questions arise concerning its application: How is the most authentic form of that text to be determined? How is it to be translated? And how is it to be interpreted?[27]

By the end of the twelfth century, all three of these questions appeared to have been settled.[28] The question of the "canon" of the Bible had been sorted out seven centuries earlier and was not seen as particularly problematic. There was a minor debate, never regarded as particularly significant, over the status of some Old Testament books that appeared in the Greek version of the Old Testament (the "Septuagint") but not in Hebrew versions. It was known that there had been some corruption in the transmission of the standard Latin translation of the Bible (discussed later here)—but it was widely believed that the thirteenth-century so-called Paris edition had eliminated most of these. The basic text of the Bible thus seemed to have been agreed upon.

The translation issue also appeared to be settled. Latin was emerging as the *lingua franca* of the West, in relation to both the church and the universities, and it was deemed entirely fitting that a Latin translation of the Bible should be regarded as definitive. This translation, often referred to as "the Vulgate," could be traced back to the time of the early church, particularly the great biblical scholar Jerome. Jerome's *editio vulgata* ("common version") of the Latin text displaced older translations and came to be regarded as an authoritative rendering of the Hebrew, Aramaic, and Greek original texts. When Western medieval Christian writers speak about "the Bible" or "Holy Scripture," they are referring to the Vulgate translation.

The issue of how the Bible was to be interpreted proved slightly more problematic. Early medieval theologians—such as Peter Abelard—were well aware that certain passages had been interpreted in different ways in the past and that much disagreement continued in the present. The issue was partially resolved through the development of certain "rules" for the interpretation of the Bible. One of the most important was known as the "Quadriga," or the "fourfold sense of Scripture." This approach held that the Bible could be read at four different levels: literally (the most basic level), allegorically (in which a text was interpreted doctrinally), tropologically (in which a text was interpreted morally), and anagogically (in which a text was interpreted as relating to the Christian hope). With the application of this method, a degree of consensus emerged over how texts were to be interpreted.

Although the problem of biblical interpretation was not insignificant for medieval Christianity, the extent of any difficulties was limited by the emerging consensus that the church itself was the supreme interpreter of the Bible. On this view of things, God had providentially endowed the church with the capacity and authority to interpret the Bible and thus to avoid confusion in matters of doctrine and morals. There were some significant debates over precisely where this authority resided within the church: With the pope himself? Or with councils of leading cardinals and theologians? Yet the general principle of the divine guidance of the church into truth was firmly established, even if the fine detail remained occasionally fuzzy.

All of this was plunged into confusion through the new interest in the Bible resulting from the rise of humanism. The term "humanism" is easily misunderstood. In the twenty-first century, this word is often used to mean something like "atheism" or "secularism" and to identify a worldview that excludes belief in—or at least reference to—the divine. At the time of the Renaissance, the word had a very different connotation. The Renaissance was a remarkable period of cultural regeneration that began in Italy in the fourteenth century and gradually spread throughout much of Europe, reaching the peak of its influence in the 1500s. Its central theme was that today's culture could be renewed by a creative engagement with the cultural legacy of the past, above all the heritage of ancient Greece and Rome.[29]

Humanism can be thought of as the worldview underlying the Renaissance. It is best understood as a quest for cultural eloquence and excellence, rooted in the belief that the best models lay in the classic civilizations of Rome and Athens. Its basic method can be summed up in the Latin slogan *ad fontes*, which can be paraphrased as "back to the sources!" A stream is at its purest at its source. Humanists argued for the bypassing of the "Middle Ages"—that telling phrase, by the way, is a humanist creation, designed to belittle this irritating historical interlude between the glories of the ancient world and their renewal in the Renaissance—in order to allow the present to be renewed and reinvigorated by drinking deeply at the wellspring of antiquity. The effects of this program can be seen at an astonishing variety of levels. Classical architectural styles came to be preferred over the prevailing Gothic. Cicero's elegant Latin style displaced the rather mechanical, barbarous form of Latin used by scholastic writers. Roman law and Greek philosophy were eagerly studied at universities. In every case, the same basic principle can be seen at work: the fountainhead of Western culture had the capacity to refresh and redirect it when it had become tired, spent, and directionless.

Most humanists of the era—such as the great Erasmus of Rotterdam—were Christians who were concerned for the renewal and reform of the church. So why not apply the same method of regeneration to Christianity? Why not return *ad fontes*, to the original sources of faith, and allow them to reinvigorate a burned-out and run-down church? Could the vitality and simplicity of the apostolic age be recaptured? It was a powerful, inspirational vision, and it captivated the imagination of many laypeople in the fifteenth and early sixteenth centuries.

But how was this to be done? What was the religious analogue of the culture of the classical world? What was the fountainhead of Christianity? Christian humanists had little doubt: the Bible, especially the New Testament. This was the ultimate source of faith. The writings of medieval theologians could be set to one side with the greatest of ease to allow a direct engagement with the ideas of the New Testament. The ecclesiastically safe and familiar interpretations of the Bible found in scholastic theology would be marginalized in favor of reading the text directly. For conservative churchmen, this was a dangerous, threatening move that had the potential to destabilize the delicately balanced theological equilibrium, achieved over many centuries.[30] The humanist demand to return to the Bible turned out to be far more radical a call than many senior churchmen could stomach.

The humanists were primarily scholars—men of letters who insisted that this systematic return to the Bible should be done on the basis of the best possible scholarship. The actual content of the Bible would have to be established by the most reliable textual methods, and it would have to be read in its original languages. Immediately, the authority of the Latin Vulgate translation came under threat. As humanist scholars began to examine the history of the text in detail, problems began to emerge. Probing questions were pressed with increasing vigor concerning its textual integrity and philological reliability. As the Vulgate text was painstakingly compared with the best Greek manuscripts, errors began to be noticed. Variant readings were identified. In 1516 Erasmus himself produced an edition of the Greek text of the New Testament that caused something of a storm. Though it had many faults, it caused a sea change in attitudes by challenging the actual Vulgate text of the Bible at several points. To put the issue as bluntly as possible: if Erasmus was right, certain statements that earlier generations had accepted as "biblical" might not be part of the original text of the New Testament at all. So what, many wondered, did this mean for those church doctrines based on such statements?

One text often used by medieval theologians to defend the doctrine of the Trinity is of particular interest: "For there are three that bear record in heaven, the Father, the Word, and the Holy Spirit: and these three are one. And there are three that bear witness in earth, the Spirit, and the water, and the blood: and these three agree as one" (1 John 5:7–8). Erasmus pointed out that the words "the Father, the Word, and the Holy Ghost: and these three are one. And there are three that bear witness in earth" are not found in any Greek manuscript. They were added later to the Latin Vulgate, probably after 800, despite not being known in any ancient Greek version. The most likely explanation is that these words were initially added as a "gloss" (a brief comment set alongside or above the text) and that a later scribe assumed them to be part of the text itself and thus included them in later Latin texts, unaware that they were not part of the original Greek text of the New Testament.[31] If this passage were to be declared "unbiblical," this most difficult of Christian doctrines might become dangerously vulnerable.

The demand that the Bible be read in its original languages found wide acceptance throughout western Europe. Those wanting to advance the ideals of the Renaissance aimed to be *trium linguarum gnarus*—that is, competent in Greek, Hebrew, and Latin. This led to the founding of trilingual colleges or, in some cases, of a chair in three languages at, for example, the Universities of Alcalá in Spain (1499), Wittenberg in Germany (1502), Oxford in England (Corpus Christi College, 1517), Louvain in modern-day Belgium (1517), and the royal Collège de France in Paris (1530).[32]

It was not long before the possibly serious translation errors uncovered in the Vulgate threatened to force revision of existing church teachings. Erasmus pointed out some of these in 1516. An excellent example is found in the Vulgate translation of the opening words of Jesus's ministry in Galilee (Matthew 4:17) as: "do penance, for the kingdom of heaven is at hand." This translation creates a direct link between the coming of God's kingdom and the sacrament of penance. Erasmus pointed out that the original Greek text should be translated as: "repent, for the Kingdom of heaven is at hand." Where the Vulgate seemed to refer to an outward practice (the sacrament of penance), Erasmus insisted that the reference was to an inward psychological attitude—that of "being repentant."

Yet there proved to be more to the humanist vision of biblical scholarship than the need for better translations. The rise of the "new learning" promoted an alternative vision of interpretative authority in the 1510s—that of the scholarly community rather than the church. The academy already held the key to the reconstruction of the biblical text and its translation into the vernacular. It would be only a small step to claim the right to interpret that text, using the new hermeneutical techniques of the Renaissance that were then emerging.[33]

"Without humanism, there would have been no Reformation." This oft-repeated slogan makes the critical point that the rise of humanism forced a more radical program of reform on the church than any had anticipated. While many believed that there was an urgent need to eliminate abuse, simplify structures, and increase levels of education within the church, others now began to suggest that another layer of review was necessary. At least some teachings of the church might rest upon less than adequate biblical foundations. People were well used to complaints about the many moral and spiritual failings of the church; this was something new, however, and it threatened to spark off deeply disturbing debates and developments that were without precedent in western Christendom.

When this call for reform of the church is linked with the new understanding of humanity to emerge around this time, an explosive mixture resulted.

THE POWER TO CHANGE THINGS:
A NEW CONCEPTION OF HUMANITY

As we have seen, the Renaissance encouraged a new level of engagement with the foundational resources of culture, urging social and intellectual renewal on the basis of classical models—including the New Testament. Yet the Renaissance also witnessed the rise of a new conception of humanity with a radically altered understanding of its place within the cosmos. To explore this, we shall consider the famous "Manifesto of the Renaissance" (1486), which resonated throughout much of Europe.

Giovanni Pico della Mirandola (1463–94), one of the leading voices of the Italian Renaissance, delivered his precocious "oration on the dignity of humanity" in 1486 at the age of twenty-four. This "Manifesto," written in highly polished and elegant Latin, depicted humanity as a creature with the capacity to determine its own identity rather than be compelled to receive this in any given fixed form. The human creature possesses no determinate image and is urged by its creator to pursue its own perfection. God, the creator of humanity, is portrayed as mandating it to shape its own destiny: "You are constrained by no limits, and shall determine the limits of your nature for yourself, in accordance with your own free will, in whose hand we have placed you."

The ideas of this oration proved to be enormously influential in the late Renaissance, and in the longer term they can be seen as setting the scene for the Enlightenment assertion of human autonomy in the eighteenth century.[34] In the short term, however, it galvanized a new understanding of human nature and capacities. There was no "fixed" order of things; everything could be changed. Humanity was mandated by God to change the social and physical world.[35] This new vision of humanity as God's agent for changing the world empowered many who felt called to transform society.

Yet the medieval church was seen to be strongly conservative, lending theological support to the existing social order. The physical and social orders were held to be fixed and permanent, sanctioned by divine command. The traditional authority of influential families, monarchs, and principalities was not to be challenged. It was a source of frustration for the entrepreneurial middle classes, who were held back by the stifling force of tradition. A religious ideology that legitimated, or perhaps even *encouraged*, change would undermine such a static worldview and open the way to a dynamic alternative.

The rise of Protestantism is widely held to be linked with the transition between a medieval notion of worldly order, founded upon an order imagined to be natural and eternal, and a modern order founded upon the acceptance, even encouragement, of change as a means of pursuing the good.[36] The medieval worldview was static: one was allocated a position within society on the basis of birth and tradition, and it was not possible to alter this situation. By the end of the fifteenth century, an ideology of transition had developed; it held that individuals could determine their social position and status by their own efforts; they were not trapped by their social origins or circumstances, but could better themselves. To an emerging entrepreneurial social class, hitherto frustrated by an inability to make significant headway in a society dominated by tradition and familial ties, the doctrine of the fundamental changeability of existing social orders opened up exciting new possibilities.

Demands for social change began to build up apace around 1500, especially in the cities. The rise of a mercantile class in cities such as Zurich posed a challenge to the power and influence of traditional aristocratic families. In the closing decade of the fifteenth century, Zurich replaced the old patrician government with a Great Council of some two hundred city fathers, chosen for life by the merchant guilds, and a Small Council of fifty, selected by the Great Council and the guilds. An expectation of change and improvement arose as a similar pattern emerged in other cities around this time.

Yet there was little in the way of a religious motivation for laypeople to become actively involved in worldly affairs, business, or social action. The church had been slow to adapt to the new economic realities of the cities and had little encouragement to offer entrepreneurial individuals.[37] Yet Protestantism would offer a theological framework that radically altered the self-perception of such individuals. Luther's cardinal doctrine of the "priesthood of all believers" marked a decisive break with the medieval idea of vocation as a calling to a monastic life; Christians were called to serve God actively in the world and its affairs. The Protestant work ethic, which emerged definitively in the 1530s, gave a new religious motivation to active lay engagement in politics, business, finance, and other professional and artistic spheres. This theology of lay empowerment resonated strongly with the aspirations of a newly emerged and increasingly confident middle class.

Protestantism thus came to be linked with the longing for social progress and reform. It is not correct to say that Protestantism caused this change, which was already under way at the time of its emergence. Nor was Protestantism caused by this shifting perception of human possibilities. The evidence points to a synergy, a confluence of Protestant religious ideas and a new set of expectations and aspirations. Many believed, not without good reason, that Protestantism was the religious counterpart of social advancement and change.[38] The scene was set for a powerful alliance of religious motivation and professional lay competency.

Erasmus's text of the Greek New Testament was published in 1516. It is perhaps no accident that the event that is traditionally regarded as sparking the birth of Protestantism took place only a year later when Martin Luther nailed a document to a church door. We must now tell the story of the origins of this spark and of how it came to ignite such a conflagration.

2

======

The Accidental Revolutionary

Martin Luther

Why do seemingly insignificant events have the capacity to spark firestorms? History is laden with seemingly minor incidents that escalated with astonishing rapidity, leading to outcomes that seemed out of proportion to the original event. Why did the assassination of Archduke Franz Ferdinand at Sarajevo in June 1914 set off the horror known as the "Great War"? How could the death of a relatively insignificant individual in an obscure part of Europe ignite such a disastrous conflict? Or, going back to an earlier age, how did Helen of Troy come to be the "face that launched a thousand ships" (Christopher Marlowe)?

The answer, as might be expected, lies not so much in the event itself, but in the greater context within which it is set. Fragilities and tensions build up, bringing events to a point at which a relatively small stimulus may trigger an explosion. Events cascade, accumulating momentum that exceeds that of any of their individual components. While historical hindsight enables us to understand how an individual event proved to be the tipping point for a seismic social shift, it is generally impossible to predict such a cause in advance. The historian is a retrodictor rather than a predictor, always put in the position of trying to explain what happened and knowing that it might not have been this way at

Uffizi, Florence, Italy; Photo: Scala/Art Resource, NY

Martin Luther and his wife, Katharina von Bora, by Lukas Cranach the Elder (1472–1553).

all. As the scientist Stephen Jay Gould commented, with the process of biological evolution in mind, such is the historical power of contingency that if we were to rewind and replay the tape of history, it would reveal a different story each time.

If the origins of the Reformation in Germany are interwoven with its distinctive cultural dynamics at that time, this does not mean that this increased appreciation of the importance of social history denies a pivotal role to individuals, either as causes or catalysts of events.[1] During the 1980s, some German social historians pointedly excluded any reference to Martin Luther from their accounts of the origins of the Reformation, holding that he was essentially irrelevant to the broader forces at work. Such a view has now been happily abandoned as unworkable. Social historians have done much in recent years to illuminate how people at this time made sense of their world, adapted to existence within it, and understood their relation with the sacred and supernatural.[2] Yet understanding a broader context does not negate the possibility of individual action within it—nor the importance of ideas in shaping the way people understand their world and act within it.

In beginning to consider the complex web of ideas, events, personalities, and social forces that constituted the crucible within which Protestantism was forged, we must turn to consider the critical role played by Martin Luther (1483–1546) in bringing the movement into existence and shaping its contours. Luther's demands for reform rested on a religious idea, which rapidly became the watchword of reforming movements in the region.[3] To understand Luther, we must grasp the power of the intellectual vision that drove him. We must therefore turn to consider the distinctive religious idea that lay behind Luther's reforming agenda—the doctrine of justification by faith.[4]

THE INTELLECTUAL POWERHOUSE: JUSTIFICATION BY FAITH

Martin Luther was born on November 10, 1483, in the German town of Eisleben, the first son of Hans and Margarette Luder (as the name was spelled at this stage; it was later Latinized to the more familiar "Luther").[5] He was named after Saint Martin of Tours, whose festival fell on the following day, when Luther was baptized. Anxious to improve his employment prospects, Hans moved the following year to the neighboring town of Mansfeld, where he established a small copper mining business. By 1500 the family had become wealthy by the standards of the region. Having himself risen from the ranks of the German peasantry, Hans was determined to see his son rise still further and bring both status and income to the family. He began to plan his son's future. He would become a lawyer—then, as now, a career with excellent financial prospects.

In 1501 Luther began his studies at the prestigious University of Erfurt, founded as Germany's third university in 1392, after Heidelberg and Cologne. Erfurt followed the traditional medieval pattern of studies based on a "lower" faculty of arts and three "higher" faculties of law, medicine, and theology. By 1505 Luther had completed the initial arts course and was in a position to move on to study law. He was clearly academically competent, being placed second in that year's class of seventeen students.

After a mere six weeks, in a dramatic reversal, Luther abandoned the study of law. As Luther himself later told the story, at some point in June 1505 he was returning to Erfurt from a visit to Mansfeld. As he drew near to the village of Storterheim, a severe thunderstorm developed. Suddenly, a bolt of lightning struck the ground next to him, throwing him off his horse. Terrified, Luther cried out, "Saint Anne, help me! I will become a monk!"

This turning point in Luther's life brought to the surface many of the personal demons that would play such an important role in his subsequent career. Lying behind Luther's cry was a mental world shaped by a number of fixed landmarks that have since crumbled over the centuries. One was a fear of death and hell, coupled with more popular beliefs about fiends and devils lurking in woods and dark places, awaiting their opportunity to snatch unwary souls and take them straight to hell.

Luther kept his word. On July 17, 1505, he entered the most rigorous of the seven major monasteries at Erfurt—the Augustinian priory. Luther's father was outraged at the decision and remained alienated from his son for some considerable time. The priory was an austere place—yet, on the basis of the theology of the day, it seemed to Luther to guarantee his place in heaven. Was not becoming a monk the surest way to avoid hell? Were there not stories about monks who had abandoned their monastic habit and been turned away from the gates of paradise because they were not properly dressed for the occasion? Luther wanted to know—and know for certain—that he would escape hell and arrive safely in paradise. What other option did he have?[6]

Luther's early career as a monk was marked by intellectual excellence, on the one hand, and a spirituality of exaggerated fastidiousness, on the other. As he later recalled, if any monk ever got into heaven by his scrupulous observance of monastic discipline, he would be that monk. A deep sense of personal unworthiness is easily discerned in Luther's attitudes and actions around this time, and some worried about his mental stability.[7] His superior, Johann von Staupitz, gently steered him away from such personal introversion, recommending the study of theology as an antidote to morbid introspection.

So Luther began the formal study of theology at Erfurt, sitting at the feet of some of the greatest German theologians of his age. By this stage, the *via moderna*—the "modern way"—had come to dominate philosophy and theology in many German universities, including Erfurt. At the theological level, this was often expressed in an understanding of salvation based upon a gracious divine response to a moral human initiative. This principle was generally expressed in the Latin slogan *facientibus quod in se est Deus non denegat gratiam,* which can be roughly translated as "God will not deny grace to those who do their best."[8] This theological principle resonated with Luther's basic psychological instincts. It seemed entirely reasonable to him at that stage that God would not reward people unless they did something to merit that action. It was certainly the academic consensus at Erfurt. It was not, however, the official teaching of the Catholic church.

During the late Middle Ages, confusion had set in over what was the private teaching of individual theologians or theological schools and what was the authorized teaching of the church. The fifteenth century is seen by some as marking a magnificent period of religious anarchy in which competing theologies vied for attention, with little official interest in adjudicating between them. The young Luther took the view that the church taught that salvation was dependent on personal austerity, discipline, and denial. If there were alternatives, they do not seem to have been known to Luther.

In 1512 Luther left Erfurt to take up a lectureship in biblical studies at the newly established University of Wittenberg, founded in 1502 by Frederick the Wise with the intention of rivaling other universities in the region. Frederick's dreams came to nothing; by the time of Luther's arrival, Wittenberg had dropped off the radar screen of prospective students and was experiencing significant recruitment problems. Its brash aspirations were not matched by its feeble academic resources. In due course, Luther would raise the university's profile enormously, although for reasons that would not entirely have pleased Frederick.[9] It was during this time that Luther developed a "wonderful new definition of God's righteousness" that would change his own spiritual world—and become a platform for renewal and reform within the church.

Enormous scholarly attention has been devoted to clarifying how Luther's reforming theology emerged during his time at Wittenberg. In what ways did he change his mind about things? When did this transition take place? And what were its implications? While there remains some uncertainty over some aspects of these questions, the broad outlines now seem reasonably well understood.[10]

The central changes in Luther's thought centered, in the first place, on how Christian theology arrives at its core ideas and, in the second, on how humanity secures salvation. By about 1516, Luther was clear that the primary source of Christian theology was not the scholastic tradition, still less the philosophy of Aristotle. It was the Bible, especially as interpreted through the writings of the early Christian theologian Augustine of Hippo (354–430). Luther increasingly came to speak of "the Bible and Augustine" as the sources of his ideas. Although the importance of the Bible had always been recognized in Christian theology, Luther began to accentuate it in a manner that would ultimately lead into dangerous new theological territory.

Yet even more dangerous was the idea that Luther developed over the period 1513 to 1516 as he wrestled with the text of the Bible, anxiously trying to discern what it really says about salvation. There are few ideas with the capacity to dismantle great institutions and invert the judgments of previous generations. For Luther, the great question of life was simple and profound: how could he find a gracious God? As a younger man, terrified of hell and convinced of his own sinfulness, Luther gave an answer that was widespread in German theological circles, as it was in popular Christian culture: if he wanted to get in with God, he had to make himself into a good person. Like other Christians of the time, he believed that humanity has the capacity to make itself righteous, that when this happens God endorses this transformation and accepts the transformed person into a relationship with him, and that this only happens through the institution of the church, which provides the God-given structures that lead securely and inevitably to salvation. By developing his doctrine of justification by faith, however, Luther would dismantle such ideas and offer a radical, alluring alternative.

Luther found at least part of this alternative idea, which he began to develop around 1516, in earlier writers of the Christian tradition, such as Augustine of Hippo. When Paul speaks of the "righteousness of God" being revealed in the gospel, he does not mean that we are told what standards of righteousness we must meet in order to be saved. Rather, we are confronted with the stunning, disarming, overwhelming declaration that God himself provides the righteousness required for salvation as a free, unmerited gift. God's love is not conditional upon transformation; rather, personal transformation follows divine acceptance and affirmation.

More radically still, Luther insisted that the believer is "at one and the same time a righteous person and a sinner (*simul iustus et peccator*)." While Luther admired Augustine for his emphasis on the unconditional love of God in justification, he suggested that Augustine had become muddled in relation to the location of the gift of righteousness. Augustine located this gift within humanity, as a transforming reality; Luther argued that it is located outside us, being "reckoned" or "imputed" to humanity, not imparted.

Perhaps the chief beneficiary of this insight was Luther himself. Convinced of his sinfulness and frustrated by his own impotence to free himself from the power of his sinful nature, Luther set out a theology of divine acceptance (Luther generally used the Pauline image of "justification") of sinners that made personal transformation and renewal the consequence, not the precondition, of God's love. Humanity, in this conception, is like a patient who is under the care of a wise physician and on the way to recovery. The decision to treat does not presuppose the desired outcome but rather brings it about.

Perhaps the most radical aspect of Luther's doctrine of justification is its conceptualization of the relationship between humanity and God. How does humanity find God and enter into a relationship with him—a relationship that delivers humanity once and for all from fear of death, hell, or damnation? Luther is adamant: this relationship is made possible through the death and resurrection of Jesus Christ and is appropriated through faith. For Luther, faith is fundamentally an attitude of trust in God that enables the believer to receive and benefit from the promises of God. But where does the institution of the church come into this?

The most radical element of Luther's doctrine of justification is its conception of salvation as a matter affecting God and the individual. The individual's relationship with God is direct, determined by faith in God's promises and the salvation procured by Christ's death and resurrection. There is no longer any need for intermediaries—for the intercession of Mary or the saints. There is no necessary role for the church, its sacraments, or its priests in the dynamic of salvation. More than that: if justification is about the reckoning of Christ's righteousness to believers, what is the point of purgatory? Does not the very idea of being accepted by God on account of Christ's perfect sacrifice on the cross lead directly to the redundancy of the intermediate state?

This was a radical idea, and once accepted, it would change everything. We are all limited and shaped by the assumptions of our culture, which are held to be self-evidently true and become absorbed as essential pieces of furniture in the mental worlds we inhabit. Yet Luther's radical new ideas would prove these seemingly unshakeable assumptions to be vulnerable. If Luther was right about justification—and his critics insisted that he was not—then the conceptual glue binding the church's rites, ceremonies, institutions, and ideas was fatally weakened. He had shown that the complex edifice of salvation, largely constructed during the Middle Ages, lacked a solid foundation.

The evidence suggests that Luther took some time to think through the implications of this idea and was even at times reluctant to accept the inner logic of his own thinking. Thus, Luther did not seem ready to abolish the institution of the church or its ministry. Yet the church would now play a subsidiary role in the dispensation of salvation, subordinate to the direct encounter between the individual human being and God. The Luther who registered his protest against the sale of indulgences—to which we shall turn in a moment—was still perfectly prepared to believe in purgatory, even if he objected most vigorously to the suggestion of Johann Tetzel (one such salesman) that divine acceptance could be purchased, as if God could be bribed, or paid for some professional service.

Others, however, were quick to see the more radical implications of Luther's core idea of justification by faith and had no hesitation in pressing those implications to their limits. Simon Fish's anticlerical tract *A Supplication for the Beggars* (1529) and similar polemical works draw upon just about every form of irony and invective to depict purgatory as a recent invention by predatory monks and friars bent on filling their coffers and satisfying their corrupt desires. Luther was reluctant to draw such conclusions; others were not. If Luther's doctrine was right, then the church's teaching and practices had been devised by clergy determined to give themselves a necessary and privileged place in the dispensation of salvation and to exploit that monopoly in every way they could. This demanded a reformation that went far deeper than mere tinkering with externals. This was a demand for reconstruction of the church from ground zero.[11]

For Luther's doctrine of justification undermined the credibility of the medieval worldview and put in its place something quite different—a way of thinking that placed the relationship between an individual and his or her God at the center of all things. This was an idea that made a powerful appeal in an increasingly individualist culture. While many in the earlier Middle Ages were content to see and define themselves in terms of their relationship to the church, the Renaissance catalyzed a new awareness of the importance of individual human existence. No longer were human beings simply to be thought of as parts of a greater whole—for example, as members of a great family, trade guild, nation, or church. They were to be valued and treated for what they were in themselves.

It was a message that was warmly received throughout much of western Europe. Those whose intellectual appetites had been whetted by Erasmus found that Luther spoke to their condition and increased their longing for reform and renewal. Yet at this stage Luther had merely changed the way he *thought*. What was it that would trigger Luther's reforming program? How did Luther's dangerous ideas begin to express themselves in concrete demands and proposals for the reform of the church?

THE TRIGGER FOR LUTHER'S REFORM: THE INDULGENCE CONTROVERSY

The event that is traditionally held to mark the beginning of the European Reformation, and hence the birth of Protestantism, took place at about midday on October 31, 1517, on the eve of All Souls' Day. Martin Luther, a lecturer in biblical studies at the recently founded University of Wittenberg, nailed a piece of paper to the main north door of the castle church of that city. The paper fluttered in the wind alongside various other academic and civic notices, probably attracting little attention at first.

Luther's notice was a request to debate a series of theological propositions about the practice of indulgences. Such debates were a regular part of the academic life of the day and rarely attracted attention beyond the limited confines of the universities. There is no evidence that his attempt to arrange a routine debate attracted any interest within the University of Wittenberg, or any attention from a wider public. It was only when Luther circulated his demands more widely that controversy began to develop.

So what was the issue at stake? The immediate cause was the visit of Johann Tetzel to Luther's hometown of Wittenberg to sell indulgences, partly in order to raise capital for the rebuilding of St. Peter's Basilica in Rome. Occupying something of a theological gray area, indulgences were popular without being entirely theoretically respectable. If there was a theological foundation to the notion, it lay in the idea that through their exemplary actions, Jesus Christ and the saints of the church had built up a "treasury of merit" on which pious Christians could draw, as and when necessary.

Over a period of time, the church had developed a complex theology of purgatory—an intermediate state in which the souls of believers were purged of their remaining sin in order to enter into the presence of God without stain or defect of any kind. This idea of an "intermediate state" could be traced back to the sixth century, although its elaboration is particularly linked with the later Middle Ages. By the early sixteenth century, a popular theology of purgatory had emerged that emphasized both the extended nature and the horrors of this refinement in purgatory—and at the same time offered a number of fast tracks through the process.[12]

One such accelerated pathway was based on prayer for the dead by the living. Throughout Europe, a whole system of intercessory foundations was created to offer prayers for souls in purgatory, including trentals (cycles of thirty requiem masses) and obits (a yearly memorial service). Chantries were established in order to ensure regular prayer for those who had died.[13] The expenses attending such cults of the dead were considerable, a fact reflected in the rise of religious fraternities dedicated to the provision of the appropriate rites of passage for their members. In times of economic hardship, at least some degree of anticlerical sentiment was thus an inevitability: the clergy could be seen as profiting from the anxiety of the impoverished living concerning their dead kinsfolk.

It was, however, a second fast track through purgatory that aroused Luther's ire. Although the theological foundations of the practice were highly questionable (it was abolished by Pope Pius V in 1567), the church began to finance military campaigns and the construction of cathedrals through the sale of "indulgences," which reduced the amount of time spent in the torment of purgatory. Johann Tetzel was a shrewd marketer and knew how to sell his product. He had crafted a catchy slogan, making the merits of his product clear even to the simplest of people:

As soon as the coin in the coffer rings,
The soul from purgatory springs!

The canny spiritual investor could thus ensure that both he and his relatives (assuming, of course, that his budget stretched that far) could miss out on the pains of purgation. Aware of the wide appeal of his product, Tetzel had developed an additional crafty marketing technique. The cost of an indulgence was tailored to individuals' ability to pay as much as to the spiritual benefits they hoped to secure.

Most people rather liked this idea, seeing it as a clever way of enjoying sin without having to worry too much about its alleged eternal consequences. Any extended experience of purgatory was strictly for those who failed to plan for the future. Yet Luther was appalled by the practice. Forgiveness was meant to be the free gift of God! For Luther, the indulgence controversy was a worrying symptom of a much deeper malaise—a loss of the foundational vision that lay at the heart of the gospel. How could the church claim to be Christian when it seemed, at least to Luther, to have lost sight of the most important of all Christian insights—that God offers salvation as a free gift? The sale of indulgences seemed to deny the essence of the Christian gospel, as Luther now understood it. And if the church denied the gospel, was it really a Christian church at all?

Armed with his doctrine of justification by faith, Luther argued that the peddling of indulgences distorted the Christian gospel into some kind of commodity. In his "Ninety-five Theses," Luther set out a series of objections to the selling of indulgences that can be reduced to two broad principles. First, they were financially exploitative of the German nation. If the pope had realized the severe poverty of the German people, he would have preferred that St. Peter's Basilica remain in ruins than that it should be rebuilt out of the "skin, flesh, and bones of his sheep." Second, Luther argued that the pope had no authority over purgatory and therefore was in no position to influence how long anyone spent there. In the highly unlikely event that he did have any such authority, surely he ought to empty the place free of charge?

These were unquestionably dangerous, subversive ideas that posed a challenge to the finances of the church as much as to its theology. Yet the reader of these theses is more likely to notice their fundamental continuity with traditional Catholicism than their explosive potential. Purgatory itself is not called into question; Luther's challenge concerned the means by which one gets out of it as quickly as possible.

The political context played an important role in fanning the flames of the ensuing controversy. A surge in German nationalism played no small role in propelling Luther's protest into the forefront of popular debate and discussion.[14] As the German ecclesiastical grievance literature of this period makes clear, intense indignation was directed against the pope, reflecting popular irritation at the manner in which ecclesiastical revenues (including the proceeds of indulgence sales) were destined for Rome and the maintenance of the somewhat extravagant lifestyles, building programs, and political adventures of the Renaissance popes. The ruling classes of Germany resented the manner in which their local political authority was compromised through papal interference in ecclesiastical and political affairs. In its appeal to nationalism and antipapalism, Luther's reforming program allowed the Reformation to ride on the crest of a wave of popular antipapal sentiment.

Luther was soon in serious trouble. Perhaps unwisely, he brashly forwarded his criticisms of the indulgence traffic to Albert, the newly installed Archbishop of Mainz. Was Luther aware, one wonders, that Tetzel's ambitious and highly inflated claims for his product were encouraged by none other than this same Albert, who would retain some of the proceeds from indulgence sales to cover the costs of securing his archbishopric? Albert would have had little time for Luther's theological critique of the idea of indulgences, seeing it as little more than pedantic intellectual sophistry that could easily be dismissed as an irrelevance. But if anyone took Luther's critique seriously, it would affect Albert's cash flow at a critical time. And he had further ecclesiastical ambitions that needed to be funded.

Albert forwarded Luther's criticism of indulgences to Rome, certain that Pope Leo X would deal with the matter. After all, Leo had authorized their sale in 1514 and would hardly be likely to overlook the financial threat posed by the upstart German theologian. In fact, however, Leo dithered. He had many other pressing matters to worry about. He was engaged in delicate political maneuvering to ensure that his preferred candidate was elected as the next Holy Roman Emperor. Three serious candidates were in the running: Henry VIII of England, Francis I of France, and Charles I of Spain. Each was a strong leader who might prove difficult to influence from Rome. Leo hoped to influence the electoral college to choose a relatively weak candidate whom he could control, and he had decided on Frederick the Wise, Elector of Saxony. Yet Frederick was sympathetic to Luther. Leo decided not to press the matter at such a sensitive moment.

He need not have bothered. On June 28, 1519, Charles was elected Holy Roman Emperor. It was no longer necessary for Leo to hold back. A year later, on June 15, 1520, Leo issued the bull Exsurge Domine ("Arise, O Lord"), which condemned Luther as a heretic. Luther famously burned this bull in public. An oak tree was later planted at the site of this dramatic event, which can be seen as a landmark. Sadly, the tree met its end during the Napoleonic wars: during a serious fuel shortage, its practical utility for heating took priority over its symbolic value. It was replanted in 1830.

Luther's public act of defiance of papal authority dramatically raised the stakes in a conflict that seemed to be escalating out of control. Undaunted, Luther began to put his ideas into action, setting out manifestos for reform. His reformation would be more than a protest against the pope; it would be a positive and constructive renewal of the church.

1520: A MANIFESTO FOR REFORM

At the time of the indulgence controversy (1517), Martin Luther was on the faculty of theology at the University of Wittenberg. It is hard to avoid retrojecting Luther's later fame into this earlier situation. Contemporary accounts make it clear that Wittenberg's best-known theologian was Andreas Bodenstein von Karlstadt, whom Luther appears to have won over to his new theology around this time. Together, the two concentrated on reforming the theological curriculum at Wittenberg. Scholastic theology and Aristotle were on their way out, displaced by a new emphasis on the Bible and Augustine.

Yet Luther realized that making changes to the theological curriculum at one of Europe's most insignificant universities was hardly likely to change the face of the church. His radical new ideas on justification needed to be proclaimed to the church at large. Luther initially had hopes that a public dispute with a leading Catholic might draw wider attention to his reforming agenda. Karlstadt and Luther duly debated the Ingolstadt theologian Johann Eck on a variety of issues in July 1519 in what is known as the "Leipzig Disputation."

Things began badly for the Wittenberg reformers. Karlstadt's ponderous and turgid performance bored the audience. The debate between Eck and Luther, however, created a buzz. Eck, a skilled debater, managed to maneuver Luther into casting doubt on the authority of the Council of Constance (1414–18) and defending some of the teachings of Jan Hus, a Bohemian reformer who had been declared a heretic at Constance. There was a long local history of hostility toward Bohemia at Leipzig, and Eck's skillful manipulation of the debate lost Luther the support of the audience. It was a profoundly uncomfortable experience for Luther, and it raised questions about whether he could advance a reforming agenda in an academic context. Yet Luther's performance at Leipzig impressed many in positions of influence. German humanists began to lionize Luther, seeing in him an articulate proponent of precisely the program of reform that they advocated. Even the great Erasmus of Rotterdam began to take an interest in this hitherto unknown figure. Luther's stock was rising.

Luther had learned from Erasmus the importance of the printing press in projecting intellectual influence within society. In 1520 he began to advance the cause of his reformation by appealing directly to the German people, over the heads of clerics and academics, through the medium of print. It was a tactic that would be imitated throughout Europe as the power of the pamphlet became obvious to all.[15] Luther now began to have the popular impact that he knew was essential if he was to change the shape of the church rather than tinker with academic niceties. *And Luther would use the vernacular.*

Why was this so important? The language of the academy, the church, and the state in western Europe throughout the Middle Ages was Latin. There was an obvious need for a common language to allow communication across this vast and diverse region of the world. Latin was the language of the great Roman poets, rhetoricians, politicians, philosophers, and highly influential Christian theologians such as Augustine of Hippo, Ambrose of Milan, and Tertullian. Luther knew that anything he wrote in Latin would be understood by the educated elite across Europe.

Yet Luther wanted to reach beyond an academic readership and touch the hearts and minds of ordinary people. Luther's decision to publish in German was iconic, in that it made a statement about the inclusive nature of the reformation he proposed to pursue. To publish in Latin was to exclude the ordinary people. To publish in German was to democratize the debate about the future of the church by including those who were traditionally marginalized by the use of the ancient scholarly language. From that moment onward, one of the hallmarks of Protestantism would be its use of the vernacular at every level. Most importantly of all, the Bible would also be translated into the language of the people.

Luther published three popular works in quick succession in 1520. *The Appeal to the Nobility of the German Nation,* widely regarded as the most important of these works, set out the case for reform of the church and argued that German nobles had every right to demand change. *The Babylonian Captivity of the Church* criticized the church's teaching on sacraments. *The Freedom of a Christian* explained Luther's views on justification in easily accessible terms.

Luther's fundamental argument in the *Appeal to the Nobility of the German Nation* was that the church had shielded itself from criticism and demands for reform by erecting defensive walls around itself. In the first place, the church drew a fundamental distinction between the "temporal" and "spiritual" orders—the laity and the clergy—and declared the government of the church to be a matter for the clergy, not the laity, whom it saw as subordinate in matters of faith. Second, it denied the laity the right to interpret the Bible, a right that ultimately rested, it said, with the pope. Third, only a pope could convene a reforming council.

Like the walls of Jericho, Luther declared, these defenses needed to be brought to the ground. The metaphorical trumpet blasts that Luther directed against these walls encapsulated some of the fundamental themes of the Reformation, which set a pattern that would gradually become normative for much of Protestantism.

Luther began his critique of the church by setting out one of the greatest themes of the Reformation—the democratization of faith. He used the German term *Gemeinde* ("community") to refer to the church so as to emphasize that the church is fundamentally a gathering of believers, not a divinely ordained institution with sacred powers and authority vested exclusively in its clergy. All believers, men and women, by virtue of their baptism, are priests. Luther noted an important corollary of this doctrine: the clergy should be free to marry, like all other Christians. This right to clerical marriage rapidly became a defining characteristic of Protestantism.

Luther grounded his doctrine of the "priesthood of all believers" in the New Testament's concept of the church as a corporate "royal priesthood."[16] There was no basis, Luther argued, for asserting that the clergy are superior to the laity, as if they are some kind of spiritual elite or their ordination confers upon them some special "indelible character." The clergy are merely laity who have been recognized by other laity within the community of the church as having special gifts and who are authorized by their colleagues to exercise a pastoral or teaching ministry among them. The authority to make such decisions thus rests with all Christians, not with an autocratic elite or putative spiritual aristocracy.

Luther developed this point with a civil analogy that is as accessible today as it was five hundred years ago. The clergy are "officeholders" who are elected by the laity as their representatives, teachers, and leaders. There is no fundamental difference between clergy and laity in terms of their status; the difference lies entirely in the former being elected to the "office" of a priest. All believers already have this status on account of their baptism. This election to office is reversible; those who are thus chosen can be de-selected if the occasion demands it.

On the basis of this doctrine of the universal priesthood of believers, Luther insisted that every Christian has the right to interpret the Bible and to raise concerns about any aspect of the church's teaching or practice that appears to be inconsistent with the Bible. There is no "spiritual" authority, distinct from or superior to ordinary Christians, who can impose certain readings of the Bible upon the church. The right to read and interpret the Bible is the birthright of all Christians. At this stage, Luther clearly believed that the Bible was sufficiently clear for ordinary Christians to be able to read and understand it. Following through on his democratizing agenda, Luther insisted that all believers have the right to read the Bible in a language they can understand and to interpret its meaning for themselves. The church is thus held accountable to its members for its interpretation of its sacred text and is open to challenge at every point.

The significance of Luther's point can hardly be overlooked. By insisting that it had a divinely ordained monopoly on biblical interpretation, the medieval church had declared itself to be above criticism on biblical grounds. No external critic had the authority to interpret scripture and thus to apply it to criticize the church's doctrines or practices. Luther's response was to empower the laity as interpreters of the Bible and to hold the church accountable *to its people* for what it taught. And if they were not satisfied with the outcome, they, as laity, had the right to demand that a reforming council be convened to address their concerns.

This final point was perhaps the most dangerous of all, as Luther seemed to have an important historical precedent on his side. Tongue placed firmly in his cheek, Luther reminded his readers that it was the Roman emperor Constantine who was responsible for summoning the Council of Nicea in 325, one of the most important councils of Christian history. If a lay ruler could summon such a council back then, why should not the German princes do the same twelve hundred years later?

In *The Babylonian Captivity of the Church,* Luther set out a series of criticisms of existing church practices and the theology on which they were based. These focused on the mass—the central rite of the medieval Catholic church, its most visible and tangible point of contact with the world of ordinary people. The changes that Luther demanded—and proposed—were nothing less than revolutionary.[17]

For a start, Luther insisted that the laity should be allowed to receive both the bread and the wine at mass. There had been a long-standing tradition, whose origins are somewhat obscure, which held that only priests should be allowed to receive both elements; the laity were only allowed bread. (Some historians speculate that early medieval problems with an enthusiastic but intoxicated laity may lie behind the practice.) Luther was adamant: the bread and wine were both signs of God's grace and love. To deny the laity access to both sacramental signs was to imply that they were also denied access to the divine realities they signified. The practice of "communion in both kinds" would henceforth be characteristic of the Reformation.

Luther also argued for other changes in practice. For example, he was critical of the practice of saying requiem masses, often carried out by mercenary "mass priests." No masses should be said for the dead by a priest alone without communicants, Luther argued, because the rite involved fellowship not only with Christ but also with believers.

Yet Luther's most radical criticism did not concern existing church practices, but the theories on which they rested. Luther denied the doctrine of transubstantiation, which held that the bread and wine of the mass were transformed into the body and blood of Christ.[18] At the moment of consecration by a priest, according to this theory, the elements of bread and wine, though retaining their accidents (that is, their outward appearance to the senses), underwent a radical change in their substance (that is, their innermost identity). The bread continued to look, taste, smell, and feel like bread; at the deepest of levels, however, it had become something utterly different—as had the wine, which now became the blood of Christ, despite a complete absence of any visible or sensible change.

Luther ridiculed this doctrine as resting on Aristotle's outmoded and invalid distinction between "substance" and "accidents." In its place, Luther proposed a doctrine now known as "consubstantiation," which asserted that Christ's body and blood were somehow received alongside the bread and wine in the communion service.

These demands for reform were not well received by the church establishment, which saw all too clearly the danger they posed for its status and power. No aristocracy, political or spiritual, feels particularly enthusiastic about demands for democracy. Summoned to appear before the Diet of Worms in 1521, Luther refused to recant his ideas or promise to conform. Luther's refusal to retract his words resounded throughout the emerging reforming movement:

> Unless I am convicted by Scripture and plain reason—I do not accept the authority of popes and councils, for they have contradicted each other—my conscience is captive to the Word of God. I cannot and I will not recant anything, for to go against conscience is neither right nor safe. Here I stand, I cannot do otherwise. God help me. Amen.[19]

At this stage, Luther had no intention of breaking away from the church. Nothing, he commented, could be achieved through schism. His hope was to reform the church from within. It was by far the best option. Yet his excommunication by Leo X in 1520 and his open condemnation by the Edict of Worms the following year seemed to rule out any such possibility.

But there was an alternative—a dangerous, radical, and groundbreaking possibility that was open to Luther only on account of the political circumstances of Germany at the time and the cautious support of his local prince. He could create a new church and start all over again. It was indeed a dangerous thought. The rules of the game had changed, and it would never be the same again.

Luther quietly slipped away from Worms before any action could be taken against him. In a piece of superb melodrama, he was kidnapped by a group of bandits and held in captivity in Wartburg Castle from May 1521 to February 1522. The "kidnapping" had been arranged by Frederick the Wise so that Luther could be protected without Frederick laying himself open to the charge of harboring a heretic. Luther used his time in the Wartburg well: he began his landmark translation of the New Testament into German, implementing his own demand that the word of God should be accessible to all. The famous legend that Luther scared off the devil at the Wartburg by throwing an inkwell at him is probably based on his statement that he had "driven the devil away with ink"—a reference to his translation of the New Testament. However, tourists who visited the Wartburg during the nineteenth century were regularly shown an ink stain on the wall and told that it marked the spot at which Satan was chased off. (What they were *not* told, of course, was that this stain was regularly touched up to preserve its fresh appearance!)

While Luther was thus engaged, events moved rapidly apace at Wittenberg. The reforms Luther had urged began to take place, without central organization or direction. Clergy began to marry. Services began to be held in German. When Luther returned to Wittenberg, no longer under the ban, he was able to resume direction of a nascent reforming movement with the potential to travel throughout Germany—and beyond.

THE FUNDAMENTAL THEMES OF LUTHER'S REFORMS

Luther's reforms, set out in 1520 and enacted at Wittenberg during the period 1522 to 1524, acted as a catalyst and role model for like-minded reforming individuals and congregations throughout Europe. This was no idealistic vision of a utopian church; it was a theological program for reform that could be implemented immediately. Luther was able to convert ideas to concrete reality. The reforms he introduced rapidly set the standards for others. The leading features of those reforms, which were characteristic of the first phase of Protestantism, can be summarized as follows.

1. *The Bible is the ultimate foundation of all Christian belief and practice.* For Luther, the Bible was central to the life and thought of the church, as it was to the personal devotion of the individual Christian. Much of Luther's early work focused on making the Bible accessible to German Christians—above all, by translating it into the German language. As it became clear that ordinary Christians experienced difficulty in interpreting the Bible, Luther produced catechisms,

devotional tracts, and biblical commentaries aimed at helping the faithful get the most from this treasure that had now been placed in their hands.

2. *The text of the Bible, and all preaching based upon it, should be in the vernacular*—the everyday language of the people, not Latin, which distanced the people from the text. Luther's fundamental concern was to break the clerical and academic monopoly on reflecting on matters of faith. When the liturgy, the Bible, preaching, and theological textbooks were all published only in Latin, ordinary Christians were excluded from reflecting on and debating about faith. Faith was to be democratized by making its foundational resources available to all who could read and by insisting that all were welcome participants in discussions about the interpretation and application of faith.

3. *Salvation is a free, unmerited gift of God, received by faith.* This notion, often referred to as "justification by faith alone," was central to Luther's reforming agenda. Every aspect of faith, Luther argued, depends on this central, controlling doctrine. If this idea is misunderstood or denied, the church loses its identity and the gospel is compromised—which was precisely what Luther believed to have taken place during the Middle Ages. Reformation was about restructuring the beliefs and practices of the church to be consistent with this core, foundational, driving belief. For Luther, it was this idea that would bring down the walls of the old Jericho and replace them. Later Protestant writers would refer to this as the *articulus stantis et cadentis ecclesiae*—the "article by which the church stands or falls."

4. *There is no fundamental distinction between clergy and laity.* This idea, articulated in Luther's doctrine of the "priesthood of all believers," had momentous implications. Clergy and laity alike, he asserted, should receive communion in both kinds. Clergy should be allowed to marry, like anyone else. Luther himself married Katharina von Bora, a former nun, who came to be regarded as a role model for women in the new Protestant order then emerging.[20] Each congregation should be able to elect its own preachers and pastors and to

de-select them if necessary. Once more, the fundamental theme is democratization—the elimination of any notion of a "spiritual elite."

5. *The reform of the church's life and thought was not about beginning* ab initio, *in a frenzy of Promethean reconstruction.* Luther was clear that his vision was to reform an existing Christian church that had lost its bearings during the Middle Ages. It was no accident that Luther summarized his reforming program as "the Bible and St. Augustine." He wanted his readers to understand that the foundation of his thought was the Bible, as read through the eyes of the great religious heroes of the past, above all Augustine of Hippo, the "doctor of grace" who had so emphasized the importance of God's graciousness toward humanity.

Luther's reforms, it is clear, were neither an opportunistic attack on the morals of the church nor a piecemeal demand for reform here and there. His fundamental conviction was that the church of his day had lost sight of some fundamental themes of the Christian gospel. After all, the theology he had been taught at Erfurt now seemed to him to be heretical, amounting to the idea of "justification by works"—the notion that humanity can achieve its own salvation by its moral or religious achievements.

Yet Luther is open to criticism here, in that he appears to have extrapolated from his own local situation to that of the entire Christian church throughout Europe. As historians have rightly pointed out, the evidence simply does not sustain Luther's picture of the medieval church as totally doctrinally corrupt or out of touch with the New Testament—a fact that helps us make sense of the mixed response to his demands for reform.

Our concern, however, is to understand Luther at this point, not to correct him. Based on his own experience of the life and thought of the German church, however idiosyncratic and unrepresentative this may now seem, Luther set out to change things. To remedy the unsatisfactory situation of the church, Luther offered a vision of the gospel that provided a comprehensive foundation for the restructuring of Christian belief and practice. Not every aspect of the church's life and thought required reform. Renewal, not innovation, was Luther's watchword. The outcome was a coherent account of an alternative vision of what a Christian church should be and do. And as his reforms at Wittenberg between 1522 and 1524 made clear, this vision could be put into practice. A template for Protestantism had been created and was being actively evaluated.

Yet however important Luther's concerns and solutions may have been, it is essential to appreciate that at this stage his was one among many local attempts to reform and renew the church.[21] Luther's growing insistence that any attempt to reform the church include reviewing its foundational doctrines was perhaps more radical than other calls for reform. What requires explanation is why *this* local reforming movement went on to achieve such significance and to play such a defining role in the shaping of Protestantism.

The importance of this question will become apparent as we turn to consider another reforming program, initially totally independent of Luther's, that began far to the south, in the Swiss city of Zurich. While Luther was still unknown, others were also agitating for reform. Yet, as we shall see, it was a rather different kind of reform from that demanded by Luther.

Huldrych Zwingli, Swiss Reformation leader, c. 1530. Anonymous, sixteenth century.

3

Alternatives to Luther

The Diversification of the Reformation

The name of Martin Luther dominates most popular accounts of the origins and development of Protestantism. By 1519 Luther's name was beginning to be known more widely, especially within humanist circles. Luther himself was somewhat despondent about the outcome of the debate with Johann Eck at Leipzig, feeling that he had been outwitted and outmaneuvered by the canny theologian from Ingolstadt. Yet humanist networks were buzzing with the news of a hitherto unknown Augustinian monk who had laid down a formidable challenge to papal authority. Luther was about to be hailed as a leading representative of the case for reform of the church and would attract support from even such a luminary as Erasmus of Rotterdam.

Yet other reforming movements were springing up elsewhere in Europe around this time, initially without any knowledge of Luther's activities and aspirations. It is now clear that uncoordinated reforming initiatives were breaking out in many parts of Europe in the 1510s, often in response to local situations or inspired by local heroes. Many of Europe's great cities became epicenters of reforming movements that responded to and addressed their local situations. Recent scholarship, in stressing the intellectual and sociological heterogeneity of the first phase of the Reformation, has made it virtually impossible to think of it as a single, coherent movement.[1]

THE HETEROGENEITY OF
EARLY PROTESTANTISM

The Reformation is best conceived as a series of initially independent reforming movements with quite distinct agendas and understandings of the nature of theology and its role in the life of the church. Through the complex networks of the interchange of people, correspondence, and publications that were characteristic of this age, these originally independent movements came to achieve at least a partial degree of alignment over the following decade. Yet this identity was not determined by the movement's origins, as if this could be frozen in time and declared to be permanently normative. In a tangled and not fully understood process of reappraisal, reorientation, and reappropriation, it would emerge over time.[2]

The concept of "Protestantism" arose from an attempt to link a series of events in the early sixteenth century to form a common narrative of transformation. For the historian, there has never been a thing called "Protestantism"; rather, there were a number of movements, each with its own distinctive regional, theological, and cultural agendas. To speak of "the rise of Protestantism" is to offer a controlling narrative that links these potentially disparate events as part of a greater, more significant movement. So persuasive was this emerging narrative that many of the reforming groups scattered across Europe realigned their sense of identity and purpose to conform to it. As these movements began to locate themselves on a historical and conceptual map, each came increasingly to identify itself in terms of what was perceived as a greater overarching movement. A subtle process of realignment led to a growing sense of institutional and intellectual identity. Yet that identity was initially conceived primarily in terms of *two* movements—the Lutheran Reformation in northeastern Germany and the Zwinglian Reformation in eastern Switzerland. The idea that these two movements were as the two sides of the same Protestant coin represents a later retrojection by historians and Protestant apologists.

The suggestion that there exists a universal notion called "Protestantism" must therefore be viewed with considerable caution, as must the traditional idea that Luther's personal religious views somehow define the essence of this putative "Protestantism." As will become clear, Protestantism designates a family of religious movements that share certain historical roots and theological resources. Luther—admired and respected in some quarters, less so in others—is certainly one of those resources. As we shall see, Protestantism developed into a coherent entity through a complicated history of negotiations and compromises in the late 1520s and 1530s, during which time it was often unclear who was "in" and who was "out," let alone what the final outcome might be. Everything was in a state of flux, and the various reforming movements of the era shared no clear sense of a common set of beliefs, values, or ways of interpreting the Bible.

In a highly insightful study on the unity of the Reformation, Dorothea Wendebourg argues that the "unity" of the Reformation emerged retrospectively, primarily in response to later Catholic criticisms of the movement.[3] Protestantism developed its sense of identity primarily in response to external threats and criticisms rather than as a result of shared beliefs. In one sense, the idea of "Protestantism" can be seen as the creation of its opponents rather than of its supporters. The history of Protestantism repeatedly demonstrates that a shared sense of identity that transcends denominational and confessional boundaries depends on there being a credible common enemy—a role that has been played, until very recently, by Catholicism.

In this chapter, we explore some of the early alternatives to Luther that sprang up throughout western Europe during the 1520s and early 1530s and the negotiations that ensued to define the characteristics of the movement and maximize the potential for collaboration in the face of shared threats and foes. We begin by noting the tensions and disagreements within the original reforming faction at Wittenberg.

WITTENBERG:
LOCAL ALTERNATIVES TO LUTHER

The Reformation at Wittenberg in the early 1520s centered on three very different dynamic and charismatic individuals: Martin Luther, Andreas Bodenstein von Karlstadt, and Thomas Müntzer. With his public profile, Luther was by far the most visible and well-known representative of the reforming movement in Germany. Yet his ideas did not find universal acceptance, even within Wittenberg itself. Luther was seen as much too conservative by Karlstadt and Müntzer, both of whom urged him to adopt far more radical reforming programs.

While Luther was in hiding in Wartburg Castle, Karlstadt began to assume leadership of the emerging reformation at Wittenberg. He had his own strong views on how the Bible was to be interpreted, and he applied these with enthusiasm. They were not, however, the same as Luther's. On Christmas Day 1521, Karlstad preached in a simple robe rather than the normal elaborate clerical dress, purged any references to a sacrifice from the text of the mass, read Christ's words of institution in German rather than Latin, and distributed both the bread and the wine to all present. The next month Karlstadt set out an agenda for even more radical reforms. All religious images were to be smashed. Did not the Old Testament forbid images altogether? Music was to be abolished altogether from churches. "Better one heart-felt prayer than a thousand cantatas of the Psalms."

This bold act of defiance alarmed Luther. On leaving the Wartburg, Luther urged caution and assumed personal direction of the reforms at Wittenberg. Many of Karlstadt's proposals were blocked with immediate effect. The issue of biblical interpretation suddenly became a source of public tension and disagreement. For Karlstadt, the Old Testament prohibited the use of religious images; Christians should therefore avoid them and destroy any that remained in churches. Luther, however, argued that such Old Testament regulations were not binding under the new covenant of grace.[4]

Karlstadt was deeply alienated by what he saw as Luther's lack of vision and nerve. He left Wittenberg and became the pastor of Orlamünde, where he was able to continue a program of radical reform, including the abolition of infant baptism as unbiblical.[5] Alarmed, Luther tried to prevent such ideas from spreading. A meeting with Karlstadt at the Black Bear Tavern in Jena failed to resolve their differences. Luther appealed to the congregation to resist Karlstadt's radical measures, but was rebuffed. They liked their new pastor and were quite happy with the direction in which he was leading them. Karlstadt subsequently moved on to Switzerland, where he developed a still more radical approach to the reform of the church.

Karlstadt regarded Luther as a compromiser, someone who had begun to reform the church but held back once things got under way.

There was a need for principled consistency, in Karlstadt's view, rather than compromising half-measures. His criticism of Luther's failure of theological nerve would reverberate throughout many other movements within Protestantism, which would see Luther as lacking the courage and integrity to follow his ideas through to their conclusions. Luther dismissed these more radical reformers as fanatics, but they were merely consistently following through on his own ideas and methods and reaching conclusions and outcomes that he personally found unacceptable.[6]

Thomas Müntzer also posed a significant challenge to Luther. Always a cautious figure, Luther was prepared to collaborate with authorities in order to secure support for his local reformation. Müntzer saw this as unbiblical, a failure to bring about the much-needed social and political reformation of society that he regarded as integral to any reformation worthy of the name. Where Luther tended to see the reformation primarily as a matter of ideas, Müntzer saw it as biblically legitimated social action. Citing the prophet Hosea, Müntzer declared that "God gave the princes and lords to the world in his anger, and intends to take them away again." Power would then be given to the "common people."[7]

These ideas would play a critical role in bringing about the Peasants' War of 1525.[8] Müntzer led the peasants at the Battle of Frankenhausen, at which they were massacred. He himself was captured and beheaded. Where Müntzer saw rebellion of the peasants against their masters as something legitimated by the Bible, Luther saw such a revolt as a metaphysical rebellion against a divinely ordained social structure, also legitimated by the Bible. It is well known that Luther's early optimism about the ability of *Herr Omnes*—his term for the German people—to interpret the Bible was severely challenged by the events of the Peasants' War.

Much, of course, could be gained through a detailed analysis and comparison of the reforming programs of Luther, Karlstadt, and Müntzer. Yet the most fundamental point is simply this: they were strikingly different. There was no single Wittenberg reforming program, no single approach to biblical interpretation and application. The fact that Luther's particular vision of reform ultimately triumphed at Wittenberg seems to the historian to be not a fundamental theological necessity but rather a matter of historical contingency, reflecting the dynamics of power and political expediency.[9] This outcome of happenstance cannot be regarded as constitutive or definitive of Protestant identity, but as representing one outcome of the many reforming agendas and programs of this formative period.

More interestingly, careful analysis of the reception of Luther's doctrine of justification by faith suggests that it was often misunderstood by the laity.[10] Luther's call to return to the Bible was often interpreted morally. The idea of the "pure gospel" led many laypeople to see the Bible as a source of instruction on behavior that was pleasing to God, or as the "law of God" illustrating how the will of God was to manifest itself in the life of human communities.[11] This conclusion led many to an understanding of the Christian life as a quest for obedience to a lawgiving God, which is some considerable conceptual distance from what Luther intended by his doctrine of justification by faith. In fact, it could be argued that this interpretation of the Bible represented a reversion to a biblical moralism that was characteristic of much medieval spirituality and led away from—rather than toward—Luther's fundamental doctrine of justification by faith.

The diversity of reforming visions becomes even clearer when we turn to consider an alternative vision of the reform of the church that was gathering pace in eastern Switzerland around the same time.

THE SWISS ALTERNATIVE: ZWINGLI AND THE CITY OF ZURICH

During the 1520s, reforming movements sprang up in many territories and cities in western Europe.[12] Our story here concerns a priest who celebrated his thirty-fifth birthday on New Year's Day 1519 by being installed as the "people's priest" at the Great Minster in the Swiss city of Zurich. Huldrych Zwingli (1484–1531) would never achieve Luther's fame and is today seen as ranking behind Luther and Calvin, in terms of both his ideas and his activities. Yet he played a vitally important part in initiating and directing the beginning of the Reformation in Switzerland—a reformation that bore little relation to Luther's.[13]

At that time, Switzerland was much smaller than it is at present. The name "Switzerland" is based on one of the three original cantons—

Schwyz, Uri, and Unterwalden—which signed a treaty of mutual defense against the Austrians in 1291. This confederation, known as the Helvetic Confederation, was gradually enlarged. In 1332 Lucerne joined the confederation, followed by Zurich (1351), Glarus and Zug (1352), and Berne (1353). When the confederation gained a historic victory over Austria at the Battle of Näfels (1388), other cantons were subsequently led to join. In 1481 the cantons of Solothurn and Fribourg joined the confederation, bringing the total membership to ten. In 1501 Basel and Schaffhausen joined, followed by Appenzell in 1513.

Zwingli was born on New Year's Day 1484 in the Toggenburg Valley in the canton of St. Gallen, in the eastern part of modern-day Switzerland. Strictly speaking, St. Gallen was not part of the Swiss confederation at that time. However, in a 1451 treaty, St. Gallen had allied itself to some of the Swiss cantons, and Zwingli appears to have always regarded himself as Swiss. He was educated at the University of Vienna at a time when the old ideas of scholasticism were being displaced by those of humanism. By the time Zwingli returned to Switzerland, he was familiar with the "new learning" and anxious to use it in reforming the church. He became linked with humanist groups in eastern Switzerland that were working for the renewal of the church, the advance of pacifism, and the development of a Swiss "republic of letters." Like many at the time, Zwingli was captivated by the humanist vision of *Christianismus renascens*—a Christianity that would be born all over again, restored to the simplicity and vitality of the apostolic age.

Zwingli's vision of reform began to develop during his time as a "people's priest" at the Benedictine monastery of Einsiedeln during the mid-1510s. In common with others beginning to think about reform around this time, Zwingli saw the Bible—or more specifically, the New Testament—as central to his program of renewal. Yet Zwingli, like so many reformers in eastern Switzerland, did not see any need for fundamental changes in what the church believed. His vision of reform was primarily institutional and moral: the church needed to return to the simple ways of the New Testament and behave according to the moral teachings of Christ. The New Testament was to be valued because of its clear teaching about Christian discipleship and ethics. Reformation was about the church and its members reshaping their lives in the light of that teaching.

On the day after his arrival at Zurich in 1519, Zwingli announced his intention of beginning a new course of sermons. He proposed to deliver a continuous course of sermons on the gospel according to Matthew. Instead of relying on commentaries, he would base his sermons directly on the scriptural text. For Zwingli, scripture was a living and liberating text by means of which God spoke to his people and enabled them to break free from bondage to false ideas and practices. In particular, he held that Christ's Sermon on the Mount set out a vision for the moral life that was binding on all Christians.

The contrast with Luther here is striking. Like the fourteenth-century English reformer John Wycliffe, Zwingli saw the Bible as setting out divine commandments for human behavior.[14] These were to be contrasted with the human commands of the papacy or state, which did not have the same divine warrant. The proper task of Christian education was to ensure that people were made aware of these divine demands and responded appropriately. For Luther, however, the Bible was primarily about the promises of God—things that God offered to do for humanity, rather than things that God expected humanity to do. (Interestingly, it seems that many misunderstood him on this point and reverted to ideas similar to those of Wycliffe.) Zwingli's reforming program makes no reference to Luther's core doctrine of "justification by faith alone." Indeed, many scholars see an explicit tension between Zwingli's moralist understanding of reformation and Luther's emphasis on the grace of God.

One of the most visible and striking divergences between the two major emerging styles of Protestantism is to be found in their differing attitudes to imagery. Where Luther was prepared to tolerate religious images in churches, Zwingli held that the Old Testament ban on images was binding on all Christians. In June 1524, the city of Zurich ruled that all religious imagery was to be removed from churches.[15] Iconoclastic riots spread throughout the region—Berne (1528), Basel (1529), Strasbourg (1530), and Geneva (1535)—marking the spreading of the Reformation by popular acts of violence and desecration.[16]

It is important to note that, throughout the entire formative period of his development as a reformer, Zwingli appears never to have heard of Martin Luther, let alone to have been influenced by him. Zwingli's distinctive approach to the reformation of the church reflected currents of thought characteristic of eastern Switzerland at that time. In common with Luther and Erasmus, Zwingli held that the church needed to realign itself with the Bible. Yet Zwingli's understanding of how that process should happen, and what form it would take, bore little relation to Luther's and was much closer to Erasmus's vision for institutional and moral reform based on an educational program grounded in the classics and the New Testament.[17]

In his 1522 treatise *The Clarity and Certainty of the Word of God,* Zwingli argued for the capacity of the Bible to interpret itself lucidly and unambivalently in all matters of importance. Like Erasmus, he insisted that the best possible aids to the interpretation of the Bible—such as a knowledge of the Hebrew and Greek languages and an understanding of the various figures of speech employed in scripture—needed to be brought to the task of establishing the natural sense of scripture.[18] Like Luther, he held that the church had no authority other than the Bible.

Despite their shared emphasis on the centrality of the Bible, Luther and Zwingli used quite different techniques of biblical interpretation. Though both appealed to the same source as authoritative, the outcomes of their engagement with the biblical text were very different—and led to very different visions of reform. Illustrating this tension is one of the most significant debates between rival camps of the Reformation during the 1520s—the controversy between Luther and Zwingli over the nature of the "real presence."[19]

In what sense, if any, is Christ really present in the bread and wine of the mass? As we noted earlier, Luther was strongly critical of the medieval doctrine of "transubstantiation," believing that it was excessively dependent on the Aristotelian philosophical notions of "substance" and "accidents." Yet his own view was that Christ is indeed present at the mass. (Luther had no difficulty in using this traditional term.) In some way, the body and blood of Christ are conveyed in, through, or under the bread and the wine. For Luther, this was the only way of interpreting Christ's words at the Last Supper, as recorded in the gospels. When Christ offered bread to his disciples, he declared that "this is my body" (Matthew 26:26). Was not the obvious, correct way of making sense of this core text that the bread in question was Christ's body? What other way could there be of interpreting this text? If this was not so, Luther argued, then the Bible could not be interpreted reliably.

Zwingli responded by pointing out that this was by no means the only way of interpreting this text. The Bible was full of statements that might seem to suggest one thing but, on closer inspection, meant another. For Zwingli, the phrase "this is my body" did not mean that the bread was identical with the body of Christ; rather, it pointed to, or signified, that body. Christ's words were to be understood as meaning that the bread of the "Supper" or "Remembrance"—Zwingli did not wish to retain the traditional term "mass"—was a symbol of Christ's body, just as the wine symbolized his blood. Christ was being remembered in his absence, and his future return anticipated.

It will be obvious that these represent totally different readings of the same text. Luther's interpretation was much more traditional, Zwingli's more radical. Which was right? And which was Protestant? We see here the fundamental difficulty that the Reformation faced: the absence of any authoritative interpreter of scripture that could give rulings on contested matters of biblical interpretation. The question was not simply whether Luther or Zwingli was right: it was whether the emerging Protestant movement possessed the means to resolve such questions of biblical interpretation. If the Bible had ultimate authority, who had the right to interpret the Bible? This was no idle question, and it lay at the heart of Protestantism's complex relationship with its core text. For this question to be answered, an authoritative rule or principle had to be proposed that stood *above* scripture—the very idea of which was ultimately anathema to Protestantism. The three leading reformers—Luther, Zwingli, and Calvin—all recognized the importance of the question; significantly, each offered a different answer.[20] Our concern here is with the influential civil political hermeneutic advocated by Zwingli.

The solution offered by Zurich was elegant in its simplicity. In January 1523, the great debate usually known as the "First Zurich Disputation" got under way. Its outcome was of great importance for the development of the Reformation. First, it was decided that the church in that city would be bound by the "word of God" and would be obedient to scripture. But who was to interpret the Bible? The pope? An ecumenical council? Zwingli himself? No. The city council, seeing itself as a duly elected representative body of the Christians of Zurich, declared that it possessed the corporate right to settle the question of the interpretation of the Bible. The interpretation of the Bible would thus be a local matter.

This was an approach that endeared itself to city councils throughout the region as the Reformation began to spread. Religious authority was transferred from the pope or local bishop to elected representatives of the people. This transfer of authority was yet another example of the "democratization of faith" that was so characteristic of the reforms then taking place, and it gave a place of no small significance to the city council within the urban "sacral community."[21] Yet it raised a major question about the coherence of the movement. If the city councils of Zurich, Basel, Bern, and Constance—to note four major cities that sided with the Reformation in the 1520s—disagreed with each other over the interpretation of the Bible, how could such a dispute be settled? Was there not a danger that it would be the political status of a council, rather than the merits of its arguments, that would determine its power to interpret? In other words, would the authority of a council to interpret the Bible end up reflecting, not its theological ability or spiritual integrity, but its political power, as reflected in the size, wealth, and might of the city itself?

This was a serious question, but not one that Zwingli chose to address in any detail. He was preoccupied with far too many other projects, including taking part in debates in other Swiss cities that would determine whether they joined the Protestant cause. In Zurich, he faced many demands to institutionalize his vision of a reformed Christian church and the new challenges this brought. Holding that clergy were free to marry if they so chose, he married the widow Anna Reinhard secretly in 1522, then publicly in 1524. He was confronted with the growing threat from more radical reformers in Zurich and was personally involved in their suppression and execution, including the 1527 execution of Felix Manz. Manz, formerly one of Zwingli's closest allies, held that there was no biblical warrant for infant baptism. Refusing to recant his views, he was tied up and drowned in the River Limmat.

Yet this internal challenge to Zwingli's form of Protestantism within Zurich was soon displaced by a much more serious external threat. The five Catholic cantons of Switzerland, increasingly alarmed at the rise of Protestantism in the region, declared war on Zurich in October 1531. No Protestant canton offered Zurich any support, leaving it to face its opponents alone. Zwingli served as chaplain to the Zurich army, inexpertly led by Georg Göldli at the critical Battle of Kappel. A chaotic situation resulted in which the Protestants were ambushed while withdrawing, and many dead and wounded were left on the battlefield—including the mortally wounded Zwingli.[22]

The result was disastrous for Zurich, which not only was forced to accept unfavorable peace terms but lost its religious leader. Some regions of Switzerland that had converted to Protestantism reverted to Catholicism. Among these was the city of Bremgarten, where Heinrich Bullinger served as pastor. Forced to leave Bremgarten on account of his emerging Protestant sympathies, Bullinger settled in Zurich at the end of October 1531. Six weeks later, he was elected to take Zwingli's place. Yet Zurich would never recover its position of prominence in the Protestant reformation. Its power and influence seeped away as other centers of activity emerged. In what follows, we consider some of the early attempts to establish commonality between the various local reformations that emerged during this fascinating, formative period in the history of Protestantism.

THE INVENTION OF PROTESTANTISM: EARLY ATTEMPTS TO UNIFY THE REFORMATION

In the 1520s, city after city in Germany and Switzerland went over to the Reformation, often as a result of public disputations followed by a vote on the part of the city council. In Germany, more than fifty of the sixty-five imperial free cities responded positively to the Reformation, with only five choosing to ignore it altogether. In Switzerland, the Reformation originated in an urban context (Zurich) and spread through a process of public debate within confederate cities such as Berne and Basel and within other centers, such as Geneva and St. Gallen, that were linked to these cities by treaty obligations.

Yet it was realized that a purely political basis for the emerging religious movement was inadequate. Political alliances would shift, the balance of power would change, princes would be subject to pressure. If the new movement was to survive, it could not be grounded merely on the contingencies and provisionalities of politics. A deeper mooring was essential. And what firmer grounding could there be than in theology? Alongside the move to build political alliances between emerging centers of reform, the movement's visionaries realized that it was essential to ground it in the firm, unchangeable realities of the will of God as revealed in the Bible.

So why did so many of Europe's great cities switch their support from traditional Catholicism to the new religion? The answer is not entirely clear, although some of the factors involved are reasonably well understood. The historian Berndt Moeller has argued that the urban sense of community was disrupted in the fifteenth century through growing social tension in the cities and an increasing reliance upon external political bodies, such as the imperial government and the papal curia. By adopting the Lutheran Reformation, Moeller suggests, these cities were able to restore a sense of communal identity, including the critically important notion of a community whose inhabitants are bound together in a shared religious life. Moeller draws particular attention to the social implications of Luther's doctrine of the priesthood of all believers, which broke down certain traditional distinctions within urban society and encouraged a sense of communal unity.[23] Other explanations could easily be added to this, some specific to local situations. Whatever the ultimate explanation may be, there was a clear perception that accepting the Reformation would lead to greater autonomy within the cities, allowing them increased control over their own affairs.

The Reformation also led, perhaps without anyone realizing it, to diversification. The emerging Protestant movement simply included too many variables to remain tightly defined. The motives of city councils for accepting the Reformation varied considerably, as did their understandings of what they were actually doing and the local situations they sought to address. Furthermore, each city had its own resident reformer—in several cases, groups of reformers—and each possessed a somewhat different vision of the nature of the gospel and its implications for individual and corporate life. With the interaction of so many factors, it is not in the least surprising that each city developed its own distinctive reformation.[24]

Some case studies illustrate the diversity of these local reformations. The great imperial free city of Strasbourg became home to one of the most politically and intellectually significant reforming movements of the 1520s. Its leading proponents included the Hebrew scholar Wolfgang Capito; Matthew Zell, the first person to preach Protestant ideas in the city; the humanist scholar Caspar Hedio; and Martin Bucer, who rapidly established a Europe-wide reputation as a scholar, theologian, and skilled ecclesiastical diplomat.[25] While they gladly followed Luther's lead in returning to scripture, their vision of reform owed more to Erasmus's concern for institutional simplicity and moral renewal than to Luther's emphasis on justification by faith.[26] While aware of Luther's emphasis on this doctrine, Bucer modified it, subtly but significantly, in order to stress the importance of moral regeneration after acceptance by God.

Zwingli's reformation at Zurich attracted much attention in his native Switzerland. After public disputations, the great cities of Berne and Basel decided to adopt the Reformation, tending to follow Zwingli's distinctive theological positions, without realizing that they were far from characteristic of the emerging movement in Wittenberg. Although Johann Oecolampadius, the reformer of Basel, was generally supportive of Zwingli, there were differences between them.[27] After Zwingli's death in battle in 1531, the religious direction of the city passed to Heinrich Bullinger.

As other cities emerged as centers of reforming action and reflection, they not only contributed to the expansion and partial consolidation of the reforming movement but also demonstrated its diversity and fundamental lack of coherent identity. At times, it seemed as if there were as many reformations as there were cities. In some cities, councils issued their own "declarations of faith," as in the Zurich "introduction" of 1523 or the Berne "theses" of 1528. These were binding locally. But what of the wider picture? What authority did these local declarations have elsewhere?

The many reforming movements began to coalesce after 1530—not without some difficulties and divergences—around two rival visions of what it meant to be Protestant. A major factor was the disagreement between Luther and Zwingli over the nature of the real presence, which drove a wedge between the German and Swiss reformations. An attempt to mediate between their rival views took place at the Colloquy of Marburg (1529), convened by Philip of Hesse and attended by such Protestant luminaries as Bucer, Luther, Philip Melanchthon, Oecolampadius, and Zwingli.

By this time, the Reformation was in trouble. It had enjoyed a period of relative tranquillity, during which it had been able to expand significantly. Yet the reason for this perhaps surprising lack of opposition was primarily that Charles V had been distracted by other, more pressing concerns from settling affairs with the Protestants. He had other crises on his hands, most notably long-standing disputes with Francis I of France, on the one hand, and Pope Clement VII, on the other. Yet suddenly, even dramatically, in 1529 these disputes were resolved within weeks of each other. Charles V was now free to give the rising threat of Protestantism his undivided attention. Suddenly, the two wings of the Reformation faced a powerful political and military threat—a threat for which they were largely unprepared.

The most obvious course of action was to settle their differences—a course of action urged by Bucer, who suggested that differences should be tolerated among Protestants, provided they agreed to recognize the Bible alone as the normative source of faith. Yet Luther and Zwingli failed to resolve their disagreements. Philip of Hesse's hope of a united evangelical front against the newly regrouped Catholic forces was dashed, and the political credibility of the Reformation seriously compromised. While some partial alignments of vision and policy were achieved, in practice these were insufficient to hold the movement together.

In early 1530, Charles V began to reassert his authority over the German Reformation. Advised by the traditionalist Lorenzo Campeggio, and imbued with a sense of destiny following his coronation by the pope at Bologna earlier that year, Charles decided the time had come to defend Catholicism against those arguing for reform. He convened the Diet of Augsburg in 1530, determined to reestablish the unity of the church. To his irritation, he found himself confronted with three quite different proposals for restoring unity.

The first was the famous Lutheran "Augsburg Confession," which Melanchthon presented to Charles V on June 25. This surprisingly conservative document gave every indication of having been designed to cause as little offense as possible to the Catholic emperor's religious sensitivities. The document made little reference to Luther's central doctrine of justification by faith alone, presumably as it was deemed too contentious for traditional Catholics. Melanchthon clearly hoped that it might provide a basis for the reunification of Christendom in Germany rather than merely as a summary of the Wittenberg reforming faction's beliefs.[28] It was a brave but ultimately forlorn hope. When the emperor summarily refused to accept it as the former, it became the latter by default.

Precisely because it was intended as an instrument of mediation, the Augsburg Confession was seen by the southern German and Swiss reformers as being far too conservative. Many began to see Luther and Melanchthon as part of the problem rather than as its solution. Zwingli presented an alternative confession to the emperor on July 8, distancing himself significantly from Melanchthon's modest proposals. Finally, on July 11, four imperial southern German cities—Strasbourg, Lindau, Memmingen, and Constance—that had declined to accept Luther's views on the "real presence" as set out in the Augsburg Confession presented a third alternative. The "Tetrapolitan Confession," written by Bucer, set out a more reformed position, particularly in relation to sacramental theology.

Charles V's refusal to take any of these confessions as the basis for reunification of the German church did more than place clear blue water between Catholics and Protestants: it also exposed the emerging differences among the latter. It was clear that at least two separate groups were crystallizing their territorial and theological boundaries. Within a decade, the Reformation had split into two. The wounds would never heal; indeed, within decades they would become even worse, when Lutherans discovered to their horror that their rivals were gaining a foothold in the German territories.

Yet the tensions within the Reformation were actually rather worse than this brief analysis suggests. The tensions that Luther experienced at Wittenberg with his more radical colleagues Karlstadt and Müntzer were being replicated throughout the reforming movement. An emerging "third way" was threatening to destabilize western European society. The name of the movement? Anabaptism.

THE RADICAL ALTERNATIVE:
THE RISE OF ANABAPTISM

The message of returning to the simplicities of the New Testament excited both intellectuals and ordinary Christians. To academics, it offered a new way of doing theology, displacing the tedium of scholasticism. It was as if a window had been opened in a smoke-filled room and a refreshing breeze had rushed in to displace and dispel the accumulated stale air. To the laity, the message offered a vision of reform, deflecting the church from its political ambitions and returning it to the simpler, more attractive institution of the New Testament. For most, this did not require any doctrinal alterations whatsoever; some, however, argued that only a reform of the church's ideas could sustain a reform of its morals.

Yet laity and academia alike wondered how far this reform should be pressed. Did a return to the world of the New Testament involve a gentle correction of errors and excesses—or was a more radical and thoroughgoing revolution required? Did existing ideas and institutions need to be totally demolished before reconstruction was possible? Although Luther's reforming program is often referred to as "radical" and "revolutionary," these are relative, not absolute, terms. We have already noted how Luther's proposals were considered rather tame and conservative by writers such as Bucer and Zwingli. To others, they were positively reactionary. Luther had betrayed the movement that he initiated. It was time for others to take control.

The central issue was the interpretation of the Bible. The debate can best be understood by considering two, quite different understandings of the all-important word *biblical*—the watchword of the reforming movements of the age.

a. Biblical means whatever is explicitly and unequivocally stated in the Bible.

b. Biblical means whatever is explicitly stated in the Bible or is consistent with this.

Which of these definitions was correct? There was no self-evidently correct answer.

Despite their severe differences on many matters, Luther and Zwingli adopted the second of these two understandings. The thought and life of the church was to be grounded in scripture, but interpreted in the dialogue with leading, reliable biblical interpreters of the past. It is important to note that Luther argued for the supremacy of Augustine as an ancient interpreter of the Bible, and Zwingli for that of Origen; these two writers had quite different, and at times diametrically opposed, theologies. Yet both Luther and Zwingli argued for continuity with the past—for retaining what was good in the medieval church and reforming what was not. (They disagreed, of course, on what these actually were.)

At both Wittenberg and Zurich, more radical reformers emerged, arguing that this represented a compromise.[29] The Bible was being shackled by the tradition of the church. What was needed was a revolution, not a reformation. Conrad Grebel at Zurich, Simon Stumpf at Hongg, and Wilhelm Reublin at Wittikon set out a program of reform embodying the first definition of *biblical*. Zwingli, they argued, had compromised reform. All that he had done was to replace the authority of the pope with that of the city council of Zurich. Zwingli was a puppet, little more than the mouthpiece of the civil authorities, in whose hands real authority now lay. The Reformation had been traduced.

So what radical program did these revolutionaries propose? Perhaps the best way of appreciating the challenge that the movement brought is to consider the question of whether infants should be baptized. This practice was common in the early church, and both Luther and Zwingli regarded it as perfectly acceptable. At no point did they make any attempt to reform what they thought of as an authentic Christian practice.

The radicals saw things very differently. At no point in the New Testament was the practice mentioned, let alone justified. (Luther and others argued that infant baptism was consistent with what was said in the New Testament, but they had to concede the absence of explicit mention of the practice, still less of any command to baptize infants.) The practice therefore had to be reformed in the light of the Bible. Only adult baptism was to be recognized. The precondition for baptism was explicit belief, something that could not be found in infants. Those who had been baptized as infants must therefore be baptized again. It was this conclusion that gave the movement the name "Anabaptism" (from the Greek term meaning "re-baptism").[30]

The radical demands went far beyond rebaptism, however, and often seemed to amount to a near-total disengagement with the present order. Many radicals saw the conversion of the Roman emperor Constantine as a watershed in the history of the church that had compromised its integrity through an accommodation with imperial power. It was imperative that this false turn—which Luther and Zwingli both regarded as legitimate—should be corrected.[31] Christians should not have to swear oaths to the secular authority or compromise themselves in any way through contamination with the fallen world of power and force. (The term "magisterial Reformation" is often used to refer to the reforming programs of Luther, Bucer, and Zwingli on account of the positive role they assigned to the magistracy and other instruments of state.) The use of violence and the bearing of weapons were forbidden. Christians should not take part in wars. The death penalty was contrary to Christian practice and should be abolished. Private property was un-Christian: did not the New Testament speak of the first Christians holding all things in common?

This radical reading of the Bible placed further strain on the already tenuous unity of the reforming movements. Most radical writers rejected Luther's doctrine of justification by faith alone, seeing it as incompatible with the New Testament's emphasis on moral regeneration.[32] More significantly, radicals began to call into question traditional doctrines that Luther and Zwingli had regarded as entirely orthodox and not in need of revision. Many radicals argued that the doctrine of the Trinity was not explicitly stated in the Bible. Far from being an authentic Christian doctrine, it reflected the later speculations and elaborations of misguided theologians. Anti-trinitarianism, already evident in the late 1520s, became a hallmark of the movement in the 1550s, causing widespread concern in both Protestant and Catholic circles.[33]

Again, the magisterial Reformation regarded traditional understandings of the identity of Jesus Christ (an area of theology known as "Christology") as not requiring further review. The "Chalcedonian Definition" that Christ was truly human and truly divine was perfectly acceptable, representing a legitimate and proper interpretation of the Bible. The radicals disagreed. This area of theology, like every other, had to be reassessed and reviewed. A variety of alternative Christologies emerged within the Radical Reformation, with writers such as Balthasar Hübmaier, Pilgram Marpeck, and Dirk Philips adopting a range of positions, none of which were entirely consistent with the traditional Christian beliefs endorsed by Luther.[34] The new radical way of interpreting the Bible, in the view of mainline reformers such as Luther, led directly to heresy. But who, we must ask, was in a position to set limits to how the Bible was interpreted? Who had the right to say that this more radical approach was *wrong?*

Anabaptists argued that they were consistent, where Luther and Zwingli were not. The latter, they argued, had arbitrarily excluded certain areas of Christian life and thought from the scope of their review and reassessment; Anabaptists were merely being consistent in carrying this program through comprehensively and coherently.[35] Lutheran terms of denigration for Anabaptists—such as the "fanatics"—seemed to reflect an assumption that there was an obvious end-point for the process of Reformation, beyond which transgression was not permitted.[36] Anabaptists held that there were no such limits—an idea that Luther and other magisterial reformers held to be dangerous and subversive. If followed through, such a position might lead to a radical overturning of the existing social and ecclesiastical order—resulting in a revolution, not a reformation.

An element of apocalyptic enthusiasm, even frenzy, began to permeate sections of the movement. Many Anabaptists read the Book of Revelation with great anticipation, seeing in it prophecies of the overthrow of the established order and the establishment of a just society.[37] Many Marxist historians of the 1970s and 1980s saw in Anabaptism the forerunners of socialism. What Marx believed would happen by a human-instigated revolution, some Anabaptists believed would take place by a divine overthrow of the corrupt world order.

It was little cause for surprise that princes and city councils regarded Anabaptism with a mixture of open contempt and hidden fear. Surely nobody would take this kind of thing seriously? But what would happen if they did and it became a mass movement capable of overturning the establishment? In Haarlem, a baker named Jan Matthys announced that he was none other than Enoch, the second witness of the Book of Revelation. The end times were coming! Such dangerous ideas were perfectly capable of initiating and sustaining a revolution.

These were particularly serious concerns in the city of Strasbourg, which was home to a particularly large community of Anabaptists. In particular, they were a cause of considerable anxiety to Martin Bucer, who realized that his own moderate vision of Protestantism could easily be radicalized by such activists. Might these radicals hijack his own more cautious reforms? In 1530 a furrier named Melchior Hoffman began to preach a millennial doctrine that predicted the imminent return of Christ and the overthrow of the city authorities. God had chosen Strasbourg as the New Jerusalem. Alarm bells began to ring throughout the city.

The event that galvanized nervous monarchs and city authorities throughout Europe took place in 1534. Jan Matthys declared that it was no longer Strasbourg that would be the site of the New Jerusalem. It was Münster.[38] Excited crowds of his supporters flocked to this unsuspecting German city and took it over. Jan van Leyden took to the streets to declare that the end was nigh, creating an atmosphere of near-hysteria. Lutherans and Catholics alike panicked and rushed to leave the city, to be replaced almost as quickly by hordes of Anabaptists eager to enter the New Jerusalem. Matthys decreed that everyone remaining in the city would have to be rebaptized or face execution. All property was to be distributed equally among the population.[39]

The seizure sent shock waves throughout the region and proved a serious setback to the cause of reform. Protestantism, it was argued, simply led to destabilization. If anyone doubted that Protestantism was a menace to social stability, the events at Münster would persuade them of its intrinsic dangers. The bishop of Münster, anxiously watched by prelates and princes throughout western Europe, laid siege to the city. It was not until the spring of 1535 that the Anabaptist seizure of Münster was ended by force, having degenerated from idealism to farce. Jan van Leyden announced that a new world order had been revealed to him and promptly began to implement it. Money was abolished; polygamy was legalized; marriage was made compulsory for women. Those who dissented faced execution. Many breathed a sigh of relief when the occupation was ended and something approaching normality was restored. It had been a dangerous moment.

Like its mainstream counterparts, the radical movement was heterogeneous and diverse, its ideas and fortunes shaped by local figures, concerns, and resources. Quite distinct forms of Anabaptism developed in Switzerland, southern Germany, and the Low Countries.[40] Yet there is no doubt that it must be considered an integral part of the reforming movements then sweeping across the cities and territories of western Europe. Anabaptists may have occupied a range of positions that some Protestants considered "extreme"; they were, however, unquestionably Protestant. The historian can only conclude that Protestantism designated a spectrum of possibilities so diverse that we must perhaps speak of "Protestantisms," each claiming to be grounded in the Bible, and the Bible alone, yet recognizing quite different authority figures, interpretative methods, and contextual constraints in their interpretation and application of that text.

By 1535 the political and theological implications of the absence of any centralized authority within Protestantism were being acutely felt. The events at Münster convinced many that the demands for reform had opened a Pandora's box of uncontrollable, unpredictable, and downright dangerous forces that threatened the stability of the region. The appeal to the Bible had once seemed so simple, so straightforward, so liberating. Now many were longing for stability and wondering whether someone might bring about the order they so earnestly desired in the midst of this theological chaos.

One possible answer began to emerge from the newly independent city of Geneva, which had declared itself a republic in 1535, not long after the end of the Münster affair. One of its reformers seemed to have answers to the questions many were pondering at this time. We now turn to the story of John Calvin and the new sense of direction and purpose he brought to many reforming movements at this time.

4

The Shift in Power

Calvin and Geneva

By the mid-1530s, two major reforming movements had become established in western Europe. The first, increasingly referred to as "Lutheranism," was geographically restricted to certain German territories and was primarily influenced by the catechisms of Martin Luther and the theological writings of Philip Melanchthon. The second, located in some of the southern German and Swiss cities and later to become known as the "Reformed" faction, adopted a program of reform that was in many ways more radical than Luther's. No single individual had anything like the personal influence of Luther over this second movement. Writers such as Huldrych Zwingli, Heinrich Bullinger (Zwingli's successor at Zurich after his death in battle in 1531), and Martin Bucer were seen as influential, rather than authoritative, within the movement. Alongside these, various other movements, more radical and often quite small, jostled for influence and power.

Lutheranism faced a series of crises in the 1540s, not least of which was Luther's death in 1546. His influence over the emergence and development of the Reformation in Germany had been immense. His death not only deprived the movement of its larger-than-life leader but threw open the question of the succession. On whom would Luther's mantle descend? How could the movement survive without clear and

Engraving of John Calvin in his study. Anonymous.

decisive leadership when it was far from clear who its new leaders would be? Yet this severe blow to Lutheranism was soon accompanied by another that placed it in a very serious dilemma.

In 1530 the Lutheran princes had presented their case for reform to Charles V at Augsburg. Determined to restore unity to his empire, Charles rejected the Augsburg Confession as a basis of faith and gave the princes until April 1531 to revert to Catholicism. The Lutheran princes responded by meeting at the Saxon town of Schmalkalden in December 1530 and creating a solemn Protestant League to oppose Charles V if he persisted with his threats.[1] As support for this Protestant League grew, Charles realized that he faced internal threats to his authority at a time when the Turkish threat to the east was becoming increasingly serious. He offered a compromise: the Lutheran princes were permitted to exercise their religion freely within their territories until the matter could be properly resolved. While some later German historians viewed this league as the potential basis of a "Protestant German empire," it was seen at the time simply as a temporary means of fending off imperial pressure.

Until 1543, it succeeded admirably. Under the leadership of Philip of Hesse and John Frederick, Elector of Saxony, Lutheranism was able to develop, virtually unchecked, within the territories of the sympathetic princes. By then, however, tensions within the league had emerged. Philip of Hesse's bigamous marriage had created a scandal. Bucer, Luther, and Melanchthon were severely criticized for sanctioning it and bringing the Reformation into disrepute. As Charles V began to regain his military strength, he entered into private agreements with local princes throughout 1546, and Philip began to realize that Lutheranism was in serious danger. He urged the formation of an alliance with Swiss Protestants before it was too late. Yet nothing came of any such plans. The Schmalkalden War broke out, pitting Charles V against a reduced group of Protestant territories. Unusually, this war proved decisive.[2] In June 1547, both Philip and John Frederick were captured and imprisoned in southern Germany. Within a year, Lutheranism had lost not merely its religious founder and leader but also its two most significant political supporters. It was a period of immense demoralization for the movement.

An iconic moment in this military defeat of Lutheranism deserves special mention. In 1547 the city of Wittenberg gave in to the inevitable and surrendered to imperial forces. Charles V entered the city personally on May 27 and rode to the Castle Church, where he stood for some moments by Luther's grave. The last time he had encountered Luther was at the Diet of Worms. What thoughts went through his mind? Might he have reflected on how he might have stopped this movement in its tracks by more aggressive action earlier? We shall never know.[3]

Charles V moved quickly to impose religious conformity on the German Lutheran territories. As the Council of Trent had only begun to respond to the challenges of the Reformation, Charles demanded interim measures that would secure religious peace until Trent's final report was published. The Augsburg Interim of 1548 allowed Lutherans to retain two of their most distinctive practices: clerical marriage and communion in both kinds.[4] In other respects, the document took a robust traditional Catholic approach to church practice. The traditional Catholic mass was to be restored, with all its ceremonial. It was as if the clock had been turned back by thirty years.

Some Lutheran princes refused to accept the Augsburg Interim and adopted instead what came to be known as the "Leipzig Interim," which was more Protestant in outlook.[5] In responding to these challenges, Melanchthon emphasized *adiaphora* ("matters of indifference"), believing that it was possible to tolerate disagreement over certain matters. Yet Melanchthon's attempt to develop a pragmatic approach, intended to safeguard as much of the Lutheran heritage as possible under the new circumstances, was regarded by many as tantamount to compromise and betrayal. His place as Luther's leading interpreter was openly challenged by those who saw him as naively accommodating Luther's vision to political expediency. Tensions grew within the movement, with the supporters of Melanchthon facing fierce opposition from a "Gnesio-Lutheran" faction that fought to retain the untainted, uncompromised doctrines of their movement's much-revered founder.

In the end, the crisis over the interims passed. The Protestants managed to regroup militarily, forcing Charles V to accept the Religious Peace of Augsburg (1555), which settled the religious shape of Germany.[6] Each territory would follow the religion of its ruler, which he could impose on his subjects. Those of his subjects who disagreed with his religious allegiance were to be free to migrate to other territories. In the imperial cities, both Catholicism and Lutheranism were to be permitted. Significantly, only these two religious options were envisaged. Anabaptism and the forms of Protestantism found in southern Germany and Switzerland were pointedly and deliberately omitted from consideration. This principle was encapsulated in the famous slogan *cuius regio, eius religio* (best interpreted as "whoever rules the region decides its religion"). Humiliated, Charles abdicated the following year. He had failed in his mission to restore Catholicism to Germany.

The Religious Peace of Augsburg gave Lutheranism a new sense of identity, partly rooted in its deep appeal to German nationalism. Yet its German moorings proved to be a major disincentive to expansion elsewhere in Europe. Lutheranism became landlocked, the prisoner of its own nationalist success. Apart from modest expansion into the Nordic countries, the movement's future expansion would in future depend primarily on emigration, chiefly to North America.[7]

But what of the other Protestant movement? Would it suffer the same fate? After all, Zwingli and other Swiss Protestant reformers were strongly committed to a nationalist agenda, seeing the rebirth of what they regarded as authentic Christianity to be linked with the cultural and political renewal of their nation.[8] Would this second form of Protestantism end up landlocked in the German-speaking cities and cantons of Switzerland, becoming, like Lutheranism, a territorial religion? Or could it develop a sense of identity, a core vision, that would allow it to transcend national boundaries and become a truly international movement? In the 1520s and early 1530s, it seemed to many that the Swiss reform movement was simply a regional religious movement whose history condemned it to a territorial future. Yet by 1560 it had become increasingly clear that this second form of Protestantism was capable of crossing political and social frontiers with ease. Something had happened to transform the movement, liberating it from such territorial limitations. But what?

The answer lay in an individual and a city, both of which played a critical role in the consolidation of Protestantism at this time—John Calvin and the city of Geneva.

THE ORIGINS OF THE REFORMATION
AT GENEVA

During the 1520s, evangelical reforming movements achieved considerable success in the cities of Switzerland. Although the movement began in Zurich, by the late 1520s it had won over some of the leading cities of the area, including Basel and Berne. Yet these were all German-speaking cities. As the decade came to an end, interest began to develop in converting some of the French-speaking regions and cities to the west of Switzerland to the reforming cause—such as the Pays de Vaud and the cities of Neuchâtel, Lausanne, and Geneva. Many of these were already linked to Swiss cities by political and commercial treaties. As those cities turned Protestant, they began to bring subtle pressure to bear on their trading partners to follow suit.[9]

Yet the evangelical emphasis on preaching in the vernacular posed a serious problem. Most of the leading reformers of the region spoke German. Where might French-speaking evangelicals be found? Some turned to Guillaume Farel, a Frenchman who had studied at Paris and been involved in reforming activities in the French diocese of Meaux.[10] Oecolampadius had welcomed him to Basel in 1524—a decision he was to regret bitterly. Farel was an abrasive, aggressive, outspoken debater who managed to alienate rather than persuade his opponents. No less a person than Erasmus himself demanded that Farel be expelled from Basel on account of the embarrassment he was causing to the great city's reputation. Eventually, Farel managed to find some support at Berne, where he was able to establish a base for his reforming activities in the region.

His greatest triumph was in 1532, when his preaching in Geneva produced positive results, eventually culminating in a great public disputation in 1535.[11] Having only won its freedom from the neighboring Duchy of Savoy that same year, Geneva was determined to mold its own future rather than be dominated by any of its neighbors. In August 1535, the city council voted that the Republic of Geneva would accept the principles of the Protestant Reformation and abolish the mass. Along with Pierre Viret, Farel found himself in charge of the direction of the religious reordering of the city.[12] It was a task for which he was not suited. He needed help. But who was there to help him?

John Calvin was born in the French cathedral city of Noyon and had attended the University of Paris before going on to study civil law at Orléans.[13] During his time at Paris, he had encountered at least some of the reforming ideas of Martin Luther, which were widely discussed in academic circles. When he returned to the city after graduating from Orléans, he became associated with reforming groups. Tantalizingly, we know very little about this period of Calvin's life; his personal papers were confiscated when the police raided his lodgings in 1533. The rector of the University of Paris, Nicholas Cop, had preached a reforming sermon that was seen as highly inflammatory by the university and city authorities (however moderate it looks to its modern readers). A copy of this sermon exists in Calvin's handwriting. Was he, many wondered, its real author?

Calvin fled before he could be arrested, eventually making his way to the Swiss city of Basel, now a bastion of Protestantism, where he sought refuge. The situation in France had deteriorated. The cause of reform had been severely injured by the "affair of the placards": anti-Catholic posters entitled "True Articles on the Horrible, Great, and Insufferable Abuses of the Papal Mass" were displayed in public places throughout Paris in October 1534. The author of the placards was unknown; many, however, believed that Guillaume Farel was involved.[14] If so, it was a political misjudgment that was typical of Farel. Francis I, once sympathetic to the cause of French reformers, was alienated overnight and became an implacable opponent of the Reformation. The Anabaptist takeover of Münster also made Francis I regard anyone interested in reform of the church as potentially seditious.

Calvin was appalled at this development. Might something be done to restore the balance? Having time on his hands while in exile in Basle, he penned a little book that set out the basic elements of the Reformed view of the Christian faith that he personally espoused. In addition to setting out his views on the Creed and the Lord's Prayer, Calvin wrote a preface, addressed to Francis I, pleading for toleration of this moderate evangelical form of Christianity and distinguishing it from the excesses and violence of Anabaptism. The *Institutes of the Christian Religion,* first published in May 1536, would eventually become one of the most influential publications of the sixteenth century—not on account of its gracious preface, but because of its lucid, systematic, and persuasive account of the basic elements of Reformed Christianity.[15] It is generally agreed that Calvin drew on both of Luther's catechisms of 1529 and his treatises on *The Freedom of the Christian* and *The Babylonian Captivity* in writing this book.

Having returned to Noyon to settle some family affairs, Calvin proceeded to Strasbourg, breaking his journey along the way. In the summer of 1536, he paused at Geneva, intending to stay only a night before moving on. Farel recognized Calvin and demanded that he stay in the city and help consolidate the reforms he had introduced. Calvin met Farel's needs in three ways: he spoke and wrote fluent French; he had just published an excellent primer in Christian doctrine, which pointed to his ability as an educationalist; and he was a graduate in civil law, able to help Geneva draft its civil ordinances. Reluctantly, Calvin agreed to stay in Geneva, where he assumed the office of "reader" (*lector*) of Holy Scripture.[16] He was never "ordained" in any sense of the term.

His rise to prominence began in September 1536. The city of Lausanne was debating whether to follow Geneva and accept the principles of the Reformation. Farel and Viret traveled to Lausanne, bringing Calvin with them, to take part in the public disputation that was now an invariable part of the decision-making process.[17] They were pitted against the local clergy, who were not noted for their academic distinction. The debate was not going well for Farel and Viret, who found themselves severely challenged by some of the questions they were forced to address.

One of those questions went to the heart of the reforming program at Geneva and raised the specter of Anabaptism. Were not Viret and Farel allowing people to interpret the Bible as they pleased, without taking the views of early church writers seriously? It was a moment of tension; the debate was in the balance. The credibility of the reformation at Geneva would be permanently damaged if any association was made with the radical cause and the social instability it was widely believed to engender. Calvin rose to answer.

Apparently quoting early Christian writers from memory, Calvin insisted that he and his colleagues took them with the greatest of seriousness and saw them as authorities of significance. The audience was dazzled by the brilliance of Calvin's presentation: he quoted the third-century writer Cyprian of Carthage to the letter ("in the second book of his letters, the third letter") and the fourth-century theologian and preacher John Chrysostom even more precisely ("the twenty-first homily, about halfway through"). By the time Calvin sat down, everyone was clear on two things: the Genevan Reformation was about the renewal and continuity of the church, and a new star had arisen in the Protestant firmament. Lausanne was won over to the Reformation, while Geneva was won over to Calvin.

Yet the relationship between Calvin and Geneva was far from relaxed. Farel was not the easiest of people to work with. More significantly, the city of Geneva, having just thrown off the political power of the Duchy of Savoy and the religious power of the papacy, was in no mood to submit itself to new strictures—especially compulsory attendance at somewhat lengthy sermons. Farel, never the most politically astute of operators, alienated so many people in Geneva that an anti-Farel faction was able to win control of the city early in 1538. In April, Farel and Calvin were expelled from the city. Calvin's correspondence suggests that he was devastated by this development. What should he do? Where could he go? In the end, he simply picked up where he had left off in the summer of 1536. He packed his bags and continued to Strasbourg, hoping to continue his work there.

Having arrived in Strasbourg two years later than he had intended, Calvin began to make up for lost time. In quick succession, he produced a series of major theological works. He produced a revised and expanded second edition of the *Institutes* (1539) and a French translation of the first edition (1541). As pastor to the French-speaking congregation in the city, Calvin was able to gain experience of the practical problems facing Reformed pastors. Through his friendship with Strasbourg's leading reformer, Martin Bucer, Calvin was able to develop his thinking on the relation between the city and the church, as well as the intellectual foundations of his reforming program. Calvin was clearly influenced significantly at points by the experienced reformer of Strasbourg, whom he playfully dubbed the "Bishop of Strasbourg." By 1541 he had gained considerable practical experience of church management and given much thought to the nature of a reformed church, especially in relation to issues of civil polity and discipline. The influence of Bucer is especially evident on these points. The reformed church and community that had existed only in Calvin's mind at Geneva in 1538 were now concrete realities. Abstract theory and pure speculation had given way to practical experience. Calvin was ready to begin all over again—but this time he was determined to get it right.

The invitation to return to Geneva finally came in the fall of 1541. In his absence, the religious and political situation had deteriorated. The city appealed to him to return and restore order and confidence. The Calvin who returned to Geneva was a wiser and more experienced young man, and far better equipped for the massive tasks awaiting him than he had been three years earlier.[18] There were tensions and controversies, not least relating to the Servetus affair, in which Calvin played a relatively minor role in securing the conviction and execution of Michael Servetus, a noted Anabaptist. Yet even this event must be seen in context: in this age, human life was routinely taken in order to maintain public order. Although Calvin would still find himself quarreling with the city authorities for more than a decade, it was from a position of strength. Geneva needed him. Finally, opposition to his program of reform died out. For the last decade of his life, he had virtually a free hand in the religious affairs of the city.

To understand Calvin's immense strategic importance to the shaping of Protestantism, we must turn to consider the book for which he is best known—the *Institutes of the Christian Religion*—and the religious system it embodies.

CALVIN'S *INSTITUTES* AND THE INTELLECTUAL MOLDING OF REFORMED CHRISTIANITY

The printed book was one of the most significant factors in molding intellectual opinion across sixteenth-century Europe. Books were easily transported, could cross national frontiers undetected, and found their way to private libraries, where they were eagerly, if secretly, devoured. The printed word was integral to the spreading of the ideas of the Reformation across the religious and political boundaries of Europe. Martin Luther never visited England, yet his ideas were brought there through books that were smuggled in through eastern ports such as Ipswich and pored over in nearby Cambridge University. Calvin's distinct and greatest contribution to the consolidation and diffusion of the

Reformed variant of Protestantism was a book that transformed the fortunes of that movement, liberating it from its earlier geographical and cultural imprisonment. The book? *Institutes of the Christian Religion.* The *Institutes* immediately became a best-seller and went through numerous, expanded editions in Latin (1539, 1543, 1550, 1553, 1559) and French (1541, 1545, 1551, 1560).

As we noted earlier, the first edition of the *Institutes* was published at Basel in 1536.[19] Modeled on Luther's influential catechisms of 1529, its six chapters included commentaries on the Ten Commandments, the Apostles' Creed, and some disputed matters of theology. Calvin revised the work substantially during his time in Strasbourg. It was the second edition that established the work as one of the most important Protestant works of the era. Completely restructured, the work's seventeen chapters set out a clear, accessible account of the basics of Christian belief, including the doctrine of God, the Trinity, the relation of the Old and New Testaments, penitence, justification by faith, the nature and relation of providence and predestination, human nature, and the nature of the Christian life. Calvin's distinctive emphases on the sovereignty of God and the authority of the Bible are evident from even a cursory reading of the work and would remain central as it underwent development in later editions.

What is so striking about this edition of the *Institutes* is not so much that it is a work of theology, but that it is a work of *pedagogy,* based on careful reflection on how to communicate and commend ideas.[20] The work offers a clear and immensely readable account of ideas that might otherwise be inaccessible and unintelligible. This concern for effective communication with a lay audience is especially evident in the French translation of the *Institutes* (1541), which shows Calvin adapting his ideas and language to his intended audience. Greek words and references to Aristotle are left out, and a healthy dose of French proverbs and idioms have been added. This translation is regularly hailed as a model of pedagogical clarity.

Yet it was not simply the many educational and presentational virtues of the book that propelled it to prominence. It addressed head-on the central weakness of Protestantism up to this point: the problem of the multiplicity of interpretations of the Bible. How can one speak of the Bible as having any authority when it is so clearly at the mercy of its interpreters? Calvin presents his *Institutes* as an authoritative guide to the correct interpretation of scripture. "My object in this work," he wrote, "is to so prepare and train students of sacred theology for the study of the word of God that they might have an easy access into it, and be able to proceed in it without hindrance."

Calvin established the credentials of his interpretations of the Bible, not by an assertion of his personal authority or wisdom, but by careful engagement with biblical passages, informed by a good knowledge of how these passages had been interpreted by well-regarded older Christian writers, such as Augustine of Hippo.[21] Readers of the work found themselves presented with reasoned, defended, and superbly presented accounts of central Christian teachings, firmly rooted in the Bible. Calvin presented and critiqued alternatives, reassuring readers of the plausibility of his own preferred interpretations in the face of these rivals. He did not merely defend his ideas; he showed how he derived them in the first place.

So what are the central ideas that Calvin developed? The most important is the fundamental assertion that a consistent and coherent theological system can be derived and defended on the basis of the Bible. Calvin's greatest legacy to Protestantism is arguably not any specific doctrines but rather his demonstration of how the Bible can serve as the foundation of a stable understanding of Christian beliefs and structures. In particular, Calvin held that the New Testament lays down a specific, defensible church order. Calvin's theology is similar to Luther's at many points, while taking a theologically subtle and diplomatic view on the issue that had caused such a furious row between Luther and Zwingli—the question of the real presence.

The growing importance of the *Institutes* led Calvin to revise and expand the work; the result was the definitive edition of 1559, consisting of eighty chapters arranged in four books. The final Latin edition was five times larger than the first. This massive expansion of the work reflects Calvin's practice of adding material relating to important controversies that had emerged since earlier editions. It must be said that some of these later additions are rather less elegant and more acerbic than earlier parts of the work and do not reflect Calvin at his best. Where Calvin earlier addressed ideas and assessed them on the basis of their intrinsic merits, he now shows a marked tendency to abuse and vilify his opponents. Calvin is believed to have suffered from irritable bowel syndrome, usually the result of stress, and this may have been the reason for this unhappy development. This final edition, however, shows a marked improvement over previous editions in that the work has been completely reorganized, allowing the inner coherence of Calvin's approach to be appreciated, while at the same time making it easier to find specific discussions.

The success of Calvin's 1559 *Institutes* gave rise to a series of publishing spin-offs designed to enhance still further the work's pedagogical excellence. In 1562 Augustin Marlorat published a set of indexes to the work that made it easy to find specific topics and questions. In 1576 Nicolas Colladon, one of Calvin's early biographers, produced an edition that included brief marginal summaries of the contents of significant passages, largely to relieve the burden on hard-worked theological students. Thomas Vautrollier, a Huguenot refugee who became one of London's more important religious publishers, printed two study guides to the *Institutes*. Edmund Bunny's *Compendium* (1576) offered simplified accounts of Calvin's main arguments. In 1583 Guillaume Delaune (a Huguenot refugee who Anglicized his name as William Lawne) produced a summary of the *Institutes* that included flowcharts and diagrams to allow readers to follow the intricate structure of the work.

Despite Protestantism's emphasis on the importance of the vernacular, Latin remained the preferred language for theological publications. Calvin's *Institutes* could be read by academics throughout Europe. However, Calvin's decision to translate the work into French showed a particular concern to communicate with the grass roots of faith. Calvin's growing appeal is evident from the appearance of vernacular translations of the *Institutes,* such as translations into Dutch (1560), English (1561), German (1572), and Spanish (1597). The impact of these translations was significant. Coherently expressed and carefully justified radical reforming doctrines had become available in a language that everyone could understand.

The response to the French translation of 1541 was noteworthy. Within a year, the Parisian authorities were insisting that all works containing heterodox doctrines, especially Calvin's *Institutes,* be surrendered to the authorities. In 1542 a martyr died at Rouen with a quotation from this work on his lips. The extent of the market for Calvin's writings can be gauged from the 1545 banning of 121 French-language titles, almost half of which were printed in Geneva. Parisian booksellers were outraged and protested vigorously: they would be ruined if they were prohibited from selling such books.

Calvin's growing appeal within many sections of Protestantism lay not in his institutional authority—he was, after all, nothing more than a pastor at Geneva, a small city by the standards of the time—but in the growing perception of his widening readership that he was serious, reliable, and trustworthy. It is generally agreed that one of the most important factors contributing to this growing reputation was the *Institutes*.

THE CONSOLIDATION AND EXPANSION OF CALVINISM IN EUROPE

Calvin's growing influence led to Geneva becoming the epicenter of the Reformed world during the second phase of Protestant development.[22] Zurich had once been that epicenter, on account of the major influence of the movement's original reformer, Zwingli. His successor, Heinrich Bullinger, did much to maintain Zurich's political and theological influence over the Reformed wing of Protestantism. However, political influence ebbed away from Zurich to the more powerful city of Berne in the early 1530s, before decisively relocating to Geneva in the 1550s.[23]

The term "Reformed" gradually became the preferred term for the form of Protestantism that emerged from this powerful crucible of ideas—partly to emphasize the movement's commitment to "reform itself according to the Word of God" and partly to distinguish itself from a rival vision of Protestantism now increasingly known as "Lutheranism." Although the term "Calvinism" is often used to refer to this type of Protestantism, on account of Calvin's influence on its emergence and consolidation, the term "Reformed" is preferred by some scholars and is widely encountered within the learned literature.

Calvin's influence and reputation led to Geneva becoming a magnet for wealthy and once-powerful religious refugees, often from France, who were determined to use their skills and wealth to advance his ideas. Printers such as Robert Estienne, lawyers such as Germain Colladon, and businessmen such as Laurent de Normandie made their home in Geneva. Calvin's position at Geneva was somewhat ambiguous in the early 1550s, owing to hostility between him and some senior members of the city council. Following the elections of 1555, in which Calvin's supporters gained a clear majority, the city of Geneva became increasingly committed to advancing the programs associated with its most famous religious leader. A significant period of expansion resulted.

One of the most obvious results of this commitment was the surge of Calvin's influence in France.[24] Calvin had been significant for French reforming movements since the appearance of the French translation of his *Institutes* in 1541. Initially, his impact was limited to his personal advice and support. Yet the burgeoning French evangelical communities needed more than this. The political and institutional support they craved was something that only the city of Geneva could offer. Prior to 1555, the city was decidedly cool about such ventures. It had no interest in becoming embroiled in Calvin's religious adventurism. Yet the city council elections of that year changed everything. In 1557 the council agreed to support Calvin's programs of reform abroad, including the infiltration of pastors into hostile parts of Europe, so long as such support could not be traced back to them.

That final clause proved to be a wise decision. In January 1561, a courier arrived in Geneva from the court of Charles IX, the new king of France, to report that the king had discovered that recent disturbances in France were linked to preachers sent from Geneva. He demanded that Geneva's agents be recalled and that no more be sent under any conditions. The council replied, truthfully, that it had sent no such individuals into France. (They saw no need to qualify this claim by adding that it was the Genevan Company of Pastors, a private ecclesiastical organization, that had done so.) A serious rupture between Geneva and France was thus averted through what was little more than a fiction.

Geneva now supplied Reformed pastors and preachers to cities and congregations throughout France. The entire operation was conducted in the greatest secrecy. Safe houses, complete with hiding places, were established in the deep valleys of Provence, set a day's journey apart. An underground network—similar to the one employed by the French Resistance during the Second World War—allowed pastors from Geneva to slip across the ill-defined frontier into France. By 1562 the number of fully established Reformed congregations in Calvin's native France had risen to 1,785.

By that time, Geneva's influence was being felt in other regions of Europe as well, including Germany. The Religious Peace of Augsburg (1555) had recognized only two religious options within the German territories—Lutheranism and Catholicism. Yet this compromise was shattered when the region of Germany known as the Palatinate, which included the city of Heidelberg, became a center of Reformed church life in the 1560s.[25] The area had originally converted to Lutheranism in the 1530s. However, Otto Henry, who held the office of elector from 1556 to 1559, died childless. As a result, the title passed to Frederick, Duke of Simmern. When a controversy broke out in 1559 over the real presence, Frederick decided to resolve it by holding a public dispute between representatives of Lutheranism and of the Reformed position. Frederick found himself persuaded by the latter, and in 1561 he set about enforcing the Reformed position in the region, assisted by theologians such as Caspar Olevianus and Zacharias Ursinus. Images of the saints, vestments, baptismal fonts, and organs were removed from the churches.

To consolidate the Reformed faith in this region, Frederick requested that a public confession of faith be devised that could be used to instruct the people in the new version of Protestantism. The result was the "Heidelberg Catechism" (1563), widely regarded as one of the finest documents of its kind.[26] Calvin's influence is everywhere apparent in this document, which did much to consolidate his influence beyond Geneva. Around this time, the term "Calvinism" was used by its opponents to refer to the Reformed type of Protestantism as a means of emphasizing that it originated from outside Germany. The term appears to have been introduced around 1552 by the Lutheran polemicist Joachim Westphal to refer to the theological, and particularly the sacramental, views of the Swiss reformers in general, and of John Calvin in particular.[27] Once introduced, the term rapidly passed into general use in the Lutheran church. In an increasingly nationalist region of Europe, it conveniently emphasized that this religious movement was foreign—unlike Lutheranism, which possessed an impeccable German pedigree.[28]

The introduction of the Reformed variant of Protestantism in a region that had hitherto been Lutheran caused major repercussions throughout Germany. Lutherans had regarded their religion as territorially sacrosanct. Now it seemed that another form of Protestantism was competing for influence within the region. The Lutherans moved to have the intruder suppressed. The crisis abated to some extent with the death of Frederick in 1576. His elder son, who succeeded him to the title, was a devout Lutheran and undid most of his father's changes. However, by then, Calvinism—as the movement was now known—had made headway.

In Scotland, Calvin's ideas were aggressively propagated by John Knox, who had fled to Geneva during the reign of Mary Tudor. Although Knox had been converted to the cause of the Reformation in Scotland around 1545, it was during his time as pastor to the English congregation in Geneva that he developed his distinctive approach to Protestantism, one that was clearly grounded in the approach then prevalent in Geneva. Knox is perhaps most famous for his 1558 work *First Blast of the Trumpet Against the Monstrous Regiment of Women,* which is by far his best-known work. (The word *regiment* here means "government.") In this work, he appeals to the Bible and the church fathers to argue that "to promote a Woman to beare rule, superioritie, dominion, or empire above any Realme, Nation or Citie is repugnant to nature, contumelie to God, a thing most contrarious to his reveled will and approved ordinance."[29]

On his return to Scotland in 1559, Knox was instrumental in the production of the *First Book of Discipline,* which can be seen as an attempt to adapt the Protestant paradigm established at Geneva to the specifics of the Scottish situation.[30] Yet Knox went further, transferring to the political sphere ideas that Calvin had limited to the sphere of church government. Taking the idea of representative government characteristic of Calvin's Reformed churches—that is, communities led by elected elders or "presbyters"—Knox applied this democratic principle at the political level—locally, regionally, and nationally.

This amounted to a virtual inversion of the traditional top-down, hierarchical model that had hitherto prevailed. Thus, the local councils ("presbyteries"), regional councils ("synods"), and national councils ("general assemblies") that presided over the faithful were made up of the people themselves, rather than representatives of the political rulers. This important transition reflected the broader impact of the ideas of the Republic of Geneva; some scholars suggest that those ideas underlay the English Civil War of the seventeenth century.

Calvin's form of Protestantism also became a significant movement in the Netherlands, at that time a Spanish province. Charles V regarded the Spanish Netherlands as an important ally in his struggle to contain Protestantism in Germany. However, Charles's abdication in 1555 began to create something of a power vacuum. The ending of the Habsburg-Valois conflict in 1559 allowed greater social mobility throughout the region, with the result that Reformed preachers were able to secure footholds in the region, most notably among the lower gentry who were angered at the state of the Catholic church. Yet at this stage, the religious views of most educated people in the region were closer to those of Erasmus of Rotterdam than those of Luther or Calvin.

Things changed when Philip II, the successor to Charles V, decided to take a strongly pro-Catholic stance in the region and enforce the decrees of the Council of Trent. His actions offended many, even the Catholic William of Orange. By 1566, Reformed Protestantism was gaining increasing support, partly as a protest against the perceived authoritarianism of Philip. Yet they needed more support. Critically, the Lutheran princes of Germany declined to become involved, having no interest in advancing the fortunes of the alternative form of Protestantism that was causing them such difficulties in their own part of the world following events in the Palatinate. Acting on Philip's instructions, the Duke of Alva marched nine thousand men from Milan to the Netherlands and set about enforcing Catholicism with a ruthlessness that outraged even its supporters. By the 1580s, much of the north of the country had adopted the Reformed faith.[31]

The fine details of this conflict are important, not least to the Dutch. For our purposes, two points about the emerging shape of Protestantism are thrown into sharp relief by this development. First, the German Lutherans declined to support the Dutch Calvinists precisely because they saw them as a potential religious threat rather than as allies with a shared faith. At this time, "Protestantism" was simply not understood as something that transcended the national and religious differences between German Lutherans and Dutch Calvinists, who were seen as two separate religious groups in competition (as events in the Palatinate indicated), and possibly even in conflict.

Second, there was significant international involvement in the Dutch revolt. French Protestant—or "Huguenot"—militias were of no small significance in the Dutch revolt against the Duke of Alva. The rise of these militias was the direct outcome of growing Calvinist influence in France. Whereas Lutheranism remained landlocked in Germany, seemingly pursuing a policy of splendid isolation, those supporting Calvin's alternative vision of Protestantism perceived an international dimension to the conflict. Calvinists shared a sense of loyalty that was not limited by political frontiers. It is an important indication of the growing capacity of Calvin's vision of the reformed Christian faith to transcend national boundaries.

The importance of this point is reinforced when it is appreciated that there was another nation that gave significant covert support to the Dutch rebellion. In 1585 England provided a force of four thousand men under the Duke of Leicester to support the rebels. England was now no friend of Spain; three years later, the island nation would face invasion from the Spanish Armada. Troops would be transported from the Spanish Netherlands to invade England and force the removal of English troops from the Netherlands. Without their support, the revolt would collapse.

CONFESSIONALIZATION: THE "SECOND REFORMATION"

At the beginning, it was all so simple. There were Lutherans, and there were Catholics, a simple binary opposition that shaped most aspects of religious life in Germany. The Council of Trent, the Catholic church's response to the Reformation, engaged seriously with Lutheran theory and practice at many points during the late 1540s; interestingly, scant attention was paid to the other form of Protestantism then consolidating itself in Europe. But once Calvin's vision of Christianity expanded beyond its original geographical limits in the 1560s and became a serious presence in Germany, the Netherlands, and France, things began to change.

The terms "confessionalization" and "the Second Reformation" are widely used to refer to the new religious situation in Germany in the 1560s and 1570s. Confessionalization is best seen as interlocking religious beliefs and practices with the objectives of the state. Central to this process was the notion of a territorial religion based on an authorized declaration of doctrines (usually referred to as a "Confession"), which would be binding on all subjects and enforced by an established church accountable to the prince or the magistrates.[32] This led to growing demand for a legally defined and enforceable system of beliefs and practices.

During this period, forms of Protestantism emerged that were largely defined by the social conditions of this part of Europe at this specific time.[33] The emergence of "state churches," defined by confessional documents, led to greater social cohesion and, in the opinion of many, the emergence of the early modern absolute state. In many ways, this can be seen as a redevelopment of the medieval idea of Christendom, now implemented at the regional, rather than continental, level. Each region was a Christendom governed by its own particular understanding of Christianity.

Many religious beliefs and practices that earlier had been considered "matters of indifference" (*adiaphora*) were now treated as criteria of demarcation between the emerging Protestant confessional churches. The need to distinguish the two confessional churches of the age—Lutheranism and Calvinism—led to a quest for differences; once identified, these differences were given an emphasis that reflected a need for social demarcation. The result was that differences in theology, liturgy, or church government became explicitly politicized as the early modern state sought to impose greater social control within its sphere of influence.

By the 1590s, there seemed little doubt as to which of the two major forms of Protestantism was gaining the ascendancy in western Europe. By 1591, Calvinism seemed to have made irreversible gains throughout Europe. The German Calvinist Abraham Scultetus (1566–1624) wrote in near-ecstatic terms of the sense of achievement, even of destiny (which Calvinist writers tended to speak of in terms of divine providence), which pervaded the movement at this time:

I cannot fail to recall the optimistic mood which I and many others felt when we considered the condition of the Reformed churches in 1591. In France there ruled the valiant King Henri IV, in England the mighty Queen Elizabeth, in Scotland the learned King James, in the Palatinate the bold hero John Casimir, in

Saxony the courageous and powerful Elector Christian I, in Hesse the clever and prudent Landgrave William, who were all inclined to the Reformed religion. In the Netherlands everything went as Prince Maurice of Orange wished, when he took Breda, Zutphen, Hulst and Nijmegen.... We imagined that *aureum seculum,* a golden age, had dawned.[34]

Yet the process also affected issues of doctrine. The rise of Calvin's vision of Protestantism forced Lutheranism to define and defend itself against two rivals instead of its traditional single opponent—Catholicism. Both Lutheran and Reformed communities now defined themselves by explicit and extensive doctrinal formulations. This can be seen as the inevitable outcome of a quest for self-definition on the part of two ecclesial bodies within the same geographical region, both claiming to be legitimate outcomes of the Reformation. At the social and political level, the communities were difficult to distinguish; doctrine therefore provided the most reliable means by which they might define themselves over and against one another. The notion of a core concept of "Protestantism," with two major branches, became difficult to sustain given the embittered hostility between the two factions and their open competition for territory and influence.

Perhaps more importantly, given the central role of the Bible for Protestantism, this new trend meant that the Bible tended to be read through the prism of "confessions"—statements of faith that frequently influenced, and sometimes determined, how certain passages of the Bible were to be interpreted. This shift was a contributing factor to the rise of "proof-texting": citing isolated, decontextualized verses of the Bible in support of often controversial confessional positions. Paradoxically, this development actually lessened the influence of the Bible within Protestantism, in that biblical statements were accommodated to existing doctrinal frameworks rather than being allowed to determine them, and even to challenge them.

As a result, pressure grew to avoid confusion by finding ways to distinguish clearly between the two forms of Protestantism. As the intellectual warfare between Lutheran and Calvinist polemicists intensified, two areas of doctrine emerged as potentially reliable demarcators: the doctrine of predestination and the concept of the "real presence." In each case, there was a clear distinction between the Lutheran and Calvinist positions.

The emergence of state churches was a response to the situation in Germany in the 1570s. Whatever the benefits of such institutions, a link was created between the church and power that would prove problematic in years to come. Protestant churches were now part of the establishment, with vested interests that might easily compromise their integrity. State churches may well have helped achieve political and social stability in the short term; in the longer term, however, they created the conditions for wars of religion, precisely on account of the interconnection of religion and natural identity, the church and the state. Theology now became a matter of political importance in that a link had been forged between theological beliefs and the state.

A further consequence of this development should be noted. When Protestant communities began to emigrate from Europe to North America, they carried with them certain apparently self-evident assumptions about how churches relate to the community at large. These assumptions, however, had been molded by forces specific to sixteenth-century Europe. The result, as we shall see later, was that American Protestantism tended to replicate the structures and habits of its European context, despite the very different social context in which it now found itself.

Having considered the three forms of Protestantism traditionally termed Lutheranism, Calvinism, and Anabaptism, we now turn to consider the emergence of another, quite distinct vision of Protestantism in England.

5

England

The Emergence of Anglicanism

The Protestant Reformation that swept across much of western Europe during the sixteenth century was far from monolithic. A mass of local factors shaped the Reformation, giving rise to patterns of reform that defied the simplifications of its more uncritical supporters and opponents alike. While shared beliefs and attitudes enabled local reformations to enjoy at least a degree of unity and direction with the larger movement, each of these smaller groups also pursued its own interests, whether subtly or more emphatically, and thus the movement's fragmentation remained a constant threat.

One of the most remarkable and, owing to the happenstances of imperial history, influential forms of Protestantism emerged in England. Careful historical analysis of the origins and development of Anglicanism has been hindered to no small extent by the lingering agendas of religiously biased writers who, in attempting to perpetuate their own accounts of the English Reformation, have been primarily motivated by vested interests over what Anglicanism ought to be.[1]

Many nineteenth-century Anglican writers sympathetic to the High Church revival movement often known as "Tractarianism" or the "Oxford Movement" were dismissive of any suggestion that this most English form of Christianity could be considered "Protestant" and pointed to the roots of their "Anglo-Catholicism" in the early seventeenth century. It is

Portrait of Henry VIII, King of England, 1540, by Hans Holbein, the Younger (1497–1543).

Galleria Nazionale d'Arte Antica, Rome, Italy; Photo: Scala/Art Resource, NY

certainly true that some significant conformist members of the Church of England during the reigns of James I and Charles I wished to lay a greater stress on its sacramental life than some of their contemporaries and were disinclined to be sympathetic toward the first generation of Protestant leaders in the English Reformation. Whereas for earlier conformists the Church of England was a champion of true religion against anti-Christian Rome, the later Jacobean and Caroline ecclesiastical establishment sought to extricate itself from the confessional struggles of European Protestantism, seeing these struggles as a liability rather than an asset. Under Charles I, this group began to gain the ascendancy: William Laud became Archbishop of Canterbury and Richard Neile became Archbishop of York. Yet such figures cannot for that reason be designated "Catholics," partly because they were generally so affirmative of their Protestant credentials, and partly because their sacramental views could easily be accommodated within the spectrum of Protestant possibilities.[2] From a historical perspective, the English national church must be regarded as a Protestant variant—the "Protestant Episcopal Church of England and Ireland," as state and parliamentary documents regularly describe it.[3]

So how did this distinctive form of Protestantism come to establish itself in England? And how did its characteristic features emerge? This chapter explores these intriguing questions.

HENRY VIII: A CATHOLIC REFORMER

One of the most remarkable developments in the recent historiography of the English Reformation under Henry VIII is the general abandonment of the term "Protestant" to refer to its leading reforming representatives.[4] English reformers simply did not refer to themselves by this term, which they tended to use instead to refer to German Lutheranism, especially seen from a political perspective. The term "evangelical" is increasingly being used to designate the English reformers of the 1520s and 1530s, who did not regard themselves as confessionally "Protestant" but rather saw themselves as "Catholics" who believed their church required reform and renewal from within.[5] Recent studies have pointed out how the Christo-centric piety characteristic of the late Middle Ages may have contributed to the continuity between pre-Reformation and evangelical piety in England.[6] The perception that England's religious reformers were Protestant dates from the reign of Edward VI and marks a significant shift of understanding in the transformation then under way within the English church.

Where some older Protestant accounts of the Reformation in England asserted that the late medieval English church was moribund and corrupt, yearning for the kind of reform that Luther espoused, recent studies of English church life on the eve of the Reformation have pointed to its vitality and diversity.[7] Often drawing heavily on local archival sources, these studies have added weight to the increasingly secure view that the English Reformation was largely, from its outset, imposed "from above" by successive governments on the English people, who were generally unsympathetic to the official "new religion."[8] There is no doubt that the English people were dissatisfied to some degree with the state of the English church in the late Middle Ages. Visitation records show a degree of concern being felt at the episcopal level over the low quality of the clergy and misgivings being expressed over various aspects of church life. There were also clear signs of hostility toward the clergy in urban contexts, most notably in London. Nevertheless, animosity toward the clergy was by no means universal. In many parts of England—especially in the west and in northern regions such as Lancashire and Yorkshire—the clergy were, on the whole, well liked, and there was no particular enthusiasm for any radical change.

As Luther's books began to be imported into England in the early 1520s—legally or otherwise—from continental ports such as Antwerp, his ideas began to be discussed. Perhaps the greatest interest in his writings at this stage was among academics, particularly at Cambridge University. The "White Horse" group, which met at a long-vanished tavern of that name, included some of the future leaders of the Reformation in England. Although it is thought that accounts of the activities and influence of this group may have been somewhat embellished, there is no doubt that Cambridge was an important early center for discussion of Luther's doctrine of justification by faith. Luther's appeal to sections of the English church may have been enhanced through the influence of Lollardy, a pre-Reformation indigenous movement that was associated with activists such as John Wycliffe and was severely critical of many aspects of church life.[9]

Nevertheless, the evidence suggests that the origins of the Reformation in England cannot be convincingly attributed either to popular dislike or criticism of the late medieval church or to a growing academic interest in Lutheranism. These factors may well have served as catalysts to that Reformation once it had begun. The evidence strongly points to the personal influence of Henry VIII on the origins and subsequent direction of the English Reformation. That influence was modulated and moderated in often subtle ways, reflecting a mixture of resistance, collaboration, and acquiescence on the part of the English population.[10]

The causes of the English Reformation, though complex and various, are widely held to be linked primarily to Henry's attempt to set up a smooth transition of power after his death by ensuring that he had a son as an undisputed legitimate heir to the English throne.[11] Henry had a daughter through his first wife, Catherine of Aragon—the future queen, Mary Tudor. Yet this marriage had not only failed to produce the requisite son and heir but also reflected the political realities of an earlier generation: an alliance between England and Spain had been seen as essential to a sound foreign policy, which was then held to depend on a secure relationship with the Holy Roman Empire. The weakness of this assumption had become clear by 1525, when Charles V declined to marry Henry's daughter by Catherine. Henry subsequently began the process by which he could divorce Catherine.

Under normal circumstances, this procedure might not have been expected to encounter any formidable obstacles. An appeal to the pope to annul the marriage could have been anticipated to secure the desired outcome. However, the situation was anything but normal. Rome was under virtual siege by the army of Charles V, and Pope Clement VII was understandably feeling somewhat insecure. Catherine of Aragon was the aunt of Charles V, and it was inevitable that the pope would wish to avoid giving unnecessary offense to the emperor at such a sensitive moment. Unsurprisingly, the petition for a divorce failed. As if to add insult to injury, Clement VII informed Henry that he would be excommunicated if he married again.

Henry's response was to assert both the independence of England—as not only a nation-state but a separate province of the church—and the autonomy of the English king.[12] The most persuasive narrative linking the various events of Henry's reign is that of a reformation imposed from above by Henry and his court, with the objective of developing an English form of Catholicism, stripped of its traditional allegiance to the pope. It is becoming increasingly clear that traditional Catholics and reforming evangelicals in England around this time shared many common religious values and that the ensuing Reformation was thus both possible and successful.[13] A nationalist agenda is easily discerned at this point: Henry wished to retain the notion of a state church as the guarantor of national unity.[14]

It is impossible to speak of any coherent English "Protestantism" at any point during Henry's reign, in that Henry appears to have had no interest in adopting either Lutheranism or Zwinglianism. Nor did evangelicals use the term "Protestant" to refer to each other. Rather, we may identify a variety of evangelical factions, which became radicalized as Henry's religious policies seemed increasingly erratic in their direction and inconsistent in their application.[15]

On November 3, 1529, Henry convened a parliament that attempted to reduce the power of both church and clergy. The initial refusal of the English clergy to concede these points prompted Henry to undertake more severe measures in order to persuade them. The most important of these took place over the period 1530–31, during which time Henry argued that the English clergy, by virtue of their support for Rome, were guilty of *praemunire*—a technical offense that can be thought of as a form of treason in that it involves allegiance to a foreign power, namely, the papacy. With this capital charge hanging over them, the clergy reluctantly agreed to at least some of Henry's demands for recognition of his ecclesiastical authority.

Henry was presented with an opportunity for advancement of his aims when the aging archbishop of Canterbury, William Warham, died in August 1532. Initially, Henry delayed appointing a replacement. However, it became increasingly clear that the resolution of his divorce from Catherine of Aragon demanded a sympathetic replacement, not least because Henry had begun an affair with Anne Boleyn. By December 1532, Boleyn was pregnant, making resolution of the issue a matter of urgency if the ensuing child was to be a legitimate heir to the English throne. Stephen Gardiner, the obvious candidate for the archbishopric, was out of favor. Henry and his adviser Thomas Cromwell identified Thomas Cranmer, who was not even a bishop at this point, as the obvious successor to Warham.

Why Cranmer? The best explanation is that he had earlier indicated his strong support for Henry's divorce proceedings. Cranmer was finally consecrated (possibly against his will) on March 30, 1533. Although the consecration was supported by papal documents, Cranmer declared that he took the obligatory oath to the pope without feeling bound by it. Henry's marriage to Catherine of Aragon was annulled by an English court in May 1533, allowing Anne to be crowned queen on June 1. Her daughter, Elizabeth Tudor, was born on September 7—a legitimate heir to the throne of England, but unfortunately for Henry (and in the light of subsequent events, even more unfortunately for Anne), not a son.

Henry's divorce of Catherine immediately led to the threat of excommunication. Henry now decided to follow through with the course of action on which he had embarked, by which his supreme political and religious authority within England would be recognized. A series of acts were imposed in 1534. The Succession Act declared that the crown would pass to Henry's children. The Supremacy Act declared that Henry was to be recognized as the "supreme head" of the English church. The Treasons Act made denial of Henry's supremacy an act of treason, punishable by death. This final act led to the execution of two prominent Catholic churchmen, Thomas More and John Fisher, both of whom refused to recognize Henry as supreme head of the English church—a title that they believed belonged only to the pope.

Henry now found himself under threat of invasion from neighboring Catholic states. The mandate of restoring papal authority would have been a more than adequate pretext for either France or Spain to satisfy their expansionist ambitions by launching a crusade against England. Henry was thus obliged to undertake a series of defensive measures to ensure the nation's safety. These measures reached their climax in 1536. The dissolution of the monasteries provided Henry with funds for his military preparations. Negotiations with German Lutherans were begun with the object of entering into military alliances. At this point, Lutheran ideas began to be adopted in some official formularies of faith, such as the Ten Articles. Nevertheless, this theological enthusiasm for Lutheranism appears to have been little more than a temporary political maneuver.

When it became clear that there was serious opposition in England to his reforming measures, Henry backtracked. The 1543 "King's Book" clearly indicates Henry's desire to avoid giving offense to Catholics. By the time of Henry's death in January 1547, the religious situation in England was somewhat ambivalent. Although Henry had made some concessions to Lutheranism, he appears to have continued personally to prefer at least some traditional Catholic beliefs and practices. For example, his will made provision for prayers to be said for his soul—overlooking, incidentally, the fact that, less than two years earlier, he had tried to close down the chantries, which existed for precisely this purpose!

From this brief account of the origins of the English Reformation under Henry VIII, it will be clear that there are reasons for supposing that Henry's agenda was political, dominated by his desire to safeguard his succession and secure his own authority throughout his kingdom. Through a series of developments, this required a schism with Rome and an increasingly tolerant attitude toward Lutheranism, in both Germany and England.[16] Yet Henry's temporary interest in Lutheranism, which peaked around 1536, does not seem to have been grounded primarily in religious considerations, but rather in the need to secure the support of reform-minded activists in England for his own distinctive style of reformation. The English Reformation was a decidedly Henrician affair, aimed at creating a confessionally unified, politically stable nation with a coherent state religion focused on the office and person of the king.

Toward the end of Henry's reign, tensions nevertheless began to emerge as warring factions began to plan for the succession. The monarch's final years were marked by political maneuvering as the increasingly confident evangelical faction within the court aimed to secure Edward's succession, which would allow them to steer England in a Protestant direction that was more explicitly confessional.[17] Indeed, Henry may even have colluded with this development, seeing it as the inevitable, if distasteful, outcome of the situation that he himself had created.

On Henry's death, England changed direction significantly. The word "Protestant" now finally became entirely appropriate to describe the new religious situation.

EDWARD VI:
THE ENFORCEMENT OF PROTESTANTISM

Henry VIII died on January 26, 1547. Under the terms of his will, his successor was beyond dispute: the nine-year-old Prince Edward, Henry's son by his third wife, Jane Seymour, was the only male Tudor heir to the throne after the death of his father. There was no question of the legitimacy of the succession. It is, however, a moot point whether one can really speak of Edward exercising kingship in either a personal or possessive sense during his brief reign.[18] Power would lie in the hands of those who advised and protected him, above all John Dudley, Duke of Northumberland, and the king's "protector," Edward Seymour, Duke of Somerset.[19] The religious changes unleashed during Edward's brief reign would have a formative impact on the shaping of the Church of England, and through it, on determining the contours of the English-speaking Protestant world.

From the outset, it was clear that Edward's reign would mark a radical break with the past. There would be no continuation of the theological ambiguities of the closing years of Henry's reign, which had left the devotional life of the English people relatively unchanged. Mass was still celebrated, and many ceremonies continued. Even where some of these were now forbidden—such as the burning of lights before images—people found convenient ways of bypassing the rules. The diocesan and parish structures of England had been left virtually as they were, particularly in relation to their forms of worship. Thomas Cranmer, Archbishop of Canterbury, might well have had ambitious ideas for the reform of the liturgy and theology of the English church, but Henry VIII gave him no opportunity to pursue them.

In marked contrast, the new king would preside over a thoroughgoing reformation of the church, modeled along the lines of continental Protestantism. As Cranmer declared at his coronation, Edward would be a Josiah, a reforming king, who would purge his kingdom of all remaining forms of idolatry.[20] Such powerful Old Testament imagery was taken further, with Edward also being portrayed as a Solomon who would build a new church. Although Cranmer and other Protestant bishops—above all, Nicholas Ridley and Hugh Latimer—are often seen as providing the driving vision for forcing through the Edwardian reforms, it must be noted that Edward himself was no passive, if approving, spectator of such developments. In 1550 Edward made his own religious views known when he personally deleted any reference to the invocation of saints in the oath of royal supremacy.

It was soon clear that Edward and his advisers were moving the English church far from the relatively modest reforms introduced under Henry. Evangelicals became Protestants and increasingly identified themselves with the narrative of events—in their view, divinely guided—already taking place on the continent of Europe. Edwardian preachers and writers were aware of the potential difficulties this might create, especially from those who might wish to present Edward as reversing his father's religious policies. The apologists for the Edwardian Reformation were careful to depict their king as the godly son of a godly father, personally and valiantly moving his nation into the natural second stage of the Reformation begun by Henry VIII. The Edwardian Reformation was simply a continuation of what had gone before, consolidating the legacy of the late monarch.

The king's Protestant Reformation—a "top-down" restructuring of the church that was generally imposed upon the English church—was in line with his vision of the godly monarch. If at times it is difficult to discern a continuous, consistent program of Protestantization during these six years of active, unsettling, and controversial Protestant Reformation, the difficulties arising from the king's youth may well be responsible. Sovereign power had to be exercised collaboratively, in the light of rival Protestant visions and aspirations associated with those who advised the new Josiah.[21]

Of these aspirations, the most important is thought to have been the revision of the *Book of Common Prayer* in 1549 and again in 1552. The use of an "authorized" prayer book for public worship proved to be a highly significant method of social and intellectual control.[22] Moreover, Cranmer's revisions would be of considerable importance, particularly in relation to eucharistic theology.[23] Although Cranmer's 1549 liturgy showed a calculated, if ultimately vague, alignment with Luther's understanding of the "real presence," by 1552 he had shifted his position and now identified with Zwingli's rather different approach. Cranmer's mature eucharistic views are best studied from his *Defense of the True and Catholic Doctrine of the Sacrament,* first published in 1550. Cranmer here argues that the eucharist represents a memorial of Christ's saving death in which believers "do spiritually eat his body, and [are] spiritually fed and nourished by him." There was, however, no mystical transformation of the bread or the wine. "The bread remains still there, as a sacrament to signify."

Cranmer was also responsible for a series of further developments designed to consolidate Protestantism in England as a long-term presence on account of its intellectual excellence rather than merely because it was enforced by royal authority and command. Recognizing that the reforms introduced to date needed firmer theological grounding, Cranmer invited leading established Protestant theologians from continental Europe to settle in England and lend a new theological direction and foundation to the English Reformation. Peter Martyr Vermigli was appointed as Regius Professor of Divinity at Oxford University, and Martin Bucer as Regius Professor of Divinity at Cambridge University. Their arrival pointed to a new determination to align the English Reformation with its European counterpart, particularly its Reformed constituency.[24]

The "Forty-two Articles" (1553) drawn up by Cranmer were strongly Protestant in orientation, as was the *Book of Homilies* (a set of approved sermons for delivery in parish churches).

The clergy would now be required to affirm their allegiance to what was clearly and emphatically a Protestant statement of faith and to preach predetermined sermons of unquestionable Protestant provenance. A close scrutiny of both the articles and the homilies suggests that the Edwardian Reformation was being positioned midway between the two visions of Protestantism then achieving dominance in Germany and Switzerland. Visitation programs led to the practical enforcement of the Protestant Reformation at the parish level, typically expressed in the destruction of images. This highly visible change to churches and worship, often enforced by vigilantes, was one of the more distinctive aspects of the emerging Reformed tradition. Its appearance in England at this time is a telling indication of the changing trajectories of theological allegiance then taking place.[25] The English church's flirtation with Lutheranism, begun largely for reasons of political expediency in the 1530s, was not yet over; however, England now began to align itself increasingly with the ideas associated with the Reformed wing of the Reformation.

So how did the English people react to such reforms, which were imposed upon them without consultation and without much obvious demand for such drastic, wholesale reform at the grassroots level? The evidence is ambivalent. There was unquestionably popular discontent during Edward's reign, but it seems to have been particularly directed against agrarian reform, above all the unpopular enclosure of vast tracts of land. With the possible exception of the "Western" or "Prayer Book" rebellion of 1549—which had to be suppressed forcibly using foreign mercenaries—there was little open public criticism of the reform measures. Yet signs of discontent were nevertheless evident. Non-attendance at church became a problem; some of those who did attend public worship were known to shun their own Reformed parishes and to frequent those offering more traditionalist forms of worship.

Edward's early death in 1553 put an abrupt end to this state-sponsored Protestantization of the English national church. To bring about a total religious conversion of England was the work of a generation, not a mere seven years. The measures, never entirely popular, had not been consolidated and could easily be reversed. Mary Tudor, who succeeded to the throne, immediately began to put in place a series of measures designed to bring about a restoration of Catholicism in England.[26] Although it can be difficult to discern the strategic goals of these moves, their object appears to have been to return England's religious life to what it had been before Henry's breach with Rome over the divorce issue. In 1554 Parliament agreed to declare void all religious legislation passed after 1529.

Protestant bishops were arrested and deposed. Cranmer, Latimer, and Ridley were arrested. The mass and clerical celibacy were restored. Married clergy would gradually be removed from office. Mary refused to accept the title of "supreme head" of the church, adopted by her father, arguing that this title properly belonged to the pope. With relations with the papacy now restored, Reginald Pole—a loyal Catholic bishop deposed under Henry VIII—was installed as Archbishop of

Canterbury. England was once more a Catholic nation. The clock had been turned back by twenty-five years.

Yet Mary's attempt to reimpose the traditional religion suffered a series of setbacks. In 1556 Pole and the pope became embroiled in controversy, souring relations between England and the papacy. The reversionary measures became particularly unpopular when Cranmer, Latimer, and Ridley were publicly burned at Oxford. Mary's diplomatic flirtations with Spain created the impression that Catholicism was a foreign religion, imposed by foreign influence.[27] Cranmer and his unfortunate colleagues were easily depicted as English patriots, murdered by a queen with Spanish sympathies.

Cranmer's fate confirmed the worst fears of many English people: it was no longer safe to be known as a committed Protestant in England. By early 1554, realizing the gravity of their situation, most Protestants with the ability and means to do so had fled England to seek refuge in Europe.[28] According to John Foxe, "Well near to 800 persons, students and others together" fled England for refuge in the Protestant havens of Europe in the first few years of Mary's turbulent reign. The favored cities of exile were Aarau, Basel, and Zurich in Switzerland; the German cities of Emden, Frankfurt, and Strasbourg; and the independent city of Geneva. Some refugees were wealthy enough to support themselves in exile; others received discreet financial support from well-wishers back home, particularly from wealthy Protestant merchants who already had extensive trading links with the cities where their protégés sought refuge. It proved to be a relatively easy matter to arrange covert support for their exiled colleagues through, for example, business deals with merchants in Strasbourg.

The Marian exiles seem to have regarded their time in the cities of Europe as paralleling a biblical event that took place two thousand years earlier—the exile of Jerusalem in Babylon. Was not this period of exile to be a time of purification and preparation for a return to their native land? And would not the returning exiles bring a purer form of religion with them? In the event, the period of the Marian exile was a mere six years, in comparison with the fifty of the biblical counterpart. Yet the exiles saw it as a period of schooling, in preparation for their return. Their time of exile allowed them firsthand experience of successful, working Protestant churches and communities and provided them with role models that would shape their vision of the new reformed Church of England they proposed to establish on their return.

The period of exile was difficult for many reasons, not least because nobody had any real idea how long it would last. Economic hardship was widespread within the small English communities, which were often treated with disinterest or hostility by their host cities. Serious divisions arose in the exiled English Protestant communities in Basel, Emden, and Frankfurt over issues of liturgy and theology, causing embitterment and demoralization. An exception to this was the English community in Geneva, which attracted approximately one-quarter of the émigrés; it was hailed by John Knox as "the most perfect school of Christ," the finest embodiment of a Christian society since the time of the New Testament. The English community in Geneva proved to be especially important in forging attitudes among the exiles that would shape the debates and tensions of Elizabethan Protestantism. The anticipation of a new era of Protestant renewal and reform in England sustained the English Protestant communities during their exile as they waited for the right time to return home.

That time came, unexpectedly and suddenly, on November 17, 1558. Mary Tudor and Reginald Pole died within hours of each other. The royal and ecclesiastical power base of the re-Catholicization program lay in ruins. Everything now depended on the religious beliefs of the remaining daughter of Henry VIII, who was the only obvious successor to Mary. But which way would Elizabeth face?

ELIZABETH I AND THE STABILIZATION OF ENGLISH RELIGION

Recognizing the need to secure religious stability in England, Elizabeth set about crafting a "Settlement of Religion" that would bring at least some degree of unity to a deeply divided nation.[29] The basic elements of the Settlement were the Act of Supremacy, which affirmed Elizabeth's sovereignty over the national church and abolished any papal power, and the Act of Uniformity, which aimed to enforce religious uniformity throughout the nation, making church attendance compulsory on Sundays and saints' days. The effect of such measures was that the queen laid down what the church should believe, how it should be governed, and how its services were to be conducted.

Elizabeth's own inclinations were unquestionably Protestant; nevertheless, she had no interest in causing offense to Catholic Spain, which might pose a significant military threat to England. This concern was probably reflected in her chosen title as "Supreme Governor" of the church: her refusal to be called "supreme head" avoided offending both Protestants (who used this title to refer to Jesus Christ) and Catholics (who used it to refer to the pope). The Church of England would be reformed in its theology yet remain Catholic in its institutions, especially its episcopacy.

Elizabeth's Settlement of Religion was always precarious, relying much on veiled promises and hints of future favors that somehow never materialized. A political rather than a theological statement, it was aimed at generating consensus and stability, assisted to no small extent by theological vagueness and evasion.[30] Elsewhere, Protestantism might be riven and cleft by theological disputes; England would be undivided, at least publicly.

Although Lutheran influence may indeed be discerned at points within the Settlement of Religion, it is clear that the balance of power had shifted decisively toward Reformed forms of Protestantism.[31] The returning Marian exiles, many of whom had spent their exile in cities such as Zurich and Geneva, included many important or soon-to-be-important English Protestant leaders, such as John Aylmer (future bishop of London), John Bale, Miles Coverdale, Richard Cox (future bishop of Ely), Edmund Grindal (future archbishop of York, then Canterbury), John Jewel (future bishop of Salisbury), and Edwin Sandys (future archbishop of York).

On the assumption that the Elizabethan Settlement was an imperfect temporary compromise, many Protestants actively supported and defended it, while waiting for the more radical measures that seemed to be imminent. Particular dissatisfaction was expressed by more radical Protestants over Elizabeth's insistence that priestly vestments revert to what they had been in the second year of the reign of Edward VI. Those who looked to Geneva or Zurich for theological guidance longed to wear black gowns and get rid of vestments altogether. Elizabeth's cryptic hint that she might alter her mind subsequently came to nothing.

The Settlement proved to be a seedbed of discontent, catalyzing growing discontent within Protestantism that subsequently led to the emergence of the Puritan party. Although the term "Puritan" is problematic for the historian, it accurately denotes a central theme of the group of Protestants whom it designates—namely, a passionate, occasionally obsessive, quest for further reformation. In the face of what they saw as Elizabeth's compromises and half-measures, they demanded a pure church, along the lines of Calvin's Geneva.[32] A turning point was reached in 1576 with the appointment of John Whitgift as archbishop of Canterbury. The Puritans realized they would never achieve their goals under Elizabeth.

One local solution was adopted by Protestant sympathizers in the Channel Islands.[33] In 1564 a French diplomatic mission to London suggested that the Channel Islands come under the ecclesiastical control of the Catholic diocese of Coutances in Normandy. After consultation with the islanders, it was ruled that they were part of the English diocese of Winchester, and hence not subject to French ecclesiastical control. However, by 1576 the islanders had established French *Reformed* beliefs and church practices in their region, claiming that they were exempt from Elizabeth's control because they were following the best practice of the French Reformed churches in the Coutances area. English religious control was not reestablished in Jersey until the reign of James I, and not in Guernsey until the reign of Charles II.

With the passage of time, the Settlement of Religion can be seen to have defined Anglicanism with reference to Catholicism, on the one hand, and to Puritans, on the other.[34] In April 1570, Pius V excommunicated Elizabeth, declaring that she was a pretender to the throne of England. The announcement placed Puritans in an impossible position, as they were obliged to defend England's Protestant queen against this act of papal aggression. Yet the papal edict united the Catholic world in the *Empresa de Inglaterra* ("the Enterprise of England")—the overthrow of the new Protestant regime. And Spain saw itself as having a leading role in this decisive event. The failure of Spain's attempt to invade England in 1588 led to a growing perception within England that it was indeed a Protestant country, facing up to the military and naval might of its Catholic opponents.

Elizabeth's long reign allowed England to emerge as a Protestant nation, its Catholic and more radical Protestant dissenters being of minor importance. Elizabeth's personal prestige enabled her to sideline dissent without undue difficulty. Although the image of Elizabeth as a militant Protestant heroine belongs to a somewhat later age, her defeat of Spain was widely seen as marking a new phase in the consolidation of Protestantism.[35] In 1600 England was emerging as a naval power of no small significance, and a powerful defender of the new religion. Under Sir Walter Raleigh, a Protestant colony was established at Roanoke Island, eventually to be known as "Virginia." Protestantism expanded into Ireland, displacing the indigenous Catholic population and laying the foundations of the religious tensions that persist to this day.

ELIZABETH AND THE INVENTION OF ANGLICANISM

In 1555 the Religious Peace of Augsburg brought at least some degree of stability to a fractured Germany. Regional rulers could choose, and then enforce, their preferred religion. Yet their choice was limited to two options—Lutheranism and Catholicism. Elizabeth failed to see why she should be limited in this way. She would choose, and then enforce, her own religious option—the reformed episcopal faith now known as Anglicanism.

The style of Protestantism that crystallized in the late Elizabethan era thus had a distinctive, even unusual identity. The form of Protestantism that began to be spread throughout the world as England expanded its naval capacity and its colonial ambitions was a distant cousin of its continental neighbors. Elizabeth desired to create a sustainable form of Protestantism, adapted to the realities of the English situation, which would represent a "middle way" between the religious extremes of her day. Although this *via media* is often described as an intermediary between Protestantism and Catholicism, a closer examination of the political and religious dynamics of the Elizabethan period suggests a desire to develop a form of Protestantism that was not identical to, but had clear points of contact with, Lutheranism and Calvinism.

Although the term "Anglican" dates from a later era, it describes this distinct form of Protestantism remarkably well. It reflects the religious instability of England as a result of the aggressive yet ultimately short-lived policies of Edward VI and Mary Tudor. Like a ship tossed about in a storm, England had first lurched sharply toward Protestantism, then equally violently toward Catholicism. Elizabeth sought to bring stability to her nation, partly through deferred promises, partly through adaptation, but above all through an insistence on her own sovereign authority in matters of religion. Anglicanism would be defined by the place of the monarch as the ground and guarantor of its religious identity and stability.

Elizabeth adopted a religion that included all the cardinal beliefs and practices of Protestantism, including the rejection of papal authority, the insistence that preaching and all public worship should be in the vernacular, the insistence upon communion in both kinds for the laity, the affirmation of the clergy's right to marry, and a set of official pronouncements of faith—the "homilies," the "Thirty-nine Articles of Faith," and the prayer book—that affirmed core Protestant beliefs (such as the sufficiency of scripture, justification by faith, and the rejection of purgatory).

It is important to judge Elizabethan Protestantism for what it actually was rather than impose the ideals of a later age upon it. Some have seen Richard Hooker (1554–1600) as reflecting the theology and ecclesiastical polity of Anglicanism at this time. Hooker's attempt to replace the "word-centered" piety characteristic of this age with one that was more "sacrament-centered" was not typical of the era, and it reflected Hooker's aspirations for the future rather than the actual situation on the ground.[36] Some Anglo-Catholic apologists of the nineteenth century tried to portray Elizabeth as constructing a reformed Catholicism at this time, but this is simply historical nonsense. By every criterion of her age, Elizabeth implanted a form of Protestantism in England—and was universally recognized at the time as having done so.

The outcome was a form of Protestantism that sought to stress its continuity with the Christian and English past, retaining a remarkable amount of organization, custom, and tradition from the pre-Reformation era. Much to the irritation of radical Protestants who had been schooled at Geneva and Zurich, Elizabeth retained bishops and insisted on distinctive clergy dress. The traditional ecclesiastical structuring of dioceses with their bishops and parishes with their parish priests continued to function. An ordered and uniform liturgy was prescribed by the *Book of Common Prayer*. The contrast with the more Genevan form of Protestantism then emerging in Scotland was obvious.

The critical role of the monarch in determining and then sustaining the character of the Church of England made a change in monarch unsettling. When Elizabeth died in 1603, there was genuine uncertainty over who would succeed her. Which way would the wind blow? When it was announced that James VI, King of Scotland, would succeed Elizabeth, the Puritan party in England was electrified. A surge of reforming anticipation swept through the movement. Would not a Scottish king reform the Church of England and create a properly Reformed church based on his own Scottish church?

REDEFINING ENGLISH PROTESTANTISM: THE RISE OF PURITANISM

In the 1580s, Geneva became for Elizabethan Puritans what Moscow was for many European Communists during the 1930s—a potent symbol of their aspirations and a source of the ideas and support that might bring them about. If Elizabeth would not allow them their demands for a purified church finally purged of its remaining vestiges of popery—such as bishops and clerical robes—then what of her successor? Elizabeth might well have suppressed serious religious dissent within her realm. But what would happen after her death? Was there not a serious danger of radical religious upheaval just over the horizon? This was certainly what many members of the Anglican establishment feared; it was also, of course, precisely what many Puritans were hoping for.

When it was announced that Elizabeth would be succeeded by James VI of Scotland, English Puritans believed their moment had come. James had earlier supported the reforms of John Knox and had created a Reformed church modeled along pure Genevan lines in his old realm. Surely he could be relied upon to do the same in England? The Puritans decided to seize the initiative and steal a march on their Anglican opponents.

On his way from Edinburgh to London in April 1603, James was met by a Puritan delegation that presented him with the "Millenary Petition," signed by more than one thousand ministers of the Church of England. Its authors went out of their way to stress their loyalty to both king and country. They had, they declared, served their church faithfully, despite their serious misgivings concerning its practices; the time had now come to change things. They demanded reforms, in particular the removal of the "burden of human rites and ceremonies" such as making the sign of the cross in baptism, wearing clerical dress, using a ring in the marriage service, and bowing at the name of Jesus. All these practices were unbiblical, they argued, and therefore could not be required of any minister of the church.

It soon became clear that James had little sympathy with such demands for reform. His personal sympathy lay with moderate Calvinist beliefs, more in line with those associated with Geneva than those now emerging from Amsterdam.[37] Ideas, however, were one thing; practices were another. James's Scottish experience had created something of an aversion on his part to the more austere forms of Presbyterian church culture and convinced him that, just as Geneva was a republic, so Calvin's followers were covert revolutionaries. His views on this matter were shaped to no small extent by some unpleasant experiences with Scottish presbyteries, particularly under Andrew Melville, a Scottish Presbyterian who had taught at the Genevan Academy and formed a close personal friendship with Calvin's protégé Theodore Beza.

At a heated encounter between the king and senior churchmen at Falkland Palace in October 1596, Melville had physically taken hold of James and accused him of being "God's silly vassal." Melville pointedly declared that while he and his colleagues would support James as king in public, in private they all knew perfectly well that Christ was the true king in Scotland, and his kingdom was the kirk—a kingdom in which James was a mere member, not a lord or head. James was shaken by this physical and verbal assault, not least because it suggested that Melville and his allies posed a significant threat to the Scottish throne.

Apologists for the Anglican establishment were quick to spot their opportunity. Richard Bancroft and others set out to persuade James that his monarchy was dependent upon the episcopacy for its future.

The ultimate goal of Puritanism, they argued, was to overthrow the monarchy altogether. Without the bishops of the Church of England, there was no future for the monarchy in England. The king's real enemies, the "Papists" and the "Puritans," had a vested interest in destroying his authority. Only a close working alliance with the bishops would preserve the status quo and allow James to exercise his (as he saw it) divinely ordained kingly role in state and church. It was a telling argument, and it hit home.

In the end, James I developed his own policy that managed to contain Puritanism's agendas without leading to any major alterations to the practices or beliefs of the established church.[38] The Puritans were offered scraps of consolation and promises of future change that either never materialized or amounted to surprisingly little. James promised a new English translation of the Bible, which some Puritans may unwisely have hoped would strengthen their position; when the famous "King James Version" was published in 1611, it turned out to use the traditional language favored by Anglicans rather than the more radical terms preferred by Puritans.

To sensitive Puritan consciences, James seemed hostile, or at best indifferent, to their concerns. Not only did the established church retain many "popish" ceremonies and practices, but James seemed to encourage cultural activities that were inconsistent with a strict interpretation of biblical commandments. One flashpoint in these "culture wars" was the "Book of Sports"; issued by James I in 1618, it explicitly authorized and encouraged the Sunday sports and rural festivals denounced by many Puritans as sinful pagan profanations of the Sabbath.[39] James countered the growing Puritan demands for rigorous observance of the Sabbath by denouncing such "Puritans and Precisians" as failing to care for human recreational needs.[40] James demanded that

> after the end of divine service our good people be not disturbed, letted or discouraged from any lawful recreation, such as dancing, either men or women; archery for men, leaping, vaulting, or any other such harmless recreation, nor from having of May-games, Whitsun-ales, and Morris-dances; and the setting up of May-poles and other sports therewith used.

While bear-baiting was forbidden on the Sabbath, the English people were permitted to enjoy a wide range of alternative recreations. Adding insult to injury, James insisted that his "Book of Sports" be read aloud from the pulpit during regular Sunday worship. For many Puritan groups, compromise seemed impossible. In 1607 a congregation from Scrooby, England, initially fled to Holland; eventually they migrated on the Mayflower to establish the Plymouth Colony on the shore of Cape Cod Bay in North America in 1620.

In the end, apart from taking the somewhat drastic step of emigrating to America, there was little that the frustrated Puritans could do other than wait for James to die and hope that his successor might open doors that, up to this point, had remained firmly closed. The shape of English Protestantism might yet be changed by royal decree. If not, there were other options. Could not a case be made for overthrowing monarchs if they stood in the way of the advance of Protestantism? It was a dangerous thought, sown in despair. Its time would come, perhaps sooner than anyone might have anticipated.

6

===

War, Peace, and Disinterest

European Protestantism in Crisis,
1560–1800

In his exploration of what gives rise to a sense of national identity, the nineteenth-century French historian and philosopher Ernest Renan (1823–92) pointed out the importance of suffering and persecution in creating a sense of solidarity and shared values: "Suffering in common," he wrote, "unifies more than joy."[1] Violence and oppression—and sometimes even the mere perception of such a threat—from a rival religious grouping help to crystallize a sense of self-identity in the face of "the other." When it comes to binding a group together, nothing is quite as effective as shared grievances, suffering, and hatred—perhaps even the hope of revenge.

This phenomenon is so well known that it needs illustration rather than justification. An excellent example lies to hand in the role of Western interventionism in politicizing and radicalizing Islam in the last hundred years. A growing Western presence and influence in Islamic regions of the world in the nineteenth and twentieth centuries has been a powerful stimulus to the development of politicized forms of Islam that derive their sense of identity and mission from hostility toward the West. For instance, an appeal to a common sense of Islamic identity is central to Osama bin Laden's ideology of "holy war." In fact,

Oliver Cromwell, c. 1649, by Robert Walker (1599–1658).

Islam is just as divided as Christianity: substantial differences exist between Sunnis and Shi'ites, not to mention the range of sects within those two broad strains, such as the Wahhabis. But the perception of a series of coordinated attacks on Islam by the United States and others was easily portrayed as an assault on "Islam" itself. Those attacks rapidly became the centers of nucleation around which a shared belief in an essential Islamic identity crystallized.

The origins of the modern Islamic movement can be traced back to about 1875, when Jamal al-Din al-Afghani urged Muslims to resist the growing Western influence in the Middle East by a reaffirmation of their Islamic heritage. He encouraged Muslims to believe that, prior to the arrival of the Westerners, a golden age of wise Islamic rule had held sway. This situation could be retrieved by a return to personal religious piety, a reform and renewal of Islamic *shariah* law, and violent resistance to the Western presence and influence in the region.[2] By defining a common enemy—the United States of America, or a specific American president—modern Islamism thus creates a sense of identity and shared goals within Islam. As we shall see, much the same process happened within Protestantism in the later sixteenth century.

PERSECUTION AND THE SHAPING OF PROTESTANT IDENTITY

As Protestantism began to expand in the early 1560s, it encountered resistance from a renewed Catholicism. The Catholic Reformation, long delayed by the Habsburg-Valois conflict, had begun to make an impact. Although some degree of internal reform had been under way since the 1490s, the rise of Protestantism catalyzed a systemic review of the church's life and thought.[3] Clerical abuses were remedied; new religious orders—such as the Society of Jesus—were established, and others reformed; and the reforming Council of Trent gave a new sense of theological direction and intellectual security to the church.

Although this renewal was partly driven by an internal agenda, based on the recognition of a need for change, the importance of external factors cannot be overlooked.[4] In northern Europe, the Catholic Reformation generally expressed itself as the Counter-Reformation, whose main concern was neutralizing and reversing the impact of Protestantism in hitherto Catholic territories. Peter Canisius's *Catechism* (1555) proved an especially effective riposte to its Protestant rivals. When the Catholic Reformation assumed this polemical nature, Protestantism was "the other." The term "Protestant" came to mean a third, deficient, and deviant form of Christianity that was neither Catholic nor Orthodox. Paradoxically, Catholics regarded the movement as an essentially homogeneous "non-church" that posed a clear and present danger to the *real* church. A group of essentially distinct, even potentially divergent, movements were thus bracketed together for essentially polemical reasons to encourage Catholic unity and vigilance. Their obvious differences were glossed over in a generally successful attempt to portray Protestantism as a single, well-defined enemy—a serious threat that demanded Catholic unity if it was to be blocked.

A similar process of mutual identification took place on the Protestant side. Especially in times of international tension, "Protestantism" became the emblematic ideal that gave a group of otherwise quite disparate religious movements a shared sense of identity—above all, through fear of a common enemy. This belief in a pan-European Protestant religious identity was at its greatest and most persuasive when the Catholic response took the form of violence. As Renan rightly noted, communal identities are forged and consolidated in many ways, but above all through a sense of solidarity in suffering.

The role of John Foxe's *Book of Martyrs* (1559) in catalyzing a sense of shared grievance and suffering illustrates this point perfectly.[5] Foxe was a Marian exile who had settled in the city of Basel. Like many at that time, he was shocked by the violence of Mary Tudor's persecution of Protestants, especially the barbaric deaths of the three leading Protestant bishops of the age—Thomas Cranmer, Hugh Latimer, and Nicholas Ridley. Many of those whom he had known personally were executed. Foxe's account of the final days of England's leading Protestant martyrs was avidly read, hardening attitudes within the community and strengthening its resolve to resist and eventually to overcome this evil. The addition of woodcut illustrations of the deaths of England's martyrs made this one of the most effective works of propaganda of the age.

The violent deaths of possibly as many as thirty thousand French Protestants (the figures are disputed and impossible to verify) in the

St. Bartholomew's Day Massacre of 1572 further radicalized many Protestants. The outrage created a powerful, if ultimately temporary, sense of shared identity between Lutheran, Reformed, and Anglican Christians, accompanied by a profound sense of grievance. Catholicism was "the other"; its violence was perceived to be directed against Protestantism as a whole. The fate of Protestantism in France did much to provoke indignation in its Protestant neighbors and create a sense of a righteous religious minority being persecuted by a Catholic juggernaut, directed from Rome. The portrayal of Protestants as the innocent victims of Catholic brutality and repression reinforced both the stereotype of Catholicism as "the other" and a sense of shared anger and solidarity throughout international Protestantism.

Protestantism's prejudices against Catholicism were reinforced by the bizarre reaction of the papacy to the massacre in France. Gregory XIII's celebration of the massacre was as jubilant as it was undiplomatic: the bells of Rome rang out to mark a public day of thanksgiving, the guns of the Castel Sant' Angelo were fired in salute, and a special commemorative medal was struck to honor the occasion. Gregory even commissioned Giorgio Vasari to paint a mural depicting the massacre. Such tactless actions could not fail to produce a reaction of total distaste and disgust, and the "anti-popery" that subsequently spread throughout Protestant regions of Europe remained a persistent element of Protestant self-definition until very recently.[6]

In England, the defeat of the Spanish Armada and the dismantling of the "Gunpowder Plot" increased the perception that Protestantism was defined primarily by its hostility to Catholicism, and especially the figure of the pope.[7] The figure of the pope thus became an icon of hostility and resistance (in much the same way that hostility toward the American president is talked up in Tehran).

Yet other conflicts led to quite different outcomes. Anabaptists were perceived as a threat by both Lutheran and Reformed Protestants, who were in turn regarded as oppressors by those who were allegedly so dangerous. As the religious geography of Germany became unsettled after the Peace of Augsburg, Lutheran and Reformed communities found themselves forced to define themselves over and against several "others." It was not merely Catholicism that threatened to overwhelm them; they faced a significant challenge from rival visions of Protestant identity. So severe were these internal tensions within Protestantism that it was at times difficult to believe that any common ideology united the factions.

The essential dynamic of Protestant identity, as disclosed by the events of the second half of the sixteenth century, was that of a fragmented and largely disunified movement that was able to set its internal divisions in their proper perspective by the very real threat of being overwhelmed by Catholicism. So great was this threat, and so fragile any sense of commonality, that the removal of this external constraint would unleash the forces, hitherto contained and constrained, that threatened to break Protestantism into warring factions. Historically, Protestantism has always needed an "other," an external threat or enemy, imagined or real, to hold itself together as a movement.

These tensions between different understandings of Protestantism finally erupted openly in the English Civil War (1642–51). Although this conflict possessed many dimensions and elements, at its heart it pitted two rival visions of Protestant identity against each other. Puritan and Anglican battled for the soul of England—and arguably, for the future direction of English-speaking Protestantism. The Puritan military victory could not be sustained politically, and Anglicanism regained the ascendancy after a remarkably short and ineffective interregnum. Yet while other intra-Protestant tensions might not have led to violence or warfare on such a dramatic scale, the tensions were real and seemed incapable of resolution. Protestantism was a house divided against itself—regionally, culturally, and theologically.

JAMES I:
THE BACKGROUND TO THE ENGLISH CIVIL WAR

Historians disagree as to whether the English Civil War should be seen as the last European war of religion or the first European revolutionary movement, presaging the French Revolution of 1789. A case can be made for each interpretation, in that at least some of their elements were unquestionably present. For our purposes, the importance of the English Civil War is that it set one form of Protestantism against another within a single nation, bringing about a major crisis of identity within the movement.[8]

The English Civil War was one of the most significant intellectual and political landmarks in the history of English-speaking Protestantism. Until the end of the Second World War, this pivotal event in English history tended to be evaluated from the perspective of the ultimate winners—the royalists and Anglicans—and thus a critical, often abusive, account of the agendas and concerns of both Parliamentarianism and Puritanism.[9] In the 1960s, the history of the English Civil War was rewritten. Puritanism, it was now believed, was a less radical force than had hitherto been believed. In line with the broader revisionist perspective that was then sweeping the field of seventeenth-century English history, Puritans were seen as deeply conservative figures who were closely allied with the political and religious establishments in England until the hostility of Charles I's regime forced them into violent opposition. Unsurprisingly, the winds of historiographical change have changed direction yet again: more recent scholarship has recovered much of the view that Puritanism was indeed a radical, even revolutionary, movement that fostered "godly discontent" to such an extent that a social and political revolution was an entirely conceivable outcome.[10]

While there were tensions between Anglicans and Puritans toward the end of the reign of Elizabeth I, these had always been held in check. The early years of the rule of James I not only exacerbated existing tensions but created new ones. After the heights of England's sense of achievement and purpose during Elizabeth's last years, a sense of disillusionment appears to have taken hold of the nation, as some of its leading figures felt increasingly undervalued and alienated.

The problems began under James I, whose somewhat extravagant notion of the "divine right of kings" caused considerable political difficulties. The idea had been around since the Middle Ages; James, however, developed it in what many regarded as an unacceptable, even downright eccentric, way.[11] The basic idea is summarized neatly in the opening sonnet of James's *Basilikon Doron* (1598), written while he was still king of Scotland:

God gives not Kings the style of Gods in vain,
For on his throne his Sceptre do they sway.

In some 1609 speeches to Parliament, James made it clear that he regarded himself as above the law, which was his instrument for ruling on God's behalf.

The king's subsequent dissolution of Parliament in 1611 was entirely consistent with his theology; it did nothing, however, to endear him to the increasingly powerful and vocal gentry. Sir Edward Coke (1552–1634) led the intellectual opposition to James's interpretation of the "divine right of kings," arguing that the king was under the law, not above it. Law was not something the king could use as he pleased to enforce his will; rather, it set limits to his actions.

The Anglican establishment felt that it had no choice but to support James in this matter. It required little critical acumen to notice that James's theology of kingship lent support to the idea of religious establishment, thus safeguarding their positions, status, and incomes at a time of uncertainty. James had made it clear that he was resolutely opposed to "Papists and Puritans" and that he intended to steer a middle way between these two camps. The theory of the divine right of kings neatly locked church and king together in a robust circle of mutual support and reinforcement, in effect making the established church impervious to significant parliamentary criticism.

Yet the most significant criticism of James's doctrine was theological. The theological foundation for the doctrine of "monarchomachy"—the idea that severe restrictions were to be placed upon the rights of kings, so that the people had both a right and a duty to resist tyrannical monarchs—was laid in France in response to the massacre of St. Bartholomew's Day in 1572. Some years earlier, John Calvin—perhaps beginning to recognize the practical and political importance of the question—had conceded that rulers might exceed the bounds of their authority by setting themselves against God; when they did so, he suggested, they abrogated their own power. These ideas were developed and extended by his French followers in the aftermath of the events of 1572. François Hotman, Theodore Beza, and Philippe Duplessis-Mornay all emphasized precisely the same point: tyrants are to be resisted.[12] The primary Christian duty to obey God is to be placed above any secondary obligation to obey a human ruler.

Puritan writers thus deconstructed the notion of the divine right of kings with theological ease and personal glee, pointing out its lack of biblical warrant. For them, the king's excesses highlighted the virtues of the republicanism of Calvin's Geneva. These virtues were emphasized by one of the most important English translations of the Bible—the so-called Geneva Bible, produced by English exiles at Geneva during the reign of Mary Tudor and published in 1560. It was probably the finest translation of its age. Yet its growing popularity in the reign of James I rested largely on an additional feature of this translation—its marginal notes.[13]

As we have emphasized time and time again, the vexed issue of biblical interpretation lies at the heart of the Protestant theological enterprise. Where earlier English Protestants, such as William Tyndale, had assumed—not a little optimistically, as it turned out—that the Bible, once translated, could easily be understood by any plowboy, the Geneva Bible explicitly recognized that there were "hard places"—that is, passages of the Bible that needed more than a little explanation. The marginal notes of the Geneva Bible provided its readers with clear explanations of the meanings of important yet potentially obscure biblical texts. Unsurprisingly, the interpretations offered were those associated with Calvin's Geneva—theologically Reformed and politically republican. And equally unsurprisingly, the notes were highly critical of any idea of the "divine right of kings."

The Geneva Bible provided powerful ammunition to those who challenged the theological basis of James's ideology of kingship.[14] Commenting on Daniel being thrown into the lions' den, the Geneva Bible notes that Daniel "disobeyed the king's wicked commandment in order to obey God." The implication is clear: God approves of those who resist the unjust demands of kings. Much the same point is made in relation to the account of the Exodus. God ended Pharaoh's oppression of his people through Moses. And God will deal in the same way with any other kings who oppress his people. It was not difficult to make the connection with James's abortive attempts to rule England.

One of the biblical texts seized upon by the supporters of the "divine right of kings" was Psalm 105:15: "Do not touch mine anointed." The meaning of the text was clear, they argued: the people are forbidden to take any form of violent action against God's anointed one—in other words, the king. The Geneva Bible interpreted this verse in a rather different way: kings are forbidden to oppress or take any violent action against God's anointed people. The implicit theological justification of republicanism could hardly be overlooked—as James himself knew.

James had encountered the Geneva Bible while in Scotland and cordially detested its marginal notes. One of his most significant religious actions as the new king of England was his 1604 command that a new English translation of the Bible was to be made—a translation that eventually appeared in 1611 and is widely known as the King James Bible. This new translation, he insisted, would have no marginal notes. Yet the new translation proved to be a commercial flop. The Geneva Bible reigned supreme until the restoration of the monarchy under Charles II—even though James banned its production in England in 1616.

THE ENGLISH CIVIL WAR:
ANGLICAN AGAINST PURITAN

The death of James I in 1625 precipitated a new wave of religious uncertainty in England. Although Charles I was widely regarded as more urbane and level-headed than his father, he was known to be much more pro-Catholic and anti-Puritan than his father. Added to that, he had married a foreign queen, Henrietta Maria of France—a Catholic. Religious criticism of the marriage surged, fueled by anxieties about what it might portend for English religious life and home and for English foreign policy.

Even the mere suggestion that Charles might marry the Spanish *Infanta* in 1623 had provoked intense criticism.[15] One court preacher was forcibly interrupted when, speaking about Solomon's marriage to an idolater, he announced his intention to "make an application to the present time." It was all too obvious what that application was going to be, and silence seemed to all present to be by far the most prudent policy. The subsequent marriage of Charles to Henrietta Maria provoked outrage in many quarters. Comparing Henrietta Maria unfavorably to Jezebel, the anonymous author of the *Sacrae Heplades* (1625) gave vent to his hope that "some Jehu" might cause her to be thrown out of her window and trodden underfoot by some passing horse.

When Charles appointed the high churchman William Laud as archbishop of Canterbury in 1633, the Puritan faction within the

Church of England was incensed.[16] At this time, Puritans were divided into factions—such as Presbyterians, Congregationalists, and Separatists. Presbyterians believed in an organic church, with a graded hierarchy of government; Congregationalists held fast to the idea of the sovereignty of local congregations. There is no greater disruptive force, no greater incentive to fragmentation, than a common creed held with a difference. The perception of a difference often leads to its accentuation, sometimes to the point where what is held in common seems to recede into the background, overshadowed by the suspicion and hostility evoked by the division. A seemingly minor divergence thus had the potential to become the cause of division and strife within Puritanism—if it was allowed to do so.

Yet the increasing perception of a dangerously hostile establishment caused Puritans to see their differences from a somewhat different perspective and to bring a sense of realism to their differences. Internecine hostilities were suspended in order to concentrate on the greater threat that confronted the movement. Puritanism became an increasingly well organized movement, alert to both dangers and opportunities. Whether, taken in isolation, that would have led to anything much remains open to question. In the context of the growing tensions between Charles and Parliament, however, the position of Puritans could be seen as much more serious.

Charles's difficulties with Parliament began early in his reign and reached a crisis in 1629, when Parliament resolved that anyone who brought religious innovations into the country was to be regarded as an enemy of the state. This thinly veiled reference to Charles's interest in Catholicism could hardly be overlooked. The king dissolved Parliament and ruled directly. The "Court of the Star Chamber" was used to dispense legal judgments, without any recourse to appeal. Like his father before him, Charles saw the ideology of the divine right of kings as conveniently legitimating his stance and abrogating fundamental legal rights. Copies of the Geneva Bible, now banned from publication in England, flowed in from the continent, especially Amsterdam. Aware of its devastating critique of this royal ideology, William Laud banned its import as well.

But it would take more than this to staunch the impact of the Geneva Bible. After reading the fine print of Laud's banning order, streetwise Puritan entrepreneurs noted a neat (though inconvenient) way of getting around it. While they were prohibited from reproducing the text of the Geneva Bible, nothing had been said about its marginal notes. Having identified this loophole, they moved quickly to exploit it. They would print the text of the new authorized version of the Bible of 1611 and *add the Genevan notes.* Since the real strength—and, for Laud, the real *danger*—of the Geneva Bible lay not so much in its translation as in the marginal notes, it seemed to all that the Puritans had gained a tactical victory.

On the political front, the Laudian attempt to maintain a national Protestant episcopal church, with the king as its supreme governor, began to encounter setbacks. Charles's hand was forced by war—first in Scotland, then in Ireland. In November 1640, he summoned the "Long Parliament" to finance the war. Sensing Charles's weakness, Parliament abolished the Star Chamber and other institutions that had been instruments of his absolutism. To demonstrate where ultimate power really lay, the Parliament also tried to impeach some of Charles's favorites. Thomas Wentworth was impeached and eventually executed for treason in 1641. Most famously, William Laud was impeached and imprisoned. He would be executed for treason in 1645.[17]

In 1641, John Pym led a parliamentary rebellion against Charles's efforts to raise an army to deal with the rebellion in Ireland; he and his followers were convinced that Charles would first use this army to crush his opponents in England before turning his attention to Ireland. Parliament issued a "Grand Remonstrance," repeating their grievances against Charles, impeaching twelve bishops, and even attempting to impeach the queen. An abortive attempt by Charles to enter the House of Commons and arrest Pym and four parliamentary acolytes polarized matters to a point at which diplomacy was impossible. In August 1642, the civil war broke out.

Initially, the war went well for Charles. Realizing the weakness of its existing military structures, Parliament revoked existing military command structures and created the "New Model Army" under Oliver Cromwell in 1645.[18] From now on, a soldier's rank would be based on ability, not social status. Then the king suffered severe military reversals. Under Sir Thomas Fairfax and Oliver Cromwell, Parliament won victories at Marston Moor (1644) and Naseby (1645). The capture of Charles's correspondence at Naseby revealed his attempts to raise foreign support for his cause, thus alienating many of his more moderate supporters. In May 1646, Charles gave himself up to the Scottish army, which eventually handed him over to Parliament. He was held captive at Hampton Court.

The death of Laud and the capture of Charles marked the end of the defining vision that had guided English Protestantism since Elizabeth I. Whatever else it may have been, the English Civil War was fundamentally a battle for the soul of English Protestantism. Both sides regarded themselves as embodying the true ideals of Protestantism. Their soldiers found passages in the Bible that seemed to support their cause.[19] Indeed, the famous "Soldiers' Pocket Bible" of 1643, intended to encourage the parliamentary army in its fight against the king, was republished fifty years later—with some significant additions—as a *royalist* tract. The defeat of Charles removed the linchpin of the now-traditional Anglican doctrine of a national Protestant episcopal church, with the monarch at its head.

As long as Charles posed a serious threat, Puritanism was forced to unite in opposition to him. Once this incentive to unity had been removed, Puritanism began to fragment. Presbyterians and Congregationalists were locked in theological combat in Parliament. The command structures of the New Model Army were threatened by the rise of "Levelers," who held that the notion of "rank" was unbiblical.[20] Irritated at the aristocratic leanings of Cromwell and his right-hand man, Henry Ireton, radical Puritans pressed for the total abolition of the monarchy and a series of constitutional rights.

In a series of meetings at the Church of St. Mary the Virgin in Putney during late October and early November 1647, radicals met Cromwell and others, pressing for more radical reformation of the English state and army. In terms that presaged those of the American Revolution, they demanded the right of all freeborn Englishmen to vote, equality before the law, and freedom of religion. Colonel Thomas Rainborough argued that every man who is ruled by a civil government ought to have a voice in that government. Cromwell demurred, insisting that this right be limited to landowners. Sensing that things were spiraling out of control, Cromwell suspended the discussions and imposed his own set of reforms. These were so badly received that they led to a near-mutiny later that month. However, the escape of Charles I from Hampton Court that same month concentrated minds. Just as quickly as the removal of any serious external threat led to fragmentation within Puritanism, its reappearance consolidated unity. Charles was recaptured. But what should be done with him?[21]

The answer was suggested by a new doctrine that had arisen within Reformed Protestantism after the death of Calvin. Though he had advocated lawful resistance to tyrants, Calvin had not endorsed the justifiable regicide—that is, the killing of oppressive monarchs.[22] Calvin's death in 1564 removed the last remaining obstacle to this new doctrine, which became increasingly significant in the late 1560s. In his *Short Treatise of Politike Power* (1556), John Ponet (1514–56) asserted that the people had the right to revolt against their oppressors—including "Kinges, Princes and other gouvernors"—and to destroy them before they destroyed the people.[23] Christopher Goodman (1520–1603) took a similar line in his *How Superior Powers Ought to Be Obeyed* (1558). Just as a surgeon might amputate a limb to save the whole body, so society ought to be able to eliminate oppressors through the death sentence.

On January 1, 1649, Charles I was charged by Parliament with being a "tyrant, traitor, and murderer." The use of these three words in the charge ensured that both a legal and a theological foundation were laid for the anticipated death sentence. The "Rump Parliament"—so-called because Cromwell had allowed only those who supported the trial to attend—duly convicted Charles, who was executed on January 30. On the evening before his death, Charles told his thirteen-year-old daughter, Elizabeth, that he was to die for "maintaining the true Protestant religion" and urged her to read the works of Lancelot Andrewes and Richard Hooker "to ground [her] against Popery." Charles saw himself as the defender of a specific form of Protestantism that was now imperiled, threatened by a rival that seemed to have triumphed at every level.

So a republic was proclaimed, and the monarchy abolished. But it was not merely the English state that was to be radically reformed. Between the years 1643 and 1647, the Church of England was systematically dismantled. Bishops, deans, archdeacons, and priests were abolished and replaced by presbyters. English Protestantism was now decisively polarized between the supporters and the opponents of episcopacy; the old middle ground occupied by consciously Reformed

Protestant archbishops after the manner of Thomas Cranmer or Matthew Parker and their Jacobean successors had vanished. For the moment, the opponents of episcopacy had won, yet their victory meant that, after the Restoration, a very different attitude toward episcopacy would emerge.

The sweeping measures brought in by Parliament to end the established church did not end with the abolition of episcopacy. Every effort was made to eradicate its instruments. The *Book of Common Prayer*, detested by Puritans, was proscribed. The celebration of any Christian festival—including Christmas Day—was prohibited. The universities were purged of those with marked Anglican sympathies. The noted Puritan writer John Owen, who managed to preach to Parliament on the day after Charles's execution without actually mentioning that not unimportant event, was appointed vice-chancellor of Oxford University. England had found its own way to Protestantism in the Elizabethan period and shaped its own distinctive form of that faith. Yet all was now changed. For the first time, England became a state modeled along the lines of Calvin's Geneva rather than contemporary Lutheranism. The radicals had won—for the time being.

Yet disenchantment and disillusion soon set in. The religious ideas might have changed, but in just about every other respect England seemed merely to have swapped one rather oppressive regime for another. The "new" national order seemed depressingly similar to the old. Some lines penned on the eve of the Puritan Commonwealth by the Puritan poet John Milton—a vigorous defender of educational and libertarian ideals—seemed to sum up the gloomy mood within Puritanism as it became increasingly obvious that the Commonwealth was imploding. Milton's twenty-four-line poem "On the New Forcers of Conscience Under the Long Parliament" (1646) argued that those who had overthrown Archbishop Laud were subverting Christian freedom, declaring the orthodox to be heretics for their own ends, and setting up a dogmatic religious institution that rivaled anything produced by the Council of Trent. The closing words of that poem would haunt the Commonwealth in its final months: "New *Presbyter* is but old Priest writ large."[24]

In the end, the Puritan Commonwealth died of exhaustion, infighting, disillusionment, and lack of vision. The decision to invite Charles II to return from exile was ultimately a counsel of despair, reflecting a wish to avoid anarchy rather than any firm conviction that it was right in itself. The Puritans had lost any popular sympathy through their religious rigidity, most famously expressed in the banning order issued against the eating of plum pudding on Christmas Day. The restoration of the monarchy unleashed a new era of social and moral experimentation, perhaps most obviously seen in the success of the bawdy "Restoration comedy."[25]

Other nations might have been tempted to experiment with atheism or agnosticism in response to the religious intolerance and bigotry of the Puritan era. The English, however, decided to reinstate the Church of England instead, presumably believing that, for all intents and purposes, this amounted to more or less the same thing. Under Charles II, who reigned from 1660 to 1685, a decidedly docile form of Anglicanism emerged as the religion of the English establishment. The Church of England would be expected to be submissive to the expectations of the people and to keep its religious beliefs to itself rather than impose them on others.

Having been suppressed for more than a decade, the Church of England was put back in place with surprising ease, not unlike that experienced by Russian Orthodoxy after the collapse of the Soviet Union. Everything abolished by the Long Parliament was restored. By 1662 a new prayer book was in place, and bishops, deans, and the clergy were back in their places in restored cathedrals, dioceses, and parishes.[26] The King James Bible, which had languished in earlier generations on account of its associations with an unpopular monarch, became a potent symbol of a new ecclesiastical stability. Who wanted to use the Geneva Bible, with its unhappy associations with the Puritan Commonwealth? It was at this point that the King James Bible began its ascent to the religious and literary heights that would make it the most revered English translation of the Bible yet to have been made.[27]

Yet Puritanism left its mark on the restored church. The concept of the divine right of kings would no longer play a significant role in English religious or political life.[28] Attempts to make Charles I into a religious martyr, evident in the royalist tract *Eikon Basilike* (1649), were subverted by Puritans. The great Puritan writer and public intellectual John Milton offered a radical deconstruction of the work to expose the vested interests of its author. The satirical writings of the Puritan poet Andrew Marvell helped shape Restoration attitudes to Charles I; by the time Marvell had finished with it, the image of Charles had been refashioned from that of "sacred icon" to "sentimental story."

Whether on account of its "precisianist" nature or through a failure to think through the practical implications of its agendas, Puritanism had failed both to uproot an older ecclesiastical system and to root itself in the hearts of the English people. Radical Protestantism would never again be a serious presence in England. Even when, for a brief period, it seemed as if Catholicism might be imposed on the nation during the short and difficult reign of James II, none seem to have entertained even the possibility of restoring Puritanism. It would, however, be permitted: the Toleration Act of 1690 gave the successors of the Puritans the right to worship, subject to certain concessions.

Yet the Toleration Act was soon seen to have an unintended consequence. Drafted to allow the English to worship in other places besides the parish churches, cathedrals, and chapels of the Church of England, it also made possible another alternative—not to worship anywhere at all.

RATIONALISM, INDIFFERENCE, REVIVAL, AND ENTHUSIASM: THE EIGHTEENTH CENTURY

By 1700 western Europe was exhausted by seemingly endless wars of religion that had caused social disintegration and economic hardship. Religious idealisms—as contradictory as they were inept—had run riot, destabilizing nations and peoples. The Thirty Years' War (1618–48) was both an international religious conflict and a German civil war, involving Lutheran, Reformed, and Catholic regions and nations. The populations of many regions were decimated by this war of attrition, and their economies brought to the brink of total collapse. The outcomes of this sterile and inconclusive conflict were meager for all concerned.[29]

When the war was finally resolved through the Peace of Westphalia (1648), any remaining enthusiasm for religious warfare had evaporated. People had had enough. A yearning for peace led to a new emphasis on toleration and growing impatience with religious disputes. The scene was set for the Enlightenment insistence that religion was to be a matter of private belief, rather than state policy. In both intellectual and political circles, religion came to be viewed as a source of international and national conflict, as a burden rather than a blessing. The emerging dislike of religious fanaticism was easily transmuted into a dislike of religion itself.

The necessity for Catholics and Protestants of various traditions to coexist throughout Europe was now so obvious that it required little argument. No one wanted a repeat of the pointless brutalization and destruction that had just ended. Yet one of the more significant outcomes of this realization, an attempt to find common ground on which all could meet, inevitably led to an emphasis on philosophy and those aspects of European culture that were not overtly religious—in other words, its secular aspects.

Unwillingly, yet unable to prevent the massive shift in the tectonic plates of western European culture, an age of faith gave way to the age of reason. The shift is evident from the political writings of each age. In 1649 the Puritan George Winstanley had set out a vision for a commonwealth in which religious values were "really and materially to be fulfilled."[30] Yet a mere forty years later, with the failed Puritan social experiment in mind, John Locke argued that the "great and chief end of men uniting into governments and putting themselves under government is the preservation of their property." The scene was set for the rise of a secular Europe.[31]

In England, the civil war was followed by a new crisis. The stability of the Restoration ended abruptly with the death of Charles II in 1685. He was succeeded by James II, a Catholic, who appointed coreligionists to prominent positions in the government, the army, and the universities. This prompted widespread concern and gave rise to furious rumors of a plot to convert England to Roman Catholicism. A new religious civil war seemed inevitable.

A characteristically English solution, however, emerged, defusing the situation. James II's daughter Mary had earlier married William III, Prince of Orange, a firmly committed Protestant with a reputation for tolerance and generosity. A secret approach was made to William: if he were to invade England, he could be assured that strategically placed well-wishers would rally the nation around him. Encouraged by such overtures, William landed in the west of England in 1688, to widespread public support. James soon realized that his cause was utterly lost. In January 1689, he fled England for France.

William and Mary were declared king and queen of England in February—but only after agreeing to sign a "Bill of Rights" that guaranteed free elections and freedom of speech. The "Glorious Revolution" had averted another civil war and neutralized the power of religion in English public life.[32] It is no accident that John Locke's famous *Letters of Toleration* were published at this precise moment, arguing for the need to tolerate diversity in religion rather than allowing it to lead to conflict. The public mood had changed.

In the intellectual sphere, this new mood was expressed in a growing interest in using human reason—rather than the contested claims of divine revelation or ecclesiastical authority—as the basis of human philosophy and ethics. Not only would the use of reason set these important areas of thought apart from the violence and fanaticism of religion, but it would place them on a single, universal basis. Reason transcended the divisions of creed, geography, and culture. Surely everyone—whether Lutheran, Reformed, Anglican, or Catholic—could agree on the power of reason to guide and illuminate? And so the movement now known as the "Enlightenment" was born.[33]

Its iconic significance for the eighteenth century is best seen from the frontispiece to Christian Wolff's *Rational Thoughts on God, the World, and the Soul* (1719). This superb piece of intellectual propaganda shows a beaming, benevolent sun smiling upon the world, removing clouds and shadows. A new age has dawned! The darkness of earlier generations will vanish, as surely as night gives way to day! This powerful vision resonated with the hopes and fears of a war-weary Europe. Might this be the way to social, religious, and political stability?

This vision also proved compelling to many conflict-weary Protestants who were deeply disillusioned by the violence and fanaticism of the recent religious past. Some Anglican clergy and bishops found its ideas compelling. Deism—a belief in a generic creator God—seemed much less intellectually demanding and tiresome than the trinitarian God of the Christian tradition. It resonated well with the new emphasis on the divine ordering of the world, now emerging from the "mechanical philosophy" of Isaac Newton and his school.[34] God could be thought of as the divine clockmaker who had constructed a particularly elegant piece of machinery and who made no demands of anyone other than a due appreciation of the beauty of the creation. Religions of all kinds now tended to be seen as corruptions of an original "religion of nature" that had no priests or creeds. Most religions were later distortions introduced by self-serving clerics who were anxious to secure their social status and exploit the gullible.

The appeal of the Enlightenment proved greatest within Reformed circles. For reasons that remain unclear, rationalism gained acceptance in many former Calvinist strongholds. Geneva and Edinburgh, both international centers of Calvinism in the late sixteenth century, were noted as epicenters of European rationalism in the late eighteenth century.[35] John Calvin and John Knox gave way to the very different worldviews of Jean-Jacques Rousseau and David Hume. In marked contrast, the Enlightenment had relatively little impact on Catholicism during the eighteenth century—unless, of course, the French Revolution (1789) is seen as a political extension of the ideas of the Enlightenment.

Yet alongside this indifference to religion and the exploration of intellectual alternatives, renewal was taking place within Protestantism. The most important of these revivalist movements, known as "Pietism," traces its origins back to the immediate aftermath of the Thirty Years' War in Germany. Faced with widespread disenchantment with the spiritually arid forms of Protestantism in this region, Philip Jakob Spener published his *Pia Desideria* ("Pious Wishes") in 1675. In this work, Spener lamented the state of the German Lutheran church in the aftermath of the Thirty Years' War (which had ended in 1648) and set out proposals for the revitalization of the church of his day. An obsession with rigid theological orthodoxy had to give way, he argued, to a new concern for the devotional life and a deeper personal relationship with Jesus Christ. Chief among his proposals was a new emphasis on personal Bible study as a means of deepening a personal, living faith in God. Bible study groups would be *ecclesiolae in ecclesiae* ("little churches within the church"), serving as springboards and catalysts for renewal. These proposals were treated with derision by academic theologians; nevertheless, they were to prove influential in German church circles, which showed a growing disillusionment and impatience with the sterility of Lutheran orthodoxy in the face of the shocking social conditions endured during the war.[36]

Pietism developed in a number of different directions, especially in England and Germany. Nikolaus Ludwig Graf von Zinzendorf (1700–1760) founded the Pietist community generally known as the "Herrnhuter"—named after the village of Herrnhut. Alienated from what he regarded as the arid rationalism and barren Protestant religious formalism of his time, Zinzendorf stressed the importance of a "religion of the heart" based on an intimate and personal relationship between Christ and the believer. A new emphasis was placed on the role in the Christian life of "feeling" (as opposed to reason or doctrinal orthodoxy), an orientation that is often seen as laying the foundations for Romanticism in later German religious thought. Zinzendorf's emphasis on a personally appropriated faith was expressed in the slogan "a living faith," an idea he contrasted unfavorably with the prevailing nominalism of Protestant orthodoxy. For orthodoxy, faith was about assent to the creeds; for Zinzendorf, it was about a personal, transforming encounter with God, with creedal assent playing a lesser role.

Zinzendorf's ideas soon began to find acceptance in England. John Wesley (1703–91) was a founder and early leader of the Methodist movement within the Church of England; that movement subsequently gave birth to Methodism as a denomination in its own right. Convinced that he "lacked the faith whereby alone we are saved," Wesley paid a visit to Herrnhut in 1738 and was deeply impressed by what he found there. Wesley found the Pietist emphasis on the need for a "living faith" and the role of experience in the Christian life to be very persuasive. His conversion experience at a meeting in Aldersgate Street, London, in May 1738—in which he felt his heart to be "strangely warmed"—led him to travel throughout England, preaching his new understanding of the Protestant religion.

Wesley's emphasis on the experiential side of Christian faith, which contrasted sharply with what he saw as the spiritual dullness of contemporary English deism, led to a minor religious revival in England during the eighteenth century.[37] Wesley was joined in his ministry by his brother Charles; between them, they wrote some of the best-known hymns in the English language, many of which express the transformative nature of faith and the need for personal conversion. It was their structured approach to Christian devotion that earned them the nickname "Methodists."

Yet this emphasis on the experiential side of religion raised the specter of "enthusiasm"—a dramatic, religiously inspired fervor, often accompanied by the agitated body movements and faintings and swoonings so devastatingly caricatured in William Hogarth's etching "Enthusiasm Delineat'd."[38] Many revivalist preachers—including John Wesley and George Whitefield—found themselves torn between sympathy for the idea that a direct experience of God might induce such dramatic effects and concern that its bizarre manifestations would alienate a religiously suspicious public. Somehow a middle way had to be found so as to avoid the religious excesses of "enthusiasm," on the one hand, and the impoverishment of "formalism," on the other.

Despite their differences, the various branches of Pietism succeeded in making Christian faith relevant to the experiential world of ordinary believers and in some ways anticipated the success of Pentecostalism two centuries later. Pietism succeeded in lodging Protestantism in the everyday realities of life for many people. It is of no small importance to note that the strongly antireligious tone of the French Revolution during the eighteenth century was partly due to the absence of any real equivalent of Pietism in French Catholicism at that time. In England and Germany, faith was being reconnected with everyday life; in France, that link appears to have been fractured—with massive implications for the future of Christianity in that region.

Initially, Methodism was organized as a group of "societies." The Wesleys discouraged their followers from leaving the Church of England, despite the hostility and general disdain they encountered from their Anglican counterparts. In part, this negative attitude reflected the sociological differences between the movements: the Wesleys were gaining a mass following within the working class, such as among miners, whereas Anglicanism tended to see itself as representing both the social and ecclesiastical establishment. After John Wesley's death in 1791, Methodism became a separate denomination organized as a "connection" made up of districts, which were divided into circuits of several churches or societies. The term "Wesleyanism" tended to be used at this stage.

The early history of English Methodism demonstrates the innate tendency to fragmentation that is characteristic of Protestantism. Divisions arose over a series of issues, including church order and discipline—though not, significantly, matters of doctrine. A dispute in the northeast of England led to the "Methodist New Connection" forming in 1797. A decade later, the "Primitive Methodists" broke away, believing that the Wesleyan connection was losing its enthusiasm for revivalism. The Bible Christian Church was founded by a Wesleyan preacher in England's west country in 1815; unusually, it made extensive use of women preachers. Other Methodist groups included the Protestant Methodists and the Wesleyan Reformers.

Yet English Methodism also illustrates Protestantism's capacity to set past controversies behind it and secure reconciliation. In 1857 three Methodist groups came together to form the United Methodist Free Churches; in 1907 these were incorporated with the Methodist New Connection and the Bible Christians as the United Methodist Church; in 1932 the Wesleyans, Primitive Methodists, and United Methodists merged to establish the Methodist Church in Great Britain.

In this chapter, we have surveyed a critically important period in the history of England—a nation destined to have a major influence on the shaping of Protestantism worldwide, particularly through its missionary enterprises in the late eighteenth and nineteenth centuries. Yet the nation that has had by far the greatest impact in recent years on the shaping of global Protestantism is the United States of America. We must now turn and explore how Protestantism came to be established in what is now regarded as this most religious of Western nations.

Cotton Mather, the leading Puritan writer who compiled one of the earliest American histories. Mezzotint by Peter Pelham, 1728.

7

Protestantism in America

Christianity was a European import to the Americas. By the end of the sixteenth century, Catholic mission stations had been established in many places colonized by France and Spain.[1] One of the first Protestant colonies in America was established in April 1562 when a group of Huguenots settled at Fort Caroline on Florida's St. Johns River. This Protestant colony did not survive long: the Spanish promptly wiped out the French Protestant refugees in 1565 and founded their own outpost at St. Augustine in its place. A more permanent French presence in America would later be established along the Mississippi Valley, the St. Lawrence Valley, and the Great Lakes. Yet vast tracts of land remained unsettled by the two great Catholic maritime powers—above all, New England.

The first English-speaking Protestant colony was established in Virginia—named after the "virgin queen" (Elizabeth I)—in 1585. The fate of this "lost colony" remains unclear. When a major English plantation—named "Jamestown" after the reigning monarch, James I—was established in Virginia in 1607, no trace could be found of the earlier settlement. Jamestown was an Anglican colony whose charter stipulated that the "religion now professed and established within our realm of England" should be regularly practiced by the colonists and spread "as much as they may amongst the savage people." One early convert was Pocahontas, daughter of the great chief Powhatan, who died during a subsequent trip to England.

Yet, despite such earlier Protestant settlements in Florida and Virginia, the history of Protestantism in America is traditionally traced to the year 1620, when the *Mayflower* docked in New England.[2] In view of the importance of this development for the shaping of Protestantism in America, we may consider it in more detail.

EARLY NEW ENGLAND PROTESTANTISM

Those who brought their form of Protestantism to New England on the *Mayflower* were not economic migrants, but rather individuals who believed that they were being persecuted or oppressed on account of their faith. They saw themselves as "called"—a notion heavily freighted with the most powerful Puritan theological themes—to establish "holy commonwealths" in a new world, free from the opposition and ridicule they had faced in England. They would be the salt of the American earth, the light of the new world.[3]

The most famous such emigration traced its origins back to 1607 or 1608, when a congregation of separatist Protestants from the Nottinghamshire town of Scrooby, weary of the hostile religious policies of James I, migrated to Amsterdam, which had by then displaced Geneva as the center of the Reformed world. In 1609 the migrants moved on to Leiden, where they developed a sense of identity as God's chosen people, as aliens in a strange land. Never regarding themselves as Dutch, and unwilling to return to the hostile ecclesiastical environment of England, they conceived a solution as desperate as it was brilliant. Those of their number who believed that they were called to do so would travel to America and establish a settlement there.

An initial attempt to sail to America in a smaller vessel, the *Speedwell,* failed when it began to leak, forcing it to dock in Plymouth and discharge its passengers. Most were able to secure passage on the larger *Mayflower,* which set sail in September 1620. Due to a navigation error, the "Pilgrim Fathers" arrived at Cape Cod, Massachusetts, in November 1620, some considerable distance north of their intended destination. A month later, they finally landed at Plymouth Rock and established a community there. The Puritan settlement of New England was under way.

Between 1627 and 1640, some four thousand individuals made the hazardous crossing of the Atlantic Ocean and settled on the coastline of Massachusetts Bay. For these settlers, there was a clear alignment between the narrative of their journey and that of the Bible. England was the land in which they struggled under oppression; America would be the land in which they found freedom. Expelled from their Egypt by a cruel Pharaoh (as they saw both James I and Charles I), they had settled in a promised land flowing with milk and honey. They would build a new Jerusalem, a city upon a hill, in this strange land. The Pilgrim Fathers were an inspiration to many who followed them to the new world.[4]

The Pilgrim Fathers were not, it must be appreciated, typical of English Puritanism at this time. They were separatists whose beliefs were more characteristic of the Anabaptists than of Calvin: they were convinced that each congregation had the democratic right to determine its own beliefs and choose its own ministers.[5] Most English Puritans of the age were Presbyterians who were committed to the notion of a single mother church with local outposts—a "universal church" with "particular congregations" bound together by shared beliefs and leaders. It was only a matter of time before the defining conflicts of the Old World would find themselves being replayed in the New. But this time, decentralization would win.

One of the most remarkable features of the early history of New England Protestantism in the 1620s and 1630s is that most Puritan communities appear to have abandoned a Presbyterian view of church government within months of their arrival and adopted a congregational polity instead. The Plymouth Colony Separatists appear to have been significant in bringing about a major shift in how congregations organized themselves and related to other congregations.[6] Reacting strongly against the rigid hierarchical structures of the European state churches, the American settlers opted instead for a democratic congregationalism. Local congregations made their own decisions. Instead of centralized authority structures—such as presbyteries or dioceses—the Puritans of the Massachusetts Bay area developed "a highly decentralized and well-nigh uncontrollable Congregational church order which licensed any individual congregation to revise Calvinist theology as it saw fit. And revise it they did."[7]

The Puritans who settled in America were far from theologically incoherent, on the one hand, or monolithic, on the other. The new situation in America, by allowing the unfettered exploration of religious possibilities that were simply unthinkable in England, led to diversification of religious beliefs and customs in response to local circumstances. The particular forms that Puritanism developed in the region are to be regarded as historical contingencies rather than theological necessities, and they generally derived from local issues of personality, power, and privilege rather than from any intrinsic "essence" of Puritan identity.[8]

Roger Williams (1603–84), one of the leading proponents of a pure separatist church, argued that the Church of England was apostate and that any kind of fellowship with it—whether in England or in America—was a serious sin. Christian believers were under an obligation to separate from apostate churches and from a secular state. Church and state should be separate; above all, the state should not be able to enforce the first four of the Ten Commandments. Disenchanted by the unwavering commitment to the mutual interpenetration of church and state in Massachusetts, Williams established the colony of Rhode Island in 1636. There he insisted upon complete religious freedom, extending this far beyond traditional Christian denominations to embrace Jews and other religious minorities.[9]

Yet further south, a somewhat different form of Protestantism had become established. Whereas Massachusetts became a hotbed of Protestant religious experimentation, with generally secondary interests in commerce, southern colonies from Delaware to Georgia were primarily concerned with trade and saw religion as peripheral to this enterprise. It was an ideal context for Anglicanism to take root and flourish, primarily as the religion of the planting class. Long used to issues of social class and distinction, Anglicanism proved an ideal provider of a veneer of religious dignity to the social structures of the plantations that continued to the dawn of the nineteenth century.[10]

THE GREAT AWAKENING

One of the most distinctive features of North American Protestant Christianity is the phenomenon of the "Awakening." To date, three Awakenings have been documented, each leading initially to religious renewal and subsequently to social change. Sociologists have noted that such religious revitalization often originates in times of cultural stress and uncertainty and leads to radical social reform and transformation.[11] The Awakening, though primarily religious in nature, has the capacity to energize the culture as a whole. The first of these religious revivals, traditionally known as the "Great Awakening," took place in New England in 1734. To appreciate its importance, we must consider the background against which it took place.

By 1700 American Protestantism appeared to be stagnant. The first generation of Puritan immigrants was possessed by a driving religious vision that was not always shared by their children. Church membership began to decline. When increased immigration from Europe led to the middle Atlantic states becoming religiously diverse to an extent without parallel anywhere else, awkward questions were raised about earlier Puritan visions of a "holy commonwealth." More significantly, a series of scandals rocked the credibility of Puritan institutions. The worst of these were the Salem witch trials of 1693; instigated by the clergy of that town, the trials led to the execution of nineteen people. Governor Sir William Phips eventually put an end to the hysteria, and the subsequent clerical apologies and recantations seriously diminished the standing and reputation of the clergy of the area.[12]

Tensions began to emerge over church membership. In the early seventeenth century, New England congregations generally had a policy of admitting to full membership only those individuals who could provide a narrative of personal conversion. As the century progressed, fewer and fewer individuals could testify to such an experience. Yet most individuals wanted some connection or association with the church, not least on account of the close ties between church membership and citizenship in most communities. As church attendance began to decline, tensions emerged between those who wanted to maintain religious purity at any cost and those who believed that the churches could survive only if they broadened their membership base by adopting less strict criteria.

A compromise was reached. In 1662 a "halfway" membership was accepted by some congregations: those prepared to accept formally the truth of Christianity and the moral discipline of the church could have their children baptized.[13] The result of this idea of a "halfway covenant" was perhaps inevitable: by the beginning of the eighteenth century, a large proportion of church members were "nominal" or "halfway" Protestants. Protestantism was on its way to becoming the civil religion of New England, with primary functions that were social and moral.

All this was changed in the Great Awakening, which is often associated with Jonathan Edwards, widely recognized as America's greatest theologian to date.[14] Edwards was born at East Windsor, Connecticut, on October 5, 1703, the son of a local pastor. In September 1716, he entered Yale College in New Haven (now Yale University), where he later served as tutor from 1724 to 1726. When he was around seventeen years of age, Edwards underwent a conversion experience. As he read 1 Timothy 1:17, he was overwhelmed by a sense of God's greatness and glory. "As I read the words," he wrote later in his journal, "there came into my soul, and it was, as it were, diffused through it, a sense of the glory of the divine Being; a new sense quite different from anything I ever experienced before."[15]

In 1726 Edwards resigned his post at Yale in order to take up a pastoral charge at Northampton, Massachusetts, as the colleague of his maternal grandfather, Solomon Stoddard. Stoddard was widely regarded as the leading spiritual authority in the Connecticut Valley—so much so, in fact, that local people called him "Pope Stoddard" behind his back. Edwards was ordained on February 15, 1727, aged twenty-three. In July of the same year, he married Sarah Pierrepont, with whom he had been in love for some considerable time. His grandfather died in February 1729, leaving Edwards in charge of one of the most important churches in the area. Reflecting on the events of those two years, Edwards noted the general absence of any real interest in religion: Northampton, like virtually all of colonial North America, "seemed to be at that time very insensible of the things of religion, and engaged in other cares and pursuits."

From about 1735 to 1745, much of New England was engulfed in religious renewal. Contemporary records speak of mass outdoor meetings that occasionally attracted twenty thousand people, open-air sermons, deserted taverns, and packed churches. Historians have pointed out that the connections between these events are often difficult to establish and that using the term "Great Awakening" retrospectively imposes a single narrative structure upon what may really have been a complex set of happenings.[16] It is, however, clear that some extraordinary events that took place at this time reversed the downward trend in church attendance and the declining public profile of religion in the region.

Edwards himself was witness to such events in Northampton during the winter of 1734–35. The final weeks of 1734 witnessed several conversions, "very remarkably and suddenly, one after another." The revival continued into the new year, reaching its peak during March and April 1735. There was hardly a household in the town that was not affected. Perhaps as many as three hundred individuals, "about the same number of males as females," appeared to have been converted.

The phenomenon of "enthusiasm" once more made an appearance, generating concern within the churches over its apparent excesses. Edwards himself was concerned that such seemingly hysterical behavior could bring the church into disrepute and even destabilize the social order.[17] Confronted with obvious evidence of ecstatic religious experiences, however, Edwards began to develop what we might now call a "psychology of religion"—an attempt to understand and make sense of ecstatic phenomena as natural responses to a sense of guilt or the realization of forgiveness. His 1741 commencement address at Yale, entitled "The Distinguishing Marks of a Work of the Spirit of God," sought to distinguish between a primary divine inspiration and a secondary human response. The latter (but not the former), he argued, could be understood in naturalist terms.

As the revival continued in New England, it was given a new sense of direction by George Whitefield, recently arrived from England.[18] England itself was then experiencing the evangelical revival associated with John and Charles Wesley as well as Whitefield. Edwards found that he himself was no longer at the forefront of the revival movement. He was also troubled by divisions within his congregation at Northampton, particularly over matters of church discipline. He moved to minister to a congregation at Stockbridge, where relatively light parish duties allowed him to write a series of major theological works that gave intellectual muscle to New England Puritanism.[19] In 1757, his reputation as a scholar firmly established, Edwards was invited to become president of the College of New Jersey in Princeton (now Princeton University). Following an unsuccessful inoculation against smallpox at Princeton, intended to demonstrate the safety of the new medical procedure to his students, he died on March 22, 1758.

The Awakening, however, continued. It was far too broad and deep to be dependent upon any one individual. By 1760 it was clear that the movement was bringing about significant changes in American Protestantism. It was not simply that people were returning to church, or that religion was playing an increasingly significant role in public life. The revival changed the nature of Protestantism, bringing about a changed perception of the relationship between the individual, the congregation, and the state.

The new emphasis on individuals having undergone a personal conversion led to the emergence of "conversion narratives" as a means of proving religious commitment and affirming personal identity.[20] Whereas in the 1630s a congregation would test an individual's beliefs to determine whether that person was indeed a truly converted, orthodox believer prior to being admitted to full membership, the emphasis now fell upon the individual's personal experience. Conversion was not authenticated by an external ecclesiastical body, but by an inward individual experience. Furthermore, these conversion narratives raised questions about the place of the precise theological formulations once favored by Puritan church leaders. It seemed to many that the convert's immediate sense of participating directly in spiritual reality was more important and significant than such rigid formulations. In short: the Awakening led to the weakening of the intellectual side of faith and shifted the emphasis to its emotional and relational aspects.

So how might such a revival be accommodated within the confines of a Calvinist theology? How could such an experiential approach to the religious life be reconciled with the theological logic of a movement often associated with intellectual rigor rather than devotional fervor? The answer lies in the dynamics of theological internalization—the process by which ideas are transmuted into attitudes.[21] The capacity of contemporary Puritanism to forge links between theology and experience must be regarded as one of its most significant characteristics, and above all in relation to explaining the origins of the Great Awakening.

Most people responded to a theology focusing on divine judgment and human sinfulness by realizing their inability to achieve self-deliverance and hence totally entrusting their destiny to the will of God. For others, a discernment of divine mercy and grace led to a joyful expectation of deliverance, often linked with moments of ecstatic perception and delight.

The Awakening also had implications for the democratization of religion. The individual experience of conversion was recognized as being open to all, whether male or female, rich or poor, ignorant or wise. Religion became "popular," in the sense that it no longer made significant intellectual demands of its adherents. Grace was something to be experienced rather than defined and articulated in the esoteric language of theology. The experience of the divine was no longer dependent upon texts or sermons. The same factors that would help make Pentecostalism the religion of the urban poor in the late twentieth century were anticipated in the Great Awakening more than two centuries earlier.

Yet the most important outcome of the Puritan commonwealths of the 1630s and their revitalization a century later was political. A radical alternative was established to the European model of Protestantism as a regional or national religion. The rise of confessionalism in Germany led to state-sponsored Protestant churches defining the religious establishment. Lutheranism was the state religion in certain parts of Germany and Scandinavia, Reformed Christianity in certain other regions of Europe, and Anglicanism in England and the British colonies—including the Carolinas and Virginia. Catholicism, of course, was firmly established as the state religion in France, Italy, Portugal, and Spain, as well as in the newly established Spanish and Portuguese colonies in Central and South America.

The congregationalism of the Puritan commonwealths offered an alternative model that had no real precedent in Europe: an understanding of religious "establishment" that did not involve preferential state support for any one specific ecclesiastical body. The Puritan experimentation in defining church-state relationships was driven as much by hatred for the English model of a state church, which both patronized and oppressed alternative forms of Christianity, as by a longing for individual and corporate freedom. Yet during the first half of the eighteenth century, this was merely a local model, appropriate to the commonwealth of Massachusetts and a few other locations in New England. It would take a revolution to make it the norm for America as a whole. As events unfolded, it turned out that such a revolution lay to hand.

PROTESTANTISM AND
THE AMERICAN REVOLUTION

The historical roots of the American Revolution are complex, and it is difficult to assign priority to any one factor as the ultimate cause of the rebellion against British rule. The burdens of taxation, the lack of due representation, and the desire for freedom were unquestionably integral ingredients in the accumulation of grievances that drove many colonials to take up arms against the king.[22] Yet religious issues also played their part, not least in intensifying a sense of injustice over the privileged status of the Church of England in the British colonies.[23] The Church of England had become established by law in the southern states of Virginia, Maryland, the Carolinas, and Georgia, and even in four counties of New York State. Although dissent was permitted, the situation rankled Baptists, Congregationalists, and Presbyterians. Opposition began to grow.

In the early 1770s, Congregationalist ministers in New England regularly preached on the theme of religious and political freedom, linking both with resisting English tyranny. Throughout Puritan Massachusetts, pamphlets appeared offering a religious justification for the use of armed force against an oppressor and urging young men to join militias.[24] The rhetoric and theology were not entirely unlike the rhetoric and theology that prevailed during the prelude to the English Civil War.

So was the American Revolution actually a war of religion? It is difficult to make the case for its being so. Religious elements were involved—above all a desire to ensure religious freedom and eliminate the privileges of the established church. Yet it would not be true to say that these concerns dominated the agenda of those driving the Revolution. The patriots came from a wide variety of religious backgrounds, only some of which were driven by the theological vision of the New England Congregationalists. The "black Regiment" of preachers such as

Charles Chauncy, Samuel Cooper, and Jonathan Mayhew (so-called on account of their clerical dress) criticized the British from their pulpits. Yet the Great Awakening had renewed a sense of vision among Lutherans, Methodists, and Baptists, and that renewal widened and diversified the theological base of the Revolution.[25] George Washington himself appears to have been somewhat unorthodox religiously and may be best described as a deist—someone who believed in a generic notion of divinity rather than the distinctively Christian conception of God.[26]

Unsurprisingly, the backbone of Protestant resistance to any form of rebellion came predominantly—though by no means exclusively—from the Church of England. Isaac Wilkens, a New York Anglican layman, decided to leave America rather than be forced into a war against England. Other Protestants, significantly drawn primarily from Anabaptist and Quaker traditions, refused to get involved in the war on either side, regarding any form of violence as unacceptable.

It is important to note that a fundamental difference existed between the American Revolution of 1776 and its French counterpart of 1789. The French Revolution was partly inspired by an antireligious agenda, with a particular animus against Catholicism.[27] While the French-language Protestant intellectual tradition may have done much to lay the foundations for the revolutionary idea of "justifiable regicide," the French Revolution appears to have harbored a generic hostility to Christianity, and many of its proponents pursed a program of "de-Christianization," which affected most churches.[28]

The American Revolution, in marked contrast, was undertaken with at least some degree of explicitly religious motivation. For many, it was a defining moment of religious purification in which the excesses and privileges of the established church could be eliminated. Yet there was no question of eliminating Anglicanism, still less Anglicans. Following the Revolution, the "Protestant Episcopal Church" was reconstituted in 1789 at Philadelphia as the successor to the Church of England in the American colonies. No Protestant denomination was designated as the "established church" in its place. The religious diversity of the newly established United States of America was such that any decision along these lines would have led to intense infighting. An alternative solution was therefore proposed.

In 1786 Thomas Jefferson's "Virginia Statute for Religious Freedom" set out the separation of church and state and ended any legal oversight or enforcement of religious belief.[29] The First Amendment to the Constitution ended the formal establishment of religion, although in terms that make its subsequent application problematic: "Congress shall make no law respecting an establishment of religion, or prohibiting the free exercise thereof." The Constitution itself makes no reference to God, Christianity, or Protestantism. Where Jefferson's "Declaration of Independence" famously invokes a "Creator" in setting out its vision of human rights, the Constitution consciously and conspicuously avoids any such references.

The new American Constitution opened the way to a radical reshaping of the nation's religious landscape by sweeping away established structures and creating new structures without parallel at that time. At one level, the constitutional separation of church and state could be seen as an attempt to marginalize religion in public life. This would, however, seem to be a mistaken perception. For many at the time, such as the Baptist minister Isaac Backus, this separation amounted to a virtual guarantee that America would be a Christian nation whose churches would be free from political interference and manipulation. And since the predominant form of Christianity was Protestantism, it seemed self-evident that the new American republic would be a Protestant bastion in the New World, like Calvin's Geneva in the Old.

But as time passed the situation began to change—and Protestantism changed with it.

TENSIONS AND REVIVAL: THE NINETEENTH CENTURY

American Protestantism underwent dramatic development during the nineteenth century, and many of the distinctive contemporary traits of the movement were forged at this time. That development was shaped by forces unique to the American situation, including the rapid expansion westward into geographical regions without any history of a Christian presence and an expanding Catholic population in what had once been a predominantly Protestant nation.

Between 1800 and the eve of the Civil War, the population of the United States expanded from about 5 million to 30 million. With the territorial expansion that accompanied this population growth, there was every risk that the nation's Christian moorings would be loosened as children sought to establish their independence from their parents and formed new communities to create new identities, far removed from those of the original colonies. Yet there is abundant evidence that many sought to cope with the radical social and political change of the times by rediscovering their religious roots and the secure sense of social location and personal identity that this entailed.[30]

Alongside such pressures that might lead to the dilution of Protestant influence, other religious groups were making their presence felt through new waves of immigration. Puritans were not the only religious minority to flee intolerance and insecurity in seventeenth-century England. In early 1634, a group of Catholic refugees settled in the Chesapeake Bay area. Maryland—named after Henrietta Maria, the wife of Charles I—became the first Catholic colony in America. Although Maryland was criticized for being a Catholic enclave in the New World, it soon established its credentials as a place of religious toleration. Under Archbishop John Carroll (1735–1815), Catholicism became increasingly accepted in American culture.

However, a fresh wave of immigration from European nations in the nineteenth century led to radical change in the nation's religious profile. Political instability and economic deprivation brought large numbers of Irish and Italian Catholics to cities such as Boston, New York, and Philadelphia. German refugees tended to settle in the upper Midwest, in centers such as St. Louis and Cincinnati. Strong ethnic loyalties led to Catholic émigrés retaining the social and religious habits of Europe and thus not integrating into American culture.[31] This rapid rise of Catholicism in cities that had hitherto been staunchly Protestant led to social and religious tension.

Protestantism itself was nothing like a coherent movement, and it is far from clear whether Anglican, Presbyterian, Baptist, Congregationalist, and Methodist congregations had any sense of a shared identity, heritage, or faith in antebellum America. Controversies within the Protestant movement—including especially ferocious and divisive divisions about slavery[32]—tended to accentuate its differences rather than identify and celebrate its commonalities.[33] Indeed, it might reasonably be argued that the rise of Catholicism in America in the nineteenth century brought a new unity to the hitherto somewhat diverse movement by providing it with a common enemy, replicating the patterns of Protestant identity maintenance that emerged in Europe during the late sixteenth century.

Despite all these difficulties, Protestant church attendance rose by a factor of ten over the period 1800 to 1860, comfortably outstripping population growth. Twice as many Protestants went to church at the end of this period than at its beginning. Why? If any factor may be identified as responsible for this development, it is the "Second Great Awakening" (1800–1830) and the new patterns of religious revivalism that this brought about. Such religious revivals not only became the defining mark of American religion but also played a central role in the nation's developing identity, independence, and democratic principles. Although the subject of criticism at the time, revivalism became deeply enmeshed within the American Protestant consciousness.[34]

The first such revival broke out in rural Kentucky in 1801 in the form of large camp meetings. The most famous of these was the "Cane Ridge" meeting, which lasted a week and was attended by at least ten thousand individuals. These meetings set a precedent for a wave of revivalist meetings throughout the frontier territories that appealed primarily to common folk and emphasized emotion rather than intellect. The outcome was the transformation of antebellum America and the emergence of the Protestant "Bible Belt."

Charles Grandison Finney (1792–1875) was the pivotal figure of the Second Awakening.[35] Following his conversion in 1821, Finney abandoned his career as a lawyer and became a Presbyterian minister. He distanced himself, however, from some aspects of the older New England Calvinism, which he regarded as in the first place unbiblical, and in the second an obstacle to effective evangelism. Finney focused on the need for people to respond to the proclamation of the gospel and on the skills that were thus required of the preacher to persuade them to do so.[36] He clearly regarded it as perfectly acceptable—perhaps even as necessary—to use every technique of persuasion available in preaching for conversion.[37]

What sort of techniques? Finney introduced many of the standard features of revivalist preaching, which rapidly became part of a largely unquestioned tradition. One such feature was the "anxious seat," a bench reserved for those who, as a result of the preacher's message, were "anxious" for their soul's safety and wanted counsel and prayer. Yet the most familiar of all Finney's innovations was the "altar call"—the invitation to come forward in response to the invitation to receive the gospel. The technique was picked up by Dwight L. Moody, the greatest revivalist preacher in the second half of the nineteenth century, and thus passed into virtually all of nineteenth- and twentieth-century revivalist preaching, from Billy Sunday through to Billy Graham.

Finney's attentiveness to controlling and directing the revival process marked a significant shift from the days of the first Great Awakening. Edwards and Whitefield had no place for "altar calls" or other such techniques. For them, revival was a matter of God's grace, which lay beyond human control or influence. For Finney, revival was "not a miracle or dependent on a miracle"; rather, it was the "result of the right use of the constituted means." Although it would be unfair to accuse Finney of reducing revival to a set of techniques, both organizational and rhetorical, those elements are certainly present in his thought.

The impact of Finney and those who developed his ministry on the shaping of modern American Protestantism was immense. The emergence of the "holiness" movement is often seen as a response to the ideas and values of revivalism. Unlike forms of Protestantism that emphasized the defense of doctrinal orthodoxy, the holiness movement was much more oriented to ethics and the spiritual life. It tended to raise ethics to the status that later fundamentalists have accorded doctrine. This emphasis on "holy living" came to be linked with support for the abolition of slavery in the antebellum period. Oberlin College in Ohio—where Finney later served as professor of theology—became a stronghold of abolitionism and a haven for those who advocated even "civil disobedience" in the face of the fugitive slave laws.[38]

The "holiness" tradition's emphasis on issues of Christian living was not limited to an attempt to end slavery. Oberlin College became the center of some serious attempts to erase racial and gender barriers within both the antebellum church and society at large. Its pioneering moves toward coeducation led to its graduating some of the most vigorous and radical feminists of the era. Antoinette Brown, the first woman to be ordained in an American church, was a graduate of Oberlin. At her ordination in 1853, Wesleyan Methodist minister Luther Lee preached on "Woman's Right to Preach the Gospel."

After the Civil War, revivalism began to develop in new directions. Revivalist rhetoric was supplemented by the emergence of a popular American hymnody. Whereas the Puritans strongly disapproved of the singing of nonbiblical texts in church, the Wesleyan revival movement in England had recognized the importance of hymns, both as a means of Christian education and as a powerful way of praising God. After the end of the Civil War, as America moved toward becoming an industrial nation, the Protestant churches were able to remain in touch with the nation's soul through the use of music. The revivalist Dwight Moody teamed up with the musician Ira David Sankey to produce a formidable double act.

The two met in 1870 after a prayer meeting for a revivalist meeting in Indianapolis.[39] The day after their meeting, Moody sent a note to Sankey, asking if they could meet on a street corner. When Sankey arrived, Moody produced a soapbox and invited Sankey to mount it and sing a hymn. Sankey—who had a magnificent voice—did so. A crowd gathered to hear him. When Sankey had finished, Moody got on the box and delivered a short sermon, inviting everyone present to follow him to the Indianapolis Opera House, where the YMCA was holding its convention. It was obvious that Finney's method had been supplemented—and bettered.

One of the most significant consequences of the rapid growth of revivalism in nineteenth-century America was the emergence of the Protestant Bible Belt—a story that needs to be told in greater detail.

THE ORIGINS OF THE BIBLE BELT

The emergence of the Bible Belt is one of the most puzzling features of American Christianity.[40] The original heartlands of Protestantism were in the greater New England area, especially Massachusetts. It was here that Congregationalism and Presbyterianism took root and quickly became the most significant and dynamic forms of Protestant self-expression in the region. The southern colonies tended to be dominated by a socially conservative and quietist Anglicanism, which lent tacit support to the hierarchical social structures that dominated their plantations and social life throughout much of the eighteenth century. The plantation aristocracy enjoyed their hunting, shooting, dueling, dancing, drinking, and gambling and tolerated Anglicanism precisely because it tolerated them. Religious commitment was low: only one in ten southerners attended church in 1776. Yet the great era of Protestant expansion and consolidation that opened up in the nineteenth century was centered in the Midwest and the South, not the original Northeast. Why?

The reasons for this development cast an interesting light on the remarkable ability of some forms of Protestantism to adapt to new situations and challenges. In her analysis of the emergence of the Bible Belt, Christine Heyrman shows that evangelical Protestants virtually reinvented their religion, setting aside any of its aspects that might alienate southern culture. By adapting to the realities of the South, evangelical Baptists and Methodists laid down the foundations of the Bible Belt. The task of adaptation and modification took over two generations. Ministers such as John Taylor, Stith Mead, and Freeborn Garrettson were able to build bridges to different cultural groups—young people, slaves, women, and, perhaps most difficult of all, white males—to defuse initial anxiety and hostility against evangelicals. Over the period 1770 to 1830, egalitarian forms of evangelicalism eventually managed to establish deep roots in southern culture, despite the tensions this created with the middle-aged white gentry.

Yet this adaptation created a form of Protestantism that stood at some distance from the forms found in the Northeast. This divergence was more than purely denominational. (In 1830 the Northeast was dominated by Presbyterians and Congregationalists, the South by Baptists and Methodists.) The new religion made its appeal primarily to individuals, focusing on the transformation of their personal lives rather than of society as a whole.[41] These characteristics appear to have persisted in the religious individualism of contemporary southern religious approaches to the reading of the Bible and the understanding of the nature of salvation.

Yet the term "Bible Belt" reflects something deeper than denominational or theological distinctions. Those observers of southern religion in the late nineteenth and early twentieth centuries who coined the phrase used it primarily to denote the remarkable religious homogeneity of the region. Once the hiatus of the Civil War had passed, allowing the South to regain religious and social stability, it became clear that southern religion had crystallized into predominantly conservative forms of Protestantism and was relatively unaffected by the social and intellectual challenges that Protestantism faced in the North, especially in urban centers.

If any religious group has an especial association with the distinctive Protestantism of this region, it is the Southern Baptist Convention, founded in Augusta, Georgia, in May 1845.[42] Up to that point, Baptist congregations in the South had operated without feeling the need for any national or regional structure, and they never thought of themselves as belonging to a "denomination." Yet there was a growing recognition that such a centralized denomination would be more efficient, more powerful, and capable of achieving greater influence. Anxious not to compromise the autonomy of local Baptist congregations, the Convention adopted a Congregationalist model of church governance: the decision of a local church in a matter of doctrine, discipline, or church order could not be overturned by any superior body, since there was no body that had authority over the local church. This principle, which was vigorously upheld by the second president of the Convention, R. B. C. Howell, during the period 1851 to 1858, is essential to any understanding of the subsequent dynamics of Southern Baptist life.

Yet the upsurge in religious interest in the South was not limited to white Americans. Black Protestantism was already a significant force in the antebellum era, even though restrictions were placed upon it—for example, worship had to be supervised by whites.[43] In Columbus, Mississippi, 80 percent of the antebellum Baptist church membership was black. In Georgia at this time, 35 to 40 percent of Baptist church members were black. The end of the Civil War brought about emancipation, and with it new possibilities for Protestantism.

With the ending of the Civil War, black Protestant churches underwent new growth—this time, under black leadership, unrestricted by white supervisors. Baptist churches quickly became core institutions of newfound black freedom, with their own styles of worship and preaching.[44] One legacy of the past was the lack of education among members of such congregations, so preachers often seemed more concerned with heightening their congregation's sense of God's love and presence than with educating them in the fundamentals of faith. Many inequities remained in the South, where blacks found themselves largely excluded from the traditional, predominantly white denominations. Yet the foundation was being laid for significant future developments.

"OPPOSITIONALISM" AND THE SHAPING OF AMERICAN PROTESTANT IDENTITY

How was a sense of identity shaped and reinforced within American Protestantism until the eve of the First World War? This important question penetrates to one of the fundamental questions probed throughout this volume—namely, what is it that actually "defines" Protestantism?

For the first Protestant settlers, their Protestant identity was what had singled them out for victimization and discrimination in Jacobean and Caroline England. Their sense of identity, already strong, was reinforced by their experience of suffering, which was frequently compared to the experiences of Israel in Pharaonic Egypt. The dangerous voyage across the Atlantic was like the crossing of the Red Sea, and the arrival at New England like the entry into the promised land of Canaan. The long history of the exodus narrative as a source of inspiration to American Protestants began with the founding of the nation.

Once settled in America, the predominantly Congregational church polity of the seventeenth century diluted a sense of Protestant identity. Memories of a European past began to fade, and the new generation knew the past indirectly, not as a lived reality or shared experience. Diaries and journals of the period certainly emphasize the importance of religious faith to many early Americans. However, this was not articulated in terms of a shared Protestant identity. The religious identity of many seems primarily to have been developed within the family, among neighbors, within the congregation, and at the level of the township. Faith was often a strongly individual commitment, expressed by church attendance and in civic responsibility.

The Great Awakening and its successor movements certainly gave a new energy and sense of direction to religious faith in America. Yet the renewal of individual faith was not linked with a deeper commitment to some pan-denominational entity called "Protestantism." My own reading of the journals and sermons of the period, while not exhaustive, suggests that a sense of transdenominational identity was articulated using the category of "the gospel," not Protestantism. In part, this may reflect growing tensions within society over the colonial question, which highlighted fissures within American Protestantism of the time—above all, between Anglicans, on the one hand, and Presbyterians and Congregationalists, on the other. At the time of the Second Great Awakening, American Protestant identity was shaped primarily by the concrete experiences of the denomination, especially its officers and structures. "Protestantism" seemed to be something ethereal and hypothetical—an abstract entity lying over the horizon of everyday church life.

If any one factor can be identified as sharpening up a sense of shared Protestant identity, it is "oppositionalism"—the belief that an outside agency threatened the future of all Protestants in America. One of the defining features nourishing and fueling a sense of Protestant identity during the period 1750 to 1960 was open hostility toward Catholicism.[45] Protestants were those who abhorred Catholicism—whether for its ideas, intolerance, oppression, or religious practices. In the eighteenth century, this opposition was often rather theoretical—there were few Catholics in America at this time—but lacked nothing in vigor for that reason. Paul Dudley (1675–1751), chief justice of Massachusetts, established the Dudleian lectures on religion at Harvard College, one of which was required to expose "the idolatry of the Romish church," including its "damnable heresies" and "abominable superstitions."[46]

When the British government extended full civil and religious freedom to Catholics in the colony of Quebec in 1774, American Protestants reacted with indignation, seeing this as legitimizing tyranny in the region. This hostility toward Catholicism was deeply ingrained across the denominations, and thoroughly embedded within American culture as a whole, shaping both the cultural and religious identity of Protestantism.[47]

Conspiracy theories mushroomed. In 1834 the somewhat incendiary Lyman Beecher published his *Plea for the West*, which portrayed the pope in cahoots with degenerate Catholic European monarchs in a plot to take over the Mississippi Valley. Tensions rose, leading to the burning of a convent in Charlestown in 1834.[48] These were given credibility as Catholic emigration to America began to surge in the second half of the nineteenth century. "Nativism" became a significant ideology, rallying those already settled in America against the newcomers, whom they believed threatened to undermine their religious and political freedoms.[49] Catholicism was regularly and aggressively portrayed as "the other" or "the threat," and as fundamentally at odds with the libertarian and republican principles of the United States. Rhetoric shaped perception, and perception became reality.

The case of late nineteenth-century Boston illustrates this trend well. In 1800 Boston, the city at the heart of the largely Puritan commonwealth of Massachusetts, was a powerful symbol of the American Yankee Protestant heritage. Yet mass immigration from Catholic Ireland from 1840 onward changed everything. In 1885 three Protestants were arrested by the police for preaching on Boston Common, sparking protests that revealed the deep levels of insecurity within the community—above all, the sense of having become aliens and strangers in what was once their heartland.[50]

Protestantism closed ranks against this growing threat. Its somewhat tenuous and fluctuating sense of shared faith and values was given both focus and substance by the perception of a serious external threat to church and nation. Other external threats helped shape the notion of a mainline Protestant identity, which had to be defended against external threats. The election of Mormon apostle Reed Smoot to the U.S. Senate in 1903 caused the mainline Protestant denominations to react against a clear threat to their ideas and values, particularly in the light of Smoot's commitment to polygamy.[51]

The decade before the First World War represents a transitional period in American Protestant history. There was little, if any, sense of a looming crisis of identity. Protestants, having always enjoyed the liberty that comes from writing the law, were confident that no difference existed between duty to the church and to the state. Yet change was under way. By about 1910, the role of government was in transition: it was turning from the enforcement of a particular moral or religious order to ensuring that competition was fair among the various concentrations of power—whether these took the form of political parties, pressure groups, business interests, or religious communities.

The scene was thus set for new tensions as American culture appeared to move in a more progressive, secular direction. The ground had been prepared for the preliminary skirmishes of the culture wars and a fundamental realignment of American Protestantism in the twentieth century—a matter to which we shall return in a later chapter.

But our attention now turns to the great events of the nineteenth century, during which Protestantism experienced massive expansion—and in growing, changed in more ways than its numerical strength. The global expansion of Protestantism reshaped its ideas and attitudes, with highly significant results for its understanding of its identity and mission.

8

The Nineteenth Century

The Global Expansion of Protestantism

By the end of the nineteenth century, Protestantism was well on its way to becoming a global faith. Catholicism had already made significant inroads in many parts of South America, Africa, and Asia, owing to the great voyages of discovery of the Portuguese and Spanish navigators. It had inflicted serious damage on European Protestantism. By 1590 roughly 50 percent of the landmass of western Europe was dominated by Protestantism; by 1690 this proportion had dropped to 20 percent. This radical curtailment was, of course, partly offset by Protestantism's growing presence in North America.

Yet Protestantism would soon make up for its European losses as it underwent global expansion. Protestantism spread, like Islam, through a complex amalgam of trading links, colonial activity, and intentional outreach. As Great Britain became a global power, establishing colonies throughout the world, a complex relationship developed between imperial ambitions and missionary activities, creating opportunities and difficulties in about equal measure for the spread of Protestantism. Yet it must be appreciated that there was considerable hostility toward any form of missionary work within Protestantism during the sixteenth and seventeenth centuries.

Religious revivals within European and American Protestantism during the eighteenth century led to the emergence of an activist

James Cook, English explorer, navigator, and hydrographer, 1775–76, by Nathaniel Dance (1734–1811).

approach to faith. Sometimes this was expressed in social action, sometimes in political activity, but above all, it was expressed in support for foreign missions. The rise of missionary societies or associations was one of the most important developments in western Protestantism and would have a defining impact on the shaping of Protestant identity outside the West.

EARLY PROTESTANT DISINTEREST IN MISSION

Protestant interest in mission overseas took some considerable time to develop. During its formative phase, Protestantism seems to have had little interest in the notions of "mission" or "evangelism." Neither John Calvin nor Martin Luther had any particular concern to reach beyond the borders of Christendom. In particular, Calvin's model of evangelism, evident in his approach to the French situation, is primarily that of the reformation of Catholics—that is to say, the conversion of people from one form of Christianity to another.

Protestantism was initially landlocked, surrounded by Catholic or Orthodox territories; reaching the heathen would have been problematic. Both Luther and Calvin were emphatic that Catholicism and Orthodoxy were Christian; what they required, they argued, was reformation. Even Calvin, who did not deny the validity of the Great Commission (the traditional term used for Christ's command to take the gospel to all nations; Matthew 28:17–20), maintained that the propagation of the Christian faith was not under the jurisdiction of the church but was the duty of the "Christian" state. After the rise of confessionalism in the 1560s, characterized by the principle *cuius regio, eius religio* ("whoever rules the region decides its religion"), the primary means of evangelism was through the activities of the local prince. Evangelism was thus seen as a function of the Christian state rather than the responsibility of the individual Christian. On this understanding, evangelism was about reaching non-Christian peoples—such as Jews, Muslims, and, most significantly, the Lapps of northern Scandinavia—within their own territories.

Catholicism was able to race ahead of Protestantism in this respect through the vast maritime exploits of its Spanish and Portuguese mariners. Franciscans, Dominicans, and Jesuits led missions to North

America, South America, India, and Japan. Even if it had missionary inclinations (which Protestants generally did not at this stage), no Lutheran or Reformed territory had any serious capacity for such voyages of exploration or evangelism; most, in fact, did not even have access to the sea. By the second half of the sixteenth century, the Christian population of the world had soared through expansion in new regions. Yet Protestantism was largely unaffected by this expansion. To some of its worried supporters, it seemed to have abdicated its missionary responsibilities.

This early Protestant disinterest in mission was first noted by Gustav Warneck in the 1880s.[1] His historical research convinced him that there was a simple explanation. Although his observations have been qualified by subsequent scholarship, they have yet to be convincingly rebutted.[2] Basing his conclusions on a careful analysis of the sources, Warneck identified three reasons for Protestantism's lack of interest in missions during the sixteenth and seventeenth centuries.

1. These early Protestants interpreted the "Great Commission"—the command to "go and make disciples of all nations" (Matthew 28:19)—as a task given to the apostles of the first century, not to their successors in the post-apostolic church.

2. They believed that the end of all things was close to hand, so that there was little point in embarking on such an ambitious undertaking.

3. It was their theological conviction that God could be relied upon to convert peoples in his own good time.

Warneck's third point is well illustrated by a famous incident involving William Carey (1761–1834), later to be one of the most important British missionaries to India. He began to frame the idea of a missionary calling after reading Captain Cook's account of his voyages in the South Seas. Yet few shared his enthusiasm. In 1792 Carey proposed—to general astonishment, it seems—that a group of Baptist ministers in Northamptonshire discuss "the duty of Christians to attempt the spread of the Gospel among heathen nations." An older minister rose and rebuked him: "Young man, sit down. When God pleases to convert the heathen, He will do it without your aid or mine." Warneck's third point precisely.

The earliest Protestant advocate of worldwide evangelization is believed to have been Adrian Saravia (1532–1613), a Flemish Reformed theologian who converted to Anglicanism and became a close associate of Richard Hooker.[3] Saravia argued "that the command to preach the Gospel to all peoples is obligatory upon the Church since the Apostles were taken up into Heaven, and that for this purpose the apostolic office is needful." This led him to insist that the obligation to evangelize all peoples rests upon the Christians of every age in history in that Christ, in giving this commission, promised to be with his disciples to the end of time. Since the apostles left the work incomplete, it is the duty of the church to carry out the Great Commission. Both Reformed and Lutheran theologians of the late sixteenth and early seventeenth centuries, such as Theodore Beza and Johann Gerhard, argued that the Commission came to an end with the close of the apostolic age. Given this hostility toward mission within classical Protestantism, the rise of missionary activity during the eighteenth century is actually quite remarkable and requires explanation. It was not until the 1830s that most mainline Protestant churches in the West regarded mission as a "good thing."

This important transition is partly explained by a classic feature of the development of Protestantism: the shifting interpretation of core biblical texts. Definitive interpretations of those texts were offered and accepted by one generation, only to be overturned by another; a new understanding of the identity and mission of Protestantism thus arose as being self-evidently correct. In this case, the text was Matthew 28:17–20, which relates how the risen Christ commissioned the apostles to take the gospel to the ends of the earth:

> Jesus came and said to them, "All authority in heaven and on earth has been given to me. Go therefore and make disciples of all nations, baptizing them in the name of the Father and of the Son and of the Holy Spirit, and teaching them to obey everything that I have commanded you. And remember, I am with you always, to the end of the age."

The command is clear—but to whom is it addressed? Who is being asked to take the gospel to all nations?

Warneck's point is that early Protestants interpreted this command as being spoken to those present on that occasion—the apostles. The task was specific to them and to their age; with their passing, the command was no longer binding on Christians. After all, the apostles had traveled to the ends of the known world to spread the gospel. That task was over. Yet when the eighteenth century revisited this interpretation of the passage, it was found to be increasingly problematic. Voyages of discovery had opened up vast new territories, unknown to the apostles. Why should not the gospel be proclaimed there?

Perhaps more significantly, Pietistic and evangelical forms of Protestantism, which emphasized personal conversion, were naturally oriented toward the idea of reaching out to those who were not converted—whether in Christianity's heartlands in western Europe, then passing through a period of religious indifference, or in the new territories being opened up through exploration.[4] German Moravian Pietists, though a small community, were engaged in missionary work in Greenland, America, and Africa by the 1750s and saw this work as the natural extension of their calling as Christians.

Yet Warneck's analysis needs expansion, and perhaps a little modification, if the surge in Protestant missionary work in the eighteenth century is to be understood. Important though the new interpretation of the Great Commission might be, this theological adjustment was inadequate in itself to transform the situation without the means to project the gospel into distant lands. The new theology might create aspirations, but it could not solve the practical problems that attended them. A Protestant mission to a region required a Protestant presence in that region. But how could Protestant churches carry out evangelism when they lacked the means to reach those parts of the world where evangelism was possible?

THE GLOBAL EXPANSION OF PROTESTANTISM

As it happened, the answers to such questions lay to hand. Two historical developments transformed the situation, allowing the evangelistic wish (stimulated, as we have seen, by evangelicalism) to become a reality: the expansion of Protestant sea power, leading to the establishment of European colonies in Asia, Africa, and Latin America; and the development of the "voluntary society," an evangelistic agency that bypassed the inertia of the churches. Each of these developments offered new opportunities.

With the expansion of Protestant sea power, Protestant European nations were able to establish colonies, which allowed the model of evangelism determined by confessionalized churches to come into operation. A colony was a region under the authority of the state; therefore, the state church was able to exercise a pastoral and evangelistic mission within this region. We have already noted this principle in operation in the establishment of the Jamestown colony in Virginia. It is thus no accident that the first major Lutheran mission, located in India, was a direct result of a Danish crown colony being created at Scrampore. After the establishment of Dutch colonies in Indonesia (then known as the "East Indies"), Reformed churches were founded in that region. However, because Britain was by far the most active colonial power, English-speaking forms of Protestantism became widely established through imperial expansion, especially in the Indian subcontinent, the Caribbean, and Australasia.

The second development, the rise of the voluntary society, led to a new model for evangelism that eventually displaced older models in American and Great Britain—but not, it must be emphasized, in Germany and other European nations.[5] Traditional models of evangelism were based on a Protestant state or denomination and thus depended on an official bureaucracy. In the second half of the eighteenth century, missionary leadership passed into the hands of entrepreneurial individuals who created dedicated missionary societies. Their members were highly motivated individuals who arranged their own fund-raising, created support groups, and identified and recruited missionaries.

For the great American missionary Rufus T. Anderson (1796–1880), such associations were critical to the success of the missionary venture.[6] Only Protestantism, he argued, could have created such missionary societies, by bringing together clergy and laity, actors and donors, for this specific purpose. "This Protestant form of association—free, open, responsible, embracing all classes, both sexes, all ages, the masses of the people—is peculiar to modern times, and almost to our age." This theme persists throughout the recent history of Protestantism, as we shall see when considering its development in North America in the twentieth century.

The origins of the London Mission Society illustrate this trend well.[7] News of William Carey's missionary work in India generated much interest in England in 1794, particularly among those working for the abolition of slavery. John Ryland, a Baptist minister, began to gather together a group of interested persons, both lay and ordained, who met in Baker's Coffee House in London to plan interdenominational missionary work. The number of supporters grew, and funds were raised. A boat was purchased, missionaries recruited, and a potentially significant mission undertaken (not, it must be said, entirely successfully) to the South Pacific.

In what follows, we shall provide a brief sketch of some features and themes of the expansion of Protestantism in the late eighteenth century and the nineteenth century, before moving on to consider some of the issues that helped shape global Protestantism at the time and their implications for the future of the movement.

Africa

Christianity became established in North Africa during the first centuries of the Christian era.[8] Churches were established along much of the North African coast in the areas now known as Algeria, Tunisia, and Libya. A particularly strong Christian presence developed in Egypt, with the city of Alexandria emerging as a leading center of Christian thought and life. Augustine of Hippo, one of the most significant Christian leaders and writers of all time, was based in this region.

Much of this Christian presence in Africa was swept away by the Arab invasions of the seventh century. Coptic Christianity survived in Egypt, although as a minority faith. The situation began to change gradually during the later sixteenth century. When Portuguese settlers occupied previously uninhabited islands off the west African coast, such as the Cape Verde Islands, they established Catholicism there. However, such offshore settlements had little impact on the mainland of Africa.

The coming of Protestantism to sub-Saharan Africa, which can be dated from the eighteenth century, was closely linked with the great evangelical awakening in England at this time. Many were appalled at the slave trade, in which British merchants bought slaves from local tribal leaders in Africa before exporting them to the plantations of the American colonies. The conversion of John Newton (1725–1807), a former slave ship captain, to evangelical Protestantism created a growing awareness of the problem. Newton celebrated his conversion by writing one of the world's best-known hymns, "Amazing Grace," which told of his spiritual transformation.[9] This same writer also wrote hymns such as "The Negro's Complaint," which spoke of the dignity conferred on all people by God, which slavery could not diminish.

Evangelical Protestants responded to this new concern for Africa in two ways: first, by working for the abolition of slavery, a project especially associated with the English politician William Wilberforce and his circle; and second, by bringing the gospel to this region of the world. These were powerful visions, and they caught the imagination of many in the 1790s. Three major British missionary societies were active in Africa during the late eighteenth and early nineteenth centuries: the Baptist Missionary Society, founded in 1792 and initially known as the "Particular Baptist Society for the Propagation of the Gospel Among the Heathen"; the London Missionary Society, founded in 1795 and initially known as the "Missionary Society"; and the Church Missionary Society, founded in 1799 and originally known as the "Church Missionary Society for Africa and the East." Each of these societies focused on a specific region: the Baptist Missionary Society on the Congo basin, the London Missionary Society on southern Africa (including Madagascar), and the Church Missionary Society on west and east Africa. All of these societies were Protestant as well as strongly evangelical in their outlook. Like John Wesley, they believed passionately in the need for conversion and regeneration and saw the overseas mission field as a priority.

Missionary work in the 1790s led to the establishment of small Christian communities among native tribes, particularly the Khoi. Gradually, surrounding tribes began to convert to Christianity. Here, as in many other situations, the motivation for conversion varied considerably.

Some conversions clearly stemmed from a deep spiritual experience; others reflected a conviction of the truth of the Christian gospel; other conversions might have been rooted in a belief that Christianity would make the benefits of Western civilization more widely available to African culture. This was particularly clear in the case of the Ganda tribe of east Africa, among whom the decision to convert to Christianity (rather than Islam) seems to have been partly influenced by the superiority of British technology and the possibility that such conversion might lead to this technology becoming more widely available to the tribe.

The dominant feature of sub-Saharan Africa in the nineteenth century was the growing presence of colonial powers in the region, some of which had Protestant state churches. Because the forms of Christianity dominant in Belgium, Britain, France, and Germany—all of which established colonies in this region during the period—varied considerably, a considerable diversity of churches became established in Africa. Anglicanism, Catholicism, and Lutheranism were all well established by the end of the century; in South Africa, the Dutch Reformed church had a particularly strong influence among European settlers. A disturbing perception arose in some quarters that Protestantism was merely the religious component of colonial power, a Western import to the region that would not survive any subsequent Western withdrawal.

Perhaps the most celebrated colonial evangelist was David Livingstone (1813–73). Livingstone was convinced of the importance of commerce in relation to the Christianization of Africa. In 1838 he offered his services to the London Missionary Society, declaring his intention to go to Africa "to make an open path for commerce and Christianity." Exploiting the British government's interest in replacing the banned slave trade with more legitimate forms of commerce, Livingstone obtained government backing for an expedition to explore the Zambezi River as a potential gateway to the interior. He believed that the interior would be capable of commercial exploitation, such as the growing of cotton, then greatly in demand by the cotton mills of Lancashire. Although the expedition was a commercial failure, it opened up the interior to missionary activity. Livingstone himself became a role model for many younger British Protestants. A series of addresses he delivered at Cambridge University led to the founding of the university's Mission to Central Africa in 1860.

Whereas the London missionary societies primarily sent white evangelists to Africa, the Protestant Episcopal Church of the United States believed that the best strategy was to send Afro-Americans to the region.[10] At least 115 black American missionaries are known to have been present and active in Africa during the period 1875 to 1899. Following the establishment of the west African republic of Liberia (1847) as a refuge for former slaves, black Protestant missionaries and church-builders went to the region, seeing their work partly as evangelism and partly as nation-building. Their work generated some friction with white missionaries in this area; nevertheless, the presence of black missionaries in Liberia was an important staging post on the road to the indigenization of mission.

Yet the rise of Protestantism caused tensions to arise within traditional African societies. An excellent example of this can be seen in the boarding school for girls established in Madagascar in 1872 by Lutherans from the Norwegian Missionary Society.[11] At that time, Christianity was becoming increasingly influential in the region. Although Madagascar became a French protectorate in 1885, the Norwegians, in part because their nation was not a colonial power, enjoyed a particular advantage in the region. The difficulty was that the Norwegian women missionaries brought contemporary Norwegian notions of domestic life to a context in which they were totally alien, thus complicating—if not compromising—their missionary agenda.

A further issue concerned marriage customs. Western Protestantism was strongly monogamist; African culture had long recognized the merits of polygamy. Increasingly, the European Christian insistence upon a man having only one wife was seen as a Western import that had no place in traditional African society. The United African Methodist Church, an indigenous church that recognized polygamy, traces its origins back to a 1917 meeting of the Methodist church in Lagos, Nigeria, at which a large group of leading laypeople were debarred from the church on account of their practice of polygamy. They responded by forming their own Methodist church, which adopted native African values frowned on by the European missionaries.

By the year 1900, Protestantism had been firmly established in many parts of sub-Saharan Africa. But there were major questions. Was its presence in the region simply a consequence of Western colonial authority? Would it disappear in the future, along with other expressions of colonialism? Similarly, the forms of Protestantism established in the region bore the unmistakable hallmarks of their predominantly European origins. The services and structures of the "Church of the Province of South Africa"—one of two Anglican organizations in the region—looked remarkably like those of British Anglicanism.[12] How would such obvious importations or transplants survive in such a different cultural context? And what would happen when the British had to go home? Could these planted churches survive without their colonial patrons?

Much the same questions were raised by Protestant attempts to expand in Asia, to which we now turn.

Asia

By the end of the nineteenth century, Protestantism had established what might best be described as a precarious presence in Asia, often protected by the diplomatic and military power of Western nations. The most significant Protestant presence was in India where Christianity is traditionally believed to have been established in the first century in the form of the "Mar Thoma" church. This group of Christians traced their origins to St. Thomas the Apostle, who was believed to have come to India within two decades of the crucifixion of Christ. According to this ancient tradition, Thomas first set foot in India at Cranganore near Cochin, at that time an important seaport on the Malabar coast with important trade connections with Palestine and its neighbors. The voyages of the Portuguese navigator Vasco da Gama (c. 1460–1524) led to the opening up of the coastal regions of the subcontinent to Catholic missionaries, with Goa as their center of operations.

Protestant missions were relatively slow to establish themselves; indeed, evangelism was often seen as subsidiary to commerce, and occasionally as an impediment to it. The first Anglican clergy in India, for example, were ship's chaplains, appointed by the English East India Company to provide pastoral care and spiritual support for the crews of their ships so that they might carry our their commercial tasks more efficiently.

However, the intrinsic importance of mission in the area was recognized by Humphrey Prideaux, the Anglican dean of Norwich (1684–

1724) who penned an *Account of the English Settlements in the East Indies, together with some proposals for the propagation of Christianity in those parts of the world.* Prideaux pointed to the need to train people for the specific work of evangelism. In his prophetic idea that a "seminary" be established in England, with a view to preparing mission workers until such time as the work could be handed over to agencies based in India itself, may be seen the basis of the missionary movement, which was destined to exercise a significant influence over Indian Christianity.[13] This new interest in evangelism was encouraged to no small extent by the 1773 decision of Pope Clement XIV to suppress the Society of Jesus, which was by then undertaking major Catholic missionary work in this region.

The first major Protestant mission to India was based at the Danish crown colony of Tranquebar on the Coromandel coast, south of Madras. Lutheran orthodoxy remained hostile to missionary activity, for reasons noted earlier in this chapter; Pietists, however, were strongly in favor. Among the German Lutheran Pietist missionaries of note in this undertaking were Bartholomäus Ziegenbalg (who directed the mission from its founding in 1706 to 1719) and Christian Frederick Schwartz (director from 1750 to 1787). Members of the Lutheran faculty of theology at Wittenberg—Luther's old university—were outraged at such a development and tried, unsuccessfully, to have it closed down.[14]

In the event, this mission bore some fruit. A Lutheran community of many thousands arose in and around the cities of the region, such as Tranquebar itself, Tanjore, Tiruchirapalli, and Tirunelveli. Danish Pietism went into decline around the year 1800, partly because of the growing influence of rationalism, and much of the work in the region was taken over by the Anglican Church Missionary Society. Around 1840, the Dresden-Leipzig Mission sent missionaries to the region, leading to many Tamil Christians reverting to Lutheranism.

The growing political power of Britain in the region, however, inevitably favored the activities of British missionaries, even though the East India Company did not want its commercial work disrupted by such activity. English Baptists began work in Bengal in 1793, settling in the Danish colonial town of Serampore, upriver from Calcutta, beyond the authority of the East India Company.[15] The founding of Serampore College in 1818 was a landmark; it was presented to its supporters back in England as an institution that would train Indians to replace Europeans completely as missionaries and so create a truly indigenous church. While this claim may have been somewhat inflated—it was designed, after all, to encourage existing donors and secure new ones—the objective was of considerable strategic importance in view of the growing suspicions about the missionaries' relationship with the British colonial authorities.

Although British missionary societies and individuals were able to operate in India without any major opposition from other European agencies from about 1775, they received no support from the British authorities. The East India Company, for example, was opposed to their activities on the grounds that they might create ill will among native Indians and thus threaten the trade upon which the company depended. However, the Charter Act, passed by Parliament on July 13, 1813, revised the conditions under which the East India Company was permitted to operate. From now on, British missionaries were given protected status and a limited degree of freedom to carry out evangelistic work on the Indian subcontinent. Their privileged status would inevitably cause them to be seen as agents of British rule and values. The Serampore program opened the way to the introduction of indigenized forms of Protestant churches.

Britain was by no means the only Western nation with missionary involvement in the Indian subcontinent. The first major American missionary undertaking had its origins at Williams College in Williamstown, Maryland, in 1810: a group of students who had been studying the history of the East India Company came to believe that they were called to serve as missionaries in the region. The General Association of Congregational Ministers of Massachusetts would form the American Board of Commissioners for Foreign Missions that same year and send a group—including some of the original Williams College students—to Calcutta.

The issue of the relation of Protestantism to Indian culture remained important throughout the nineteenth century. It seemed to many that Protestantism was not only alien to India but insensitive to its cultural values and norms. The "Sepoy Mutiny" of 1857 is often seen as a revolt against alleged attempts to Westernize Indian culture as much as a rebellion against colonial rule.[16] Christians and Christian institutions were targeted precisely because they were seen as the instruments or outcomes of Western culture.

A similar situation arose in China. A Christian presence had been established in China in 1294 when Franciscan missionaries reached the country. However, the church never achieved any great success in conversions. One of the many effects of the Opium War of the 1840s was to open the "Middle Kingdom" up to Western missionaries. China had been isolated from the West until the nineteenth century, when growing interest in commerce opened up the region to Western missionaries, predominantly from America and Britain. Hampered by a lack of knowledge of the written or spoken language, these missionaries labored under immense difficulties.[17] One of these missionaries, the Englishman James Hudson Taylor (1832–1905), may be singled out for special comment.

Hudson Taylor was initially a missionary with the Chinese Evangelization Society. Dissatisfaction with this organization led him to found the China Inland Mission in 1865. This mission was unusual in several aspects, not least its willingness to accept single women as missionaries and its interdenominational character. Hudson Taylor showed an awareness of the cultural barriers facing Christian missionaries in China and did what he could to remove them—for example, he required his missionaries to wear Chinese, rather than Western, dress. The China Inland Mission stood virtually alone among missionary societies at this time in recognizing the need for its missionaries to be taught Mandarin in schools especially established for this purpose. Other missionary societies merely provided their workers with language manuals and advice from native speakers.

The Western powers gained major footholds in China as a consequence of the Opium War (1839–42). Under the Treaty of Nanjing (1842), China was forced to make major concessions to Britain, including the granting of "extraterritoriality" (that is, exemption from Chinese laws) to British nationals. This proved to be the first of a number of "unequal treaties" that were imposed upon China by Western powers and led to growing Western influence in the region. During the period 1861 to 1894, the "Self-Strengthening Movement," championed by Qing Dynasty scholars and officials such as Li Hongzhang (1823–1901) and Zuo Zongtang (1812–85), attempted to achieve a confluence of Western technology with traditional Chinese culture. Western missionaries were generally welcomed, not least on account of their perceived potential as educators.

However, China's defeat by Japan in the disastrous Sino-Japanese War of 1895 led to new tensions. A new conservative elite gave support to the anti-foreign and anti-Christian movement of secret societies that came to be known as "the Boxers." In 1900 Boxer bands were active throughout north China. Christianity was seen as something Western and hence un-Chinese. Foreign Christian missionaries were particularly at risk, as were any buildings associated with Christianity. Chinese Christians were massacred in many areas. Such was the scale of the action that foreign concessions in Beijing and Tianjin were besieged in June 1900, and eventually the Western powers were provoked to make an armed intervention. At this point, the Qing court formally took command of the Boxer forces and led a coordinated yet ultimately unsuccessful program of resistance to the Western relief army. The Peace Protocol imposed upon the Qing court on September 7, 1900, marked a final humiliation for the dynasty. It did nothing, however, to advance the cause of Christianity, which was clearly identified as a Western import.[18]

In Japan, Christianity first gained a presence in 1549, when the Jesuit missionary Francis Xavier landed at Kagoshima. The small church in Japan experienced a long period of isolation from the West during the Tokugawa shogunate. When Japan finally opened its doors to the West in 1865, the continuing presence of about sixty thousand Christian believers in the country was revealed. During the Meiji period (1868–1912), Protestantism gained a growing following in the country.[19] However, it never achieved the significant growth that some anticipated. For many Japanese, Christianity, like butter, was seen as a Western import: the colloquial Japanese term for Christianity can be translated as "it tastes of butter."

The South Pacific

The term "Oceania" is now generally used to refer to the 1,500 or so islands in the Pacific Ocean. Oceania is further subdivided into three regions. "Polynesia" designates the group of islands stretching from

Hawaii (known as the "Sandwich Islands" in earlier centuries) in the north to New Zealand in the south, including Tahiti and Pitcairn Island. "Micronesia" refers to the group of small islands between Hawaii and the Philippines, including the Caroline, Gilbert, and Marshall Islands. "Melanesia" refers to the group of islands south of Micronesia and north of Australia, including Fiji, the Solomon Islands, and the New Hebrides. The population of this vast and dispersed region is relatively small; however, it was considered by nineteenth-century Protestant missionaries to be of major importance. Indeed, the predominant form of Christianity initially established in the region in the early nineteenth century was English-speaking Protestantism.

Missionary interest in the region was first awakened by reports of the voyages of Captain Cook during the eighteenth century. In 1795 the London Missionary Society was founded with the primary objective of sending missionaries to "the islands of the South Sea." The first major missionary expedition to the region set off in August 1796 when thirty missionaries of the London Mission Society set sail for Tahiti. Although this mission faced considerable difficulties—not least of which related to the very different sexual mores of England and Tahiti—it can be seen as marking the beginning of a sustained effort to establish Christianity in the region.

The geographical nature of the region made one of the most reliable means of evangelization—the establishment of mission stations—impossible. The populations of the islands were generally too small to justify the building and maintenance of such settlements. The most successful strategy to be adopted was the use of missionary vessels, which allowed European missionaries to direct and oversee the operations of native evangelists, pastors, and teachers in the region.

The most significant Christian missions in the South Pacific were located in Australia and New Zealand, which eventually came to serve as the base for most missionary work in the region. Christianity came to Australia in 1788. The circumstances of its arrival were not entirely happy. The fleet that arrived in New South Wales was transporting convicts to the penal settlements that were being established in the region. At the last moment, William Wilberforce persuaded the British naval authorities to allow a chaplain to sail with the fleet. With the dramatic increase in immigration to the region from Britain in the following century, the various forms of British Christianity became established in the region. The formation of the "Bush Brotherhoods" in 1897 laid the basis for the evangelization of the interior of the continent.

The first missionaries arrived in New Zealand in 1814. A small group of missionaries, sponsored by the Church Missionary Society and led by Samuel Marsden, made contact with the Maori people and secured a positive response to Christianity. By the 1830s, many Maori had converted to Protestantism, while adapting it to reflect their own distinctive values. However, when serious tensions arose after the arrival of large numbers of colonists in the 1850s, many Maori reasserted more traditional forms of religion in reaction to the excesses of the British émigrés. The consolidation of Christianity in the region was largely due to the efforts of Bishop George Selwyn (1809–78), who was appointed missionary bishop of New Zealand in 1841. During his time in the region, he had a marked impact on the development of Christianity, particularly in relation to education.[20]

Throughout the South Pacific region, a major issue has been the relation of Christianity to the native peoples of the region, particularly the Australian Kuri (often still inappropriately referred to as "Aborigines") and New Zealand Maori peoples. For some, Christianity is a Western colonial phenomenon to be rejected as destructive of indigenous culture; for others, Christianity has no necessary connection with Western culture or power and can be put at the service of indigenous peoples and cultures. The use of Christian rituals throughout the region to reaffirm traditional social and cultural values has been particularly significant.[21]

PROTESTANT MISSION AND NATIVE AMERICANS

While the predominant model of Protestant mission in the late eighteenth century and the nineteenth century involved missionaries working abroad, it is important to appreciate that a quite different model emerged in North America as Protestant settlers encountered Native American cultures. Missionary work began in New England in the seventeenth century as Puritan settlers made contact with local tribes. The Puritan missionary John Eliot (1604–90) became interested in the culture and language of the Native Americans who lived around Roxbury, and he learned Natic (as this regional variant of Algonquin was known) to preach to them. He was able to attract support for his missionary work in the region and in 1649 gained parliamentary approval for the establishment of the Society for the Propagation of the Gospel in New England. Between 1661 and 1663, he translated and produced a Natic-language Bible, using a professional printer, Marmaduke Johnson, sent over from England in 1660 on a three-year contract.

In the eighteenth century, mission work shifted into a higher gear as the Great Awakening kindled interest in spreading the gospel among Native Americans. Various groups were involved in this enterprise, including European émigrés influenced by the revivals in Germany and England. Unusually, Moravian settlers were prepared to live among, and even marry, Native Americans, much to the concern of the British colonial authorities. This special relationship with Native Americans proved to be of particular importance evangelistically.[22]

A quite different form of engagement emerged in the early nineteenth century in response to the religious changes of that era. The revivalism that developed in Kansas during the Second Great Awakening led to growing interest in evangelization of the native tribes of the area. Baptists and Methodists—the two denominations most affected by the Awakening—undertook major missionary enterprises at this time.

One of the most significant and effective forms of missionary work was education.[23] Baptist workers set up a training school near Topeka, which became a major center for evangelism in the 1850s.[24] Medical missions also played an important role. Jotham Meeker (1804-55) combined his professional expertise as a printer with a somewhat amateur interest in medicine, using both as a way of establishing contact and trust with the Shawnees, Stockbridges, and Ottawas during the 1830s and 1840s.[25]

The motivation of these Protestant missionaries to evangelize Native Americans was complex. Virtually all of the missionaries I studied in preparing this section believed deeply and passionately that the coming of the gospel would enlighten and liberate the people to whom they were ministering. Yet other motivations can be discerned, paralleling rather than contradicting their primary concern. One such motivation was a desire to preserve the identity and interests of Native Americans in the face of rapid social change. At times, this motivation was accompanied by a naïveté that led to serious misjudgments—such as Isaac McCoy's belief that reservations held the key to the safeguarding of the cultural identity of Native Americans.[26]

The case of the Canadian Baptist missionary Silas T. Rand (1810–89) illustrates this concern well, while also demonstrating the importance of Protestant missionaries for historical anthropology.[27] Rand had aspirations to serve in foreign mission fields. However, his missionary interests were redirected in 1846. While ministering in Prince Edward Island, he became familiar with the Micmac language. Although the Micmac people of the Maritimes had already encountered Catholicism, Rand believed that he had a mission to them, and he was supported in this goal by a somewhat aggressively anti-Catholic group of supporters in Nova Scotia.

Rand believed that Christianity would deliver the Micmac from the predations and depravations of white culture, and he came to love and respect the Micmac language and folklore. Determined to preserve both, he acted as an advocate for the Micmac people in land rights disputes and published both the original texts and translations of their oral traditions. He was heavily criticized for doing so: why, a strict Baptist newspaper demanded, was Rand concerning himself with such "fables" when he was meant to be preaching the gospel? Here, as in so many other cases, our knowledge of the traditions, customs, and languages of America's first peoples were preserved and transmitted by missionaries, many of whom developed a deep respect for the cultures within which they were working.

Similarly, the Hawaiian language was preserved because missionaries in the 1820s insisted on learning the native language in order to explain the gospel—and then came to see its preservation as an important issue in itself. Hiram Bingham (1789–1869) even refused to teach the islanders English, believing that this would destroy their linguistic—and hence their cultural—identity.[28]

A similar pattern can be seen in the ministry of Asher Wright (1803–75), a missionary to the Seneca people in Buffalo Creek, New York. After graduating from Andover Seminary, Wright joined the Buffalo Creek mission and would spend forty-four years working with the Seneca. His missionary work was not especially successful; however, his commitment to the people and knowledge of their language and customs led to the preservation of their distinctive features.[29] Wright's ministry is one of many examples that raise questions about the "colonial" stereotype of missionaries, until recently widely encountered in accounts of the Protestant missions of the nineteenth century.

COLONIALISM, IMPERIALISM, AND PROTESTANT MISSIONS

There has been a surge of interest in the history of Protestant missions in recent years on account of its multiple facets. The study of these missions possesses the capacity to illuminate a wide variety of issues—such as the history of specific Protestant denominations, the relation of mission to the practically simultaneous global expansion of capitalism and imperialism (summed up for many in David Livingstone's slogan "Christianity, commerce, and civilization"), and the place of Christianity in the development of the religious and cultural histories of indigenous peoples.[30] Each of these areas of research proves to be more complex and nuanced than previous generations of scholars had appreciated.

Until recently, it was common to argue that Protestant missions created a "state of colonialism" that was the precursor to the advent of a colonial state.[31] On this view, the colonization of a region began with the assertion of the superiority of the values and ideas of the missionaries, which created a state of cultural subservience that was amenable to colonialist exploitation. The missionaries prepared the way for Western imperial rule by undermining native confidence in their own ideas, values, and civilizations. Such studies tend to be based on local situations—often in Africa—that are detached from the astonishingly broad range of Protestant missionary enterprises of the nineteenth century.

Yet this traditional view has now been challenged by detailed scholarship that has exposed its many flaws. Many missionaries attempted to subvert the "colonial mentality" that depersonalized indigenous Africans and often viewed them as little more than economic commodities. Perhaps the most interesting example of this is provided by Franz Michael Zahn (1833–1900) of the Bremen Mission in the German west African colony of Togo in the closing years of the nineteenth century. An aristocratic Pietist colleague of Gustav Warneck's, Zahn energetically defended the right of the indigenous population to use their own language, against the opposing views of the colonial authorities, and sought, on the basis of his theological convictions, to reaffirm the basic humanity of the colonized.[32]

A study of the work of the London Mission Society among the Khoi people of southern Africa has proved particularly important in undermining the simplistic set of binary oppositions set up by the now-discredited "mission as colonialism" approach.[33] Far from propounding colonialism, they provided the Khoi with an ideology of resistance against their Afrikaner masters. Furthermore, Protestant missionaries were active in many parts of the world that never came under imperial rule—indeed, in some of these cases missionaries worked to subvert any such possibility.[34] It is impossible to present any one case as "typical," as if there were a single controlling narrative.

There is now abundant evidence to suggest that Protestant missionary undertakings were far from the imperialist adventures that older research suggested they were, whether by accident or design. The thesis that Protestant missionaries colluded with or collaborated in the enterprise of empire has a certain superficial plausibility, yet ultimately it rests on a series of problematic assumptions about cause and effects, actions and identity, and above all on a failure to engage with the many agents in such a narrative. It was inevitable that British, German, Dutch, and Danish missionary enterprises would become entangled with the dynamics of empire. And while the clarification of the origins, mechanisms, and outcomes of such interconnections is historically important, it has not shown Protestant missionaries as half-witted colluders with the *imperium*, far less as its willing accomplices.

The nineteenth-century Protestant missionary encounter with other cultures had a significant impact on Protestant identity, and it is important to reflect on how this took place. The interaction of missionaries with culture is typically presented as one-way: the missionary, through an act of intellectual and culture imperialism, imposes his or her views on a native culture. This stereotype of the missionary still lingers in the darker recesses of cultural anthropology, some of whose practitioners persist in portraying them as rigidly ethnocentric.[35]

The reality is otherwise. While exceptions can easily be identified—and presented as the norm by those with vested interests—it is clear that missionaries were "far from being rampant cultural imperialists" and instead were usually "extremely diffident about imposing their own views."[36] The essential point is that the missionary enterprise has always been dialogical and interactive—that is, the missionary physically and mentally inhabits the world of the group to which he or she feels called. The seeds of the notion of cross-cultural mission were laid in this great era of missionary expansion, even if the lessons learned were implicitly absorbed by individual missionaries rather than explicitly stated and analyzed by their successors.[37]

Moreover, the alleged universality of the Enlightenment, which had been assumed by many Protestant missionaries of the eighteenth and nineteenth centuries, began to lose its plausibility.[38] Increased understanding of non-Western cultures began to expose the wide variety of cultural and intellectual norms that existed across the world. Eighteenth-century advances in physical geography had not been accompanied by a mapping of the world's rationalities and moralities, which proved to be far from universal. Cultural geography thus proved to be at least as important as its physical counterpart. Indeed, the reports of missionaries in such regions did much to advance the discipline of cultural anthropology, which insisted that each ethnic group had its own essential characteristics that could not be shoehorned into preconceived molds.

The high point of this era of Protestant missions was the World Missionary Conference, held at Edinburgh in 1910. This conference represented a serious attempt to reflect on what had been learned to date and to consider how these lessons might be applied to the future. Enormous effort had been directed into preparation for the conference. There was a sense of urgency and excitement as insights and visions were shared and networks were shaped and expanded.[39] Yet with the benefit of hindsight, the conference can be seen to have reinforced existing Protestant paradigms of mission at a time when redirection and review were increasingly necessary.

The missionary movement's best analysts and thinkers worked on the assumption that there was a reasonably homogeneous Christian world, primarily in Europe and North America, that was fully evangelized; beyond it lay at best a partially evangelized world, with many regions that had yet to be evangelized at all, such as Latin America.

While the movement recognized the emergence of a "Native Church" in parts of the world, it saw that church as a tender plant in need of supervision from the West as much as Western resources. Evangelism would remain the business of the "Home Church"—in other words, the spiritually and numerically robust churches of the West. The paradigm of a church-shaped mission remained unaltered, even though increased interdenominational collaboration had broadened the base of the "church" in question. The tasks of mission produced a remarkable consensus among those who attended the conference, which is often regarded, for good reason, as the seed of the subsequent ecumenical movement.

But other, perhaps wiser, voices were not heard. Gustav Warneck did not attend the conference, partly in protest against the preponderance of American and British delegates and theological viewpoints. Warneck and other German thinkers and practitioners regarded the Anglo-American approach as culturally simplistic, being linked as it was to the conversion of individual souls rather than committed to the creation of indigenous churches grounded in the cultural and social realities of the region.[40] The church could not be based on Western models, still less embody or proclaim Western norms; instead, the gospel had to be related to and expressed through indigenous social and cultural institutions.

But little came of these ideas. Other, more pressing matters intruded to force them to the margins of Protestant reflections. The great era of Protestant missions came to an end in 1914 with the outbreak of the Great War, as it was then known (now referred to as the First World War). Many of the tentative patterns of collaboration between missionaries across national and denominational boundaries were overwhelmed by a tidal wave of nationalism unleashed by the war and the economic and political uncertainties that ensued.[41]

It is entirely fitting to regard the outbreak of the First World War as bringing down the curtain on the classic era of Protestantism, when a set of seemingly secure and settled beliefs and assumptions prevailed. As events proved, the twentieth century would see greater change in the movement than ever before—a matter to which we return in the third part of this study. It is now appropriate, however, to probe the inner identity of Protestantism in far greater detail, and so we turn to consider its ideas and attitudes in some depth.

PART II

Manifestation

In exploring the development of Protestantism thus far, we have noted the multiplicity of possibilities that the word "Protestant" denotes. Each of these possibilities—whether Lutheran, Reformed, Congregationalist, Baptist, Anglican, or Methodist—has its own sense of identity and right to belong within the Christian tradition and especially its Protestant constituency. Each has its own understanding of how to read the Bible, conduct worship, organize its churches, and engage with the world. Each has its own tensions, debates, and authority figures, some of which carry greater weight in the Protestant community or in the Christian church in general. In more recent years, however, these Protestant traditions have been supplemented by newer arrivals, of which the most important by far is Pentecostalism.

As our narrative of the development and expansion of Protestantism has proceeded, a number of major questions about Protestant beliefs and attitudes have emerged. So what are those beliefs and attitudes? How has the history of Protestantism been shaped by them? How do they arise in the first place? How can such a wide range of beliefs and attitudes be accommodated within a single movement called "Protestantism"? The sheer observable, historical diversity of Protestantism is a constant source of frustration to those who like everything to be rigorously and clearly defined—and a source of inspiration to those who believe that diversity encourages creative innovation and experimentation.

This section explores some fundamental questions concerning the identity of Protestantism. It examines how Protestantism has arrived at its distinctive ideas in the first place, noting the particular importance that it attaches to the Bible and how this text is to be interpreted and applied. Particular attention is paid to the major differences over biblical interpretation within Protestantism and their implications for an appeal to the Bible as the supreme arbiter of doctrinal disputes. Some fundamental Protestant ideas are then considered, along with some of the internal debates within Protestantism that these have generated and the tensions they have caused. We then move on to look at how Protestant ideas manifest themselves—in how Protestants worship and work, in their interaction with culture, and in their attitudes to the arts and sciences.

We begin with the central focus of Protestant theology and spirituality—the Bible.

9

The Bible and Protestantism

One of the most enduring descriptions of Protestantism comes from the English theologian William Chillingworth (1602–44). In his *The Religion of Protestants the Safe Way to Salvation* (1637), he famously declared that "the Bible, the Bible alone, is the religion of Protestants." This is perhaps one of the most familiar statements of one of the slogans that emerged from the early Reformation and is characteristic of Protestantism as a whole—the Latin phrase *sola Scriptura* ("by Scripture alone").[1] At its heart, Protestantism represents a constant return to the Bible to revalidate and where necessary restate its beliefs and values, refusing to allow any one generation or individual to determine what is definitive for Protestantism as a whole.[2]

This might suggest that Protestantism is a text-centered religion like Islam. It is important to appreciate from the outset that this idea can be misleading. There are indeed parallels between the two, particularly in relation to how texts are interpreted and the problems that arise through an absence of centralized authority figures and structures. While some very conservative Protestants do treat the Bible as if it were the Christian Qu'ran, the majority are clear that the Bible has a special place in the Christian life on account of its witness to Jesus Christ rather than its specific identity as a text. For Martin Luther, the purpose of scripture was to "inculcate Christ," who is the "mathematical point" of the Bible.

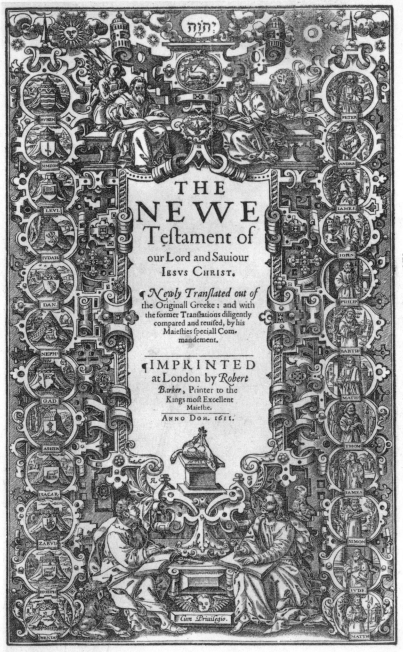

Title page to the New Testament, from the King James Bible. London:
Robert Barker, 1611.

The real contrast is thus actually between the Qu'ran and Jesus Christ, not the Qu'ran and the Bible. When the first generation of Protestants spoke of the "authority of the Bible," this was to be understood as "the authority of the risen Christ, mediated and expressed through the Bible."[3]

Protestantism shares with other forms of Christianity an emphasis and focus upon the historical figure who stands at its center—Jesus Christ. As Stephen Charles Neill, a Protestant missionary-scholar with vast firsthand experience and knowledge of the religions of India and Africa, once commented, "The historical figure of Jesus of Nazareth is the criterion by which every Christian affirmation has to be judged, and in the light of which it stands or falls."[4] For Protestantism, Christ is both the focus and foundation of the Bible.

Precisely because Jesus Christ stands at the heart of the Christian faith, Protestants argue, so must the Bible. There is the most intimate interconnection between the Bible and Christ in the Protestant tradition. The Bible is the means by which Christ is displayed, proclaimed, and manifested. Why read scripture? For Calvin, the answer was as clear as it was simple: because by doing so we come "to know Jesus Christ truly, and the infinite riches which are included in him and are offered to us by God the Father." Karl Barth, widely regarded as Protestantism's greatest theologian of the twentieth century, made much the same point: "From first to last, the Bible directs us to the name of Jesus Christ."[5]

THE PLACE OF THE BIBLE IN PROTESTANT THOUGHT

The first generation of Protestants regarded an appeal to the supreme authority of the Bible as both theologically correct and ecclesiastically liberating. The authority of the pope could be resisted, even undermined, through the programmatic assertion that all are ultimately under the authority of the Word and are to be judged by it. The slogan *Verbum Domini manet in aeternum* ("The Word of the Lord abides in eternity") became emblematic for Lutheranism in the 1520s.[6] Lutherans literally wore their ecclesiological hearts on their sleeves by embroidering the letters VDMA on their garments and even carving them on household implements.[7]

Given the importance of the notion of the "Word of the Lord" for the fledgling movement, it is not surprising that the first phase of Protestantism saw the appearance of a wide variety of resources designed to enable and encourage ordinary believers to become familiar with the Bible. Aware of the difficulties that many experienced in reading and making sense of the Bible, Protestant theologians and pedagogues produced a rich range of material that aimed to make an engagement with the Bible as simple and productive as possible. The role of the printing press in allowing the ready production and dissemination of these resources was of critical importance to the success of the Protestant enterprise at this point. There were four main categories of resources:

1. *Biblical translations:* Although a number of vernacular translations of the Bible were produced during the Middle Ages, these were often unreliable and occasionally even illegal. The democratizing agenda of Protestantism demanded that every believer have access to the text of the Bible; this necessitated its translation into the vernacular.

2. *Biblical commentaries:* From the outset, Protestantism produced a wide range of study aids for the interpretation of the Bible, of which the Bible "commentary" remains one of the most enduring. These works explained difficult ideas, commented on translation issues, addressed theological issues, and made practical applications. Some were primarily academic in tone; others were more devotional.

3. *Lectionaries:* Protestant sermons often take a strongly expository form, working through a biblical book and making connections between the text and the life of the church. Protestant churches that observe a liturgical year, such as Lutheranism and Anglicanism, use a "lectionary," which identifies biblical readings that are especially appropriate for the season of the year—Christmas, Easter, Pentecost, and so forth—and are intended to serve as the basis for preaching.

4. *Works of biblical theology:* Calvin's *Institutes of the Christian Religion* was intended to be a guide to the ideas of the Bible that would allow its readers to build up a systematic overview of Christian doctrine through an engagement with the biblical text. Many others have fol-

lowed in its wake, aiming to weave together the themes of the Bible in order to give a systematic and coherent account of the themes of the Christian faith.

The Protestant *sola Scriptura* principle is linked with two subsidiary ideas. The "sufficiency of scripture," already noted, affirms that no doctrines other than those clearly set out in the Bible are necessary for salvation. The Anglican "Thirty-nine Articles" (1571) set out this position with classic precision in article 8: "Holy Scripture containeth all things necessary to salvation: so that whatsoever is not read therein, nor may be proved thereby, is not to be required of any man, that it should be believed as an article of the faith, or be thought requisite or necessary to salvation." Or, as the Princeton theologian Alexander Archibald Hodge put it: "[Protestants] affirm that every essential article of faith and rule of practice is clearly revealed in Scripture, or may certainly be deduced therefrom."

The second idea is that of the "clarity of scripture," sometimes also referred to as the "perspicuity of scripture."[8] This holds that the basic meaning of the Bible can be ascertained by ordinary Christians. The perspicuity of scripture affirms the basic principle that its core teachings are clear and that those parts of it that are harder to understand can be interpreted in the light of clearer passages.

During the first phase of Protestantism, both of these ideas were vigorously disputed by Catholic writers. The Spanish Dominican writer Melchior Cano (1525–60) argued that the Bible is far from clear and that ordinary people need help with its interpretation. Protestantism, he argued, ends up making the individual believer the judge of the meaning of the Bible and has no place for the corporate judgment of the church. A similar criticism was made by Roberto Bellarmine (1541–60). It is obvious, he argued, that the Bible is difficult to interpret, a fact that Protestantism tried to conceal by following a herd instinct and pretending that this amounted to divine guidance.

There are some serious issues here, and we consider these later in this volume. It is a simple fact of Protestant history that in four major areas of biblical interpretation, the consensus has shifted between 1500 and 2000. We have already noted one of these—the changed understanding of Matthew 28:19. Were the apostles being charged with the task of evangelization (a virtually universal interpretation in sixteenth-century Protestantism), or was this responsibility being passed on to individual Christians in later generations (the dominant view since the nineteenth century)?

A further notion of importance is that of "adiaphora," or "matters of indifference." This basic concept, articulated out of necessity by Philip Melanchthon during the crises faced by Lutheranism in the late 1540s, acknowledges that sometimes the interpretation or application of the Bible is not clear. The first decades of the Reformation threw up many such issues: What form of dress should the clergy wear? What forms of worship should be adopted? Should hymns be sung in church? In such cases, Melanchthon argued, Protestants must be free to make their own judgments, while being respectful of the views of others. As the Puritan writer Richard Baxter (1615–91) put it: "In necessary things, unity; in doubtful things, liberty; in all things, charity." We shall return presently to consider how Protestants interpreted and applied the Bible.

It is important to appreciate that Protestant readings of the Bible are often shaped by past controversies. An excellent example is to be found in Protestant attitudes to Mary, the mother of Jesus of Nazareth. Luther gave Mary a significant role in evangelical devotion, seeing her as an exemplary model of Christian discipleship.[9] Yet Protestantism as a whole has been wary of giving Mary a significant role in the lives of believers, despite the New Testament's positive statements concerning her. Indeed, many scholars argue that Protestantism is characterized by the modesty, even ambivalence, of its statements about Mary. Why? The reason is simple: Protestants have reacted to what they have seen as Catholic overstatements about Mary, particularly in relation to her role in salvation.

This situation is now changing. As we pointed out earlier, Protestant perceptions of "the other," which have played a critically important role in shaping Protestant self-definition, have changed since 1960. No longer is Catholicism the enemy. As a result, Protestants have shown themselves willing to reexamine the Bible and, where necessary, correct any past interpretations of scripture that can now be seen to represent polemical reactions against Catholicism rather than faithful and obedient renderings of the text.[10] The result has been a cautious yet decisive willingness to give Mary a place in Christian devotion—above all, at

Christmas, Good Friday, and Easter—that is more in line with the New Testament witness than with past Protestant polemics.

Changing attitudes among Protestants toward Mary is one sign of the greater openness among Protestants to Roman Catholicism in general, on the one hand, and on the other, remaining faithful to the fundamental Protestant principle of constantly reexamining existing readings of the Bible to ensure that these are faithful. Though some may find this paradoxical, the emerging interest in Mary is entirely consistent with Protestantism considered as a way of doing theology, even though it may cause tensions with Protestantism considered as a fixed body of attitudes from the past.

Although Protestants have always regarded the Bible as authoritative, various attempts have been made to formalize this authority by developing theories that would explain precisely what it is about the Bible that gives it such an authority.[11] These theories date mainly from the later nineteenth century, when the proclamation of the dogma of papal infallibility in 1870 put Protestants under pressure to clarify their understanding of authority. One of the most influential such theories was set out by the Princeton Reformed theologian Benjamin B. Warfield.[12]

For Warfield, the unique authority of the Bible lay in the fact that it is inspired. "Inspiration is that extra-ordinary, supernatural influence ... exerted by the Holy Ghost on the writers of our Sacred Books, by which their words were rendered also the words of God, and, therefore, perfectly infallible." (It may be noted that Warfield's use of the term "infallible" to refer to the Bible may represent a response to the First Vatican Council's insistence that the pope is infallible.) Although Warfield is careful to stress that the humanity and individuality of biblical writers were not abolished by inspiration, he nevertheless insists that their humanity "was so dominated that their words became at the same time the words of God, and thus, in every case and all alike, absolutely infallible." Other theories of inspiration located this authority elsewhere.[13] What is important, however, is that recognition of the authority of the Bible preceded any attempt to formalize that authority theoretically.

Yet this raises an important question, one that has been the subject of considerable debate between Catholics and Protestants since the sixteenth century. What range of writings does the canon of the Bible embrace?

THE SHAPE OF THE BIBLE:
THE OLD TESTAMENT AND THE APOCRYPHA

The rise of Protestantism forced reconsideration of what had up to that point been a relatively unproblematic question: what specific texts does the phrase "the Bible" denote? At a fairly early stage in its history, the Christian church had to make some important decisions as to what the term "scripture" actually designated. The first major phase in the history of the church, often referred to as the "patristic period" (c. 100–c. 450), witnessed the setting of the limits to the New Testament—a process usually known as "the fixing of the canon." The word "canon" derives from the Greek word *kanon,* meaning a "rule" or "reference point." The phrase "the canon of scripture" thus refers to a limited and defined group of writings that are accepted as authoritative within the church.

What criteria were used in drawing up this canon? The basic principle underlying this process appears to have been that of the *recognition* rather than the *imposition* of authority. In other words, the works in question were recognized by Christians as already possessing authority; they did not have an arbitrary authority imposed upon them. For the early church father Irenaeus, the church does not create the canon of scripture; it acknowledges, conserves, and receives canonical scripture on the basis of the authority already inherent to it. Some early Christians appear to have regarded apostolic authorship as of decisive importance; others were prepared to accept books that did not appear to have apostolic credentials. Although the precise details of how this selection was made remain unclear, it is certain that the canon was closed within the Western church by the beginning of the fifth century. The issue of the canon would not be raised again until the dawn of Protestantism.

At the time of the Reformation, a major debate broke out over whether some works accepted by the medieval church as canonical really deserved this status. It must be emphasized that the debate centered on the Old Testament; the canon of the New Testament was never seriously questioned, despite Martin Luther's misgivings about the canonicity of the letter of James and three other shorter letters.

While all the New Testament works were accepted as canonical—Luther's misgivings would gain little support—doubts were raised concerning the canonicity of a group of Old Testament works. A comparison of the contents of the Old Testament in the Hebrew Bible, on the one hand, and in the Greek and Latin versions (such as the Septuagint and the Vulgate), on the other, shows that the latter contain a number of works not found in the former. Following the lead of Jerome, the reformers argued that the only Old Testament writings that could be regarded as belonging to the canon of scripture were those originally included in the Hebrew Bible.

Protestants thus drew a distinction between the Old Testament and what they termed the "Apocrypha." The former consisted of texts found in the Hebrew Bible, while the latter consisted of text found in Greek and Latin versions of the Bible but *not* in the Hebrew Bible. While some reformers allowed that the apocryphal works made for edifying reading, there was general agreement that these works could not be used as the basis of doctrine. However, Catholic theologians of the Middle Ages, followed by the Council of Trent in 1546, defined the Old Testament as "those Old Testament works contained in the Greek and Latin bibles," thus eliminating from the outset any distinction between "Old Testament" and "Apocrypha."

From the beginning, therefore, Catholics and Protestants have had quite different understandings of what the term "the Bible" means, and this difference persists to the present day. A comparison of current Protestant versions of the Bible—the two most important being the New Revised Standard Version (NRSV) and the New International Version (NIV)—with their Catholic counterparts, such as the Jerusalem Bible, reveals these differences.

One practical outcome of this sixteenth-century debate was the production and circulation of authorized lists of books that were to be regarded as "scriptural." The fourth session of the Council of Trent (1546) produced a detailed list that included the works of the Apocrypha as authentically scriptural, while Protestant congregations in Switzerland, France, and elsewhere produced lists that either totally omitted any reference to these works or indicated that they were of no importance in matters of doctrine.

PROTESTANT INTERPRETATIONS OF
THE *SOLA SCRIPTURA* PRINCIPLE

At the Diet of Worms, held April 18, 1521, Martin Luther famously declared: "My conscience is captive to the word of God." In its formative phase, Protestantism was characterized by a belief—a radical, liberating, yet *dangerous* belief—that scripture is clear enough for ordinary Christians to understand and apply without the need for a classical education, philosophical or theological expertise, clerical guidance, or ecclesiastical tradition, in the confident expectation that difficult passages will be illuminated by clearer ones. Although some early Protestants appear to have believed that it would be possible to develop a single, well-defined biblical theology and church practice, it soon became clear that additional constraints would be needed.

This point has been recognized since the 1520s. Martin Bucer, alarmed at the needless tensions that were emerging within Protestantism on account of the violent disagreement between Luther and Zwingli over sacramental theology, proposed that Protestantism simply declare that it would respect a reasonable degree of theological diversity, since this appeared to be the inevitable outcome of biblical interpretation.[14] So long as it could be shown that a given doctrine was adequately justified on the basis of the Bible, Bucer asserted, it should be accepted as lying within the spectrum of Protestant thought.

In the end, Bucer's irenic approach was not adopted because it was seen as vague and imprecise. Yet Bucer, one of the most perceptive Protestant thinkers during this formative age, had appreciated the fundamental problem of Protestant theological identity—namely, that the movement was primarily about a certain way of doing theology that could lead to an uncontrollable diversity of outcomes. To illustrate the issue, we may consider a question of no small relevance to tensions within North American culture at present.

What do Protestants believe about the creation of humanity, especially in the light of Charles Darwin's theory of evolution? This is a significant, highly contentious question, and we consider its importance in more detail in a later chapter. As someone with a specialist interest in this area, I can easily identify at least nineteen distinct Protestant answers to this question, each claiming to be the correct interpretation of the Bible. So which is the Protestant answer? Which one is right?

The first question can be answered quite simply. All nineteen positions represent answers that have been shaped by what is clearly a Protestant approach to the interpretation of scripture. The nineteen approaches may well be different, but each one has every right to call itself Protestant and to be recognized as such by other Protestants. The question of which approach is *right* is rather more difficult!

Since every Protestant has the right to interpret the Bible, a wide range of interpretations cannot be avoided. And since there is no centralized authority within Protestantism, this proliferation of options cannot be controlled. Who has the right to decide what is orthodox and what is heretical? For many early Protestants, this was a dangerous idea that opened the floodgates to a torrent of distortion, misunderstanding, and confusion.

So what could be done to limit the range of biblical interpretations? This was a pressing question, since the more radical thinkers within Protestantism chose to interpret the Bible in ways that seemed to many to lie beyond the pale of orthodoxy. John Dryden, writing in the seventeenth century, pointed out that both heretics and the orthodox appealed to the Bible. They happened to interpret it in different ways. And if there was no Protestant equivalent of the *magisterium*, the centralized teaching authority of the church, how could these positions be defined as heretical? Or even as un-Protestant?

> For did not Arius first, Socinus now
> The Son's eternal Godhead disavow?
> And did not these by Gospel texts alone
> Condemn our doctrine and maintain their own?
> Have not all heretics the same pretence,
> To plead the Scriptures in their own defence?
> "The Hind and the Panther," part 2, lines 150–55

Over the years, each strand of Protestantism developed its own way of understanding and implementing the *sola Scriptura* principle.[15] Each accorded primacy to scripture yet recognized a number of additional resources—such as tradition, reason, and experience—that might serve in connecting scripture with the intellectual and experiential world of every generation. Two approaches, both affirming the important role of the Christian community in interpreting scripture, proved to be of particular importance. The first stressed its *synchronic* role—in other words, the role of the present-day community of believers in seeking to understand a text. The second emphasized its *diachronic* role, looking to the testimony of believers in the past as an aid to the present-day task of interpretation.

The first approach stressed that biblical interpretation is ultimately a corporate, rather than an individual, matter. Individual believers have every right to ask for an explanation or defense of the views of the wider body, according to this approach. While the Holy Spirit has indeed been given to all believers—partly to illuminate their reading of scripture—the community of faith has a vital role in checking misperceptions or misreadings. Questions of doctrine are to be settled, however, by the community of faith as a whole, not by a single person. Anabaptism, often regarded as the form of Protestantism that gave individuals the greatest degree of freedom in this respect, generally emphasized the importance of the congregation in determining how to interpret scripture.[16] Similarly, American Baptist theologians respect the judgments of earlier luminaries within their tradition, regarding them as important dialogue partners in the contemporary task of explicating and applying the Bible.[17]

The second approach emphasized the role of the past in interpreting scripture. The mainline reformers argued that since Protestantism represented the continuation and renewal of apostolic Christianity, it was able to share in the early Christian community's decisions concerning norms of faith and that community's identification of heresies and other inauthentic forms of faith. Most Protestants therefore accepted the traditional ecumenical creeds, regarding these as publicly authorized and endorsed interpretations of scripture. This approach was generally not adopted by sixteenth-century Anabaptist communities, which had serious reservations concerning the authenticity of earlier forms of Christianity, even during the patristic period. However, modern Anabaptist theologians take their own tradition with the greatest seriousness in attempting to fashion an appropriate engagement with the Bible in the light of today's questions and issues.[18]

The form of Protestantism that probably exemplified this approach best was early seventeenth-century Anglicanism. Francis White (1564–1638), sometime Bishop of Ely, was a leading representative of early seventeenth-century Anglican theology, which represented a classic statement of the "reformed Catholicism" of the Church of England at this time, combining the Reformation's insistence on the theological priority of scripture with a Catholic understanding of the institutional mediation of scripture through the church.[19]

For White, the church constructs "her faith and religion upon the sacred and canonical Scriptures of the Holy Prophets and Apostles, as upon her main and prime foundation."[20] Yet White insisted on the need for an agreed, consensual means by which the Bible might be interpreted, and he found this in "the consentient testimony and authority of the Bishops and pastors of the true and ancient Catholic church," which were to be set over and against innovations resulting from individualist speculation.

In effect, White distinguished between two sources of authority—one magisterial, the other ministerial; one sovereign, the other subordinate. The former is scripture; the latter is the "voice and testimony of the Primitive Church," which acts as "a ministerial and subordinate rule and guide, to preserve us and direct us in the right understanding of the Scriptures."

The recognition that the church has a role to play in the interpretation of the Bible in no way invalidates the *sola Scriptura* principle. William Whitaker (1547–95) echoed a general Protestant consensus when he stated: "For we also say that the church is the interpreter of Scripture, and that the gift of interpretation resides only in the church: but we deny that it pertains to particular persons, or is tied to any particular see or succession of men."[21] This naturally leads us to consider the role of tradition as an aid to the interpretation of scripture.

THE BIBLE AND TRADITION

The word "tradition" comes from the Latin term *traditio*, which can be understood to mean both the "act of handing over" and "what is actually handed over." The idea is found in the New Testament itself, as when Paul speaks of handing over to the church at Corinth teachings about Jesus Christ that had originally been handed over to him (1 Co-rinthians 15:1–4). The mainline reformers believed that the Bible had been honored, interpreted, and applied faithfully in the past and that Protestant theologians were under an obligation to take their reflections into account as they interpreted the Bible in the present day.[22] Luther insisted that tradition—understood as ideas inherited from the past—operated in a ministerial, not magisterial, mode, serving not directing the church.

There is genuine disagreement within Protestantism over the relation of the Bible and tradition. The Anabaptist wing of the Reformation argued, not entirely without justification, that the only consistent way in which the *sola Scriptura* principle could be applied was to limit Protestant belief and practice to what was explicitly taught in scripture. Since the practice of infant baptism was not mentioned in the Bible, it was therefore to be rejected as unbiblical. Similar anxieties were expressed by some radical writers about the doctrine of the Trinity.

The mainline reformers, such as Luther and Calvin, held that upholding the supreme authority of the Bible did not mean rejecting the church's past history of biblical reflection as a God-given resource to help with its present-day interpretation.[23] As we noted earlier, Luther styled his reforming program at Wittenberg as a return to "the Bible and Augustine" and regarded Augustine as something of a theological lodestar. Luther's colleague Philip Melanchthon developed similar arguments, most notably that the Reformation could be seen as a return to the consensus of the early church, especially as found in the writings of Augustine and Ambrose. Calvin insisted that the Reformation was about a return to the doctrinal purity of the early church, corrected as necessary against the Bible. Like Luther, he had an especially high regard for Augustine of Hippo.[24]

The fundamental idea here is that the past can be a resource for the present. Where radical writers such as Sebastian Franck dismissed patristic writers such as Augustine as servants of anti-Christ, mainline Protestantism valued them and saw itself as a continuation and expansion of all that was good about the early church. This allowed early Protestants to make a critical apologetic point. In response to their Catholic critics who declared that Protestantism was an innovation—

where was your church before Luther?—they replied that they stood in continuity with the early church. The Catholic church, they argued, had itself distorted the early church's teachings during the Middle Ages.

At the Council of Trent (1546), Catholicism responded by arguing that Protestantism had lost its theological moorings. It valued the Bible, which was good in itself, but failed to recognize that the church possessed unwritten traditions, passed down from one generation to the next, on central themes of the Christian faith. The principle of *sola Scriptura* simply cut off Protestantism from these necessary truths, and hence from the full riches of the Christian faith. Trent developed a "two-source" theory of tradition that regarded the Bible and unwritten tradition as sources of equal value for doctrine and morals. By denying tradition as a source of revelation independent of the Bible, Protestantism had cut itself off from the apostolic period, and hence from Christ himself.[25]

Protestant attitudes to tradition are deeply revealing about the movement's self-understanding. Mainline Protestantism was emphatic that it was not a new church brought into existence by the circumstances of the sixteenth century. It represented a reform and renewal of Christianity, implying and affirming continuity with the great historic tradition of Christian faith and stretching back through the patristic era to the apostles themselves. Protestantism saw itself as a purified and renewed vision of Christian identity and pointed to historical landmarks in the past—such as the Pelagian controversy—that indicated that a similar process of criticism and regeneration was built into the fabric of faith.[26]

Anabaptists, however, preferred not to speak of the "reformation" of the church, in that this implied that a Christian church existed before the Reformation—a belief that Luther and Calvin regarded as historically and theologically self-evident and unproblematic. For more radical Protestants, the church needed to be re-created from its very foundations. This Promethean reconstruction of the church from ground zero was better expressed as a "restoration" of the church rather than a "reformation."

THE TRANSLATION OF THE BIBLE

Whereas Islam insists that the Qu'ran must be read in its original Arabic, there is no requirement in the Bible that it be read, other than for reasons of scholarly accuracy, in its original languages. During the Middle Ages, the laity was largely disconnected from the Bible. Many monastic orders—such as the Benedictines—placed a high value on detailed, extensive study of the Bible. Yet such a knowledge of the text was simply impossible for most ordinary Christians, most of whom could neither read nor afford to buy a manuscript of the Bible. The advent of printing would alleviate the latter problem, although Johann Gutenberg's first printed Bibles cost far more than large houses of his day.

Things began to change in England in the late Middle Ages, even though the translation of the Bible into English was illegal at this time. John Wycliffe, the English religious reformer of the fourteenth century, is often referred to as the "morning star of the Reformation." It is an appropriate, if not totally accurate, designation. One of Wycliffe's best-known slogans, shamelessly plagiarized by Abraham Lincoln, affirms the fundamentally democratizing consequences of giving people access to the Bible: this book would give rise to "government of the people, by the people, and for the people."

Wycliffe himself made no small contribution to this development, although he appears to have inspired others to translate the Bible into English rather than to have done so himself.[27] The fourteenth-century Wycliffite translations into English were based on the Latin Vulgate translation of the Bible rather than the original Hebrew and Greek texts. It was not until the year 1516 that new possibilities opened up, when Erasmus of Rotterdam published the Greek text of the New Testament. It is no accident that this landmark event took place so close to the dawn of the reforming challenges to the established social, religious, and intellectual orders of the day.

Luther demanded that all Christians should be able to read the Bible for themselves. Lay access to the Bible was about power as much as it was about encouraging personal spirituality. The pressure to place the Bible in the hands of the ordinary person was an implicit demand for the emancipation of the laity from clerical domination. Always a realist in matters of human nature, Luther knew that it was a waste of time demanding that everyone learn the original biblical languages. The needs of the situation demanded action on his part. The Bible had to be translated into ordinary German! But that would take time—something that Luther simply did not have in 1520.

Then events took an unexpected turn, and Luther suddenly found himself with an abundance of time on his hands. Following his condemnation at Worms, Luther was "kidnapped" in May 1521 by his friends and placed in safe custody in Wartburg Castle. "Junker Jörg" (Sir George)—as Luther was known during this period of enforced isolation—spent his first eleven weeks translating the New Testament into German. The "September Testament" was edited by Melanchthon and others and published in 1522. It created a sensation and had a permanent effect on the shaping of the modern German language.[28]

Others were inspired by this effort and longed to do the same. William Tyndale even traveled to Wittenberg in order to benefit from both Luther's personal example and his translation of the New Testament.[29] Perhaps as many as three thousand copies of Tyndale's English translation of the New Testament were printed in great secrecy in the German city of Worms and imported shortly afterward into England, where they caused a sensation. The bishop of London ordered that every available copy be seized and burned.

Why was the translation regarded as so dangerous? Two reasons stand out. First, any English translation was dangerous because it enabled ordinary Christians to carry out a reality check on the teaching and morality of the church. It was a disconcerting, even threatening, development. Second, Tyndale's translation used vocabulary that threatened to undermine traditional authority structures within the church. An example will make this point clear.

The English church had had priests since anyone could remember. Yet Tyndale's New Testament rendered the Greek word *presbyteros*, traditionally translated as "priest," as "senior." The English word "priest" should, he argued, be reserved solely for translating the Greek term *hiereus*, used in the New Testament exclusively to refer to Jewish or pagan priests or to Christ himself. The Greek term *ekklesia*, traditionally translated as "church," was now translated as "congregation." Sections of the New Testament that could have been taken as endorsing the institution of the church were now to be understood as referring to local congregations of believers. In both cases, the new translation threatened to subvert the existing structures of the church by implying that they were not found in the New Testament itself.

Realizing that they could not prevent such translations from getting through to England, where they would secure a ready and enthusiastic readership, the authorities reluctantly decided they would have to authorize and produce their own English translations of the Bible. Far better, they reasoned, to have a translation they could control than to try to fight off subversive translations. A series of English Bibles thus appeared over the next eighty years, battling it out for the loyalty of the English public.[30] We have already noted the importance of the unauthorized Geneva Bible (1560), produced by Protestants in Geneva. Yet perhaps the greatest English translation of the Bible was the King James Bible of 1611, also known as the "Authorized Version."

The origins of this version can be traced back to the first year of the reign of James I. Anxious to secure religious peace in England, James authorized the production of a new English translation of the Bible early in his reign. The fifty translators were divided into six "companies," two based at Westminster, two at Oxford, and two at Cambridge. Each was allocated a section of the Bible, including the Apocrypha. They were given strict instructions about how they were to proceed with the translation. They would make no marginal notes; they would use traditional English ecclesiastical language (for example, "church," not "congregation"); and they would draw upon earlier English translations as appropriate. The new translation would be conservative theologically while maintaining complete accuracy by the standards of its day.

The resulting translation, published in 1611, eventually became a religious classic—even if it did take about eighty years for it to be fully accepted as such. The impact of the King James Bible on the English language was decisive. Countless phrases originally deriving from Hebrew—such as "to fall flat on one's face," "the skin of one's teeth," "to stand in awe," and "to lick the dust"—now found their way into everyday English. The impact of such translations on the shaping of national languages and cultures has been immense. The English Bible, above all the King James Bible, has shaped "the common code of the English-speaking world," almost as if it were some kind of linguistic DNA.[31]

Yet the most interesting section of the King James Bible is now generally omitted, owing to lack of space. Miles Smith, writing on behalf of the translators, provided a preface that offered an account of the benefits of biblical translation to the people of God. It allowed them to gain access to the spiritual nourishment found in the Bible. Translation opened a window and let in the light; broke the shell that we might eat the kernel; drew aside the curtain that we might look into the most holy place; removed the cover of the well that we might drink of its water, "even as Jacob rolled away the stone from the mouth of the well, by which means the flocks of Laban were watered [Genesis 29:10]." To translate the Bible was an act of service to the people of God.

By 1900 the King James Bible was firmly established as a religious classic. Several North American religious groups have regarded it as the definitive translation of the Bible and refused to countenance others.[32] Many have felt that this text, like Shakespeare's works, is vested with the dignity and sanctity of a classic and therefore cannot be revised.

It is beyond doubt that the King James Version of the Bible was an outstanding translation by the standards of 1611 and beyond. Yet translations eventually require revision, not necessarily because they are defective, but because the language into which they were translated changes over time. Translation involves aiming at a moving target that has accelerated over the centuries. Living languages are developing more quickly today than at any time in their previous history. Some words have ceased to be used, while others have changed their meanings. For example, consider this sentence from the King James translation:

> For this we say unto you by the word of the Lord, that we which are alive and remain unto the coming of the Lord shall not prevent them which are asleep. (1 Thessalonians 4:15)

A modern reader would find this puzzling, in that the 1611 meaning of "prevent"—"to go before" or "to precede"—is different from its modern sense of "to hinder." Linguistic change makes classic translations—such as the King James Bible—capable of misleading and confusing readers. When a translation itself requires explanation, it has ceased to function as a working translation.

This point has considerable relevance to late twentieth-century American debates over the place of the King James translation. Those who insist on retaining the King James Bible as the only acceptable English translation of the Bible actually betray the intentions and goals of those who conceived and translated it—namely, to translate the Bible into living English.[33]

ISSUES IN BIBLICAL INTERPRETATION

How is the Bible to be interpreted? This unavoidable question lies at the heart of Protestantism. In virtually every debate that takes place within the Protestant community of faith—whether concerning the origins of humanity, the ministry of women, the nature of the end times, or the legitimacy of abortion—all sides will make an appeal to the Bible. One side will accentuate one set of texts and the other side another set, or both will appeal to the same basic texts yet interpret them differently.[34] The outcome is a range of interpretations of the Bible. Some issues on which Protestants have offered—and continue to offer—significantly different readings of the Bible include:

1. Should infants be baptized?

2. Is Jesus Christ really present in the bread and wine?

3. Does baptism *effect* or *signify* the forgiveness of sins?

4. Should women exercise leadership roles in churches?

5. Was the world created in six periods of twenty-four hours?

6. Should Christians fight in wars?

7. What is the most authentically "biblical" form of worship?

8. Are Catholics Christians?

Other issues can easily be added to this list, which is clearly illustrative, not exhaustive.

The vast majority of Protestant theologians do not regard this diversity of biblically based beliefs and practices as compromising the principle of the perspicuity of scripture. The essential point made by this principle is that, at any given point in the church's history, scripture is both clear and sufficient in all things that are necessary to salvation. As early as the 1520s, irenic Protestant theologians, such as Martin Bucer, were stressing the importance of learning to live in a community that was producing important differences of biblical interpretation and thus different conclusions drawn from the same foundational document.

In part, the issue has to do with the identity of Protestantism itself. It is not difficult to identify specific groups within Protestantism according to their relatively well-defined and well-defended—yet *different*—ways of interpreting the Bible. In the United States on the eve of the First World War, for example, relatively coherent and distinctive belief systems, each rigorously based on the Bible, were associated with Presbyterianism, Methodism, the Southern Baptist Convention, Episcopalianism, and Lutheranism. Reinforced by dedicated seminaries, denominational theological textbooks, and preachers, each group defended its specific reading of the Bible against the alternatives.

The difficulty emerges if one imagines that there exists a universal category called "Protestantism" that is embodied in each of these groups. The reality is that Protestantism has always been a somewhat diffuse notion, whereas each of the individual religious groupings just named— to which others, such as Pentecostalism, could easily be added—are living social realities. Sociologically, it is easy to show that Americans in the years immediately before the First World War may have been vaguely committed to the greater, overarching notion of "Protestantism" but defined themselves primarily in terms of their own denominations. Even as late as 1960, most Americans had serious misgivings about worshiping at Protestant denominations other than their own, feeling that this compromised their religious identities. Their loyalty was primarily—and in many cases exclusively—to the specific beliefs, structure, and life of a particular denomination. If the category of "Protestantism" is proposed as the primary category of identification, a significant degree of diversity on such matters as church order, doctrinal standards, and sacramental practice arises, precisely on account of the different historical traditions that make up the greater category of "Protestantism."

In practice, this has not troubled most Protestants, who are sufficiently historically literate, on the one hand, to realize the inevitability of this problem and sufficiently tolerant, on the other, to cope with the varieties of beliefs and practices that arise from this situation. Such limited diversity has been present from the outset within Protestantism and is arguably the inevitable outcome of its shared commitment to the authority of the Bible and its special place in Christian life and thought.

The same phenomenon arises within Islamic interpretation of the Qu'ran, which shows important parallels to—with equally important divergences from—Protestantism's engagement with the Bible. Although there are some shared assumptions that govern Qu'ranic interpretation within Islam, this has not led to anything approaching uniformity within the movement. Is the Qu'ran a document of its own age that must be interpreted within that historical context? Or is it a timeless document, liberated from the specifics of its history?[35] To what extent can one break with traditional interpretations of the Qu'ran in facing new contexts and challenges?[36] Islam, like Protestantism, faces increasing diversification as new contexts and issues emerge, demanding new interpretations of the Qu'ran and placing older, traditional interpretations under increasing conceptual and ethical strain.[37]

Yet this historical diversity of biblical interpretation has been the cause for some concern and even distress for those who believe that Protestantism ought to be characterized by a homogeneous, monolithic belief system. Mistakenly believing that even a modest diversity of biblical interpretation compromises the notion of the "clarity of scripture," they have sought ways of securing and enforcing a single, unambiguous interpretation of the Bible at every point. In effect, the equivalent of a "Protestant papacy" has been proposed, by which the correct interpretation of the Bible might be laid down by decree. Such efforts have not proved successful, for two main reasons. First, they involve the imposition of single meanings on clusters of core passages, but it is clear that a diversity of interpretations has existed throughout Protestant history. Second, the nature of Protestantism is such than no one has the right or authority to speak for Protestantism in this way. Indeed, the Reformation itself, by insisting on the right of all believers to read and interpret the Bible for themselves, can be seen as a revolt against this quasi-papal centralization of authority.

One strategy of particular interest emerged during the 1980s, when some conservative Protestants, particularly in the United States, began increasingly to characterize the Bible as "infallible" or "inerrant."[38] In doing so, they were picking up some themes from the nineteenth-century writings of Benjamin Warfield, while giving them a new and significant emphasis. Yet this claim did not, as some had hoped, solve the problem of multiple interpretations. It is perfectly possible for an inerrant text to be interpreted incorrectly. Asserting the infallibility of a text merely accentuates the importance of the interpreter of that text. Unless the interpreter is also to be thought of as infallible—a view that Protestantism has rejected, associating it with Catholic views of the church or papacy—the issue of determining the "right" meaning of the Bible is not settled, or even addressed, by declaring that the sacred text is infallible. The Jehovah's Witnesses, for example, regard the Bible as infallible, yet interpret core passages in a way that most Protestants find unacceptable, especially in relation to the identity of Jesus of Nazareth.

Debates about biblical interpretation take place in every Christian community, not merely Protestant ones. What distinguishes Protestantism at this point is its principled refusal to allow any authority above scripture, such as a pope or council. This principle is often affirmed using the Latin slogan *Scriptura ipsius interpres* ("Scripture is its own interpreter"). Whereas Catholicism resolves such tensions through magisterial pronouncements on the part of the teaching authority of the church, Protestantism recognizes no such authority above scripture. Such tensions must be resolved by means that will command support within Protestantism on account of their intrinsic merits, including their intellectual plausibility and their consonance with the biblical witness as a whole.

The classic Protestant approach has been well defended in recent years by J. I. Packer, an Oxford-educated theologian who spent the most significant part of his career teaching at Regent College in Vancouver. Packer argues that two principles are essential to a Protestant approach to the interpretation of the Bible:

> Scripture yields two basic principles for its own interpretation. The first is that the proper, natural sense of each passage (i.e., the intended sense of the writer) is to be taken as fundamental; the meaning of texts in their own contexts, and for their original readers, is the necessary starting-point for enquiry into their wider

significance.... The second basic principle of interpretation is that Scripture must interpret Scripture; the scope and significance of one passage is to be brought out by relating it to others.[39]

Packer emphasizes that the "natural" or "plain" sense of a passage depends on whether that passage was intended to be read as history, prophecy, poetry, narrative, or teaching. Not every biblical passage can be forced into the same preconceived mold; each must be interpreted on its own terms.

So what are the issues that arise in biblical interpretation? How do these affect the beliefs, values, and actions of Protestants, whether as individuals or as communities? The best way of dealing with such questions is to explore some general issues that arise in biblical interpretation and then see how these relate to contemporary or classic debates. Here we look at four issues. There are others—including how to resolve apparent conflicts between biblical texts—that fully deserve to be discussed but have been omitted simply on account of space constraints.

The Relation Between the Old and New Testaments

Protestants regard the Bible as having two major sections—the Old and New Testaments. Following John Calvin, most Protestants affirm the theological continuity between the two Testaments: both are the work of the same God, setting out the same fundamental themes of creation, grace, sin, judgment, redemption, and consummation. At the theological level, the New Testament states more clearly and more fully what is sometimes set out more opaquely in the Old. This basic theme is often summarized in a slogan of Augustine of Hippo: "The New Testament is hidden in the Old; the Old is made accessible by the New."

But what of the Old Testament's moral commands? For example, the Old Testament commands that the Sabbath (Saturday) be kept holy and prescribes the death sentence for those who defile it. Virtually every Christian community, including Protestantism, insists that a distinction must be made between the "cultic" and the "moral" commandments. Where the Old Testament lays down a general moral principle—such as "You shall not murder"—this is binding on Christians. Where it lays down a command linked with the Old Testament cult—for example, relating to sacrifices, the priesthood, or the worship of the Temple—this is not binding. On this reading, the command to observe the Sabbath is a cultic requirement and is therefore open to reinterpretation by Christians.

This issue has become of major significance in recent debates over homosexuals and the ordained ministry. Those who oppose the ordination of active homosexuals often appeal to texts in the "holiness code" of the Book of Leviticus that condemn homosexuality. This section of the text deals with eating blood (17:10–11; 19:26), proper sacrifices (17:2–8; 19:5–8), incest (18:6–18; 20:17), menstrual uncleanness (18:19), adultery (18:20; 20:10), homosexuality (18:22; 20:13), Sabbath keeping (19:3, 30), and unclean animals (20:25). Most interpreters have regarded the "holiness code" as mingling cultic and moral issues, in that the Old Testament makes no distinction between them, whereas Christians regard the distinction as significant.

Debates within Protestantism over the question of homosexual ordination thus tend to focus on the question of whether its prohibition in the Old Testament is cultic or moral. Those in favor regard the prohibition as cultic; those who are opposed see it as moral.

The Status of Biblical Language: Literal, Metaphorical, Poetic, or Accommodated?

The Bible frequently makes statements of the form "A is B." Debate has often arisen over whether the deceptively simple word "is" means "is literally identical with" or something rather more nuanced, such as "is like" or "points to." We have already seen how precisely this kind of debate fractured both the personal relationship between Luther and Zwingli and that between the German and Swiss Reformations. That debate was over this statement made by Jesus of Nazareth at the Last Supper: "This is my body" (Matthew 26:26). For Luther, this statement was literally true; for Zwingli, Jesus was using a figure of speech meaning "this represents my body."

Protestant fundamentalism is often portrayed as interpreting the Bible literally at every point. It requires only a modest familiarity with the writings and sermons of fundamentalists to realize how inaccurate this characterization is. Fundamentalists undoubtedly regard as literally true certain texts that other Protestants might interpret symbolically or allegorically—for example, the visions of the Book of Revelation. Yet fundamentalists interpret other texts spiritually—such as the prophecies of the liberation of the poor and oppressed (Isaiah 61), which they generally take to mean "spiritually impoverished and oppressed." Untidy though it may seem, all Protestants agree that some texts are to be interpreted literally and others metaphorically. The problem is that there is no universal agreement on which texts should be allocated to each category.

John Calvin introduced another category that proved to be influential at this point. Noting that classical orators adapted or accommodated their language and imagery to their intended audience, Calvin argued that God adapts or accommodates revelation to the abilities of those toward whom it is directed.[40] God might use strongly realist imagery—such as the "arm of the Lord"—to enable effective communication to its recipients. Biblical statements that at first sight appear to be literally true might therefore be "accommodated" and might need to be interpreted in this light. This issue would become of major importance in the Protestant reaction to the Copernican model of the solar system, which we shall consider later.

A related issue concerns the literary genre in which a given text is located. For example, the Psalms declare that "the mountains skipped like rams, the hills like lambs" (Psalm 114:4) in response to the great saving acts of God. Is that to be taken as literally true? Most Protestants have argued that it should not. It is a poetic statement, pointing to the exultation of all of nature at the redemptive action of the creator.

While this point might seem straightforward in theory, it is rather more problematic in practice. Who decides what literary genre a given section of the Bible belongs to? Protestants often find themselves in disagreement over how to categorize a section of the Bible. For example, is Genesis 1 to be understood as history, myth, or poetry? Each position has found its advocates within the Protestant tradition, with important implications for how the passage is interpreted, especially in relation to the Darwinian theory of evolution—a point of no small importance to which we shall return in a later chapter.

New Testament Commands:
Universal or Specific to the Original Audience?

A third problem concerns the intended audience of a biblical passage. Earlier, we saw that for its first two centuries Protestantism tended to interpret the "Great Commission" as a mandate delivered to the apostles, not their successors (Matthew 28:17–20). As a result, Protestants saw little reason to pursue missionary work—until the end of the eighteenth century, when the passage in question was "read" in a different way. The passage clearly demanded that the gospel be proclaimed; its interpretation was not in dispute. The debate concerned who was being commanded to proclaim it—the apostles at a specific period in history or all Christians throughout history?[41]

The same issue occurs repeatedly throughout the Bible. One issue that has caused some division within Protestantism is the ministry of women. In 1 Corinthians 14:34, Paul states that women should be silent in church: if they have theological questions, they should ask their husbands when they get home. Is this meant to be a universal principle, binding on all Christians at all times, or a specific instruction to the Corinthian church at that specific moment in its history, given the particular difficulties it was known to be experiencing?

The text can be interpreted in very different ways. Some might argue that it demonstrates that women cannot exercise any ministry, and therefore they interpret it as a universal ruling. Others see it as illustrating the problems at that specific juncture in the church's history on account of the newfound freedom that women then enjoyed through the rise of Christianity. On this reading, married women were disrupting the service by asking questions of their husbands, so they were instructed to wait and ask their questions at home. Which is right? Both sides of this debate are well represented within Protestantism's ample girth.

Perhaps the most significant case of such a question concerns the question of spiritual gifts, a cause of much comment in Paul's letters, especially the Corinthian correspondence. Paul affirms the importance of such gifts, while at the same time urging restraint and caution in exercising them—an attitude neatly summed up as "Cool it, don't kill it."

But were those gifts given for all time, or were they specific to the apostolic era and so have now died out? Was the pattern of spiritual gifts that was shown, for example, on the Day of Pentecost (Acts 2) specific to the needs and opportunities of the first years of the church—or was it valid for all time? The New Testament offers no unequivocal answer, although its interpreters have been known to suggest otherwise.

The belief that such gifts had died out (known as "cessationism") was widespread within mainline Protestantism from the sixteenth to the end of the nineteenth century. There was no reason to think otherwise, in the absence of any significant evidence of such spiritual gifts being experienced within the church. The outbreak of charismatic phenomena—such as speaking in tongues—on the first day of the twentieth century in the United States, followed by sustained global growth in such phenomena, raised questions about cessationism and convinced many that such spiritual gifts remained at the disposal of the church. Here, the decisive factor in changing the corporate mind of Protestantism over the best part of a century was not a new way of interpreting the Bible but renewed experience of something that had been believed to be extinct. Experience forced revision of existing ways of reading and interpreting the Bible.

Biblical Values and Ethics: Culturally Contingent or Universal?

A fourth area of debate in biblical interpretation concerns whether the cultural norms assumed within the biblical narrative were endorsed by the biblical writers. The case of slavery is of particular importance, and we consider this in more detail later. This question has been particularly significant in recent discussions about Christian attitudes toward homosexuality. Although the Bible makes surprisingly few unequivocal references to homosexual practices, those that can be identified are uniformly negative: "You shall not lie with a male as with a woman; it is an abomination" (Leviticus 18:22). While Jesus of Nazareth makes no reference to the subject, Paul explicitly condemns homosexual practice in his letter to the Romans (Romans 1:26–27). So how are these verses to be interpreted?

A traditionalist reading of these texts holds that they represent unequivocal, clear, and unambivalent condemnations that are therefore valid and binding on the church for all time. A liberal reading argues that it is important to discern the intention that lies behind these prohibitions and to distinguish this intention from the actual condemnations, which reflect issues in the culture of the ancient world (for example, the influence of paganism) that do not apply today.[42]

This brief account of four of the issues that have arisen in biblical interpretation—some of which have played a significant role in shaping the present form of Protestantism—helps explain the historical and contemporary diversity within Protestantism. It also leads us to reflect on an important consequence of the dangerous idea at the heart of Protestantism, an issue to which we now turn—namely, who decides what is orthodoxy and what is heresy.

THE PROBLEM OF HERESY FOR PROTESTANTISM

"Heresy" is one of the most ominous terms in the vocabulary of Christendom. The Christian usage of the word can be traced back to the New Testament itself, where it is used to designate a sect, faction, or grouping (see, for example, Acts 24:5; 28:22). Similarly, the great Jewish historian Josephus applies the term (*airesis*) to the three religious sects prevalent in Judea in his day: the Sadducees, the Pharisees, and the Essenes. At this stage, the term did not have the strongly negative associations that later developed; these, however, were not long in emerging.[43]

By the second century, "orthodoxy" and "heresy" were emerging as significant ideas.[44] The term "heresy" was used to designate deficient, and potentially vulnerable, understandings of the Christian faith that were to be rejected.[45] The identification of heresy was seen as a corporate judgment by the church that rested on a consensus that such views were unsatisfactory, fallacious, and misleading. Yet it is essential to appreciate that heresies were ultimately *unacceptable interpretations of the Bible.*

This can be seen by considering the fourth-century movement known as Arianism, widely seen as the most important early Christian heresy.[46] Arius and his followers held that Jesus of Nazareth could not be regarded as divine in any meaningful sense of the word. He was "supreme among God's creatures," but a creature nonetheless. This doctrine was severely criticized by writers such as Athanasius of Alexandria for undermining the internal coherence of the Christian faith. Yet both Arius and Athanasius based their ideas on substantially the same biblical texts, which they interpreted in different ways.[47]

The essence of heresy can therefore be located in flawed biblical interpretation. But who decides which biblical interpretations are flawed and which are orthodox? If all Christians have the right to interpret the Bible as they see fit, how can heresy be identified, let alone combated? If the Bible alone is the supreme rule of faith, how can any authority beyond that text be recognized as its authoritative interpreter? It is at this point that the distinctive approach of Protestantism encounters a seemingly formidable obstacle, in that it seems to undermine the very idea of an authoritative interpretation of the Bible—in other words, the notion of orthodoxy.

This already significant problem was made acute by the unusual social and intellectual conditions of the sixteenth century, catalyzed by the spirit of inquiry of the Renaissance. This era of scientific and intellectual restlessness was marked by a determination to explore new options and reevaluate old ones. Some of these were local heterodoxies, whose ideas had little impact at the time, even though they may have caused frissons of intellectual anxiety.[48] Among those, we may include the Italian village miller Domenico Scandella from the mountain village of Montereale, who took the view that the world arose from chaos, just as "cheese is made out of milk, and worms appeared in it, and these were the angels."[49] A surge of alternative viewpoints emerged, posing a powerful challenge to the religious and political stability of late Renaissance Europe. The authorities, political and religious, did what they could to limit their impact by branding such ideas as magic or heresy. Among these new movements, of course, was Protestantism itself—or perhaps we should say, many of the various tributaries that flowed into its vortex.

From its outset, Protestantism was branded as a heresy by the Catholic church. Protestants responded with indignation, retorting that they had recovered orthodoxy from its medieval distortions. What was Protestantism if not the recovery of the orthodox faith of the early church?[50] Yet Catholics had little difficulty in arguing that, while Protestantism might be perfectly capable of recovering earlier biblical interpretations, it lacked the means to determine whether what it had retrieved was orthodox or heterodox. And lacking any such capacity to discriminate between such interpretations, Protestants were obligated to repeat the judgments of the Catholic church on these matters. In their turn, Protestants argued that, since they were committed to restoring the authentic teaching of the early church, this naturally extended to its views on orthodoxy and heresy. In the end, the arguments were not decisive. However, the debate highlighted the potential danger for Protestantism arising from competing biblical interpretations. Who had the right to decide which were orthodox and which heretical?

This led to a further difficulty as divisions emerged within Protestant constituencies. Itself partly a consequence of the intellectual ferment of the Renaissance, Protestantism found that it could not check this innovative and critical tendency within its own ranks. It had merely been relocated, not neutralized. One particular difficulty was the rise of anti-trinitarianism in Italian Protestant circles, a movement that rapidly gained a following in northern Europe.[51] For Juan de Valdés and others, the doctrine of the Trinity was simply not to be found in the Bible, nor could it be defended on biblical grounds. Protestants who were faithful to the Bible not only were therefore under no obligation to accept this doctrine but had a responsibility to challenge it as a distortion of biblical truth. Forced out of Italy by the Inquisition, many anti-trinitarians settled in the independent republic of the Grisons in southeast Switzerland, where their influence upon Reformed Protestantism began to grow.

In this case, Protestantism was able to deal with such heterodox trends by appealing to the consensus of faith of the church, as set out in the Councils of Ephesus and Chalcedon. Christianity as a whole had declared such teachings to be heretical; Protestantism thus endorsed this pattern of traditional teaching and, in doing so, rejected anti-trinitarianism as heretical. But what of other dissident voices within Protestantism that urged teachings that had never been declared heretical in the past by the church as a whole but were nevertheless regarded with intense animosity within certain sections of the movement?

For instance, the major controversy that arose over the doctrine of predestination led to a fundamental bifurcation between Calvinism and Arminianism.[52] Each accused the other of being heretical. Yet in reality, each was a coherent interpretation of the Bible that happened to differ substantially from the other, both in terms of basic ideas and implications for the Christian life. There was—and is—no higher Protestant authority that can declare one or the other to be in the right. In the end, the only means of deciding the question was a vote within the constituency in question—as, for example, at the Synod of Dort, which established the boundaries of Calvinist orthodoxy. Orthodoxy thus ran the risk of being defined as the theology with the most votes within a given constituency, and heterodoxy as the minority voice.

The problem here is that "heresy" is ultimately a teaching judged unacceptable by the entire church; the term is not properly applicable to either Calvinism or Arminianism, which are each subdivisions of one constituency of Protestantism. One can certainly speak of heresy arising within Protestantism—for example, the revival of Arianism in seventeenth- and eighteenth-century Anglicanism.[53] In this case, ideas that the entire church regarded as heretical made a reappearance. Yet the nature of Protestantism makes it very difficult to use the term "heresy" to refer to divergent schools of thought within that movement, unless they reproduce ideas that the church as a whole has agreed are unorthodox. The problem is that of competing orthodoxies, each with its own grounding in the Bible, its own understanding of the internal dynamics of faith, and its own parameters of adjudication as to what is acceptable and what is not.

The problems that Protestantism faced here were famously set out by John Dryden in his satirical poem *Religio Laici* (1682). In this poem, whose title is best translated as "A Layperson's Religion," Dryden argues that the great Protestant emphasis on the Bible has merely led to the proliferation of heresy, owing to the absence of any universally acknowledged authoritative interpreter. The dangerous idea that underlies Protestantism, for Dryden, not merely leaves it powerless to resist heresy but actually encourages its emergence, through its naïve idea that ordinary Christians will be led, inerrantly and inevitably, to the gentle uplands of orthodoxy as they browse its pages. In a swipe at more radical Protestant approaches, he comments that the spirit gives the "doctoral degree" that qualifies believers as biblical authorities.

The Book thus put in every vulgar hand,
Which each presumed he best could understand,

The common rule was made the common prey,
And at the mercy of the rabble lay. (400–403, 406)

Dryden points out that orthodoxy and heterodoxy are both merely interpretations of the same text, which each regards as its own orthodoxy.[54] The text of scripture was open to all, but what of the rule by which it was to be interpreted? Protestants agreed on and respected a common authority, but they had no shared notion of meta-authority.

Dryden invites us to imagine an orthodox Protestant, convinced that the Bible clearly teaches the divinity of Christ, yet disturbingly confronted with another Protestant who interprets those same passages purely in terms of Christ's humanity—the Socinian heresy, a subtle reworking of Arianism.

We hold, and say we prove from Scripture plain,
That Christ is *God;* the bold Socinian
From the same Scripture urges he's but *man.*
Now what appeal can end th' important suit;
Both parts talk loudly, but the Rule is mute? (311–15)

Scripture did not disclose, clearly and unambiguously, the rule by which it was to be interpreted. And as there was no authority higher than scripture, how could Protestantism discriminate between orthodoxy and heresy? It was a dangerous vulnerability, and many believe that it remains at best incompletely resolved.

This naturally raises a question that merits further exploration. What place is there within Protestantism for "authority" figures who claim to offer definitive, orthodox, or reliable interpretations of the Bible when many feel overwhelmed by "option overload"? We consider this question in what follows.

THE GUARDIANS: AUTHORITY WITHIN PROTESTANTISM

One of the most important findings of modern social psychology concerns the mechanisms by which ideas and values are absorbed and assimilated so that they appear "natural," despite actually being nothing of the sort. It is widely conceded that the plausibility, legitimacy, and coherence of belief systems are *created* through social and cultural means.[55] For religious believers of any persuasion, their faith engenders a sense of what is "natural" or "real" that structures their engagement with and understanding of the world. Yet the transmission and validation of religious ideas depend on a complex process of socialization in which certain institutions, authorities, and networks of relationships shape the way in which people think about and engage the world. It is impossible to understand any religious movement, including Protestantism, without exploring at least some aspects of this socialization and the mechanisms it involves.

Any movement—whether religious, political, or cultural—has both its "standard bearers" and its "scouts." The standard bearers are those who see themselves as charged with the responsibility of maintaining traditional values and ideas; the scouts are those who are anxious to explore new frontiers and develop new ideas. Both are necessary, in that no movement can retain its core identity by freezing its ideas and values; there is a need for dynamic review in which the creative work of discernment of earlier ages is continued in the future. Paradoxical though it may at first sight appear, to stay the same, a movement must change. So what are the dynamics of this process within Protestantism? Above all, who are the "guardians" of its ideas and values?

We have already noted the fundamentally democratic nature of Protestant theology: it is an enterprise that may be undertaken by any person, on the basis of a publicly available resource—the Bible. There is no question of any one interpretation being "privileged" or of any secret additional sources of divine knowledge that are accessible only to the initiated and upon which salvation ultimately depends. Nor is there any idea of a spiritual elite: no group of believers has the right to impose its views, whether on account of academic qualifications (the German Lutheran writer Martin Kähler described this as "a papacy of the professors") or institutional seniority. Protestantism is adamant that the officeholders of the church are accountable to the church's members for the interpretations of the Bible they offer in their preaching and teaching and that they may be challenged and corrected on its basis.

This approach is subversive of the authority of individual preachers and theologians, no matter how venerable, in that it insists that their views must be judged in the light of the Bible. Protestantism ultimately grounds itself in the Bible alone, not in any specific interpretation of the Bible. Perhaps anxious that some might come to regard Martin Luther as an infallible guide to Christian doctrine, Lutherans drafted the "Formula of Concord" (1577), which insists that no interpretation of scripture can be defined as normative. "Other writings, whether of the fathers or more recent theologians, no matter what their names may be, cannot be regarded as possessing equal status to Holy Scripture. All must be considered to be subordinate to it, and to witness to the way in which the teaching of the prophets and apostles was preserved in post-apostolic times and in different parts of the world."[56]

So how can any Protestant claim to speak with "authority" when Protestantism subverts that claim by insisting that all Christians are priests and that no case can be made for the present existence or future emergence of any kind of "spiritual elite" who are placed above others? The Protestant understanding of the place of the Bible in the Christian life is utterly and irreconcilably opposed to placing any human figure, agency, or institution above it. This would seem to lead to the conclusion that Protestantism is a democratic faith: because the views of every believer are of equal value, it is impossible for authority figures to emerge.

The logic may be sound, but the reality is somewhat different. In practice, authority figures play an important role in Protestantism. The denominations in which the "priesthood of all believers" is most vigorously upheld as a matter of principle, such as the "Open Brethren," tend to lie outside the mainstream of Protestantism. The Open Brethren movement does not recognize an ordained ministry, although the New Testament offices of elder and deacon are retained. "Gifted brothers" and "gifted sisters" play an important role in the leadership of these communities, but these persons are not understood to be ordained. Yet even in such a denomination, certain figures emerge and come to be regarded as authoritative by others.[57]

In the next section, we first of all consider who these authority figures are, and second, how they emerge.

INSTRUMENTS OF AUTHORITY:
CREEDS AND CONFESSIONS

Protestantism regards itself as Christian and thus accepts the two great creeds of the Christian church—the Apostles' Creed, which dates from the eighth century in its final form, and the fourth-century Nicene Creed. These creeds, which are both minimalist, set out fundamental landmarks for Christian belief—such as the "two natures" of Jesus Christ—while merely affirming other areas of faith or leaving them altogether undefined. For example, the creeds set out no doctrine of the church or sacraments.

While regarding such creeds as fundamental, each Protestant grouping has its own statement of belief—often referred to as a "confession of faith"—that supplements the brief statements of the creeds and sets out a precise statement of that group. Such confessions, many of which were drawn up in the sixteenth and seventeenth centuries, often include both affirmative and negative elements: they set out the beliefs of the group while criticizing those of other groups that the group regards as unacceptable. The Thirty-nine Articles of Faith, set out by the Church of England in 1572, spells out the distinctive beliefs of Anglicanism while criticizing Catholics and Anabaptists on a number of points.

So what is the status of these confessions? Protestantism regards the Bible as being of supreme authority and understands the creeds to be reliable, communal statements of faith that are subordinate to the Bible. The creeds set out the beliefs of Christianity; confessions set out the distinctive beliefs of a specific form of Protestant Christianity. In terms of a hierarchy of authority, the situation can therefore be represented as follows: Bible → creeds → confessions.

The confessions are regarded as defining the shape of the form of Protestantism that created them. They serve as important historical benchmarks and theological points of reference for determining whether a given belief is typical of, or acceptable to, that form of Protestantism. Whereas all Protestants regard the Bible and creeds as authoritative, they do not extend such recognition to the confessions of other Protestants. Thus, Lutherans do not regard the Anglican Thirty-nine Articles, nor Anglicans the Lutheran Augsburg Confession, as having any particular authority within their own community.

Whereas Lutherans regard only one confessional document—the Augsburg Confession (1530)—as having particular significance, most other denominations, such as the Baptists and Methodists, define themselves with reference to a multiplicity of confessions. The Reformed churches have produced more confessions of faith than most churches. Each region that adopted a form of Calvinism expressed its fundamental themes in ways adapted to its own situation, often with subtle theological variations. Some were written by single authors, others by committees.[58] The most important such regional Reformed confessions are the following:

Confession	Date	Region
Gallic	1559	France
Scottish	1560	Scotland
Belgic	1561	the Lowlands
Second Helvetic	1562	Switzerland
Westminster	1646	England

Although several of these confessions had their origins in regional Reformed churches, they were so well regarded that they began to be used elsewhere. The Second Helvetic Confession, for example, was widely used in many parts of Germany. The Westminster Confession of Faith, drawn up by the assembly of Puritan divines during the period of the Commonwealth, found wide acceptance in Presbyterian circles in North America and throughout the English-speaking Protestant world.

As Karl Barth rightly observes, these confessions were provisional, spontaneous, and practical documents that came into being as a direct response to a challenge of the moment.[59] They were the product of local Christian communities that took the view that confessions of faith were far from having absolute authority and were subject to review and revision by succeeding generations. For Pierre Maury, confessions "are given by the Holy Spirit out of the pressure of a living, historical situation" that raises certain questions that demand answers. In 1966 the World Alliance of Reformed Churches declared that it "could not treat as absolute any of the structures and confessions which we inherit," but that it must be prepared to "go wherever the Spirit leads, even if it be through that death that leads to new life."

As the original confessions recede into the past, some Protestant denominations have found themselves debating their continuing role in a significantly changed social and cultural environment. The Church of England, for example, has seen sustained internal debate since about 1850 over whether the Thirty-nine Articles should continue to have a significant role in determining and communicating Anglican identity.[60]

PERSONS OF INFLUENCE:
THEOLOGIANS AND PREACHERS

Protestantism has been shaped to no small extent by individuals who rose to prominence and influence and became accepted and recognized as leading interpreters of its traditions. In the formative phase of Protestantism, theologians such as Martin Luther, Huldrych Zwingli, Philip Melanchthon, John Calvin, Theodore Beza, Thomas Cranmer, Balthasar Hübmaier, and Menno Simons played leading roles in shaping and articulating the ideas of the emergent Protestant groupings. The rise of new forms of Protestantism in the seventeenth and early eighteenth centuries brought Puritan writers such as John Owen, Richard Baxter, and Jonathan Edwards to prominence, alongside Pietist thinkers such as John Wesley.

Since the eighteenth century, the increasing professionalization of academic theology has opened up a widening gulf between academic theology, as taught in a university context, and a theology oriented toward the mission and ministry of the church. More recent Protestant theologians to have exercised significant influence within Protestantism as a whole have included F. D. E. Schleiermacher, Karl Barth, Emil Brunner, Wolfhart Pannenberg, and Jürgen Moltmann.

Yet it is important to appreciate that Protestants are stimulated and guided in their reflections about faith by writers who are not traditional theologians. The centrality of the Bible for Protestants has given particular prominence to the biblical commentator. One of the most widely revered commentators in recent Protestant history was William Barclay (1907–78), whose commentaries were hugely popular and influential in both conservative and liberal Protestant circles. Barclay was professor of New Testament at the University of Glasgow and a minister of the Church of Scotland. Although his academic credentials were impeccable, his reputation rested on his ability to communicate and explain—qualities that endeared him to millions of readers.[61] The seventeen volumes of his "Daily Study Bible" became an authoritative guide to the New Testament for many.

Yet Protestantism's most influential authority figures have been the preachers. For Protestantism, the sermon is a means for opening up the biblical text and exploring its rich intellectual landscape in order to make connections with issues of spirituality and ethics. As a result, preachers have played a critically important role in shaping Protestantism's sense of identity and advancing its theological, social, ethical, and political agendas. An excellent example is provided by the great Victorian Baptist preacher Charles Haddon Spurgeon, who established himself as the foremost pulpit orator of his age.

At the age of twenty, Spurgeon became pastor of New Park Street Church, one of London's most important Baptist churches. As his reputation as a preacher grew, the expanding congregation was forced to move to increasingly larger premises, before moving permanently to the newly constructed Metropolitan Tabernacle in 1861. Widely distributed in pamphlets and books, Spurgeon's sermons were of huge importance in shaping Baptist identity in the nineteenth century. Though many of his admirers, especially in North America, were puzzled by his love of cigars, Spurgeon's reputation and influence remained enormous for a generation after his death, consolidated to no small extent by the founding of Spurgeon's College, London, designed to mold future preachers after his likeness.

How did these persons come to have such influence over Protestantism? How did they rise to such positions of prominence? These individuals were not imposed upon Protestantism; nobody had to go to hear Spurgeon preach, or read the commentaries of William Barclay. They developed their influence partly through being excellent communicators, but more fundamentally through being trusted and respected by their audiences, who recommended them to their friends by word of mouth.

Protestantism's fundamentally democratic nature was easily translated into an essentially consumerist approach to matters of theology, spiritual direction, and pastoral care: individual Protestants followed the teachings of those whom they believed were worthy of trust and respect. The figures in question—Spurgeon, Barclay, and countless others too numerous to list—often had surprisingly little authority within their own denominations. Their influence, however, was all the more powerful because it was seen as *personal*, not *institutional*. Personal authority carried with it the capacity to transcend denominational and sectarian boundaries. Spurgeon was read and admired by many who were not Baptists, just as Barclay was loved and respected by many who were not Presbyterians.

The best theoretical model to account for this development—which remains fundamental to Protestantism—is Antonio Gramsci's idea of the "organic intellectual."[62] Although a Marxist, Gramsci found the Protestant idea of the "priesthood of all believers" to be a powerful conceptual foundation for mobilizing political activism. Gramsci drew a sharp distinction between an "organic intellectual" and a "traditional intellectual," the latter generally being someone who is imposed upon people by an external authority and is seen to be linked with the preservation of the interests of that authority—for example, bishops in the Catholic church. In marked contrast, the "organic intellectual" is one whose authority emerges from within the community as a consequence of the growing respect and trust in which he or she is held. The community comes to accept this individual as its representative and spokesperson. The organic intellectual is not imposed upon the community; rather, having discerned that person's merits, people choose to submit to his or her authority. This point is of fundamental importance in understanding the emergence of some highly influential personal ministries that have reshaped Protestantism during the twentieth century.

It would be impossible, and not a little irresponsible, to discuss the Protestant approach to authority without noting the considerable dangers that it creates. In his essay "The Sociology of Charismatic Authority," Max Weber noted that when traditional power structures seem to be in decline or confusion, people are disposed to seek out authority elsewhere.[63] When society seems confused about its moral values, or traditional academic institutions seem muddled over questions of truth, people look for—and find—those who speak with a clear voice and offer crisp, neat, and authoritative solutions. Protestant preaching of the form we have noted in this section owes some of its power to the force of its conviction—that is, perhaps it is not so much the *views* held by the preacher, or the *doctrines* preached, but the *conviction and authority* with which they are held and preached. This sort of preaching is clearly open to abuse, running the risk of becoming manipulative and exploitative.[64]

The dangers of such a Protestant personality cult were explored by Sinclair Lewis in his famous novel *Elmer Gantry*.[65] The central figure of the novel is an evangelical preacher whose highly profiled public posture of self-righteousness and virtue masks an inner life of deception and fraud. Lewis's novel spawned the popular image of TV evangelists that has become a cultural cliché of our time. Protestantism as a whole is vulnerable at this point, needing to ensure accountability on the part of its authority figures so that such influence is always exercised responsibly and carefully.

Yet Protestantism already possesses the resources it needs to deal with this difficulty, which is bound to arise from time to time given Protestantism's loose and fluid authority structures. The problems really start to arise when such "guardians" see themselves as the masters, rather than the servants, of the people of God and come to regard themselves as divinely appointed judges in matters of doctrine and morality. The doctrine of the "priesthood of all believers" reaffirms the central place of the community of believers, extended over time and space, who are guided by both scripture and the Holy Spirit and serve as a theological jury to whom all judges are ultimately subordinate.

This theme is found in the writings of most major Protestant writers but was set out with particular clarity in a lecture given in Paris on April 14, 1934, by the great Swiss Protestant theologian Karl Barth. Barth stressed the importance of theology in safeguarding the vision and identity of the church. Positive, yet critical, theology serves the church and keeps it faithful to its calling. And who is authorized to "do" theology? Barth had no hesitation in reaffirming the great Protestant theme of the democratization of faith:

> Theology is not a private subject for theologians only. Nor is it a private subject for professors. Fortunately, there have always been pastors who have understood more about theology than most professors. Nor is theology a private subject of study for pastors.

Fortunately, there have repeatedly been congregation members, and often whole congregations, who have pursued theology energetically while their pastors were theological infants or barbarians. Theology is a matter for the Church.[66]

NETWORKS: THE POWER OF ALIGNMENT AND ASSOCIATION

One of the most important tools for shaping Protestant identity emerged in England and America during the late eighteenth and early nineteenth centuries—the voluntary society. We have already noted its significance in developing a mission agenda. This same mechanism came to be of major importance in shaping Protestant identity. A group of like-minded individuals would come together to promote a shared concern or interest—for example, to encourage the spread of the gospel in Oceania, to promote the King James Bible at a time when other translations were gaining the upper hand, or to ensure that the ideas of premillennialism were more widely understood. These often became pressure groups that lobbied churches and seminaries in order to persuade them to change their policies on certain issues. They gathered support from like-minded individuals and, as a result, were able to exercise greater influence.

The pattern is familiar from many areas of life, particularly the political sphere. Yet the voluntary society has played a particularly significant role in the shaping of Protestantism in that this form of Christianity has been particularly supportive of entrepreneurialism. An excellent example is provided by the Dallas Theological Seminary, which was founded in 1924 as the Evangelical Theological College by the Presbyterian Bible teacher Lewis Chafer (1871–1952). Chafer's objective was to establish an institution that would promote dispensationalism—a specific way of interpreting the Bible—thus ensuring a supply of pastors who would preach this approach.

There can be no doubting the success of that vision, given the subsequent growth of the Dallas Theological Seminary and the impact of its alumni. The important point to appreciate is that the same fundamental pattern can be seen throughout Protestant history since about 1800. There has been a surge of organizations, networks, seminaries, and other institutions dedicated to advancing a particular emphasis or doctrine within Protestantism. At times, critical observers have expressed concerns about these developments, suggesting that they are about naked political power. Yet it is an important reality of Protestant life that needs to be understood—without necessarily being endorsed—if the development of the movement is to be understood.

In this chapter, we have explored how Protestantism has understood its relationship with the Bible and how this affects its life and thought. Yet we have only begun to explore the many questions raised by this symbiotic relationship of people and book, faith and text. In the next chapter, we explore the impact of the Protestant emphasis on the Bible on its worship and preaching.

Memling Museum, Sint-Janshospital, Bruges, Belgium; Photo: Scala/Art Resource, NY

St. John the Evangelist on the island of Patmos,
by Hans Memling (1435/40–94).

10

Believing and Belonging

Some Distinctive Protestant Beliefs

What do Protestants believe? And how do those belief commitments show themselves in the values and actions of Protestant communities? How do Protestant ideas manifest themselves? The historical narrative already presented has highlighted at least some of the main themes of Protestant belief, while hinting at an endemic diversity that is essential to the movement's origins and development. This chapter explores some of the beliefs that have been characteristic of Protestantism throughout its history and briefly describes some of the more distinctive ideas and emphases of the various groups within the movement.[1]

Yet it is not enough simply to describe these ideas. A deeper question must be addressed: What *difference* do they make? What role have they played in shaping Protestantism, in aiding or hindering its advance, and in determining its characteristic concerns? Ideas shape actions and attitudes. In this chapter, we examine the ways in which specific Protestant ideas have influenced the development of the movement.

One of those beliefs has already been considered in great detail in the previous chapter—the fundamental, identity-giving Protestant emphasis on the supremacy of the Bible, traditionally stated using the Latin slogan *sola Scriptura*. While this "scripture principle" is not intended to exclude other theological resources, it makes absolutely clear that scripture is the ultimate foundation and the final court of appeal for Protestant belief and action. Other resources may be useful and helpful; they do not, however, possess the same weight as scripture. The Westminster Confession of Faith summarizes this position well:

> The whole counsel of God, concerning all things necessary for his own glory, man's salvation, faith and life, is either expressly set down in Scripture, or by good and necessary consequence may be deduced from Scripture; to which nothing at any time is to be added, whether by new revelations of the Spirit, or traditions of men. (I, 6)

It is important to appreciate from the outset that the Protestant strategy of prioritizing an engagement with the Bible has led to a multiplicity of belief outcomes. In one sense, "Protestantism" designates a way of doing theology rather than any given set of possible or specific outcomes. The question of which is the "right" interpretation of the Bible raises a series of fundamental issues about who has the authority to make such a judgment—about who owns Protestantism. There is no equivalent within Protestantism of the pope, the Vatican, or the "Congregation of the Faith"—to mention the centralized authorities within Catholicism—even though individual denominations, organizations, societies, and networks recognize certain "authority figures" within their own ranks. It is clearly inappropriate to try to homogenize this complex picture or impose a doctrinal uniformity upon the components of global Protantism when this clearly does intellectual violence to them.[2]

In general terms, Protestantism reaffirmed the core beliefs of Christian orthodoxy as these were set out by the Council of Chalcedon (451), particularly the "two natures" of Jesus Christ and the doctrine of the Trinity. Although the Reformation of the sixteenth century subjected the entire gamut of Christian belief to critical reexamination in the light of biblical foundations, these two core areas were found not to require reformation by the mainline reformers.

Nevertheless, some radical reformers, regarding these beliefs as being inadequately grounded in the Bible, spawned movements, however small—such as evangelical anti-trinitarianism—at this early stage. A reaffirmation of the core dogmatic beliefs of the early church may be characteristic of Protestantism, but it has never been univocal. A significant minority—and they cannot be dismissed as a "lunatic fringe"—have had other views. The radical wing of the Reformation argued, not without reason, that mainline reformers such as Luther, Zwingli, and Calvin had been inconsistent and failed to apply their biblicist reforming agenda to all areas of the church's life and thought. If the use of the term "radical" implies that there were obvious limits to the application of the *sola Scriptura* principle overlooked by those in this camp, it must be noted that they merely advocated consistent usage of the principle. The category of "radical Protestant" is thus more than a little problematic, its legitimacy depending on whose perspective is taken.

It is, of course, possible to argue that the anti-trinitarian movements of the sixteenth century were not Protestant. Such an argument, however, introduces a prescriptive component into any account of the movement, by which the agendas of power groups intrude into a serious historical investigation of what, as a matter of fact, Protestants actually believed.

The present chapter is deliberately subtitled "Some Distinctive Protestant Beliefs" to make the point that, while Protestants share certain core beliefs with other styles of Christianity, there are points at which they diverge. C. S. Lewis offered an image that may be helpful at this point. In his influential *Mere Christianity*, Lewis suggests that we think of a great house in which a large hall has a number of rooms leading off to its sides. The hall is the Christian faith, and the rooms are its different constituent elements—Catholicism, Orthodoxy, and so forth.

In one sense, Protestantism belongs to Lewis's broad category of "mere Christianity" in that it shares the core beliefs of Christianity as a whole—such as belief in God, the hope of heaven, and so on. Our concern in this chapter is to explore the rooms leading off from this hall that contain beliefs specific to Protestantism, or versions of more general Christian beliefs that are held in a specific form within Protestantism. To understand Protestantism, it is important to understand at least some of these beliefs. This chapter identifies and explores some—but not all—of these beliefs as a means of grasping what Protestantism is all about.

In the previous chapter, we noted that diversity has arisen within Protestantism as a result of differing approaches to biblical interpretation, or because of multiple outcomes of essentially the same approach. The agreement of all Protestant groups on the priority of the Bible does not—and indeed could not—lead to a homogeneity of interpretations. The importance of this becomes clear at many points throughout this chapter.

JUSTIFICATION BY FAITH ALONE

One of the most distinguishing features of Western Christianity is its insistence that the basis of salvation is not any form of human privilege, merit, or achievement, but the graciousness of God. The idea is found throughout the New Testament, particularly in the letters of Paul: "By grace you have been saved through faith, and this is not your own doing; it is the gift of God—not the result of works" (Ephesians 2:8–9).

The implications of these ideas were explored and clarified during the Pelagian controversy, which pitted Augustine of Hippo against the Rome-based British theologian Pelagius. Where Pelagius argued that humanity is required to do certain things and behave in certain ways to secure God's favor, Augustine argued that such actions and behavior are the result, not the cause, of being accepted by God. Divine acceptance is an act of total grace that leads to the moral and spiritual transformation of the sinner.[3]

Although little interest in these matters was shown by the early Swiss Reformation, which was primarily concerned with the renewal and reform of the life and morality of both the church and individual Christians, these issues lay at the heart of the emerging evangelical reformation at Wittenberg. Throughout the late 1510s, Luther and his colleagues Andreas Karlstadt and Nikolaus von Amsdorf sought to renew Augustine's reforming agenda in the face of what they believed to be a fresh outbreak of Pelagianism in the contemporary church. Although historians have noted the unacceptable generalization in their thinking—Luther and his colleagues were extrapolating, with no justification, from a local situation to the entire church—there is little doubt that they had some valid grounds for concern.

What gave the Lutheran Reformation its distinctive character was its decision to change the terminology in which the question of human salvation was conceived. Up to this point, the Christian tradition had focused on the Pauline notion of "salvation by grace" (Ephesians 2:8) and used this vocabulary in its discussion of how humanity is reconciled to God. Luther and his colleagues now used a different Pauline category to express substantially the same notion: "justification by faith" (Romans 5:1). The reasons for this shift in vocabulary are not fully understood.

This change in terms defined the contours of Protestantism. From now on, Protestant writers would discuss how the individual secures salvation using the specific terminology of "justification by faith" and would tend to regard any other form of words as unacceptable. Initially, their Catholic opponents followed suit: the Council of Trent chose to address its opponents using their own terminology. However, by the middle of the following century Catholicism had reverted to the traditional means of discussing the question in terms of salvation by grace. The prioritization of the idea of justification by faith was now a Protestant distinctive.

As we noted earlier, the doctrine of justification by faith was central to Luther's reforming agenda.[4] This concern was often summed up in the Latin slogan *sola fide*, "by faith alone." It is important to appreciate that this concept is notionally independent of the early Reformation emphasis on the supreme importance of the Bible. The Reformation in eastern Switzerland, though rigorously focused on the Bible, did not develop any such doctrine of justification *sola fide*.

Luther was adamant that the doctrine of justification by faith was fundamental to the recovery of Christian identity and integrity at the time of the Reformation.[5] If humanity became righteous in the sight of God because of its good actions, the whole gospel of grace was compromised. Salvation was a gift, not something that was earned through achievements or merit. Arguing that contemporary Catholicism taught "justification by works," Luther insisted that Paul's doctrine of "justification by faith" was definitive for Christianity. And to make sure that there were no misunderstandings about this, he added the word "alone," lest anyone see faith as one among a number of causes of justification—including works.

This addition caused a furor. Catholics pointed out that the New Testament nowhere taught "justification by faith alone"; indeed, the

Letter of James explicitly condemned this idea. Luther responded by making the point that his slogan encapsulated neatly the substance of the New Testament, even if it did not use precisely its original words. And as for the Letter of James, was it not "an epistle of straw" that ought not to be there in the New Testament anyway? This second argument caused considerable unease within Protestant circles and was not maintained by Luther's successors.

Luther's doctrine of justification won wide—but not universal—acceptance within early Protestantism. Zwingli and other eastern Swiss reformers of the late 1510s clearly entertained a vision of reformation that did not entail this idea and may even have been contradicted by it. Many Swiss and Rhineland reformers of the 1520s were nervous about the idea, believing that it suggested that Christians were relieved of any obligation to do good works. Bucer, perhaps showing his ethical sympathies with Erasmus of Rotterdam, set out a doctrine of double justification, which ensured a robust link between God's act of gracious acceptation and the human response of grateful moral action.[6] Some Anabaptist writers also distanced themselves from it, again expressing anxieties about its biblical foundations and moral implications.

Luther responded by calming such fears—particularly in his "Sermon on Good Works"—arguing that all he was saying was that good works are the natural result of having been justified, not the cause of that justification. Far from destroying morality, Luther simply saw himself as setting it in its proper context. Believers perform good works as an act of thankfulness to God for having forgiven them, rather than in an attempt to persuade or entice God to forgive them in the first place.

These ideas were consolidated by Luther's colleague Philip Melanchthon, who drew a distinction between justification (the act in which God accepts a sinner as righteous) and sanctification (the process in which God transforms and renews the sinner). Developing the idea of "forensic justification," Melanchthon argued that God imputes Christ's righteousness, won by his obedience on the cross, to individual sinners, so that they are vindicated or acquitted of sin in the heavenly courtroom. There is thus no need for any notion of "purgatory," because the believer is now clothed with the perfect righteousness of Christ.

At one level, the Reformation can be seen as a replay of some of the leading themes of the Pelagian controversy between Augustine of

Hippo and Pelagius. Although the debate was wide-ranging, one of its central themes was the human capacity to do good without the assistance of God's grace. Pelagius held that humanity can fulfill the divine law unaided; God created humanity with the capacity for perfection, and they are thus under obligation to achieve it. Augustine argued that God's grace is essential at every stage in the Christian life. Humanity is fallen, damaged and wounded by sin, and needs healing and restoration—something they cannot achieve themselves. God's gracious assistance can be discerned in operation from the beginnings of faith to its fulfillment.

Following Luther and Calvin, mainline Protestantism sided with Augustine in this dispute, regarding him as a generally trustworthy interpreter of the Bible and defender of divine grace. Melanchthon saw the Reformation as recycling this older controversy, with Protestantism playing Augustine's role and Catholicism Pelagius's—a suggestion that was not well received by Catholics, who emphasized their shared opposition to Pelagianism.

It is important, however, to note the dissident voices within Protestantism on this matter. Zwingli and other Swiss reformers of the late 1510s, followed by some Anabaptist leaders of the 1520s and 1530s, saw their reforming work primarily in terms of the renewal of morals and set out reforming agendas that were closer to Pelagius's ideals than many realize.[7] Later, John Wesley suggested that Pelagius's idea of "Christian perfection" was laudable and ought to be pursued by Christians.

The Council of Trent responded by criticizing the emerging Protestant consensus on justification at a number of levels. First, Trent insisted that the notion of justification by "faith alone" was unacceptable in that it failed to do justice to the New Testament emphasis on the place of love in the Christian life. More significantly, Trent argued that justification is a complex process, enfolding both acceptance and subsequent transformation by God. In other words, Trent insisted that the word "justification" denoted what Melanchthon understood by both "justification" and "sanctification," rolled into a single concept. This argument was a recipe for confusion, and it almost certainly underlies the popular nineteenth-century Protestant misunderstanding that Catholicism taught "justification by works."

The Protestant doctrine of justification had implications for the traditional Catholic cult of the saints. The saints were believed to work wonders, and their relics were highly prized. Most importantly, they were understood to play a role in ensuring the salvation of individuals through their righteous and effective prayer.[8] The doctrine of justification rendered the cult of the saints redundant. They would add nothing to what Christ had done; there was nothing they could achieve that had not already been secured through Christ's saving death.

That having been said, a growing body of evidence points to early Protestant leaders being treated as if they were traditional saints during the first phase of the movement.[9] Both Melanchthon and Luther became the object of stories of miraculous events—such as the village whose well dried up after Luther's censure of its citizens for supporting Karlstadt. Luther's birthplace in Eisleben began to attract pilgrims and was rumored to have miraculously survived destruction by fire several times. These ideas seem to have persisted into the seventeenth century—perhaps confirming the views of those who suggest that humanity is intrinsically religious.

Since the Second World War, there has been growing hesitation within many sections of Protestantism concerning its traditional way of speaking about salvation.[10] While some have insisted that Protestants are bound by their tradition to speak and think in this manner, others have expressed anxieties over its continued use, especially in the light of a growing consensus among New Testament scholars that the notion of "justification by faith" is not as central to the thought of the New Testament, or even Paul himself, as Luther and others appear to have believed.[11] Many follow Albert Schweitzer, who suggested that the idea of justification was only a "subsidiary crater" in Paul's thought, rather than constituting its core and center. Why, many Protestant scholars have asked, should the movement be obliged to replicate Luther's interpretation of Paul when it appears questionable at points? Are not Protestants meant to constantly reexamine their ideas in the light of the biblical material rather than accept interpretations inherited from the past, however venerable or influential? Others have expressed concern that the phrase "justification by faith" is virtually unintelligible to modern secular humanity, and they suggest that other biblical concepts might be redeployed to remedy the situation.[12] It remains to be seen where this debate will lead in the future.

So why did this doctrine play such an important role in the first phase of Protestantism? After all, the basic ideas underlying the doctrine were known in earlier periods of the history of Christian thought. The answer to this question is complex and nuanced and relates particularly to the emergence of the idea of the "individual." Although the origins of a sense of individual, personal identity, one that could be affirmed over and against one's place as a member of society at large, can be traced back to the early Middle Ages, there is no doubt that Renaissance humanism gave this notion a new sense of importance, as well as an injection of intellectual energy.[13]

The doctrine of justification made a powerful appeal to this emerging sense of individual identity. One's relationship to God was a *personal* matter, involving the creator and the creature. Justification was an act of personal graciousness and acceptation of the sinner by a God who promised to forgive sins and renew human nature. Each individual believer mattered profoundly to God and could not be reduced to an ecclesiastical statistic. Luther's doctrine of justification by faith was widely understood to mean that the individual relates directly to God, without having to involve the institution of the church or its priests or rites. The doctrine resonated profoundly with the notion of a privatized, personal faith. This is not what Luther intended; it was, however, how he was understood by his appreciative readers throughout Europe during the 1520s.

This individualist understanding of the doctrine of justification became so influential that second-generation Protestants felt the need to restore the balance and remind their followers of the corporate dimensions of faith. Christianity was not just about the individual's personal relationship with God; it had implications for an individual's existence in the community. Calvin's comments on the role of the church can be seen as an important corrective to a radically individualist reading of Luther. God uses certain definite earthly means to work out the salvation of his elect; although he is not absolutely bound by these means, he normally works within them. The church is thus identified as a divinely founded body within which God effects the sanctification of his people. "You cannot," Calvin argued, "have God as your father unless you have the church for your mother."

This naturally leads us to consider Protestant reflections on the nature of the church itself and its importance for the development of Protestantism.

THE CHURCH AS THE BEARER OF THE WORD

One of the most significant and distinctive Protestant beliefs concerns the nature of the church. As we saw earlier, the medieval church in western Europe offered a strongly institutionalized account of how salvation was effected. There was no salvation outside the institution of the church; it was by membership in the sacral community and observation of its rites that the individual secured salvation. Continuity with the apostles was safeguarded by historical institutional continuity, which was transmitted by the laying on of hands and passed down from one generation of the successors of the apostles to the next. This strongly institutionalized vision of the church was often defended by citing a maxim of the third-century martyr Cyprian of Carthage: "Outside the church, there is no salvation." Anyone who wanted to be saved had to belong to the Catholic church.

The detachment of the fledgling Protestant churches from this body was thus fraught with theological peril. Were these breakaway communities *really* Christian churches? Could they offer the same salvation and spiritual security as the Catholic church? These were no academic questions, but matters of ultimate significance. Salvation was a serious matter in the sixteenth century.

The Protestant response to these entirely proper questions was to offer a new vision of what it meant to be a "Christian church." As we shall see, the new theory removed any necessity for institutional continuity with the medieval church. It opened the way for the radical proliferation of "churches" in the modern period by laying the conceptual foundations for a way of thinking about the nature of the church that encouraged entrepreneurs to set up their own churches, breaking away from older communities if necessary. To understand Protestant theorizing about the church is to gain insights into the remarkable ecclesiastical diversification and fragmentation that subsequently took place throughout the West.

For the mainline reformers, there were two—and only two—essential elements of a Christian church: the preaching of the word of God and the proper administration of the sacraments. As Calvin put it:

> Wherever we see the Word of God purely preached and listened to, and the sacraments administered according to Christ's institution, it is in no way to be doubted that a church of God exists. For his promise cannot fail: "Wherever two or three are gathered in my name, there I am in the midst of them" (Matthew 18:20).[14]

Calvin's definition is significant as much for what it does *not* say as for what it does explicitly affirm. There is no reference to the necessity of any historical or institutional continuity with the apostles. For Calvin, it was more important to teach what the apostles taught than to be able to show an unbroken line of institutional continuity with them. (It should be remembered here that Calvin himself was never ordained; he was simply licensed as a pastor by the city council of Geneva.) After all, does institutional continuity guarantee intellectual fidelity? For Calvin, the Catholic church had suffered from institutional drift and lost its grounding in the fundamental ideas of the apostles—which were, of course, expressed in the Bible.

This radical new understanding of the church in effect envisaged the church as a community that gathers around the preaching of the word of God and celebrates and proclaims the gospel through the sacraments. Where the gospel is truly preached, there a church will gather. Protestant theologians, sensitive to the charge that this new approach represented a distortion of a proper theology of the church, pointed to a classic statement of the first-century Christian writer Ignatius of Antioch: "Wherever Christ is, there is also the church (*ubi Christus ibi ecclesia*)." Gathering together in the name of Christ ensures his presence—and with that presence, a church comes into being.

Although this distinctive and characteristic Protestant doctrine of the church dates from the early 1500s, its full significance only became clear in the nineteenth and twentieth centuries. With no universally accepted authority structure within Protestantism, enterprising individuals, often fired up by a vision of a specific form of ministry, could start their own congregations, or even their own denominations. It is certainly true that many Protestant churches moved quickly to establish authority structures that embodied their specific visions of Protestantism, thus exercising control over their ministers and members. But the very nature of Protestantism is such that these can only hope to define specific *forms of* Protestantism, not Protestantism itself. Individuals might break away from parent churches or start new churches altogether.

Sometimes a movement's strength is also its weakness, and vice versa. This distinctive aspect of Protestant identity holds the key to understanding the proliferation of churches, the fragmentation of denominations, and the inflation of church networks that is so characteristic of modern Protestantism. Many would see this as a weakness. There might well be one universal church to which all Christians belong—but there are countless local churches, each embodying a distinctive idea of what it means to be a Christian.

The outcome of this doctrine was inevitable: a consumerist mentality developed as Protestants felt able to pick and choose the local church that suited their needs, beliefs, and aspirations. And if they didn't find one that was just right, they could establish their own. Catholic critics of Protestantism often point to its innate tendency toward schism, which they regard as showing a lack of concern for the fundamental unity of the church. While this congregational inflation is unquestionably problematic, it has two strengths, both of which are of decisive importance for the future of Protestantism.

First, it allows Protestantism to deal with rapid social and cultural change, which otherwise often leaves churches locked into the realities of a bygone age. Entrepreneurial pastors and preachers can easily recast a vision of the gospel, adapting it to the new situation—in much the same way as older visions were adapted to their situations—and thus preventing Protestantism from becoming trapped in a time warp. Willow Creek Community Church, located just outside of Chicago, is an excellent example of this kind of adaptation that was made possible and legitimate by the fluid Protestant understanding of the church. More particularly, this adaptability enables Protestants to respond to perceived needs for specialist ministries to specific groups through the formation of voluntary societies, which often come to exercise a para-church role.

Second, Protestant congregational variety enables Protestant churches to deal with situations in which the denominational leadership is seen to be radically out of touch with its membership—typically, by pursuing theological agendas or cultural trends that are not accepted by the majority of their congregations. It does not matter whether these agendas are right-wing or left-wing, conservative or liberal. Protestantism empowers the congregation, first, to protest against their leaders; second, to remove them; and third, to form another congregation elsewhere, *while still remaining a Christian church*. While some Protestant denominations attempt to shield themselves against such accountability to their membership, these fundamental rights remain, in principle, as part of the movement's core identity. One can leave one denomination and join another—while still remaining a Protestant.

It is not unfair to suggest that the Protestant vision of the church unleashes a Darwinian process of competition and survival in which maladapted churches are gradually eliminated and what survives is better suited to the needs and opportunities of the day. Using an essentially economic model, Laurence Iannaccone and Rodney Stark argue that the European state churches have created a religious monopoly, leading to a radical restriction of religious options for its people. In marked contrast, the United States offers an open market of religious options, with none either sanctioned or restricted by the state.[15] Commitment to organized religion is higher in countries such as the United States because religious pluralism encourages market responsiveness to the religious consumer. In Europe, they argue, the institutional churches have seen little purpose in identifying and meeting the needs of their parishioners.

If Iannaccone and Stark are right, Protestantism flourishes in the United States on account of open competition, which forces churches to take the needs and aspirations of their members seriously. In contrast, the privileged position of state churches in Europe has often led to the entrenchment of outdated approaches and attitudes, and above all a neglect of the religious consumer by leaders who are often wedded to the convenient certainties of the past. In America, competition encourages religious entrepreneurship and vitality. As Steve Bruce, professor of sociology at the University of Aberdeen, points out: "Free-market capitalism explains why Americans are rich; free-market religion explains why Americans are church-going."[16]

Yet Protestants found themselves in disagreement about the church in the sixteenth century, and they remain in disagreement today. One particularly significant disagreement that pitted mainline reformers against their radical counterparts concerned whether the church was a "mixed body" or a "pure body." This controversy was also a replay of an earlier controversy involving Augustine of Hippo. In the fourth century, the Donatist movement began to raise fundamental questions about the identity of the church.[17] Following a series of lapses on the part of Christian leaders in North Africa in response to Roman persecutions, questions began to be raised about the qualities required of Christian leaders and their congregations. The fourth-century Donatist movement—so named after Donatus, one of its early leaders—took a rigorist position, arguing that the church had every right to expect moral and doctrinal purity on the part of its members.[18] The church was to be conceived as a "pure body."

Augustine took the view that human frailty was such that the church could not achieve such a goal in practice. He cited one of Jesus of Nazareth's parables to make his point. A farmer woke up one morning to find weeds growing in his field of wheat. Being unwilling to pull out the weeds, which would have damaged the wheat growing alongside them, he decided to wait until the harvest and then separate the wheat and the weeds (Matthew 13:24–30). For Augustine, that parable referred to the church: it was a "mixed body" of wheat and weeds, saints and sinners. Separation could wait until the final judgment.

The same controversy flared up during the early years of Protestantism. Luther and Calvin adopted Augustine's model of the church as a "mixed body." In his characteristically racy manner, Luther spiced up Augustine's imagery. Where Augustine spoke of "weeds among the wheat," Luther spoke of "mouse-droppings among the peppercorns." This intriguing image underlies an understanding of the church adapted to the realities of European politics of the sixteenth century, just as Augustine accounted for the Roman imperial situation of the late fourth century. The political realities of the western European situation in the sixteenth century called for state churches in some shape or form, especially as the phenomenon of confessionalization began to take root in the 1560s. A theory of the church that could not accommodate the requirement that a church engage positively yet critically with the state would have created serious difficulties for such a vision of Protestant Christendom.

Anabaptists and other radicals, however, held that this doctrine of the church represented a compromise with power and a loss of the defining vision of the gospel. Many Anabaptists saw the conversion of Constantine, who went on to become the first Christian Roman emperor, as a disaster. Christianity was disfigured and damaged by its collusion with power and status. When it became the official religion of the Roman Empire, it lost its cutting edge and moral underpinnings.

Adopting something very similar to a Donatist understanding of the church, many Anabaptists insisted that the church should have no dealings with the corruption of political life. The swearing of oaths, the use of coercive force, the taking of life, and the authority of the magistrate were all sinful, worldly intrusions into the Christian life. The church should be separate from such pollution, untainted by the compromises of the world. The pacifism that was characteristic of Swiss humanism in the 1510s and 1520s came to be an integral element of Anabaptist thought, grounded in the New Testament's witness to Jesus of Nazareth. The clearest statement of the general Anabaptist attitude toward secular authority may be found in the "Schleitheim Confession" (1527), which taught that coercion has its place "outside the perfection of Christ"; inside the community of faith, physical force has no place. Christians should therefore not hold public office, since doing so would involve collusion with power and violence.

The Anabaptist concern for the doctrinal and moral purity of the church led to a corresponding emphasis on the importance of discipline within the church. Anabaptism maintained discipline in its communities through "the ban"—a means by which church members could be excluded from Anabaptist congregations. This means of discipline was regarded as essential to the identity of a true church. Part of the Anabaptist case for radical separation from the mainstream churches (a practice that continues to this day among Amish communities in the

United States) was the perceived failure of those churches to maintain proper discipline within their ranks.

These concerns were developed during the seventeenth century within Puritanism, in both England and North America. Richard Baxter laid considerable emphasis upon the importance of doctrinal and moral purity within the church and had no hesitation about devising disciplinary procedures to ensure that such purity was maintained.[19]

Underlying both the Anabaptist and Puritan vision of Protestantism was an idea that would come of age in a later era—the notion of the church primarily as a "fellowship of believers." Turning their backs on traditional hierarchical models of the church, both movements moved toward more participative, democratic models of church government in which individual congregations had the right to determine their own identity and future. Not only did this trend anticipate—some argue that it was an important factor in causing—the emergence of democracy at the political level, as in the American Revolution, but it bypassed the traditionally conservative ecclesiastical hierarchies, which were often locked into older ways of thinking and acting.

In the twentieth century, this approach began to accelerate, initially within North American Protestantism. The "congregationalization" of American Protestantism after the Second World War allowed entrepreneurial church leaders to develop new models of the church that were unimpeded by the restraining hand of an episcopacy or denominational hierarchy. As we shall see later, this proved to be a decisive factor in the reshaping of Protestantism at this time.

THE SACRAMENTS

The great tumult of the early sixteenth century that gave birth to Protestantism was not simply about how ideas are developed or what those ideas might be. It concerned actions—the way in which the Christian faith was manifested through the worship of the church in a series of rites that were held to be of particular importance to affirming the identity of the Christian faith, the place of the church in the scheme of salvation, and the deepening of faith and commitment on the part of the individual Christian. These rites are traditionally known as "sacraments."[20]

The word "sacrament" needs an explanation. The word comes from the Latin term *sacramentum,* meaning "something that is consecrated." The word was regularly used in the church to refer to a series of rites or ordinances that were regarded as having special spiritual qualities, such as the ability to convey the grace of God. In secular Roman use, the term had come to mean "a sacred oath" sworn by soldiers and state officials. The word "sacrament" is not found in the Bible, although most Protestants were content to retain the term while reinterpreting it in ways they regarded as consistent with the Bible.

So what is a sacrament? That is precisely the question raised during the Reformation, which witnessed a major debate over how a sacrament was to be defined. During the Middle Ages, Catholicism set out a comprehensive view of the ministry of the church that recognized seven sacraments: the mass, baptism, confirmation, ordination, marriage, penance, and unction (anointing with oil). These played a significant role in how the church was experienced by ordinary people—in other words, in how the church manifested itself.

To reform the sacraments was thus to make obvious changes to the life of the church and community. For most laypersons, the main point of contact with the church was through church services on Sundays. The pulpit was one of the most important public platforms of the medieval period for this very reason—hence the desire of both reformers and city councils to control what was said from the pulpit. Yet the church's impact on the people transcended preaching; by far the most important experience for laypersons was the rite or sacrament universally known as "the mass."

By the end of the 1520s, two fundamental changes to existing understandings of sacraments had emerged within Protestantism and achieved widespread consensus throughout the movement.

1. The number of sacraments was reduced from seven to two—the mass (but now generally known by other names) and baptism.

2. Whereas Catholicism allowed the laity to receive only bread at the mass, Protestantism insisted that the entire people of God should be allowed to receive both bread and wine.

Martin Luther argued that a sacrament is essentially an outward and visible sign of an inward and invisible grace. The core component of a sacrament is a physical sign that points to a promise on God's part— such as forgiveness of sins, or the hope of eternal life. Yet while all sacraments might be signs, not all signs are sacraments. In his *Babylonian Captivity of the Church* (1520), Luther argued that a sign can only be regarded as a sacrament if there was an explicit command from Jesus of Nazareth that his followers undertake such an action. Applying this criterion, Luther declared that there were only two sacraments of the Christian gospel—the mass and baptism.

Luther's defense of the principle of "communion in both kinds"— that is, the laity being allowed to receive both bread and wine—is based on his theology of how signs work. The bread and the wine, he argued, are signs of God's grace and forgiveness. To deny the laity access to a sign is tantamount to denying them the greater reality to which the sign points. In addition to lacking biblical warrant, the practice of "communion in one kind" appeared to imply that the laity are excluded from at least some aspect of God's promises of grace and are thus to be regarded as second-class Christians. Since Luther's doctrine of the "priesthood of all believers" affirmed the equal spiritual dignity and value of all Christians, this medieval practice was to be rejected as unacceptable.

Yet while consensus was achieved on these two highly significant matters, Protestantism found itself unable to agree on a wide range of additional issues, some of which became so controversial that they occasionally caused, and regularly contributed to, divisions between denominations. Once more, the divisions primarily concerned the interpretation and application of the Bible to the social contexts in which Protestantism found itself.

First, Protestants were agreed that Christians should meet regularly to share bread and wine, as Jesus of Nazareth had commanded, but what was this practice to be called? Luther was prepared to retain the older term "mass" (the Latin term *missa* literally means "a service"), regarding it as unproblematic if properly explained. Most Protestants, however, held that the word "mass" carried baggage with it from medieval Catholicism and was best discontinued. The New Testament did not prescribe any specific terms for such gatherings, tending to use simple terms like "breaking bread," so there was no obvious alternative. A number of terms were explored, including the Lord's Supper, communion (or Holy Communion), eucharist (from the Greek verb *eucharistein*, "to give thanks"), and remembrance. A less significant disagreement emerged over the word "sacrament," which some found to be too heavily freighted with Catholic assumptions to be acceptable; the term "ordinance" was proposed as an alternative.

Second, a major debate erupted during the 1520s—and continues unresolved to this day—over how the bread and wine relate to the spiritual realities they represent. Luther held that the bread and the wine are the body and blood of Christ; Zwingli held that they are symbolic representations.[21] Other Protestant writers took intermediary positions—for example, Theodore Beza proposed the notion of an "efficacious sign." The serious dispute between Luther and Zwingli raised serious questions about the clarity of scripture: how could the Bible be "clear" when such totally different understandings were defended by leading Protestants on the basis of the same biblical texts?

Third, Protestants found themselves unable to agree on how often Christians should gather to break bread and drink wine. The New Testament gave no explicit ruling on the matter. The history of the early church strongly suggested that this gathering had rapidly become the main worship event of the church, taking place every Sunday. Luther retained this practice; Zwingli suggested that it was such a solemn event that it should be commemorated three or four times a year. Once more, Protestant writers have positioned themselves at various points on a spectrum of possibilities. The Church of England followed Zwingli's pattern until the nineteenth century, when the rise of the High Church "Oxford Movement" laid the foundations for reverting to the more ancient Christian practice of weekly celebration.

Other lesser debates concerning this sacrament may be noted in passing. Given that a sermon was invariably preached on these occasions, a debate arose over the relative importance of the sermon and the sacrament. Which took priority? Luther integrated the two superbly, speaking of the "ministry of the word" and the "ministry of the sacrament"; others, however, took different views. Another debate arose over concerns about whether the administration of wine to the laity might encourage alcohol addiction. Many Protestant groups thus stipulate that the "juice of the grape," not wine, should be administered at communion services. A further debate concerned whether there should be a common cup from which all would drink or whether the wine (or grape juice) should be administered in a separate vessel for each communicant. And should communion be open to all (a policy sometimes known as the "open table) or limited to those who had been properly instructed and admitted to full membership in their churches?

A further major debate developed within early Protestantism concerning the sacrament of baptism. Should infants be baptized? The historical evidence indicates that the church began baptizing the infants of Christian parents at a very early stage. The practice is not explicitly mentioned in the New Testament, although it is possible that references to the baptism of "households" (Acts 16:15, 33; 1 Corinthians 1:16) might include children. The mainline reformers regarded infant baptism as a thoroughly authentic Christian practice and commended and practiced it. They did so, however, for different reasons. Luther regarded infant baptism as the means by which God brought about faith in individuals. For Luther, baptism was the cause of faith. Zwingli, on the other hand, saw it as a sign of the covenant between God and the church. Anabaptism regarded the practice as completely without biblical warrant. At no point, they argued, did the New Testament instruct Christians to baptize infants. Baptism was to be restricted to believing adults who were capable of making a confession of faith.

These differences led to a clear divergence within Protestantism on this matter, with important implications for the life of the church. The Church of England, for example, baptizes infants by the sprinkling of water. Since the infant cannot make promises of faith, "godparents" are selected to ensure that the infant grows up within the Christian faith, until they are ready to confess that faith for themselves. At this point, they are admitted to full membership in the church through confirmation.

Baptists, following their Anabaptist forebears, reject infant baptism. James Robinson Graves (1820–93), probably the most significant intellectual force in the early period of the Southern Baptist Convention, argued that only confessing believers should be baptized and that this baptism should take the form of total immersion.

A wide variety of attitudes toward the sacraments can be seen within Protestantism, and it is very difficult to see how any of these can be regarded as "definitive" for the movement. Lutheranism and sections of Anglicanism give particular emphasis to the importance of sacraments, stressing the interconnectedness of the ministries of the word and sacrament. Luther refused to accept any notion of either baptism or the Lord's Supper that saw them simply as external signs; to him, any such teaching was a gross distortion of the biblical witness. Luther's views, however, were regarded as dangerously close to those of Catholicism by many of his contemporaries within the Swiss wing of the Reformation, and in later Protestantism. The radical divergence within Protestantism on this point can be seen from the famous declaration of the great Victorian Baptist preacher Charles Haddon Spurgeon that the idea of baptismal regeneration was a "deceitful invention of Anti-Christ."

The dominant—but not exclusive, nor even characteristic—tendency within Protestantism has been to see the sacraments as signs that point to the greater spiritual realities that lie beyond them but are not actually contained in them. This view can be seen as part of the tendency to "desacralize" the world, which writers such as Max Weber came to see as characteristic of Protestantism. Nature in itself cannot be seen as sacred; at best, it can point beyond itself to the realm of the divine or transcendent. Nature has been "disenchanted"; it can only play a symbolical role in reminding people of sacred realities or act as a signpost to where those realities may be found and encountered.

This position is seen at its most consistent in the theology of Huldrych Zwingli, who had a considerable impact on many sections of Protestantism. Zwingli's theology presupposes a fundamental separation of secular reality and sacred significance—a development that Charles Taylor has described as the "great disembedding."[22] Zwingli subtly converted the sacraments from manifestations and disclosures of the sacred to communal signs of corporate allegiance. The idea of a "sacral society" was reinterpreted as membership in a covenantal community, and the sacraments as pledges toward that community.

Zwingli therefore tended to use political or social analogies for the sacraments, stressing in particular their role in fostering social cohesion and a sense of belonging to the community. A disconnection between the "spiritual" and the "secular" was presupposed from the outset. Whereas Luther saw the sacraments as proclaiming and confirming the commitment of God to believers, Zwingli tended to accentuate a somewhat different aspect of the sacraments—namely, the fostering of social cohesion and the confirmation of mutual loyalty within the community.

This trend is important because it points to one of the most significant, yet inadequately understood, aspects of the style of Protestantism that emerged from Zwingli's Zurich, and later from Calvin's Geneva—namely, a way of conceiving the world, the state, and religion that assumes that the "spiritual" or "sacred" cannot be directly encountered but are known indirectly, primarily in a logocentric manner, through personal reading of the Bible and the hearing of sermons on its themes.

It is instructive to consider changing attitudes toward the sacraments within English Protestantism, where the question of their symbolic and ceremonial role came to be of particular importance in the early seventeenth century. While most Elizabethan Protestants were happy to follow continental ideas, especially those of Calvin, their Jacobean and Stuart successors were increasingly aware of the need to symbolize the interaction and interpenetration of the sacred and secular. The poetry of George Herbert can be seen as an attempt to retain an essentially Calvinist theology of the sacraments, while developing its capacity to promote the church's social and confessional cohesion.[23]

This decoupling of the sacred from the quotidian, characteristic of certain types of Protestantism, accelerated the rise of a functionally atheist worldview in which God was not regarded as an active participant in the world.[24] It is no accident that two sixteenth-century European centers of Calvinism—Geneva and Edinburgh—had become centers of rationalism two centuries later.

We shall have more to say about this development later. Yet it is important to appreciate here that one of the most fundamental characteristics of Pentecostalism is its insistence that the divine may be encountered in the secular realm. Its astonishing success points to the reversal of this trend and the emergence of a new form of Protestantism characterized by its expectation of the direct experience of the spiritual within the mundane.

PREDESTINATION

From the outset, Protestantism has found itself divided by certain issues—such as the nature of the presence of Christ in the bread and wine. One of the most contentious debates has been centered in the area of theology known as "predestination."[25] The question at issue concerns the way in which God and humanity are involved in salvation. Is salvation something that humanity freely chooses? Or is it something that is chosen for humanity by God? The matter was debated extensively in the fifth, ninth, and fourteenth centuries, and it became a topic of fresh disagreement in the early sixteenth century, when a significant division opened up between the Lutheran and Calvinist wings of the Reformation.

We shall explore the nature of this division shortly. It is important to appreciate, however, that the emergence of this serious disagreement coincided with the rise of confessionalism, which put Lutheranism and Calvinism in competition for the loyalty of princes in many regions of Germany. One of the functions of Christian doctrine is to act as a social demarcator—in other words, to distinguish groups that are otherwise very similar.[26] Predestination was propelled to the forefront of debate because it became the litmus test that distinguished Lutheranism and Calvinism—two otherwise very similar movements.

So what were these two differing positions? In general terms, the best way of understanding the differences that were so important at this time is to consider doctrines of predestination as falling into two broad categories:

1. *Single predestination* holds that since all people have sinned on account of the Fall, they are unable to save themselves. In a single act of divine election, God chooses to save some people and to pass over others. Predestination is thus "single" in that there is no deliberate act of rejection, only a single decision to save certain individuals.

2. *Double predestination* holds that God elects, from all eternity, to save certain individuals and condemn others. Predestination thus involves a double act of election in which God actively chooses to save certain individuals and actively chooses to condemn others.

Although Luther inclined toward the second of these options in his famous debate over free will with Erasmus of Rotterdam in 1525, his successors endorsed the first.[27] The "Formula of Concord" sets out this position with admirable clarity:

> In his eternal counsel, purpose, and ordinance, God has not only prepared salvation in general, but he has also graciously considered and elected to salvation each and every individual among the elect who are to be saved through Christ.... God wills by his grace, gifts, and effective working to bring them to salvation, and to help, further, strengthen and preserve them to this end.

For Lutheranism, God chooses to save the elect and foresees—but does not cause—the condemnation of those who are not of the elect. Predestination is single in that there is no negative dimension to God's election. Those who reject the gospel are held to be responsible for their own fate.

Reformed theologians followed the lead of John Calvin, who argued that predestination involves a double decision—a positive decision to election and a negative decision to reprobation. In his brief discussion of the doctrine, Calvin defines predestination as "the eternal decree of God, by which he determined what he wished to make of every man. For he does not create everyone in the same condition, but ordains eternal life for some and eternal damnation for others." God, in a demonstration of his sovereignty and power, determines the eternal destiny of every individual. Calvin is not introducing a hitherto unknown notion into the sphere of Christian theology; similar ideas were propounded by some late medieval writers, such as Gregory of Rimini and Hugolino of Orvieto, who also taught a doctrine of absolute double predestination—that God allocates some to eternal life and others to eternal condemnation without any reference to their merits or demerits.[28] People's fate rests totally upon the will of God rather than on their individuality.

These viewpoints are radically different and involve significantly divergent readings of core biblical texts. Nor has the force of these disagreements diminished over time. If we leave behind sixteenth-century Europe and consider twentieth-century America, we find the same debate being replayed. Consider this discussion of predestination set out in the "Brief Statement" of the Lutheran Church (Missouri Synod), which was adopted in 1932.[29] The statement insists that salvation takes place "by grace alone, for Christ's sake, and by way of the means of grace." Here we have a reaffirmation of some of the great slogans of the Reformation—by grace alone, by Christ alone, by faith alone. But what of those who are not saved? On this point, the Lutheran church makes its opposition to the Reformed doctrine of double predestination unequivocally clear:

> There is no election of wrath, or predestination to damnation. Scripture plainly reveals the truth that the love of God for the world of lost sinners is universal, that is, that it embraces all people without exception, that Christ has fully reconciled all people unto God, and that God earnestly desires to bring all people to faith, to preserve them therein, and thus to save them, as Scripture testifies, 1 Timothy 2:4: "God will have all to be saved and to come to the knowledge of the truth." No one is lost because God has predestined him or her to eternal damnation.

Once more, this radical divergence points to the genuine difficulties and uncertainties attending the process of biblical interpretation. This is not a recent development, but an issue that emerged as deeply divisive during the emergent phase of Protestantism. On a naïve, simplistic understanding of the "clarity of scripture," these two positions cannot both be right: either one is wrong and the other right, or they are both wrong and there exists a third alternative. Yet a more nuanced interpretation of this principle would point to the fundamental truth that both the Lutheran and Reformed communities affirm, despite their differences—namely, that, in the words of the "Brief Statement," "the eternal election of God not only foresees and foreknows the salvation of the elect, but is also, from the gracious will and pleasure of God in Christ Jesus, a cause which procures, works, helps, and promotes our salvation and what pertains thereto; and upon this our salvation is so founded that the gates of hell cannot prevail against it."

This historic debate of the sixteenth century was deeply divisive. It is perhaps little wonder that the Anglican "Thirty-nine Articles of Religion" chose to speak of the topic in such Delphic and opaque terms, avoiding taking sides in such a contentious debate. Yet the debate continued still further as a major split developed within the Reformed camp over the matter. The debate is especially associated with Calvinism in the Lowlands and is often referred to as the "Arminian" controversy, after Arminius (1560–1609).

To understand the debate, we must introduce a further set of divisions into Protestant thinking on predestination. Earlier, we explored the importance of the categories of "single" and "double" predestination; now we must consider an additional question. Is predestination about God's election of a people or election of individuals? At first sight, the question is impossible to answer on its own terms, as the obvious answer is "both." Did not God call the people of Israel? And then the church? And did not God also call individuals, such as Abraham, the prophets, and Paul? While this may indeed be the case, this distinction is essential to appreciate the difference between Calvinism and Arminianism, and we must therefore explain the two options.

1. An *individualist approach* to predestination holds that God's decision concerns a single, named person. God may make many decisions to elect—but each of these decisions concerns a single individual. Calvin's definition of election, provided earlier, clearly belongs to this category.

2. A *corporate approach* to predestination holds that God elects a group of people to salvation. Arminius held that God predetermines that the people who have been elected in this way are those who have faith. Therefore, Arminius argued, in order to be saved, it is necessary to join this group of people—in other words, to have faith.

Arminius held that humanity has the capacity to respond to God's grace or to resist it. God has made salvation possible, as an act of total grace. Yet the decision as to whether to accept that salvation lies with the individual. Calvinism taught that divine grace is irresistible; whoever is elected by God cannot resist the transformative work of grace. Arminius insisted that God offers grace but does not impose it. Christ made salvation possible for all people. It is up to them whether they respond to it or not.[30]

The Synod of Dort (Dordrecht), meeting in 1618–19 in the Lowlands, set out the definitive Calvinist response to Arminianism. As a result, many Calvinists regarded Arminianism as a heresy. The basic teachings of the Synod of Dort are often referred to as the "Five Points," and they are often memorized using the acronym TULIP—highly appropriate for English-language Calvinism, given the long-standing association between the Netherlands and tulips.

T *Total* depravity of sinful human nature

U *Unconditional* election (humans are not predestined on the basis of any foreseen merit, quality, or achievement)

L *Limited* atonement (Christ died only for the elect)

I *Irresistible* grace (by which the elect are infallibly called and redeemed)

P *Perseverance* of the saints (those who are truly predestined by God cannot in any way defect from that calling)

Yet Arminianism reappeared in the English-speaking world, in a new, reinvigorated form, through the preaching of John Wesley. Wesley's "optimism of grace" proved highly effective when wedded to his theology of evangelism.[31] God has done everything possible to make salvation possible, as a gracious gift; all people need to do is to respond to it—to accept God's gift. This theology played an important role in the Second Great Awakening in the United States and probably lies behind the "altar call" practice that became such a distinctive feature of American revivalism.

In this section, we have noted three major positions on the question of predestination within historic and contemporary Protestantism: Lutheranism, Calvinism, and Arminianism. All three remain significant options for Protestants today, and the passage of time has eroded neither the credibility of any one of them nor the tensions they generate within the wider Protestant movement. All affirm central biblical themes—yet in different ways, and with different outcomes.

This could easily lead to tensions, not to mention crude theological vilification, particularly between Calvinists and the followers of John

Wesley, who took an Arminian view on this matter. Yet it is possible for Protestants to reflect graciously on these differences, respecting the personal integrity of those who hold different views. The greatest English Calvinist writer of the nineteenth century was the famous Baptist Victorian preacher Charles Haddon Spurgeon, who commented thus on his attitude toward John Wesley:

> Most atrocious things have been spoken about the character and spiritual condition of John Wesley, the modern prince of Arminians. I can only say concerning him that, while I detest many of the doctrines which he preached, yet for the man himself I have a reverence second to no Wesleyan; and if there were wanted two apostles to be added to the number of the twelve, I do not believe that there could be found two men more fit to be so added than George Whitefield and John Wesley.[32]

As the famous "Down-Grade" controversy of the 1890s makes clear, Spurgeon was prepared to dissociate himself from individuals or organizations—such as the Baptist Union—if he believed they were heretical or unorthodox. He did not see this debate as touching upon such matters.

Each of the approaches noted here has significant consequences for the shaping of Protestant thought, expectations, and aspirations. One may be singled out for mention—the Calvinist belief that, like Israel, they were a "chosen people" who had been called by God to be a light to the nations. This strong sense of divine calling and commission gave direction and motivation to the Puritans then leaving England to settle in the New World. England was their Egypt, and America their promised land.

THE LAST THINGS

A final theological debate that has been important in shaping contemporary Protestantism concerns the "last things" or "end times," an area of theology sometimes referred to as "eschatology." Protestantism shares many of the traditional Christian beliefs about the afterlife, especially the hope of heaven.[33] Many Protestant writers have understood the Christian life in the classical terms of a pilgrimage from their exile in this world to their true destiny and home in the New Jerusalem. The most familiar example of this approach is found in John Bunyan's famous religious allegory *The Pilgrim's Progress*.[34] Bunyan established the journey from the "city of destruction" to the "heavenly city" as a framework for making sense of the ambiguities, sorrows, and pains of the Christian life, especially in times of doubt, persecution, and difficulty. His powerful appeal to imagery, coupled with a masterly use of narrative, ensured that the imagery of the New Jerusalem would have a profound and permanent effect on popular Protestant spirituality.

As understandings of the relation between the individual and corporate aspects of faith have changed over the years, and with changes in political and social circumstances as well, Protestant understandings of the nature of heaven have shifted. The "classic" Protestant conception of heaven is probably most clearly stated in the writings of Puritans, such as Richard Baxter, who emphasize that the primary characteristic of heaven is a total and reverential focus on God. In his *The Saints' Everlasting Rest*, Baxter argues that the worship of God is the supreme activity of the saints in heaven. Nothing can distract them from the adoration of the God who created and redeemed them and finally brought them to eternal rest in the heavenly places. This concept of heaven remains firmly embedded within Protestantism.

During the nineteenth century, alternative visions of heaven began to emerge, especially in the aftermath of the American Civil War. This war saw unprecedented levels of casualties and caused distress and mourning throughout the nation. A new interest in spiritualism flourished as anguished families sought to reestablish contact with relatives who had died on the field of battle. The new genre of "consolation literature" reconceived heaven primarily as a reencounter with loved ones.[35] In *The Gates Ajar* (1868), Elizabeth Stuart Phelps (1844–1911) rejects the traditional idea of heaven as "harping and praying" and argues that it is about the restoration of life and relationships. Heaven is portrayed in this book as an extended nineteenth-century family in which little children are busy "devouring heavenly gingersnaps" and playing rosewood pianos, while the adults listen to learned discourses from glorified philosophers and the symphonies of Beethoven.

Protestantism's attitudes to hell reflect, again, the Christian tradition in general. The traditional Christian view of hell as a sulfurous inferno of eternal torment emerged during the Middle Ages, and it continued to be found in many Protestant writings of the eighteenth and nineteenth centuries.[36] The most famous exposition of this classic Protestant idea is found in Jonathan Edwards's sermon "Sinners in the Hands of an Angry God," preached in Enfield, Connecticut, on July 8, 1741. Edwards is clear about what unrepentant sinners can expect to encounter: "The wrath of God burns against them, their damnation does not slumber; the pit is prepared, the fire is made ready, the furnace is now hot, ready to receive them."

Since the nineteenth century, however, this concept of hell has come under criticism within many sections of Christianity, including Protestantism, as representing a medieval expansion of the biblical material. Many Protestants have expressed puzzlement about the moral purpose of eternal punishment and uneasiness about the traditional answers offered, including the idea that such punishment glorifies God. One response, widely advocated within sections of English Protestantism in the 1880s and now found increasingly within American evangelicalism, is a reappropriation of the patristic idea of "conditional immortality," which holds that human souls are created with the capacity for immortality, but that this capacity is actualized only through repentance and faith.[37]

This uneasiness about the idea of hell has had a significant impact on some evangelical approaches to evangelism. One common evangelistic strategy of the eighteenth and nineteenth centuries was to present the gospel as the only way of escaping the horrors and pain of hell. Edwards's famous sermon ends with a plea to those who have not yet come to faith to "awake and fly from the wrath to come." Echoes of this approach can be found in the early preaching of Billy Graham, widely regarded as the twentieth century's most prominent Protestant evangelist. Yet the weakening of the cultural belief in hell—which is generally regarded as having been in decline in the West since the 1960s[38]—has diminished the power of this approach. In response to this development, many Protestant evangelists now base their appeal primarily upon the love of God or the capacity of the gospel to make sense of life and transform it. It makes little sense, they argue, to have to persuade people of the existence of hell before they can be persuaded of the relevance of the gospel.

While Protestantism follows traditional Christian views at many points concerning the "last things," it has generally rejected the notion of an "intermediate state," or purgatory, holding that this traditional Catholic idea is not adequately grounded in the Bible and is in any case made redundant by the doctrine of justification by faith. The believer does not need to be purified by fire, precisely because Christ has already purified the believer through his death—an idea often expressed in popular Protestant spirituality in terms of "being washed in the blood of the Lamb." The imagery of the believer being able to approach God, enfolded in Christ's righteousness, is perhaps most familiar from Charles Wesley's famous hymn "And Can It Be?"

No Condemnation now I dread,
   Jesus, and all in Him, is mine.
Alive in Him, my Living Head,
   And clothed in Righteousness Divine,
Bold I approach th' eternal Throne,
And claim the Crown, through Christ my own.

A final area of interest in Protestant eschatology concerns the details of the end times. Christians have always enjoyed speculating about origins and endings, and it is hardly surprising that this area of theology proved to have the capacity to engage the popular imagination.[39] Early Protestantism was reluctant to engage with such issues, believing that speculation about when the end of the world might take place was likely to inflame passions and distract people from the more serious business of reforming the church and sorting out the problems of contemporary society. However, the debate flared up again in the nineteenth century, particularly within American Protestantism, and it has continued unabated since then.

Much of the debate has centered on the "millennium," an idea mentioned in the Book of Revelation, which brings the New Testament canon to its close (Revelation 20:2–5).[40] The millennium refers to the hope of a restored earthly kingdom lasting for a period of one thousand years and separating the second coming of Christ and the subsequent establishment of a totally new cosmic order. Although some early Christian writers—such as Irenaeus of Lyons—interpreted this passage literally, a consensus developed that it should be understood figuratively. The reference to a period of a thousand years should not be understood as a literal prediction of the chronological duration of an earthly kingdom, but as an allegorical indication of the grandeur of the heavenly kingdom.

One of the most distinctive features of contemporary American conservative Protestantism is its rediscovery of the idea of the millennium, which it has understood in three ways—again, reflecting different approaches to the interpretation of the Bible. The traditional Protestant disinclination to speculate about the end times is now named the "amillennial" approach and is contrasted with two approaches that make much greater use of the notion of the millennium.

The postmillennial viewpoint was particularly influential in American Protestantism during the nineteenth century. It holds that Christ will return at the close of a long period (not necessarily lasting one thousand years) of righteousness and peace, commonly called the millennium. Leading conservative Protestant theologians, such as the Princeton academics Charles B. Hodge (1797–1878) and Benjamin B. Warfield (1851–1921), took the view that God is bringing about his purposes through steady human progress over evil that will progressively lead to a Christianized world. Postmillennialism sees the church as playing a major role in transforming whole social structures before the Second Coming of Christ and endeavoring to bring about a golden age of peace and prosperity with great advances in education, the arts, the sciences, and medicine. During this process, the church will rise in power, influence, and integrity, serving as the standard bearer for the coming kingdom of God on earth. Its credibility was severely damaged by the suffering and damage of the First and Second World Wars, both of which increased the appeal of premillennialism, especially in North America.

The premillennial viewpoint holds that the figure known as "the Antichrist" will appear on earth, ushering in a seven-year period of suffering known as "the Tribulation." This great period of destruction, war, and disaster will finally be ended by God defeating evil at the battle of Armageddon. After this, Christ will return to earth to rule for a period of a thousand years (the millennium), during which time the forces of evil will finally be subdued and conquered.

Premillennialism offers the strongly pessimistic view that things are deteriorating on earth and will go on doing so until God brings history to an end. This view resonates deeply with the sense of cultural alienation shared by many conservative American Protestants, especially its belief that anti-Christian forces are gaining the upper hand in America, as in the world in general. But since premillennialists see the degeneration of the world as a sign that the end of the world is near, they can view this negative development as a harbinger of something positive.

Beliefs about the end times have had a major impact on American popular Protestantism, as is evident from the huge sales of fiction and nonfiction works reflecting these standpoints. Hal Lindsey's end-times book *The Late Great Planet Earth* (1970) was one of the best-selling novels of that decade. More recently, the best-selling "Left Behind" novels, written by Tim LaHaye and Jerry Jenkins, have ensured that premillennial ideology retains a high profile across America. In a similar vein, John Hagee, senior pastor of an evangelical mega-church in San Antonio, Texas, has penned a series of end-time novels, including *Devil's Island* (2001), that reflect a fascination with the interconnection between the politics of the Middle East and the end of the world.

The brief engagement with some aspects of Protestant teachings offered in this chapter has touched on some of its most distinctive beliefs, while at the same time noting the diversity within the movement. The movement's shared commitment to the authority of the Bible does not lead to a common mind on how the Bible is to be interpreted. This is not seen as a particular problem, except for those who mistakenly hold that the principle of the "clarity of scripture" demands total uniformity of interpretation on all matters.

So what is the impact of Protestant attitudes and beliefs on everyday life? What difference do they make? In the following chapter, we consider how these ideas shape Protestant life and worship.

Interior of the Oude Kerk *(Old Church) at Amsterdam,*
by Emmanuel de Witte (1617–92).

I I

The Structures of Faith

Organization, Worship, and Preaching

In the words of Jean Monnet, who had so much to do with achieving European unity in the twentieth century, "Rien n'est possible sans les hommes, rien n'est durable sans les institutions."[1] Monnet's point is simple: individuals make things happen, but for those things to survive, institutions are required. No movement can exist without structures. As Protestantism emerged and consolidated itself in the 1520s, the question of how its core ideas could be sustained in the longer term became increasingly pressing. At first, this matter was not seen as critical; as time passed, however, it could not be ignored.

Many of the first generation of Protestants believed that their separation from the Catholic church was temporary. It was only a matter of time before that church would concede the need for reform and those who had been forced to leave could return. This rather pleasing aspiration was certainly plausible throughout much of the 1520s and 1530s. In the 1540s, however, it became clear that separation and alienation were likely to be permanent. The failure of the Colloquy of Regensburg (1541), which had brought together like-minded senior Catholics and Protestants to explore possibilities of rapprochement, was an important straw in the wind.[2] More significantly, the Council of Trent—the foundation of the Catholic Reformation—sent out signals at a very early stage that it was not concerned with seeking reconciliation with Protestantism but rather with offering a robust restatement of the Catholic position, coupled with explicit criticism of Protestant views, particularly those on the relation of the Bible and tradition and the doctrine of justification by faith.[3] The countering of the Protestant Reformation would be an explicit part of the renewal of Catholicism. The Catholic Reformation would thus also be a Counter-Reformation.

From the late 1540s, institutional questions assumed a new priority within Protestantism. By this stage, however, Luther was dead and his mantle had passed to his successors. The fixing of denominational structures would be a task for the second generation of Protestants. The first generation had hoped this would never be necessary, believing that provisional interim arrangements would suffice until reunion took place. By 1550 it was evident that a reunion would never take place.

PROTESTANT DENOMINATIONAL STRUCTURES

In this chapter, we consider the emergence of the structures of Protestantism, from the time of its origins to the more recent period. The essential point that emerges from any historical analysis of the emergence of these structures is that they are remarkably fluid. While older Protestant groups, particularly those that trace their origins back to the sixteenth century, have often found themselves trapped within inflexible institutional structures, more recent groupings have developed leaner, more efficient, and above all more responsive structures.

The three traditional types of Protestant church organization may be designated as episcopal, presbyterian, and congregational. Each of these was developed within a European context and has subsequently been transplanted to American, African, and Asian contexts—not always with total success—as Protestantism has expanded. One of the challenges faced by Protestantism in the twentieth century was rethinking these European prototypes for church order, most of which emerged during the sixteenth and seventeenth centuries.

Many Protestant churches cannot easily be assigned to any of these three broad categories. For example, Methodism embraces a family of denominations that possess a rich variety of traditions. Some—such as the United Methodist Church—can be regarded as essentially episcopal; others, however, place greater emphasis on the autonomy of the local congregation. Even denominations that appear committed to one specific model often display a far greater variation than might be expected. Anglicanism, for example, is rightly regarded as an episcopal form of Protestantism. Yet in practice, many evangelical Anglicans adopt a congregationalist approach to church order, regarding bishops as possessing a purely symbolic function rather than exercising genuine authority or leadership. Nevertheless, despite being so obviously porous, these three categories are helpful in exploring the shaping of Protestantism and understanding its distinctive forms.

In the 1520s, the first evangelical groups began to emerge in Germany and Switzerland. While reforming factions, such as the Waldensians, had existed throughout the Middle Ages, these tended to be movements existing within the church—not always with its permission and blessing. These pressure groups acted as lobbyists, advocating reform and redirection. On occasion, they posed such a threat to vested interests within the church that they were designated as heretical, even though their religious views often fitted comfortably within the ample theological girth of the medieval church. The real threat lay in the challenge they posed to papal authority.

The emergence of Lutheran and Zwinglian factions *as distinct ecclesial groups* changed things significantly. Not only were Protestants placed under some external pressure by their critics to justify such acts of schism, which seemed to deny them access to any of the benefits of the Christian faith, but they also experienced internal pressure from their supporters to clarify how these communities were to be structured and organized.

The simplest option emerged in England during the 1530s. Henry VIII's reformation of the English church involved the relatively simple measure of replacing the authority of the pope with that of the monarch, making as few doctrinal adjustments as possible, and leaving ecclesiastical structures unchanged. Even after the major changes wrought during the reigns of Edward VI, Mary Tudor, and Elizabeth I, much the same self-understanding of the English church remained: it retained its traditional Catholic structures—such as dioceses, provinces, archbishops, bishops, archdeacons, priests, and deacons—but these enfolded an essentially Protestant understanding of the Christian faith.

As British influence increased in the eighteenth and nineteenth centuries, colonial churches were established throughout its empire; based on English models, these churches defined their identity through an episcopal church structure and the doctrinal and liturgical formulations of the *Book of Common Prayer* (1662). The adoption of the name Protestant Episcopal Church in the United States of America (PECUSA) was intended to emphasize the distinctive feature of this version of Protestantism—its episcopal form of church government.[4] The use of the King James Bible (1611) for the public reading of scripture reinforced this sense of a distinct global Protestant church communion. This sense of shared identity was further strengthened when the archbishop of Canterbury agreed to summon all 144 Anglican bishops to a "national synod of the bishops of the Anglican Church at home and abroad" to meet under his leadership at Lambeth Palace in London in 1867.

The episcopal model is primarily used by those Protestant denominational families that have the closest historical roots to the medieval church and that saw reformation as applying primarily to doctrine and liturgy and only secondarily to church structures. This form of church government sits uneasily with some core Protestant principles, especially the "priesthood of all believers." Many Protestants in episcopal denominations argue that the structure locates an excessive amount of power in the person of the bishop, opening the way to the reemergence of the medieval "prince-bishop."

Luther's reformation of church structures, though more radical than its English counterpart, was conservative by broader European standards.[5] It seems that Luther did not deem it necessary to be unduly specific in matters of church structure or organizations. Luther regarded the organization of the church as a matter determined by historical contingency, with no need for theological prescription. For Luther, the church was not about institutional structures but about the "sheep who hear the voice of their shepherd."

Luther's successors could thus see themselves as free to develop church structures that would be best adapted to their situations. Luther himself did not envisage retaining bishops. Elsewhere in Europe, however, most Lutheran churches were episcopal—that is, governed by bishops.[6] In North America and elsewhere, Lutherans would adopt congregational and synodical forms of government, in which local churches link together for common purposes. In the United States, Lutherans gradually coalesced into three distinct bodies: the Lutheran Church in America, the Lutheran Church—Missouri Synod, and the American Lutheran Church. The American Lutheran Church, the Lutheran Church in America, and a third group, the Association of Evangelical Lutheran Churches, united in 1987 to form the Evangelical Lutheran Church of America. The Lutheran World Federation, founded in 1947, aims to provide a forum in which the world's diverse Lutheran bodies can discuss issues of mutual concern.

We see here the emergence of the notion of a "denominational family"—a group of churches that arose from a common Protestant origin through schism, division, or geographical separation. These churches within the same denominational family generally form alliances, confederations, and other joint groups for consultation and the sharing of resources. A good example is the Geneva-based World Alliance of Reformed Churches, a fellowship of 75 million Reformed Christians in 218 churches in 107 countries. Other examples include the Baptist World Alliance, the World Lutheran Federation, and the World Methodist Council. These bodies seek to sustain a distinctly denominational vision of Protestantism while allowing their member churches to remain flexible in actualizing that vision in their local situation.

John Calvin was responsible for the most significant development in sixteenth-century Protestant thinking on the structures of the church. Whereas most earlier Protestant writers had assumed that the New Testament did not lay down any specific form of church structure, giving each church a significant degree of freedom to reform or redevelop existing historical models, Calvin insisted that a highly specific form of ministry was stipulated by scripture—and should therefore be embodied at Geneva.

Calvin identified a fourfold structure of pastors, teachers, elders, and deacons in the New Testament. Pastors were called to preach and teach, to administer the sacraments, and to visit the sick.[7] The teachers (or "doctors") were to instruct their congregations in those things that were necessary to salvation. The elders (or "presbyters"), who were to be elected within the congregation, were to ensure good order within the church.[8] (The importance attached to the role of the elder [*presbyteros* in Greek] in church government lies behind the use of the word "presbyterian" to describe this distinctive approach.) Finally, the deacons were called to care for the sick and support the poor.[9]

As a result, Calvin's reformation possessed a distinctive church structure that proved well adapted to the situation of Geneva itself, and—although this cannot have been in Calvin's mind at the time—to the new challenges and opportunities that subsequently arose in the New World. Even by the time of Calvin's death in 1564, Calvinism had become established as the most formidable alternative to Roman Catholicism in western Europe, assisted to no small extent by Calvin's brilliance in recognizing the importance of ecclesiastical organization and structuring to the survival of a movement. His successors recognized the importance of applying this idea to his religious thought as well, that is, to supplement Calvinist ecclesiastical institutions with equally resilient intellectual structures.

The presbyterian system of church government has proved highly influential in modern-day North America and Korea, while its impact on European Protestantism has been much less marked. Many Presbyterians of the sixteenth and seventeenth centuries held that they were restoring the original form of church government, but this position would not be vigorously defended by many Presbyterians today. While insisting that Presbyterianism is a biblically warranted form of church government, most writers within this tradition accept that patterns of church order have undergone historical development and that a variety of valid church orders may be recognized.

Presbyterianism now designates a congregational family, not a single denomination. In the United States, the largest such group is presently the Presbyterian Church (USA), headquartered in Louisville, Kentucky. This congregation was formed in 1983 as a result of a reunion between the predominantly southern Presbyterian Church in the United States (PCUS) and the predominantly northern United Presbyterian Church in the USA (UPCUSA). Other Presbyterian denominations in the United States currently include the Presbyterian Church in America, the Cumberland Presbyterian Church, the Orthodox Presbyterian Church, and the Associate Reformed Presbyterian Church.

Yet many regarded presbyterianism as giving too much power to the pastor. Such disagreements emerged forcefully during the period of the Westminster Assembly, when even John Milton was led to set to one side his "calm and pleasing solitariness" in order to become a voice in the "troubled sea of noises and hoarse disputes" then taking place. For Milton, the new ascendant presbyterianism simply replicated the authoritarianism of the old episcopal structures. "The episcopal arts begin to bud again," he grimly remarked. For such reasons, many preferred an alternative that they regarded as entirely consistent with the Reformed tradition and well grounded in the New Testament—congregationalism.

The essence of the congregational model is that of local, autonomous congregations that are not under any centralized control. For congregationalists, the New Testament era knew only individual congregations that were not subject to episcopal or presbyterial control. The idea emerged toward the end of the sixteenth century. It can be seen in Robert Browne's 1582 treatise *Reformation Without Tarrying for Any*, which affirms the principle of the gathered church, its independence from bishops and magistrates, and its right to ordain its own ministers. By locating power within the church firmly in its membership, the doctrine of the "priesthood of all believers" can be upheld. Ministers, while called to lead, are fundamentally understood to act in a ministerial, not magisterial, role. Congregationalists are generally reluctant to demand assent to specified confessions of faith, believing that such a requirement undermines the independence of the local congregation.

Although congregationalism had its origins in England, it has been most significant in the religious life of the United States.[10] The Puritan congregations in the Massachusetts Bay area in the early seventeenth century generally adopted a congregationalist church polity because they were anxious to avoid the problems with authority they had experienced in England. The most significant manifestation of a congregational polity today, however, is found in the Southern Baptist Convention, which represents a voluntary association of individual Baptist congregations, each retaining its own identity and sovereignty. So influential has this group become within American Protestantism that many outsiders fail to appreciate that the term "Baptist" designates a much broader range of options, both religiously and politically.[11]

From its foundation in 1845 until 1925, the Southern Baptist Convention (SBC) avoided adopting any centralized belief system. In 1846

William B. Johnson, the first president of the SBC, published *The Gospel Developed Through the Government and Order of the Churches of Jesus Christ,* in which he argued that Baptists, because they are governed by the Bible, do not need creeds or confessions. "Why not," Johnson asked, "use the Bible as the standard? Can man present God's system in a selection and compilation of some of its parts, better than God has himself done it, as a whole in his own book?" This strong statement of the autonomy of each local congregation under the Bible remains central to the SBC today. However, that position has been supplemented by statements that some Baptists believe might represent "creeds" or "confessions" and thus undermine their congregationalist ethos.

In 1925 the SBC produced its "Statement of the Baptist Faith and Message." Although the SBC was emphatic that this document was descriptive and not prescriptive, to some it represented a centralizing trend that corroded the SBC's fundamental commitment to congregational sovereignty.[12] To most Baptists, however, the statement—which has since been modified on a regular basis, to respond to new developments within the church and society—is not a document that imposes a centralized authority but one that offers guidance. In setting out its 2000 revision, the SBC reaffirmed that "Baptists cherish and defend religious liberty, and deny the right of any secular or religious authority to impose a confession of faith upon a church or body of churches. We honor the principles of soul competency and the priesthood of believers, affirming together both our liberty in Christ and our accountability to each other under the Word of God."

The emergence of Pentecostalism in the twentieth century has reopened the question of Protestant structures. For many Pentecostals, structures are an impediment to the movement and action of the Holy Spirit. Excessively rigid and unresponsive structures might hinder or even "quench" the work of the Spirit, on which the worship and mission of the church ultimately depend. Whereas Catholics tend to discuss their identity in terms of ecclesiology, and classic Protestants in terms of their doctrine of the "Word of God," Pentecostals tend to identify themselves primarily (some possibly exclusively) in terms of their doctrine of the Holy Spirit. Everything else—including both the practicalities and theories of church structures—are seen as secondary to a right understanding of how the Holy Spirit operates and is experienced. Where Protestants and Catholics tend to develop ecclesiologies based on Ignatius of Antioch's maxim "Wherever Christ is, there is also the Church," Pentecostals tend to be guided by a maxim of Irenaeus of Lyons: "Where the Spirit of God is, there is the Church, and all grace."[13]

THE REUNIFICATION OF PROTESTANTISM?

This brief analysis of some of the major constituent elements of modern Protestantism raises an important question: might the denominations representing these elements settle their differences someday and form one large Protestant mega-church? The vision of a reunited Protestantism has captivated the imaginations of many Protestants, especially when the movement has felt itself to be under threat and in need of reaffirming its unity. Two threats in particular have brought home the importance of collaboration between the divergent Protestant groups.

In the West, the rise of secularism since the 1960s has brought home the need for Protestant unity in the face of this new threat. Secularism takes various forms: in the United Kingdom, secularism is basically an aspiration toward the elimination of any religious *influence* on public institutions; in the United States that aspiration takes the form of eliminating any religious *presence* in public institutions. In the face of this threat, increased collaboration between Protestants is to be expected. As we have constantly stressed in this work, "the other" is no longer Roman Catholicism but secularism. The threat of Catholicism once drew Protestants together; now the threat that predominantly catalyzes such collaboration and sets intra-Protestant differences in their proper perspective is the one coming from those opposed to religion.

A similar increase in cooperation among Protestants is occurring in the developing world, where there has also been a fundamental change in the identity of the "other" that is posing a common threat. Once it was Catholicism; now it is Islam, especially in its militant fundamentalist forms. Benjamin Franklin's famous quip at the signing of the Declaration of Independence on July 4, 1776, has become a harsh reality for many Protestants: "We must indeed all hang together, or, most assuredly, we shall all hang separately."

These pressures might be expected to encourage denominational mergers. In fact, they have not, owing in part to widespread dissatisfaction in most parts of Protestantism with the most ambitious such ecumenical project to date—the World Council of Churches, headquartered in Geneva. The first assembly of the World Council of Churches, held in August 1948 in Amsterdam, was seen as a beacon of hope for postwar Europe.[14] Its founders had no doubt that a landmark had been achieved in the history of Protestantism. The main Protestant churches had covenanted to work together and to stay together.

Yet when the time came to mark the World Council of Churches' golden jubilee in 1998, nobody felt there was all that much to celebrate. The group seemed to have lost its way, having fallen victim to institutional navel-gazing and become preoccupied with its closed circles of meetings, committees, reports, and publications. However noble its intentions, the organization had become bogged down in internal debates and ceased to play a credible role in bringing Protestants together. The beautiful princess had become a Cinderella. Yet this does not mean that Protestants have lost interest in each other or in working to deepen their unity. A different style of ecumenism has triumphed instead.

The new style of ecumenism that has swept through Protestantism since about 1990 is based on the grass roots of the movement, not its institutions. The World Council of Churches wanted "visible unity"— that is, either the uniting of denominations in a single global church or at least a reduction in the number of denominations through mergers.[15] With the passing of time, it has become clear that this vision was quite unrealistic and failed to take seriously the realities of church life. What ordinary Protestants wanted was better working relationships with their fellow Christians of other denominations. They did not want their denomination to be swallowed up by someone else, nor did they want to take anyone else over. They just wanted to understand and get on with each other at both the individual and institutional levels.

In the United States, this grassroots ecumenism went further than anyone had expected. The election of Bill Clinton as president in 1992 was seen by many Americans as marking the rise of secularism and hostility toward Christianity in the public arena. Though this turned out to be a misjudgment, the threat seemed real enough at the time. It persuaded some senior evangelical Protestants and Catholics that the time had come to do some serious talking.

It was an astonishing development. Could there be two more different groups? Yet there was enough shared ground to make this a positive and significant discussion. Both groups were conservative theologically. They certainly disagreed on a number of matters—such as the authority of the pope and whether there is a place called purgatory (and whether it matters). But they also shared certain core Christian beliefs, over and against a secular culture and a liberal bias in the mainline Protestant denominations.

What else, the leaders of this movement argued, could they do? They could refuse to have anything to do with each other on account of the continuing doctrinal disagreements associated with the agenda of the Reformation. Yet should feuds between Christians be allowed to help secularism win? A divided Christianity was simply a weakened Christianity. In the end, they agreed to collaborate with each other on a limited range of issues, while acknowledging that differences remained on others. The document "Evangelicals and Catholics Together" (1994) created a minor sensation. Many evangelicals and Roman Catholics were puzzled, and some outraged, that such discussions should be taking place at all. After all, the agenda of the Reformation remained and had not been resolved. So how could such collaboration be taking place?[16]

Since then, there has been a growing groundswell of support for collaboration between Roman Catholics and evangelicals while at the same time recognizing the doctrinal differences that remain between the two groups. In 1995 discussions began to bring Orthodox Christians into the collaborative networks that were being set up. It remains to be seen where this grassroots ecumenism leads in the future.

Protestants now find it easier to collaborate with each other than ever before, both in the West and in the developing world, as they huddle together for fellowship and mutual support in the face of real threats. Since neither secularism nor Islam seem likely to disappear in the foreseeable future, Protestantism can be expected to shrug off some of its historic debates and differences, in the interest of mutual survival.

THE STYLES OF PROTESTANT WORSHIP

For most people, Protestantism is encountered primarily through the regular acts of worship of its churches. Protestantism is most regularly experienced and encountered as a living reality through its Sunday worship and its marriages, baptisms, and funerals. Any account of how Protestantism manifests itself must therefore include description and analysis of Protestant worship.

Yet this is not the easiest of tasks, mainly because of the astonishing variety of forms of worship now encountered within Protestant worship. This diversity is evident even within Protestant denominations, such as Anglicanism. Anglican congregations that worship in the Anglo-Catholic tradition, influenced by the Oxford Movement of the nineteenth century, generally have the eucharist (often referred to as the "mass") at the heart of their worship. The eucharist is typically celebrated with elaborate rituals and settings reminiscent of Catholicism prior to the Second Vatican Council, by priests who are often sumptuously attired in stoles and chasubles. The order of worship follows a fixed liturgy, with set prayers for each Sunday and seasonal variations for Advent, Christmas, and so forth.

Anglican congregations that worship in the evangelical tradition, in marked contrast, tend to focus on the reading and preaching of the word of God, and their ministers (note the terminology) either wear the clerical robes specified during the Elizabethan era or abandon robes altogether in favor of suits. The eucharist (usually referred to as the "Lord's Supper") is generally seen as an occasional event that serves as a reminder of the death of Christ. The worship is often informal, without any set liturgy.

While there is an astonishing diversity of worship forms within classical Protestantism, three features almost invariably lie at their heart: the use of the vernacular, the public reading of scripture, and a sermon or homily based on that text.[17] These features may be *characteristic* of Protestantism; however, they are no longer *distinctive.* Since the Second Vatican Council, the structure of Catholic worship has become much more similar to that of its Protestant counterparts, especially Lutherans and Anglicans. The mass is no longer said in Latin, scripture is more extensively read, and sermons are more biblical.

There are, of course, significant differences within Protestantism over all these matters, particularly since the emergence of Pentecostalism, with its highly distinctive, nontraditional worship styles. Some Protestant congregations follow a lectionary, which allocates set biblical readings for each Sunday of the year; others choose to work through specific books of the Bible, generally chosen by the clergy—the practice developed by Calvin and known as *lectio continua*.

Some historical controversies may help illuminate some Protestant concerns about worship. Without doubt, the most contentious issue to divide Protestantism was whether prayer and worship should be extempore and informal or follow a set form. This debate lay behind the famous "Troubles of Frankfurt" of 1554. During the troubled reign of Mary Tudor, many English Protestants fled to the safety of European cities, including Frankfurt. They began to meet regularly for worship. But how were they to worship?

A major disagreement erupted over whether the congregation should use the 1552 prayer book, drawn up by Thomas Cranmer during the reign of Edward VI. John Knox, then serving as one of the pastors of the church, refused to use the prayer book and wrote to Calvin for advice.[18] From that letter, it is possible to work out the points of contention: the minister being required to wear a surplice; the use of appointed lessons, prescribed prayers, and fasts; the inclusion of high feasts and holidays; and the use of the sign of the cross in baptism. Some English Protestants, including Richard Cox, wanted "Protestantism with an English face"; others, including Knox and William Whittingham (who was later responsible for the Geneva Bible), believed that the prayer book both limited Protestant freedom to worship and included practices of highly questionable provenance. Knox hinted darkly that it appeared to include some material that was little more than superstitious.

In its place, Knox proposed a form of common worship to be used by the English congregation at Geneva. This was adopted, with some modifications, when Knox moved to Scotland. Although this form of worship is often referred to as a "liturgy," it is more a directory, stipulating the overall shape that worship should take. The order of worship for the weekly service on the Lord's day was determined to be: an opening congregational prayer for confession of sin; the congregational singing of a psalm; a prayer before the sermon; the sermon itself, along with the biblical passage on which it was based; a prayer for the church; the congregational singing of a second psalm; and the minister pronouncing a blessing (taken from scripture) upon the congregation.

So what role did the laity play in worship? In recent years, growing attention has been paid to the practice in early Protestant churches of involving the laity in worship through "prophesying."[19] This is generally interpreted as an attempt to involve the laity in public worship so as to affirm the doctrine of the "priesthood of all believers" in the face of the rise of a new professional class of preachers and ministers, which seemed to pose a threat to the fundamental principles of Protestantism. Although lay involvement appears to have been common in some churches during the 1550s, in the end these "prophesyings" were brought to an end because they were regarded as disruptive and unhelpful. They have reemerged, however, in recent years in Pentecostalism, which is committed to the all-important notion of the "prophethood of all believers."

We have already hinted at the importance of preaching for Protestant worship. Since it plays such an important role in maintaining Protestant identity, it merits much more detailed discussion.

PREACHING IN THE PROTESTANT TRADITION

Christianity has always valued preaching as an important means of teaching congregations, offering them guidance on practical issues, and encouraging them to remain faithful. The sermon served an important devotional role during the Middle Ages, particularly in a monastic context.[20] But sermons were not limited to the monastic world. A homily would be (or was meant to be) preached in each parish church at Sunday mass. These sermons were often based on biblical passages, but a tension can be discerned, particularly in England—namely, the desire to get across a particular, authorized interpretation of a biblical passage or narrative, without allowing the laity to get hold of the full biblical text itself.[21]

The rise of biblical humanism in the 1520s saw increased attention being paid to the sermon as a means by which the wisdom of the Bible could be conveyed to the people eloquently and accurately.[22] Erasmus of

Rotterdam played a major role in encouraging this development, which was designed to increase lay access to the Bible—a program that Erasmus had set out in his *Handbook of the Christian Soldier*. Yet the rise of Protestantism gave a new status to the sermon, with important consequences for the shaping of the movement. While a number of factors contributed to this development, two are of particular importance.

In the first phase of Protestant history, the justification for the breach with the medieval church was of paramount importance. Congregations needed to be reassured that this schism was justified and that the salvation of their souls was not imperiled by the breach with Rome. Although the essence of Protestantism was arguably the recovery of Christian authenticity (both in life and thought), the ideological agendas of its first period led early Protestant preachers to portray Catholicism as "the other," or "the enemy." Not surprisingly, the popular conviction arose that the essence of Protestantism was anti-Catholicism, whereas in fact anti-Catholicism was merely a situationally specific expression of Protestant identity, not that identity itself.

A second reason for the growing importance of the sermon was the emerging belief that it was, in some sense of the term, the "Word of God." The sermon was the means by which God spoke to his people. This idea, which emerged at a very early stage in Protestantism, is often linked to Heinrich Bullinger, Zwingli's successor as the religious leader of Protestant Zurich. For Bullinger, "the preaching of the word of God *is* the Word of God."[23] Although this idea can be discerned within both early Lutheranism and early Anglicanism, it is particularly associated with the Reformed tradition within Protestantism. As the office of the preacher came to be regarded with especial importance, a number of other significant developments would shape the form that Protestantism took.

The most significant of these changes concerned church architecture. Initially, Protestantism took over existing church buildings, adapting them to its basic principles and beliefs. The modifications introduced by Protestants are very revealing. The interiors of the churches of the United Provinces, as painted by Emmanuel de Witte, Hendrick van Vliet, Gerrit Beckheyde, and Gerrit Houckgeest, make it clear that the pulpit was the central focus of the building, reflecting the new importance of preaching.

The greatest ecclesiastical structure in Geneva is St. Peter's Cathedral, which dominates the old city and dates back to 1160. The interior of the building was totally reordered in the late 1530s, in line with Calvin's vision of reform. The altar was removed, and a pulpit, raised high above the congregation, was installed. All frescoes, statues, and any other forms of religious imagery were removed. The focus of the building was once the altar; now it was the pulpit. A substantial shift in theology underlies this tactile transition. God was now to be encountered indirectly, through the preaching of the word, not substantially or mystically through the sacrament of the bread and wine. The clergy were now to be regarded as authoritative spokesmen for a distant God rather than as a wonder-working priesthood who ensured the direct presence of God within the everyday material world.

The layout of St. Peter's reflects the reordering of an existing building. What happened when a building was specially commissioned, purposely built to meet the agenda of Protestantism? The first such building is thought to be the chapel of the castle of Hartenfels in Germany, which was formally inaugurated by a sermon preached by Luther on August 5, 1544.[24] The chapel takes the form of a simple rectangle with four bays, surrounded by a two-story stone gallery. The focal point of the chapel is the elevated pulpit, decorated with biblical scenes. In his sermon, Luther declared that "the purpose of this new building" was "that nothing else may ever happen in it except that our dear Lord himself may speak to us through his Holy Word, and we respond to him through prayer and praise."

Reformed Protestantism displaced all forms of secular and ecclesiastical authority with an appeal to the word of God—to the Bible. Yet the Bible required authoritative interpretation and application to the situations faced by believers. Protestantism placed the preacher as the intermediary between God and the congregation, charged with the sacred task of interpretation and application of the Bible. Armed with a theology that insisted that obedient and faithful preaching was an authorized channel of divine communication and instruction, the preacher was clearly placed in a position of some authority and power within the community of faith. So how could abuse be avoided?

The classic response was simple: what preachers say must be *controlled*. This concern about limiting the freedom of the preacher was evident in England during both the Edwardian and Elizabethan eras. The *Book of Homilies* set out prefabricated, centrally approved sermons that preachers were required to deliver. The Puritans were incensed; they regarded this practice as a human distortion of the word of God and sought to establish "lectureships" that would allow them to preach what they believed the biblical text said, rather than what the authorities wished them to believe.[25]

The real question, however, was deciding who could be said to be *authorized* to preach. State churches retained a tight control over those who were permitted to preach, fearful of the threat of sedition, unrest, or scandal. The issue was important in other contexts as well. During the period of the Puritan Commonwealth, the Westminster Assembly accepted the need for a "directory for preaching." While insisting that it was Christ who called preachers and endowed them with the gift of his Spirit, the *Westminster Larger Catechism* stipulated that only those who were "duly approved and called to that office" could be permitted to preach in public. Preachers were to be "ordained"—that is to say, authorized. The fifth commandment—"You shall honor your Father and Mother"—was interpreted by the Westminster Assembly to extend beyond physical parents and to refer particularly to those who, "by God's ordinance, are over us in place of authority" (q. 124). The preacher was thus firmly embedded in the authority structures of Puritanism.

The Westminster Assembly also set out a specific theology of preaching that emphasized its unique character and its special place in the Christian life. How, asked the *Westminster Larger Catechism,* was the "word made effectual to salvation"? While reading the Bible was helpful, the *Catechism* emphasized that preaching was the supreme means by which the Holy Spirit enlightens, convinces, and humbles sinners (q. 155). To help audiences gain the most from such sermons, the *Catechism* also recommended that they "attend upon it with diligence, preparation, and prayer" and "receive the truth" that it conveyed (q. 160).

So how is a sermon to be structured? Does its efficacy depend on following a set formula—and if so, who has the right to determine it? This question has been debated and discussed throughout Christian history. A particularly influential model of preaching was set out in the thirteenth century by Robert of Basevorn, based on the sermons of

Jesus, Saint Paul, Augustine of Hippo, Gregory the Great, and Bernard of Clairvaux.[26] Robert recommended using various forms of ornamentation to hold the audience's interest, including vocal modulation, humor, and gestures. The debate flared up in the early years of Protestantism as controversy raged over whether the Bible itself defined a specific pattern of preaching. The debate, though lengthy, was inconclusive. Should a "plain style" of preaching be used, so that nothing distracted the listener from the simple truths that were being proclaimed and applied? Or might an "ornamented style" be used, to hold the interest of the audience? The difference is easily appreciated by comparing seventeenth-century Anglican and Puritan sermons.

An Anglican sermon—as preached, for example, by that prince of the pulpit, Lancelot Andrewes—would often open with the statement of a theme, generally linked to a biblical verse. The preacher would then launch into an exploration of the wording and imagery of the text, using each as the starting point for a remarkable piece of verbal or conceptual embroidery, weaving together a rich web of allusions and associations. Although the text was the ultimate foundation of all that was said, it was often used as little more than the occasion for the preacher's rhetorical flourishes and elaborate ornamentations. Eventually, the sermon would come to its triumphant conclusion, having steadily gained verbal and conceptual momentum as it proceeded.

A Puritan sermon—as exemplified by William Perkins, who did much to shape this genre—tended to consist of three essential components: doctrine, reason, and use.[27] The sermon would open with a reading of the text, followed by brief comments that restated its verbal imagery in more prosaic terms, set the context of the passage, and explained difficult terms. The sermon would then turn to the first of its three points, setting out the basic doctrine contained in the text. The preacher would use the same flat tone of voice throughout, trusting in the power of his message rather than relying upon any rhetorical skills. Having explained the doctrine, he would move on to consider its proofs, usually set out as numbered points, before finally turning to apply the doctrine to his audience. That being done, the sermon would end.

Substantially the same debates about sermons remain significant within Protestantism to this day. In the Victorian age—regarded by many as the golden age of Protestant preaching—these debates were supplemented by an additional controversy: should sermons be read from a full text or delivered extempore?[28] One side argued that written sermons were generally better organized and more logically sound than extemporaneous ones; the other side recognized that written sermons were often less powerful than those delivered without the impediment of a full text. Those committed to preaching without notes argued that passion was more important than precision and that extemporaneous sermons had "more life, vigor, and power" than those that had been committed to writing and were merely being read aloud in church.

From what has been said, it will be clear that the preacher has played a major role in maintaining and developing the ethos and identity of Protestant groupings. Anglican, Lutheran, Calvinist, Methodist, and Baptist churches have all seen preaching as playing a determinative role, often exceeding the influence of authorized denominational officials or directives. Preachers are the "guardians" of the various Protestant traditions, acting as centers of nucleation, purification, and growth for what is perceived to be reliable, relevant, persuasive, and powerful statements of their positions.

It is no accident that probably the most influential Baptist of the nineteenth century was Charles Haddon Spurgeon and that the most influential British evangelicals of the twentieth century were Martyn Lloyd-Jones and John Stott. All three were highly effective preachers who extended their influence through their published sermons and related works. Each was based at a large London church—the Metropolitan Tabernacle, Westminster Chapel, and All Souls' Church in Langham Place, respectively—that rose to prominence through their preaching. Each continues to be regarded as an authority within his constituency, and occasionally beyond it.

PROTESTANT VIEWS ON MUSIC IN WORSHIP

Modern Protestant worship makes extensive use of music, especially hymns, choruses, and worship songs. Indeed, Protestants have become so used to singing hymns as part of their worship that many have no idea that this practice was late to develop and was accompanied by much controversy. In this section, we explore how the place of hymns in worship was significantly affected by characteristically Protestant debates about how to understand and apply the Bible.

Luther saw no difficulty with using music in the public worship of the church.[29] "Next to the Word of God, music deserves the highest praise," he wrote. "I do not believe that all the arts should be removed or forbidden on account of the Gospel, as some fanatics suggest. On the contrary, I would gladly see all arts, especially music, in the service of Him Who has given and created them." Himself a skilled musician, Luther urged others within the reforming movement to write hymns based upon the Psalms in order that the whole of Christendom might be enlightened and inspired.[30] Luther's best-known hymn is a paraphrase of Psalm 46, which opens with the words "God is our refuge and strength, a very present help in trouble." Luther's work, set to a tune of his own composing, became a landmark in Christian hymnody: "A Mighty Fortress Is Our God."[31]

This work is important in another respect: it represents an example of Luther's most significant liturgical innovation—the "chorale." This was a piece of German-language verse written in stanza form, generally set to music similar to popular German secular songs of the period, and sung by the whole congregation during church services. The first such collection appeared in 1524 as the *Little Book of Spiritual Songs,* which includes "A Mighty Fortress." Like John Wesley after him, Luther had no difficulty with appropriating well-known songs and changing the words to suit his religious needs. Thus, the popular ballad "I Must Leave You, Innsbrück" became "I Must Leave You, O World." The chorale tradition was raised to new heights in later Lutheranism by Johann Sebastian Bach.

Whereas Lutheranism developed a rich tradition of vernacular hymns in the sixteenth century—some written by Luther himself—the emerging Anglican and Reformed traditions took the view that God had provided his people with a perfectly adequate set of inspired hymns in the Bible, especially in the Psalms.[32] English Protestantism, following the Reformed rather than Lutheran model, dismissed the idea of worship hymns as implying that God's work was incomplete or inadequate. Worship might therefore include a psalmody, but not a hymnody. Furthermore, early English psalmody was almost exclusively vocal. Most Reformed clergy believed that instruments were appropriate only for secular music, not for public worship. The Psalms were therefore sung without accompaniment—not unlike the plainchant of medieval monasteries.[33]

Wherever possible, the Church of England directed that the words of the Psalms would be chanted, not paraphrased, despite the metrical difficulties thus created for singing. This nonmetrical approach preserved the integrity of the actual words of scripture and required no alteration of the biblical text—always a theologically sensitive issue in the Reformed tradition. In the forms of Anglican chant that developed to meet this theological sensitivity, the first portion of a line was sung on a sustained pitch with harmonic support, with the final syllables resolving in a short series of chords. This form of chant had the advantage of preserving the Hebrew parallelism of the psalms, but was clearly better suited for choirs than for congregational singing.[34]

Nevertheless, the fundamental Protestant desire to involve all believers in the worship of the church soon led to the development of paraphrased Psalms that could be sung by congregations to easily learned tunes.[35] The Psalm text was now retranslated, not in order to achieve total verbal accuracy but to render it in a poetic meter so that it could be sung to tunes. The simplicity of these metered tunes made it easier to sing *and remember* the Psalms—one of the key goals of Protestants.

In his draft ecclesiastical ordinances of 1537, John Calvin proposed that the liturgy could be appropriately enriched by the congregational singing of Psalms. During his period in Strasbourg (1538–41), Calvin managed to find about a dozen Psalms translated into French and versified by Clément Marot. These "metrical Psalms" rapidly became the norm for Reformed Protestantism. The *Geneva Psalter* (1542) included thirty metrical Psalms by Marot, with accompanying musical settings by Louis Bourgeois.[36] Because each Psalm had its own distinct melody, a close correlation could be established between each text and its corresponding tune, which was composed with the specific structure of that Psalm in mind. The *Psalter* was gradually expanded as additional metrical Psalms were added after Marot's death in 1544, by which time he had managed to versify only fifty-two of the Psalms. The remainder of the work was completed by Theodore Beza between 1551 and 1562.

In England, John Day produced a *Book of Psalms* (1562), based on Psalm texts translated by Thomas Sternhold, John Hopkins, and others, with tunes drawn from both the *Geneva Psalter* and familiar English sources, including popular ballads.[37] Day's *Psalms* remained in general use for more than 250 years and is thought to have gone through more than five hundred editions. It later came to be known as the *Old Version* when Nahum Tate and Nicholas Brady brought out their *New Version of the Psalms* (1696). Such was its influence that three of its most common settings—common meter (8.6.8.6), short meter (6.6.8.6) and long meter (8.8.8.8)—became standard, exercising a significant influence on the development of later English hymnody.

Some of these paraphrases became landmarks in their own right. William Kethe (died 1594) wrote a paraphrase of Psalm 100 that was included in Day's *Psalms* and remains widely sung in Christian churches throughout the world:

> All people that on earth do dwell,
> sing to the Lord with cheerful voice:
> Him serve with fear, his praise forth tell,
> come ye before him and rejoice.

Yet perhaps the most famous paraphrase of all is found in the *Scottish Psalter* of 1650, authorized for general use by the Church of Scotland. This collection of paraphrases of all 150 Psalms includes the familiar version of Psalm 23.

> The Lord's my shepherd, I'll not want.
> He makes me down to lie
> In pastures green: he leadeth me
> the quiet waters by.

This paraphrase is often sung to the tune "Crimond," which was composed around 1870 by Jessie Seymour Irvine (1836–87). Happily, the editors' introduction to the Psalm, which somewhat cryptically invites congregations to "be as a daughter of the horse-leech" in their devotion to God, has long since been forgotten.

The work of Isaac Watts (1674–1748) marks a watershed in the development of English worship.[38] Watts, a Congregationalist divine, believed that contemporary worship was in serious need of enrichment.

"The singing of God's praise is the part of worship most clearly related to heaven," he remarked, "but its performance among us is the worst on earth." The problem was not entirely difficult to locate: the Anglican and Reformed use of paraphrases was, in his view, excessively restricted and ill suited to congregational singing. In his *Psalms of David Imitated in the Language of the New Testament* (1719), Watts broke with the long-standing tradition of "close-fitting" paraphrases and produced hymns that were still paraphrases of the biblical Psalms, but much more attuned to the poetic possibilities of the English language. Watts also had theological difficulties with the prevailing approach to the Psalms, which he believed did not do justice to the New Testament theme of Christ as the fulfillment of Israel's hopes. For Watts, it was both necessary and appropriate to incorporate elements of the Christian gospel into his Psalm paraphrases.

Watts's genius is best appreciated by comparing his rendering of Psalm 90 with that of the prevailing "gold standard"—the *Scottish Psalter* (1650):

Scottish Psalter
Lord, thou hast been our dwelling-place,
in generations all.
Before thou ever hadst brought forth,
the mountains great or small.

Watts
O God, our help in ages past,
Our hope in years to come.
Our shelter from the stormy blast,
And our eternal home.

Yet Watts was not content merely to paraphrase the Psalms. In a marked break with the English Protestant tradition of his day, he composed hymns that focused on great theological themes, including the death of Christ. Though saturated in the ideas and phraseology of the Bible, the hymns were not literally biblical, nor could they be described as mere paraphrases. They were independent compositions, written in order to be sung, to be memorable, and above all to be spiritually effective.

Watts's breakthrough was generally ignored by Anglicans and Presbyterians, though taken up with increasing enthusiasm by Congregationalists. Yet his greatest achievement was arguably to lay the
groundwork for perhaps the most significant development in English
hymnody—the work of John and Charles Wesley, who recognized the
role that hymns could play in fostering personal devotion and theological understanding. The evangelical revival of the eighteenth century saw
the hymn transformed into an engine of devotion, renewal, and understanding, appealing to the heart and the mind.

John Wesley (1703–91) had no hesitation in using secular models for
his hymns; these models, he believed, enabled his hymns to relate better
to his audience. An excellent example can be found in his hymnodic
parody of the "Song of Venus," one of the great odes from John
Dryden's patriotic drama *King Arthur* (1691):

Fairest Isle, all isles excelling,
Seat of pleasures, and of loves;
Venus here will choose her dwelling,
And forsake her Cyprian groves.

Exploiting the powerful language and imagery of the ode, Wesley converted it into one of his best-known hymns:

Love divine, all loves excelling,
joy of heaven, to earth come down,
fix in us thy humble dwelling,
all thy faithful mercies crown!

Yet one of Wesley's most significant achievements was to make the
hymn an instrument of theological education. Recognizing that a good
hymn was memorable as well as inspirational, he developed their potential as catechetical aids, combining finely polished phrases with
highly accessible theology. His brother Charles Wesley (1707–88) produced a collection of "Hymns on the Lord's Supper" that served as both
devotional aids and theological explanations of their themes.

The success of the Wesleys was such that the potential of the hymn
could no longer be ignored. From the end of the eighteenth century

onward, hymnody became widely accepted in Anglican and Presbyterian circles, as both an enrichment to worship and an aid to Christian education. A series of landmark publications ensured that Christian worship would be provided with a rich range of resources. The most famous of these in its time was *Hymns Ancient and Modern* (1861), the result of a conversation between two clergymen during a journey on the old Great Western Railway.

In Germany, theological divisions within Protestantism over the role of church music caused no small problems for professional musicians, not least of whom was Johann Sebastian Bach (1685–1750). As Bach's career led him throughout Germany, the musical implications of German confessionalization became increasingly clear. *Cuius regio, eius religio*—and confessional differences entailed radically different attitudes toward music. Himself a devout Lutheran, Bach saw his task as setting the Bible to music in such a way that its meaning and power might be fully appreciated by congregations.[39]

By this time, Lutheranism had developed a rich musical tradition, which Bach augmented, particularly through his cantatas and passions. Bach's last and greatest appointment was as organist and choirmaster at the Lutheran Thomaskirche in Leipzig. His major works that date from this period include the *Magnificat in D*, the *St. John Passion*, the *St. Matthew Passion*, the *B-Minor Mass*, and the *Christmas Oratorio*. But not all of Bach's appointments were in Lutheran contexts.

From 1717 to 1723, Bach served at the Reformed court of Anhalt-Köthen. Though the court was strongly supportive of music, their Reformed outlook was inconsistent with the use of music in public worship. Bach thus found himself focusing on secular works during this period and was unable to express his musical talents liturgically. Undeterred, Bach wrote the six Brandenburg Concertos for the Margrave Christian Ludwig of Brandenburg and the first book of the Well-Tempered Clavier. It proved to be an enormously productive period of his life, even if he was not able to exercise his art in his own favored context—congregational worship.

A more complex situation had arisen earlier, when Bach was appointed organist at Mühlhausen in 1707. Here religious tensions were seething between orthodox Lutheranism and Pietism. Pietism emphasized musical simplicity and had no place for anything other than unadorned motets and musically simple hymns—the musical equivalent of the "plain style" of preaching so favored by English Puritanism. In particular, Pietists were implacably opposed to the cantata, which they regarded as modeled on opera, the most secular of all secular models. For the Pietists, the cantata represented the secularization, even desecration, of sacred music. Unsurprisingly, Bach stayed a mere nine months in Mühlhausen before moving on to more congenial surroundings.

Since then, church music has become increasingly important throughout Protestantism. Its origins have come to mean less than how it enhances worship or reaches out to society at large. The increased acceptance of pipe organs in church enhanced the musical quality of congregational worship, until such forms of worship were regarded as the norm by the beginning of the twentieth century. Once more, this was not without controversy. The installation of an organ in 1828 at Brunswick Methodist Chapel in Leeds caused significant division within the denomination. The fact that the inaugural recital was given by Samuel Sebastian Wesley, one of the most renowned organists of the day and the grandson of Charles Wesley, one of the founders of Methodism, did nothing to abate the storm that ensued.

American Protestantism was slower than its English counterpart to realize the importance of hymnody.[40] Early American Puritan efforts at biblical paraphrasing, though suitable for congregational singing, were not entirely felicitous. Cotton Mather (1663–1728), who was involved in the infamous Salem witch trials, attempted to paraphrase the Psalmist's urging of all creatures of the seas to praise their creator in a hopelessly pedestrian way that nowadays evokes more amusement than reverence:

> Ye monsters of the bubbling deep,
> Your Maker's praises spout;
> Up from the sands ye codlings peep,
> And wag your tails about.

It certainly rhymes. But it's not exactly inspirational. Nevertheless, by the nineteenth century American Protestantism had caught up with its European counterparts and had managed to better them at points. The famous Christmas carol "O Little Town of Bethlehem" was penned in

1868 by Phillips Brooks (1835–1903), an Episcopalian rector in Philadelphia, following a visit to the Holy Land.

American Protestantism produced new genres of religious music for use in worship that were without real parallel in Europe. One of the most remarkable of these was the African American tradition of hymnody, which brought a new dimension to worship.[41] Music now addressed the suffering, deprivation, and hopelessness of life, offering solace. Words and music stressed the consolation brought by the gospel to the marginalized and oppressed:

> There is a balm in Gilead,
> To make the wounded whole;
> There is a balm in Gilead,
> To heal the sin-sick soul.

The African American "spiritual" came into its own after the Civil War, when it began to attract wider attention within the Protestant community.

Equally significantly, the revivalist tradition within American Protestantism realized the importance of hymnody in worship as a means of reaching out beyond the Christian community. Revivalist services used the congregational singing of hymns, psalms, and spirituals to create an awareness of the presence of God and the potential of transformation through the gospel. Dwight L. Moody and Ira David Sankey pioneered the "gospel song"—which could be sung to or sung by the congregation—as a means of teaching and evangelism. Perhaps the most famous of these gospel songs was penned by Robert Lowry (1826–99) in 1864, while he was a pastor in Brooklyn, New York.

> Shall we gather at the river,
> Where bright angel-feet have trod,
> With its crystal tide forever
> Flowing by the throne of God?
>
> *Chorus:*
> Yes, we'll gather at the river,
> The beautiful, the beautiful river;

Gather with the saints at the river
That flows by the throne of God.

Gospel songs were more accessible than the more theologically and musically sophisticated hymns then being written within mainline Protestantism. Revivalism recognized that popular hymnody had the potential to connect with a wide audience, both churched and unchurched.[42] The use of the chorus came to be excoriated as excessively popularist by the more sophisticated within Protestant communities. Yet the chorus proved to be a powerful way of affirming the involvement of everyone in worship, reasserting the principle of the "priesthood of all believers," and, perhaps most importantly, proclaiming the availability of the gospel to all.

This kind of accessible worship song became more and more popular during the twentieth century as the great hymns of the Victorian era began to appear tired and dated. Writers such as Graham Kendrick (born 1950) have pioneered new styles of worship songs that appeal directly to the emotions and imagination and are well adapted to the cultural changes of the age. The rise of the charismatic movement has been accompanied by an intuitive—if not necessarily theologically reflective—awareness of the power of music to assist both worship and devotion, and worship songs have been written for this form of worship.[43] These often lack the theological depth and verbal richness of the hymns of a writer such as John Wesley; nevertheless, they are widely experienced as heightening the congregation's awareness of God in their midst.[44]

The essential point is that Protestantism came into being with a profoundly ambivalent attitude toward music but would later come to embrace it wholeheartedly. The two most significant strands of Protestantism in the 1540s—Lutheranism and the Reformed tradition—had quite different attitudes to the place of music in worship, but as time passed, and the merits of music became increasingly clear, Protestantism as a whole moved decisively and, it seems, irreversibly toward uses of music that some of its sixteenth-century forebears would have regarded as little more than paganism.

This change in attitude toward music is a classic example of the malleability of Protantism. Where multiple interpretations or applications of the Bible are possible, the outcomes are often determined mainly by pragmatic considerations. The sheer utility of hymns, gospel songs, and other forms of music in worship swamped the remaining theological anxieties. Although it is still possible to encounter small traditionalist congregations that tenaciously and defiantly hold fast to early seventeenth-century Puritan forms of worship, these are now rare. The entrepreneurial activities of innovators such as Isaac Watts, John Wesley, and their modern successors have transformed Protestant worship and will continue to do so in the future. Given the nature of Protestantism, it seems certain that its forms of worship will continue to adapt to both the tastes of the moment and the needs of the church.

WORSHIP AND THE VISUAL IN PROTESTANTISM

The medieval Catholic church had a strong sense of the importance of the visual in church life, in relation to both worship and Christian education. Gospel scenes were often painted on church walls to act as visual aids for the illiterate. Altarpieces that provided vivid depictions of the crucifixion enabled worshipers to appreciate the suffering of Christ and the benefits resulting from his death. These were supplemented by panel paintings, decorated pulpits, and pictorial epitaphs, all of which represented the core Catholic understanding of the creation, salvation, and future judgment of the world in a powerful visual manner that captured the imagination.

Early Protestantism was divided over how to use the visual in relation to worship.[45] The emerging Reformed tradition took the view that all images were prohibited by the Bible. Images distracted from the preaching and could easily become objects of worship in themselves. The iconoclasm of this wing of the Reformation was conceptual as much as physical: it was not merely that Reformed churches rejected physical religious images and statues, but that they rejected the very idea that images could serve a fundamental theological role—an idea deeply embedded within Catholicism—as a return to paganism.

Reformed Protestantism had no difficulty with the verbal images of scripture. These, however, were logocentric: they used the word of God as a means to govern and control the human imagination. Images such as God as shepherd (Psalm 23:1) were developed and amplified by the written and spoken word, always under the authority and control of the Bible. Puritan preachers in particular were anxious about what would happen if the untutored imagination of the laity were to encounter visual representations of the divine. Such encounters, they believed, would inevitably lead to idolatry (through confusing the image and its referent) or heterodoxy (through misinterpreting the image).

This point was set out with theological precision by the *Heidelberg Catechism* (1563), which rapidly established itself as normative in matters of Reformed life and thought. This catechism developed the idea that images of God are neither necessary nor helpful for Christian believers. There is an interesting parallel with Islam here, in that both Islam and Reformed theology are concerned that images of God meant to aid in the worship of God could become objects of worship in themselves. The traditional question-and-answer format that follows is characteristic of Protestant catechisms of the age. The discussion is based on the Second Commandment, which is translated in the Geneva Bible (1560) as: "Thou shalt make thee no graven image, neither any similitude of things that are in heaven above, neither that are in the earth beneath, nor that are in the waters under the earth" (Exodus 20:4).

Question 96: What does God require in the next commandment?
Answer: That we should not portray God in any way, nor worship him in any other manner than he has commanded in his Word.

Question 97: So should we not make any use of images?
Answer: God cannot and should not be depicted in any way. As for creatures, although they may indeed be depicted, God forbids making use of or having any likeness of them, in order to worship them or to use them to serve him.

Question 98: But should we allow pictures instead of books in churches, for the benefit of the unlearned?
Answer: No. For we should not presume to be wiser than God, who does not want Christendom to be taught by means of dumb idols, but through the living preaching of his Word.

The *Heidelberg Catechism* emphasized that knowledge of God and the presence of God are mediated through the word—through the reading of the Bible and preaching. This strongly logocentric understanding of the mediation of the divine held that anything that distracts from attentive listening to the public reading of the Bible and the exposition of its contents is to be removed as a matter of principle.

For instance, the internal walls of Calvinist churches were whitewashed. This practice seems to have served three functions. First, it eliminated distractions. Where pre-Reformation churches were being converted for Protestant use, existing murals or ornamentation were simply blotted out. Second, the use of whitewash symbolized cleansing and purification. This was an important principle in the first phase of Reformed church practice. For Zwingli, whitewashing the pagan art of Catholic churches was a visible sign of their having been cleansed and rededicated to the worship of the true God.[46] Third, whitewash symbolized light; in much the same way the Reformed churches preferred clear glass in church windows, whitewashed walls were devoid of distracting ornamentation or illustration.

At times, the Reformed attitude toward images verges on iconophobia—a fear that the open, conceptually porous nature of images lacked the closed, conceptual precision of tight theological arguments.[47] Although the historical context of Calvinism limited its engagement with Orthodoxy, there is no doubt that its fundamental theological trajectory was hostile to the use of icons in worship or personal devotion.[48]

Lutheranism took a fundamentally different approach from the outset. While Luther may have objected to some of the themes depicted in the ornamentation of Catholic churches, he had no problems with the medium itself. Many traditional Catholic images were abandoned, most notably Mary and the saints. In their place, Lukas Cranach the Elder and his school developed altarpieces and other visual forms that affirmed Lutheran themes. Alongside traditional depictions of the crucifixion, we find representations of the dialectic between the law and the gospel. Those who found this polarity difficult to assimilate at the conceptual level could enjoy—and even understand—the idea when expressed visually.[49] The law is portrayed as barren, leading only to death and condemnation; the gospel, however, brings life and hope.

The subsequent development of Protestant attitudes to the use of the visual arts in church architecture in general, and to worship in particular, shows a pattern not dissimilar to that observed in relation to music. Most Protestants, especially Puritans in both the Old and New Worlds, remained hostile toward any form of visual adornment or ornamentation of churches and to the use of visual aids to worship or devotion.[50] Yet as time passed theological resistance to the use of such devices began to wane. Stained-glass windows began to appear in Reformed churches. The importance of ecclesiastical architecture in enhancing the experience of worship began to be appreciated. Especially within Lutheranism and Anglicanism, an understanding developed that the beauty of a church interior could be seen as a mirror of the beauty of God.

Yet one point must be made in closing these reflections on the place of the visual in Protestant worship. During my frequent trips to Zurich to research the origins of the Reformation, I have been a regular visitor to the city's "Great Minster," which abuts the libraries in which I have conducted much of my research. I have often sat within this spacious building, which dates back to the twelfth century and was totally reordered under Zwingli. Its brilliantly, almost clinically, white interior is austere. The size and location of the great pulpit expresses the theology of Zwingli and his successors: God is known and encountered through a text—the Bible. The forbidding, frigid elegance of the building gently insinuates the inadequacy and illegitimacy of expecting to encounter God in any other place and in any other way.

I admire that simplicity and elegance, and I understand both its historical origins and its symbolism. Yet today, when that history has largely been forgotten and the symbolism has ceased to be meaningful for so many, the building seems instead to point to an absent God, a God who does not speak, a God who cannot be experienced. It is not unlike the poetry of the Anglican priest-poet R. S. Thomas (1913–2000), who found the silence of an empty church to be a disturbing expression of the absence of God.[51]

As the English rationalist critic Thomas Hobbes pointed out, this Protestant God might as well not exist, since his supposed existence seems to make very little difference to anything. A permanently absent God is about as much use as a dead God. If the existence of God makes little or no impact upon the experiences of everyday life, the business of living might as well be conducted without reference to him. Hugo Grotius (1583–1645), the great Dutch Protestant lawyer, noted that the end result of all this was a world in which people lived *etsi Deus non daretur*—"as if God did not exist."

The problem for this strand of Protestantism is that its alternatives represent God as being accessible, capable of being encountered and experienced in the here and now. For example, seventeenth-century Catholicism offered an imaginative alternative to this aesthetically severe Protestant approach to sacred spaces. Once the Council of Trent had countered the theological threat posed by Protestantism, Catholicism turned its attention to exploiting its aesthetic deficiencies. One of its chief weapons was the development of the Baroque style, which flourished during the period 1600 to 1750.[52]

Baroque churches were much larger in scale than their predecessors, and their interiors were sumptuously decorated with sculpture and paintings. Baroque church interiors were designed to elicit an immediate, emotional response from congregations and visitors through their dramatic lighting effects, symmetry, dynamic architectural forms, and lavish decoration. The idea was that a church interior should be a visible, tangible embodiment of the glory of God, seamlessly integrated with the preaching and sacramental life of the church. When this style of architecture was integrated with the baroque musical style, the holistic vision of the beauty of God and the gospel thus presented posed a formidable challenge to forms of Protestantism that remained suspicious of any use of music or visual arts in worship.

The challenge to this form of Protestantism was not limited to Catholicism. The rise of Pietism in the seventeenth and eighteenth centuries posed an internal threat. This Protestant style, in reaction against the indirect, word-centered approach to Christian spirituality, held that the essence of a "living faith" was direct experience of God. This emphasis on the existential certainty of knowing God is expressed in Charles Wesley's hymn *Free Grace*, written shortly after his conversion in 1738:

> Still the small inward Voice I hear,
> That whispers all my Sins forgiv'n;

Still the atoning Blood is near,
    That quench'd the Wrath of hostile Heav'n:
I *feel* the Life his Wounds impart;
    I *feel* my Savior in my Heart.

The weight given to the subjective perception of the living Christ in the believer ("I *feel* my Savior in my heart") was a corrective against what was seen in sharp contrast as a somewhat cerebral "book-knowledge" of God. A very similar point must be made concerning Pentecostalism, a more recent form of Protestantism that insists on the immediate accessibility of God through the Holy Spirit. We consider the implications of the dramatic rise of Pentecostalism in the final part of this work.

In this chapter, we have considered the internal aspects of faith, examining how the life of Protestantism has been shaped by its controlling beliefs and values. But what of the society within which Protestantism is located? In what way do its beliefs and values influence culture in general? Our attention now turns to the complex interaction between Protestantism and Western culture.

I 2

Protestantism and the Shaping of Western Culture

Christianity has always had an ambivalent relationship with its cultural context. As Christianity became a growing presence within the Roman Empire during the first three centuries of its existence, it was regularly regarded with hostility and suspicion and occasionally even persecuted by the authorities.[1] So how were Christians, who often held high public office, to understand their relationship with the culture at large?

The rise of monasticism was a particularly significant development in shaping Christian attitudes toward culture. Antony of Egypt and others believed that life in the world distracts people from the love and praise of God and leads to their corruption rather than salvation. With-drawal from the world was the only solution. These attitudes are expressed in the title and contents of Thomas à Kempis's spiritual classic, *The Imitation of Christ and of Contempt of the World and All Its Vanities.*

As Protestantism gained prominence in western Europe and beyond, it was forced to address the question of how it interacted with its cultural environment. The question had, of course, never been entirely absent from Protestant reflection. Martin Luther's theology of "the two kingdoms" can be seen as an attempt to give intellectual justification to his own somewhat complex relationship with Frederick the Wise, just

The burning of Thomas Cranmer, Archbishop of Canterbury, 1563. From "Actes and monuments" by John Foxe (1516–87).

as John Calvin was obliged to develop a theology that was consistent with the social realities of Geneva. Neither Luther nor Calvin, of course, could control his cultural context; each was obliged to work within that context, while aspiring to its transformation. Anabaptism found itself in conflict with sixteenth-century culture at large and believed that its own identity and agendas were best served through withdrawal and disengagement with the world.

Those tensions remain today. In twenty-first-century America, many Protestants are involved in cultural activities and debates, while others withdraw from these entirely, seeing them as "worldly" or leading to compromise. Today Protestantism displays perhaps the greatest range of attitudes to culture of any religious group, Christian or otherwise. To understand the variety of Protestant attitudes to culture at large, we shall explore a number of "models" of how Christianity relates to culture that have been adopted by Protestants. Each is based on a particular reading of the Bible, and each leads to quite a different attitude toward culture at large.

So what is "culture"? The word is often used in a neutral sense to mean something like the integrated system of learned behavior patterns that are characteristic of the members of a society, or the total way of life of a people.[2] The word can also be used in a more nuanced sense, as in T. S. Eliot's famous remark, "Culture may even be described simply as that which makes life worth living."[3] For our purposes in this discussion, we take the word in its neutral sense to refer to the intellectual and social environment within which humanity exists. In a later chapter, we consider Protestantism's relationship with culture in Eliot's sense of the term.

RELIGION AND CULTURE: PROTESTANT MODELS OF INTERACTION

The classic analysis of the types of relationships to emerge between Christianity and its cultural context was the work of the American Protestant theologian Richard Niebuhr (1894–1962). In 1951 Niebuhr published *Christ and Culture,* which sets out five models that historic Christianity developed in reflecting on its relationship to its environment.[4] Although Niebuhr clearly had a preference for the fifth of these models (to be described later), his work gave an empathetic account of all the existing possibilities, identifying both their biblical foundations and the nature of their application.

Niebuhr was concerned with Christianity as a whole, not specifically with Protestantism. Yet a close reading of the book reveals an important point that has been confirmed by all subsequent scholarship. *Protestantism did not introduce any new models for understanding its interaction with culture.* It worked within existing Christian paradigms, adapting and developing them to meet its concerns—but not developing new models of its own. Protestantism may prefer certain models over others, allowing differences of emphasis to be identified. Yet there is no sign of radical innovation in this area.

In what follows, we consider each of the five models identified by Niebuhr, noting the Protestant writers and movements that embraced them and attempting to describe their implications for Protestantism's broader relationships with society at large.

Christ Against Culture

This model asserts that there is a fundamental opposition between Christianity and culture. The relationship is one of antagonism, whether arising from culture's hostility toward the church or the inverse. Such attitudes were found in some early church writers, such as Tertullian, and in monasticism. In the Protestant tradition, this attitude was initially associated with the Radical Reformation and writers such as Menno Simons and Jakob Hutter. The instinct to separate from a fallen culture is particularly well exemplified in some contemporary American Protestant movements that trace their origins back to the Radical Reformation.

The best known of these is the Amish, a diverse group of communities originating from the teaching of Menno Simons but given a new sense of direction under Jakob Amman in the seventeenth century.[5] Their rejection of contemporary American culture led them to retain many aspects of late seventeenth-century rural European communities. This ethos is not primarily based on nostalgia or on a particular affection for an identity-giving past. It is best seen as a way of developing practices and behaviors that isolate the Amish from modern American culture and hence make a pointed statement about their identity and values. The best-known Amish communities are located in Lancaster County, Pennsylvania; other Amish groups exist elsewhere.

This attitude toward culture is also found within modern American Protestant fundamentalism. The roots of this attitude can be traced back to John Nelson Darby (1800–1882), who founded the Plymouth Brethren and exercised a significant influence within conservative Protestant circles in the United Kingdom and North America. The rise of fundamentalism is best seen as due to social and political circumstances peculiar to the United States in the 1920s (we consider this movement in more detail later). For our purposes in this section, the important point is that this group is perhaps the best example of a community whose attitudes and values are shaped by the "Christ against culture" model.

The Christ of Culture

This model argues that the Christian faith represents what "the world values most dearly," and its aim is to adjust and accommodate Christianity to be in tune with cultural norms. "Christ is identified with what men conceive to be their finest ideals, their noblest institutions, and their best philosophy." As such judgments are inevitably historically contingent and subject to cultural geography, this approach is probably best regarded as leading to temporary adjustments that are modified still further over time.

The best example of this assimilationist approach is the movement generally referred to as "liberal Protestantism," which began to emerge in Germany at the beginning of the nineteenth century. Initially associated with the great Berlin theologian F. D. E. Schleiermacher, the movement achieved its most significant successes under A. B. Ritschl and Adolf von Harnack. Classic liberal Protestantism arose in response to a growing perception that Christian faith and theology alike required reconstruction in the light of modern knowledge, attitudes, and values. To use Niebuhr's language, the "finest ideals" of the nineteenth century seemed very different from those of the sixteenth century. Protestantism needed to adapt if it was to survive. The increasingly positive reception given to Charles Darwin's theory of natural selection (popularly known as the "Darwinian theory of evolution") in the 1870s created a climate in which some elements of traditional Christian theology (such as the doctrine of the seven days of creation) seemed to be increasingly untenable.

Leading liberal Protestant writers argued that a reconstruction of belief "in the light of modern knowledge" was essential if Christianity was to remain a serious intellectual and cultural option in the modern world. For this reason, they demanded a degree of freedom in relation to the doctrinal inheritance of Christianity, on the one hand, and traditional methods of biblical interpretation, on the other. Where traditional ways of interpreting scripture, or traditional beliefs, seemed to be compromised by developments in human knowledge, it was imperative that those interpretations be discarded or adapted to bring them into line with what was now known about the world.

The theological implications of this shift in direction were considerable. A number of Christian beliefs came to be regarded as seriously out of line with modern cultural norms; these beliefs were either abandoned, as resting upon outdated or mistaken presuppositions, or reinterpreted in a manner more conducive to the spirit of the age. For example, the traditional Christian doctrine of the divinity of Christ was reinterpreted as an affirmation of Jesus exemplifying qualities that humanity as a whole could hope to emulate. Jesus thus differed from humanity in degree, not in kind.

These ideas proved to be very influential in Germany, England, and the United States.[6] Their critics regarded them, however, as a dilution of the essence of Protestantism that reduced it to a mere endorsement of prevailing cultural norms. All that remained of classic Protestantism, they suggested, was "an aroma from an empty bottle" (Erik Peterson). Liberal Protestants retorted by arguing that they had rescued the church from cultural and intellectual irrelevance.

Christ Above Culture

The third approach identified by Niebuhr tries to synthesize the Protestant faith with contemporary culture norms. Whereas liberal Protestantism tends to accommodate its ideas and values to those of secular culture, the "Christ above culture" approach aims to subordinate those ideas to Christian concerns. This view holds that the relation between Christ and culture takes the form of a convergence of nature and grace, without significant cultural Christian accommodation and reduction of the nature of Christ or the gospel to contemporary norms. Niebuhr argues that this approach, which he finds particularly in the writings of the great scholastic theologian Thomas Aquinas, synthesizes elements from the gospel and the culture into a single structure of thought and conduct.

One exponent of this approach identified by Niebuhr is the American Protestant theologian Paul Tillich, who set out to correlate the fundamental questions asked by contemporary culture with the answer provided by the Christian revelation.[7] Tillich's synthesis is set out with particular clarity in an essay of 1956 in which he explored the relation of the church and culture: "The Church judges culture, including its own forms of life. For its forms are created by culture, as its substance makes culture possible. The Church and culture are within, not alongside each other. And the Kingdom of God includes both while transcending both."[8] The basic features of the "Christ above culture" approach can be seen clearly in this extract. Niebuhr himself expressed concerns about this approach, noting in particular its tendency toward cultural conservatism and the risk of institutionalizing Christ and the gospel.

Christ and Culture in Paradox

The fourth approach identified by Niebuhr holds that individual Christians and the church exist in a tension with the world, as a result of its fallenness. The Christian must be thought of as belonging to two, quite distinct realms, usually designated as "the temporal" and "the spiritual." Christians cannot evade the resulting tension between these two authorities. Niebuhr sees this approach exemplified in Luther, particularly his doctrine of "the two kingdoms."[9]

As noted earlier, Luther rejected the medieval distinction between the "temporal" and "spiritual" estates. In its place, Luther developed an alternative theory of spheres of authority, based upon a distinction between the "two kingdoms," or the "two governments," which refer to the "spiritual" and the "worldly" government of society. God's spiritual government is effected through the word of God and the guidance of the Holy Spirit. God's worldly government is effected through kings, princes, and magistrates and through the use of the sword and the civil law. Whether these princes or magistrates are true believers or not, they still perform a divine role (Romans 13:1–7; 1 Peter 2:13–14).

Luther insists that God has ordained that order shall be imposed upon creation, for the maintenance of peace and the repression of sin. There are three hierarchies, or "orders," within a Christian society: the household or family, with the father as the head (reflecting the paternalism of Luther's age); the princes and magistrates, who exercise secular authority; and the clergy, who exercise spiritual authority. All these are founded on the word of God and reflect the divine will for the structuring and preservation of the worldly realm.

In the end, Luther's social ethic seems to suggest that two totally different moralities exist side by side: a private Christian ethic, reflecting the rule of love embodied in the Sermon on the Mount; and a public morality, based upon force. The tensions are manifest, and the result is a permanent tension.[10] For Luther, that is the inevitable outcome of the nature of reality. This approach does, however, raise some difficult questions, as we shall see when we consider the German church crisis of the 1930s, which many commentators argue arose directly from Luther's inadequate social ethic.

Christ the Transformer of Culture

Niebuhr's fifth and final category is clearly the one that he himself preferred. Here the theme is conversion. Although Niebuhr includes Augustine in this category, most of those he cites are Protestants—John Calvin, John Wesley, Jonathan Edwards and the Puritan tradition, and the Swiss theologian Karl Barth. All of these "try to convert the values and goals of secular culture into the service of the kingdom of God." Here Christ is seen as converting people within their cultures and societies, not apart from them. This approach rejects isolating the church from the world without accommodating central Christian truths to the values of contemporary culture. While taking a more positive attitude toward culture than the paradoxical dualists, it holds that culture stands under God's judgment.

This fifth category can be seen in the works of one of the twentieth century's most significant Protestant missionary theologians—Lesslie Newbigin.[11] In his 1952 Kerr Lectures, Newbigin commented on the significance of the breakdown of Christendom for Christian life and witness.[12] For Newbigin, the notion of "Christendom" meant "the synthesis between the Gospel and the culture of the western part of the European peninsula of Asia" that had developed during the Middle Ages and remained in place, though in a weakened form—in other words, Niebuhr's "Christ above culture" model. Newbigin argued that Christianity had become so domesticated within European culture that it had become little more than a form of folk religion. To remedy the situation, Newbigin called for the rediscovery of a missionary perspective aimed at the conversion of culture.

Given this diversity of attitudes toward culture on the part of Protestants, both historical and contemporary, it is to be expected that a similar range of attitudes should be expected in relation to the question of social engagement. To what extent should Protestants become engaged with social issues? And which side should they take? We consider some instructive examples in what follows.

PROTESTANTISM AND SOCIAL ENGAGEMENT

Recent studies have noted that most of the intellectual and spiritual leaders of medieval Christianity were monastic, isolated from many of the harsher realities of everyday life by the walls of their monasteries and convents. Protestantism chose to inhabit the more dangerous world of the city and marketplace, exposing its thinkers to pressures and problems that their Catholic forebears had not been required to consider. It is of the utmost importance to appreciate that the intellectual lights of the first phase of Protestantism—Martin Luther, Huldrych Zwingli, Martin Bucer, Heinrich Bullinger, and John Calvin—lived, thought, and wrote in the midst of urban society, producing theology that possesses a refreshingly earthly quality.

Yet the transition from the monastery to the marketplace was dangerous. Protestantism was exposed to precisely the dangers, threats, and problems that had led to the emergence of the monastic movement in the first place. How could Christianity maintain its integrity when it was now immersed in, and confronted with, the challenges of the world? As Roland Bainton, one of the most distinguished analysts of the early sixteenth century, remarked, when Christianity takes itself seriously, it must either renounce or master the world.[13] Given the political realities of the age, Protestantism could only aspire to mastery; unlike Islam, it never achieved religious mastery of the secular but was obliged to work with more or less sympathetic secular rulers.

At first sight, this last statement may seem puzzling to those familiar with some popular accounts of Calvin's Geneva. Surely this was a theocracy in which Calvin ruled the city with a rod of iron? This outdated stereotype is in need of radical revision. Those who speak loosely about Calvin's "theocracy" in Geneva need to be reminded that all secular power, and not a little religious power, remained firmly in the hands of the city council throughout his lifetime. Calvin's successes and failures at Geneva can be accounted for largely through his shifting relationships with the real source of authority within the city. Calvin's idea of "theocracy" was intellectual, not practical or institutional; it related to the idea that all power and authority are derived from God. But God, as Calvin knew perfectly well from his New Testament, was prepared to work through secular rulers, then as now.

The real problem for Protestantism can be explored using a biblical analogy that featured prominently in the movement's reflections on the issues. Jesus of Nazareth declared that his followers were the "salt of the earth." But what, he asked, if that salt were to lose its saltiness (Matthew 5:13)? It was no longer of any use. Perhaps Jesus was referring to rock salt, whose saltiness can be leeched out by dampness. But whatever the real-life model for the image, its power is undeniable. What if a movement whose identity depends upon its distinctiveness loses precisely that distinguishing mark of identification? What if engagement with the world led Protestantism to become indistinguishable from the world, with only traces of its saline origins remaining? How could Protestantism remain in the world without becoming of the world—adopting the world's standards, norms, language, and values and losing its own, whether accidentally or deliberately?

Two Protestant strategies for coping with the problematic of the ordinary emerged in its first formative period and have remained characteristic of the movement ever since. Each has its strengths and weaknesses. In what follows, we consider each of these strategies before going on to consider some illuminating case studies of Protestant engagement with society and the issues that these raised.

The first strategy, initially associated primarily with the Anabaptists, can be seen as a continuation of the monastic model, though with subtle modifications. As Anabaptism became the object of increasing suspicion on the part of monarchs, city councils, and mainline Protestant leaders in the late 1520s, its instinct was to form a counterculture. Anabaptists rejected the coercive structures of contemporary society, refusing to swear oaths, hold any magisterial office, serve in any military capacity, or bear arms.

Such a radically apolitical and world-renouncing attitude inevitably entailed separation from the world. Perhaps using as a model the pre-Constantinian church—which existed within, but not as part of, the Roman Empire—the radicals often conceived of their communities as an "alternative godly society" within, but not part of, the greater society surrounding them. Like Israel before them, they insisted on separating from the nations, for fear of becoming like them.[14] Purity and integrity were best—indeed only—maintained by withdrawal from a fallen world, which would otherwise absorb them utterly, leeching out their saltiness.

Similar approaches can be found in certain—but certainly not all—forms of Pietism. It must be stressed that many Pietists were social activists, as the history of early Methodism makes abundantly clear.[15] Yet one of the traits that came to be associated with many Pietists was what might be termed the "privatization of religion"—that is, the restriction · of religious involvement to matters of spirituality. This approach holds that involvement in social or political issues is "worldly" or "corrupting." Discipleship entails disengagement from the world. The approach is particularly associated with Protestant fundamentalism in the early twentieth century, which emphasized the need for a dividing wall between church and society in the face of the increased secularization of the United States.

The strengths of this approach must be acknowledged immediately. It unquestionably serves to maintain Christian distinctiveness and integrity by relieving Christian communities of any sense of obligation to mimic the language, values, or customs of the world. As the recent works of Stanley Hauerwas and John Howard Yoder have demonstrated, such approaches have enormous potential for the life and thought of the church.[16] One particular strength of this approach lies in the possibilities it offers for exploring nonviolent approaches to social existence—or, indeed, aspects of Christian theology that have often rested on an analysis of violence, such as theories of the atonement.[17]

Yet there are weaknesses and risks to this approach. These are best illustrated by the concerns that led to the emergence of "neo-evangelicalism" in the United States during the late 1940s, in response to the perceived failures of fundamentalism. As we shall see later, fundamentalism arose in reaction to secularism within American culture in the 1920s and led many conservative Protestants to withdraw from any form of social or cultural engagement. In his *Uneasy Conscience of Modern Fundamentalism* (1947), Carl F. H. Henry argues that fundamentalism was too otherworldly and anti-intellectual to gain a hearing among the educated public and that it was also unwilling to concern itself with exploring how Christianity related to culture and social life.[18]

The latter failing had simply led to the exclusion of any Christian presence in culture and society. This essay in fundamentalist self-criticism saw Henry—writing as a fundamentalist—expressing considerable misgivings about the directions the movement had taken and about its obvious failure to achieve its goals. As Millard J. Erickson points out, it had become increasingly clear that fundamentalism totally failed to turn back the rising tide of modernism, that it had not achieved any significant impact upon the thought-world of its day, and that it had spurned the social problems of its time.[19] The watchword of the "new evangelicalism" would be *engagement*—cultural, social, and intellectual.

With the benefit of hindsight, this can be seen as having done much to shape the contemporary political landscape of the United States. The emergence of the "Religious Right" is one of many important results of this new attitude, which led politically conservative Protestants of the 1980s to emulate the political engagement of left-leaning activists of the 1960s.[20] The election of George W. Bush as the forty-third president of the United States was widely interpreted by political commentators as the outcome of a new commitment to political activism on the part of Protestants who had hitherto regarded it as pointless or a distraction from the real business of life.

The program advocated by the new evangelicalism in 1947 was, in many ways, a return to the approach advocated by the mainline Protestant constituency throughout the 1540s and 1550s. Here we find an emphasis on engagement subtly balanced by an insistence on maintenance of identity. Protestants can be active in the world, while being safeguarded in their identity and calling through the preaching and support of the church. If the world is a wasteland, the church is the oasis. If the world is desalinated and desalinating, the church is the saltcellar.

The theological foundations of this delicate balancing act were developed by Calvin, who constructed a sophisticated dialectic between faith and the world that allowed scope for positive action in the world while identifying and averting the risks such action entailed.[21] In Calvin's thought, Christians should be encouraged to invest in and commit themselves to the world. There was no place in his thinking for the medieval monastic attitude toward society, which led to individuals renouncing the world while the institutions they served affirmed it. Yet Christians, he warned, while immersing themselves in the affairs and anxieties of the world, must learn to keep it at a critical distance. Outward investment in and commitment to the world must be accompanied by inward detachment and the fostering of a critical attitude toward the secular. Believers must immerse themselves in the secular sphere, but not allow themselves to be submerged by it. "We are to learn to pass through this world as though it were a foreign country, treating lightly all earthly things and declining to set our hearts upon them."[22]

Yet the weakness of this strategy is clear and cannot be evaded. Those who seem to master the world are often those who have actually been mastered by it. Those who are counted successes by the world are often those who have capitulated to its norms. Latent within Calvinism is a purely profane approach to life, in that the failure to maintain a proper dialectic between God and the world leads to the collapse of the divine into the secular. Calvinist moral, economic, social, and political structures and values, although firmly grounded in theology, could all too easily become detached and independent from those theological foundations. The emancipation of such structures and values from faith itself through cultural erosion is one of the most significant aspects of the Western reception and assimilation of Calvinism, especially in North America. We shall have occasion to return to this point when considering a possible link between Protestantism and secularization.

We have considered the two families of attitudes that emerged within Protestantism as it sought to maintain its identity and fulfill its calling in the modern world, and the analysis thus far calls out for some examples to illustrate the points being made. In what follows, we offer a brief consideration of some illuminating episodes from Protestant history. We begin by considering Protestant attitudes to slavery.

The issue of slavery was at the heart of one the most important and difficult debates within American Protestantism in the nineteenth century. It proved immensely divisive, causing political tensions and bringing some denominations to the point of near-schism. At the heart of the debate lay a fundamental issue of biblical interpretation. Did the Bible legitimize slavery? Most Protestants in antebellum America assumed it did. Did not Noah's curse on Ham (Genesis 9:25) justify the practice?[23] The Bible did not condemn slavery; it merely regulated it. Little wonder that Jefferson Davis (1808–89), president of the Confederate States of

America, could declare that slavery was "sanctioned in the Bible, in both Testaments, from Genesis to Revelation."

Abolitionism had gained ground in England in the late eighteenth century, aided to no small extent by growing Protestant opposition to the practice. William Wilberforce was a particularly significant and influential voice in the debate.[24] Were not all peoples created in the image of God? The idea of a person being treated as "chattel" seemed increasingly unacceptable in the opening decades of the nineteenth century.

In the United States, a significant polarization emerged. The northern states moved to abolish slavery in the years following the American Revolution as increasing numbers of former slave owners, such as Benjamin Franklin, changed their views on the matter. The Second Great Awakening, which rekindled religious fervor in much of the nation, saw new religious pressure for abolition. Oberlin College in Ohio was founded as an abolitionist institution. In the South, abolitionists broke away from mainline Methodism to form the Free Methodist Church. African American Christians were a particularly significant voice urging the churches to read the Old Testament in the light of the New and abolish slavery.

Yet the dominant position in the South was strongly pro-slavery, and the Bible was used to defend this entrenched position. Theologically, the arguments used by the pro-slavery lobby represent a fascinating illustration and condemnation of how the Bible may be used to support a notion by reading the text within a rigid interpretative framework that forces predetermined conclusions on the text.[25]

The defeat of the Confederacy in the Civil War inevitably led to the final abolition of slavery throughout the Union. Yet a lingering question remains, which hangs awkwardly over Protestantism. Many respected Protestant intellectuals and statesmen of the nineteenth century—including Princeton's venerable theologian Charles B. Hodge—supported slavery *on biblical grounds,* often dismissing abolitionists as liberal progressives who did not take the Bible seriously. Might not the same mistakes be made all over again, this time over other issues?[26]

A second example illuminates the tensions resulting from tendencies within Protestantism that pull in opposite directions. As we shall see presently, the emergence of a strong "work ethic" during the formative phase of Protestantism led to an emphasis on moral activism that approved the generation of wealth but not its expenditure. One outcome was the rise of a "spirit of capitalism"; another, although in this case less direct, was the notion of a "gospel of wealth." This latter belief held that prosperity was a sign of divine favor. Although this often represented little more than a loose assumption on the part of some Protestants, it was actively developed by some into what is widely known as the "health and wealth" movement.[27] The Bible is interpreted to mean that financial success and personal well-being are the direct results of God's approval of an individual.

So what of the poor? Is their plight the result of God's disfavor? What about the many biblical texts that emphasize God's special care and love for the widowed, orphaned, impoverished, and dispossessed? Is the alleviation of poverty tantamount to the subversion of God's will? For some (wealthy and healthy) Protestants in the 1890s and beyond, this was indeed the case. Leave things alone, they argued.

Others disagreed, seeing themselves as driven and compelled by the biblical testimony to work for the relief of the poor. The origins of the Salvation Army lie in such concerns for the poor, whose situation its founders believed could be alleviated by combining evangelism and social action. William Booth's remarkable book *In Darkest England* drew attention to the social deprivation experienced by millions in England in the 1890s.[28] After the movement became established in the United States in 1880, it pursued its twin tacks of revivalist evangelism and social action. Salvation Army bands marched through the main thoroughfares of Chicago and New York, its preachers proclaimed the good news of redemption, and its social workers cared for unwed mothers and women who had been deserted by their husbands.[29]

The "Social Gospel" movement in the United States also attempted to address these issues.[30] Many Protestant clergy were concerned at their churches' failure to care for the urban poor. Washington Gladden (1836–1918) and Walter Rauschenbusch (1861–1918) both took the view that unrestricted capitalism was the cause of urban poverty, which in turn caused other social problems. Rauschenbusch published what is now widely seen as the manifesto of this movement—*The Social Gospel* (1908).[31] Although political socialism never gained a significant following in the

United States, the attitudes of the Social Gospel movement paralleled those of the movements generally known as "Christian socialism" elsewhere.

Social concern within Protestantism has been forged and developed in other contexts as well. The most important of these in recent years has been the emergence of Pentecostalism, which is often characterized by a strong sense of social concern for the marginalized and the poor.[32] Although this is especially evident in Pentecostal ministries in the developing world, it has also become characteristic of such ministries in urban America. The 23,000-member West Angeles Church of God in Christ is heavily involved in social outreach programs focusing on low-income housing, the care of seniors, and recovery ministry. Such social engagement is not seen as peripheral or supplementary to gospel concerns, but as integral to the Christian vision of healing and renewal—a characteristic emphasis of Pentecostal spirituality.

These examples illustrate both the possibilities and the tensions that accompany Protestant attempts to engage society—above all, the difficulties that arise from interpreting and applying the biblical material to social issues. The nature of Protestantism is such that these difficulties can be expected to continue, precisely because of the lack of any widespread agreement over the principles that should govern its engagement with society. Similar problems also arise in relation to an issue of ongoing significance for Protestantism, to which we now turn—the question of the relationship of church and state.

PROTESTANTISM ON CHURCH AND STATE

The birth of Protestantism coincided with the beginning of the end of Christendom—the great medieval vision of the essential unity of church and state, with individual monarchs ruling their territories, all presided over by the pope. From the outset, Protestantism was bound to cause political ripples. Perhaps it should be no cause for surprise that the first mainline Protestant reformers adopted models for understanding the relation of church and state that were adapted to the political realities of their regions.

Luther's doctrine of the "two kingdoms" gave the state (especially "the godly prince") a major say in the running of the church. Zwingli adopted an approach to authority and government within the church that bore a remarkable resemblance to the civic authority structures at Zurich in the 1520s. Calvin's strong republican convictions may have been connected to the fact that the city of Geneva, where he ministered from 1536, had declared itself a republic in 1535. English Protestantism gladly recognized the monarch as the "head of the church," until a theologically prudent Elizabeth I changed the terminology as a matter of theological diplomacy. She and her successors would be the "supreme governors" of the national church.

We see here the political realism of early Protestantism. The price paid in order to secure its reforming measures was to give religious legitimacy to existing authorities. They, in their turn, averted the risk of revolution—always seen as a possibility after the seizure of the German city of Münster by radicals in 1534—but at the price of giving protection to the new religious authorities and enforcing their wishes when this was deemed necessary or expedient. The political conservatism of sixteenth-century Protestantism has often been noted; it is not difficult to understand it. Only the Anabaptists chose to stand apart from this cozy relationship of church and state, believing that something vital had been compromised. The church, they believed, had lost its way after Constantine, the first Christian Roman emperor. A fundamentally corrupting alliance had been forged then between the church and political power.

This point is of major importance in relation to the rise of atheism in western Europe, which was often a consequence of the perception that the Protestant churches enjoyed a disproportionate status and influence.[33] Karl Marx's criticism of German Lutheranism during the 1840s is a particularly significant example. Protestantism was seen to be privileged and powerful; what better way was there to undermine its conservative political influence than to destroy the ideas upon which it ultimately rested?

The situation in the United States, following the Revolution of 1776, was quite different. The constitutional separation of church and state prevented any Protestant denomination from gaining "established" status and created a level playing field for Christian groups. Alexis de Tocqueville noted the implications of this fact and suggested that the American separation of church and state was directly related to the

American interest in religion—in stark contrast with the situation he knew back in Europe.

The serious consequences of Protestantism's ambivalent relationship with power are best seen in the German church crisis of the 1930s. Adolf Hitler came to power in Germany in 1933 and promptly set about the "Nazification" of German culture. This was relatively easily presented in terms of the renewal of German culture, an effort welcomed by some within liberal Protestantism, which assumed a close link between religion and culture. Nazi rule was at first welcomed by many German churchmen, partly because it offered a bulwark against the ominous state atheism sponsored by the Soviet Union, and partly because it seemed to offer a new cultural role for religion. Indeed, many churchmen—such as Paul Althaus, Emanuel Hirsch, and Gerhard Kittel—supported Hitler.[34]

A furious debate broke out between the "Confessing Church," led by figures such as Martin Niemöller, who were not willing to cooperate with Hitler in church matters, and the "German Christians," who saw Hitler as the savior of the German nation and church. There were unquestionably many Protestants who took a courageous stance against the Nazi regime, including Dietrich Bonhoeffer, who was executed in the final phase of the Second World War. Yet the Protestant churches as institutions are widely criticized for having failed to provide a credible and cogent alternative to Nazism.

The Nazification of German culture showed up the fatal vulnerability of any form of Christianity that took its lead from contemporary cultural norms. Since liberal Protestantism mirrored the norms of contemporary culture, it had no adequate basis for critiquing that culture. Protestant writers such as Karl Barth and Dietrich Bonhoeffer vigorously opposed this trend, arguing that Christianity and the churches should seek their norms and legitimation in Jesus Christ and the Bible, not in cultural norms. But they were a decided minority.

It is therefore not surprising that many Protestant thinkers found both Bonhoeffer and Barth immensely congenial resources as they struggled with similar issues. For example, John de Gruchy, Professor of Christian Studies at the University of Cape Town, pointed out the important of Bonhoeffer for Christians in South Africa at the time of apartheid. Bonhoeffer, he argued, provided a model for challenging prevailing cultural norms and taking a stand against a state that enjoyed a substantial degree of support from the established church of the region—in this case, the Dutch Reformed Church.

Barth and Bonhoeffer vigorously contested any Faustian pact between the church and state, between Christianity and culture. Although both writers had clear political commitments of their own, they regarded these as subservient to the overriding task of remaining faithful to Jesus Christ. A church that smells the powerful fragrance of power and influence shows a worrying ability to become accommodating and flexible on matters some might regard as nonnegotiable. How serious a risk is this? For example, the Church of England is the established state church of England. Might it not run the risk of simply regurgitating the policies and values of successive British governments? That risk is certainly there; it must not, however, be overstated. Even in the depths of the Second World War, some bishops of the Church of England (particularly George Bell) spoke out against the inhumanity of massive Allied bombing raids against German cities, incurring the wrath of the British political establishment in doing so.

The growth of the Religious Right in the United States is often seen as representing a Faustian pact between faith and politics. The rise of this grouping, which is widely held to be linked with the Republican Party, was stimulated by a series of major Supreme Court decisions that the movement perceived as threats to traditional American patterns of social life, perhaps most notably *Engej v. Vitale* (1962), which banned prayer in public schools.[35] To its critics, this association represents precisely the kind of unholy alliance that Christians ought to avoid. In response, the Religious Right argues that many mainline denominations have already fallen into precisely the same kind of alliance with the Democratic Party, leading to an institutionalization of liberalism within these denominations—for example, the Episcopal Church in the northeastern states. Although the Constitution prohibits any alliance of church and state, this has clearly not prevented more informal alliances from taking place. To an outside observer, the United States seems to embrace a variety of "culture Protestantisms," each comfortably attached to a political and social agenda.

PROTESTANTISM AND ECONOMICS

One of the most visible differences between Protestant and Catholic Europe in the early seventeenth century was the marked economic superiority of the former over the latter. For example, consider Flanders, which was torn apart in the second half of the sixteenth century by Protestant revolt and Catholic reconquest by the Spaniards. For the best part of two hundred years thereafter, the Protestant zone was bustling and prosperous, and the Catholic area depressed and unproductive. Even in robustly Catholic nations, such as France and Austria, economic entrepreneurialism was primarily due to Calvinists. Capitalism and Calvinism were virtually coextensive by the middle of the seventeenth century.

This observation is easily made; explaining it is somewhat more difficult. It is impossible to engage with this topic without mentioning, however briefly, the "Weber thesis," developed by the German sociologist Max Weber (1864–1920).[36] Weber set out a complex argument, not entirely justified by the evidence he assembled, to the effect that a new "spirit of capitalism" emerged in the early modern period and seemed to be associated with Protestantism—more specifically, with Calvinism.[37]

Weber set out to identify the characteristics of "modern" capitalism by comparing it with what he termed the "adventurer" capitalism of the medieval period. This earlier form of capitalism, he argued, was opportunistic and unscrupulous; it tended to consume its capital gains in flamboyant and decadent lifestyles. The forms of capitalism that emerged in the early modern period, however, possessed a strong ethical basis, which was often linked to personal asceticism in respect to material goods.

Under Catholicism, the accumulation of capital was seen as intrinsically sinful; under Calvinism, it was seen as praiseworthy. In Weber's view, this fundamental change in attitude was particularly well illustrated by a number of seventeenth-century Calvinist writers such as Benjamin Franklin, whose writings combined commendation of the accumulation of capital through engagement with the world with criticism of its consumption. Capital was seen as something to be increased, not something to be consumed. Calvinism, according to Weber, thus generated the psychological preconditions essential to the development of modern capitalism.

Weber's argument linked the rise of the "spirit of capitalism" with Calvinism through the concept of predestination. Weber argued that Calvin's predestinarianism created religious anxiety on the part of those wondering whether they were truly elect. In attempting to overcome this anxiety, Weber argued, Calvinists such as William Perkins developed a heightened sense of a moral obligation to work, the conviction that a person's election by God was authenticated by his or her activism, and a pervasive ethos of living thriftily off the proceeds from such work, with the remainder being saved, invested, or simply given away.

The "spirit of capitalism" thus arose from the quest for the assurance of salvation—which Calvin's theological system accentuated but did not itself resolve.[38] This has proved to be an influential, yet not an ultimately persuasive, argument.[39] What is clear, however, is that the emergence of modern Western capitalism has a connection with Calvinism—whether as cause or effect, or whether as shared elements of a cultural syndrome. Whereas Karl Marx had argued that the emergence of modern capitalism brought Protestantism into being, Weber argued precisely the reverse. Calvinism made commercial success respectable by declaring that the virtues that lay behind it—such as thrift, austerity, and discipline—were themselves acceptable in God's sight.

Calvinism is clearly linked to the rise of modern capitalism in other respects. The most important of these is Calvin's attitude toward usury—lending money at interest with a view to making a profit on the loan. Throughout the patristic era and the Middle Ages, the entire consensus of the church had been that usury was a mortal sin.[40] This was no peripheral matter, no matter of theological vagueness. The credit markets of western Europe, like those of Islamic nations today, were held back by a belief, reinforced by church legislation, that usury was contrary both to the gospel and to natural law.

The Old Testament explicitly prohibited this practice.[41] Throughout the patristic and medieval periods, this prohibition was both reinforced and clarified. In a series of sermons, Ambrose denounced the taking of interest on a loan, arguing that such usury was a violation of the law of God and was prohibited by both "the Old and Divine law."[42] Jerome defined usury as "collecting more than one has given," something that is explicitly prohibited by the law and prophets. Did not Luke 6:35 explicitly state that Christians should "lend, expecting nothing in return"?

Three medieval councils—the Second and Third Lateran Councils (1139 and 1179) and the Council of Vienna (1314)—reinforced the Old Testament ban, even stipulating that usurers were to be denied a Christian burial.[43] In 1140 the great medieval authority on canon law, Gratian of Bologna, declared that:

> To demand or receive or even to lend expecting to receive something above the capital is to be guilty of usury; usury may exist on money or something else; one who receives usury is guilty of rapine and is just as culpable as a thief; the prohibition against usury holds for laymen as well as clerics but, when guilty, the latter will be more severely punished.

Yet while Christians were prohibited from lending money at interest, Jews were explicitly exempted from this ban. This exemption led to the emergence of the stereotype of the Jew as an avaricious moneylender, famously exemplified in Shakespeare's Shylock in *The Merchant of Venice*.

These views were not challenged in the first phase of Protestantism. Martin Luther regarded the biblical prohibition of usury as permanently binding. In his 1524 sermon on trade and usury, Luther lashed out at any attempt to charge interest. In his view, Christians "should willingly and gladly lend money without any charge." The Elizabethan Protestant bishop John Jewel reflected the views of his age when he raged from his pulpit against the iniquities of usury. "It is theft, it is the murdering of our brethren, it is the curse of God and the curse of the people."[44] This uncompromising opposition to usury was embodied in a statute passed by the English Parliament in 1571, which had the unforeseen and unintended effect of *legitimating* usury at a fixed rate of 10 percent.

Yet the lending of money at interest was essential to the emergence of modern capitalism. A steadily increasing hunger for capital led many in both church and state to turn a blind eye to moneylending and to reconsider the entire theological basis of the prohibition of usury. Calvin could not have been unaware of these problems. The survival of the city of Geneva depended on being able to sustain and develop its urban economy and remain independent of potentially dangerous neighbors.

In 1545 Calvin wrote to his friend Claude de Sachin, setting out his views on usury. The letter was not published until after Calvin's death (1564), when Theodore Beza decided to make its contents generally known in 1575. At one level, this letter can be read as a total inversion of the teaching of the Old Testament; a more attentive reading confirms this suspicion but discloses the sophisticated lines of argument that led Calvin to his surprising conclusion. So how could Calvin reinterpret the Old Testament's explicit statements that usury is prohibited to mean that it is actually permitted?[45]

Calvin's letter of 1545 reinforces the importance of biblical interpretation to Protestantism. In one respect, Calvin reaffirmed the general Protestant idea that not all the rules set out for Jews in the Old Testament were binding upon Christians; in these instances, the Old Testament offered moral guidance only, not positive prescriptions for conduct. Yet this way of interpreting the Old Testament had been applied to cultic issues—such as the Old Testament's demand for animal sacrifices. Calvin's extension of the principle to usury broke new ground.

A fundamental theme recurring throughout the letter was that things had moved on. The situation in sixteenth-century Europe was not the same as that in ancient Israel. As Biéler points out in his magisterial study of Calvin's economic thought, the new realities of financial life in the early modern period made the uncritical application of such Old Testament texts highly problematic.[46] The new economic realities of the sixteenth century made it possible to view interest as simply rent paid on capital. Calvin therefore argued for the need to probe deeper and ascertain the general principles that seemed to underlie the Old Testament ban on usury in its original context. It was the *purpose* of the prohibition, not the prohibition itself, that had to govern Protestant thinking on this matter. "We ought not to judge usury according to a few passages of Scripture, but in accordance with the principle of equity." For Calvin, the real concern was the exploitation of the poor through high interest rates. This, he argued, could be dealt with in other ways—such as the fixing of interest rates at communally acceptable levels. Calvin's willingness to allow a variable rate of interest showed an awareness of the pressures upon capital in the more or less free market of the age.[47]

Calvin's views, which were seen by many as running counter to the clear meaning of the Bible, took some time to become accepted. By the middle of the seventeenth century—more than one hundred years after Calvin's groundbreaking analysis—usury was finally regarded as acceptable. Protestant jurists such as Hugo Grotius and Samuel Pufendorf supplemented Calvin's theological analysis with clarifications of economic concepts, especially in relation to price and value, that finally removed any remaining scruples about lending money at interest. The Catholic church did not legitimate usury, however, until 1830, apparently in response to the widespread acceptance of the practice within predominantly Protestant western Europe.

Yet Protestantism did more than bring about the theological adjustment that opened the way to a modern capitalist economy; its early development in the cities of Europe, especially in Switzerland, created the economic conditions that made such a change inevitable and essential. During the period 1535 to 1540, an economic recession descended on the area around Geneva. Despite this downturn, Geneva was able to survive and to go on to benefit from the subsequent recovery throughout the region, which lasted from 1540 to 1555. It is now thought that one of the prime reasons for Geneva's resilience during this period was the emergence of the Swiss banking system, which allowed Basel and other major Swiss Protestant cities sympathetic to Calvin's religious agenda to bail him out through large loans.[48] The Swiss banking system emerged as a direct response to a shared sense of identity throughout the Protestant cantons of Switzerland and neighboring cities—including Geneva.

By the early 1540s, Geneva was a city without an economic hinterland, and it faced considerable pressure from the growing number of religious refugees, often fleeing from persecution in France. Its survival increasingly came to depend on the generation of new markets and industries. As many refugees brought manufacturing and marketing skills with them, the scene was set for economic expansion.[49] Geneva's fabled connection with the watchmaking industry began with the arrival of French refugees who specialized in this area. A significant publishing industry developed, along with ancillary industries, such as papermaking and the production of printing type. The immigration of French families associated with the cloth and drapery trades—such as the Bordiers and Mallets—led to the expansion of these industries at Geneva. With the abolition of the old seigneurial ecclesiastical and guild system—the final obstacle to "modern capitalism"—these newcomers could set up business and begin manufacturing and trading without serious restrictions.

The raising of capital for economic expansion thus became imperative for Geneva around this time. Calvin's removal of the remaining theological impediments to the practice of usury was not merely religiously progressive; it was essential if his version of Protestantism was to survive. So intimate was the connection between the religious system of Calvinism and the city of Geneva that the collapse of the latter would have had disastrous implications for the former.

Economic activism subsequently came to be associated with Puritanism in England, Scotland, and the United States in the late sixteenth and seventeenth centuries.[50] Welsh Calvinists who settled in Ohio in the nineteenth century brought their faith and their capitalism with them to the region.[51] Although there is some evidence that an ethos of hard work and the prudent use of resources may have become a culturally embedded tradition rather than an instinct that arose naturally from personal religious convictions, there is clear evidence that Calvinism's later representatives saw an obvious link between their faith and capitalism.

There is another component of Weber's argument that we must consider here—the notion of "calling." Max Weber suggested that the idea of the call played a critical role in shaping Protestantism, and above all in shaping its characteristically entrepreneurial attitudes.[52] In view of the importance of this notion to the Protestant work ethic, we consider it separately in some detail, without any commitment to the specifics of Weber's occasionally problematic analysis.

THE PROTESTANT WORK ETHIC

The phrase "the Protestant work ethic" is widely used in contemporary Western culture to designate the belief that work has intrinsic value in its own right and for its own sake.[53] This, it must be noted, represents a secularized version of this work ethic; it might more accurately be described as "the post-Protestant work ethic." Protestantism's own rigorously theological reevaluation of the place of work in human life and culture, however, would continue to influence Western culture—albeit in a largely secularized form.

To appreciate the significance of the emergence of the Protestant work ethic, it is necessary to understand the intense distaste with which classical culture regarded work.[54] The social patricians of ancient Rome regarded work as something incompatible with their social status. This negative attitude toward work was reflected in early Christianity, especially in the emerging monastic movement. For Eusebius of Caesarea, the perfect Christian life was one devoted to serving God, untainted by physical labor. Those who chose to work for a living were second-rate Christians. To live and work in the world was to forfeit a first-rate Christian calling, with all that this implied. Work was often seen as a debasing and demeaning activity. Such attitudes probably reached the height of their influence during the Middle Ages.

The monastic spirituality of the medieval period generally regarded work as degrading. This widespread stigma against manual labor was pervasive, but not universal. Benedictine spirituality, for instance, created a genuine spiritual place for work within the monastic life.[55] Yet the more widespread medieval attitude was that found in Chaucer's Pardoner, who boasts that he will not stoop so low as to weave baskets with his own hands. As the Italian historian of culture Adriano Tilgher concluded in his definitive study of work in the Western world, monastic spirituality never regarded everyday work in the world as anything of value.[56] Those who chose to live and work in the world were, at best, "regarded with indulgent charity." Those who committed themselves—either by choice or through lack of serious alternatives—to living and working in the everyday world were regarded as inferior, devoid of any "calling." The Latin term *vocation* was understood to mean a call to the monastic life that involved leaving the world behind.

From the outset, Protestantism rejected the critical medieval distinction between the "sacred" and "secular" orders. While this position can easily be interpreted as a claim for the desacralization of the sacred, it can equally well be understood as a claim for the sacralization of the secular. As early as 1520, Luther had laid the fundamental conceptual foundations for created sacred space within the secular. His doctrine of the "priesthood of all believers" asserted that there is no genuine difference of status between the "spiritual" and the "temporal" order. All Christians are called to be priests—and can exercise that calling within the everyday world. The idea of "calling" was fundamentally redefined: no longer was it about being called to serve God by leaving the world; it was now about serving God in the world.[57]

God calls his people, not just to faith, but to express that faith in quite definite areas of life. This idea of a "double calling" played a particularly important role in the thought of William Perkins, who insisted that one is called, in the first place, to be a Christian, and in the second, to live out that faith in a certain sphere of activity in the world.[58] Luther stated this point succinctly when commenting on Genesis 3:19: "What seem to be secular works are actually the praise of God and represent an obedience which is well pleasing to him." There were no limits to this notion of calling. Luther even extolled the religious value of housework, declaring that although "it had no obvious appearance of holiness, yet these very household chores are more to be valued than all the works of monks and nuns." Luther's English follower William Tyndale commented that while the "washing of dishes and preaching the word of God" clearly represented different human activities, he insisted that, "as touching to please God," there was no essential difference.

The historical transformation of the status of work through this ethic is quite remarkable. In his magisterial study of the status of work from Aristotle to Calvin, Vittorio Tranquilli showed how Calvin's theology led directly from a view of work as a socially demeaning, if pragmatically necessary, activity, best left to one's social inferiors, to a dignified and glorious means of praising and affirming God in and through his creation while adding further to its well-being.[59] It is no accident that those regions of Europe that adopted Protestantism soon found themselves prospering economically—a spin-off rather than an intended and premeditated consequence of the new religious importance attached to work.

The Protestant work ethic is nowadays often described in terms of an "ethic of self-reliance"; in this view, work is a thing that is good in itself. The concept of "vocation" or "calling" has been desacralized and now refers to whatever it is that an individual wants to do with his or her life. Yet the post-Protestant secular variant of the work ethic is open to criticism, not least because it has been held to lead to the addictive patterns of behavior often referred to as "workaholism." If work is seen as an end in itself, a distorted set of priorities ensues, with inevitable negative outcomes for social, family, and personal relationships.[60] It can be argued that this problem arose from later Puritanism, which often identified people's God-given vocation with work, at the expense of their other involvements and responsibilities in society, family, and church.

Nevertheless, the original Protestant work ethic is itself in need of revision in the light of changing social structures and work patterns. In recent years, it has become clear that the notion of "a job for life" is no longer the only, or even the best, option. Both Luther and Calvin, it can be argued, linked people's work to their existing station in life rather than to the particular gifts God gave them to use. They defined work, in other words, in terms of social function, not personal gifts.

This socially static concept of work or vocation was relatively unproblematic for much of the nineteenth and twentieth centuries; it has now become significantly deficient. One response has been a reworking of the Protestant work ethic to emphasize the importance of individual gifts and their potential actualization in many spheres of life.[61] Individuals may thus engage in a variety of "works" throughout their lifetimes, seeing their God-given calling as capable of transfer to different contexts.

The Protestant work ethic finds its application in many contexts in the twenty-first century. Perhaps the most obvious is the phenomenon of "faith-based activism": religious groups using their faith both as a platform and a guiding principle for social engagement and voluntary work.[62] Although this is no longer a distinctively Protestant phenomenon, the history of its development makes clear its strong, intentional connections with mainline Protestantism, especially in the United States. Protestant activism, expressed in the Protestant work ethic, is clearly a resource that is likely to play a more significant role in the future if government funding for social welfare programs is reduced.

PROTESTANTISM AND EDUCATION

As it began to gain influence in western Europe, Protestantism discovered the importance of education. Populations had to be persuaded of the folly of their older religious ways and beliefs and assisted in gaining a firm grasp of the principles of the new form of Christianity that was gaining influence and momentum. The development of the educational form of the "catechism" was an important response to this need: congregations could be encouraged to learn these by heart. Luther's Catechisms of 1529 proved particularly effective and established the question-and-answer format as normative. Yet more was clearly required. Luther recognized the potential importance of the public school system for educating children in the ways and ideas of Protestantism, yet lacked the professional expertise necessary to exploit this resource.[63]

As time passed and Protestantism became more securely established, the home began to emerge as the primary focus of intergenerational transmission of faith.[64] Family Bible reading and prayer became an important daily routine, cementing the family's unity as much as its religious devotion.[65] The late eighteenth century saw the emergence of the family Bible with notes, which was an important source of religious education within the family, not to mention a significant influence on the shaping of social attitudes in relation to issues of gender.[66]

The rise of the Sunday school in the late eighteenth century proved to be a significant means of consolidating Protestant influence. This was initially seen as a means of providing suitable occupation for the urban poor, who would otherwise merely cause trouble. However, Sunday schools quickly developed into an important agency of Protestant education in the cities of the United States. There students were encouraged to memorize verses of the Bible, an exercise seen as fundamental to a religious upbringing.[67] By 1820 there are known to have been several hundred Sunday schools in the United States. All gave priority to religious instruction over reading and writing, although most taught the latter subjects as a means of inculcating the former. Many schools used a "ticket reward" system: students were given a blue ticket for every ten verses they memorized, traded six blue tickets for one red, and eventually cashed in the red tickets at a value of one-half cent each toward purchasing Sunday school books or tracts. Some expressed anxieties over this mercenary aspect of the educational process; others relished the fact that it seemed to work so well.

Yet the most significant way in which Protestantism shaped education was through the founding of colleges, seminaries, and universities. Recognizing the importance of well-educated pastors and other church leaders, Protestantism saw investment in education as essential to its survival. Calvin realized the need for such facilities in 1541; owing to political disagreements in Geneva, however, it was not until 1559 that the Geneva Academy was inaugurated, with Theodore Beza as its first rector.[68]

Yet the new academy was soon upstaged. As Calvinism became an international movement, an increasing number of universities became favorably disposed toward the new religion. Leiden and Heidelberg rapidly gained an international reputation, eclipsing Calvin's personal foundation. These new seats of learning were supplemented by the new Calvinist academies located strategically at German cities such as Herborn in Hanau, and especially those founded in France after the Edict of Nantes—Montauban, Saumur, and Sedan.

The founding of what became known as Harvard College in 1636 established the intellectual hegemony of Calvinism in New England. Following the founding of Harvard would be the establishment of a series of colleges and seminaries dedicated to the propagation of the Protestant faith in church and society. From its outset, Harvard saw itself as dedicated to the goal of a Protestant education. As the Statutes of 1646 put it, the chief object of its education would be "to know God and Jesus Christ which is eternal life." This goal was admirably summarized in the college's motto of 1692: *Veritas Christo et Ecclesiae* ("Truth for Christ and the Church"). Other schools followed this trend, usually emphasizing denominational distinctions alongside a general desire to deepen personal faith and piety.

It was a powerful, yet ultimately vulnerable, vision. The American Revolution caused significant modifications to the founding ideals of many such institutions on account of the constitutional separation of church and state.[69] Yet the real issues began to emerge in the late nineteenth century, and especially in the twentieth, when colleges with Protestant religious foundations began to wonder whether they were prisoners of their past. Was their Protestant commitment deterring potential applicants? Might these be barriers to funding? A slow, complex, and seemingly irreversible process of secularization began as colleges across the United States chose to marginalize their religious heritages.[70] In a deeply symbolic move, Harvard changed its motto to the single word *Veritas*. Most colleges and universities that began with specific Protestant faith commitments have now given up on these.[71]

This phenomenon of institutional drift in American Protestant educational institutions has taken place at three different, though clearly interconnected, levels.

1. A denominational or sectional identity has been lost, in order to achieve a broader appeal within the wider Protestant community. Recent changes in seminary names are indicative of a desire to relocate institutions on conceptual maps without necessarily changing theological identity.

2. A generally Protestant identity has been lost, in order to serve a wider constituency within the Christian churches. The rise of ecumenism, especially at the grassroots level, in the final decades of the twentieth century has accelerated this trend.

3. A specifically Christian identity has been lost, either in order to focus on religion in general, without any specific commitment to its Christian form, or in order to focus on other disciplines for which Christian identity either confers no advantages or is seen to be an impediment. The pressures created by the need for academic accreditation from secular agencies has played no small role in catalyzing this transition.[72]

While all institutions of education founded on a specifically religious basis face similar challenges, it seems that Protestantism has been particularly vulnerable to an erosion of vision and loss of focus. One possible explanation lies in the influence of Pietism within Protestant institutions. The traditional Pietist emphasis on a "religion of the heart" easily leads to a neglect of theology and a disregard for the church. This expresses itself in religious anti-intellectualism, which has little time for the intellectual content of faith and makes little attempt to correlate it with other academic disciplines. The outcome has been a religious disengagement with learning. Faith was a matter of the heart, not the mind. The outcome was predictable: apart from an emphasis on nourishing personal devotion to Christ, educational programs at such institutions became indistinguishable from those offered at secular institutions. The Pietist element came to be regarded as academically risible by academics in such institutions and often fell into disrepute.

Faced with this phenomenon of institutional drift, Protestants have sought to find ways of either enforcing the religious identity of their institutions or making this a selling point. The former approach generally involves a "statement of faith," which all trustees and faculty members are required to sign as a condition of service. These statements are seen as safeguarding the institution's core identity from erosion or redirection. Although these are generally quite broad—often affirming little more than what C. S. Lewis would term "mere Christianity," though sometimes with specific denominational emphases or issues—they have occasionally been the source of tension within institutions, particularly if long-standing faculty members change their religious views—for example, through converting to Catholicism or Orthodoxy.

With the resurgence of interest in religion in North America since about 1980, this latter option has become entirely realistic. The Council for Christian Colleges and Universities (CCCU) was founded in 1976 with the objective of advancing "the cause of Christ-centered higher education" and "faithfully relating scholarship and service to biblical truth." The Council offers support to the presidents and faculties of its member institutions in order that they might retain their distinct identities and agendas and engage positively with the increasingly competitive higher education market.[73]

Yet Protestantism has continued to expand its educational vision, especially in North America. Fuller Theological Seminary, now one of the world's most prestigious institutions of theological education, was founded in Pasadena, California, in 1947 by evangelicals who were anxious to establish evangelicalism's intellectual credentials in the wake of the damaging fundamentalist controversies of the previous decades.[74] Regent College in Vancouver opened its doors in 1970 and is now Canada's largest institute of theological education, with a significant global reach. Both schools are interdenominational and evangelical. The age of Protestant commitment to education is far from over; indeed, it seems to be entering a new phase.

The rapid expansion of Protestantism in Africa, Latin America, and Asia in the twentieth century has led to some remarkable new educational developments. Korea now has some of the largest Protestant seminaries and universities in the world, reflecting both that nation's valuing of learning and the remarkable advances of Protestantism there since 1900.

PROTESTANTISM AND WOMEN

In recent years, there has been a concerted effort to rediscover the role played by women in the religious and social life of the later Middle Ages, the Renaissance, and the Reformation.[75] There is a clear consensus that the agendas and interests of earlier (largely, it must be admitted, male) historians of these movements may have minimized the significance of these writers, whether unconsciously or deliberately. The retrieval of such forgotten or repressed histories has renewed interest in the new possibilities created for women by the new religious movements of the age.

The emergence of Protestantism was of considerable significance for women, even if the actualization of the promise of the movement proved rather more problematic than some had hoped. Above all, Luther's doctrine of the "priesthood of all believers" affirmed that all Christians—whether male or female—possessed the status of priests within the corporate priesthood of the people of God. If pursued consistently, this line of thought led inexorably to women being able to exercise the same ministerial functions as men.

Yet Luther was conservative in both his theology and his practice and appears to have been reluctant to follow through his radical affirmation to its ecclesiological conclusions. Indeed, Protestantism did not even allow women the subsidiary clerical roles that nuns had earlier performed. While Calvin held that the Pauline admonition that women should be silent in church is a matter of time-bound apostolic advice rather than divine law for all time, there is little evidence that he believed the time was right to make changes there and then.

Nevertheless, it is clear that he was open to such major changes in the future.[76]

Others were more radical—or, as they would see it, more consistent. On February 1, 1532, the Parisian faculty of theology issued its condemnation of a series of subversive doctrines propounded by the Protestant Étienne Le Court, including his radical suggestion that, "now that God has willed that the Bible should be in French, women will take over the office of bishops, and bishops the office of women. Women will preach the gospel, while bishops will gossip with young girls."[77]

The problem of this failure was accentuated by Protestantism's removal of one (and occasionally both) of the two realms in which women were able to exercise genuine leadership and authority during the medieval period—the monarchy and the convent.[78] The early Protestant critique of the monastic life, though not always totally negative, regarded it as isolating Christians from the world. The closure of the convents denied to women the leadership roles evident in Catholic women writers such as Teresa of Ávila and Catherine of Siena, both of whom were declared to be "doctors of the church" in 1970.

Early Protestantism downplayed the spiritual roles of women in other, more subtle ways. The Protestant rejection of the "cult of the saints" eliminated a series of role models known to have been important to women during the Middle Ages—such as Saint Anne, mother of Mary and the patron saint of pregnant women. Religious processions and other rituals that gave women clear functions of their own were now discontinued, as were female religious confraternities.[79]

In part, such losses were remedied through the early Protestant relocation of the concept of calling for women within the family. One of the most significant consequences of the Protestant rejection of the idea of clerical celibacy—which was in any case widely flouted—was a new emphasis on the importance of marriage as a covenant relationship. The deliberate decisions of Martin Luther and Martin Bucer to marry former nuns was a clear statement of the transference of vocation from the convent to the home. The family was to be the new unit of religious calling and nurture.[80]

Protestantism is often held to be responsible for the emergence of the characteristic Western notion of the "nuclear family." In the Middle Ages and the Renaissance, individuals belonged to multiple families, including confraternities, guilds, corporations, and religious orders. The "family" was a diffuse and extended notion involving multiple loyalties and associations, and it included the dead as well as the living. Although there was no Protestant "theology of the family," a number of theological and social factors that were clearly of Protestant provenance—such as a disinclination to pray for the dead and the abolition of confraternities—led to the family becoming an increasingly important social unit. The family was now understood to be defined by *biological and physical proximity*—that is, a group of people closely related by blood and living in the same place.[81]

This new respect for the family and motherhood marked a significant break with the existing consensus. Medieval Catholicism tended to laud the virtues of celibacy and virginity and regarded the decision of those who chose to marry and bear children as an unfortunate consequence of original sin. The need to procreate and have legitimate heirs was, of course, entirely understandable, not least for monarchs. Yet it was seen as an unfortunate necessity, a means of taming physical lust rather than the fruit of Christian piety. While this public praise of celibacy was often accompanied by clandestine affairs, little attention was paid to those who chose to marry and bear children. By doing so, they had lost their spiritual credibility and degenerated to the spiritually debased category of the ordinary.

It is easy to point to Protestant works emphasizing the importance of women in the family and arguing for an enhanced valuation of their role. Johann Steinbach, in his *Household of Women* (1561), argued that women should play a much greater role in the running of households. Johann Freder's *Dialogue in Honor of Marriage* (1543) advocated greater parity between the genders on the grounds that women had the same noble and rational souls as men.[82] Yet other forces were at work that would ultimately subvert these developments.[83] In the end, sixteenth-century Protestantism altered the perception of women without necessarily effecting the transvaluation and transformation of social roles that this would have seemed to entail.

Individual Protestant women achieved significant prominence in the following centuries. Anne Bradstreet (1612–72) played an important role in the spiritual affairs of Puritan New England, not least through her religious poetry. Phoebe Palmer (1807–74) was at the center of Methodist holiness revivalism in the United States, especially during the 1850s. The Anglican Cecil Frances Alexander (1818–95) penned some of the classic hymns of the English language, including *There Is a Green Hill, Once in Royal David's City*, and *All Things Bright and Beautiful*. Her American counterpart Fanny J. Cosby (1820–1915) wrote *Blessed Assurance* and *To God Be the Glory*.

Elizabeth Cady Stanton and others produced *The Women's Bible* (1895), which set out to use the Bible itself to liberate women from the straitjacket that had been placed around them by institutionalized Protestantism. "Paul, in speaking of equality as the very soul and essence of Christianity, said, 'There is neither Jew nor Greek, there is neither bond nor free, there is neither male nor female; for ye are all one in Christ Jesus.'... [With] this declaration of the equality of the sexes in the New, we may well wonder at the contemptible status woman occupies in the Christian Church of to-day." Cady's well-turned phrases and careful arguments did much to raise concern about Protestantism's traditional attitudes toward women.

In the end, the radical changes in Protestant attitudes toward women in the twentieth century must be judged to be primarily the result of the greater acceptance of women's roles in society as a whole, rather than the outcomes of a theologically driven agenda. In this case, theology showed an intriguing tendency to follow public opinion, not to shape it. Women received the right to vote in many Western nations—including Great Britain and the United States—after the end of the First World War in 1918. Yet it was not until the 1950s, in the aftermath of the Second World War, that Protestantism as a whole began to explore the place of women in ordained ministry with any great seriousness.

Since then, those denominations ordaining women to full leadership positions have seen their numbers mushroom. In the United States between 1977 and 1997, the number of ordained women in the Baptist churches increased from 157 to 712; in the Episcopal church from 94 to 1,394; and in the United Methodist church from 319 to 3,003. In June 2006, the General Convention of the American Episcopal Church elected Bishop Katharine Jefferts Schori of Nevada as its new presiding bishop. By 2005 more than 50 percent of the students in American Protestant seminaries were women. In the Church of England, which voted to ordain women as priests in 1992, the number of women being ordained is now equal to that of men and is expected to surpass that number in the future. This has alarmed traditionalists, who see this change as the "feminization" of the priesthood. Others suggest that it is the inevitable and welcome outcome of the fundamental doctrine of the "priesthood of all believers."

From the material presented in this chapter thus far, it will be clear that the relationship between Protestantism and its social context cannot be defined in terms of some "universal Protestantism" shaping its social context in an ideologically controlled or predetermined manner. The relationship was mutual, in that social factors shaped Protestantism as much as Protestantism molded its context. The significant differences in styles of Protestantism, when linked with the substantial cultural and political variations between nations and regions, led to a multiplicity of interactions.

Yet in the twentieth century, Protestantism expanded far beyond its original homelands in the West, taking root in Asia, Africa, and Latin America. This has generated new concerns and debates, as will become clear from what follows.

BEYOND THE WEST: NEW CULTURAL CONCERNS

In the past, discussions about Protestantism and culture have been shaped by Western concerns—precisely because of the widely held assumption that Protestantism is a Western religion, located in Western culture. The twentieth century has challenged both assumptions, not only through the emergence of Protestantism outside the West but also—and perhaps more significantly—through the transformation of Protestantism in those other regions as its foundational legacy of theological and cultural recalibration is carried out there. To put it bluntly, Protestantism is no longer a "Western" religion.

In the twentieth century, Protestantism found itself caught up in the "clash of civilizations."[84] Thinkers of the Enlightenment assumed that there was a moral and intellectual system common to all peoples and that its universal extension to all was simply a matter of time. Its ideas and values were already embodied in the West; globalization—which was simply the extension of Western values to the world at large—would lead to the universal triumph of those ideas and values in due course.

This is no longer believed to be the case. Political and cultural resistance to the West has grown significantly in recent years, and Islamic and Asian nations have reasserted their value systems. Thus, Western human rights policies have been seen as "power politics in disguise"—an instrument for the covert advancement of Western political and economic interests.[85] The impact of the reassertion of traditional Asian, African, and Islamic values in the many regions of the world where Protestantism is a growing presence is significant.

Demonstrating this impact is the issue of the ordination of homosexuals, which has been the subject of debate within many Protestant denominations since 1990. The issue has proved especially divisive within Anglicanism. In the United States, the Episcopal church has seen itself as spearheading a progressive agenda that embodies the best of American liberal values. The ordination of homosexuals has been seen there as tantamount to a human rights issue. Although the debate has proved divisive within the Episcopal church, it is strongly in line with the American liberal ethos that the Episcopal church has come to represent since the 1960s.

Yet Anglicanism is now a form of Protestantism that is predominantly located in the developing world. There are more Anglicans in the west African state of Nigeria than in the United Kingdom, the United States, Canada, Australia, and New Zealand *put together*. Nigerian Anglicans see no need whatsoever to endorse what they see as the intrusion of liberal American cultural values into the church. Within the Nigerian cultural context, in which Islam is a major presence, homosexuality is regarded as a cultural abomination.

Paradoxically, an approach that affirms that Protestantism should reflect the cultural norms of its environment thus leads to totally different outcomes in New England and in Nigeria. The tensions over this issue are now so great that it is difficult to see how these two churches can remain in the same denomination. The only realistic outcome is for Anglicanism to follow the trend already established by Presbyterians, Baptists, and Methodists and recognize a "denominational family," with tensions and fissures over significant issues.

The ordination of homosexuals, however, is only one issue among many to confront Protestantism in its new phase of development. Demands for the "de-Westernization" of Protestantism are growing, both as the strength of the movement in the developing world increases and as the spiritual and theological robustness of the Western churches seems to decline in comparison with the rest of the world. A new agenda is developing, and it can only lead to the transformation of Protestantism. Global Protestantism is leaving the traditional agenda of the West behind as it reflects on its engagement with Islam, its relationship to traditional Chinese religion and customs (such as "grave-sweeping"), its attitudes toward indigenous tribal practices in the Amazonian rain forests, and the use of Taoist or Hindu ideas as points of contact for the proclamation of the gospel.

What the discerning observer notices is the emergence of local Protestantisms that seek to interpret and apply the Bible within their own cultural contexts, without feeling any pressing need to introduce Western assumptions, ideas, or values into their reflections.[86] In many ways, this represents a return to the first days of Protestantism, when Luther and Zwingli faced the challenge of trying to apply their vision of the gospel to the very different situations in Wittenberg and Zurich. Their twenty-first-century descendants are trying to do exactly the same thing, yet in contexts that Luther and Zwingli could not have imagined.

Protestantism, as we have stressed throughout this book, is above all a method rather than a fixed set of outcomes, and it is capable of rapid and extensive adaptation to new situations without loss of its original core vision. Its detachment from Western culture appears to have led to its growth and the development of new forms that often bear a remarkable resemblance to what we know of the church in the first three centuries of its existence. Might the development of Protestantism in these new contexts, set free from its cultural imprisonment in the West, let us see it as if for the very first time?

Thus far, we have considered how Protestantism relates to culture in the most general sense of that word. But what of its relationship to culture in T. S. Eliot's subtly developed sense of the word? Or in Matthew Arnold's sense of the term, summed up in his famous definition of culture as "the best which has been thought and said in the world"? What of more recent extensions of this theme that hold that culture is defined and manifested, more broadly, in terms of the embodiment of its values in sport? In the following chapter, we consider the ambivalence of Protestantism's involvement in the development of the arts, sports, and natural sciences.

The Alchemist, *by David Teniers the Younger (1610–90).*

13

Protestantism, the Arts, and the Natural Sciences

An ominous cloud of suspicion hovers over the issues to be discussed in this chapter, casting a shadow over its themes. It is impossible to ignore the brute historical fact that, virtually from the inception of the movement, certain sections of Protestantism unleashed a wave of destruction of religious art. How can we even begin to explore the relationship of Protestantism to the arts in the light of such a violent and destructive past? Was not the Welsh poet R. S. Thomas right when he castigated Protestantism as "the adroit castrator of art"? And what of sport, widely regarded by its supporters as an art form, which was so famously detested by the Puritans?

The situation seems just as troubling in relation to the natural sciences. Surely the infamous Scopes "monkey" trial of 1925 made clear Protestantism's outright hostility to the entire scientific enterprise, especially when this seemed to pose even the slightest challenge to the literal reading of the Bible? And what about Calvin's outright opposition to Copernicus when he lambasted the Polish astronomer for daring to place his own authority over that of the Holy Spirit? Did not the Bible declare that "God has established the world; it shall never be moved" (Psalm 93:1)?

These concerns are entirely understandable, and reflect the deep ambivalence within certain sections of Protestantism in relation to both the arts and sciences. Nevertheless, the situation is much more complex and nuanced, not to mention more *interesting,* than prevalent stereotypes suggest. This chapter explores the origins and emergence of Protestant attitudes to the arts and sciences, attempting to document and account for a wide variety of viewpoints. There is no single, definitive "Protestant" attitude toward any of these matters; instead, we find a surprisingly wide range of approaches, each of which is consistent with the specific vision of Protestantism that underlies it. As there are many such visions, it is only to be expected that a correspondingly broad range of attitudes have emerged.

In his famous Rede Lecture at Cambridge University entitled "The Two Cultures and the Scientific Revolution," C. P. Snow (1905–80) lamented the growing divide he discerned within Western culture between what he called "the literary intellectuals" and "the scientists." These two groups, he remarked, had "a curiously distorted image of each other" and were separated by a "gulf of mutual incomprehension." It may seem inappropriate to include two such variegated domains in a single chapter. However, since the object here is to explore the interaction of Protestantism with modern intellectual culture, it is both convenient and imperative to treat them together. We begin by considering the relationship between Christianity and the arts.

PAINTING:
PROTESTANTISM AND ICONOCLASM

Ordinary people encountered the medieval Catholic church not so much in the form of its abstract ideas but through its practices and images. The liturgy of the church, especially the mass, enacted the theology of the church, setting out dramatically a visual "grand narrative" of human history and experience. The church's ritual observances and symbolic gestures shaped the congregation's perception of the world and their own location within it. It offered spectacle and instruction, theater and dogma, in a form that reaffirmed the medieval worldview and the necessary place of the institutional church as an instrument and vehicle of salvation.[1] Outside that church, there was no salvation.

The drama of the liturgy was supplemented by images, often images of gospel scenes—painted on church walls, illustrating gospel scenes for the benefit of those who could not read—or images of saints, especially Mary, whose intercessory powers were affirmed and proclaimed by the church. Saints were mediators of divine grace who would hear and mediate the prayers of ordinary people.[2] In churches throughout western Europe, the cult of the saints was represented iconically—through paintings, altarpieces, and statues.[3] These images expressed and transmitted a theology, but one that Protestantism regarded as fundamentally misguided.

The rise of Protestantism represented a break with the past. The nature and extent of that rupture was understood in different ways within the movement. For radical reformers, a Promethean reconstruction of the church from ground zero was required; for Luther and Calvin, the church was capable of being reformed and purged of its defects. Yet in every case a break with the past was presupposed. So how could that rupture be defended and explained?

Protestants moved swiftly to neutralize the imaginative power of the Catholic church by abolishing the mass and destroying its images. The theological break with the past necessitated an imaginative counterpart in order to bring home to ordinary people—Luther talked about "Herr Omnes," or "everyman"—that something radical had taken place. The old actions and images would disappear and be replaced by their Protestant alternatives. Statues of saints were smashed, relics destroyed, altars overturned, paintings defaced or eventually whitewashed, and clerical vestments ripped apart.

The early Protestant hostility toward religious imagery around the year 1500 is thus to be understood primarily—but not exclusively—as a reaction against the theology that this imagery mediated. For deep within the Protestant psyche, a deeper sense of anxiety had emerged—that the new importance attached to the Ten Commandments negated the use of images altogether. Whereas Luther believed that one could identify the principle of the Old Testament prohibition against the use of "graven images" (Exodus 20:4; Deuteronomy 5:8), and retain the practice with appropriate safeguards, Zwingli and Calvin believed this was a compromise. Images had to be abolished altogether. Underlying the Reformation reaction against images was a new theology that demanded the resignification of the sacred.[4]

This led to a fundamental iconic divergence between Lutheranism and the versions of Protestantism associated with Zwingli and Calvin—usually referred to as "Reformed." Lutheranism chose to retain religious imagery while redirecting its subject. Recognizing the imaginative and pedagogical power of images, Lutheranism used them extensively in churches, as noted earlier. Reformed churches were notable for the absence of any form of imagery in them. One entered the building and walked into a whitewashed space where daylight entered unmodulated through clear rather than stained glass. The imagery was that of illumination, simplicity, and purification. ("The unfolding of your words gives light"; Psalm 119:130.)

Some have argued that this hostility toward the visual image is not to be seen as a Protestant distinction, still less as an affectation. Until recently, it was a commonplace to suggest that Christianity itself was opposed to the use of images in sacred contexts, particularly worship.[5] Yet the view that early Christianity represented "a fundamentally and irrevocably aniconic form of religiosity" rests on a superficial engagement with primary sources, and can no longer be defended. In any case, the iconoclastic elements within early Protestantism did not undertake detailed research into primary Christian sources in developing their views. These emerged immediately, from a reading of the Ten Commandments and an inspection of what they regarded as idolatrous material in the churches of their day. The remedy, it seemed to them, was straightforward and thoroughly practical. And so the destruction of the images began.

One fundamental question emerges from this historical analysis: was this hostility toward images specific to this era tactical rather than strategic? Once the break with the past had been made, physically and iconically, would a different attitude emerge as medieval Catholicism became a memory, not a living threat? On the basis of the evidence available, the best answer that can be given is that, within Reformed Protestantism—but not in other forms of the movement—this hostility was ultimately seen as grounded in theology, not the contingencies of a specific historical moment.

Lutheranism and Anglicanism went on to make extensive use of religious imagery, particularly as they moved away from their historical origins and the needs of the moment became of more pressing importance. Images had power—indeed, images might even, in some situations, have greater power than words.[6] The simple fact was that no Protestant writer could ignore the power of images. Images simplified and reified: they expressed complex ideas in simple, memorable ways, and they represented complex, abstract principles in concrete, personalized form. In 1545 Luther sponsored the production of a crude and vivid series of ten woodcuts entitled *The True Depiction of the Papacy*.[7] The first of these depicted the "Pope-Ass," an image created in 1520 by Lukas Cranach the Elder, which represented the pope as a monstrous ass in human form.

The complex issues of the emergence of Protestantism were here drastically reduced to a simplistic struggle—freedom rather than oppression, good rather than evil, and God rather than Satan. Luther's own theological works do not legitimate such simplistic reductions, yet the propaganda issued on his behalf went far beyond his cautious statements, apparently representing a gross distortion rather than a popular simplification of his ideas. Was the use of such crude imagery a tacit admission that theology had failed to deliver? That its complex, abstract ideas had not been grasped? That images were needed where arguments had failed?

Although Reformed Protestantism would not allow images in church, it had no doubt of their power. We have already noted the importance of the Geneva Bible (1560), which added marginal notes to help its readers understand what it euphemistically termed "the hard places." Yet this Bible went even further by adding illustrations to help the reader make more visual sense of some difficult passages (such as the vision of Ezekiel) or to depict scenes from biblical narratives (such as the "garments of the high priest," described in Exodus 28). Those who created the Geneva Bible had clearly absorbed Calvin's famous theological principle of divine accommodation. If God "accommodated himself to human capacity" in communicating with humanity—for example, by using visual images, such as "God as shepherd"—why should not the Bible follow this excellent precedent?

Images of any kind would be rigorously excluded from Reformed churches. However, the Reformed hostility to pictorial representations of God was fundamentally theological in its foundation and did not extend to other subject matters. No significant restrictions were placed upon the activities of Reformed artists outside the specific sphere of ecclesiastical ornamentation. John Calvin was perfectly clear on this matter: painting and sculpture were perfectly permissible—he even called them "gifts of God"—provided that the objects represented were "visible to our eyes." Calvinist painters might thus well find themselves having serious theological misgivings about representing God in their paintings; they had no such difficulties with the enterprise of painting itself. After all, artists were among the earliest supporters of the Protestant Reformation in the Lowlands.[8] Other possibilities lay wide open to them as the emerging interest in landscapes, townscapes, domestic scenes, and portraits characteristic of seventeenth-century Flemish art makes clear.

Yet alongside the absence of prohibition of such natural objects, another force of significance must be noted.[9] Market forces were becoming increasingly important in predominantly Reformed parts of Europe by 1600.[10] Protestantism turned out to have unleashed forces that it could not ultimately control. Indeed, the growing wealth of Reformed communities, not totally unconnected with their association with capitalism, led to the emergence of patterns of artistic patronage similar to those associated with the Italian Renaissance. The wealthy Calvinist burghers of Flanders appear to have been just as aware of the importance of decorating buildings and homes as their Renaissance predecessors.

As the epicenter of English Protestantism gradually shifted from Luther's Wittenberg to Calvin's Geneva, hostility toward images deepened. Puritanism maintained the prohibition against any visual aids to worship, while extending it to personal devotional aids. The period of the Puritan Commonwealth witnessed an outbreak of iconoclasm on a scale exceeding anything seen at the time of the Reformation. A Puritan raid on the chapel of Clare College, Cambridge, yielded more than one thousand religious "superstitious" images, including images of God the father, Jesus Christ, and the Holy Spirit "like a dove with wings."[11] The same severe attitudes were characteristic of American Puritanism throughout the seventeenth century.

Yet lying alongside this uniform hostility toward religious imagery within Reformed Protestantism—and raising questions about its long-term viability—are discernible tensions, anxieties, and even inconsistencies. One is a simple fact of human psychology—the need to visualize the abstract, and above all the divine. Attention is often drawn to a fascinating feature of Emmanuel de Witte's picture of the south aisle of the *Oude Kerk* (1660) in Amsterdam, which was purged of its images in 1566 when the wave of iconoclasm in the southern Netherlands swept north. At the center of the painting, Witte placed an icon of the Holy Face—a cultic representation of the face of Christ.[12] Was this an act of memory or of protest?

Puritan preachers and pastors might well be iconophobic; they were also, however, human beings who could not ignore the imaginative capacity and needs of their minds. A leading feature of Puritan spirituality was the longing ultimately to see God, when at present God could not be seen. Many Puritan sermons preached on Psalm 27:8—"Your face, Lord, do I seek!"—urged their congregations to "see" (that is, form a mental image of) the face of God, and prescribed a number of spiritual disciplines that might assist in doing so.[13] As many recent scholarly studies of Puritan attitudes toward images have stressed, the movement found itself in the ambivalent position of both needing images and needing to deny them.[14]

This ambivalence remains a potent element in contemporary Reformed reflection on the arts. Many mainline Protestant leaders now have no difficulty in valuing art in itself as a human activity directed toward the praise of God and filling an invaluable role in fostering an imaginative encounter with God.[15] Public worship, private devotion, and the public communication of faith are all enriched by the sensitive and judicious use of imagery. Yet within the Reformed tradition, attitudes remain ambivalent toward visual art, which is viewed as something that can mislead as much as it can serve as an aid to piety.[16]

POETRY:
PROTESTANTISM AND VERBAL CREATIVITY

Early Protestantism developed an antipathy toward poetry that was typical of its age, rather than demonstrating any particular distinguishing theological roots. The early Christian writer Tatian (born c. 120) was skeptical concerning the merits of classic rhetoric and poetry, both of which he regarded as encouraging deception and a disregard for matters of truth. Plato's severe censure of poetry was widely accepted within early Christian circles and percolated into the Christian tradition.

The Protestant debate about the merits of poetry began to take its distinctive form in England during the 1590s as the case for poetry began to be made seriously in the writings of Sir Philip Sidney. Aware of the religious hostility toward the notion, Sidney was obliged to combine his intellectual defense of poetry with a certain amount of political diplomacy as he sought to position himself in relation to the religious critics of this emerging art form.[17] Sidney was aware of the immense influence of Stephen Gosson's *Schoole of Abuse* (1579), which followed Plato in arguing that poetry and drama were morally disruptive and should therefore be banned from "a reformed commonwealth."

The nub of Gosson's case against poetry and drama was that they were sensuous, indulgent, flamboyant forms of art that lacked the simplicity and rigor of plain words. Using a culinary metaphor, Gosson suggested that poetry and drama were like rich, extravagant food that gave rise to pleasure—contrasting with the Protestant moral values of frugality and personal discipline.[18] Drama, he argued, forced the players to be tricksters, "telling lies by counterfeiting of other personalities than their own." These arts were out of place in a Protestant commonwealth because they propagated fiction and deceit instead of concentrating human minds upon the elegant simplicities of truth.

In responding, Sidney was obliged to take into account Gosson's Puritan reworking of Plato's fundamental charge that poetry was an inferior and deceptive mimesis, lacking rigor and honesty in comparison with philosophy. It was a charge that could be met by pointing to poetry's capacity to transform, while shrewdly observing that Plato condemned the abuses of poetry, not the art form itself. However, poetry's association with generating pleasure on the part of the reader proved much more difficult to rebut, partly because Sidney himself clearly regarded this as one of poetry's chief virtues. In the end, Sidney was able to turn Gosson's argument against himself by arguing that the pleasure offered by poetry was actually profit and improvement.

A close reading of Puritan critiques of poetry suggests that the basic objection lay in rooting religious discourse in what Samuel Mather termed "our own fancies and imaginations" rather than in the divine "types" revealed in scripture or in the created order of nature.[19] Poetry and drama alike proceeded from the imagination and were therefore fictions. This is certainly the view that we find in the noted Puritan writer Richard Baxter, who argued that literature actively promoted a culture of falsehood that "dangerously bewitcheth and corrupteth the minds of young and empty people."

Yet the Protestant critique of poetry began to lose its edge as more and more Protestants broke rank and wrote poetry that was well received within their communities. In Puritan America, the most conspicuous example was Anne Bradstreet (1612–72), one of the most important figures in the history of American literature, and considered by many to be the first American poet.[20] Her poems, written in a deceptively simple style, rest on a rigorous Puritan theological foundation, while being firmly anchored in the realities of American colonial life of that age.

In England, Anglicans served as trailblazers for religious poetry. John Donne (1572–1631) and George Herbert (1593–1633) both demonstrated the potential of the poetic genre to communicate theology through an essentially imaginative engagement. Each proved that it was possible to communicate—and commend—Protestant ideas through the poetic medium. George Herbert's poem *The Elixir* represents a powerful statement of the transforming impact of Christ upon mundane human life, allowing the Protestant work ethic to be set out with a new vitality:

> A servant with this clause
>   Makes Drudgerie divine:
> Who sweeps a room, as for thy laws,
>   Makes that and th' action fine.[21]

John Donne was able to use the same medium to set out the Protestant doctrine of the bondage of the will through sin that requires God to "batter down" human resistance to the transforming power of grace:

> Batter my heart, three-person'd God; for you
>   As yet but knock; breathe, shine, and seek to mend;
> That I may rise, and stand, o'erthrow me, and bend
>   Your force, to break, blow, burn, and make me new.[22]

The two intellectuals who played an important role in directing the course of Oliver Cromwell's Puritan Commonwealth—Andrew Marvell (1621–78) and John Milton (1608–74)—both demonstrated that Puritans could write poetry just as good as anyone else's, and poetry would give their ideas a way to reach new audiences.

Yet important though these stimuli were to the development of Protestant poetics, the most significant catalyst was the rise of hymnody in the eighteenth century. Hymns were religious poems set to music and intended to edify and inform congregations. Suddenly, poetry was seen to have a thoroughly acceptable Protestant function— not the generation of aesthetic pleasure—always frowned on by the more austere forms of Protestantism—but the education and shaping of minds. Protestantism may not itself have yielded a vast poetic heritage; its function has been more to shape the minds and outlooks of poets than to produce poets.[23]

DRAMA:
PROTESTANTISM AND THE STAGE

In the sixteenth century, the image of the "theater" came to play a potent role in public symbolism, religious or otherwise. John Calvin famously declared that the world was a "theater of the glory of God," in which the divine works of creation and redemption were displayed for the benefit of humanity, who were invited to become participants within, rather than mere observers of, what they saw.[24] This suggests that Calvin and his successors might have warmed to the theater as an art form capable of communicating the gospel in dramatic form—not unlike the highly successful medieval mystery plays. In fact, they did nothing of the sort. The early Protestant hostility toward the theater was striking.

While there are notable exceptions, such as Martin Bucer's *De ludis honestis* ("On the propriety of plays," 1551), a predominantly negative tone had set in by about 1560.[25] Anti-theatrical tracts poured from the presses: John Northbrooke's *A Treatise Against Dicing, Dancing, Plays, and Interludes* (1577), Gosson's *Schoole of Abuse* (1579), Philip Stubbes's *Anatomie of Abuses* (1583), and John Rainold's *Overthrow of Stage-Players* (1599) castigated the stage and its players.[26]

Why this hostility? The answer once more lies in the Protestant anxiety about both the fictionality of drama and the implied deception on the part of actors. Drama was about fabrication, falsity, and the feigning of truth—behaviors that were clearly out of bounds for pious Protestants.[27] Others added to the litany of complaints: the play was a "bastard of Babylon" (William Crashawe) in that it displayed examples of evil, thus encouraging others to emulate them. In his *Histrio-Mastix* (1632), the Puritan moral fanatic William Prynne (1600–1669) argued that "popular stage-playes are sinfull, heathenish, lewde, ungodly spectacles, and most pernicious corruptions." Its 1,100 pages castigated every form of drama, arguing that they represented a vile degradation of true Christian piety.[28] Prynne had an especial animus against women actors, whom he described as "notorious whores." The work is perhaps notable chiefly for its length, its bilious tone, and its virtual ignorance of contemporary drama. (Prynne confesses that he was lured into attending four plays by degenerate colleagues—clearly four too many for his taste.) Interestingly, his main criticism of Shakespeare was that his works were printed on better-quality paper than most Bibles.

Yet despite this clamor of criticism, English Protestantism was not united in adopting such critical attitudes toward the stage. Might not the drama be put to religious use? Was it not a vehicle that, despite its faults, could be used to advance religious debates and agendas?[29] A case can certainly be made that popular theatrical performances under Elizabeth I and James I could be seen as reflecting themes of English Protestantism with an intention of shaping Protestant habits of mind.[30] Others have seen intra-Protestant debates surfacing in the drama of the period. Is Shakespeare's rollicking, drunken Sir John Falstaff based on Sir John Oldcastle, a proto-Protestant martyr?[31]

Where the other major writers of his age became involved in the great religious debates of the age—Ben Jonson became a Catholic and ended up in prison, while Christopher Marlowe dabbled in a little Protestant espionage here and there—Shakespeare, Protestant England's greatest playwright, kept his own counsel. We know little of his personal religious views, even though the subject has attracted much attention.[32] Yet rumors persisted that Shakespeare was more Catholic than Protestant. Richard Davies, a Protestant, commented in the early seventeenth century that "Shakespeare dyed a papist." This possibility must be kept open. There is much in his dramas that sits uneasily alongside Protestant doctrine.

The most debated example concerns the Ghost in *Hamlet*.[33] It is quite clear that Shakespeare intends us to understand that the Ghost has come from purgatory. The term is never mentioned, presumably because it would never have got past the vigilant Elizabethan censor. But it is there, unmistakably, in the imagery that Shakespeare uses (1.5.11–14). The Ghost is:

> Doomed for a certain term to walk the night
> And for the day confined to fast in fires,
> Till the foul crimes done in days of nature
> Are burnt and purged away.

The Ghost thus inhabits the vast imaginative space left empty by English Protestantism's final banishment of purgatory in 1563. The Ghost returns from purgatory and by doing so brings purgatory back into the English public domain in a fictionalized and thereby transformed shape. Shakespeare's *Hamlet* participates in a dangerous, forbidden, exotic "cult of the dead"—and enables the audience to do so as well by stepping back in time, when such beliefs were the norm.[34]

Protestantism having taken the drama and spectacle out of religious life by abolishing Catholic ritual, England was troubled by a cultural void—a sensory vacuum that needed to be filled. In one sense, Shakespeare's dramas moved in to occupy the space left vacant by the banishment of Catholic ritual. At several points, Shakespeare seems to echo hints of long-suppressed Catholic rituals, evoking their rich memory to highlight the aesthetic austerity of their Protestant equivalents.

An instance of this can be found in the brief final act of *The Merchant of Venice*. The passage is so beautifully constructed that the audience is likely to fail to notice that it is apparently irrelevant to the plot. Yet the passage contains an astonishing number of allusions to the Easter Triduum of the Catholic church—as if Shakespeare is deliberately evoking its memory and its rich symbolic allusions. As the liturgy celebrates Christ's death, burial, and resurrection, it sets out a number of images and formulas: the Easter moon; solemn music in the open air; a single candle; the veneration of the cross; the refrain "This is the night" repeated eight times. The same elements are present in this brief final act: moonlight, a single candle dispelling the darkness, the playing of music, the phrase "in such a night" repeated eight times; kneeling at holy crosses.[35]

Under the Puritan Commonwealth, music and drama went into decline. Even as early as 1641, a Puritan-dominated Parliament passed legislation closing down all of London's theaters. With the restoration of Charles II in 1660, the theaters came to life again. The bawdy Restoration dramas of this era represented both a reaction against the moral censoriousness of the Puritan age and a celebration of the looser moral codes of the new monarchy.

In America, however, the Puritan influence continued to be strong, at least in the northern states. The founder of Pennsylvania, William Penn (1644–1718), had little time for the theater. He dismissed it with a rhetorical question: "How many plays did Jesus Christ and his apostles recreate themselves at? What poets, romances, comedies, and the like did the apostles and the saints make or use to pass their time withal?" The answer was obvious, and as far as Penn was concerned, that ended the discussion. Pennsylvania's "Frame of Government" (1682) laid down that "stage-plays" and related activities were to be prevented, since they "excite the people to rudeness, cruelty, looseness and irreligion."

Those who had hoped that the American Revolution would bring about a transformation of attitudes were doomed to disappointment. Meeting in Pennsylvania in 1774, the Continental Congress declared that it would "discourage every species of extravagance and dissipation, especially all horse-racing, and all kinds of gaming, cock fighting, exhibition of shews, plays, and other expensive diversions and entertainments." Four years later, Congress tightened up its hostility to the performance of plays still further by laying down that "any person holding an office under the United States, who shall act, promote, encourage, or attend such plays, shall be unworthy to hold such office, and shall be accordingly dismissed."

FICTION: PROTESTANTISM AND THE NOVEL

As we have seen, early Protestants disliked both drama and opera, seeing these as extravagant, fictional, illusory art forms devoted to amusement rather than education. Protestantism's similarly hostile attitudes toward the literary category of the novel reflect this pervasive, characteristic distrust of fiction as a form of cultured deceit.[36] For Puritan writers, ample literary satisfaction was to be had from the literary genre of "conversion narratives."[37] Why read fiction when real life was more interesting, instructive, and inspirational?

The breakthrough in Protestant attitudes came with a landmark work of religious allegory that contains a sustained narrative that has led many to characterize it as one of the earliest novels. John Bunyan (1626–88), perhaps one of the best-known Puritan writers of the seventeenth century, became involved with the Puritan cause during the English Civil War. With the establishment of the Puritan Commonwealth, Bunyan turned his attention to preaching and became the minister of an independent congregation in Bedford. His Puritan sympathies caused him to be out of favor when the English monarchy was restored in 1660, with the result that he spent many years inside Bedford jail. Bunyan used his time in prison to write his autobiography, *Grace Abounding to the Chief of Sinners,* and to begin work on his best-known work, *The Pilgrim's Progress,* the first part of which appeared in 1678, and the second in 1684.

The central narrative of *The Pilgrim's Progress* concerns its hero, Christian. Initially bowed down with a burden of sin upon his back, Christian flees from the City of Destruction and seeks eternal life. He thus sets out on a long and arduous pilgrimage, which eventually leads him over the bridgeless River of Death to be received in the Celestial Jerusalem. The characters Christian meets along the way—with names such as "Faithful," "Hopeful," and "Mr. Worldly Wiseman"—embody abstract qualities and defects, virtues and vices. These characters, who speak in the simple, lively, humorous language of ordinary people, were almost certainly modeled on the men and women Bunyan knew. Perhaps it is no surprise that the work went on to become one of the most widely read works in the English language, reaching the height of its popularity in the Victorian period.

This early novel sanitized the genre by constructing a fictional narrative that clearly embodied biblical images and reified the abstract concepts central to Christian discipleship—such as faith, doubt, and pride. Bunyan's own credentials as a Puritan activist, imprisoned for his beliefs, helped reassure his reading public that the work was religiously sound and could be used for entertainment as much as for education.

This was followed by *Robinson Crusoe,* a work of fiction that gained respectability partly by being based on fact and partly by representing a version of the conversion narrative genre. Its author, Daniel Defoe (1660–1731), was a "dissenter"—that is, a Protestant outside the English religious establishment—who attended the Academy for Dissenters in Stoke Newington, now a suburb of London. There he was taught by Reverend Charles Morton, who later went on to become the first vice president of Harvard College. Although Defoe wrote at least five hundred known books, many of which were political pamphlets arguing for greater religious toleration, he is remembered today mainly for the work of fiction written in his sixtieth year and published in 1719.

Robinson Crusoe, which tells the story of a shipwrecked mariner, is loosely yet recognizably based on the true story of Alexander Selkirk. The main action of the story takes place in 1659, when Crusoe is shipwrecked on an uninhabited island. With great skill, Defoe explores how Crusoe's intuition and skills allow him to survive in his new situation. Crusoe is portrayed as a man who had made his fortune as a trader but now finds himself in a situation in which goods and money are of no value to him. The novel's exploration of the consequences of this "inversion of values" is widely regarded as compelling.

Alongside this, we find an exploration of Crusoe's inner feelings, especially his attitude toward God. Defoe tells a story of a personal and inward journey that leads to spiritual renewal, paralleling the account of the self-sufficiency that allows Crusoe to survive at the physical level. The journal entries for June 16 through July 4, 1660, make it clear that a spiritual rebirth follows this inversion of values. Discovering tobacco and a Bible in an old sea chest, Crusoe begins to browse through the latter and is eventually—like Augustine of Hippo before him—brought to the point of conversion:

> I threw down the Book, and with my Heart as well as my Hands lifted up to Heaven, in a Kind of Extasy of Joy, I cry'd out aloud, Jesus, thou Son of David, Jesus, thou exalted Prince and Saviour, give me Repentance!

Robinson Crusoe is a remarkable novel that can be read at several levels—as an Enlightenment account of the individual's self-discovery and self-actualization, as a Protestant account of the awakening of the soul through the encounter with the word of God, or as a theological exploration of a radically individualist reading of the Bible, without any guidance or assistance from church or tradition. Yet its real significance was in awakening Protestant interest in the novel as a literary form with apologetic and didactic potential. It would be some time before its full potential was realized; the process of exploration and reflection, however, had unquestionably begun.

A further landmark in the growing Protestant acceptance of the novel was the publication of Charles Sheldon's *In His Steps*.[38] Sheldon arrived as pastor of the Central Congregational Church in Topeka, Kansas, in 1888 to find depressingly small congregations on Sunday evenings. In an attempt to attract newcomers, he began reading chapters of novels he had written to his congregation. When this approach met with a positive response, he was encouraged to develop it. In October 1896, he began reading chapters from *In His Steps*.

The novel invites its readers to imagine the quandary faced by a clergyman and his congregation when a thirty-year-old stranger arrives in their midst, clearly in need of help. They resolve to ask themselves the fundamental question: what would Jesus do? As its central characters consider this question, they find themselves changed utterly. A newspaper editor decides not to print accounts of prize fights or local society gossip; nor will he run liquor or tobacco ads. A talented singer decides that she will use her beautiful voice for gospel singing rather than opera performances.

The work was accessible and inspirational, and it rapidly garnered a huge readership.[39] Nobody has the slightest idea how many copies it sold, but the figure is believed to be in excess of ten million copies. Why does nobody know? Because Sheldon sold the rights to a religious magazine, the *Advance*, which published it in book form. The publisher inadvertently failed to file enough copies of the book with the copyright authorities, with the result that copyright protection was not obtained. The work passed into the public domain and could be reprinted by anyone. Its continuing potency can be seen today in the sports armbands and bracelets bearing the letters WWJD—an abbreviation, of course, for What Would Jesus Do?

More recently, the power of the novel to convey Protestant ideas has been appreciated and developed within conservative American communities, particularly those with strongly apocalyptic views of the end times.[40] Frank Peretti's two spiritual warfare novels *This Present Darkness* (1988) and *Piercing the Darkness* (1989) captivated their readerships, offering a vivid and dramatic account of the spiritual geography of a fallen world. The first of these follows an intrepid born-again Christian preacher and a newspaper reporter as they unearth a New Age plot to take over the local community and eventually the entire world. Described by some critics as "sanctified Stephen King," the novels demonstrate the capacity of the genre to mediate theology and suspense in about equal measure. A similar success has been enjoyed by the apocalyptic "Left Behind" series by Tim LaHaye and Jerry Jenkins.

In Britain the role of the novel in developing the Christian imagination was developed by the Anglican writer C. S. Lewis. Lewis's own severely austere Protestant upbringing in Northern Ireland, especially when coupled with periods of solitariness following his mother's death, led to his discovery of the power of the imagination to console and to excite, often through the creation and inhabitation of imaginary worlds. Following his conversion at Oxford in 1929, Lewis began to explore the power of fiction to communicate truth through the imagination. In doing so, he drew on the writings of the Scottish Protestant preacher and writer George MacDonald (1824–1905). The outcome was initially *The Pilgrim's Regress* and eventually the series of children's novels for which he is best known—the "Chronicles of Narnia" series.

Lewis's exploration of the use of narrative to develop the religious potential of the imagination raised hackles in some Protestant circles. Yet the overwhelmingly positive reaction to his books has long since eclipsed such criticisms and concerns. The imaginative impoverishment of Protestantism, widely cited as a major contributing cause to the rise of secularism, appears to have been reversed through the impact of

Lewis and others. Just as Iris Murdoch demonstrated the potential of the novel to explore philosophical themes, Lewis and others have firmly established the potential of the novel to engage with theology. That exploration has only just begun; its further exploration is likely to yield some fascinating outcomes and insights.

SPORT: THE ORIGINS OF "MUSCULAR CHRISTIANITY"

The emergence of a symbiotic relationship between Protestantism and sport dates to the nineteenth century. If Puritanism can be judged to be representative of the movement as a whole, early Protestantism was characterized by a virtually unrelenting hostility toward any form of sport, which was seen as a waste of time and effort and a diversion from the more serious things in life.[41] Yet such a uniformly negative attitude eventually proved unsustainable as the value of sport for public health and personal development became increasingly accepted. During the nineteenth century, a new attitude toward sport began to emerge in both Britain and the United States as its potential as a tool of Christian witness and social formation came to be appreciated.[42]

The term "muscular Christianity" appears to have first made its appearance in England during the late 1850s to describe the values embodied in two Victorian novels: Charles Kingsley's *Two Years Ago* and Thomas Hughes's *Tom Brown's School Days*. The British popular press picked up the phrase, using it to refer to adventure novels that advocated and exemplified high moral principles and manly Christian heroes. A new paradigm of Christian existence was emerging as Protestants broke free of the somewhat sentimental attitudes toward religion that had settled in within much of Victorian church life.

In part, this development reflected a growing concern that Christianity was becoming feminized. Church congregations seemed increasingly to be made up of women—an observation that led many men to wonder what role masculine values might play in the ministry and mission of the church.[43] Alarmed by statistics in the early 1890s suggesting that the membership of Protestant denominations was becoming increasingly female, many pastors wondered how the church could be reconnected with masculine values. For some critics, including powerful lay figures such as Theodore Roosevelt and John D. Rockefeller, the problem lay with the pastors themselves, who were seen by some as little more than "thin, vapid, affected, driveling little doodles" who found it easier to take tea with women than to encounter men on their own territory. What congregations needed, they said, were more "men whose blood coursed strong and hot through their veins, fine specimens of muscular, soldierly Christianity."[44] Protestant clergy and lay leaders of the "muscular Christianity" movement abandoned the sentimentality and "feminine" forms of religion that had gained the upper hand in the Victorian era, opting for a new model that stressed action rather than reflection and "masculinity" rather than gentility. An active Christian presence in sport seemed to be the answer to this problem.

The origins of this perhaps surprising development—given the long-standing Puritan hostility toward sport—lay in the English love for cricket, and especially the social respect given to its heroes. In the late nineteenth century, three gentleman Victorian cricketing brothers demonstrated the potential of sport as a means of Christian outreach. The three Studd brothers were all educated at Eton and Cambridge University, which was at that time experiencing an evangelical revival, partly through the activities of the Cambridge Inter-Collegiate Christian Union, founded in 1877.[45] Sir John Edward Kynaston Studd (1858–1944), George Brown Studd (1859–1945), and Charles Thomas Studd (1860–1931) were all converted in the summer of 1878 during the Moody-Sankey missionary campaign in England. All were gifted cricketers, each captaining the Cambridge University cricket team in successive seasons from 1882 to 1884.

Their importance to the history of English cricket is legendary, not least on account of Charles's involvement in the famous Ashes test match against Australia in 1882. Yet their greater significance for our narrative is in their forging of a link between sporting excellence and evangelistic outreach in the United States, where sport increasingly became seen as a socially acceptable means of developing personal fitness and discipline and propagating the faith. The most significant developments followed in the wake of John Studd's visit to America in 1885, when he toured various American colleges and planted the basic ideas of "muscular" Christianity. (It must be remembered that cricket was widely played in the United States at the time; its total displacement by baseball as America's preferred team sport had yet to take place.⁴⁶) The values of muscular Christianity resonated well with the YMCA's emphasis on physical well-being as a goal of the Christian life and helped create a more positive and accommodating attitude toward sport within conservative Protestantism and the broader American culture. The association of healthy bodies with healthy faith inevitably pointed to sport as a means of physical and spiritual enrichment.

The YMCA itself gave rise to one of America's most popular sports—basketball. This was invented in December 1891 by James Naismith, a physical education teacher at the YMCA International Training School at Springfield College in Springfield, Massachusetts. Confronted by bored students unable to undertake sports outside in the cold weather, Naismith developed an indoor ball game suited to the limitations of a gymnasium, based on some articles he had read in a Christian missionary magazine about traditional Mesoamerican ball games.

Not content with inventing this new sport, Naismith developed the notion of coaching, which he viewed as a form of spiritual mentoring or discipling. During his time at the University of Kansas, Naismith did much to lay the intellectual and spiritual foundations of the notion of coaching. It is easy to argue that there is a direct link between the evangelical origins of basketball coaching and the values seen in the career of a Bill McCartney—the evangelical University of Colorado football coach who founded the "Promise Keepers" movement.⁴⁷

Naismith's philosophy was based on the idea that sport was in itself an activity embodying the values of Protestantism, so that basketball could be seen as a means of transferring, actualizing, and nourishing Christian character within a masculine context. While this ethos persists, it has arguably been displaced by growing interest in using sport as a gateway into the Christian faith. Gil Dodds, one of the preeminent American runners of the 1940s, became part of Billy Graham's outreach team and used sporting prowess as a means of commending the gospel. Similarly, Bill Glass, the former member of the Detroit Lions and the Cleveland Browns, evangelized his fellow sportsmen and saw football as an effective means to reach American youngsters.⁴⁸

So is this emphasis on sport alien to the spirit of Protestantism? Its advocates rightly point out that the New Testament frequently uses sporting illustrations and metaphors to encourage discipleship—such as running a race (1 Corinthians 9:24; Hebrews 12:1). Yet the link between Protestantism and sport has not been without its problems and dangers. Activism, after all, is not a purely male concern. The same dynamic that gave rise to the Boy Scouts also gave rise to its female equivalent. Nor is sport a purely Protestant concern: Catholicism can equally well be said to promote muscular Christianity, at least to some extent, through the athletic programs of such leading schools as the University of Notre Dame in Indiana.

There are deeper issues that should also be noted. After the First World War, American Protestant leaders such as Harry Emerson Fosdick and Sherwood Eddy blamed muscular Christianity for encouraging militarism and thus contributing to the disaster of the war. The new world order seemed to demand a more accommodating, less aggressive attitude on the part of men.[49] It has also been pointed out that during its early years in America muscular Christianity existed in a tense and often ambivalent relationship with regnant ideologies of male domination and white supremacy. Equally significant, in more recent times Protestantism's relationship with sport has proved to be akin to riding a tiger: sport, in the view of some cultural analysts, has emerged as a religion (or at least a religious activity) in its own right, threatening to displace Protestantism in the struggle for the soul of the American male.

Conservative American attitudes toward sport can be seen as a mirror of its relationship with culture in general. While all generalizations are open to criticism, three broad phases can be discerned since 1890. In the first period, which flourished until the end of the First World War, evangelical Christians were encouraged to take part in competitive sport and to bear witness to the gospel, both through their sporting prowess and their moral integrity. The rise of fundamentalism led to a major disengagement with sport throughout the 1930s; this period of disengagement did not come to an end until the Second World War ended in 1945. Thereafter, the diminishing influence of fundamentalism and the rise of neo-evangelicalism led to the emergence of a wide range of sport-identified mission organizations (including Sports Ambassadors, the Fellowship of Christian Athletes, Campus Crusade for Christ, and Athletes in Action), sports chaplaincies (such as Baseball Chapel and Pro Athletes Outreach), and sports programs at evangelical mega-churches. In Britain, Christians in Sport has played a significant role in advocating a Christian presence across the spectrum of sporting activities. Protestant attitudes toward sport, as toward culture in general, seems dependent on its prevailing theological and cultural assumptions. It is therefore unsafe and unwise to predict what the future holds.

Having considered the complex and constantly changing interaction between Protestantism and the arts, we now consider its relationship with the natural sciences.

PROTESTANTISM AND THE EMERGENCE OF THE NATURAL SCIENCES

To some, the notion of any positive link between religion and science seems highly improbable from the outset. Surely science and religion have always been locked in mortal combat? Yet the stereotype of the "warfare of science and religion" is a product of the social conditions of the late nineteenth century and is now regarded as historically unacceptable.[50] The interaction of science and religion is far too complex and interesting to be represented in such a simplistic, inaccurate way. The massive advances made in the history of science now allow the early relationship of science and Protestantism to be seen in a much more persuasive light.[51]

It is often noted that the emergence of the natural sciences is specifically linked with the Christian intellectual environment of western Europe. Less obvious, however, is a theoretical explanation for this that is firmly anchored to the historical evidence. A good case can be made for arguing that the Christian doctrine of creation affirmed that the universe was regular and ordered and that the study of nature was an indirect way of recognizing and honoring the divine wisdom, as seen in the order of things.

In recent years, however, a growing body of scholarly work has emerged arguing that the decisive contribution to the emergence of the natural sciences came not from Christianity in general but from Protestantism in particular. A major factor in this argument concerns changes in how the Bible was interpreted, a process in which Protestantism played a strategic role.[52] The fundamental change emerged in the first years of Protestantism, whose new approach to the biblical text brought about a hermeneutical revolution that led to a new approach to natural objects. This arose from the new meaning that approach lent to the old and religiously appealing "two books" metaphor: God as the author of both a "book of words" (the Bible) and a "book of works" (nature).[53]

Early Christian writers were well aware that the "book of nature" could be "read" in various ways. The great Alexandrian theologian Origen held that the visible world is invested with symbols that, if correctly interpreted, teach the diligent observer about God. To understand these, however, the reader needed to penetrate beyond the material appearances of the creatures and discover their deeper and more profound meanings. The same attitude was adopted toward reading the Bible, which was widely held to possess a superficial "literal" or "historical" sense as well as deeper symbolic meanings accessible to discerning readers. Both the Bible and nature possessed deeper symbolic meanings.

In the Middle Ages, these symbolic meanings tended to be given the greater weight. Natural objects were understood in terms of how they fitted into a complex web of theological and spiritual symbolism, rather than being treated as "natural" objects in their own right. Similarly, the allegorical reading of the Bible was held to disclose deeper truths than might be possible by a literal reading of the text.

It is at this point that the significance of Protestantism can be appreciated. Although Luther and early Protestants were fully aware of the importance of symbolic and spiritual meanings of texts, they emphasized literal or historical readings.[54] What, they asked, was the *natural* sense of a biblical passage? This way of reading the book of scripture led, when transferred to reading the book of nature, to a way of engaging with the natural order that emphasized a direct, "natural" account of things. The new hermeneutical strategies promoted by the first Protestants were thus of central importance in establishing the conditions that made the emergence of modern science possible.

This literalist mentality toward the Bible was transposed into an insistent empiricism in the field of science. Both religious and scientific truth were held to arise from the immediate, literal sense of what met the human eye. No professional intermediaries, sacred or secular, were required in either case. Science and religion alike were democratized. In his *History of the Royal Society* (1667), Thomas Sprat perceptively remarked that, just as there were two "books," so there were also two "reformations," each prizing direct engagement with God's two books without the need for scholars or priests.

This emerging tendency to see nature as "natural" was linked with the Protestant hostility toward images, which further reinforced the demise of the symbolic conceptions of the natural order. Protestant iconoclasm deeply distrusted objects that were asserted to have significance as religious symbols. The same line of thought that held that human artifacts could not mediate or symbolize the divine led to natural objects and phenomena being stripped of their symbolic associations—and hence allowed to become objects of scientific investigation.

This theme of the "desacralization" or "disenchantment" of nature has been studied in depth by scholars of the early modern period who have noted its implications for the emergence of the natural sciences—and also for secularism and atheism. Peter Berger's analysis of the role of Protestantism in causing secularization deserves mention at this point.[55] For Berger, Protestantism can be thought of as having caused "an immense shrinkage in the scope of the sacred in reality." Protestants did not see themselves as living in a world that was "ongoingly penetrated by sacred beings and forces." Instead, they understood their world to be "polarized between a radically transcendent divinity and a radically 'fallen' humanity" that was devoid of any sacred qualities or connections. Catholicism had contained secularizing forces through its deeply symbolic understanding of the natural world and humanity's place within it. Without realizing what it was doing, Protestantism, for Berger, opened the floodgates of the forces that would shape modernity and ultimately cause Protestantism such grief in its heartlands.

Yet Protestantism created a new motivation—or perhaps, some might argue, enhanced an existing one—for the scientific study of nature. A persistent theme throughout the works of John Calvin was that the wisdom of the invisible and intangible God might be discerned and studied through his works—such as the created order. Calvin thus commended—and even ventured to express some little jealousy of—natural scientists, who were able to experience and appreciate the beauty and wisdom of God through what God had created and molded.

This fundamental motivation for the scientific study of nature has since pervaded Protestantism. It can be seen in many confessional documents of the Reformed church in western Europe. For example, the Belgic Confession affirmed that nature is set "before our eyes as a most beautiful book, in which all creatures, great and small, are like so many characters leading us to contemplate the invisible things of God" (2). The trajectory of thought could not be clearer: reading the "book of nature" enhances our appreciation of what is known of God through the "book of scripture."

Others have noted that the Protestant motivation for studying science was not limited to factors that emerged as significant during the sixteenth century. In 1938 the sociologist Robert Merton (1910–2003) suggested that certain types of Protestantism played a significant role in consolidating a scientific culture in seventeenth-century England. At the heart of the "Merton thesis" is a variation of Max Weber's famous theory concerning Protestantism and the rise of the "spirit of capitalism." The Protestant ethos—especially that found in English Puritanism and German Pietism—stimulated scientific research by giving it a religious dimension.[56]

In our discussion thus far, we have emphasized that changing fashions in the interpretation of the Bible underlay, at least to some extent, the rise of the natural sciences in western Europe. This in itself is an important witness to the importance of the Protestant enterprise in that it demonstrates that the reexamination of traditional interpretations of the Bible often stimulated new ways of envisaging and investigating the natural world.

Yet there is more—considerably more—than this to the relationship between the natural sciences and Protestant approaches to biblical interpretation. In the view of a growing number of Protestant theologians and scientists, especially during the seventeenth century, the natural sciences offered a means of providing the church with the best possible system of biblical interpretation. Might the manner in which the scientist interpreted the book of nature provide a paradigm for the way in which the theologian interpreted the book of scripture?

Although it has become something of a scholarly habit to speak of the "scientific revolution" of the early modern period, this expression reflects the perspective of today's scholars. At the time, contemporary observers often spoke of the emergence of the natural sciences as a "reformation," and they drew an explicit parallel between the reformations in religion and science. Using the imagery of "God's two books" of nature and the Bible, it was easy to suggest that the remarkable successes and advances made in the interpretation of the former might also assist with the cognate biblical undertaking.[57] Might the somewhat precarious enterprise of biblical interpretation be placed upon a new, rigorous intellectual foundation firmly grounded in the order of things?

It was an idea that entranced many, including Isaac Newton. Yet its appeal to the wider Protestant community soon paled as it became clear that this new method of biblical interpretation led into the byways of heterodoxy. Newton's reformation in science-based biblical interpretation led him to reject the Trinity, although he was careful not to draw attention to this fact during his lifetime.[58] The new strategies seemed to lead to deist readings of the Bible and were treated with growing suspicion by orthodox Protestant writers.

It is thus important to note that the issue of heterodoxy makes the link between Protestantism and the scientific revolution more complex.[59] Earlier, we noted that Protestantism is thought to have emerged in part because of the intellectual turbulence of the early sixteenth century, when new options for understanding the world of culture and nature were being eagerly explored and evaluated. Many of those Protestants who were at the forefront of the scientific movement were of questionable theological orthodoxy. Newton, for example, was associated with anti-trinitarianism and Arianism, both of which could be accommodated without difficulty to his system of natural philosophy.[60] Joseph Priestley, the discoverer of oxygen, saw scientific advance as a means of securing religious reform—including the revision of traditional theology along more rational lines.[61]

The history of the Protestant interaction with the emerging natural sciences is thus neither simple nor uniformly positive. To understand the complexity of the interaction, we shall consider two landmark areas of debate in which Protestantism found itself in an ambivalent relationship with the sciences—the Copernican controversies of the sixteenth century and the Darwinian controversies of the nineteenth and twentieth centuries.

COPERNICUS: BIBLICAL INTERPRETATION AND THE SOLAR SYSTEM

One of the fundamental principles of Protestantism is its insistence that all interpretations of the Bible must be regarded as provisional, not final; part of the task of the church is continually to reexamine previous ways of interpreting scripture to ensure that they have not lapsed into uncritical, unthinking, or simply *wrong* ways of interpreting this foundational text. During the Middle Ages, the Bible was interpreted on the basis of a set of assumptions that were assumed to be secure and permanent. One of them was that the sun and all other heavenly bodies revolved around the earth. The outcome was inevitable: the Bible was interpreted in the light of this assumption, with the result that the Bible was held to endorse a geocentric model of the solar system.

In the 1540s, this fundamental assumption of the medieval era was called into question by the Polish astronomer Nicolas Copernicus. *De revolutionibus orbium coelestium* ("On the revolutions of the heavenly bodies") was published after Copernicus's death in May 1543. The work caused a minor sensation in that it set out a heliocentric model of the solar system. Copernicus argued that the best explanation of a vast body of astronomical evidence was that the planets revolve around the sun and only the moon revolves around the earth. There were some loose ends in his analysis; the final acceptance of the model would have to wait for the detailed work by Johannes Kepler (1571–1630) in the first two decades of the seventeenth century.

Early published defenses of the Copernican theory (such as G. J. Rheticus's *Treatise on Holy Scripture and the Motion of the Earth*, which is widely regarded as the earliest known work to deal explicitly with the relation of the Bible and the Copernican theory) thus had to deal with two issues. First, they had to set out the observational evidence that led to the conclusion that the earth and other planets rotate around the sun. Second, they had to demonstrate that this viewpoint was consistent with the Bible, which had long been read as endorsing a geocentric view of the world.

There is no doubt that the rise of the heliocentric theory of the solar system caused both Catholic and Protestant theologians to reexamine traditional interpretations of certain biblical passages. It is still widely believed that John Calvin refused to accept the heliocentric model of the solar system because it allegedly contradicted the Bible. The source of this idea is Bertrand Russell's hastily written *History of Western Philosophy*, in which he declared that Calvin "demolished Copernicus with the text: 'The world also is stablished, that it cannot be moved' (Psa. xciii.1), and exclaimed: 'Who will venture to place the authority of Copernicus above that of the Holy Spirit?'"[62] This statement has been widely cited ever since, often without acknowledgment and usually without any critical investigation.

Which is a pity. The "quotation" is a complete fabrication whose true source has yet to be identified with certainty. Calvin wrote no such words, which are in any case inconsistent with his approach to theology.[63] Russell appears to have borrowed the passage from Andrew Dickson White's hopelessly inaccurate work *History of the Warfare of Science with Theology in Christendom* (1896) without bothering to check White's sources.

In fact, the Copernican controversy largely vindicated Protestantism's theological method as developed by Calvin. Some biblical passages seem to suggest that the sun rotates about the earth. Calvin argued that these passages were "adapted" or "accommodated" to the ways of thinking of primitive people and had to be interpreted in that light. His fundamental point was that divine revelation takes place in culturally and anthropologically conditioned manners and forms, with the result that it needs to be appropriately interpreted. This approach has a long tradition of use within Judaism and subsequently within Christian theology.[64]

Calvin argued that God adjusts himself to the capacities of the human mind and heart. God paints a portrait of himself that we are capable of understanding. The analogy behind Calvin's thinking at this point is that of a human orator. A good speaker knows the limitations of his audience and adjusts how he speaks accordingly. God, in revealing himself to us, has accommodated himself to our levels of understanding and our innate preference for pictorial means of conceiving him. God reveals himself, not as he is in himself, but in forms adapted to our human capacity. Thus, scripture speaks of God having arms, a mouth, and so on—but these are just vivid and memorable metaphors, ideally suited to our intellectual abilities. The Bible might seem to speak of the sun revolving around the earth—but this is to be interpreted as an "accommodated" way of speaking, adapted to the way of thinking of long ago.

The impact of these ideas upon English scientific theorizing, especially during the seventeenth century, was considerable. For example, Edward Wright defended Copernicus's heliocentric theory of the solar system against biblical literalists by arguing, in the first place, that scripture was not concerned with physics, and in the second, that its manner of speaking was "accommodated to the understanding and way of speech of the common people, like nurses to little children." Both of these arguments derive directly from Calvin.

Yet although the Copernican debates led to a generally positive and helpful outcome, giving the science of Protestant biblical interpretation a much needed stimulus, a much more difficult debate over biblical interpretation lay ahead. This time the question concerned how the early chapters of the Book of Genesis were to be interpreted—a question brought into sharp focus by the Darwinian theory of evolution, to which we now turn.

DARWIN: BIBLICAL INTERPRETATION AND THE ORIGINS OF HUMANITY

One of the most vigorous debates within modern Christian thought concerns the implications of Darwinism for religious belief. It is a debate that is by no means limited to Christianity, as is evident from the generally hostile reaction to Darwinism in the Islamic world. So what is Darwinism? While the term is often used to refer specifically to the views set out by Charles Darwin in his *Origin of Species*, it is more widely used to refer to the theories that emerged from Darwin's work and have since been developed and modified.

The publication of Charles Darwin's *On the Origin of Species* (1859) is rightly regarded as a landmark in nineteenth-century science. Darwin held that all species—including humanity—result from a long and complex process of biological evolution.[65] The religious implications of Darwin's theory will be clear. Traditional Christian thought regarded humanity as set apart from the rest of nature, created as the height of God's creation, and alone endowed with the "image of God." Darwin's theory suggested that human nature has emerged gradually over a long period of time and that no fundamental biological distinction can be drawn between human beings and animals in terms of their origins and development.[66]

This idea caused considerable anxiety to many Christians at the time. In traditional Christian theology, humanity was located within the created order as a whole, but stood above it on account of its unique relationship to God, articulated in the notion of the *imago Dei*. Yet Darwin's *Origin of Species* posed an implicit—and his *Descent of Man* (1871) an explicit—challenge to this view. Humanity had emerged, Darwin asserted, over a vast period of time from within the natural order. This posed a powerful challenge to popular Protestant ideas and soon led to heated controversy.

One popular Protestant account of the origin of species, widely supported by the English religious and academic establishment of the early nineteenth century, held that God somehow created everything, in all its intricacy, more or less as we now see it. The success of this view owed much to the influence of William Paley (1743–1805), Archdeacon of Carlisle, who, in promulgating this view, compared God to one of the mechanical geniuses of the industrial revolution.[67]

Paley's *Natural Theology* (1802) had a profound influence on popular English religious thought in the first half of the nineteenth century, and Darwin is known to have read it. Paley was deeply impressed by Newton's discovery of the regularity of nature, which allowed the universe to be thought of as a complex mechanism operating according to regular and understandable principles. Nature consists of a series of biological structures that can be thought of as "contrived"—that is, constructed with a clear purpose in mind. Paley argued that the present organization of the world, both physical and biological, can be seen as a compelling witness to the wisdom of a creator god. Yet Paley's argument depended on a static worldview and simply could not cope with the dynamic worldview underlying Darwinism.

It is important to note that Darwinism became most worrisome to Christians in cultures that had been particularly influenced by literal readings of the Book of Genesis. Such readings are known to have been widespread within popular Protestantism in Britain and the United States in the first half of the nineteenth century, even though more nuanced interpretative schemes had been proposed by Protestant academics in both countries. Despite these more sophisticated interpretations of the Genesis creation accounts, at the popular level it was widely assumed that a commonsense reading of the Bible led to an understanding that the world and humanity had been created in six days.

Darwinism posed a significant challenge, both to this specific reading of the Book of Genesis and to existing models of biblical interpretation in general. Were the six days of the Genesis creation account to be taken literally as periods of twenty-four hours each? Or as indefinite periods of time? And was it legitimate to suggest that vast periods of time might separate the events of that narrative? Or was the Genesis creation account to be interpreted as a historically and culturally conditioned narrative reflecting ancient Babylonian myths, which could not be taken as a scientific account of the origins of life in general and humanity in particular? The debates were many, and they continue to this day.[68]

It is important to note that these challenges to existing biblical interpretations have occurred in a characteristically Protestant context: an ongoing dialogue between the community of faith and its foundational text. The history of Protestantism has been one of constantly revisiting and reevaluating existing interpretations of the Bible, a process that has been precipitated and catalyzed by many factors—including scientific advance.

Although these debates were well under way within English Protestantism by the late nineteenth century, they have become of especial importance in twentieth-century American evangelicalism, especially in its fundamentalist forms. Interestingly, early fundamentalism does not appear to have had any particular difficulties with Darwinism; opposition was a later development that gained sympathy after the celebrated Scopes "monkey" trial of 1925.[69] In May 1925, John T. Scopes, a young high-school science teacher, fell afoul of a recently adopted statute that prohibited the teaching of evolution in Tennessee's public schools. The American Civil Liberties Union moved in to support Scopes, while William Jennings Bryan served as prosecution counsel. The trial proved to be something of a public relations disaster for fundamentalism.

Bryan, who had billed the trial as a "duel to the death" between Christianity and atheism, was totally wrong-footed by the celebrated agnostic attorney Clarence Darrow. Bryan was called to the stand as a witness for the defense and interrogated concerning his views on evolution. Bryan was forced to admit that he had no knowledge of geology, comparative religions, or ancient civilizations, and he showed himself to have hopelessly naïve religious views. In the end, Bryan won the trial but lost the public relations war. Fundamentalists were easily portrayed as ignorant of both science and the problems of biblical interpretation.

So what of the issue today? Some North American evangelicals—such as those generally described as "creationists"—remain adamant that all forms of the theory of biological evolution are contrary to the teaching of the Bible. This was certainly the view taken in the nineteenth century by the highly influential conservative Protestant writer Charles Hodge, for whom Darwinism was simply a form of atheism. It must, however, be pointed out that Hodge drew a distinction between "Darwinism" and "evolution" and regarded the Darwinian viewpoint as unacceptable on account of its apparent rejection of the notion of divine design. Hodge was prepared to accept evolution, not as a random process, but as one in which the guiding hand of God could be discerned.

Nevertheless, this has not been the only view within evangelicalism on this matter, as can be seen from the writings of Benjamin B. Warfield and James I. Packer, widely regarded as the most significant evangelical writers of the nineteenth and twentieth centuries, respectively.[70] In an 1888 essay on Darwin, Warfield set out his view that the Darwinian doctrine of natural selection could easily be accommodated by evangelicals as a natural law operating under the aegis of the general providence of God. Packer followed Warfield at this point, insisting that he could not see that anything, "in the first chapters of Genesis or elsewhere, bears on the biological theory of evolution one way or the other."[71] Again, following the lead of Warfield, Packer argued that interrogating biblical statements concerning nature in the light of scientific knowledge might help toward attaining a more precise exegesis of them. For though exegesis had to be controlled by the text itself, not shaped by extraneous considerations, the exegetical process was constantly stimulated by questioning the text.

The views of Packer and Warfield have not met with universal assent. Creationists such as Henry Morris have somewhat hastily dismissed the approach adopted by Warfield as a clear case of "pervasive theological apostasy." However, Packer's and Warfield's views are illustrative of a major trend within historical evangelicalism—seeking to reconcile the biblical creation accounts with the insights of the natural sciences. Creationist writers have attempted to suppress or dismiss this prominent section of the evangelical movement, often insisting that an openly anti-evolutionary stance is an essential element of evangelical identity.[72] The reality is otherwise.

Four major positions are now found on this matter within modern American evangelicalism; each position is linked with a specific way of interpreting the Bible, on the one hand, and of engaging with science, on the other.[73] Each can be further subdivided, yielding up nineteen possible Protestant interpretations of the origins of humanity. In what follows, we limit ourselves to identifying four broad categories. Readers might note that the first two are often brought together and treated under the single category of "creationism." Because there are such great variations within this movement, it seemed appropriate to make a distinction between its "young-earth" and "old-earth" variants.

Young-Earth Creationism

Young-earth creationism represents the continuation of the "common reading" of Genesis, which was widely encountered in popular and at least some academic writing before 1800. On this view, the earth was created in its basic form between six thousand and ten thousand years ago. Young-earth creationists read the first two chapters of the Book of Genesis in a way that allows for no living creatures of any kind before Eden, and no death before the Fall. Most young-earth creationists hold that all living things were created simultaneously, within the time frame proposed by the Genesis creation accounts, with the Hebrew word *yom* ("day") meaning a period of twenty-four hours. The fossil records, which point to a much longer time frame and the existence of extinct species, are understood by many young-earth creationists to date from the time of Noah's flood. This viewpoint is often, but not universally, stated in the form of a 144-hour creation and a universal flood.

Old-Earth Creationism

Old-earth creationism, which has a long history, is probably the majority viewpoint within conservative Protestant circles. It has no particular difficulty with the vast age of the world and argues that the young-earth approach requires modification in at least two respects. First, the Hebrew word *yom* may need to be interpreted as an "indefinite time participle" (not unlike the English word "while") signifying an indeterminate period of time that is given specificity by its context. In other words, the word "day" in the Genesis creation accounts is to be interpreted as a long period of time, not a specific period of twenty-four hours. Second, this view proposes that there may be a large gap between Genesis 1:1 and Genesis 1:2. In other words, the narrative is not understood to be continuous but to make way for the intervention of a substantial period of time between the primordial act of creation of the universe and the emergence of life on earth. This viewpoint is advocated by the famous Scofield Reference Bible, first published in 1909, although the ideas can be traced back to writers such as the earlier nineteenth-century Scottish divine Thomas Chalmers.

Intelligent Design

The intelligent design movement, which has gained considerable influence in the United States in recent years, argues that the biosphere is possessed of an "irreducible complexity" that makes it impossible to explain its origins and development using any other theory besides "intelligent design."[74] Intelligent design does not deny biological evolution; its most fundamental criticism of Darwinism is teleological—that evolution has no goal. The intelligent design movement argues that standard Darwinism runs into significant explanatory difficulties that can only be adequately resolved through the intentional creation of individual species. Its critics argue that these difficulties are overstated, or that they will be resolved in due course by future theoretical advances.[75]

Although the movement avoids identifying this intelligent designer directly with God (presumably for political reasons), it is clear that this assumption is intrinsic to its working methods.

Evolutionary Theism

A final approach argues that evolution is to be understood as God's chosen method of bringing life into existence from inorganic materials and creating complexity within life. Whereas Darwinism gives a significant place to random events in the evolutionary process, evolutionary theism sees the process as divinely directed. Some evolutionary theists propose that each level of complexity is to be explained on the basis of "God working within the system," perhaps at the quantum level. Others, such as Howard van Till, adopt a "fully-gifted creation" perspective, arguing that God built in the potential for the emergence and complexity of life in the initial act of creation, so that further acts of divine intervention are not required.

From this survey of Protestant attitudes to Darwinism, it will be clear that some of the movement's constituent elements retain a degree of suspicion, even hostility, toward the sciences, especially in relation to questions of origins. This is traditionally interpreted as a problem for Protestantism. There is some truth in this view, provided the various constituencies within Protestantism are disentangled, and their numerical strengths and theological positions understood. *But it is also a problem for the sciences.* Recent polemical works from aggressively atheist scientific popularizers, such as Richard Dawkins and Daniel Dennett, have created the quite false impression that study of the natural sciences necessitates an atheist worldview.[76] Many American Protestants accept the idea of intelligent design, not on a scientific basis, but because it affirms the legitimate place of God within the greater scheme of things.

As the Darwinian philosopher Michael Ruse pointed out, Dawkins and Dennett have been "absolute disasters" for the sciences in that they have predisposed many Protestants—not to mention other Christians—against the sciences, reinforcing some of the oldest and deepest prejudices of the movement against scholarly advance and new insights.[77] Some serious building of bridges and mending of fences clearly needs to be done. It is utterly pointless to alienate nearly one billion individuals from the sciences on the basis of a highly questionable, perhaps even totally spurious, interpretation of the religious implications of the sciences.[78]

With this sobering reflection, we end this survey of the beliefs and cultural manifestations of classic Protestantism. We now turn to document the remarkable changes of the twentieth century, which saw the movement change beyond recognition in many regions of the world. In part 3 of this work, we shall examine the transformation of Protestantism in the twentieth century arising from the global dominance of the cultural influence of the United States of America, the astonishing rise of Pentecostalism, and the burgeoning of Protestantism in the global South.

PART III

===

Transformation

The twentieth century witnessed many events in the history of Protestant-ism—some inspirational, some deeply disturbing, and others merely signifi-cant. One of those events was the inexorable rise of the economic, military, and cultural power of the United States of America, which has had incalcu-lable consequences for Protestantism.[1] The phenomenon now described as "globalization" was well under way by the middle of the century, with the result that Protestant ideas originating in the United States have been "sub-ject to constant reappropriation, repackaging, and dissemination into the transnational realm."[2]

This can be seen at every level of Protestant identity—including ecumen-ism, theology, missionary activity, the forging of new models of ministry, and spirituality. In my own specialty—the discipline of "systematic theol-ogy"—the intellectual lead has passed decisively from its 1900 epicenter in Germany to the United States. Christian theology was dominated from 1900 to about 1970 by German-language writers, including Karl Barth, Emil Brunner, Adolf von Harnack, Jürgen Moltmann, and Wolfhart Pannenberg. Yet since about 1980, the intellectual lead has passed to America.

Yet one development that played a critical role in the global shaping of twentieth-century Protestantism is too easily overlooked—as, indeed, it was at the time. With hindsight, it is possible to see that a series of seemingly unimportant events in the early 1900s pointed the way to the changing of the Protestant world in the twentieth century. As might be expected, the most famous of these took place in the United States—not in any great city or university, but in a town in the rural state of Kansas that was still recovering from the economic depression of the 1890s, and in a run-down, near-derelict church in San Francisco where the congregation sat on planks to pray.

Late in the evening on the first day of the twentieth century—January 1, 1901—an event took place at Bethel Bible College in Topeka, Kansas. The institution had been founded in the holiness tradition the previous October by Charles Fox Parham (1873–1929), a former pastor in the Methodist Episcopal church. Topeka had already attracted wide attention through the novels of its Congregationalist pastor Charles Sheldon, author of In His Steps. *As an exercise, Parham asked his students to investigate the New Testament evidence for the continued activity of the Holy Spirit in the Christian life.*

It was seen as an empty, pointless question by many. The theological wisdom of the day took the form of "cessationism," which was widely taught by Protestant theological heavyweights. In this view, the active gifts of the Holy Spirit, such as "speaking in tongues," belonged to the age of the New Testament and were no longer available or operational.[3] *The New Testament was thus read from within a somewhat rationalist framework, reflecting the ideas of the Enlightenment, which had already determined that such spiritual phenomena were things of the past. Parham was not so sure. Within his own holiness tradition, reports were circulating of what seemed to be charismatic phenomena. He asked his students for their views.*

Their response—perhaps too easily dismissed as naïve and simplistic—was that a straightforward reading of the biblical texts suggested that this charismatic gifting was still a possibility and that it could be identified by speaking in other tongues. Impressed by the clarity of this response, Parham joined his students for a prayer vigil that began on December 31, 1900, in the hope that the gift might be renewed. At eleven o'clock the following evening, when the new century was less than a day old, one of Parham's students, Agnes Ozman, had such an experience. A few days later others, including Parham himself, followed suit.

Parham and his students began to tell others about this apparent recovery of the gift of tongues. One of those who heard Parham speak in 1905 was the African American preacher William J. Seymour (1870–1922), who was forced by the southern segregationist policies of that period to listen to Parham's lectures through a half-opened door. Sadly, Parham—noted for his white supremacist views—did nothing to break down this racial wall of separation. Inspired, Seymour went on to open the Apostolic Faith Mission in a dilapidated church, then used only for storage, at 312 Azusa Street in Los Angeles in April 1906.

Over the next two years, a major revival broke out at Azusa Street, characterized by speaking in tongues. The movement began to be characterized by the term "Pentecostalism," which came from "the Day of Pentecost"—the occasion, according to the New Testament, when the phenomenon was first experienced by the early Christian disciples (Acts 2:1–4). Significantly, at a time of ruthless racial segregation in American culture brought about by the notorious Jim Crow segregation laws, the Azusa Street mission pointedly ignored racial issues.[4] A black man was leading a diverse ministry team comprising white people, black people, and Hispanics. As historian of Pentecostalism Frank Bartlemann put it, alluding to a great revivalist theological theme, "the color line was washed away with the blood."

Through events like this, not limited to the United States, a new Protestant movement was born in the first decade of the twentieth century. One hundred years after its birth, it is estimated that at least half a billion people are Pentecostals—the largest Christian group of any kind other than Catholicism. Its emergence and consolidation has transformed Protestantism and raised the possibility that the twenty-first century will be shaped decisively and permanently by this new, dynamic, populist form of Christianity. It forms the backdrop against which the story of Protestantism in the twentieth century must be told—and on which its future may well depend.

Yet we must begin our account of the remarkable reconfiguration of Protestantism in the twentieth century by considering its development in the nation that stamped its presence and influence on that era—the United States of America.

A nineteenth-century American camp meeting. Thousands of these took place, especially in the southern states, helping to shape the emergence of the "Bible Belt." Lithograph by Hugh Bridport, c. 1829.

14

The Changing Shape of American Protestantism

As the twentieth century dawned, it seemed to many American Protestants that something troubling was happening to their nation. Its Protestant foundations seemed threatened by erosion in some quarters; in others they were regarded as insignificant. With the benefit of hindsight, we can see that the exchange by the American academy and body politic of one orthodoxy for another was well under way. This process would culminate by the late twentieth century in the predominance of a strictly secular understanding of human existence, a commanding status that earlier had been granted to forms of mainline Protestant orthodoxy. The situation was made worse by German biblical criticism, whose growing impact on Protestant seminaries seemed to be eroding traditional attitudes toward the authority of sacred text. Things seemed to be going wrong for Protestantism. So what would happen next?

FUNDAMENTALISM: WITHDRAWAL FROM THE MAINSTREAM

What should be done? One answer was given in a series of pamphlets published during the years 1910 to 1915 entitled "The Fundamentals: A

Testimony to the Truth." These essays, drawn from a range of conservative Protestant writers, set out a classic statement of Protestant teachings from a generally Reformed perspective. By an accident of history, they gave birth to the term "fundamentalism," which was first used in 1920 by the journalist Curtis Lee Laws to designate those who were ready "to do battle royal for the Fundamentals."

Since then, fundamentalism has regularly been presented as an unthinking, uncritical, highly dogmatic form of Protestantism. While there is some truth in this generalization, it fails to penetrate to the heart of the matter. The essence of all forms of religious fundamentalism is an *oppositionalist mentality* arising in response to a major threat.[1] To treat fundamentalism simply as conservative religion confuses the characteristic and the distinctive. As Martin Marty has written, "Fundamentalism in any context takes form when members of already conservative or traditional movements experience threat." In this case, the threat did not come from Catholicism, as in the past, but from secularizing forces within American society at large.

Protestant fundamentalism is thus best seen as a specific reaction to developments in the world of early twentieth-century America and is thus, in one sense of the word, thoroughly "modern." It was from its outset, and has remained, a countercultural movement that uses central doctrinal affirmations as a means of defining cultural boundaries. Whereas most nineteenth-century forms of American evangelicalism were culturally centralist, committed to engaging with culture in order to transform it through the gospel, the fundamentalist reaction against modern secularism has entailed a separatist attitude toward culture. Certain central doctrines—most notably, the absolutely literal authority of scripture and the idea of the premillennial return of Christ—have been treated as barriers; they are intended as much to alienate secular culture as to give fundamentalists a sense of identity and purpose.

Controversies broke out within many American denominations over the issues raised by fundamentalism. The debate within Presbyterianism was particularly painful and divisive, and it seriously wounded the denomination.[2]

In 1922 a sermon by the Baptist preacher Henry Emerson Fosdick (1878–1969) originally entitled "Shall the Fundamentalists Win?" was distributed throughout the United States under the new title "The New Knowledge and the Christian Faith." Then serving at First Presbyterian Church in New York, Fosdick noted the emergence of conservative and liberal positions within the churches and pleaded for inclusiveness and mutual respect for each position. A fundamentalist riposte soon followed from across the Hudson River—Clarence Edward Macartney's tract "Shall Unbelief Win?" The situation rapidly polarized, and oppositionalist mentalities on both sides of the debate framed the issue in black-and-white terms: Presbyterians were forced to decide whether they were "unbelieving liberals" or "reactionary fundamentalists."

Yet the situation was far more complex than these simple characterizations suggest. It is often forgotten, for example, that in 1935 Fosdick himself shocked his progressive colleagues with a sermon entitled "The Church Must Go Beyond Modernism." Drawing on the emerging neo-orthodox theologies of Karl Barth and Reinhold Niebuhr, he criticized liberalism's habit of changing beliefs to accommodate culture, softening the reality of God, and downplaying the themes of personal and social sin. Although Fosdick disliked fundamentalism's rigidity, dogmatism, and aggressiveness, he did not consider all of its ideas mistaken. Fosdick was a voice in the wilderness at this point, however, drowned out by the clamor of battle.

Positions were clarified, crystallized, and then petrified. Fundamentalists came to believe that the best way of fighting the "culture wars" that emerged in many denominations in the 1920s and 1930s was to disengage, leave their—as they saw it—liberalized and secularized denominations behind, and found new, pure denominations. By the 1930s, when it became painfully clear that reform from within could not prevent the spread of modernism in the major northern denominations, more and more fundamentalists began to declare that separation from America's major denominations was an article of faith.[3] It was a strategy that failed. Why?

Two main problems emerged. First, an oppositionalist mentality, once acquired, proves to be extremely difficult to shake off. Having broken away from traditional denominations over points of doctrine, fundamentalists now continued those debates with equally great ferocity in the supposedly pure denominations that had just been formed by their secession. Having got so used to fighting their opponents, they now started fighting each other. This pervasive infighting simply weakened the movement and prevented it from even beginning to achieve its goals.

One example concerns the great critic of Presbyterian liberalism of this era, J. Gresham Machen (1881–1937).[4] Convinced that the official Presbyterian Board of Foreign Missions failed to do justice to the uniqueness of Christianity, Machen formed the Independent Board for Presbyterian Foreign Missions in 1933. Those who joined him in this venture shared his opinion. As time went on, however, it became painfully clear that they had little else in common. Divisions over other issues, such as a simmering controversy between strict Calvinists and dispensationalists, soon emerged. Machen was ousted as the president of the board in 1936; worn out by the arguments and dissent within a supposedly "doctrinally pure" body, he died a few months later, in January 1937. By that time, the board had virtually ceased to exist in anything but name. It had simply imploded as a result of controversy and tensions.

The second problem was that fundamentalism's decision to break away from mainline denominations and isolate itself from a tainted, fallen culture simply put it in the position of having no influence over either church or society. It was powerless to oppose the changes it so detested in both the churches and society at large. As time passed, it became clear that fundamentalism had committed a fundamental strategic error by disconnecting itself from any positions of power or influence. Conservative Protestantism seemed to have painted itself into a corner by accomplishing what its opponents had expected to happen only after major battles—its own total marginalization. The enormity of the error soon became apparent. It was only a matter of time before another strategy would emerge.

NEO-EVANGELICALISM: REENGAGEMENT WITH THE MAINSTREAM

The battles of the Second World War diverted American Protestantism from its internal feuds and set them in a not altogether unhelpful context. Once the war was over, new voices began to emerge within conservative Protestantism, urging fundamental changes of direction. The emergence of evangelicalism as a distinctive Protestant position dates to 1942 and the formation of the National Association of Evangelicals, with its principled attempt to distinguish evangelicalism from fundamentalism.⁵ In contrast to the dogmatic fundamentalist insistence on separation from modern culture, the "new evangelicals"—led by E. J. Carnell, Harold Ockenga, Carl Henry, and Billy Graham—were committed to a positive engagement with culture in an attempt to transform it through the gospel.

Billy Graham is probably the best-known representative of this new movement on account of his worldwide evangelistic ministry, which began in the late 1940s. Graham came to regard traditional fundamentalist "oppositionalism" as a barrier to the preaching of the gospel. In 1956 the popular fundamentalist magazine *Christian Life* published an article entitled "Is Evangelical Theology Changing?" It argued that the fundamentalist old guard was committed to the slogan "earnestly contend for the faith," whereas the new generation preferred "you must be born again." A heated controversy resulted.

Three months later, the same journal published an interview with Billy Graham in which he declared that he was "sick and fed up" with such controversies and just wanted to get on with preaching the gospel. For Graham, fundamentalism led to interminable, sterile theological conflicts at a time when there was important evangelistic work to be done. The growing alienation of Graham from fundamentalism was publicly demonstrated when he accepted an invitation in 1955 to hold a crusade in New York City. The invitation came from a coalition of Christian churches, many of which were not in any way fundamentalist. By the time the crusade opened to massive publicity in the spring of 1957, fundamentalism seemed to be consigned to the past.⁶ Although Graham was unquestionably a conservative Protestant, that did not make him a fundamentalist.

Carl Henry (1913–2003) illustrates the character of the new movement particularly well, especially its attitude toward culture at large. In his *Uneasy Conscience of Modern Fundamentalism* (1947)—the "manifesto of neo-evangelicalism" (Dirk Jellema)—Henry argued that fundamentalism presented and proclaimed an impoverished and reduced gospel that was radically defective in its social vision. Fundamentalism, he suggested, was too otherworldly and anti-intellectual to gain a hearing with the educated public. It showed no interest in exploring the relationship between Christianity and culture and social life.

Yet Jean Monnet's admonition now came into play: without institutions, nothing survives. The new movement required *institutions*—in this case, both a seminary and a journal—to consolidate its influence. The founding in 1947 of Fuller Theological Seminary, which quickly (and controversially) aligned itself with the "new" evangelicalism rather than fundamentalism, ensured its institutional survival.[7] Henry's experience as a journalist led to an invitation from Billy Graham and L. Nelson Bell to edit a new journal then being launched. As editor-in-chief of *Christianity Today* from 1956 until 1968, Henry did much to establish the profile, concerns, and credibility of the "new evangelicalism."

The success and possible downside of the forms of cultural engagement advocated by evangelicalism can be seen in the ministry of Billy Graham.[8] Although Graham's relationship with President Harry Truman was tentative and uncertain, he succeeded in building a good working relationship with President Dwight "Ike" Eisenhower. His relationship with John F. Kennedy was ambivalent, but he consolidated his emerging role as unofficial pastor and spiritual adviser to the White House with Lyndon B. Johnson and Richard Nixon, and he would retain that role until the end of the Clinton administration. Graham thus enjoyed a privileged relationship with nine presidents over a period of nearly fifty years, virtually becoming a chaplain to the presidency.

Yet this high degree of political acceptance was not without its costs. Graham felt that he could not openly criticize those whom he served in this way, and as a result he failed to carry out the prophetic ministry many believed he was uniquely placed to exercise. He offered support for the Vietnam War effort under Johnson and was surprisingly unforthcoming over the moral failures of several presidencies—most notably the Watergate scandal that engulfed Nixon and the sexual intrigues of the Clinton presidency. To its critics, the increasing social acceptability of evangelicalism was the reverse side of evangelicalism's increasing acceptance of wider cultural norms: through such acceptance, it had lost its moral cutting edge.[9]

One clear area of divergence between fundamentalism and evangelicalism concerned social action. The impact of earlier revivals had led to new interest in engaging with society. By the middle of the nineteenth century, it had become assumed that those who had experienced some spiritual renewal should straightway take part in the various efforts to help the less fortunate in the community. Yet in the 1920s and 1930s, fundamentalism turned its back on any attempt at social outreach. For reasons that are not entirely persuasive and rest more on imagined associations than on demonstrable convergences, many influential fundamentalists saw efforts to help the poor as betraying a commitment to liberal theology. After all, were not the proponents of the "social gospel" during the modernist controversy of the 1920s theological liberals?[10] Until recently, fundamentalists tended to see Christian social action as limited purely to struggles for religious freedom and against abortion. For evangelicals, in contrast, the gospel clearly calls Christians to fight racism, sexism, and poverty as well.

Other changes and realignments taking place around this time were further altering the nature of Protestantism. Once more, those changes centered on Protestantism's relationship to culture.

A NEW REFORMATION?
REVISIONIST PROTESTANTISM, 1960–1990

During the 1960s, Western society underwent a series of convulsions that called the settled assumptions of the past into question with unprecedented vigor. It was as if there was an unrelenting impatience with the ways of the past, a sense of dissatisfaction with existing ideas and values, and a strong belief that a new beginning lay just around the corner. The cultural mood of the period is caught well by Tom Wolfe in his essay "The Great Relearning."[11] It was all about sweeping everything aside and starting all over again, "following a Promethean and unprecedented start from zero." Perhaps a clean sweep appealed more to the imagination than to the reason—but it certainly captured the mood of the moment.

Protestantism could not help but be caught up in this "great relearning." Its fundamental mandate was, after all, to reexamine itself constantly, asking whether its present institutional forms and distinctive beliefs represented the most authentic and reliable interpretations of the Bible. Yet during this period a growing number of Protestant intellectuals began to ask even more radical and dangerous questions—such as whether the Bible could be taken seriously in modern culture.

Demands for a "new Reformation" gathered momentum. The "old Reformation," it was argued, was based on the Bible; what was now needed was something more radical than had ever been proposed before. Writers such as John Shelby Spong, the Episcopal bishop of Newark, declared that this new Reformation would abandon obsolete ideas—such as a transcendent God, the resurrection of Jesus Christ, and a reliable revelation of God in the Bible. Although these revisionist ideas had been around since the early Enlightenment, they had tended to exercise influence primarily within radical groupings outside the church. In the late twentieth century, however, they became an integral part of the agenda of revisionist Protestantism.

So if the Bible was not to be trusted, what was? By the late 1960s, the Enlightenment suggestion that reason could be trusted where the Bible could not was being abandoned as unworkable. Other alternatives were therefore proposed. Those who were perhaps the most influential argued that Protestantism should take its leads from the ideas and values of Western culture. The intellectual origins of this trend could be traced back to the great liberal Protestant writers of the nineteenth century, such as A. B. Ritschl (1822–89). Yet it was a risky strategy. As William Ralph Inge (1860–1954) once quipped, whoever married the spirit of the age today would be widowed tomorrow. Cultural change erodes culturally based theologies. And in the 1960s, Western culture went into convulsion.

The outcome was a series of suggestions that now seem a little extravagant, perhaps even mildly hysterical. The best known of these was the "death of God" movement, which made the front cover of *Time* magazine on April 8, 1966. The funereal black cover was emblazoned with three words: "Is God dead?" Books with titles such as Paul van Buren's *Secular Meaning of the Gospel* (1963) and Thomas J. J. Altizer's *Gospel of Christian Atheism* (1966) cornered headlines in a puzzled yet fascinated secular press. Altizer's legendary inability to express himself clearly just puzzled them more.

A much more coherent statement of this agenda was set out when Harvey Cox—newly arrived at Harvard Divinity School—published his book *The Secular City* (1965). The book, which became a best-seller, took its stand on a series of incontrovertible core beliefs. "Secularization rolls on, and if we are to understand and communicate with our present age we must learn to love it in its unremitting secularity. We must learn, as Bonhoeffer said, to speak of God in a secular fashion and find a non-religious interpretation of biblical concepts." Secularism was here to stay; God was dead; Christianity would have to accommodate itself to modern thought and values; religion was about humanity, not God. "As Bonhoeffer says, in Jesus God is teaching man to get along without Him, to become mature, free from infantile dependencies, fully human." The book proved to be a landmark in the "secular Christianity" movement.

Similar ideas were expressed by the English bishop John Robinson in *Honest to God* (1963), which questioned whether the notion of a transcendent God could be taken seriously by "modern man." John Shelby Spong developed these ideas in the 1990s, extending Robinson's critique to many additional elements of Protestant beliefs.[12] Catholicism, which was undergoing its own internal convulsions at that time as a result of the Second Vatican Council (1962–65), was not affected by these social trends to anything like the same extent.

Many of the more radical religious writings of the 1960s proposed agendas based on the assumption that the prevailing cultural trends represented permanent changes in Western culture. That was a hasty and incorrect judgment. With the benefit of hindsight, this fascinating, turbulent period witnessed what was no more than a temporary change of cultural mood, but some were unwise enough to treat it as a fixed and lasting change in the condition of humanity. John Robinson's *Honest to God* ultimately represents a modernist take on traditional Christianity.[13] So what happens when modernism gives way to postmodernism, which rejects or inverts most of modernism's fundamental ideas? A generation later, Robinson's work feels like an exhibit in a museum of historical theology—a fascinating account of the cultural mood of a bygone era and the failed strategy to respond to it.

Others, taking their lead from postmodernity, argue that Protestantism must revise its ideas to accommodate the cultural insight that nothing can be known for certain and no reliable closure can ever be secured. The English theologian Don Cupitt illustrates this trend well, particularly in his assertion, "We alone improvise our knowledge about everything—including even ourselves." In *The Time Being* (1992), Cupitt insists that the "world of signs" is endlessly transient, making it impossible to reach firm and permanent conclusions.[14]

These strongly revisionist approaches are part of the inevitable free market of ideas that shape Protestant identity. Protestantism is not a static entity, but a living entity whose identity mutates over time. Yet that mutation leads to a variety of outcomes—among which some flourish and others wither. While such revisionist approaches have found some support within sections of Protestantism in the West—especially the left wing of American culture—they have not attained the wide acceptance found by other new developments, such as Pentecostalism, which addresses the postmodern context on a very different intellectual basis and using a hermeneutical method.

Most commentators on recent American cultural history take the view that God, declared somewhat prematurely dead in 1966, underwent an intellectual and political resurrection in the following decades.[15] As the president of America's Skeptics' Society, Michael Shermer, commented recently, never in history have so many, and such a high percentage of the American population, believed in God.[16] Not only is God not "dead," as the German philosopher Friedrich Nietzsche prematurely proclaimed, but he never seems to have been more alive.

There is perhaps no more telling witness to this than the same Harvey Cox who published *The Secular City* in 1965. Some twenty years later, he followed this with *Religion in the Secular City*.[17] Far from endorsing the views he expressed earlier, Cox argued that religion is—and would continue to be—a significant force in society. "With the passing of the modern age, the epoch of 'modern theology' which tried to interpret Christianity in the face of secularization is also over." Cox pointed to the current vitality of Catholicism in Latin America and Protestant fundamentalism in the United States as signs that the long-predicted triumph of secularism was simply not going to happen.

Cox moved the goalposts still further in 1995 when he published *Fire from Heaven*.[18] The central argument of this book represents a near-total inversion of Cox's judgments of 1965. The twenty-first century, he asserts, will belong to Pentecostalism, not secularism. Pentecostalism is "a spiritual hurricane that has already touched nearly half a billion people, and an alternative vision of the human future whose impact may only be in its earliest stages today." And what is the secret of its success? Cox is clear: it lies in its fundamental conviction "that the Spirit of God needs no mediators but is available to anyone in an intense, immediate, indeed interior way." The evidence suggests that Cox may well be right in this judgment, at least in the short term. We return to consider this new movement in the following chapter.

THE FUTURE OF THE PROTESTANT DENOMINATION

As we noted earlier, the Protestant denomination is essentially a European phenomenon that reflects the shifting patterns of church life and controversy in western Europe from the sixteenth century to the eighteenth. Patterns of religious affiliation and belonging that derived from the general situation of western Europe—and often the very specific conditions of religious life in England—were thus exported to the United States as self-evidently correct forms of Christian association. As a result, the emerging church life of North America was significantly shaped by the historical contingencies of western Europe.

This transplantation of European religious ideas to America must not, however, be seen as an unthinking and wooden undertaking with no attempt at modification or indigenization. We have already noted that seventeenth-century Puritanism in the Massachusetts Bay area shifted from the predominantly presbyterian model of church polity that was the norm in many parts of England to a congregationalist model. The simplest explanation for this development is that this model was better adapted to the American context. Again, the emergence of the Southern Baptist Convention can be seen as reflecting the local credibility of the voluntary association or voluntary society and the realization of its ecclesiological potential. The fact remains, however, that in many if not all respects most American denominations retained a surprising degree of continuity with their European pasts.

In 1929 H. Richard Niebuhr published a study of the origin of modern American religious denominations.[19] They were, he argued, a distinguishing mark of American religious life, and they were here to stay, in that they were rooted in historical differences of social class, wealth, national origin, and race. Denominational diversity was thus the by-product of wider social divisions. This approach has been criticized for placing too much causal weight on existing social differences in shaping denominational identity when it is known that other factors are significant in shaping both denominational rupture or schism, on the one hand, and merger, on the other.[20] Nevertheless, the merits of Niebuhr's argument were widely conceded.

Niebuhr's analysis pointed to the continuing importance of denominationalism in the United States in that it was sustained by deeper social causes. To belong to a specific denomination was often to make a statement about one's historical origins or social status rather than one's theological beliefs. The predominance of Christianity in the United States seemed to ensure that Protestant denominations, while separate from the state, would form what was almost a cultural establishment in their own right. The future of the denominations seemed secure.

Even in the 1950s, the position of the Protestant denominations seemed secure. The membership figures of the five major Protestant denominations—Baptists, Congregationalists, Episcopalians, Presbyterians, and Methodists—increased each year. Social surveys made it clear that each denominational family saw itself as self-contained and sovereign. A 1955 Gallup poll showed that 96 percent of the adult population attended a church of the same denomination their parents attended. In another poll the following year, 80 percent of Episcopalians seemed to believe that it was wrong to worship with other Christian groups. The old demarcations were still firmly embedded in the fabric of Protestantism. As Will Herberg pointed out in his classic study of the American religious establishment at that time, the denominational system had become part of the basic assumptions of Protestants about America, as it had become part of the basic assumptions of all Americans about themselves.[21]

Yet by the year 2000 it was clear that things had changed. In 2004 researchers Tom W. Smith and Seokho Kim of the National Opinion

Research Center at the University of Chicago released a report, *The Vanishing Protestant Majority*, which showed that the number of Americans identifying themselves as "Protestant" fell from 63 percent in 1992 to 52 percent in 2002.[22] The report pointed to a fundamental failure on the part of most Protestant denominations to evangelize and assimilate their own youth and young adults. It also observed that in recent years immigrant groups have not followed the older pattern of eventual identification with the nation's Protestant majority.

The mainline Protestant denominations are still there, but now they coexist uneasily with a growing group of churches that are clearly Protestant in their outlook but are also of very recent origin and see no reason to regard themselves as defined by the past. The entrepreneurial spirit that is so characteristic of Protestantism seems to have been redirected to activities outside, rather than within, the traditional denominational structures.

A group of factors seems to be implicated in this erosion of specifically denominational understandings of Protestantism, although it is not always clear which is cause and which effect. Here we briefly consider four of those factors before moving on to consider two that have had a particularly significant impact on the shaping of American Protestantism since about 1970.

In the first place, most Americans no longer regard a denominational marque, or "badge," as something that makes a significant statement about their historical origins or social identity. With the emergence of a consumerist mentality in American Protestant culture since about 1980, the driving issue is where to find the best preaching, the best Christian education, or even the best parking facilities. This mentality may lead a Protestant family to attend, say, a Baptist church in Florida, a Methodist church upon moving to California, and a Presbyterian church after finally settling in Chicago. The issue is not denominational identity but local pastoral excellence. In marked contrast, their grandparents would have sought out the local church of their own denomination wherever they went.

The second point follows on immediately from this. The emphasis upon the local facilities offered by individual churches leads Protestants to be more than willing to contribute financially and personally to church outreach and social welfare programs. Yet this often strong sense of belonging and commitment to the local congregation is rarely extended to the denomination as a whole, which is likely to be viewed as an inefficient and redundant bureaucracy that makes serious financial demands of local congregations while giving little in return. This perception is exacerbated where local congregations are in dispute with the mainline denomination over issues such as sexuality in ministry, and these conflicts often lead to local withholding of funds from the central structures. More seriously, even as the general decline in membership of many mainline denominations inevitably leads to reductions in financial support, the costs of maintaining denominational structures are rising. Many denominations are facing up to the fact that centralized downsizing and rationalization may be the only way ahead.

A third factor has to do with the rise of evangelicalism and the charismatic movement, which are both transdenominational in character.[23] Both movements tend to prioritize fellowship and collaboration with other evangelicals and charismatics, irrespective of their denominational allegiance. Anglican evangelicals often feel more at home with Baptist evangelicals, despite the substantial differences between their denominations over matters of church structure and polity. This is seen in the rise of "para-church" organizations—such as Youth with a Mission or the InterVarsity Fellowship—which transcend denominational structures and divisions in order to pursue a cross-denominational agenda. This development has led to a slight blurring of denominational boundaries. Yet much more importantly, it has also led to the relativization of the denomination, which is often seen as a barrier to inter-Protestant or inter-Christian collaboration that must be transcended in the service of the gospel.

A fourth factor that has been identified as of significance by sociologists with a particular interest in Protestant denominations is the rise of "lay liberalism," which erases the clear boundaries separating believers from unbelievers.[24] Where evangelicalism emphasizes the distinctiveness of Christianity, this pragmatic, laid-back lay liberalism feels able to renegotiate Christian moral and theological principles in the light of prevailing social norms. This has led to an erosion of the boundary between "church" and "world"—but also between Protestant denominations. Without clear "faith boundaries," identification with any particular form of Protestantism—indeed, even with Christianity itself—becomes socially meaningless.

These four significant factors suggest that traditional Protestant denominations may come under still further pressure in the future. It is far too early to speak responsibly of a "crisis" in mainline Protestantism. However, it is clear that forces are at work that will force redefinition and reconception of the traditional denomination. In addition to the four points just noted, we must examine two other, arguably more significant, factors that are essential to an understanding of the recent fortunes of American Protestantism—the rise of new ways of "being church" and the redefinition of "the other." In view of their importance, we consider these in some detail.

NEW MODELS OF THE CHURCH

The limitations of the traditional denomination were being felt by some by the late 1950s.[25] Some strongly entrepreneurial Protestants found themselves increasingly frustrated by the institutional inertia of denominational structures, which increasingly appeared to them to be unresponsive bureaucracies that were uninterested in local initiatives or innovations.

Such frustration, of course, is not new. The great Protestant preacher Harry Emerson Fosdick, who played such an important role in the great fundamentalist controversies of the 1920s, once made the astonishing revelation that he had once considered leaving "the historic Christian organizations" in order to start his own "independent movement."[26] Fosdick was dismissive of those who demanded ecclesiastical loyalty, holding that his only loyalty was to Christ. Yet despite his frustrations, he never set up his own church, even though his personal reputation was such that its future would have been secure. After all, he was widely regarded as the greatest preacher of his age and was regularly introduced to clergy conferences as "Dr. Fosdick, whose sermons you will have read and preached."

Yet deep in the heart of the Protestant understanding of God's dealings with humanity lay precisely the idea that would give a new sense of direction to those who shared Fosdick's frustrations but not his patience. Protestant understandings of the nature of the church locate its identity as a Christian body, not in its institutional history or connections, but in its fidelity in preaching and ministering the sacraments. So why not break free of such denominational control and establish congregations that were open to new ways of embodying Protestantism? They could preach and administer the sacraments just as well as before, but they would be free to develop new pastoral and evangelistic ministries.

These were dangerous thoughts as far as the mainline denominations were concerned. Yet the entrepreneurial individuals asking these questions could not be held back forever. Their sense of theological vision, coupled with a can-do mentality that was nourished and inspired by the Protestant work ethic, eventually drove them to achieve their goals outside the traditional denominations. Like Luther, they did not want to work outside their mother churches, but the needs and realities of the situation seemed to provide them with no alternatives. The outcome was a surge of new initiatives that met needs largely ignored by mainline denominations and set new patterns for how churches work, develop, and organize themselves.

The first wave of new developments took place in the 1960s. It was a time of ferment and demands for change. The strongly countercultural "Jesus movement" was widely seen as a protest against the social conservatism and institutional preoccupations of traditional Protestant worship that had led many to conclude that change was needed. Several major new Protestant movements trace their roots back to this time, including Calvary Chapel.

Calvary Chapel began in 1965 when Chuck Smith began to pastor a church of that name in Costa Mesa, California. The congregation grew quickly, reaching two thousand by 1967. The church reflected the informal, anti-establishment views of the Jesus movement. Guitars displaced pipe organs; robed choirs disappeared; instructions about when to stand, sit, recite, or read were dropped; and clergy dispensed with robes and dressed informally. Although traditional theologically, the mode of expression of that theology was quite different. The new emphasis of worship, especially of its music, was on deepening the individual's personal relationship to God.[27]

Yet the most interesting aspect of Calvary Chapel was its growth and its implications for denominational structure. At present, more than five hundred churches are affiliated with Calvary Chapel, mostly in California. Calvary Chapel insists that it is not a "denomination," but a "fellowship of churches." Where traditional denominations establish churches using a corporatist model of "branches" or "offices" of the central organization, Calvary Chapel's approach is more that of a franchise, an organizational form that avoids the financial and administrative overheads of traditional denominations. Any congregation prepared to accept the "Calvary Chapel Distinctives" can become a member of this fellowship and identify itself as such.

A similar model is used by the Vineyard Churches, which originated in Anaheim, California, and are particularly associated with John Wimber (1934–97). The Vineyard movement grew out of the Calvary Chapel network: Wimber led a breakaway group that was concerned in part that Calvary did not give sufficient attention to the role of spiritual gifts. The charismatic movement was becoming a significant presence in California in the 1970s, and Wimber had been involved in its development, teaching a controversial course on "signs and wonders" at Fuller Theological Seminary. Like Calvary Chapel, the Vineyard movement does not regard itself as a denomination, but as an association or fellowship. It has no centralized structures or authority figures.

The impact of such movements goes beyond the reshaping of denominational options and structures and the provision of new and less centralized models of the church. Developments such as these within Protestantism have led to new and informal worship styles, an explosion in "worship songs," a new concern about the dynamics of worship, and an increasing dislike of the traditionalism of formal liturgical worship, especially the cumbersome use of hymn books and service books, which many see as culturally alienating to "seekers" from within secular American culture.

This is perhaps seen most clearly in the emergence of the Willow Creek network, which traces its origins back to 1981. Founded in South Barrington, Illinois, just outside Chicago, Willow Creek Community Church aimed to present the Christian faith without the baggage of Protestant ecclesiastical tradition—such as clerical robes, hard pews, collection plates, and old-fashioned hymns. "Seeker-sensitive" worship would take place in an environment in which "unchurched" individuals could feel at home while learning about the Christian faith. Founding pastor Bill Hybels wanted Willow Creek to be "a safe place where seekers can hear the very dangerous, life-changing message of Jesus Christ."

Its success encouraged many other churches to use its methods. Once more, any suggestion that Willow Creek represented a new denomination was avoided. Individual congregations could associate themselves with Willow Creek; there would, however, be no centralized structures. Willow Creek—like Calvary Chapel and the Vineyard—has spawned a global network of churches that look to it for guidance.

The phenomenon of the "community church" allows entrepreneurs to develop their gifts in ways that would be impossible within the confining and restricting structures of most traditional denominations. These churches are strongly sensitive to the needs of their local communities, and their local grounding and knowledge inform their strategies and agendas. Most community churches are nondenominational and eschew the byzantine labyrinth of ecclesiastical politics. They see themselves as existing primarily for their members, and they have no great interest in supporting or sustaining the unwieldy and increasingly self-serving denominational hierarchies.

Perhaps the most celebrated recent example of a community church was established at Saddleback Valley in Orange County, California, in 1980 by Rick and Kay Warren, who had just graduated from Southwestern Baptist Theological Seminary in Texas. It aimed to reach out to those who did not traditionally attend church, in a way that was seeker-sensitive, on the one hand, and theologically conservative, on the other. The vision was to establish "a place where the hurting, the depressed, the frustrated, and the confused can find love, acceptance, help, hope, forgiveness, guidance, and encouragement." Warren's best-sellers *The Purpose-Driven Church* (1995) and *The Purpose-Driven Life* (2002) have had a significant impact on the reshaping of Protestant attitudes toward creating community, evangelism, pastoral care, and outreach—all unimpeded by any denominational apparatus.

So is this the future? There will be other big community churches that develop distinctive ministries that work well and draw the attention of would-be imitators. A major transformation of the religious life of the United States is under way: the mega-churches are, in effect, becoming the new dioceses, with large numbers of orbiting planets. They are more responsive to social changes, easier to manage, and cheaper to run than traditional denominations. Just as the great medieval monasteries planted smaller monasteries ("daughter houses") in outlying regions, resourced by the mother house until they were deemed strong enough to be self-sufficient, so the mega-churches are spreading. The future of Protestant denominations in America will be deeply shaped by this major new trend.

The longer-term outcome, however, remains uncertain. Historians of American religion, such as Philip Jenkins, point out that certain cyclical trends can be seen at work over generations in the past, and these may well be repeated in the future with these new styles of Protestantism. As such groups become more established, they become more respectable. Their emerging leaders attend seminaries that become more liberal, with the result that the denominations themselves become more liberal in the next generation. This then leads to division within the denomination and the breaking away of groups to form more conservative or fundamentalist denominations, often with their own accredited seminaries. The future is far from clear.

REDEFINING "THE OTHER": CHANGING ATTITUDES TOWARD CATHOLICISM

As we have stressed throughout this work, Protestantism gains its sense of identity through both internal and external factors. Internally, this sense of common identity arises from a shared commitment to certain beliefs and norms—such as the centrality of the Bible. Yet Protestantism has also been shaped by the perception of a common threat from a significant enemy—Catholicism. From its beginnings until very recently, this has been an integral aspect of Protestant identity.

The importance of "binary opposition" in shaping perceptions of identity has been highlighted in recent years, not least on account of the major debate between different schools of critical thought over whether such "oppositions" determine and shape human thought or are the outcome of human thought.[28] A series of significant binary oppositions are held to have shaped Western thought—such as "male-female" and "white-black." Binary oppositions lead to the construction of the category of "the other"—the devalued half of a binary opposition when applied to groups of people. Group identity is often fostered by defining "the other"—as, for example, in Nazi Germany, with its opposition "Aryan-Jew."

In the case of Protestantism, the main binary opposition has been Catholic-Protestant. Its plausibility has been enormously enhanced by the fact that Catholicism adopted precisely the same opposition. Protestantism was not a significant presence in regions of the world where Orthodoxy was dominant, but this binary opposition came to be perceived as normative elsewhere. Each side saw its opponent as "the other," a perception that was relentlessly advanced by novelists and other shapers of public opinion.[29] Media reporting of the social unrest in Northern Ireland from 1970 to 1995 reinforced this opposition.

It is a simple fact of history that Protestantism has defined itself against this significant "other." While European Protestantism was haunted by this specter for many years, the lack of a significant Catholic presence in many parts of North America during the colonial era led many Protestants to search, not entirely successfully, for alternative "others." Then waves of Catholic immigration from Europe in the nineteenth century revitalized the traditional perception that the enemy was Catholicism. "The other" had reemerged and proved of decisive importance in shaping American Protestantism's sense of identity.[30]

The identification of Catholicism with "the other" was pervasive in American Protestantism in the late nineteenth century and can be summed up in the famous comments of a delegate to the Evangelical Alliance meeting in New York in 1873: "The most formidable foe of living Christianity among us is not Deism or Atheism, or any form of infidelity, but the nominally Christian Church of Rome." As the twentieth century opened, this perception seemed permanent and normative. At one level, Protestantism was defined by anti-Catholicism.

Yet the twentieth century has seen this perception change, to the point that it now lingers on only in some parts of American Protestantism, and then more as a historical memory than a current reality. Anti-Catholicism is arguably now more characteristic of political pressure groups and media gurus who resent the continuing moral and political influence of Catholicism in America.[31] "The other" is being redefined. No longer is Catholicism the enemy for conservative Protestants; it is the perceived secularism and incipient atheism of America's cultural opinion makers. Socially conservative Protestants and Catholics thus see each other as natural allies in a struggle against a secularizing government, despite the obvious tensions within that working agreement.

This is not to say that Protestants no longer regard Catholicism with suspicion, or even hostility. For many Protestants, the agenda of the European Reformation remains a live issue and has not been resolved to this day.[32] The point here, however, is more subtle: it is that secularism has surfaced as *the* major concern of many Protestants. This does not mean that other concerns or threats have been eliminated, or are even seen to have been eliminated. It represents a communal shift in many Protestant circles concerning the identity of the most pressing challenge of the moment.

What of liberal Protestants, still a very significant constituency within the American religious scene? On the whole, these Protestants do not regard secularizing forces in America as an enemy, being broadly sympathetic to their goals, if occasionally uneasy over their fine detail. Protestants in this constituency tend to regard conservative Christians, irrespective of denominational allegiance, as "the other" and occasionally use the term "fundamentalist" in a purely derogatory sense to stigmatize them.[33] This points to the fragmentation of "the other" within Protestantism as a whole.

Yet while many Protestants no longer regard Catholicism as an enemy, it is still widely seen as a rival. This perception has been catalyzed by a significant development since about 1990—prominent Protestants, including evangelicals, have been converting, either by "crossing the Tiber" to Catholicism or "crossing the Bosphorus" to Orthodoxy. In 1990 the leading Lutheran theologian Richard John Neuhaus converted to Catholicism, setting a trend that has escalated since then. Recent defections from the Evangelical Lutheran Church of America (ELCA) illustrate this trend well. Robert Wilken, a leading Lutheran patristics scholar teaching at the University of Virginia, became a Roman Catholic. The preeminent church historian Jaroslav Pelikan, Sterling Professor of Ecclesiastical History at Yale University, became a member of the Orthodox Church. Leonard Klein, pastor of Christ Church, a large

Lutheran parish in York, Pennsylvania, and sometime editor of *Lutheran Forum,* converted to Catholicism with his family and is studying for the priesthood. Bruce Marshall, one of American's most significant younger Lutheran theologians, recently converted to Catholicism. The list goes on.

What is causing these conversions? It is clear that a variety of factors are involved. One of the reasons so many evangelicals are "crossing the Bosphorus" is that they are alarmed at evangelicalism's lack of historical roots and institutional continuity with the New Testament and they see Orthodoxy as having particularly strong credentials in this area. Other Protestants are uneasy about the biblical foundations of one of the core ideas of the first phase of the Reformation—the doctrine of justification by faith alone. Catholic critics regularly argue that this is unbiblical: not only, they insist, is there no New Testament passage that affirms this idea, but one passage explicitly condemns the idea.[34] A third group is concerned about developments within their denominations that they regard as departing from historic Christianity; therefore, they have transferred to churches with a strong record of defending the tradition.

The long-term implications of this trend, if continued, remain uncertain. Yet all the indications are that it has not led to increased hostility between Catholicism and Protestantism but is actually the outcome of increased understanding, which makes such ecclesiastical transitions easier. While the evidence is that some Catholics do convert to forms of Protestantism, the traffic appears to be primarily in the other direction.

Finally, we must note that this shift in the perception of Catholicism came about through changes in American culture at large, not in response to Protestantism's understanding of its internal marks of identity. "The other" is determined culturally. When there were hardly any Catholics in America, "the other" was often identified as Protestants with differing views on church polity. The massive immigration of Catholics—a social development—altered that perception. The rise of secularism changed it still further. But what lies in the future? Will "the other" be redefined still further? To Protestants in many parts of Africa and Asia, "the other" is radical Islam, which is widely regarded as an intellectual and physical threat to Protestantism. It must be noted that America is not typical of global Protestantism and that its culturally determined perceptions of "the other" do not resonate with the experience of coreligionists in other parts of the world.

With that point in mind, we shall presently turn to consider the remarkable transformation in Protestant identity that took place in the twentieth century as Protestantism became a significant living presence in Africa, Asia, and Latin America. However, we must now address a new form of Protestantism that emerged in the twentieth century and has now become the largest single constituency of the movement—Pentecostalism.

The Descent of the Holy Spirit, *by Marcos de Escamilla (sixteenth century).*

15

Tongues of Fire

The Pentecostal Revolution in Protestantism

The charismatic movement is the most rapidly growing element of Christianity today. Pentecostalism in its various forms is now the largest single Christian group apart from Catholicism and outnumbers the sum total of all other forms of Protestantism. Although numerical estimates of its strength are unreliable, the movement grew from ground zero in 1900 to at least half a billion in 2000. Its historical origins and fundamental beliefs locate it firmly within the bounds of Protestantism. Yet its astonishing growth, spiritual vitality, and capacity to adapt to local situations are forcing Protestantism to review both its center and its limits. The numerical growth of Pentecostalism, primarily among the urban poor and the socially marginalized of Asia, Africa, and South America, is transforming Protestantism.

A few examples may help readers who are unfamiliar with the scale and significance of this movement to gain a sense of the cumulative seismic impact it is having on world Christianity.[1] The Yoido Full Gospel Church is a Pentecostal church based in the Yoido district of Seoul in the Republic of Korea. When the church began in ex-army tents in the slums of Seoul in 1958, it emphasized the transformative impact of the gospel through the empowerment of the Holy Spirit in the face of the adverse social and economic conditions of depressed postwar Korea. Today the church has a membership of 700,000. Its main place of worship can hold 25,000 people, but it must still hold multiple services on Sundays.

The city of Lagos in the former British west African colony of Nigeria is widely regarded as the Pentecostal capital of the world—despite the fact that Pentecostalism in that nation traces its origins back only to small-scale projects in the 1970s. Today the Faith Tabernacle can accommodate 50,000 worshipers in its stadium-like auditorium. The Redeemed Christian Church of God now has 4,000 parishes throughout Nigeria. The movement has achieved such prominence that traditional Protestant denominations in the region now incorporate charismatic elements into their worship. The somewhat staid forms of Anglican worship that predominated during the colonial era have simply been displaced by worship forms that emphasize African cultural roots and the transforming power of the Holy Spirit.

So what is this new form of Protestantism? Where did it come from? Why has it proved so attractive? What challenges does it raise for more traditional forms of Protestant life and thought? And most important of all, what are its implications for the future of Protestantism? In this chapter, we reflect on these issues.

THE GROWTH OF AMERICAN PENTECOSTALISM

The origins of the Pentecostal movement are traditionally held to lie in the United States. Although the roots of the movement are particularly to be found in the holiness tradition, the movement took on its distinctive form in the first decade of the twentieth century, primarily through the influence of the African American preacher William J. Seymour.

Seymour was born in Centerville, Louisiana, in 1870, the son of former slaves, Simon and Phyllis Seymour. After a period working as a railroad porter in Indianapolis, he moved in 1900 to Cincinnati, where he joined the Evening Light Saints, a Christian group noted for its radical holiness theology, including the doctrine of "second blessing entire sanctification," premillennialism, and the promise of a worldwide revival through the Holy Spirit before the rapture. In 1903 Seymour moved to Houston, Texas, where he joined a small holiness church pastored by a black woman, Lucy Farrow, who put him in touch with Charles Fox Parham. On hearing Parham's descriptions of speaking in tongues in 1905, Seymour set out to spread the word, based at the church he founded, the Apostolic Faith Mission on Azusa Street in Los Angeles.[2]

Primarily (though not exclusively) from this California base, Pentecostalism spread rapidly in America. It appealed particularly to the socially marginalized, especially through Seymour's important concept of an ecstatic egalitarian ecclesiology.[3] Unusually, it seemed to appeal to and be embraced by both white and African American Christian groups. It was regarded as eccentric, even dangerous, by American culture at large, as newspaper headlines in Los Angeles in April 1906 made clear: "New Sect of Fanatics Is Breaking Loose," and "Wild Scene Last Night on Azusa Street."

Popular journalism around the time of the Azusa Street revival made clear the antipathy felt toward the movement, which aroused both racial and theological prejudices: "Colored people and a sprinkling of Whites compose the congregation, and night is made hideous in the neighborhood by the howlings of the worshippers who spend hours swaying forth and back in a nerve-racking attitude of prayer and supplication." The key role played by women in the revival was out of line with contemporary cultural norms and once more attracted negative media coverage.[4] More significantly, the charismatic experiences reported seemed to many to represent a new outbreak of the "enthusiasm" that mainline Protestantism had regarded with intense suspicion, laced with not a little cultural disdain, since the eighteenth century.[5]

It is also important to appreciate that Charles Parham had no intention of adopting the racial inclusiveness proclaimed and practiced by Seymour and Azusa Street. In an abortive and counterproductive move, Parham, who was particularly disturbed by its commitment to interracial fellowship, attempted to take control of the Azusa phenomenon.[6] Among other things, Parham later went on to teach that white Anglo-Saxon Protestants were the privileged descendants of the lost tribes of Israel, and he spoke in glowing terms of the Ku Klux Klan. He was never reconciled with Seymour and eventually died in disgrace.[7]

Although Pentecostalism can be thought of as traditionalist in its Christian theology, it differs radically from other Christian groupings in its emphasis on speaking in tongues and its forms of worship. These are strongly experiential and involve prophesying, healings, and exorcisms. The Pentecostal worldview includes elements that relate easily and naturally to the folk religions of many regions of the world, especially in Africa and Latin America, such as the casting out of demons (a practice that tends to make Western academic theologians cringe with unease). The movement's populist worship style and apparent lack of intellectual sophistication have caused mainline denominations and the academy either to ridicule or ignore it. Yet Pentecostalism began a new phase of expansion after the Second World War, paving the way for its massive growth in the second half of the twentieth century. Even in the United States, Pentecostalism has overtaken most of the mainline denominations that dominated the American religious landscape from 1800 to 1950.[8]

Pentecostalism began to become respectable and accepted in white middle-class America through the neo-charismatic renewal of the 1960s. In part, this change in attitude can be put down to the upward social mobility, greater disposable income, and suburbanization that followed the Second World War. Yet the decisive factor was the emergence of charismatic phenomena typical of Pentecostalism—hitherto seen as a distinct Christian group—within the historic Protestant denominations. The incident that is traditionally identified as having brought Pentecostalism to wider public attention in the United States took place in Van Nuys, California, in 1960, when the rector of the local Episcopalian church, Dennis Bennett, told his congregation that he had been filled with the Holy Spirit and spoken in tongues. Reaction varied from bewilderment to outrage; the local Episcopalian bishop promptly banned speaking in tongues from his churches. However, it soon became clear that others in the mainline denominations had shared Bennett's experience. They came out of their closets and made it clear that they believed that they had experienced an authentic New Testament phenomenon that would lead to the renewal of the churches.

By the late 1960s, it was evident that some form of renewal based on charismatic gifts (such as speaking in tongues) was gaining hold within Anglican, Lutheran, Methodist, and Presbyterian circles. Through this development, Pentecostal themes and emphases became increasingly acceptable within American Protestantism, even if that acceptance took rather longer in some denominations than in others—the Southern Baptist Convention, for example, has not been significantly affected by the charismatic movement. Of equal importance, a charismatic movement began to develop within the Roman Catholic church. The Catholic Charismatic Renewal movement started in Pittsburgh, Pennsylvania, in 1967 among students and faculty of Duquesne University.

In an influential study of the development of charismatic movements in the United States during the twentieth century, church historian Peter Wagner distinguished three "waves" of the movement.[9] The first such wave took the form of classic Pentecostalism, which arose in the early 1900s and was characterized by its emphasis on speaking in tongues. The second wave took place in the 1960s and 1970s, mainly within mainline denominations as they appropriated spiritual healing and other charismatic practices. This second wave transformed public perceptions of the movement and began its move away from the periphery of American religious life and toward the center.

The third wave, exemplified by John Wimber, emphasized "signs and wonders." Through the Spirit, he argued, a new wave of supernatural power had been unleashed upon the churches to enable healing, victorious living, and the defeat of evil spiritual powers. The idea of "spiritual warfare"—that is, the Christian's spiritual battle against evil spirits—played a particularly important role in Wimber's thought.[10]

This third wave caused considerable controversy during its early period in the 1980s. Wimber and Wagner taught a course popularly known as "Signs and Wonders" at Fuller Theological Seminary from 1982 to 1986, when faculty and trustee pressure closed it down for a year; it was reinstated, with a markedly lower profile, a year later. Wimber went on to lead the Vineyard Fellowship, which has proved one of the most significant global agencies in developing this approach to the Christian life.

Using the term "Pentecostal" to describe all these movements has now become problematic. The term is generally used today to refer to a family of churches—such as the Assemblies of God—that particularly emphasize speaking in tongues. The term "charismatic" is now used to refer to movements within the mainline churches based upon the ideas and experiences of the Pentecostal movement. Charismatic renewal within the mainline churches has led to new and informal worship styles, an explosion in "worship songs," a new concern for the dynamics of worship, and an increasing dislike of the traditionalism of formal liturgical worship.

The Pentecostal movement—which must now be taken to include charismatic groups within mainline churches—has changed considerably since the Second World War. The most obvious change is the massive surge in its numbers. It is now estimated that there are more than 500 million Pentecostals in the world, with a very wide geographical distribution. This movement that some argue has its origins primarily within African American culture has now taken root in South America, Asia, Africa, and Europe. But there have been other, more subtle changes in the movement that reflect its remarkable ability to adjust to the social dynamics and realities of its increasingly diverse environments. The absence of any centralized authority within Pentecostalism has removed the inflexibility that has so hampered mainline Protestant attempts to indigenize the gospel outside the West.

Some significant divergences have emerged within the movement, especially between charismatics working within mainline Protestant denominations and those in specifically Pentecostal contexts. The former, with the theologies and sacraments of their parent denominations on which to draw, often are more developed in these areas than their Pentecostal counterparts. Pentecostals, on the other hand, tend to adopt intuitive, pragmatic attitudes toward the church, believing that its structures and forms are capable of infinite adaptation through the leading of the Holy Spirit.

The American origins of the movement have led some to suggest that its success is ultimately linked with American power and influence.[11] There is some truth in this observation, in that American Pentecostalism has been immensely influential in beginning other movements worldwide. However, two cautionary comments are in order. First, American Pentecostals have not been close to their nation's government, power, or influence. Even until 1960—by which time the global "planting" of Pentecostalism was well under way—the movement was seen as lying on the margins of American society and was virtually devoid of cultural credibility, academic respectability, economic power, or political influence.

Second, Pentecostalism developed in ways adapted to its new global environments, with leadership rapidly passing to indigenous pastors. The case of Korea is instructive. In 1952 the American Assemblies of God sent Abner Chesnut to Korea as their first missionary. The Korean Assemblies of God was organized in 1953 and opened its first Bible school the following year. Paul Yonggi Cho—who went on to found the Yoido Full Gospel Church—was one of its first students. The form of Pentecostalism that Cho developed was clearly influenced by Presbyterianism (the dominant form of Christianity in Korea) and by worship traditions originating from the revivalist and holiness traditions. Yet it was unquestionably Korean, having adapted to its local context rather than retained the forms of those who planted it.

The spread of Pentecostalism is not due primarily to the projection of American influence but to the capacity of what was projected to take root in new situations. The ministry of Carlos Alberto Annacondia, who was converted in Buenos Aires in 1979 through the ministry of the Panamanian evangelist Manuel A. Ruiz, indicates how an essentially Latin American Pentecostalism has developed by propagating and transforming itself through indigenous agencies. The revival that swept through Argentinean Protestant communities in 1982, primarily through Annacondia's ministry, was thoroughly homegrown, having supplanted the old missionary gospel with a new, culturally resonant package of beliefs and social outreach.

Yet there is another response that may be made to the charge that Pentecostalism is essentially an American export. This involves a more attentive study of its origins, which reveals that its history is far more complex than has been appreciated. In what follows, we note some insights emerging from the new quest for the origins of Pentecostalism.

THE NEW QUEST FOR THE ORIGINS OF PENTECOSTALISM

The traditional account of the origins of Pentecostalism, which we set out earlier in this chapter, tends to portray it as an American phenomenon that gradually spread throughout the world, partly by active transfer, partly by passive diffusion. On this view, Azusa Street was the Jerusalem from which the message of God's gift of the Spirit went out to the nations. There is certainly some truth in this account: twenty-six Pentecostal denominations trace their historical origins back to Azusa Street. Nevertheless, this hugely influential (especially in the United States) account is increasingly recognized to be incomplete in the light of a wealth of material now being uncovered by historians.

More significantly, the traditional theory demands a model of Pentecostal development that is essentially that of the adaptation of an American model to other contexts. The question that the historian is forced to consider is why and how an American model was changed to suit other locales. What if the phenomenon had multiple origins, most of which were outside the United States? What if Pentecostalism was already present in India (to give only one possibility) before Azusa Street and developed its own independent trajectory in that region?[12]

The explosion of scholarly interest in Pentecostalism that has arisen in the last twenty years has begun to cast light on the complex origins of the movement that forces revision of the traditional model.[13] Major studies of the origins of the movement in Argentina, Chile, Ghana, Korea, the Philippines, South Africa, and South India have forced historians to make essential revisions to the earlier paradigms. The historical origins of Pentecostalism now seem as complex as those of the original Protestant Reformation itself. A number of roughly contemporary movements with recognizable shared beliefs and expectations emerged in the first decade of the twentieth century, but without any obvious indication of reciprocal causality.

The picture that is now becoming clear is that of a series of local "Pentecostalisms" emerging in the first decade of the twentieth century. The 1906 revival at Azusa Street was one of them. So was the 1903 revival in Pyongyang, Korea; the 1905–7 revival at Pandita Ramabai's Mukti Mission in Poona, India; the Manchurian revival of 1908; the revival in Valparaiso, Chile, in 1909; the revival that broke out in the Ivory Coast, the Gold Coast, and the Liberian Kru in 1914; and other revivals in Norway, China, Venezuela, and elsewhere. Each of these revivals demonstrated Pentecostal characteristics, though there was no clear connection between them. What we can now recognize as Pentecostalism was well established in India before anyone there had heard of Charles Parham, Azusa Street, or William Seymour.[14]

The parallel with the emerging scholarly understanding of the origins of Protestantism in the early sixteenth century is striking. Once more, multiple sources for the movement have had to be recognized as the historical evidence mounts for the fundamental historical and intellectual heterogeneity of the movement—whose manifestations nevertheless share enough common ground to allow collaboration, negotiation, and mutual support. And the same mechanisms that led to the consolidation and significant—but not total—convergence of individual reformations to yield "the Reformation" led to the collaboration and even convergence of these emergent Pentecostalisms. The American model may have been more influential than some in shaping the emerging movement's thought, structures, and expectations—but it cannot be said to be the cause or source of the movement.

As this more complex picture has emerged, Pentecostal historians have begun to interpret it in terms of the providential dispersal of essentially the same divine gift throughout the world in a relatively brief period of time.[15] Yet for our purposes, this increasingly complex and nuanced picture allows a critically important point to be made: the theme of "diversity within unity" was present from the origins of the movement. It was not a later development that resulted from an essentially American movement being forced to reconsider its strategies, objectives, and approaches in the light of its encounter with non-American situations. Rather, it was integral to the historical emergence of the phenomenon that we now call "Pentecostalism" but that had no shared name or sense of identity until people began to compare notes, often stimulated by the fame of events at Azusa Street.

PENTECOSTALISM: ITS DEFINING CHARACTERISTICS

In many respects, Pentecostalism accepts the basic themes of Protestant theology, but with a significant addition that leads to modifications of doctrinal emphasis at some points and different patterns of worship at others. The term "Pentecostal" takes its name from the Jewish festival of Pentecost, during which, the New Testament records, the apostles were "filled with the Holy Spirit and began to speak in other tongues" (Acts 2:4). Traditional Protestant theology had regarded this phenomenon as unique to the age of the apostles; adapted and necessary to the first phase of the expansion of the church, it was not, on this view, requisite or active thereafter.

The defense of this "cessationist" position was not without its difficulties, beginning with the fact that any consistent application of this argument threatened to make large sections of the New Testament irrelevant to modern Protestantism. In practice, of course, no such argument has ever been made. When all the theological accretions are swept away from the argument, it reduces to one very simple point: the Holy Spirit is not experienced in the church today as it was by the apostles on Pentecost. The significance of the events in Topeka, Kansas, in January 1901, and then at Azusa Street in Los Angeles in April 1906, was that they suggested that things might have changed. And if they had, a lot of theological rethinking would have to be done. We see here a classic example of what the historian of science Thomas Kuhn famously described as a "paradigm shift" in the development of the natural sciences—the emergence of new approaches when the capacity of older theories to account for new experiences and observations is seen to be defective.

The feature that both characterizes and distinguishes Pentecostalism from all other forms of Christianity is its insistence and emphasis upon an immediate encounter with God through the Holy Spirit and the ensuing transformation of individuals. Although Pentecostals and other charismatics do not always agree on how best to articulate theologically this understanding of the role of the Holy Spirit, they share a common expectation of certain patterns of divine action. The "full gospel," Pentecostals insist, must include the gift of tongues. Yet there is more to this characteristic of Pentecostalism than this brief statement might suggest. Pentecostalism does not simply believe in speaking in tongues; it provides a social context that reinforces a sense of expectation that speaking in tongues will take place, thereby creating the social structures that sustain and extend the phenomenon.[16] Pentecostal communities embody this social expectancy, which provides an important support against criticisms of the phenomenon as "abnormal" or "improper" from outside.

So what exactly is this gift? The New Testament draws a distinction between *xenolalia* ("speaking in foreign languages") and *glossolalia* ("speaking in tongues"). Most early Pentecostals, such as Charles

Parham, insisted that believers have been given the power to speak in foreign languages; most of them subsequently came to the view, however, that the Spirit causes speaking in tongues for personal edification. The classic Pentecostal view has come to be that this phenomenon is a consequence of the presence of the Spirit in believers.[17]

So just what is "speaking in tongues"? In trying to answer this question, it is helpful to draw a distinction between a description of the phenomenon and its theological interpretation. The phenomenon usually takes the form of an intense religious experience expressing itself in ecstatic speech, typically during a period of worship or open prayer that is perceived to have great personal meaning for the individual worshiper. The "speech" in question corresponds to no known language and is generally unintelligible to external observers.[18] Charismatic theologians interpret this phenomenon as corresponding to the experience of the early Christian communities, as recorded in the New Testament, particularly in Paul's Corinthian correspondence. It is seen as a sign of the living presence of God within individuals, offering both reassurance of salvation and guidance to individuals and the community as a whole.[19]

The phrase "baptism in the Spirit" has come to be especially important for Pentecostalism. It refers to a special divine anointing, gift, or blessing subsequent to conversion, which is demonstrated by speaking in tongues. Classical Protestantism held that all necessary resources were given to the believer at baptism or conversion. The continuity of Pentecostalism with the holiness tradition is clear at this point: sections of the movement recognize a "second blessing" in which believers receive a special anointing from God to enable them to live a victorious life, triumphing over sin and temptation. The holiness movement recognized a postconversion enhancement of an individual's personal spirituality, which was often described as the "second blessing." The baptism of the Spirit is seen as the fulfillment of this "second blessing."

Writers such as A. J. Gordon and Reuben A. Torrey began to speak of a "baptism of the Holy Spirit" in the 1880s and 1890s. However, this was conceived primarily as the empowerment of the individual through an increase in the personal indwelling of the Holy Spirit. An excellent example of this phenomenon can be seen in the ministry of the noted evangelist Dwight L. Moody, who experienced this form of personal renewal in 1870. Yet—and this is of critical importance—there was no suggestion that this "second blessing" or "baptism in the Holy Spirit" led to speaking in tongues. It was all about empowerment and encouragement.

The suggestion of a theological link between "baptism in the Spirit" and "speaking in tongues" was first made by Parham in 1901, and that link has remained typical of Pentecostalism ever since. Refinements introduced since that time include the distinction between speaking in tongues as a universal sign and as a specific gift. On this view, all true believers are able to speak in tongues as a sign of their baptism in the Spirit, and some have the gift of being able to use this in public worship. The evidence of this "second blessing" is the ability to speak in tongues.

This has important implications for the understanding of the identity and significance of Jesus Christ in Pentecostal thought. Whereas traditional Protestantism tends to think of Christ as having secured forgiveness of past sins and an assurance of eternal life through his death on the cross, Pentecostalism has developed a fourfold understanding of his significance that is often referred to as the "foursquare" gospel, following the approach developed by the American Pentecostal leader Aimee Semple McPherson (1890–1944). While preaching in California in 1922, she had a vision based upon four symbols—a cross, a crown, a dove, and a cup. She took these to be symbols of the central themes of evangelism, empowered by the Holy Spirit, and used them as the theological basis of her International Church of the Foursquare Gospel.[20]

The "foursquare" interpretation of evangelism emphasizes what Christ presently does within the lives of believers. While retaining the traditional Protestant teaching of the past and future dimensions of salvation—the forgiveness of past sins and the future hope of resurrection—McPherson stressed the transformative impact of Christ upon individuals and communities here and now. On this approach, Jesus Christ is to be understood as:

1. Savior—the one who delivers individuals from their sins

2. Healer—the one who delivers from illness and the power of Satan

3. Baptizer in the Spirit—the one who empowers ordinary people to bear witness to the gospel to the ends of the earth

4. The coming King—the one who is preparing the way within the church for his coming return in glory

Although the basic beliefs of the foursquare gospel are not universally acknowledged within Pentecostalism, they illustrate one of the movement's most significant characteristics—the affirmation that Jesus Christ may be experienced at the present moment and has the power to heal and transform people and communities at their point of need and in their moment of need.

THE APPEAL OF PENTECOSTALISM

Why is Pentecostalism so appealing, especially to those who find themselves on the margins of society? The best answer seems to be its emphasis upon personal spiritual empowerment, through which the status of individuals is not determined by their sociological location or their intellectual ability, but by their gifting by the Holy Spirit. This radical shift in the frames of reference by which individuals are evaluated is strongly evident in the egalitarianism of Seymour's Azusa Street ecclesiology (but not, it must be emphasized, in Parham's Topeka ministry).

This is a point of no small importance. Robert Beckford, a British black Pentecostal scholar, has argued that the egalitarian phenomenon of speaking in tongues at Azusa Street signified more than any baptism in the Spirit. It was an expression of the community's commitment to a "radical social transformation" that placed it in direct continuity with the egalitarianism shown by the New Testament community of faith in the aftermath of its experience of the Holy Spirit.[21] God speaks to and through all true believers. While this egalitarian ethos has been lost in many sections of Pentecostalism through the rise of various forms of elitism, it remains an ideal that challenges and attracts in about equal measure. Where the first generation of Protestants spoke of the "priesthood of all believers," the Pentecostal equivalent would be the "prophethood of all believers."[22]

Alongside this tendency toward egalitarianism—and possibly as its fundamental condition—Pentecostalism insists upon the universal accessibility of the divine. Experience of God is not restricted to a spiritual elite; it is not dependent on intellectual or academic excellence; nor is it something that is unattainable in the present, being postponed until a postmortem encounter with God in the heavenly realms. Like certain forms of Pietism or sections of the holiness tradition, Pentecostalism accentuates the reality of this experience of God and its importance for spiritual growth and theological reflection. A "living faith" (to borrow the language of the Pietist tradition) is not about doctrinal rectitude or theological precision, but about the experience of God as a living reality in the believer's soul.

Yet this accessibility applies to the means as much as to the goal of the spiritual life. Pentecostalism uses a language and form of communication that enable it to bridge cultural gaps with great effectiveness. Walter Hollenweger, one of the most distinguished historians of the movement, points to the importance of this use of readily accessible means of communication to the success of the movement:

> [Pentecostalism] is an oral religion. It is not defined by the abstract language that characterises, for instance, Presbyterians or Catholics. Pentecostalism is communicated in stories, testimonies and songs. Oral language is a much more global language than that of the universities or church denominations. Oral tradition is flexible and can adapt itself to a variety of circumstances.... When you become a Pentecostal, you talk about how you've been healed, or how your very life has been changed. That's something that Pentecostals talk about over and over, partly because people are interested in hearing that sort of thing. Pentecostalism today addresses the whole of life, including the thinking part. More mainline forms of Christianity address the thinking part first, and that often affects the rest of life—but not always.[23]

Such reflections led an earlier generation of Pentecostals to be suspicious of academic study and to wear their anti-intellectualism as a badge of honor. Yet the increasing sense of confidence within the movement has led it to become more interested in technical questions of biblical interpretation, systematic theology, and broader cultural issues. Pentecostals are increasingly aware of the potential of their tradition to deal with interpretative issues that deadlocked American Protestantism in the early twentieth century.[24] It remains to be seen whether this intellectual and cultural engagement will dull Pentecostalism's cutting edge or increase its capacity for self-actualization in new contexts.

THE IMMEDIACY OF GOD: PENTECOSTALISM AND THE TRANSCENDENT

In an earlier chapter, we noted that traditional Protestantism's emphasis upon an indirect knowledge of God, mediated through reading the Bible, led to "desacralization"—the creation of a culture with no sense or expectation of God's presence in its midst. This point has been stressed by a series of sociologists—including Max Weber, Charles Taylor, and Stephen Toulmin—who have, in their different ways, shown that Protestantism was the means by which a society that originally possessed a strong sense of the sacred became "disenchanted." The inevitable result of this was secularization—the final elimination of God from the world. As Francis Fukuyama points out in his *End of History and the Last Man* (1992), "the generally accepted agent for this secularization in the West was Protestantism."[25]

Historically, it is clear that a major determinant for the emergence of atheism as a serious cultural force is whether a culture has lost a sense of the divine. The absence of any expectation of encountering the divine *directly* through nature or in personal experience inevitably encourages belief in a godless world—the kind of culture that lives *etsi Deus non daretur* ("as if God did not exist"). By limiting knowledge of God to what can be known about God's words and God's will, some classic forms of Protestantism have in effect placed an embargo on any direct knowledge or experience of God.

Indeed, some sections of Protestantism, often deeply influenced by the rationalism of the Enlightenment, continue to this day to emphasize "theological correctness" by stressing the overarching importance of having right ideas about God. These correct notions of God are to be determined by a reading of the Bible, which is understood primarily as a doctrinal handbook. Faith thus becomes an *indirect* knowledge of God, stated in terms of beliefs about God that, however correct they may be as far as they go, convey the impression that Christianity is little more than abstract theorizing about a God whose will is revealed in the Bible.

It is a danger that is well recognized within mainline Protestantism, and it was partly addressed through the rise of Pietism. The noted American Presbyterian writer James Henley Thornwell (1812–62) had no doubts about the danger of excessively rationalist or cerebral approaches to theology:

> It gave no scope to the play of Christian feeling; it never turned aside to reverence, to worship, or to adore. It exhibited truth, nakedly and baldly, in its objective reality, without any reference to the subjective conditions which, under the influence of the Spirit, that truth was calculated to produce. It was a dry digest of theses and propositions—perfect in form, but as cold and lifeless as a skeleton.[26]

Such an approach to theology divorced it from the realm of experience—and hence from the reality of everyday Christian life, especially among believers who did not find intellectual analysis natural or easy.

This is precisely what Harvey Cox describes as "text-orientated believers"—that is, those Protestants who believe that God can only be accessed (and then to a limited extent, in the form of abstract religious ideas) through reading the Bible or hearing an expository sermon. For Cox, Pentecostalism celebrates the resurgence of "primal spirituality" and absolutely refuses to allow experience of God to be limited to the rarefied world of abstract ideas. God is experienced and known as a personal, transformative, living reality.

The contrast with Pentecostalism on this point could not be greater. Pentecostalism's emphasis on a direct, immediate experience of God avoids the rather dry and cerebral forms of Christianity that many find unattractive and unintelligible. It is thus significant that Pentecostalism has made huge inroads in working-class areas of Latin America, Africa, and Asia, in that it is able to communicate a sense of the divine and its implications without the need for prayer books and the other traditional paraphernalia of Protestant culture. Pentecostalism eschews the aridity of dogmatic theology and sets in its place the personal renewal of the believer through the Spirit—something that can be narrated and proclaimed rather than logically dissected and analyzed.

Pentecostalism declares that it is possible to encounter God directly and personally through the power of the Holy Spirit. God is to be known immediately and directly, not indirectly through study of a text. Whereas traditional Protestantism is wary of allowing any such immediate experience of God, Pentecostalism celebrates it and makes it a hallmark of Christian living. God has an impact upon the totality of existence and is not confined—as in some traditional Protestant traditions—to the world of the mind.

So why is this so important? These observations need to be set against one of the most dramatic developments to take place globally in the aftermath of the Second World War—the spread of Marxism. Although imposed by force in many parts of eastern Europe and central Asia, Marxist ideas proved inspirational to many groups in Latin America, Africa, and Asia that were disillusioned with the existing social order and wanted to change it radically. Marxism offered a worldview that promised to transform society—and it was a worldview without God.

In Latin America, Marxism quickly gained the initiative, with Cuba emerging as a revolutionary template. In Brazil, Marxism adapted to the local situation, and theorists such as Caio Prado (1907–90) presented its socioeconomic vision as the remedy for the nation's ills. Recognizing the importance of dealing with the social issues this reflected, some prominent Catholics in the region developed "liberation theology," which emphasized the transformative social vision of the gospel.[27] Liberation theology was not, however, compelling. Part of its problem was that it offered a vision of social transformation in which the individual seemed to have no particular role. Pentecostalism, in marked contrast, offered a vision of *personal* transformation in which individuals sorted out their own lives, then those of their families, and then moved on to broader social issues.

Pentecostalism creates a strong sense of expectation of a direct, personal, transformative encounter with God in the worship of the church and in personal experience. Personal transformation subsequently leads into social concern. Far from being oppressive or fraudulent (as Marxism argued), belief in God has been liberating and transforming. How could God's existence be doubted when God is such a powerful reality in people's lives? And how could God's relevance be doubted when God inspires people to care for the poor, heal the sick, and work for the dispossessed? The outcome of this movement has been remarkable. Pentecostalism is displacing Marxism as the solace and inspiration of the urban poor.

Important though this development is, the relevant point in this section is Pentecostalism's resacralization of everyday life. A permanently absent God can quickly become a dead God. If the existence of God makes little or no impact upon the experiences of everyday life, the business of living might as well be conducted without reference to God. By opening up again the possibility of a transcendent reality virtually closed off by modernism, Pentecostalism injects the presence of God into everyday life—through social action, politics, and evangelism.

The rise of Pentecostalism thus represents a challenge to the more cerebralized forms of Protestantism. It urges them to reconsider their excessive intellectualism and to discover the forbidden realms of imagination, emotion, narrative, and experience. This kind of experiential and transcendent impoverishment of faith is partly due to early trends in sections of Protestantism, which are open to challenge and correction, and partly due to the excessive influence of modernism upon the movement as a whole, which is subject to historical erosion as well as principled rejection. Protestantism is not wedded to such a distancing from the transcendent; the rise of Pentecostalism may yet prove to be the stimulus for it to reconsider this question—to the enrichment of the movement as a whole. Protestantism, after all, is a work in progress that subjects itself to constant review and is willing to correct mistakes and wrong turnings.

Yet many mainstream Protestants feel that Pentecostalism itself might represent precisely such a mistake and a wrong turning. We must therefore move on to consider some tensions between the movements and their implications for the future of both movements.

TENSIONS WITH TRADITIONAL PROTESTANTISM

The rapid rise of Pentecostalism has not been without controversy. The movement is unquestionably a form of Protestantism: it emerged historically from the American holiness tradition, and it emphasizes the place of the Bible in Christian life and tradition. Like all Protestant groups, Pentecostalism affirms the authority of the Bible with a specific and distinctive way of interpreting the text that attaches particular importance to the role of the Holy Spirit in interpreting the Bible and in guiding and empowering the individual. Pentecostalism regularly affirms a commitment to the acceptance of the real and present work of the Holy Spirit through gifts and signs as imparted to believers for service and witness.

This commitment has given rise to a tension that is often characterized as "word *versus* spirit." Classical Protestantism holds that God's will and purposes are revealed only through the written text of the Bible; Pentecostalism recognizes the role of "words of knowledge" to individual believers, which may be important for the community as a whole. For traditional Protestants, this approach seems to devalue the place of the Bible in the Christian life; for Pentecostals, the older approaches limit God's capacity to reveal himself to individuals through his Spirit.

Classical Protestantism is also uneasy about Pentecostalism's idea of "baptism in the Spirit," which it regards as inadequately grounded in the Bible. Most charismatics believe that a Christian receives the Holy Spirit at conversion but does not receive the fullness of the Spirit until later, through baptism in the Holy Spirit, in which he or she receives a full empowerment for Christian service. Baptism in the Holy Spirit is thus seen as a second work of grace after conversion. Traditional Protestant theology does not accept this framework, which is also encountered in the holiness tradition, holding instead that all Christians are baptized in the Holy Spirit at conversion.

A more serious concern has arisen over what many traditional Protestants see as the non-trinitarian understandings of the Holy Spirit associated with one or two Pentecostal groups. Although these groups are not typical of the movement as a whole, their critics regard them as indicative of the movement's theological trends and patterns of thought. "Oneness" Pentecostals—sometimes referred to as "Jesus Only" charismatics by their critics—insist upon the unity of God (as seen in the "Shema"; Deuteronomy 6:4) and regard the classical idea of the Trinity as introducing division within the Godhead.

The United Pentecostal Church International (UPCI) thus differs significantly from the Assemblies of God (AoG) and other classic Pentecostal churches through its declaration that it "views the Trinitarian concept of God, that of God eternally existing as three distinctive persons, as inadequate and a departure from the consistent and emphatic biblical revelation of God being one." In its place, the UPCI offers a doctrine of God that classical Protestantism—and the vast majority of Pentecostals—regard as a form of modalism, a trinitarian heresy rejected by the early church. Thus, the UPCI states that "God is manifested as Father in creation and as the Father of the Son, in the Son for our redemption, and as the Holy Spirit in our regeneration"—a view usually referred to and rejected as "Sabellianism."[28]

A final area in which traditional Protestantism has expressed concern about Pentecostalism concerns a strand of thought that has emerged in a significant number of its churches—namely, that being right with God ensures health and wealth. Leading American exponents of this approach within the Pentecostal tradition include Oral Roberts and Benny Hinn. This "prosperity gospel" is capable of being stated in a number of ways; its most fundamental theme, however, is that "being poor or ill is a sin, when God promises prosperity and health."[29] This "name-it-and-claim-it" theology causes many, both Pentecostals and traditional Protestants, serious theological problems. After all, Jesus Christ was not wealthy in any sense of the term, and his crucifixion is hardly consistent with the idea that God blesses the faithful with long lives and the evasion of suffering.

While many traditional Protestants are uneasy about the rise of Pentecostalism, there is a growing appreciation of its merits and a willingness to work with it in programs of outreach, pastoral care, and political and social action. This naturally leads us to explore what the longer-term impact of the movement on Protestantism might be.

THE SIGNIFICANCE OF PENTECOSTALISM
FOR PROTESTANTISM

Many see the advent and advance of Pentecostalism in the twentieth century as no less important than the Reformation of the sixteenth century, And some even describe the emergence of Pentecostalism as a "second Reformation," or a "new Reformation." Both of these labels, though understandable, are inappropriate. The term "second Reformation" was widely used in scholarly studies of an earlier generation to refer to what is now more accurately and helpfully known as "confessionalization." This was not understood as a "second" or "new" Reformation, but as a second phase in the continuing process of recalibration and reformulation that lies at the heart of the Protestant enterprise.[30]

Pentecostalism is to be seen as part of the Protestant process of reflection, reconsideration, and regeneration. It is not the consequence of a "new Reformation," but a legitimate outcome of the ongoing program that has characterized and defined Protestantism from its outset. Like most other movements within Protestantism, it builds upon what has gone before. Its spiritual egalitarianism is clearly both a recovery and a restatement of the classic Protestant doctrine of the "priesthood of all believers." Its emphasis upon the importance of experience and the need for transformation can be traced back to earlier Pietism, particularly as developed within the holiness tradition. Yet it has welded and wedded these insights into its own distinctive vision of the Christian life and of how God is encountered and proclaimed. It offers Protestantism a new paradigm of self-expression that was once regarded as marginal and slightly eccentric by the Protestant mainstream; one hundred years later, Pentecostalism is increasingly coming to define and determine that mainstream itself.

So what might this movement have to say to other Protestants? At one level, the movement has brought about renewal within mainline Protestantism through its "worship songs." The history of Pentecostalism in France—one of Europe's most secular countries—illustrates this well. Evangelical and charismatic churches grew from 800 registered congregations in 1970 to 1,800 in 2000. This growth is widely attributed to the charismatic movement, which has not only become a significant

Protestant group in itself but also revitalized worship in many mainline denominations. While noncharismatic Protestant churches appear to be stagnant or in decline, charismatic sectors of the Protestant community are growing and taking advantage of a subtle yet growing interest in spiritual matters among French youth.

Yet there are deeper issues here, one of which is of particular interest. In that Pentecostalism is a late arrival on the Protestant scene, it has forged its ideas and approaches without being molded by past controversies, constraints, and traditions. One of the most distinctive features of Pentecostalism is its total disconnection with any notion of "Christendom." This paradigm shaped Western Christian thinking about its social identity from the onset of the Middle Ages (some would argue since the conversion of the Roman emperor Constantine) until the end of the First World War.[31] It is based on the notion of geographical regions that possess a religious and cultural identity determined by the Christian faith.

Although this notion has been in decline in western Europe since the eighteenth century, Protestantism emerged in an era when this notion was still dominant. Protestantism has never entirely shaken off its lingering memory, and over the years it has acquired habits of action and thought that reflect its social origins in western Europe. Whether the Protestant communities have been inclined to accept or reject the model of Christendom, it was the constant backdrop to their reflections.

Much the same is true of the Enlightenment and the rise of modernity, which have had a decisive effect on the shaping of Protestantism and made no small contribution to the tensions, confusion, and disagreements over how to respond to postmodernity. Wolfhart Pannenberg has persuasively argued that much Western Protestant theology has been shaped by the rise of the natural sciences and the secular critique of authority.[32]

Pentecostalism emerged in the first years of the twentieth century and blossomed from about 1950. It was never subject to the controlling assumptions about what was "reasonable" or "normal" that so shaped earlier Protestant communities. Sociologically, it was a religion of the poor, marginalized, and dispossessed, who had little interest in matters of theology or church politics. Without having its ideas and expectations molded by the notion of Christendom and traditional Protestant responses to this, Pentecostalism was free to develop its own post-Christendom paradigms and often retrieved pre-Christendom strategies without even realizing it.

Similarly, Pentecostalism adapted to postmodernity without having first been molded by modernism. Its emergence at a cultural junction allowed it to adapt as it saw best to the prevailing local cultures without having to discard or modify an inherited set of assumptions and attitudes that traditionalists tended to regard as normative. Pentecostalism was thus able to respond rapidly and sympathetically to local cultures without being restrained by modernist Western assumptions about how this should be done. Pentecostalism, as has often been observed, is the global religion best adapted to the globalization process itself.[33]

We see here an emerging form of Christianity that has skipped the agenda of a past generation and is able to construct its outlook and strategic policies without reference to a period of history that was of such importance in the West. There is an obvious technological analogy to hand in the emergence of cell-phone technology. Many Africans now have cell phones without having had traditional landlines in the past. Technology has simply skipped an intermediate generation in this region. No one needs to have used a landline telephone to understand or use a cell phone. Seeing no need to engage with past memories of Christendom or modernity, Pentecostals proceed directly to the next generation of ideas and approaches.

Some have suggested that Pentecostalism was deliberately conceived as a postmodern form of Protestantism. The historical evidence for this is simply not compelling. It is far more accurate to suggest that the movement emerged with an outlook that proved—by accident rather than design (although Pentecostals would speak of "divine providence" in this regard)—to be exceptionally well adapted to the new cultural mood emerging in the West in the late twentieth century and to the premodern mood prevalent throughout the global South. This is a resonance of happenstance, not a carefully crafted strategy of adaptation. Yet for Pentecostals, this is a matter of God's providence and planning and must be discerned as such.

Pentecostalism's resonance with postmodernism is probably best seen in the field of biblical interpretation. Pentecostals, while affirming the traditional Protestant notion of the accessibility of the Bible and the right of every believer to interpret this text, stress the multiple dimensions of meaning that arise—not on account of the indeterminate nature of the text, but on account of the "leading of the Spirit" into the true meaning of the text, which that same Spirit originally inspired.

We must now consider the global growth and diversification of Protestantism in the twentieth century, a process in which Pentecostalism has played a significant role. Yet while Pentecostalism is by far the most numerous component of the worldwide Protestant movement at present, there are other significant players and factors that have made significant contributions to its dynamics in the opening years of the twenty-first century. In the following chapter, we consider some of these trends and their possible implications for the future.

16

The New Frontiers of Protestantism

The Global South

The transformation of Protestantism in the twentieth century was the outcome of many forces, social and cultural as much as theological, that combined to give a new lease of life and sense of identity to a movement that seemed to some to be about to run into the enfolding sands of history in the aftermath of the First World War.

The shaping of Protestantism in the later twentieth century was dominated by the United States, which became the intellectual and entrepreneurial powerhouse of the movement after the Second World War. Yet the recent history of Protestant America is only part (although a very important part) of the greater story of the movement as a whole. For one of the most intriguing aspects of the transformation of Protestantism as the twentieth century proceeded was that America—and indeed, the entire Western homeland of Protestantism—began to lose its preeminence as other regions began to rise. Three factors combined to bring about this development.

First, the numerical center of Christianity, including Protestantism, shifted decisively away from the West between 1900 and 2000.[1] Christianity is now predominantly a religion of the global South. Population growth in these areas, when set alongside the evangelistic and missionary

Smithsonian American Art Museum, Washington, DC;
Photo: Smithsonian American Art Museum, Washington, DC/Art Resource, NY

Mount Cavalry, *1944, by William H. Johnson (1901–70).*

successes of the twentieth century, has ensured that an increasing proportion of increasingly large populations are now Christian. For example, in
1900 the population of Africa was 10 million people, of whom 9 percent
were Christian; in 2005 the population was more than 400 million, of
whom 46 percent were Christian.

Second, the styles of Christianity developing in Asia, Latin America,
and Africa are noticeably different from those found in the United
States, and even more different from those found in western Europe.
The Protestantism of the global South tends to be more charismatic or
Pentecostal, to maintain traditional moral values, and to have little time
for the modernist modes of reading the Bible that have dominated the
West until recently. As a result, the Protestant denominations of the
global South tend to have more in common with each other than with
their counterparts in America or Europe. African Lutherans tend to
have more in common with African Methodists than with American

Lutherans, despite the denominational link. This is especially evident in the case of Anglicanism: the totally different social mores and theological presuppositions of African and American Anglicans are causing serious, possibly irreconcilable, tensions within that denomination.

Finally, a new form of Christianity has emerged in the twentieth century, and it has now surged ahead in terms of its popular appeal, social impact, and, increasingly, its theological acumen. As noted in the previous chapter, Pentecostalism's capacity to engage the urban poor and make Christianity accessible to the illiterate has led to the demographical transformation of Protestantism in many parts of the global South. Although the movement grew slowly until the late 1950s, it experienced sustained and spectacular growth thereafter, possibly unparalleled in the history of religion.

It is impossible in the scope of a single chapter to provide anything more than a sketch of the diversity, fecundity, and vitality of Protestant Christianity in the emerging world. In what follows, we highlight some of the most interesting developments and assess their implications both for an understanding of Protestant identity and for its future prospects and shape.

THE WESTERN RECOGNITION OF THE NEED FOR INDIGENIZATION

At the dawn of the twentieth century, Protestantism was at best a minority presence outside the West, sustained largely by Western missionaries. The great Edinburgh mission conference of 1910 had set an agenda that was interrupted by the outbreak of the First World War. Once the war was over, Western Protestants turned their attention to renewing and reinvigorating the missionary enterprise.[2] Yet it soon became clear that things were changing. The war—which had seen death and devastation on an unprecedented scale—created serious difficulties for the entire missionary enterprise. How could Christianity be commended to the world when Christian nations had caused and participated in so scandalous a war?

From about 1920, a new mind-set began to emerge. Christianity had to be divested of its unhelpful associations with Western culture. This pragmatic response to the scandal of the war cleared the ground for more serious reflection on the theology of indigenization—that is, how the Christian faith might take root in new cultural contexts in ways that were sensitive and adapted to those situations.[3] Rather than impose Western models of church order, it was necessary to discern what forms of Christian thought and life were appropriate to the local culture. This new theme, developed in works such as Daniel Fleming's *Whither Bound in Missions* (1925), involved drawing a sharp distinction between Christ and Western culture.

This trend was assisted by the theology of mission championed by the Edinburgh Conference of 1910. Some conservative Protestants had adopted a "theory of degeneration," which held that a primordial global monotheism had been corrupted and distorted in non-Christian contexts. Their more liberal counterparts often adopted a more Darwinian approach, which held that Christianity was the supreme religion, and Western civilization its greatest achievement. The inferiority of other religions was demonstrated by their social inadequacy. Though very different, both these theologies encouraged a triumphalist and negative attitude on the part of Christian missionaries toward native cultures.

In marked contrast to both these approaches, Edinburgh adopted a fulfillment theology of mission that saw Jesus Christ as the "fulfillment of other religions." Holding that "all religions await their fulfillment in Christ," the Edinburgh Conference gave its missionaries a mandate to respect and engage with native cultures, seeing these as capable of being fulfilled in and through Christ.[4] This led to a new interest in finding "points of contact" between indigenous cultures and the gospel.[5]

The term "indigenization" proved unpopular. In Africa it was quickly replaced by terms such as "adaptionism," which gave intellectual legitimacy to the use of African thought forms in Christian theology and of African rituals in the liturgy. Those of a more Catholic persuasion came to adopt "incarnationism," some missiologists preferred "translation," and the World Council of Churches adopted the preferred terminology of the Taiwanese theologian Shoki Coe (Chang Hui Hwang, 1914–88)—"contextualization."[6] Yet the same basic theme can be discerned throughout—the need to express and embody the gospel in a manner appropriate to a local culture rather than imposing a certain vision of the gospel upon that culture.[7]

Although this trend was not without importance in the period between the two world wars, the scholarly consensus is that the history of global Christianity began to move in significant new directions after the Second World War. Some of the most prominent activists for political independence in both sub-Saharan Africa and India were Christian; they saw the achievement of a proper national identity as essential for the establishment of a viable local theology instead of the culturally implausible Western impositions.

Some sociologists argued that Christianity in non-Western contexts, especially Africa, was sustained by the presence of the Western colonial power, and therefore, they predicted, the demise of Christianity would follow the withdrawal of this political support. Not for the first time, a theory proved misguided: the removal of Western power actually removed Western constraints that had been preventing the emergence of more culturally adapted forms of Christianity. The withdrawal of colonial powers—such as Britain and France—from their former territories allowed local churches to develop theologies, ministries, and styles of worship that were adaptations to their contexts rather than poor copies of the churches found in the colonial homelands. In most cases, the departure of the colonial power was followed by renewal as the cultural restraints on indigenous variants of Christianity were finally removed. Political independence rapidly led to ecclesiastical independence and the ending of the paternalist suppression of indigenous theologies and worship patterns.

Unsurprisingly, much of the emerging theology of Africa and Asia has reacted against Western Christian models. A revolt against the "colonization of the mind" demands self-definition and affirmation of identity over and against the colonizing "other." With the end of the colonial era, therefore, we may say that a new understanding of Protestant identity and a new style of Protestant theology began to emerge. No longer, for example, did Singaporean Anglicanism look like that of Surbiton incongruously transplanted to the tropics; it developed its own ethos and identity—and began to grow.

Throughout these declarations of intellectual, ecclesiastical, and political independence, the churches of the global South maintained the fundamental Protestant principle of constant reexamination, reassessment, and restatement, thus allowing the Bible and the historical Protestant tradition to be brought to bear on their situation. Instead of importing ready-made theologies, liturgies, and handbooks of evangelism from the West, its increasingly confident indigenous practitioners were now prepared to create their own. Western influence on churches in the global South remains: many of its leaders have studied at British or American universities and seminaries and have been shaped at least to some extent by the Western ethos. Yet this influence now seems ministerial, not magisterial—a relation of committed partners, not of master and servant.

Before considering the impact of the new dynamics of Protestantism in the global South on Protestantism as a whole, we consider some individual cases as well as some more general trends to illustrate what is happening on the ground, giving an account that is often overlooked by the Western media and intelligentsia alike. In what follows, we present a survey of developments, not in order to provide a detailed analysis of the situation, but to show how Protestantism has been transformed in the twentieth century—in ways that would have been unpredictable at the beginning of that era.

AFRICA: ENGAGING TRADITIONAL RELIGION AND CULTURE

Early missionaries tended to regard traditional African religions as evil, primitive, and superstitious, and they extended this negative attitude toward African culture as a whole. The Ghanaian writer Kwame Bediako points out that African Christians were thus often put in the intolerable position of being obliged to turn their backs on their own traditions and culture and rely on an imported European heritage.[8] This served to reinforce the perception that Christianity was culturally alien to Africa—a perception that was particularly acute in the case of Anglicanism, which retained many outward manifestations of its English origins (for example, the virtually universal use of the *Book of Common Prayer* until the Second World War). Catholic missionaries, often armed with a "natural theology" that encouraged them to find and value "points of contact" between the gospel and African culture, were rather more positive about cultural engagement. Protestants, often inculcated against "primitive superstition" by the culture of the Enlightenment rather than by Christianity itself, were much more censorious.[9]

The outcome was predictable. Africans who converted to Protestantism read the Bible through African eyes, not through the modernist prism of Western missionaries.[10] African Protestants saw little difficulty in reading parts of the Bible in a literalist way, and so they alarmed the enlightened missionaries by taking literally gospel commands such as to heal and cast out demons. This was not to be seen as a "primitive" way of reading the Bible, but a rejection of the habits of interpretation that had emerged in the West as a result of the Enlightenment's rationalist worldview, which held that "demons" and "spirits" were irrational beliefs. African converts had no difficulty in accepting their reality, and they relished the gospel's direct engagement with these core elements of their worldview. As Elizabeth Isichei comments in her masterly history of Christianity in Africa, such converts

> found in the world of the Bible, a world of victory over sickness and death, of mastery over evil spirits.... The emphasis on healing and miracles was not wholly absent from the mission churches, but, typically, they interpreted disease in a rationalist-scientific way, and relied more on hospitals than prayer to solve health problems.[11]

More significantly, African converts to the historical Protestant mission churches held that many traditional African practices—such as polygamy—should be regarded as permissible under the gospel.

The outcome of these tensions was the formation of a wide range of African Initiated Churches (AICs), which are virtually entirely Protestant.[12] African Protestants knew enough about the history of their movement to draw the conclusion that it was perfectly legitimate to break away from parent denominations when these were seen to fail or fall short at critical points. AICs are strongest and most numerous in southern Africa, west Africa, the Congo Basin, and central Kenya. Three major categories of AICs can be identified.[13]

"Ethiopian" and "African" Churches

AICs that do not claim to be prophetic or to offer special manifestations of the Holy Spirit have been referred to as "Ethiopian" or "Ethiopiantype" churches in southern Africa and as "African" churches in Nigeria.

Generally earlier in origin than the other two types, these churches arose primarily as a political and administrative reaction to European mission-founded churches. For this reason, Ethiopian or African churches are very similar to the historical Protestant churches from which they emerged. For example, they usually practice infant baptism, read set liturgies, wear European clerical vestments (often black), and use forms of worship that are less enthusiastic or emotional than the forms of worship in other AICs.

"Prophet-Healing" and "Spiritual" Churches

"Prophet-healing" or "spiritual" churches are AICs that have historical and theological roots in the Pentecostalist movement and emphasize the working of the power of the Spirit in the church. This is the largest grouping of AICs, and it includes a wide variety of some of the biggest churches in Africa. It includes the Kimbanguist movement and the African Apostolic church in central Africa, the Aladura and Harrist churches in west Africa, and the Zion Christian church and the Amanazaretha in southern Africa. The theology of these churches tends to be more precisely formulated than in European mission-founded churches, and the differences in belief systems, liturgy, and prophetic healing practices are often considerable. The most obvious distinguishing feature of these churches throughout most of Africa is the almost universal use of uniforms for members, often white robes with bright sashes.

"New Pentecostal" Churches

"New Pentecostal" churches, which are of more recent origin (mostly after 1980), also emphasize the power and the gifts of the Holy Spirit. Probably the fastest-growing expression of Christianity in Africa today, these churches burst onto the African religious scene about 1975, and their explosive growth since then has challenged many previously accepted assumptions about the character of African Protestantism. The difference between these churches—examples of which are the Deeper Life Church in Nigeria, the Zimbabwe Assemblies of God African, and Grace Bible Church in South Africa—and those of Western Pentecostal origin has mainly to do with their form of church government. Leadership in the new churches is entirely black and essentially local and autonomous, with no organizational links with Pentecostal denominations outside Africa.

The surge of spiritual and intellectual energy now animating African Protestantism can be seen from one of the most significant publications of the opening years of the twenty-first century. The *Africa Bible Commentary* (2006) is a 1,600-page commentary on the entire text of the Bible, with the African horizon in mind.[14] Western academic questions and agendas are gently set to one side in order to allow the text to address and engage the living issues of Africa, here and now—such as HIV/AIDS, demons and exorcisms, funeral and burial rites, the care of widows and orphans, and responses to persecution. A French edition is scheduled for release in 2007, with editions in Amharic, Portuguese, and other regional languages to follow.

KOREA: THE FIRST ASIAN PROTESTANT NATION

At the beginning of the twentieth century, the only predominantly Christian nation in Asia was the Philippines, which was a strongly Catholic country with a small Protestant minority. At the end of the twentieth century, Korea has established itself as a largely Christian nation, with Protestantism—especially Presbyterianism—being by far the largest Christian group.

Yet in 1901, only a tiny proportion of the Korean population was Christian—perhaps 1 percent. How did a country with virtually no Christian presence come to be, in effect, a Christian nation? The answer is complex. The Pyongyang revival of 1907 was one of a series of essentially independent Pentecostal movements of the first decade of the twentieth century and is known to have been a significant force in bringing about conversions among the native population.

A further point of importance is that Christianity came to be perceived as an ally rather than an enemy by Koreans in the twentieth century. Korea was annexed by Japan in 1910 and remained under Japanese rule until the end of the Second World War. Unusually, Christianity was seen as allied with Korean nationalism, especially in the face of Japanese oppression. Elsewhere in Asia, Christianity was easily depicted by its critics as the lackey of Western imperialism. In Korea, however, the enemy was not the West but Japan. Throughout this time, Christians played an active role in the Korean independence movement, out of all proportion to their numbers. Of the 123 people tried for insurgence by the Japanese in the 1911 popular revolt against Japanese rule, 98 were Christians. At this time, Christians made up just over 1 percent of the Korean population. The significance of this point could hardly be overlooked.

Following the Second World War, Korea underwent partition into a Communist north and democratic south following the Korean War, which broke out on June 25, 1950. The heavy involvement of Christian missionary agencies in the relief programs that followed the ending of the war created a powerful stimulus to the development of Christianity, which was catalyzed still further by the Korean churches' programs of social action during the 1960s. Growth continued unabated, especially within Korean Protestantism. In 1957 there were about 800,000 Protestants in Korea. This figure had more than doubled by 1968 (1,873,000) and soared even further by 1978 (5,294,000). The Catholic church also enjoyed a surge in its growth, rising from 285,000 (1957) to 751,000 (1968), then to 1,144,000 (1986).

Today Korea sends out Christian missionaries to nations throughout Asia, and increasingly to the large Korean diasporas of major Western cities, from Sydney to Los Angeles, from Melbourne to New York. These missionaries are now closely linked with a network of churches that increasingly serve as a focal point for community action, mutual support, and spiritual nourishment. In 1979 Korean churches sent 93 missionaries overseas. In 1990 that number had increased to 1,645; in 2000 it stood at 8,103.[15] South Korea is today home to some of the world's largest Protestant churches.

And as North Korea shows every sign of being about to collapse, economically and politically, the question of the future religious development of this hard-line Communist state remains completely open. The anecdotal evidence suggests that Christianity has already made deep inroads among the population, and it is expected to grow further in the next decade.

The rise of Korea to prominence within global Protestantism is an important reminder of how situations change, often quite rapidly.

Korea is overwhelmingly Presbyterian, although with a rich diversity of expressions not found elsewhere. Other versions of Protestantism are also found in Korea, including a small Anglican community of about 50,000 that traces its origins back to 1890. One of the most significant distinctive features of Korean Protestantism is its commitment to theological education, evident in its many colleges, seminaries, and universities. The oldest of these—the Presbyterian College and Theological Seminary—was founded in 1901 in Pyongyang; it relocated to an eastern district of Seoul following the Communist takeover of the north.

Korea is an example of an essentially Buddhist nation that has come to be predominantly Protestant. Yet Protestantism has also been gaining ground in other regions of the world, including some that until recently were regarded as uniformly Catholic. In what follows, we consider the astonishing rise of Protestantism in Latin America and its implications for Protestantism itself and the global dynamics of Christianity as a whole.

IS LATIN AMERICA TURNING PROTESTANT?

Latin America was colonized by Spain and Portugal during the sixteenth and seventeenth centuries, with the result that Catholicism became the established religion of the area. The five-hundredth anniversary of the discovery of the Americas by Christopher Columbus in 1492 was the subject of some controversy within the region, with many Catholic bishops and laity expressing unease over any form of celebration of the European presence in the Americas, owing to the abuses committed during and after the conquest.

European immigrants, particularly from Germany, founded small Protestant communities in many parts of the continent during the nineteenth century. An Anglican church was established in Buenos Aires in 1821. Yet Protestants—*evangélicos*—were generally seen as an elite minority, standing slightly outside the religious mainstream. They were never seen as a threat to the Catholic establishment, since they seemed content to retain their historic denominational beliefs and practices, usually imported from Europe, without attempting any form of outreach to the local population.

The situation of historical Latin American Protestantism has not changed significantly since the nineteenth century.[16] The rise of liberation theology in the late 1960s brought some Protestant theologians in the region to wider prominence. Although liberation theology is widely regarded as a Catholic phenomenon, it is easily forgotten that some of its most prominent thinkers were Protestant—such as the Argentinean Methodist theologian José Míguez Bonino. Historic Protestants have been content to maintain their denominational identity and traditions and have not seen any significant growth in their numbers throughout Latin America. Nevertheless, they have exercised an influence far in excess of their numerical strength, partly on account of their entrepreneurial attitudes, which ultimately reflect the Protestant work ethic.

A significant debate within historic Protestantism in this region, particularly during the late 1940s, was the question of whether the Protestant community should see itself as Anglo-Saxon or as Latin. At a conference in Buenos Aires in 1949, Protestants resolved to commit themselves to work and witness within the Latin context—in effect indigenizing themselves. Yet this development had little impact on the numerical strength or missionary activity of Protestantism in Latin America.

The rise of Pentecostalism in the region, which dates from the first decade of the twentieth century, changed everything. The revival that broke out in the Methodist church at Valparaiso, Chile, in 1909 set the scene for a series of indigenous Pentecostal events throughout the region. Although this was assisted, especially in the aftermath of the Second World War, by missionaries from Pentecostal denominations in the United States, Latin American Pentecostalism has retained its own distinctive identity.

Why has Pentecostalism exploded in Latin America? Some Catholic and Marxist historians with axes to grind have had a quick and easy answer: American imperialism. Pentecostalism was the religious vanguard of a socioeconomic assault on the identity and values of Latin America. There were even dark rumors that the spread of Pentecostalism was due to the work of the Central Intelligence Agency during the Reagan era. However, more careful studies by sociologists and religious historians have established beyond doubt that the religious trends in question were in place long before this time.[17]

Careful sociological studies suggest that the accelerated transformation of Pentecostalism in Latin America has a number of causes, including its adaptive openness—characteristic of Protestantism—to local cultural beliefs and values and political issues. Yet the determining issue often seems to be accessibility. "Whereas nineteenth-century Protestant movements represented a religion of the written word, of civil and rational education, the current popular Protestant movements constitute an oral religion that is unlettered and lively."[18]

The rise of Latin American Pentecostalism has transformed the religious dynamic of the region. In Brazil, Chile, Guatemala, and Nicaragua, Pentecostals now far outnumber all other Protestant groups, and on some projections, they may soon constitute the majority of the population. Pentecostalism is also growing rapidly in areas adjacent to Latin America, such as the Caribbean, where Jamaica, Puerto Rico, and Haiti have seen large increases in Pentecostal congregations. These developments, although noted in many research publications, have taken many in the West by surprise. Only the most obtuse could fail to realize what David Stoll's well-researched 1990 book *Is Latin America Turning Protestant?* was all about.[19]

The greatest transformation of the Latin American religious landscape in the last fifty years—if not in the last five hundred years—is the transition from a monopolistic religious economy to a free-market one. Protestantism had been a small yet significant presence in Latin America since the early nineteenth century—yet it did not flourish, even with the disestablishment of Catholicism as the official state religion throughout Latin America between the middle of the nineteenth century and the first quarter of the twentieth. It was only with the development of Pentecostalism in the first decades of the twentieth century that the popular classes had a culturally appropriate alternative to Catholicism. The implications for Catholicism are obvious and have been noted with concern by the bishops of the region.

One significant response has been to develop contemporary worship styles that mimic the informality of evangelicalism and Pentecostalism while retaining the basic structure and content of Catholic worship. Neocharismatic elements within the Catholic church have shown that the needs and expectations of many who might otherwise be drawn to Pentecostalism can be met through Catholicism. The rise of Pentecostalism outside the church has thus proved a potent catalyst for the development of the charismatic movement within it. After four centuries of religious monopoly, the Catholic church has had to get used to competition—but the indications are that it is rising to the challenge.[20]

The implications for classic forms of Protestantism in the region are no less significant. Having also enjoyed something of their own kind of religious monopoly for a century, traditional Protestant denominations have found themselves confronted with an alternative model of ecclesiology and spirituality that challenges some of their core presuppositions. The most important of these concern word-centered preaching and spirituality and an essentially static conception of the denomination that creates no anticipation or expectation of church growth. Latin American Protestantism has a long and distinguished record of social involvement with the poor and marginalized—but not of evangelizing them. One of the most significant outcomes of Pentecostal growth within such socio-economic groups has been the challenge to this non-evangelistic conception of mission.[21] Yet there are other challenges. The many charismatic groups in Latin America have opened up new opportunities for spiritual leadership on the part of women, challenging the male-dominated church culture of historical Protestantism in the region.[22]

The unexpected developments in Latin America during the twentieth century raise some significant questions. One of them has to do with the future religious shape of the United States of America. Hispanics are already the largest ethnic minority in the United States, and they are predicted to become the majority within the next fifty years. It has traditionally been assumed that this will lead to the United States becoming increasingly Catholic. Yet recent developments in Latin America call any such assumption into question. The religious future of the United States remains far more open than many realize.

Perhaps a more intriguing question to emerge from the rapid growth of Protestantism in Latin America is whether this same phenomenon might occur elsewhere in the future. Might there be predominantly Catholic nations elsewhere in the global South that will experience a surge in Protestant growth as Pentecostalism expands still further? In what follows, we consider one nation where such a trend might well develop within the next two generations: the Philippines.

WILL THE PHILIPPINES TURN PROTESTANT?

In 1521 the great Spanish explorer Ferdinand Magellan discovered a group of some 3,141 islands. The islands, now known as "the Philippines," became a Spanish colony. Under Spanish rule, a program of evangelization was undertaken by various religious orders, especially the Franciscans and Dominicans. The islands were annexed by the United States in 1898. The Philippines are unusual in that they constitute the only predominantly Christian country in Southeast Asia. Although Catholicism is the dominant form of Christianity in the Philippines at present, many Protestant missionary societies established a presence there following the end of Spanish rule. While various forms of Protestantism are now firmly rooted in the region, they constitute a minority. A 1970 survey suggested that, even after seventy-five years of American missionary presence, fewer than 1 percent of the population had turned Protestant.

In part, this must be regarded as the outcome of a series of lost opportunities, including a curious failure on the part of Protestant missionaries to appreciate the strategic importance of the emergence of the Iglesia Filipina Independiente at the beginning of the twentieth century.[23] Furthermore, most American missionaries adopted a woodenly hostile approach to Catholicism, reflecting the defining Protestant ideology of the age—namely, that Catholicism was "the other." In the end, this approach merely resulted in open confrontation with Catholicism, which achieved little in the way of results.

To add to the catalog of failures, the American missionaries of the early twentieth century took a radically individualist approach to matters of faith, a strategy that totally failed to connect with the strongly communal outlook of the Philippines, where the family plays an especially important practical and symbolic role. The predominance of a modernist worldview within the missionary community led to a somewhat rationalist and cerebral understanding of faith that failed to appreciate the imaginative, emotional, and communitarian aspects of Christian faith—aspects already well developed within Filipino Catholicism.[24] In the end, American missionaries managed to export the old controversies of the Reformation and the newer battles of the fundamentalist-modernist debate more effectively than they did the gospel itself.

Protestant churches in Manila were in open competition with each other from the first decade of the twentieth century and spent more time and effort wooing members from each other than reaching out to the culture at large.[25] Altogether, the missionary experience in the Philippines represents a textbook case of the imposition of Westernized forms of Protestantism in a culturally inappropriate and insensitive manner. Protestant churches in Manila and elsewhere have certainly grown since the end of the Second World War, yet this growth is primarily to be attributed to biological reproduction, not conversion or outreach.[26]

With such an unimpressive track record, it might seem unwise, even unrealistic, to speak of the Philippines as being poised to become a significant player in global Protestantism. Yet there are powerful points of comparison to be made to the situation in Latin America. Both regions were Hispanic colonies in which Catholicism enjoyed a virtual religious monopoly until about 1900.[27]

The real issue here is that certain critical changes that have taken place suggest that this is a genuine possibility. The most important of these is that Pentecostalism—the engine of Protestant growth in Latin America—is now a growing presence within the nation, especially in metropolitan Manila. Historical analysis indicates a multiplicity of historical originations of Pentecostalism in the Philippines, including through Filipino laborers and students returning home after working in the United States and encountering Pentecostalism during their stay.[28] Although the forms of Pentecostalism introduced to the Philippines from the late 1920s onward were American in provenance, many adapted to the local culture, especially its ready acceptance of a "spirit world."

The classic Pentecostalist denominations—such as the Assemblies of God and the Foursquare Church—were well established in Manila by the 1950s. These were supplemented by a number of groups that are best described as "independent" churches—such as the "Jesus Is Lord" church, founded in 1978, the Bread of Life movement (1982), the Christ's Commission Fellowship (1982), and the Victory Christian Fellowship (1984). These movements have grown rapidly, in a manner similar to their Latin American counterparts. One of the factors that undergirds this growth is the use of cells as a means of pastoral care and outreach. The "cell" model of the church, which originated in East Asia, builds on the strong sense of group identity associated with the family in this region of the world. This way of conceiving the identity and function of the church sits uneasily with traditional Protestant models and represents yet another area in which Protestantism is being forced to reexamine existing paradigms and practices in the light of developments in the global South.

As developed by Lawrence Khong in Singapore or the Christ's Commission Fellowship in Manila, the church is understood to be a "church of cells."[29] The basic idea behind the movement can be found in the patterns of church life described in the New Testament, especially in the Acts of the Apostles (for example, Acts 2:42–46). Like the early church, the movement forms small cells, sometimes called "basic Christian communities," which are typically based in members' houses. The life of the church lies in the cells, which are seen as primary; the gathered congregation on Sundays is secondary. The phrase "church of cells" is preferred, as it emphasizes the primacy of the cell; the alternative "church with cells" implies that the cells are secondary.

In what follows, we describe the cell church model found in the Christ's Commission Fellowship, which is based on the "Discipling of Twelve" (D–12) model of church growth.[30] The cells generally start off with six to eight people and then grow over a period of weeks or months to twelve. At this point, each cell splits into two smaller groups and grows again, before dividing again. New members are drawn into the group through personal friendship, witness, or evangelism and are cared for within the group. The primary purpose of the cell is often described as edification and multiplication—that is, to build up believers and to enable them to reach out into their communities and bring new converts into the church.

"Cell multiplication" is the watchword of this community-based approach to evangelism. The cells gather together for "celebration" on Sundays, but the real pastoral work and outreach takes place within the cells themselves. The church leaders emphasize the proper training of cell group leaders, which they see as critically important to support and outreach. Sundays are viewed as an opportunity to offer "seeker-friendly" services; additional services are held on Wednesday or Thursday evenings for the committed. (The influence of the Willow Creek approach is evident here.)

The significance of this development for the traditional Western notion of the "Protestant denomination" is clear. The cell church movement avoids the costly bureaucracies and committee-ridden structures of traditional denominations. Instead, this movement empowers the leadership of individual cells, while relieving the church leadership team of the administrative burdens normally associated with churches of this size. This new way of conceiving the church not only creates new possibilities for pastoral care and outreach but also creates a significant leadership role for the laity within the cells.

So what of the future? Neither the Catholic church, which is used to operating within a monopoly of religious influence, nor traditional Protestantism appears to have been able to match the growth rates in the newer forms of Protestantism that began to emerge in the Philippines in the late 1970s. As in Latin America, Protestant growth has primarily taken place within Pentecostal groups, both those with historic roots in America (such as the Assemblies of God) and the local movements that have emerged in the Filipino context. Although charismatic elements have emerged within the Filipino Catholic church, these tend to be initiated and led by laity; located outside the church's hierarchy, charismatics are thus isolated from power and influence in the church.[31] It is uncertain where these trends will lead. Present growth patterns, however, point to the significant theoretical possibility that a large portion of the Filipino population will be Pentecostal in the future.

THE GLOBAL SOUTH AND THE TRANSFORMATION OF PROTESTANTISM

In this chapter, we have sketched some of the developments taking place within Protestantism beyond the traditional heartlands of the West. A fuller analysis would consider many other regional developments, each fascinating and significant in itself, yet precluded from discussion owing to lack of space. The growth and transmutation of Protestantism in Hong Kong during its period as a British colony,[32] in

China,[33] and in Indonesia[34]—each has its proper place in the greater narrative of which this book can only tell part. Similarly, there is much that can be learned from the present failure of Protestantism to emulate such patterns of growth and development in other regions of the world, such as Japan, where many Protestant denominations and representative groups remain suspicious of Pentecostalism.[35]

So what can be learned? What conclusions can be drawn? The most obvious point is that a Darwinian restlessness is evident within Protestantism. New forms are emerging in response to rapidly changing cultures and environments and the religious and social needs of the moment. In Western cultures, where historical constraints—such as state churches or a de facto religious establishment—are operational, such developments can be controlled or marginalized. But in the global South, especially since decolonization, such restraints generally do not exist. Only in Islamic nations is such a degree of enforced political control of Christianity now possible.

The result has been an unprecedented outbreak of entrepreneurial adaptation, leading to the emergence of new ways of conceiving the gospel. And as traditional control mechanisms begin to crumble in the West, partly under consumerist pressures, new possibilities for "being church" are beginning to emerge. Many in the West are exploring the cell church model, despite the fact that it originated as an analogue of the family in a social context in which the family plays a much more significant social role than it does in the West.

Yet whether this specific model of the church finds wider acceptance or not, Protestantism in the global South is forcing a radical rethinking of Protestant theories of the church (ecclesiologies) in the West. As we noted earlier, the core elements of all such theories are the proclamation of the gospel and the proper administration of the sacraments. Everything else is negotiable. Yet over the years, certain habits of mind and action have led Protestant ecclesiologies to remain shaped by the assumptions and norms of long-dead leaders and long-past social contexts. Above all, they have been dominated by the assumption that the church's task is primarily educational, social, and pastoral. This was indeed the function of the church in an era when Christendom was still a plausible notion.

Protestantism in the global South has long since learned to work within a "post-Christendom" model of the church in which evangelism and the cultivation of discipleship are seen as integral to the mission of the church, alongside social outreach, pastoral care, and teaching.[36] It has developed ecclesiologies that are adapted to the realities of their day and age, not to those of sixteenth-century Geneva or Elizabethan England. The basic aim has been to construct "local theologies" in which the "seed of faith is allowed to interact with the native soil, leading to a new flowering of Christianity, faithful both to the local culture and to the apostolic faith."[37] As secularism continues to be a significant presence in the West, the retrieval of this kind of ecclesiology is essential to Western Protestantism's conception of its identity and tasks. What the church believes it *is* determines what it *does* as it shapes its priorities and agendas.

These developments are not geographically limited to the global South. Immigration from the south to the north has led to the emergence of these trends within Protestantism in its Western homelands. An excellent example is the arrival of the "new Pentecostal" African Initiated Churches in London, which have experienced significantly greater growth than older forms of black Pentecostalism. Of these, the Redeemed Christian Church of God (RCCG) is the largest and most successful in terms of membership growth. The RCCG planted its first church in Britain back in 1985, with just four people attending the first service. Today it has fifty churches of varying sizes, with a membership somewhere in the region of 200,000—mostly in London and the Midlands, but also with sizable representation in a number of Britain's larger urban areas. In part, this growth may be put down to the historic need to provide social support structures in an alien culture.[38] Yet the question remains: why *this* form of Pentecostalism rather than the older forms? And will the AICs penetrate the mainstream of British Christianity, or will they continue to be seen as a west African phenomenon? Many in these churches see themselves as missionaries to British culture as a whole, not simply to its immigrant communities.

The forms of Protestantism now emerging in the global South also pose a powerful challenge to traditional Western notions of theology. To Protestant leaders and pastors in the South, Western Protestantism has suffered from an overintellectualized theological tradition and a weakened spirituality. In their view, this has weakened Protestantism's capacity to transform individuals and society in the West; furthermore, its well-meaning efforts to impose the same approaches on emerging churches without regard to their very different situations may have undermined their capacity for growth.

The challenge to Western Protestantism at this point is clear. Since Christians outside of Europe and North America live their faith in different historical, political, socioeconomic, and religious contexts, the kinds of questions they are asking are substantially different from those asked in the Western tradition. As the great South African church leader Desmond Tutu once remarked, Western theology has some splendid answers—but they are answers to questions that no one else seems to be asking.

The Three Kings, *1958, by Carlos Merida.*

17

Protestantism

The Next Generation

This study has woven together many histories to create a "grand narrative" of the origins and development of Protestantism. Like a plant, the movement has grown rapidly, and in unexpected ways. Perhaps the biological notion of mutation offers the best model for understanding the growth of Protestantism. In biological mutation, small changes in genetic codes lead to the emergence of new forms. Some of these prove poorly adapted to survival and die out; others prove highly adapted and flourish, transmitting their genes to future generations. While there is a very high degree of genetic continuity between these forms, they are not identical. Moreover, environmental factors have caused unpredictable changes in the genetic code.[1]

Although clearly continuous with and related to other versions of Christianity, Protestantism arose as a new way of reading the Bible. Yet Protestantism has mutated over time as new forms emerged that shared a high degree of continuity—*but not absolute identity*—with what went before them. The "genetic codes"—in the case of Protestantism, the set of instructions for interpreting the Bible—have changed over time, even though they are nearly identical with those of other versions of Protestantism. Yet these small changes have brought about significant differences, over long periods of time. Some of these turned out to be unsuccessful and gradually faded away. Yet others proved highly adapted and went on to experience growth, thus passing their distinctive understanding of the patterns of Christian truth on to future generations.

Pentecostalism represents the outcome of a seemingly small change in how Protestantism reads the Bible—recognizing, even expecting, that the Holy Spirit remains active today in much the same manner as in the apostolic era. Yet that seemingly small change in the genetic code has led to a dramatically altered understanding of the dynamics of the Christian life and reshaped the contours of the Christian faith.

Biological models have their limitations in explaining religious phenomena.[2] Nevertheless, the concept of mutation is a useful model to account for the development of Protestantism because it highlights two points.

1. While new developments within Protestantism can be accounted for after they have happened, they cannot be *predicted*. The intrinsic proclivity toward reformulation, exploration, and adaptation demonstrated by its history suggests that this pattern of development will continue in the future. Its results, however, cannot be predicted.

2. The biological concept of mutation links survival with a capacity to change, on the one hand, and a competition for survival, on the other. On a Darwinian approach, it is only the best adapted forms that survive and pass their genes on to a future generation. The forms of Protestantism that have emerged from this historical process of testing and elimination are thus likely to cope with the intense pressures of the contemporary religious marketplace precisely because they have shown that they are able to prosper in such environments. The biological analogy of halophilic bacteria comes to mind: in hostile biological environments with very high salt concentrations, certain types of bacteria (more strictly, *Archaea*) have emerged that can survive and reproduce under these conditions.[3] Protestantism shows that same capacity to adapt—and hence to proliferate through diversification.

So what might the future of the movement look like? Three major trends can be identified, each of which emphasizes the movement's capacity to adapt and change: changing understandings of Protestant identity; changing patterns of biblical interpretation; and a continuing shift away from a controlling institutional centralism. We consider each of these trends in what follows.

THE PROBLEM OF PROTESTANT IDENTITY

What is the essence of Protestantism? What gives it its inner identity? On a critical historical reading of the development of Protestantism, the movement has been characterized from its outset by divergence and difference. Protestantism came into being as a diverse entity shaped by a multiplicity of different driving agendas, cultural contexts, intellectual resources, and directing visions. There is no question of a "lost primal unity" of Protestantism, a golden age of unity that quickly shattered into fragments. Its multiple geographical, cultural, and historical origins made Protestantism diverse from the beginning.

The origins of Protestantism lie in what was ultimately an uncontrollable burst of creative energy directed toward the intellectual and spiritual renewal and institutional reform of the church. That creative burst gave birth to a solar system of planets of various sizes revolving around a biblical sun at different distances and in orbits of varying eccentricity; there was no single, unambiguous Protestant template, gene, or paradigm controlling their formation. A plurality of related though competing biblical interpretations jostled for space, attention, and influence in many parts of western Europe.

One pattern that emerges from the development of Protestantism is what seems to be an endless cycle of birth, maturing, aging, and death, leading to renewal and reformulation. The relentless energy and creativity of one generation gives rise to a new movement; a later generation, anxious because the original dynamism and energy of the movement appears to be dissipating, tries to preserve it by petrification—that is, by *freezing* the original vision in the hope that its energy will thus be preserved. Yet all too often, petrification leads to the conservation of only a structure, not the life-giving vision itself. However perfectly preserved in the entomologist's specimen room, the butterfly is still dead.

Classically, this is held to have happened in the rise of orthodoxy within Protestantism after the deaths of Luther and Calvin. As the geopolitical aspects of the Reformation became increasingly important, the rise of confessionalism led to a politically enforced uniformity within the movement in many regions of Germany. The use of "confessions of faith" as a means of preserving the foundational insights of Lutheranism and Calvinism led, in the view of concerned Protestant activists, to the emergence of a conformist attitude toward religion expressed in formal acceptance of statements of faith rather than in a living and trusting faith in God. This concern inevitably led to growing demands for reform and renewal as faith became increasingly a matter of outward observance, without any inward spiritual reality. Pietism attempted to renew the relational aspects of faith by giving priority to an understanding of faith as personal trust in God, rather than as formal assent to doctrinal statements. The great revivals within American Protestantism showed very similar patterns.

For the historian, such cycles of review and renewal seem to be an integral aspect of Protestant identity. The development of Pietism, the emergence of the American holiness tradition, and the rise of global Pentecostalism can all be understood as the outcomes of this ongoing renewal of older traditions and development of new understandings of what it means to be a Protestant. A similar process can be seen at work within Anglicanism, a form of Protestantism that is capable of accommodating a significant number of traditional "Catholic" notions—such as the use of liturgy and architecture to communicate the truths of faith—without losing its Protestant identity. This process of review and development has not stopped, and all the indications are that further changes lie ahead in the future.

The pressure of these changes has created a furious debate within sections of Protestantism, leading to a confrontation between two very different visions—one static, the other dynamic—of Protestant identity. On the one hand are Protestant traditionalists who hold that the essence of Protestantism can only be preserved by "freezing" defining moments in the past—for example, the clerical dress, cultural attitudes, and worship styles of sixteenth-century Calvinism, seventeenth-century Puritanism, or eighteenth-century English evangelicalism. For such traditionalists, fidelity to the past is the touchstone of authenticity and integrity.

On the other hand are those who argue that Protestantism is not, and never has been, defined in this way, but locates its identity in its constant self-examination in the light of the Bible and in its willingness to correct itself when it takes wrong turns or situations change. This second approach—often summarized in the slogan *semper reformandum* ("always being reformed")—defines the distinctive identity of Protestantism as a *method,* not as any one specific historical outcome of the *application* of that method.

Protestantism is thus seen as applying the Bible to new situations in which one may learn from past applications but is not obligated to repeat them. It is this vision of Protestantism that has gained the upper hand in the late twentieth century and captured the imaginations of strongly entrepreneurial individuals—precisely because it creates conceptual space for the innovation, development, and experimentation that are virtually precluded by the older, more static model. Pentecostalism is perhaps the supreme example of this second Protestant paradigm that is now clearly in the ascendancy in many parts of the world.

This second model of Protestant identity has major implications for the future of the movement. By refusing to regard any past expression of Protestantism as normative, this approach has liberated the movement from its captivity to the cultural habits of early modern western Europe. Why should twenty-first-century Presbyterian ministers in Kenya wear the black gowns favored by sixteenth-century Geneva? Why should Western cultural norms be preferred over their African equivalents? Why should Asians have to read the Bible through Western eyes? This assertion of the cultural independence of the global South has led to significant shifts in understanding and opened the way to rapid Protestant expansion outside its traditional homelands in the West. Each region now sees itself as free to find its own form of Protestant identity, grounded in a local interpretation and application of the Bible.

The twentieth century thus saw a rediscovery of the radical, dangerous Protestant principle of starting all over again, wherever necessary dismantling outmoded approaches and forging new ones, shaped by the biblical witness. It has become increasingly clear that some traditional Protestant ideas about church architecture, denominational structures, worship patterns, and even moral values were often little more than cultural constructs, reflecting a bygone era in western European culture. The capacity of the Protestant template to respond and adapt to new environments has given it a new lease of life as it expands into new regions of the world and faces new challenges and opportunities.

This naturally leads us to consider how the Bible continues to shape Protestant identity and development.

PROTESTANTISM'S CHANGING INTERPRETATIONS OF SCRIPTURE

In 1620 the great Puritan theologian John Robinson preached a sermon to those about to leave for the New World aboard the *Mayflower*. His powerful address portrayed the pilgrims as setting out on a voyage that would lead them not only to a new world but to a new grasp of truth. They would be spiritual and theological pioneers exploring not only the new world of the Americas but the new insights they would find in the Bible as they sought to plant the kingdom of God there. One phrase from that sermon has rebounded down the ages: "I am verily persuaded the Lord hath more truth yet to break forth out of His Holy Word."

Robinson's words are a fitting epigram to the entire Protestant engagement with the Bible. Some have argued that this task is completed and that closure has been secured. Protestantism's task is merely to repeat the ideas and values of its definitive shapers, such as Luther and Calvin. Most, however, hold that this argument is quite contrary to the ethos of Protestantism. To be a Protestant is to set out on an intellectual and spiritual pilgrimage that is never completed. Every location, every generation, every challenge forces the community of faith to reread the Bible, asking what it might have to say in *this* situation that it did not say in other situations. For Robinson, no person, no age, could ever fully plumb the depths of scripture. Through the guidance of the Holy Spirit, new challenges would lead to new insights, above all in relation to church structures and policy. What might be right in one situation or for one era might not be so in another.

As we have seen, the capacity to adapt is the birthright of Protestantism. The contrast with both Catholicism and Orthodoxy could not be greater at this point. Although both consider the wooden repetition of yesterday's certainties to be inadequate, preferring to work with the idea of a "living tradition" that is capable of at least a degree of development, both equally emphasize the fixity of their doctrinal and institutional forms. For the noted Catholic apologist Jacques-Bénigne Bossuet (1627–1704), the Catholic deposit of faith is the same yesterday, today, and forever. Protestant innovations and heretical degradations—religious categories that tended to elide in Bossuet's judgment—could be identified without undue difficulty precisely because they represented change.[4] John Henry Newman had no doubt that each generation could wrest further insights from the Catholic tradition; its substance, however, would not change.

From its outset, Protestantism stated its identity in terms of a method rather than its outcome—a means by which ideas would be generated and governed, not a specific set of ideas resulting from its application. The Protestant principle of grounding matters of doctrine and ethics in the Bible and subjecting these to constant review immediately generated controversy. Luther and Calvin argued that this method led to the reestablishment of the fundamental truths of the Christian faith, on the one hand, and the reformation of areas in which the medieval church had gone astray through inadequate attention to scripture, on the other. These doctrinal outcomes were expressed as "confessions of faith," which were understood as local, provisional, and revisable statements of faith, not to be confused with the universal and final statements of Christian faith contained in the creeds.

Their radical Protestant critics suggested that this represented an inconsistent reading of the Bible; a more radical—or, better, a more *consistent*—reading of the text led to skepticism concerning traditional doctrines such as the Trinity and more recent innovations such as Luther's doctrine of justification by faith alone, which they held to lack biblical warrant. Yet such debates were ultimately healthy in that they encouraged theological vigilance and avoided the premature foreclosure of important debates.

This had three significant results. First, a number of ways of interpreting the Bible emerged as characteristic of Protestant traditions, and those traditions then felt obliged to defend their way of interpreting scripture. One can easily speak of a Lutheran tradition of interpretation of Paul's doctrine of justification, or a Reformed tradition of interpretation of the concept of the kingdom of God. Second, the debate led to changing patterns of biblical interpretation over time as constant review led to revision of the original judgments of the founders of Protestantism. Third, it resulted in a variety of approaches to biblical interpretation within specific Protestant groupings, thus forcing a difficult discussion of the acceptable limits of diversity. When did diversity degenerate into deviation, hence forcing the exclusion of those who would then go on to form new Protestant groupings, further contributing to the fragmentation of Protestantism?

In considering such difficult questions, it is important to note that biblical interpretation is partly a socially constructed enterprise that rests on inherited assumptions concerning what is "natural" or "obvious" within a community. Individuals experience part of the complex process of socialization by growing up within such an interpretative community, absorbing its values and approaches.[5] Judgments as to what is the "natural" way of reading a biblical passage rest partly (but not exclusively) on the prevailing consensus within that community, which often assumes that the familiar and traditional are equivalent to the self-evidently correct. The theological notion of the "natural sense of scripture," not unlike its cultural cousin "common sense," is a communal notion that is shaped partly by the happenstances of history and is sustained and sanctified through constant repetition and application.[6]

As the history and experience of a community develop, traditional ways of reading scripture are reviewed and revised in the light of new challenges, experiences, and encounters—such as the rise of a capitalist economy, a growing awareness of the existence of vast geographical regions untouched by the Christian gospel, or spiritual experiences that appear to replicate those described in the New Testament. All of these can be shown to have been important factors in encouraging Protestant engagements with the Bible and shaping their outcome.

Even the briefest account of Protestant biblical interpretation during the first five hundred years of its existence shows shifting understandings of what the Bible says and how it is to be read, and these shifts are laden with significance for the identity of the movement. If Protestantism is held to be defined by a set of specific interpretations of the Bible, then, in addition to being pluriform from the outset, it has undergone significant changes since its emergence.

Four examples of shifting Protestant understandings of the meaning of the Bible may be noted, all of which have been discussed in this work. In each case, the settled interpretation of earlier generations underwent significant modification as opinion shifted decisively toward a rather different view.

1. *Is usury allowed?* The consensus throughout the first age of Protestantism, on the basis of the unconditional Old Testament prohibition of the practice, was that usury was not permissible. Yet Calvin's creative and highly original argument of 1545 that this specific biblical mandate could be overlooked in order to fulfill more fundamental biblical principles introduced a new way of thinking. It took more than a century for Protestantism as a whole to come around to this new way of thinking. Yet such is the widespread acceptance of the practice today that most contemporary Protestants would be surprised to learn that this was ever an issue for their forebears.

2. *Are Christians meant to evangelize?* The predominant interpretation of the gospel imperative to "make disciples of all nations" (Matthew 28:19) in the sixteenth century was that this command was addressed to the apostles, not to subsequent generations. It was not until the late eighteenth century that this view began to be challenged successfully, particularly through the growing influence of missionary societies in England. By the end of the nineteenth century, most Protestants considered the passage to be an obvious and clear call to all Christians to evangelize and to support the work of missions.

3. *Will there be a millennium at the end of time?* The belief that there would be a period of one thousand years—the millennium—during which Christ would reign on earth immediately before the end of history was widespread in the early church. Writers such as Irenaeus and Tertullian regarded this as the clear and obvious meaning of Revelation 20:2. Yet from the time of Augustine onward, this way of reading this text was abandoned in favor of the "amillennial" view that Christ presently reigns from heaven. This view was upheld by mainline Protestantism until the middle of the nineteenth century, when a "premillennial" reading of the text began to gain a significant following. Today premillennialism, espoused by Pentecostals and

many American evangelicals, is the numerically predominant way of reading the text.

4. *Do charismatic phenomena happen today?* While all early Protestants agreed that such phenomena as speaking in tongues took place in the early church, as recorded in the New Testament, there was a consensus that these ceased with the ending of the apostolic age. Although occasionally raised as a possibility by some marginal groups, this "cessationist" view was totally predominant within Protestantism for the first four hundred years of its existence. Today it is the minority view. Pentecostalism's insistence that such phenomena happen today is now dominant within Protestantism.

Alongside these significant shifts in patterns of biblical interpretation over the last five hundred years, a number of debates have continued, repeating the debates of past years with occasional extensions. Of these, the most famous is the long-standing debate over how to interpret the words of Jesus of Nazareth at the Last Supper: "This is my body" (Matthew 26:26). Here the main positions taken in the first age of the Reformation remain contested to this day, and the debate still circles well-established landmarks and authorities. No Protestant now seriously expects these debates to be resolved; indeed, many now regard them as lying beyond resolution, having become so deeply ingrained within the traditions that make up contemporary Protestantism that they cannot be disentangled from those traditions' sense of identity and historical rootedness.

Yet other debates have opened up, extending debates over biblical interpretation. Debates about the ministry of women and homosexuals have opened up new questions and given new urgency to old ones—such as the passionate and often vitriolic debate within American Protestantism during the first half of the nineteenth century over whether the Bible sanctioned slavery. These debates, which often involve complex and controversial judgments about the role of cultural norms in biblical interpretation, often point up significant divergences within global Protestantism, especially over issues of sexuality.

DECENTRALIZATION AND
THE FUTURE OF DENOMINATIONS

The history of twentieth-century Protestantism confirms that the movement is in the middle of a clear and irreversible process of congregationalization, in which central authority is ebbing away from denominational bureaucracies and becoming concentrated in individual congregations. Since the 1980s, the growth of market-shaped or market-driven congregations in American Protestantism has forced denominational leaderships to determine whether they will be regulatory or consultative in nature. While this development can be seen as a pragmatic response by successful congregations to increasingly unwieldy central structures, it can equally well be seen as the late flowering of one of the most fundamental themes of early seventeenth-century American Protestant theology—"the principle that a corporate body is created by the consent of constituent members," in the words of the historian Perry Miller.[7]

In noting the fundamental themes of Protestant models of the church, we have emphasized the absence of any necessary institutional component. Institutions might be useful; they are not, however, essential to the identity of a Protestant congregation. Many Protestant writers draw a pointed distinction between what is necessary for the *esse*, and what is appropriate for the *bene esse*, of a church.[8] No specific institutional structure is required if a group is to be recognized as a church; certain structures might, however, be helpful in enabling congregations in their mission and ministry.

This theory of the church enables radical entrepreneurial activity. In the seventeenth century, it found expression in the idea of the local congregation as a covenanted community. In the eighteenth and early nineteenth centuries, the model of the voluntary society gained wide acceptance and was found in various forms in the emergence of British Methodism and the Southern Baptist Convention in the United States. More recently, two other models have begun to emerge, both of which have their origins in the business world: the church as franchise and the church as a small business. Both models give considerable scope to entrepreneurial activity, personal initiative, and creativity on the part of leaders and allow them to circumvent the often cumbersome procedures and high overheads of traditional denominations.

The best-known example of the franchise model is Calvary Chapel, begun by Chuck Smith in the 1960s and now boasting five hundred affiliated congregations throughout the United States, especially in California. Congregations that wish to be known as "Calvary Chapel" may apply for a local franchise, which is granted subject to certain conditions, of which the most important is conformity to the distinctive ethos of the parent body. A slightly different model was developed by Willow Creek Community Church, which founded the Willow Creek Association in 1992. Once more, congregations opt in to what is essentially a franchising operation.

Yet the model that has proved most successful in driving Protestant expansion in recent years is based on the analogy of starting your own business—the dream of many would-be entrepreneurs who find themselves frustrated by the unimaginative and unresponsive attitudes of their companies. On this model, individuals set up their own churches and rely on growth in reputation and congregational numbers to secure their future. Though laden with risk, the model offers pastors with a strong sense of vision the opportunity to develop a ministry that meets a specific need they believe is not being adequately met elsewhere. Calvary Chapel, Willow Creek Community Church, and Saddleback Church are all examples of successful churches built on the visions of their founders. The same phenomenon can be seen in large Pentecostal churches in Asia and the more recent African Initiated Churches, which often trace their origins and driving visions to a founding pastor.

This phenomenon is set to increase, partly owing to the inexorable dispersion of power from the center to the periphery of traditional denominations, but more significantly on account of the responsiveness of such decentralized models to their environments. With no centralized Protestant validating agency equivalent to the Vatican, there is no enforceable means by which this phenomenon of innovation can be controlled. The downside is obvious: being accountable to no external authority, the pastor is often responsible only to congregation members for the theological direction of the church. Yet the upside can hardly be ignored, especially when the approach meets a real need on the part of enthusiastic pastors and receptive congregations.

The impact of this accelerating trend is perhaps most obvious in the case of Anglicanism, which has in the past defied the decentralizing trend seen within other Protestant denominations. A number of factors have accounted for this surprising cohesion within Anglicanism—the British colonial legacy, maintained more recently through the British Commonwealth of Nations; the British crown as a symbol of unity; the English language as the Anglican Communion's *lingua franca;* the King James Bible of 1611 and the *Book of Common Prayer* of 1662 as unifying texts. Yet all of these have been subject to historical erosion; the growing cultural, linguistic, and political diversity within Anglicanism has gradually eaten away at any sense of a shared identity. Although recent debates over homosexuality have exacerbated this process, they have not been its cause.

It is to be expected that Anglicanism will go the way of other Protestant groups and transmute into a denominational family characterized by a federalist structure and perhaps presided over by a symbolic figure of unity, almost certain to be the Archbishop of Canterbury. The cultural differences between North American liberalism and West African traditionalism may well catalyze this process of fissure, and the absence of strong leadership makes the situation worse than it need be. Yet these tensions have simply highlighted the theological fissures and fatigues that have been part of Anglicanism from its origins.

Weaknesses and vulnerabilities in a tradition or institution often lie unnoticed until new stresses and pressures place them under such strain that they finally rupture. From the 1990s, Anglicanism has been confronted with the contradictions inherent in its own heritage, long shielded from view by a benign and static cultural environment. Happily, this confrontation does not mean the end of Anglicanism, nor even the beginning of a decline. It need do no more than usher in a period of alternative models of the church, each faithful to the Protestant tradition and adapted to its own specific environment. Paradoxically, the future of Anglicanism is thus likely to be characterized by overall growth rather than contraction.

THE CRITICAL ANALOGY BETWEEN
PROTESTANTISM AND ISLAM

In recent years, reform movements have arisen within non-Christian religions, particularly Nichiren Buddhism, which bears clear resemblances to Protestantism.[9] An excellent example of this trend is provided by the Soka Gakkai, a Japanese lay reformist Buddhist organization that emphasizes social engagement.[10] Yet the most striking and interesting parallels exist between Protestantism and the world's second-largest religious movement—Islam.

As is well known, the Muslim world is divided into a number of factions, the two largest of which are the Sunni and the Shia. It is often suggested that Protestantism has certain affinities with the Shia. However, the truth is more complex. Islam *as a whole,* precisely because it is a logocentric, text-based religion, bears many similarities to certain forms of Protestantism.

The parallel is not exact. Some forms of Protestantism—such as Lutheranism, or certain forms of Anglicanism—are focused primarily upon the person of Jesus Christ and give weight to the Bible insofar as it gives access to him. Although the Bible is regarded as fundamental, such Protestants place Christ where Islam places the Qu'ran. Yet other forms of Protestantism—particularly within fundamentalism and various forms of evangelicalism—see the Bible as standing at the center of all things. These groups share Islam's suspicion of imagery of the divine, preferring to focus on the preaching and proclamation of the word. For such Protestants, the differences between Christianity and Islam lie in the question of which text they regard as authoritative: the Qu'ran or the Bible?

Like many forms of Protestantism, Islam focuses on a central text—the Qu'ran. And as with Protestantism, the question of who has the right to interpret the Qu'ran, and hence to define the nature of Islam, has become of critical importance.[11] There has never been a "Muslim pope" or the Islamic equivalent of the Vatican. Authority has traditionally resided with certain clerical institutions.

Yet in the late twentieth century, something along the lines of an "Islamic Reformation" from below can be seen emerging. Highly charismatic individuals outside the clerical establishment—such as Osama bin Laden—have offered their own interpretations of Islam. The popular support they have garnered within the global Muslim constituency has undermined the authority of traditional Islamic institutions and laid the foundations for a radical, even dangerous, debate over the essence of Islam. Just as printing spread the ideas of the Protestant Reformation across Europe, so the Internet allows the ideas of the new Islamic radicals to spread globally, challenging traditional Islamic beliefs and values.

The four accepted Sunni schools of Qu'ranic interpretation—Hanafi, Shafi'i, Maliki, and Hanbali—are facing a major challenge from a rising generation of Muslims who are impatient with the conservatism of these schools and prefer the radicalism of alternatives. Each of these schools can be likened to a branch of Protestantism: each is based on the same text, yet offers different interpretations and implementations. New schools are emerging, however, precisely because of a growing realization that the contingencies of history prevent their number from being fixed. More radical schools argue for the need to refer directly to the Qu'ran and Hadith to discover the doctrines and rites of religion rather than trust in the traditions of the past. New possibilities will emerge, along with new schools. Like Protestantism, Islam will face increasing fragmentation as it enters into new cultural contexts in which the restraints of past convention are no longer decisive. Islam's growing presence in the West is opening the door to precisely these reinterpretations, catalyzed by new assumptions about texts, new challenges and pressures, and increasing historical and cultural distance from the Arabic homelands of Islam.

The same patterns can be seen within Protestantism. The settled consensus of an older generation is overthrown by a rising generation who bring new interpretations to the same texts. The emergence of Pentecostalism—easily the most significant development within Protestantism in the twentieth century—illustrates this perfectly. In the nineteenth century, Protestantism's authority figures were more or less unanimous: charismatic phenomena belonged to the apostolic age and had now ceased. That judgment is now the minority report. Patterns of biblical interpretation have changed—and with those changes in biblical interpretation have emerged radical new forms of Protestantism.

The argument that "Islam traditionally teaches this" now carries little weight when authority structures are shifting and a new generation is developing new interpretations of the Qu'ran or reclaiming older interpretations that have been marginalized by the Islamic establishment. Within Islam, older Islamic scholars often cite interpretations of the Qu'ran that a more militant grassroots constituency rejects—most notably in relation to the idea of the *jihad*.

Might there be further changes? Islam's well-known opposition to usury has spawned a minor *sharia*-compliant financial industry in some parts of the world. Yet Protestantism emerged with precisely the same hostility toward usury, based on its foundational religious text. As we have seen, that judgment was open to challenge, and ultimately total reversal. Might Islam do the same?

There is a deeper question here. Is Islam about to go through the convulsions that shook Western Christianity in the sixteenth century and led to social and political instability for more than a century? And what might be the implications of such a development for the West? Exploring the development of Protestantism may not entirely answer this question. But it certainly maps out some possibilities and raises questions that Western political and religious leaders cannot afford to overlook or ignore.

PROTESTANTISM, RELIGION, AND WORLD POWER

The world is changing rapidly, leaving many puzzled by its twists and turns. One of the settled assumptions of Western thought during the period 1960 to 1990 was that religion was of diminishing importance in world affairs. Paul Kennedy's magisterial *Rise and Fall of the Great Powers* (1988) mentions Islam only incidentally, and then links it particularly with the fortunes of the Ottoman Empire.[12] There is no hint, no anticipation, of the importance of Islam as a political force to be reckoned with in the "new world order" following the collapse of the Soviet Union. As was pointed out some time ago by the Washington-based Center for Strategic and International Studies, the foreign policy of the United States has consistently underestimated the importance of religion as a political force.[13] Democratic and Republican administrations alike have seriously misread the growing importance of religion as a global force.

The development is obvious to those who have eyes to see. Religion has the capacity to transcend national and cultural barriers, uniting Muslims in Britain in a powerful bond of sympathy with their coreligionists in Palestine, Jews in New York with those in Israel, and Catholics in Boston with those in Northern Ireland. As both Christianity and Islam continue their global expansion, the question of their frontiers and boundaries is becoming increasingly sensitive—witness the serious tensions in both Nigeria and the Sudan between the predominantly Muslim north and predominantly Christian south. If Western statecraft is to deal with these developments, it needs to be realistic about the strategic importance of religion instead of relying on the wisdom of the late 1960s, which held that religion was dying out and would be replaced by a secular liberal world order in both the East and West.

But an objection might be raised at this point. Granted that religion is becoming more important as a global factor—surely this hardly applies, however, to Protestantism, which has shown relatively little inclination to political activism throughout the twentieth century?

The analysis of this book suggests that this is a dangerously simplistic judgment. It is of the essence of Protestantism to reexamine and renew itself, responding to its environment, on the one hand, and its own reading of the Bible, on the other. Protestantism has undergone massive change in the twentieth century—change that would have been unpredicted and unanticipated in the closing years of the nineteenth century. Protestantism is uncontrollable. As with Islam, there is no centralized power, no institutionalized authority to regulate or limit its development. Protestantism is increasingly open to political radicalization, with unforeseeable implications.

That process is already under way. There are telltale straws in the wind for those who are willing to look and listen. In 1960 it would have been unthinkable for conservative American Protestants to become actively involved in politics. Faith was a private matter, confined to the home and church. Politics was seen as "worldly," something that corrupted faithful believers and led them away from the straight and narrow path. As late as 1965, Jerry Falwell distinguished between "Ministers and Marchers," arguing that "the duty of the church is to preach the Word, not focus on externals." Yet even then there was a growing realization of the need for political engagement and activism on the part of many around him. By the late 1990s, even the most conservative Protestants were politically engaged, determined to redirect their nation, religiously and politically. There are many who dislike their politics; their importance, however, can hardly be overlooked.

So what has changed? George Marsden and other historians are clear that a critical factor was the perceived drift of American political culture in a secular or antireligious direction. Reacting against such developments, conservative Protestants realized the importance of religiously motivated political engagement. The fundamental theme was that of "a proclamation of reclaimed authority over a sacred tradition which is to be reinstated as an antidote for a society that has strayed from its cultural moorings."[14] Just as Western secularism and political adventurism in the Middle East contributed to the rise of radical Islam, so its counterpart back home may well have begun an equivalent process within Protestantism. The political impact of this development, if it continues, will be incalculable. Protestantism has the innate capacity to reclaim its older self-understanding as a political as much as a religious entity. Whether that happens depends largely on whether Western culture creates the conditions that will bring it about—for it is primarily a *reactive* process.

So what of the future of Protestantism? Those who base their answer on its fortunes in western Europe, its original heartlands, may offer a somewhat negative answer. But for those who have reflected on its remarkable advances elsewhere, such an answer is inadequate. Yes, the sun may set on a movement—but it is too easily forgotten that the sun rises again the next day. Protestantism has had its moments in the past; it will have them again in the future.

Those who are anxious about the future of Protestantism often urge that radical change in its self-understanding is necessary if it is to survive, let alone prosper. *Tempora mutantur, nos et mutamur in illis* ("Times are changing, and we change with them"—Ovid). The historical and theological analysis presented in this book offers a rather different answer. We have seen that Protestantism possesses a unique and innate capacity for innovation, renewal, and reform based on its own internal resources. *The future of Protestantism lies precisely in Protestantism being what Protestantism actually is.*

Notes

INTRODUCTION

1. Diarmaid MacCulloch, *Thomas Cranmer* (New Haven, CT: Yale University Press, 1996), 196.
2. This is not to say that this idea was not encountered in other periods of Christian history, where it was associated with individual writers or sectarian groups. The point is that this marginal idea became mainline as it moved from the fringes of respectable church life to take a central place in the major religious transformations of the sixteenth century.
3. For some of the issues, see Marcus Walsh, "Profession and Authority: The Interpretation of the Bible in the Seventeenth and Eighteenth Centuries," *Literature and Theology* 9 (1995): 383–98.
4. *The Vanishing Protestant Majority,* GSS Social Change Report 49 (Chicago: National Opinion Research Center, University of Chicago, 2004).
5. Outstanding recent studies of the history of the Reformation include: Euan Cameron, *The European Reformation* (Oxford: Clarendon Press, 1991); Carter Lindberg, *The European Reformations* (Oxford: Blackwell, 1996); and Diarmaid MacCulloch, *Reformation: Europe's House Divided, 1490–1700* (London: Allen Lane, 2003).
6. The older generation of such studies includes: John Dillenberger and Claude Welch, *Protestant Christianity Interpreted Through Its Development* (New York: Scribner, 1954); J. S. Whale, *The Protestant Tradition: An Essay in Interpretation* (Cambridge: Cambridge University Press, 1955); Louis Bouyer, *The Spirit and Forms of Protestantism* (Westminster, MD: Newman Press, 1956); Émile G. Léonard, *A History of Protestantism* (London: Nelson, 1965); Charles W. Kegley, *Protestantism in Transition* (New York: Harper & Row, 1965); Jerald C. Brauer, *Protestantism in America: A Narrative History* (Philadelphia: Westminster Press,

1965); Martin E. Marty, *Protestantism* (New York: Holt, Rinehart, and Winston, 1972).

7. Andrew Pettegree, "Reformation Europe Re-formed," *History Today* 49, no. 12 (1999): 10–16.

8. Mack P. Holt, "The Social History of the Reformation: Recent Trends and Future Agendas," *Journal of Social History* 37 (2003): 133–44.

9. Lucy E. C. Wooding, *Rethinking Catholicism in Reformation England* (Oxford: Clarendon Press, 2000).

10. Volker Leppin, "Wie reformatorisch war die Reformation?" *Zeitschrift für Theologie und Kirche* 99 (2002): 162–76; Martin Ohst, "'Reformation' Versus 'Protestantismus'? Theologiegeschichtliche Fallstudien," *Zeitschrift für Theologie und Kirche* 99 (2002): 441–79.

11. Thomas J. Davis, "Images of Intolerance: John Calvin in Nineteenth-Century History Textbooks," *Church History* 65 (1996): 234–48. For the lingering influence of this stereotype of Calvin, see Will Durant's comment that "we shall always find it hard to love the man who darkened the human soul with the most absurd and blasphemous conception of God in all the long and honored history of nonsense"; Will Durant, *The Reformation* (New York: Simon & Schuster, 1957), 490.

12. Petegree, "Reformation Europe Re-formed," 16.

13. Murray W. Dempster, Byron D. Klaus, and Douglas Petersen, eds., *The Globalization of Pentecostalism: A Religion Made to Travel* (Carlisle, UK: Regnum Books International, 1999).

14. See the important points made by Mark A. Noll, "The Contingencies of Christian Republicanism: An Alternative Account of Protestantism and the American Founding," in *Protestantism and the American Founding*, edited by Thomas S. Engeman and Michael P. Zuckert (Notre Dame, IN: University of Notre Dame Press, 2004), 225–56.

15. Alister E. McGrath, *Luther's Theology of the Cross: Martin Luther's Theological Breakthrough* (Oxford: Blackwell, 1985).

16. Alister E. McGrath, *Iustitia Dei: A History of the Christian Doctrine of Justification*, 3rd ed. (Cambridge: Cambridge University Press, 2005).

17. Alister E. McGrath, *The Intellectual Origins of the European Reformation*, 2nd ed. (Oxford: Blackwell, 2003).

CHAPTER 1: THE GATHERING STORM

1. For studies illuminating aspects of these roles, see Colin Morris, *The Papal Monarchy: The Western Church from 1050 to 1250* (Oxford: Oxford University Press, 1991); Eamon Duffy, *The Stripping of the Altars: Traditional Religion in England c. 1400–c. 1580* (New Haven, CT: Yale University Press, 1992); R. N. Swanson, *Church and Society in Late Medieval England* (Oxford: Blackwell, 1993); Carl A. Volz, *The Medieval Church: From the Dawn of the Middle Ages to the Eve of the Reformation* (Nashville: Abingdon Press, 1997).

2. George Holmes, ed., *Oxford Illustrated History of Medieval Europe* (Oxford: Oxford University Press, 1988); Robert Bartlett, *The Making of Europe: Conquest, Colonization, and Cultural Change, 950–1350* (Princeton, NJ: Princeton University Press, 1993).

3. See James C. Russell, *The Germanization of Early Medieval Christianity: A Socio-historical Approach to Religious Transformation* (Oxford: Oxford University Press, 1994).

4. Kathleen Cushing, *Papacy and Law in the Gregorian Revolution* (Oxford: Oxford University Press, 1998).

5. Jane Sayers, *Innocent III, Leader of Europe, 1198–1216* (New York: Longman, 1994).

6. The classic account of the early phase of this development remains Brian Tierney, *Foundations of the Conciliar Theory: The Contribution of the Medieval Canonists from Gratian to the Great Schism* (Cambridge: Cambridge University Press, 1955). For its later development, see Brian Patrick McGuire, *Jean Gerson and the Last Medieval Reformation* (University Park: Pennsylvania State University Press, 2005).

7. For an accessible account, see Yves Renouard, *The Avignon Papacy, 1305–1403* (London: Faber and Faber, 1970).

8. The flavor of the debates of that era can be sensed from J. H. Burns and Thomas M. Izbicki, eds., *Conciliarism and Papalism* (Cambridge: Cambridge University Press, 1997). For the later debate, see Katherine Eliot van Liere, "Victoria, Cajetan, and the Conciliarists," *Journal of the History of Ideas* 58 (1997): 597–616.

9. Caroline M. Barron and Jenny Stratford, eds., *The Church and Learning in Later Medieval Society* (Donington, UK: Shaun Tyas, 2002).

10. See Peter L. Berger and Thomas Luckmann, *The Social Construction of Reality: A Treatise in the Sociology of Knowledge* (New York: Anchor Books, 1990).

11. David S. Peterson, "Out of the Margins: Religion and the Church in Renaissance Italy," *Renaissance Quarterly* 53 (2000): 835–79.

12. Jean-Maurice Rouquette, *Provence romane: La Provence rhodanienne,* 2nd ed. (La Pierre-qui-Vire: Zodiaque, 1980), 50.

13. Francis Sullivan, *Salvation Outside the Church? Tracing the History of the Catholic Response* (Mahwah, NJ: Paulist Press, 1992).

14. On the Borgias, see Joachim Brambach, *Die Borgia: Faszination einer Renaissance-Familie* (Munich: Diederichs, 1995).

15. For comment, see Wendy Scase, *Piers Plowman and the New Anticlericalism* (Cambridge: Cambridge University Press, 1989); Peter A. Dykema and Heiko A. Oberman, eds., *Anticlericalism in Late Medieval and Early Modern Europe,* 2nd ed. (Leiden: Brill, 1994); Geoffrey Dipple, *Antifraternalism and Anticlericalism in the German Reformation: Johann Eberlin von Günzburg and the Campaign Against the Friars* (Aldershot, UK: Ashgate, 1996).

16. For comments on the growth of piety in England around this time, see Andrew Brown, *Popular Piety in Late Medieval England: The Diocese of Salisbury, 1250–1550* (Oxford: Clarendon Press, 1995); Susan S. Morrison, *Women Pilgrims in Late Medieval England: Private Piety as Public Performance* (London: Routledge, 2000); Mary C. Erler, *Women, Reading, and Piety in Late Medieval England* (Cambridge: Cambridge University Press, 2002); Kathleen Kamerick, *Popular Piety and Art in the Late Middle Ages: Image Worship and Idolatry in England, 1350–1500* (New York: Palgrave Macmillan, 2002).

17. For a fascinating analysis of peasant beliefs on this matter, see Carlo Ginzburg, *The Night Battles: Witchcraft and Agrarian Cults in the Sixteenth and Seventeenth Centuries* (Baltimore: Johns Hopkins University Press, 1992).

18. See Anne Clark Bartlett and H. Bestul Thomas, *Cultures of Piety: Medieval English Devotional Literature in Translation* (Ithaca. NY: Cornell University Press, 1999).

19. Robert Stupperich, "Das *Enchiridion Militis Christiani* des Erasmus von Rotterdam nach seiner Entstehung, seinem Sinn und Charakter," *Archiv für Reformationsgeschichte* 69 (1978): 5–23.

20. For points of connection, see Heinz Holeczek, *Humanistische Bibelphilologie als Reformproblem bei Erasmus von Rotterdam, Thomas More, und William Tyndale* (Leiden: Brill, 1975).

21. The classic study remains Elizabeth L. Eisenstein, *The Printing Press as an Agent of Change: Communications and Cultural Transformations in Early-Modern Europe* (Cambridge: Cambridge University Press, 1997). For a careful study of the gradual change from manuscript to printed books, see David McKitterick, *Print, Manuscript, and the Search for Order, 1450–1830* (Cambridge: Cambridge University Press, 2003).

22. For some of the developments, see John W. O'Malley, *Giles of Viterbo on Church and Reform: A Study in Renaissance Thought* (Leiden: Brill, 1968); Barbara McClung Hallman, *Italian Cardinals, Reform, and the Church as Property* (Berkeley: University of California Press, 1985).

23. For an accessible account of these reforms and their impact, see Sara Tilghman Nalle, *God in La Mancha: Religious Reform and the People of Cuenca, 1500–1650* (Baltimore: Johns Hopkins University Press, 1992), 3–31.

24. For the background, see John Edwards, *The Spain of the Catholic Monarchs, 1474–1520* (Oxford: Blackwell, 2000); Charles A. Truxillo, *By the Sword and the Cross: The Historical Evolution of the Catholic World Monarchy in Spain and the New World, 1492–1825* (Westport, CT: Greenwood Press, 2001).

25. Gabriel Audisio, *The Waldensian Dissent: Persecution and Survival, c. 1170–c. 1570* (Cambridge: Cambridge University Press, 1999). Note also the alternative spelling "Waldesian." For a more popular account of this important movement, see Giorgio Tourn, *I Valdesi: La Singolare vicenda di un popolo-chiesa (1170–1976)* (Turin: Editrice Claudiana, 1977).

26. The best study of this movement is Marie F. Viallon, *Italie, 1541, ou l'unité perdue de l'Église* (Paris: Éditions CNRS, 2005).

27. For analysis of this important issue, see Joseph T. Lienhard, *The Bible, the Church, and Authority: The Canon of the Christian Bible in History and Theology* (Collegeville, MN: Liturgical Press, 1995); Stephen E. Fowl, ed., *The Theological Interpretation of Scripture: Classic and Contemporary Readings* (Oxford: Blackwell, 1997).

28. For a full scholarly account of the developments noted in this section, see Alister E. McGrath, *The Intellectual Origins of the European Reformation*, 2nd ed. (Oxford: Blackwell, 2003).

29. For introductions, see Roberto Weiss, *The Renaissance Discovery of Classical Antiquity* (Oxford: Blackwell, 1988); Charles G. Nauert, *Humanism and the Culture of Renaissance Europe* (Cambridge: Cambridge University Press, 1995); Jill Kraye,

ed., *The Cambridge Companion to Renaissance Humanism* (Cambridge: Cambridge University Press, 1996).

30. See, for example, Robert Coogan, *Erasmus, Lee, and the Correction of the Vulgate: The Shaking of the Foundations* (Geneva: Librairie Droz, 1992).

31. Erasmus actually included this in his text of the New Testament, for reasons that are not entirely persuasive; see Charles Augrain, "À propos du Comma Johanneum," *Moreana* 35 (1998): 87–94.

32. See the classic study of P. S. Allen, "The Trilingual Colleges of the Early Sixteenth Century," in *Erasmus: Lectures and Wayfaring Sketches* (Oxford: Clarendon Press, 1934), 138–63.

33. For some of these approaches, see Kathy Eden, *Hermeneutics and the Rhetorical Tradition: Chapters in the Ancient Legacy and Its Humanist Reception* (New Haven, CT: Yale University Press, 1997).

34. See the discussion of Pico's influence in Stephen A. McKnight, *Sacralizing the Secular: The Renaissance Origins of Modernity* (Baton Rouge: Louisiana State University Press, 1981), 50–70.

35. Charles Trinkaus, "Cosmos and Man: Marsilio Ficino and Giovanni Pico on the Structure of the Universe and the Freedom of Man," *Vivens Homo* 5 (1994): 335–57.

36. Skinner sees this idea as linked with Calvinism; see Quentin Skinner, *Foundations of Modern Political Thought*, 2 vols. (Cambridge: Cambridge University Press, 1978), 2:219–40.

37. See the comments of Lester K. Little, *Religious Poverty and the Profit Economy in Medieval Europe* (Ithaca, NY: Cornell University Press, 1983).

38. A point stressed by Michael Walzer in *The Revolution of the Saints: A Study in the Origins of Radical Politics* (Cambridge, MA: Harvard University Press, 1982).

CHAPTER 2: THE ACCIDENTAL REVOLUTIONARY: MARTIN LUTHER

1. For excellent recent studies, see Susan C. Karant-Nunn, *The Reformation of Ritual: An Interpretation of Early Modern Germany, Christianity, and Society in the Modern World* (London: Routledge, 1997); Steven E. Ozment, *Flesh and Spirit: Private Life in Early Modern Germany* (London: Penguin, 2002).

2. Early works of this nature include Natalie Z. Davis, *Society and Culture in Early Modern France* (Stanford, CA: Stanford University Press, 1975); Keith Thomas, *Religion and the Decline of Magic: Studies in Popular Beliefs in Sixteenth- and Seventeenth-Century England* (London: Penguin, 1978). For a survey of more recent studies, see Mack P. Holt, "The Social History of the Reformation: Recent Trends and Future Agendas," *Journal of Social History* 37 (2003): 133–44.

3. For a vigorous reassertion of the religious roots of the Reformation, focusing particularly on its impact on individuals, see Steven E. Ozment, *Protestants: The Birth of a Revolution* (New York: Doubleday, 1992).

4. The standard account of this doctrine is Alister E. McGrath, Iustitia Dei: *A History of the Christian Doctrine of Justification*, 3rd ed. (Cambridge: Cambridge University Press, 2005).

5. The best critical biography is Martin Brecht, *Martin Luther*, 3 vols. (Minneapolis: Fortress Press, 1990–94).

6. This theme is prominent in the important biography of Heiko A. Oberman, *Luther: Man Between God and the Devil* (New York: Doubleday, 1989).

7. See the classic, though deeply flawed, account of this in Erik H. Erikson, *Young Man Luther: A Study in Psychoanalysis and History* (New York: Norton, 1958).

8. For the development and significance of this idea, see McGrath, Iustitia Dei, 107–17.

9. Jens-Martin Kruse, *Universitätstheologie und Kirchenreform: Die Anfänge der Reformation in Wittenberg 1516–1522* (Mainz: Philipp von Zabern, 2002).

10. Alister E. McGrath, *Luther's Theology of the Cross: Martin Luther's Theological Breakthrough* (Oxford: Blackwell, 1985); Bernard Lohse, *Martin Luther's Theology: Its Historical and Systematic Development* (Philadelphia: Fortress Press, 1999).

11. It is interesting to speculate whether Luther's early critics entirely appreciated this point: see David V. N. Bagchi, *Luther's Earliest Opponents: Catholic Controversialists, 1518–1525* (Minneapolis: Augsburg Fortress, 1991).

12. The best study is Stephen Greenblatt, *Hamlet in Purgatory* (Princeton, NJ: Princeton University Press, 2001).

13. Howard Colvin, "The Origin of Chantries," *Journal of Medieval History* 26 (2000): 163–73.

14. For the background to this issue, see Kurt Stadtwald, *Roman Popes and German Patriots: Antipapalism in the Politics of the German Humanist Movement from Gregor Heimburg to Martin Luther* (Geneva: Librairie Droz, 1996).

15. For an excellent study of the use of pamphlets in England, see Joad Raymond, *Pamphlets and Pamphleteering in Early Modern Britain* (Cambridge: Cambridge University Press, 2003).

16. Norman E. Nagel, "Luther and the Priesthood of All Believers," *Concordia Theological Quarterly* 61 (1997): 277–98.

17. For analysis and comment, see Hermann Sasse, *This Is My Body: Luther's Contention for the Real Presence in the Sacrament of the Altar* (Minneapolis: Concordia, 2003).

18. See the useful background material in Josef Wohlmuth, *Realpräsenz und Transsubstantiation im Konzil von Trient: Eine historisch-kritische Analyse* (Bern: Peter Lang, 1975).

19. It must be noted that the famous phrase "Here I stand, I cannot do otherwise" is not included in the official transcript of the proceedings at Worms and may have been added to Luther's words by a printer; see the discussion in Oberman, *Luther: Man Between God and the Devil*, 35–40.

20. The best study is Jeanette C. Smith, "Katharina von Bora Through Five Centuries: A Historiography," *Sixteenth Century Journal* 30 (1999): 745–74.

21. This point is stressed in Berndt Hamm, "Einheit und Vielfalt der Reformation– oder: Was die Reformation zur Reformation machte," in *Reformationstheorien: Ein kirchenhistorischer Disput über Einheit und Vielfalt der Reformation*, edited by Berndt Hamm, Bernd Moeller, and Dorothea Wendebourg (Göttingen: Vandenhoeck & Ruprecht, 1995), 57–127.

CHAPTER 3: ALTERNATIVES TO LUTHER: THE DIVERSIFICATION OF THE REFORMATION

1. See Hans-Jürgen Goertz, "Eine 'bewegte' Epoche: Zur Heterogenität reformatorischer Bewegungen," in *Wegscheiden der Reformation: Alternatives Denken vom 16. bis zum 18. Jahrhundert*, edited by Günter Vogler (Weimar: Bohlaus Nachfolger, 1994), 23–56; Alister E. McGrath, *The Intellectual Origins of the European Reformation*, 2nd ed. (Oxford: Blackwell, 2003), 182–89.

2. For a collection of excellent attempts to make sense of what happened, see Bruce Gordon, ed., *Protestant History and Identity in Sixteenth-Century Europe*, 2 vols. (Aldershot, UK: Ashgate, 1996).

3. Dorothea Wendebourg, "Die Einheit der Reformation als historisches Problem," in *Reformationstheorien: Ein kirchenhistorischer Disput über Einheit und Vielfalt der Reformation*, edited by Berndt Hamm, Bernd Moeller, and Dorothea Wendebourg (Göttingen: Vandenhoeck & Ruprecht, 1995), 31–51.

4. Carlos M. N. Eire, *War Against the Idols: The Reformation of Worship from Erasmus to Calvin* (Cambridge: Cambridge University Press, 1986), 65–73.

5. Ulrich Bubenheimer and Stefan Oehmig, eds., *Querdenker der Reformation: Andreas Bodenstein von Karlstadt und seine frühe Wirkung* (Würzburg: Religion & Kultur Verlag, 2001).

6. The same criticism would be directed against Zwingli's limited reforms in Zurich, even though these were more radical than Luther's; see Andrea Strübind, *Eifriger als Zwingli: Die frühe Täuferbewegung in der Schweiz* (Berlin: Duncker & Humblot, 2003), 79–119.

7. For an excellent analysis, see Abraham Friesen, *Thomas Müntzer, a Destroyer of the Godless: The Making of a Sixteenth-Century Religious Revolutionary* (Berkeley: University of California Press, 1990), 33–52.

8. Peter Blickle, *Der deutsche Bauernkrieg von 1525* (Darmstadt: Wissenschaftliche Buchgesellschaft, 1985).

9. For an analysis of some of these factors, see Berndt Hamm, "Reformation 'von unten' und Reformation 'von oben': Zur Problematik der reformationshistorischen Klassifizierungen," in *Reformation in Deutschland und Europa: Interpretationen und Debatten*, edited by Hans R. Guggisberg and Gottfried G. Krodel (Gütersloh: Mohn, 1993), 256–93.

10. See especially Franziska Conrad's study of the reception of reforming ideas in Alsace, *Reformation in der bäuerlichen Gesellschaft: Zur Rezeption reformatorischer Theologie im Elsass* (Stuttgart: Steiner Verlag, 1984).

11. A point stressed in Peter Blickle, *Gemeindereformation: Die Menschen des 16. Jahrhunderts auf dem Weg zum Heil* (Munich: Oldenbourg, 1987).

12. Berndt Hamm, *Bürgertum und Glaube: Konturen der städtischen Reformation* (Göttingen: Vandenhoeck & Ruprecht, 1996).

13. The best study of this fascinating movement is Bruce Gordon, *The Swiss Reformation* (Manchester, UK: Manchester University Press, 2002).

14. For a comparison of the divergent hermeneutical approaches of Luther and Zwingli, see McGrath, *The Intellectual Origins of the European Reformation*, 153–66.

15. For popular demands for iconoclasm elsewhere in the region, see Paul A. Russell, *Lay Theology in the Reformation: Popular Pamphleteers in Southwest Germany, 1521–1525* (Cambridge: Cambridge University Press, 1986), 56–79.

16. For reflections on the role of riots in spreading Protestantism, see Natalie Z. Davis, "The Rites of Violence: Religious Riot in Sixteenth-Century France," *Past and Present* 59 (1973): 51–91.

17. Christine Christ, "Das Schriftverständnis von Zwingli und Erasmus im Jahre 1522," *Zwingliana* 16 (1983): 111–25.

18. See here the excellent study of Ralf Hoburg, *Seligkeit und Heilsgewissheit: Hermeneutik und Schriftauslegung bei Huldrych Zwingli bis 1522* (Stuttgart: Calwer Verlag, 1994).

19. See Eberhard Grötzinger, *Luther und Zwingli: Die Kritik an der mittelalterlichen Lehre von der Messe, als Wurzel des Abendmahlsstreites* (Zurich: Benziger Verlag, 1980).

20. See Rupert E. Davies's classic study, *The Problem of Authority in the Continental Reformers: A Study in Luther, Zwingli, and Calvin* (London: Epworth Press, 1946).

21. The role of this notion, along with other "communal" concepts, is contested; see Robert W. Scribner, "Communalism: Universal Category or Ideological Construct? A Debate in the Historiography of Early Modern Germany and Switzerland," *Historical Journal* 37 (1994): 199–207.

22. The best study is Walter Schaufelberger, "Kappel: Die Hintergründe einer militärschen Katastrophe," *Schweizerisches Archiv für Volkskunde* 51 (1955): 34–61. The mortally wounded Zwingli was run through with a sword by Captain Fuckinger of Unterwalden after refusing to make confession.

23. See Berndt Moeller, *Imperial Cities and the Reformation* (Durham, NC: Labyrinth Press, 1982). Note also the analysis in Alister E. McGrath, "Justification and the Reformation: The Significance of the Doctrine of Justification by Faith to Sixteenth-Century Urban Communities," *Archiv fur Reformationsgeschichte* 81 (1990): 5–19.

24. For an excellent account of the issues underlying these developments, see Andrew Pettegree, *Reformation and the Culture of Persuasion* (Cambridge: Cambridge University Press, 2005).

25. Lorna Jane Abray, *The People's Reformation: Magistrates, Clergy, and Commons in Strasbourg, 1500–1598* (Ithaca, NY: Cornell University Press, 1985).

26. See Friedhelm Kruger, *Bucer und Erasmus: Eine Untersuchung zum Einfluss des Erasmus auf die Theologie Martin Bucers* (Wiesbaden: Franz Steiner, 1970); Beate Stierle, *Capito als Humanist* (Gütersloh: Mohn, 1974).

27. T. A. Fudge, "Icarus of Basel? Oecolampadius and the Early Swiss Reformation," *Journal of Religious History* 21 (1997): 268–84.

28. For the Catholic response to the Augsburg Confession at this point, see the magisterial study by Vinzenz Pfnür, *Einig in der Rechtfertigungslehre?: Die Rechtfertigungslehre der Confessio Augustana (1530) und die Stellungnahme der katholischen Kontroverstheologie zwischen 1530 und 1535* (Wiesbaden: Steiner, 1970).

29. The best study is George H. Williams, *The Radical Reformation*, 3rd ed. (Kirksville, MO: Sixteenth Century Journal Publishers, 1992).

30. Arnold Snyder, *Anabaptist History and Theology: An Introduction* (Kitchener, ON: Pandora Press, 1996).
31. For the impact of such ideas on one group, see Donald B. Kraybill, *The Amish and the State*, 2nd ed. (Baltimore: Johns Hopkins University Press, 2003).
32. The best study is Alvin J. Beachy, *The Concept of Grace in the Radical Reformation* (Nieuwkoop: De Graaf, 1977).
33. See, for example, Mihály Balázs, *Early Transylvanian Anti-trinitarianism (1566–1571): From Servet to Palaeologus* (Baden-Baden: Valentin Koerner, 1996).
34. The best study is John D. Rempel, *The Lord's Supper in Anabaptism: A Study in the Christology of Balthasar Hubmaier, Pilgram Marpeck, and Dirk Philips* (Scottdale, PA: Herald Press, 1993).
35. See the discussion in Stuart Murray, *Biblical Interpretation in the Anabaptist Tradition* (Kitchener, ON: Pandora Press, 2000).
36. For some reflections, see Paul L. Maier, "Fanaticism as a Theological Category in the Lutheran Confessions," *Concordia Theological Quarterly* 44 (1980): 173–81. Luther used the term *Schwärmerei* to refer to just about any Protestants who transgressed his own theological boundaries, including Zwingli, Karlstadt, Müntzer, and the Anabaptists.
37. For the history of the interpretation of this biblical work—a favorite with marginalized groups—see Kenneth G. C. Newport, *Apocalypse and Millennium: Studies in Biblical Eisegesis* (Cambridge: Cambridge University Press, 2000).
38. Anthony Arthur, *The Tailor-King: The Rise and Fall of the Anabaptist Kingdom of Münster* (New York: St. Martin's Press, 1999).
39. Sigrun Haude, *In the Shadow of "Savage Wolves": Anabaptist Münster and the German Reformation During the 1530s* (Boston: Humanities Press, 2000).
40. Claus-Peter Clasen, *Anabaptism: A Social History, 1525–1618: Switzerland, Austria, Moravia, South and Central Germany* (Ithaca, NY: Cornell University Press, 1972).

CHAPTER 4: THE SHIFT IN POWER: CALVIN AND GENEVA

1. For the background, see Gabriele Schlütter-Schindler, *Der Schmalkaldische Bund und das Problem der causa religionis* (Frankfurt am Main: Peter Lang, 1986).
2. See the comments of Frank Tallett in *War and Society in Early Modern Europe, 1495–1715* (London: Routledge, 1992), 51.
3. A series of legends have arisen around this event, none with any reliable historical basis. The best known is that, on being urged to burn Luther's bones to demonstrate he died as a heretic, Charles answered: "He has met his judge. I only wage war on the living, not on the dead."
4. For an excellent study, see Oliver K. Olson, *Matthias Flacius and the Survival of Luther's Reform* (Wiesbaden: Harrassowitz, 2002).
5. Nathan Baruch Rein, "Faith and Empire: Conflicting Visions of Religion in a Late-Reformation Controversy: The Augsburg Interim and Its Opponents, 1548–1550," *Journal of the American Academy of Religion* 71 (2003): 45–74.
6. See Axel Gotthard, *Der Augsburger Religionsfrieden* (Münster: Aschendorff, 2004).

7. For details of Lutheranism's expansion into Nordic countries, see Ole Peter Grell, *The Scandinavian Reformation: From Evangelical Movement to Institutionalization of Reform* (Cambridge: Cambridge University Press, 1995).

8. For reflections on the general issue of nationalism in relation to the Reformation, see Bob Scribner, Roy Porter, and Mikulás Teich, eds., *The Reformation in National Context* (Cambridge: Cambridge University Press, 1994).

9. For good analyses, see André Holenstein, "Reformierte Konfessionalisierung und bernischer Territorialstaat," in *Territorialstaat und Calvinismus,* edited by Meinrad Schaab (Stuttgart: Kohlhammer, 1993), 5–33; Heinrich Richard Schmidt, *Dorf und Religion: Reformierte Sittenzucht in Berner Landgemeinden der frühen Neuzeit* (Stuttgart: Fischer, 1995).

10. Farel Comité, *Guillaume Farel, 1489–1565: Biographie nouvelle* (Geneve: Slatkine Reprints, 1978).

11. Henri Delarue, "La Première offensive évangélique à Genève," *Bulletin de la Société et d'Archéologie de Genève* 9 (1948): 83–102.

12. For a good introduction to Viret, see Georges Bavaud, *Le Réformateur Pierre Viret, 1511–1571: Sa théologie* (Geneva: Labor et Fides, 1986).

13. The best recent biography is Bernard Cottret, *Calvin: A Biography* (Grand Rapids, MI: Eerdmans, 2000).

14. For an account of the event and theories of the placards' authorship, see Gabrielle Berthoud, *Antoine Marcourt: Réformateur et pamphlétaire, du "Livre des marchans" aux Placards de 1534* (Geneva: Droz, 1973).

15. For an analysis of its contents, see Ford Lewis Battles, *Analysis of the Institutes of the Christian Religion of John Calvin* (Grand Rapids, MI: Baker Book House, 1980).

16. For the best account of the Reformation at Geneva and Calvin's role in its implementation, see Henri Naef, *Les Origines de la réforme à Genève,* 2 vols. (Geneva: Droz, 1968).

17. Eric Junod, ed., *La Dispute de Lausanne (1536): La Théologie réformée après Zwingli et avant Calvin* (Lausanne: Presses Centrales Lausanne, 1988).

18. For an excellent analysis of this phase, see William G. Naphy, *Calvin and the Consolidation of the Genevan Reformation* (Louisville, KY: Westminster John Knox, 2003).

19. Albert Autin, *L'Institution chrétienne de Calvin* (Paris: Malfere, 1929).

20. For a good discussion of this point, see Alexandre Ganoczy, *The Young Calvin* (Philadelphia: Westminster Press, 1987), 137–68.

21. For the importance of this point, see A. N. S. Lane, *John Calvin: Student of the Church Fathers* (Edinburgh: T. & T. Clark, 1999).

22. See the material gathered in Menna Prestwich, ed., *International Calvinism, 1541–1715* (Oxford: Clarendon Press, 1986).

23. Gottfried W. Locher, "Von Bern nach Genf: Die Ursachen der Spannung zwischen zwinglischer und calvinistischer Reformation," in *Wegen en gestalten in het gereformeerd protestantisme: Een bundel studies over de geschiedenis van het gereformeerd protestantisme,* edited by W. Balke, C. Graafland, and H. Harkema (Amsterdam: Ton Bolland, 1976), 75–87.

24. The best study of Geneva's role in this development remains Robert M. Kingdon, *Geneva and the Coming of the Wars of Religion in France, 1555–1563* (Geneva: Droz, 1956).

25. The best study is Volker Press, *Calvinismus und Territorialstaat: Regierung und Zentralbehörden der Kurpfalz, 1559–1619* (Stuttgart: Klett, 1970).

26. For comment, see Lyle D. Bierma, *The Doctrine of the Sacraments in the Heidelberg Catechism* (Princeton, NJ: Princeton Theological Seminary, 1999).

27. See Ernst Bizer, *Studien zur Geschichte des Abendmahlstreits im 16. Jahrhundert* (Gütersloh: Mohn, 1940); Josef Bohatec, "'Lutherisch' und 'Reformiert,'" *Reformiertes Kirchenblatt für Österreich* (January 28, 1951): 1–3.

28. The classic study remains Hans Leube, *Kalvinismus und Luthertum im Zeitalter der Orthodoxie I: Der Kampf um die Herrschaft im protestantischen Deutschland* (Leipzig: Deichert, 1928). For more recent perspectives, see Bodo Nischan, *Lutherans and Calvinists in the Age of Confessionalism* (Aldershot, UK: Ashgate, 1999).

29. Knox has, of course, Mary, Queen of Scots, in mind: see Sydney H. Wood, *Mary Queen of Scots and the Scottish Reformation, 1540–1587* (London: Collins, 1999).

30. For a thorough analysis, see Ian B. Cowan, *The Scottish Reformation: Church and Society in Sixteenth-Century Scotland* (London: Weidenfeld and Nicolson, 1982).

31. See Jonathan I. Israel, *The Dutch Republic: Its Rise, Greatness, and Fall, 1477–1806* (Oxford: Clarendon Press, 1995); R. Po-chia Hsia and Henk F. K. van Nierop, eds., *Calvinism and Religious Toleration in the Dutch Golden Age* (Cambridge: Cambridge University Press, 2002).

32. See Alois Schröer, *Die Reformation in Westfalen: Der Glaubenskampf einer Landschaft* (Münster: Aschendorff, 1979); Michael G. Müller, *Zweite Reformation und städtische Autonomie im königlichen Preussen: Danzig, Elbing, und Thorn in der Epoche der Konfessionalisierung (1557–1660)* (Berlin: Akademie Verlag, 1997).

33. See John M. Headley, Hans Joachim Hillerbrand, and Anthony J. Papalas, eds., *Confessionalization in Europe, 1555–1700: Essays in Honor and Memory of Bodo Nischan* (Aldershot, UK: Ashgate, 2004).

34. H. J. Cohn, "The Territorial Princes in Germany's Second Reformation, 1559–1622," in *International Calvinism, 1541–1715,* edited by M. Prestwich (Oxford: Oxford University Press, 1985), 135–65, 135.

CHAPTER 5: ENGLAND: THE EMERGENCE OF ANGLICANISM

1. Diarmaid MacCulloch, "The Myth of the English Reformation," *Journal of British Studies* 30 (1991): 1–19.

2. It is, in fact, quite difficult to find a satisfactory label for these forerunners of the nineteenth-century Anglo-Catholics other than the vague description "High Church," which can be applied equally to Presbyterians in comparison with Congregationalists. In his excellent account of this period, Anthony Milton has suggested the term "avant-garde conformists" to refer to this trend; see Anthony Milton, *Catholic and Reformed: The Roman and Protestant Churches in English Protestant Thought, 1600–1640* (Cambridge: Cambridge University Press, 1995).

3. See, for example, the "Bill for the Relief of His Majesty's Roman Catholic Subjects" of March 24, 1829.

4. See especially Alec Ryrie, *The Gospel and Henry VIII: Evangelicals in the Early English Reformation* (Cambridge: Cambridge University Press, 2003), xv–xvi. Older studies remain important, such as Greg Walker, *Persuasive Fictions: Faction, Faith, and Political Culture in the Reign of Henry VIII* (Aldershot, UK: Scolar, 1996), 136–37.

5. Peter Marshall, *Religious Identities in Henry VIII's England* (Aldershot, UK: Ashgate, 2006), 4–8.

6. Christine Peters, *Patterns of Piety: Women, Gender, and Religion in Late Medieval and Reformation England* (Cambridge: Cambridge University Press, 2002), 60–96.

7. See especially Eamon Duffy, *The Stripping of the Altars: Traditional Religion in England, c. 1400–c. 1580* (New Haven, CT: Yale University Press, 1992); Felicity Heal, *Reformation in Britain and Ireland* (Oxford: Clarendon Press, 2003).

8. Norman L. Jones, *The English Reformation: Religion and Cultural Adaptation* (Oxford: Blackwell, 2002).

9. Ryrie, *The Gospel and Henry VIII*, 233–37. The role of Lollardy is contested; see the more negative assessment in Richard Rex, *The Lollards* (Basingstoke, UK: Palgrave, 2002).

10. See the documentation of this point in Ethan H. Shagan, *Popular Politics and the English Reformation* (Cambridge: Cambridge University Press, 2003).

11. For the theological motifs linked to this concern, see Alec Ryrie, "Divine Kingship and Royal Theology in Henry VIII's Reformation," *Reformation* 7 (2002): 49–77.

12. G. W. Bernard, *The King's Reformation: Henry VIII and the Remaking of the English Church* (New Haven, CT: Yale University Press, 2005).

13. See especially Marjo Kaartinen, *Religious Life and English Culture in the Reformation* (Basingstoke, UK: Palgrave, 2002).

14. For the argument that English nationalism emerged in the 1520s, see Liah Greenfeld, *Nationalism: Five Roads to Modernity* (Cambridge, MA: Harvard University Press, 1992). The situation is more complex, however, than Greenfeld suggests, as shown by Gillian E. Brennan, *Patriotism, Power, and Print: National Consciousness in Tudor England* (Pittsburgh: Duquesne University Press, 2003).

15. Ryrie, *The Gospel and Henry VIII*, 8–10.

16. For the fortunes of Lutheranism in England, see Alec Ryrie, "The Strange Death of Lutheran England," *Journal of Ecclesiastical History* 53 (2002): 64–92.

17. For comment, see Rory McEntegart, *Henry VIII, the League of Schmalkalden, and the English Reformation* (Woodbridge, UK: Boydell Press, 2002); Peter Marshall, *Reformation England: 1480–1642* (London: Arnold, 2003), 197–98.

18. The issues are explored in Stephen Alford, *Kingship and Politics in the Reign of Edward VI* (Cambridge: Cambridge University Press, 2002).

19. W. K. Jordan, *Edward VI, the Young King: The Protectorship of the Duke of Somerset* (Cambridge, MA: Belknap Press of Harvard University Press, 1971); Alford, *Kingship and Politics in the Reign of Edward VI*, 65–99.

20. Diarmaid MacCulloch, *Thomas Cranmer* (New Haven, CT: Yale University Press, 1996), 364–65.

21. The best study is Diarmaid MacCulloch, *Tudor Church Militant: Edward VI and the Protestant Reformation* (London: Allen Lane, 1999).

22. For a study of the development of these texts and their impact, see the elegant study by David N. Griffiths, *The Bibliography of the Book of Common Prayer, 1549–1999* (London: British Library, 2002).

23. Julia Houston, "Transubstantiation and the Sign: Cranmer's Drama of the Last Supper," *Journal of Medieval and Renaissance Studies* 24 (1994): 115–30; Judith H. Anderson, "Language and History in the Reformation: Cranmer, Gardiner, and the Words of Institution," *Renaissance Quarterly* 54 (2001): 20–35.

24. Basil Hall, "Cranmer, the Eucharist, and the Foreign Divines in the Reign of Edward VI," in *Thomas Cranmer: Churchman and Scholar,* edited by Paul Ayris and David Selwyn (Woodbridge, UK: Boydell, 1993), 217–58.

25. See Carlos M. N. Eire, *War Against the Idols: The Reformation of Worship from Erasmus to Calvin* (Cambridge: Cambridge University Press, 1986), 76–83, 304–5.

26. D. M. Loades, *The Reign of Mary Tudor: Politics, Government, and Religion in England, 1553–1558,* 2nd ed. (London: Longman, 1991).

27. For analysis of the Spanish religious connection and its impact at this time, see John Edwards and R. W. Truman, eds., *Reforming Catholicism in the England of Mary Tudor: The Achievement of Friar Bartolome Carranza* (Aldershot, UK: Ashgate, 2005).

28. Claire Cross, "No Continuing City: Exiles in the English Reformation, 1520–1570," *History Review* 32 (1998): 17–22.

29. For the process, see William P. Haugaard, *Elizabeth and the English Reformation: The Struggle for a Stable Settlement of Religion* (Cambridge: Cambridge University Press, 1970).

30. See Norman L. Jones, *Faith by Statute: Parliament and the Settlement of Religion, 1559* (London: Royal Historical Society, 1982).

31. Hirofumi Horie, "The Lutheran Influence on the Elizabethan Settlement, 1558–1563," *Historical Journal* 34 (1991): 519–37.

32. For the origins of this demand for institutional, doctrinal, and personal purity, see Theodore Dwight Bozeman, *To Live Ancient Lives: The Primitivist Dimension in Puritanism* (Chapel Hill: University of North Carolina Press, 1988).

33. C. S. L. Davies, "International Politics and the Establishment of Presbyterianism: The Coutances Connection," *Journal of Ecclesiastical History* 50 (1999): 498–522.

34. See the comments of Diana Newton, *Papists, Protestants, and Puritans, 1559–1714* (Cambridge: Cambridge University Press, 1998).

35. Susan Doran and Thomas S. Freeman, eds., *The Myth of Elizabeth* (Basingstoke, UK: Palgrave Macmillan, 2003). For alternative evaluations, see Julia M. Walker, *Dissing Elizabeth: Negative Representations of Gloriana* (Durham, NC: Duke University Press, 1998).

36. See Peter Lake, *Anglicans and Puritans? Presbyterianism and English Conformist Thought from Whitgift to Hooker* (London: Unwin Hyman, 1988); and especially Daniel W. Doerksen, *Conforming to the Word: Herbert, Donne, and the English Church Before Laud* (Lewisburg, PA: Bucknell University Press, 1997).

37. See Charles and Katherine George, *The Protestant Mind of the English Reformation, 1570–1640* (Princeton, NJ: Princeton University Press, 1961); Patrick Collinson, *The Religion of Protestants: The Church in English Society, 1559–1625* (Oxford: Clarendon Press, 1982); Nicholas Tyacke, *Anti-Calvinists: The Rise of English Arminianism,*

c. 1590–1640 (Oxford: Clarendon Press, 1987); Peter White, *Predestination, Policy, and Polemic: Conflict and Consensus in the English Church from the Reformation to the Civil War* (Cambridge: Cambridge University Press, 1992).

38. For details, see Kenneth Fincham and Peter Lake, "The Ecclesiastical Policy of King James I," *Journal of British Studies* 24 (1985): 182–86; Kenneth Fincham, *Prelate as Pastor: The Episcopate of James I* (Oxford: Clarendon Press, 1990).

39. The text is more properly known as the "Declaration to His Subjects." For this and other works, including the famous "Directions to Preachers" (1622), see Neil Rhodes, Jennifer Richards, and Joseph Marshall, eds., *King James VI and I: Selected Writings* (Aldershot, UK: Ashgate, 2003).

40. For the controversies, and their continuation in North America, see Theodore Dwight Bozeman, *The Precisianist Strain: Disciplinary Religion and Antinomian Backlash in Puritanism to 1638* (Chapel Hill: University of North Carolina Press, 2004).

CHAPTER 6: WAR, PEACE, AND DISINTEREST: EUROPEAN PROTESTANTISM IN CRISIS, 1560–1800

1. Ernest Renan, "What Is a Nation?," in *Nation and Narration,* edited by Homi K. Bhabha (London: Routledge, 1990), 8–22, 19.

2. For an excellent analysis, see Nikki Keddie, *An Islamic Response to Imperialism: Political and Religious Writings of Sayyid Jamal al-Din al-Afghani* (Berkeley: University of California Press, 1983).

3. Robert Bireley, *The Refashioning of Catholicism, 1450–1700: A Reassessment of the Counter Reformation* (Basingstoke, UK: Macmillan, 1999).

4. R. Po-chia Hsia, *The World of Catholic Renewal, 1540–1770,* 2nd ed. (Cambridge: Cambridge University Press, 2005).

5. For the sources of this remarkable work, see Susan Wabuda, "Henry Bull, Miles Coverdale, and the Making of Foxe's *Book of Martyrs,*" in *Martyrs and Martyrologies,* edited by Diana Wood (Oxford: Blackwell, 1993), 245–58.

6. Peter Lake, "Anti-popery: The Structure of a Prejudice," in *Conflict in Early Stuart England: Studies in Religion and Politics, 1603–1642,* edited by Richard Cust and Ann Hughes (London: Longman, 1989), 72–106.

7. See David Cressy, *Bonfires and Bells: National Memory and the Protestant Calendar in Elizabethan and Stuart England* (London: Weidenfeld and Nicholson, 1989).

8. The phrase "Wars of the Three Kingdoms" is sometimes used to indicate that the English Civil War also affected Ireland and Scotland. Until the Act of Union (1801), these three countries could not be regarded as a single political entity. For background, see Conrad Russell, *The Origins of the English Civil War* (Basingstoke, UK: Macmillan, 1973); Norah Carlin, *The Causes of the English Civil War* (Oxford: Blackwell, 1998).

9. See the analysis in Roxane C. Murph, *The English Civil War Through the Restoration in Fiction: An Annotated Bibliography, 1625–1999* (Westport, CT: Greenwood Press, 2000).

10. See especially the essays gathered in Laura Lunger Knoppers, ed., *Puritanism and Its Discontents* (Newark, NJ: University of Delaware Press, 2003).

11. For an important study, see Richard McCoy, *Alterations of State: Sacred Kingship in the English Reformation* (New York: Columbia University Press, 2002).

12. R. E. Giesey, "The Monarchomach Triumvirs: Hotman, Beza, and Mornay," *Bibliothèque d'Humanisme et Renaissance* 32 (1970): 41–56. For the later development of this point, see W. J. Stankiewicz, *Politics and Religion in Seventeenth-Century France: A Study of Political Ideas from the Monarchomachs to Bayle* (Westport, CT: Greenwood Press, 1976).

13. Dan G. Danner, "The Contribution of the Geneva Bible of 1560 to English Protestantism," *Sixteenth Century Journal* 12 (1981): 5–18.

14. For an exploration of the central role of the Bible at this time, see Christopher Hill, *The English Bible and the Seventeenth-Century Revolution* (London: Penguin Books, 1993).

15. For the political background to these negotiations, see Glyn Redworth, *The Prince and the Infanta: The Cultural Politics of the Spanish Match* (New Haven, CT: Yale University Press, 2003).

16. On this fascinating figure, see the classic study of Hugh R. Trevor-Roper, *Archbishop Laud, 1573–1645*, 3rd ed. (Basingstoke, UK: Macmillan, 1988).

17. The definition of "treason" at this time is not without interest. Originally understood as a personal crime against the person of the monarch, treason was redefined as a crime against an impersonal state. The issue was of special importance in the charge of treason laid against Charles I by Parliament. For an excellent account of this development, see D. Alan Orr, *Treason and the State: Law, Politics, and Ideology in the English Civil War* (Cambridge: Cambridge University Press, 2002).

18. For critical accounts of Cromwell's religious and political significance, see Christopher Hill, *God's Englishman: Oliver Cromwell and the English Revolution* (London: Penguin, 2000); Antonia Fraser, *Cromwell: Our Chief of Men* (London: Phoenix, 2002).

19. See the fascinating study by Robert Thomas Fallon, *The Christian Soldier: Religious Tracts Published for Soldiers on Both Sides During and After the English Civil Wars, 1642–1648* (Tempe: Arizona Center for Medieval and Renaissance Studies, 2003).

20. The best account is Michael Mendle, *The Putney Debates of 1647: The Army, the Levelers, and the English State* (Cambridge: Cambridge University Press, 2001).

21. For some aspects of the debate, see Graham E. Seel, *Regicide and Republic: England, 1603–1660* (Cambridge: Cambridge University Press, 2001).

22. Quentin Skinner, *The Foundations of Modern Political Thought*, 2 vols. (Cambridge: Cambridge University Press, 1978), 2:193.

23. See the older study by Winthrop S. Hudson, *John Ponet (1516?–1556), Advocate of Limited Monarchy* (Chicago: University of Chicago Press, 1942).

24. Others went further: Cromwell, they argued, had simply assumed the role of the king. For the apparent merging of protectoral and monarchical iconography, as reflected in contemporary portraits of Cromwell, see John Cooper, *Oliver the First: Contemporary Images of Oliver Cromwell* (London: National Portrait Gallery, 1999).

25. J. Douglas Canfield, *Tricksters and Estates: On the Ideology of Restoration Comedy* (Lexington: University Press of Kentucky, 1997).

26. John Morrill, "Life After Death? The Survival of the Church of England in the Seventeenth Century," *History Review* 30 (1998): 18–23.

27. For a study, see Alister E. McGrath, *In the Beginning: The Story of the King James Bible* (New York: Doubleday, 2001).

28. See McCoy, *Alterations of State*, 108, 135–37.

29. Geoffrey Parker, *The Thirty Years' War*, rev. ed. (London: Routledge & Kegan Paul, 1987).

30. For a study of how such a radicalized social vision arose within English Puritanism at this time, see Nicholas McDowell, *The English Radical Imagination: Culture, Religion, and Revolution, 1630–1660* (Oxford: Clarendon Press, 2003).

31. This is the thesis of Christopher Dawson, *The Dividing of Christendom* (New York: Sheed & Ward, 1965), 9–11. Cf. his earlier work, *The Judgment of the Nations* (New York: Sheed & Ward, 1942), 103–4. However, recent studies have stressed that a Christian—rather than a secular—agenda undergirded Locke's approach; see especially Jeremy Waldron, *God, Locke, and Equality: Christian Foundations of John Locke's Political Thought* (Cambridge: Cambridge University Press, 2002).

32. Ole Peter Grell, Jonathan Irvine Israel, and Nicholas Tyacke, eds., *From Persecution to Toleration: The Glorious Revolution and Religion in England* (Oxford: Clarendon Press, 1991).

33. See the analysis in Louis K. Dupré, *Passage to Modernity: An Essay in the Hermeneutics of Nature and Culture* (New Haven, CT: Yale University Press, 1993).

34. See the arguments of Margaret C. Jacob, *The Newtonians and the English Revolution, 1689–1720* (Ithaca, NY: Cornell University Press, 1976).

35. See the classic essay of H. R. Trevor-Roper, "Religious Origins of the Enlightenment," in *Religion, the Reformation, and Social Change* (London: Macmillan, 1967), 193–236.

36. For useful surveys, see F. Ernest Stoeffler, *German Pietism During the Eighteenth Century* (Leiden: Brill, 1973); Harry Yeide, *Studies in Classical Pietism: The Flowering of the Ecclesiola* (New York: Peter Lang, 1997).

37. J. Munsey Turner, *John Wesley: The Evangelical Revival and the Rise of Methodism in England* (Peterborough, UK: Epworth Press, 2002).

38. For the best study of this phenomenon, see Ann Taves, *Fits, Trances, and Visions: Experiencing Religion and Explaining Experience from Wesley to James* (Princeton, NJ: Princeton University Press, 1999), 13–117.

CHAPTER 7: PROTESTANTISM IN AMERICA

1. For the best survey of the emergence of American Christianity, see Mark A. Noll, *The Old Religion in a New World: The History of North American Christianity* (Grand Rapids, MI: Eerdmans, 2002).

2. Virginia DeJohn Anderson, *New England's Generation: The Great Migration and the Formation of Society and Culture in the Seventeenth Century* (Cambridge: Cambridge University Press, 1991).

3. For useful studies, see Peter N. Carroll, *Puritanism and the Wilderness: The Intellectual Significance of the New England Frontier, 1629–1700* (New York: Columbia University Press, 1969); Stephen Foster, *The Long Argument: English Puritanism and the Shaping of New England Culture, 1570–1700* (Chapel Hill: University of North Carolina Press, 1991).

4. Harry S. Stout, *The New England Soul: Preaching and Religious Culture in Colonial New England* (New York: Oxford University Press, 1986).

5. See the classic study by Barry R. White, *The English Separatist Tradition: From the Marian Martyrs to the Pilgrim Fathers* (London: Oxford University Press, 1971).

6. Lazar Ziff, "The Salem Puritans in the 'Free Aire of a New World,'" *Huntington Library Quarterly* 20 (1956–57): 373–84; John M. Bumstead, "A Well-Bounded Toleration: Church and State in the Plymouth Colony," *Journal of Church and State* 10 (1968): 265–79.

7. Allen C. Guelzo, *Abraham Lincoln: Redeemer President* (Grand Rapids, MI: Eerdmans, 2003), 11.

8. This point is stressed by Louise A. Breen, *Transgressing the Bounds: Subversive Enterprises Among the Puritan Elite in Massachusetts, 1630–1692* (New York: Oxford University Press, 2001). Her suggestions of alternative outcomes, though historically tentative, reflect the diversity of visions of Puritanism in the region and the fragility of certain balances of power.

9. See Martin E. Marty, *Anticipating Pluralism: The Founders' Vision* (Providence, RI: John Carter Brown Library, 1986); Edwin S. Gaustad, *Liberty of Conscience: Roger Williams in America* (Grand Rapids, MI: Eerdmans, 1991).

10. The situation in South Carolina is especially illuminating; see Robert Olwell, *Masters, Slaves, and Subjects: The Culture of Power in the South Carolina Low Country, 1740–1790* (Ithaca, NY: Cornell University Press, 1998).

11. As pointed out by William G. McLoughlin, *Revivals, Awakenings, and Reform: An Essay on Religion and Social Change in America, 1607–1977* (Chicago: University of Chicago Press, 1978).

12. For an account of this appalling episode, see Frances Hill, *A Delusion of Satan: The Full Story of the Salem Witch Trials* (New York: Doubleday, 1995).

13. The best study remains Robert G. Pope, *The Half-Way Covenant: Church Membership in Puritan New England* (Princeton, NJ: Princeton University Press, 1969).

14. For what follows, see Joseph A. Conforti, *Jonathan Edwards, Religious Tradition, and American Culture* (Chapel Hill: University of North Carolina Press, 1995).

15. For comment on this theme, see Linda Munk, "His Dazzling Absence: The Shekinah in Jonathan Edwards," *Early American Literature* 27 (1992): 1–30.

16. See the study by Frank Lambert, *Inventing the "Great Awakening"* (Princeton, NJ: Princeton University Press, 1999).

17. Ann Taves, *Fits, Trances, and Visions: Experiencing Religion and Explaining Experience from Wesley to James* (Princeton, NJ: Princeton University Press, 1999), 34–41.

18. Frank Lambert, *"Pedlar in Divinity": George Whitefield and the Transatlantic Revivals, 1737–1770* (Princeton, NJ: Princeton University Press, 2003).

19. For studies, see Robert W. Jenson, *America's Theologian: A Recommendation of Jonathan Edwards* (New York: Oxford University Press, 1988); Leon Chai, *Jonathan Edwards and the Limits of Enlightenment Philosophy* (New York: Oxford University Press, 1998).

20. The best study is Bruce D. Hindmarsh, *The Evangelical Conversion Narrative: Spiritual Autobiography in Early Modern England* (Oxford: Oxford University Press, 2005).

21. See especially Michael McGiffert, *God's Plot: Puritan Spirituality in Thomas Shepard's Cambridge* (Amherst: University of Massachusetts Press, 1994), 42–48.

More generally, see Charles Lloyd Cohen, *God's Caress: The Psychology of Puritan Religious Experience* (New York: Oxford University Press, 1986).

22. Andrew S. Walmsley, *Thomas Hutchinson and the Origins of the American Revolution* (New York: New York University Press, 1999).

23. Page Smith, *Religious Origins of the American Revolution* (Missoula, MT: American Academy of Religion, 1976).

24. Dale S. Kuehne, *Massachusetts Congregationalist Political Thought, 1760–1790* (Colombia: University of Missouri Press, 1996). For examples of such sermons, see Marie L. Ahern, *The Rhetoric of War: Training Day, the Militia, and the Military Sermon* (Westport, CT: Greenwood Press, 1989).

25. John W. Thornton, ed., *The Pulpit of the American Revolution: or, The Political Sermons of the Period of 1776* (New York: Franklin, 1970).

26. The religious diversity of the leading figures of the American Revolution is explored in David L. Holmes, *The Faiths of the Founding Fathers* (Oxford: Oxford University Press, 2006).

27. For the origins of this animus against religion, see Charles A. Gliozzo, "The Philosophes and Religion: Intellectual Origins of the De-Christianization Movement in the French Revolution," *Church History* 40 (1971): 273–83.

28. Dale K. Van Kley, *The Religious Origins of the French Revolution: From Calvin to the Civil Constitution, 1560–1791* (New Haven, CT: Yale University Press, 1996).

29. H. J. Eckenrode, *Separation of Church and State in Virginia: A Study in the Development of the Revolution* (New York: Da Capo Press, 1971).

30. There is a large literature: see John L. Brooke, *The Heart of the Commonwealth: Society and Political Culture in Worcester County, Massachusetts, 1713–1861* (Cambridge: Cambridge University Press, 1989); Randolph A. Roth, *The Democratic Dilemma: Religion, Reform, and the Social Order in the Connecticut River Valley of Vermont, 1791–1850* (Cambridge: Cambridge University Press, 1987); Curtis D. Johnson, *Islands of Holiness: Rural Religion in Upstate New York, 1790–1860* (Ithaca, NY: Cornell University Press, 1989).

31. Jay P. Dolan, *In Search of an American Catholicism: A History of Religion and Culture in Tension* (Oxford: Oxford University Press, 2004).

32. For the background, see Peter Kolchin, *American Slavery, 1619–1877* (New York: Hill and Wang, 2003).

33. The divisions went far beyond traditional denominational disputes. For some of the factors, see Susan Juster and Lisa MacFarlane, eds., *A Mighty Baptism: Race, Gender, and the Creation of American Protestantism* (Ithaca, NY: Cornell University Press, 1996).

34. James D. Bratt, *Antirevivalism in Antebellum America: A Collection of Religious Voices* (New Brunswick, NJ: Rutgers University Press, 2005).

35. The best study is Charles E. Hambrick-Stowe, *Charles G. Finney and the Spirit of American Evangelicalism* (Grand Rapids, MI: Eerdmans, 1996).

36. See David B. Chesebrough, *Charles G. Finney: Revivalistic Rhetoric* (Westport, CT: Greenwood, 2002).

37. See the judgment of William G. McLoughlin, *Modern Revivalism: Charles Grandison Finney to Billy Graham* (New York: Ronald Press, 1959), 86: "[Finney] and his followers believed it to be the legitimate function of a revivalist to utilize

the laws of mind in order to engineer individuals and crowds into making a choice which was ostensibly based upon free will."

38. Robert Samuel Fletcher, *A History of Oberlin College from Its Foundation Through the Civil War,* 2 vols. (Oberlin, OH: Oberlin College Press, 1943). On the college's later influence, see John Barnard, *From Evangelicalism to Progressivism at Oberlin College, 1866–1917* (Columbus: Ohio State University Press, 1969).

39. Don Cusic, *The Sound of Light: A History of Gospel Music* (Bowling Green, OH: Bowling Green State University Popular Press, 1990), 59–60.

40. For what follows, see Christine Leigh Heyrman, *Southern Cross: The Beginnings of the Bible Belt* (Chapel Hill: University of North Carolina Press, 1997).

41. See the excellent analysis in John B. Boles, *The Great Revival: Beginnings of the Bible Belt* (Lexington: University Press of Kentucky, 1996).

42. Arthur Emery Farnsley, *Southern Baptist Politics: Authority and Power in the Restructuring of an American Denomination* (University Park: Pennsylvania State University Press, 1994), 2–10.

43. Paul Harvey, *Redeeming the South: Religious Cultures and Racial Identities Among Southern Baptists, 1865–1925* (Chapel Hill: University of North Carolina Press, 1997), 45–50. It must be pointed out that there appears to have been little attempt by such white supervisors to control antebellum black congregations.

44. William E. Montgomery, *Under Their Own Vine and Fig Tree: The African-American Church in the South, 1865–1900* (Baton Rouge: Louisiana State University Press, 1993).

45. Richard Carwardine, *Evangelicals and Politics in Antebellum America* (New Haven, CT: Yale University Press, 1993), 80–84.

46. Mary Augustina Ray, *American Opinion of Roman Catholicism in the Eighteenth Century* (New York: Octagon Books, 1974), 128.

47. For an excellent study, see John T. McGreevy, *Catholicism and American Freedom: A History* (New York: Norton, 2003).

48. For the background, see Nancy L. Schultz, *Fire and Roses: The Burning of the Charlestown Convent, 1834* (New York: Free Press, 2000). Many believed that Beecher's inflammatory preaching contributed to this act of mob violence.

49. John Higham, *Strangers in the Land: Patterns of American Nativism, 1860–1925* (New York: Atheneum, 1963).

50. For the incident and its significance, see Margaret Bendroth, "Rum, Romanism, and Evangelism: Protestants and Catholics in Late Nineteenth-Century Boston," *Church History* 68 (1999): 627–47.

51. Kathleen Flake, *The Politics of American Religious Identity: The Seating of Senator Reed Smoot, Mormon Apostle* (Chapel Hill: University of North Carolina Press, 2004).

CHAPTER 8: THE NINETEENTH CENTURY: THE GLOBAL EXPANSION OF PROTESTANTISM

1. Gustav Warneck, *Abriss einer Geschichte der protestantischen Missionen von der Reformation bis auf die Gegenwart: Ein Beitrag zur neueren Kirchengeschichte,* 5th ed. (Berlin: Martin Warneck, 1899).

2. The best response is from the Swedish scholar Ingemar Oberg, *Luther och världsmissionen* (Abo, Finland: Abo Akademi, 1991). Yet Oberg merely shows that the

basic elements of a missionary theology are present in Luther, not that they were assembled and put to use for this purpose by Luther himself or his immediate followers. Although there is no doubt that the basic elements of a missionary theology can be found in the writings of both Luther and Calvin, they were like vestigial organs—present, but not perceived to be useful.

3. For an introduction to his thought, though, sadly, it fails to emphasize this point, see Willem Nijenhuis, *Adrianus Saravia (c. 1532–1613): Dutch Calvinist, First Reformed Defender of the English Episcopal Church Order on the Basis of the* Ius Divinum (Leiden: Brill, 1980). The Lutheran writer Justinian von Weltz (1621–68) should also be noted as an early example of a Protestant who explicitly advocated missionary work and evangelism.

4. One of the best studies of the motivations for this surge of missionary enthusiasm remains Johannes van den Berg, *Constrained by Jesus' Love: An Inquiry into the Motives of the Missionary Awakening in Great Britain in the Period Between 1698 and 1815* (Kampen: Kok, 1956).

5. Andrew F. Walls, in *The Missionary Movement in Christian History* (Maryknoll, NY: Orbis, 1996), speaks of the "fortunate subversion" of the church by such societies (241–54).

6. For a detailed analysis, see Paul William Harris, *Nothing but Christ: Rufus Anderson and the Ideology of Protestant Foreign Missions* (New York: Oxford University Press, 1999).

7. The best account is still Richard Lovett, *The History of the London Missionary Society, 1795–1895,* 2 vols. (London: Oxford University Press, 1899).

8. The best history is Elizabeth Isichei, *A History of Christianity in Africa from Antiquity to the Present* (London: SPCK, 1995).

9. For the importance of such hymns, see Donald E. Demarey, *The Innovation of John Newton (1725–1807): Synergism of Word and Music in Eighteenth-Century Evangelism* (Lewiston, NY: Edwin Mellen Press, 1988).

10. J. R. Oldfield, "The Protestant Episcopal Church, Black Nationalists, and Expansion of the West African Missionary Field, 1851–71," *Church History* 31 (1988): 31–45.

11. Line Nyhagen Predelli, "Sexual Control and the Remaking of Gender: The Attempt of Nineteenth-Century Protestant Norwegian Women to Export Western Domesticity to Madagascar," *Journal of Women's History* 12 (2000): 88–103.

12. The CPSA was sympathetic to the Oxford Movement, which was fundamentally a Catholic renewal movement within the Church of England that sought to deny, or at least downplay, the Protestant origins and character of that church.

13. Stephen Charles Neill, *A History of Christianity in India,* 2 vols. (Cambridge: Cambridge University Press, 1984–85).

14. Werner Raupp, *Mission in Quellentexten: Geschichte der Deutschen Evangelischen Mission von der Reformation bis zur Weltmissionskonferenz Edinburgh 1910* (Erlangen: Verlag der Evangelisch-Lutherischen Mission, 1990).

15. For an excellent account of the background, see D. Dennis Hudson, *Protestant Origins in India: Tamil Evangelical Christians, 1706–1835* (Grand Rapids, MI: Eerdmans, 2000).

16. John Kaye, *Kaye's and Malleson's History of the Indian Mutiny of 1857–1858* (London: Longman, Green & Co., 1889), 5: 279–95. "The mutiny of the army and

the insurrection in the provinces ... were the natural consequences of an attempt to govern a great Eastern empire according to purely Western ideas."

17. For a very critical assessment of these missionaries, see Eric Reinders, *Borrowed Gods and Foreign Bodies: Christian Missionaries Imagine Chinese Religion* (Berkeley: University of California Press, 2004).

18. Joseph Tse-Hei Lee, *The Bible and the Gun: Christianity in South China, 1860– 1900, East Asia: History, Politics, Sociology, Culture* (New York: Routledge, 2003).

19. Aasulv Lande, *Meiji Protestantism in History and Historiography: A Comparative Study of Japanese and Western Interpretation of Early Protestantism in Japan* (Frankfurt am Main: Peter Lang, 1989).

20. For discussion of this era, see Allan K. Davidson, "The Interaction of Missionary and Colonial Christianity in Nineteenth-Century New Zealand," *Studies in World Christianity* 2 (1996): 145–66.

21. For example, see Elizabeth M. Roach, "Transformation of Christian Ritual in the Pacific: Samoan White Sunday," *Missiology* 16 (1988): 173–82.

22. Karl-Wilhelm Westmeier, "Becoming All Things to All People: Early Moravian Mission to Native North Americans," *International Bulletin of Missionary Research* 21 (1997): 172–76.

23. Steven J. Crum, "Henry Roe Cloud, a Winnebago Indian Reformer: His Quest for American Indian Higher Education," *Kansas History* 11 (1988): 171–84.

24. Thomas P. Barr, "The Pottawatomie Baptist Manual Labor Training School," *Kansas Historical Quarterly* 43 (Winter 1977): 377–431.

25. Charles R. King, "Physician to Body and Soul: Jotham Meeker—Kansas Missionary," *Kansas History* 17 (Winter 1994–95): 262–73.

26. George A. Schultz, *An Indian Canaan: Isaac McCoy and the Vision of an Indian State* (Norman: University of Oklahoma Press, 1972).

27. Virginia P. Miller, "Silas T. Rand, Nineteenth-Century Anthropologist Among the Micmac," *Anthropologica* 22 (1980): 235–49.

28. G. S. Parsonson, "The Literate Revolution in Polynesia," *Journal of Pacific History* 2 (1967): 39–57.

29. William N. Fenton, "Toward the Gradual Civilization of the Indian Natives: The Missionary and Linguistic Work of Asher Wright (1803–75) Among the Senecas of Western New York," *American Philosophical Society Proceedings* 199 (1956): 567–81.

30. The best analysis of these factors is John D. Y. Peel, *Religious Encounter and the Making of the Yoruba* (Bloomington: Indiana University Press, 2000).

31. For example, see John L. Comaroff and Jean Comaroff, *Of Revelation and Revolution: Christianity, Colonialism, and Consciousness in South Africa* (Chicago: University of Chicago Press, 1991).

32. See Martin Pabst, *Mission und Kolonialpolitik: Die Norddeutsche Missonsgesellschaft an der Goldküste und in Togo bis zum Ausbruch des Ersten Weltkrieges* (Munich: Verlagsgemeinschaft Anarche, 1988); Werner Ustorf, *Die Missionsmethode Franz Michael Zahns und der Aufbau kirchlicher Strukturen in Westafrika: Eine missionsgeschichtliche Untersuchung* (Erlangen: Verlag der Evangelisch-Lutherischen Mission, 1989).

33. Elizabeth Elbourne, *Blood Ground: Colonialism, Missions, and the Contest for Christianity in the Cape Colony and Britain, 1799–1853* (Montreal: McGill-Queen's University Press, 2002).

34. See the evidence assembled in Andrew N. Porter, *Religion Versus Empire?: British Protestant Missionaries and Overseas Expansion, 1700–1914* (Manchester, UK: Manchester University Press, 2004).

35. Claude E. Stipe, "Anthropologists Versus Missionaries: The Influence of Presuppositions," *American Anthropologist* 35 (1980): 165–79.

36. Nigel Barley, *The Innocent Anthropologist: Notes from a Mud Hut* (London: Penguin Books, 1986), 28–29.

37. Andrew F. Walls, *The Cross-Cultural Process in Christian History: Studies in the Transmission and Appropriation of Faith* (Maryknoll, NY: Orbis Books, 2002).

38. See the material gathered in Brian Stanley, ed., *Christian Missions and the Enlightenment* (Grand Rapids, MI: Eerdmans, 2001).

39. See, for example, J. Stanley Friesen, *Missionary Responses to Tribal Religions at Edinburgh, 1910* (New York: Peter Lang, 1996).

40. See, for example, the ideas of Christian Keysser, including the critical notion of the *Volkskirch*—a community based on local social realities and open to the work of the Holy Spirit; see Timothy Yates, *Christian Mission in the Twentieth Century* (Cambridge: Cambridge University Press, 1994), 34–56.

41. Richard V. Pierard, "Shaking the Foundations: World War I, the Western Allies, and German Protestant Missions," *International Bulletin of Missionary Research* 22 (1998): 13–19.

CHAPTER 9: THE BIBLE AND PROTESTANTISM

1. Ulrich Luz, "Was heisst 'sola scriptura' heute? Ein Hilferuf für das protestantische Schriftprinzip," *Evangelische Theologie* 57 (1997): 28–35.

2. On Calvin's views on this matter, see H. Jackson Forstman, *Word and Spirit: Calvin's Doctrine of Biblical Authority* (Stanford, CA: Stanford University Press, 1962).

3. Calvin's analysis merits close consideration; see John D. Morrison, "John Calvin's Christological Assertion of Word Authority in the Context of Sixteenth-Century Ecclesiological Polemics," *Scottish Journal of Theology* 45 (1993): 465–86. For a related approach that stresses the "authority of God," see N. T. Wright, *Scripture and the Authority of God* (London: SPCK, 2005), 17–25.

4. Stephen Charles Neill, *Crises of Belief* (London: Hodder & Stoughton, 1984), 23.

5. Karl Barth, *Church Dogmatics,* 14 vols. (Edinburgh: T. & T. Clark, 1936–75), II/2:52–54.

6. Frederick Stopp, "'Verbum Domini Manet in Aeternum': The Dissemination of a Reformation Slogan, 1522–1904," in *Essays in German Language, Culture, and Society,* edited by Siegbert Salomon Prawer, R. Hinton Thomas, Leonard Wilson Forster, and Roy Pascal (London: University of London Institute of Germanic Studies, 1969), 123–35.

7. Their Catholic opponents wryly suggested that the words meant *Verbum Domini manet in Ärmeln*—"the word of the Lord stays on sleeves."

8. For a rich account of this idea, see John Webster, "Biblical Theology and the Clarity of Scripture," in *Out of Egypt: Biblical Theology and Biblical Interpreta-*

tion, edited by Craig Bartholomew (Carlisle, UK: Paternoster Press, 2004), 352–84. See also James P. Callahan, "*Claritas Scripturae:* The Role of Perspicuity in Protestant Hermeneutics," *Journal of the Evangelical Theological Society* 39 (1996): 353–72.

9. Beth Kreitzer, *Reforming Mary: Changing Images of the Virgin Mary in Lutheran Sermons of the Sixteenth Century* (Oxford: Oxford University Press, 2004). For Zwingli, see Emidio Campi, *Zwingli und Maria: Eine reformationsgeschichtliche Studie* (Zurich: TVZ Theologischer Verlag, 1997).

10. See especially Beverly R. Gaventa and Cynthia L. Rigby, eds., *Blessed One: Protestant Perspectives on Mary* (Louisville, KY: Westminster John Knox Press, 2002); Tim Perry, *Mary for Evangelicals: Towards an Understanding of the Mother of Our Lord* (Downers Grove, IL: InterVarsity Press, 2006).

11. H. D. McDonald, *Theories of Revelation: An Historical Study 1700–1960* (Grand Rapids, MI: Baker Book House, 1979); W. J. Abraham, *The Divine Inspiration of Holy Scripture* (Oxford: Oxford University Press, 1981).

12. K. R. Trembath, *Evangelical Theories of Biblical Inspiration* (Oxford: Oxford University Press, 1987).

13. A. C. Sundberg, "The Bible Canon and the Christian Doctrine of Inspiration," *Interpretation* 29 (1975): 352–71; Paul Achtemeier, *The Inspiration of Scripture: Problems and Proposals* (Philadelphia: Westminster, 1980).

14. For an excellent survey of the debates at the time, see Richard A. Muller and John L. Thompson, eds., *Biblical Interpretation in the Era of the Reformation: Essays Presented to David C. Steinmetz in Honor of His Sixtieth Birthday* (Grand Rapids, MI: Eerdmans, 1996).

15. For some of these issues, see Hans Heinrich Schmid and Joachim Mehlhausen, eds., *Sola scriptura: Das reformatorische Schriftprinzip in der säkularen Welt* (Gütersloh: Mohn, 1991); Hans-Ulrich Gehring, *Schriftprinzip und Rezeptionsästhetik: Rezeption in Martin Luthers Predigt und bei Hans Robert Jauss* (Neukirchen-Vluyn: Neukirchener, 1999).

16. Stuart Murray, *Biblical Interpretation in the Anabaptist Tradition* (Scottdale, PA: Herald Press, 2000).

17. Timothy George and David S. Dockery, eds., *Theologians of the Baptist Tradition* (Nashville, TN: Broadman & Holman, 2001).

18. See, for example, the excellent studies of Robert Friedmann, *The Theology of Anabaptism: An Interpretation* (Scottdale, PA: Herald Press, 1973); A. James Reimer, *Mennonites and Classical Theology: Dogmatic Foundations for Christian Ethics* (Kitchener, ON: Pandora, 2001).

19. For comment on this specific approach, see the classic study by H. R. McAdoo, *The Spirit of Anglicanism* (London: A. & C. Black, 1965).

20. Francis White, *A Treatise of the Sabbath Day* (London: Richard Badger, 1635), 11–12.

21. William Whitaker, *A Disputation on Holy Scripture* (Cambridge: Cambridge University Press, 1849), 411.

22. David C. Steinmetz, "Luther and Calvin on Church and Tradition," in *Luther in Context* (Bloomington: Indiana University Press, 1986), 85–97.

23. David W. Lotz, "*Sola Scriptura:* Luther on Biblical Authority," *Interpretation* 35 (1981): 258–73.

24. Luchesius Smits, *Saint Augustin dans l'oeuvre de Jean Calvin* (Assen: Van Gorcum, 1956).

25. See the important study of Joseph Ratzinger, "On the Interpretation of the Tridentine Decree on Tradition," in *Revelation and Tradition*, edited by Karl Rahner and Joseph Ratzinger (New York: Herder & Herder, 1966), 50–68.

26. See Irena Backus, *Historical Method and Confessional Identity in the Era of the Reformation (1378–1615)* (Leiden: Brill, 2003). See also the classic study by Peter Fraenkel, *Testimonia Patrum: The Function of the Patristic Argument in the Theology of Philip Melanchthon* (Geneva: Droz, 1961).

27. Anne Hudson, *The Premature Reformation: Wycliffite Texts and Lollard History* (Oxford: Clarendon Press, 1988).

28. See *Neues Testament und Psalter in der Sprache Martin Luthers für Leser von Heute* (Hamburg: Friedrich Wittig, 1982).

29. The best study remains David Daniell, *Wiliam Tyndale* (New Haven, CT: Yale University Press, 1994).

30. See the superb account of this process in Cameron A. MacKenzie, *The Battle for the Bible in England, 1557–1582* (New York: Peter Lang, 2002).

31. This is the thesis of David S. Katz, *God's Last Words: Reading the English Bible from the Reformation to Fundamentalism* (New Haven, CT: Yale University Press, 2004), x–xi.

32. For an introduction to this somewhat ill-tempered debate, see D. A. Carson, *The King James Version Debate: A Plea for Realism* (Grand Rapids, MI: Baker Book House, 1979).

33. For the issues, see Peter J. Thuesen, *In Discordance with the Scriptures: American Protestant Battles over Translating the Bible* (New York: Oxford University Press, 1999).

34. For specific issues, see Joseph A. Burgess, "Lutheran Interpretation of Scripture," in *The Bible in the Churches: How Various Christians Interpret the Scriptures*, edited by Kenneth Hagen (Milwaukee: Marquette University Press, 1998), 101–28; Marion L. Soards, "Reformed Interpretation of Scripture," in ibid., 159–74.

35. For some aspects of this debate, see J. J. G. Jansen, *The Interpretation of the Koran in Modern Egypt* (Leiden: Brill, 1980), 60–69.

36. See the material in Albert Hourani, *Arabic Thought in the Liberal Age (1798–1939)* (Cambridge: Cambridge University Press, 1988).

37. Similar debates have, of course, taken place within Judaism; see David W. Halivni, "Plain Sense and Applied Meaning in Rabbinic Exegesis," in *The Return to Scripture in Judaism and Christianity: Essays in Postcritical Scriptural Interpretation*, edited by Peter Ochs (New York: Paulist Press, 1993), 107–41.

38. Donald W. Dayton, "The Battle for the Bible: Renewing the Inerrancy Debate," *Christian Century* (1976): 976–80.

39. J. I. Packer, *"Fundamentalism" and the Word of God* (London: InterVarsity Press, 1959), 101–14. For an alternative view, see Kathryn E. Tanner, "Theology and the Plain Sense," in *Scriptural Authority and Narrative Interpretation: Essays on the Occasion of the Sixty-fifth Birthday of Hans Frei*, edited by Garrett Green (Philadelphia: Fortress Press, 1987), 59–78.

40. David F. Wright, "Accommodation and Barbarity in John Calvin's Old Testament Commentaries," in *Understanding Poets and Prophets*, edited by A. Graeme

Auld (Sheffield, UK: JSOT Press, 1993), 413–27. More generally, see Stephen D. Benin, *The Footprints of God: Divine Accommodation in Jewish and Christian Thought* (Albany: State University of New York Press, 1993).

41. Kevin J. Vanhoozer, "The Reader in New Testament Interpretation," in *Hearing the New Testament: Strategies for Interpretation,* edited by Joel B. Green (Grand Rapids, MI: Eerdmans, 1995), 301–28.

42. For different perspectives on this debate, see the material gathered in Eugene F. Rogers, *Theology and Sexuality: Classic and Contemporary Readings—Blackwell Readings in Modern Theology* (Oxford: Blackwell, 2002).

43. Marcel Simon, "From Greek *Hairesis* to Christian Heresy," in *Early Christian Literature and the Classical Intellectual Tradition,* edited by William R. Schoedel and Robert L. Wilken (Paris: Beauchesne, 1979), 101–16.

44. H. E. W. Turner, *The Pattern of Christian Truth: A Study in the Relations Between Orthodoxy and Heresy in the Early Church* (London: Mowbray, 1954), 81–94.

45. For magisterial surveys of this development, see Robert M. Grant, *Heresy and Criticism: The Search for Authenticity in Early Christian Literature* (Louisville, KY: Westminster/John Knox Press, 1993); Arland J. Hultgren, *The Rise of Normative Christianity* (Minneapolis: Fortress Press, 1994).

46. The best study of this movement is Rowan Williams, *Arius: Heresy and Tradition,* 2nd ed. (London: SCM Press, 2001).

47. See the important study by T. E. Pollard, *Johannine Christology and the Early Church* (Cambridge: Cambridge University Press, 1970).

48. See the impressive list of *novateurs* provided by Gabriel Naudé, *Apologie pour tous les grands personages qui sont faussement soupçonnez de magie* (Paris, 1625).

49. Hence the title of the work by Carlo Ginzburg, *The Cheese and the Worms: The Cosmos of a Sixteenth-Century Miller* (Baltimore: Johns Hopkins University Press, 2003), which explores the intellectual world of this era.

50. For Melanchthon's important statement of this position, see the classic study by Peter Fraenkel, *Testimonia Patrum.* This analysis has been extended in Backus, *Historical Method and Confessional Identity.*

51. For details, see Massimo Firpo, "The Italian Reformation and Juan de Valdés," *Sixteenth Century Journal* 27 (1996): 353–64.

52. Other controversies of relevance here include the dispute between the Arminians and the Gomarists; see Jonathan Israel, *The Dutch Republic: Its Rise, Greatness, and Fall, 1477–1806* (Oxford: Oxford University Press, 1996), 411–63.

53. See Maurice Wiles, *Archetypal Heresy: Arianism Through the Centuries* (Oxford: Clarendon Press, 1996).

54. Oscar Kenshur, "Scriptural Deism and the Politics of Dryden's *Religio Laici,*" *English Literary History* 54 (1987): 869–92.

55. See especially Benjamin Beit-Hallahmi and Michael Argyle, *Acquiring Religious Beliefs: Socialization and Continuity* (London: Routledge, 1997), 97–113.

56. *Epitome,* 1–8, in *Die Bekenntisschriften der evangelisch-lutherischen Kirche,* 2nd ed. (Göttingen: Vandenhoeck & Ruprecht, 1952), 767–69.

57. See, for example, Henry Pickering, *Chief Men Among the Brethren* (Neptune, NJ: Loizeaux, 1918).

58. See the useful material in Thomas F. Torrance, *The School of Faith: The Catechisms of the Reformed Church* (London: James Clarke, 1959).

59. For what follows, see Alan P. F. Sell, *A Reformed, Evangelical, Catholic Theology: The Contribution of the World Alliance of Reformed Churches, 1875–1982* (Grand Rapids, MI: Eerdmans, 1991), 73–78.

60. W. J. Sparrow-Simpson, *Assent to the Articles: A Short History of Subscription to the XXXIX Articles of the Church of England* (London: SPCK, 1925).

61. Clive L. Rawlins, *William Barclay: The Authorized Biography* (Grand Rapids, MI: Eerdmans, 1984).

62. The key work is Antonio Gramsci, *Gli intellettuali e l'organizzazione della cultura*, 6th ed. (Milan: Giulio Einaudi Editore, 1955). For an introduction, see David Harris, *From Class Struggle to the Politics of Pleasure: The Effects of Gramscianism on Cultural Studies* (London: Routledge, 1992).

63. Max Weber, "The Sociology of Charismatic Authority," in *From Max Weber: Essays in Sociology*, edited by H. H. Gerth and C. Wright Mills (London: Oxford University Press, 1946), 246–52. For a critical assessment of this famous axiom, see Rongfen Wang, "Cäsarismus und Machtpolitik: Eine historisch-biobibliographische Analyse von Max Webers Charismakonzept," *Kölner Zeitschrift für Soziologie und Sozialpsychologie* 55 (2003): 136–51.

64. For the issues in biblical interpretation, see Gale A. Yee, "The Author/Text/Reader and Power: Suggestions for a Critical Framework for Biblical Studies," in *Reading from This Place*, vol. 1, *Social Location and Biblical Interpretation in the United States*, edited by Fernando F. Segovia and Mary Ann Tolbert (Minneapolis: Fortress Press, 1995), 109–18.

65. Sinclair Lewis, *Elmer Gantry* (New York: Dell, 1954).

66. Karl Barth, "Theology," in *God in Action* (Edinburgh: T. & T. Clark, 1936), 39–57.

CHAPTER 10: BELIEVING AND BELONGING: SOME DISTINCTIVE PROTESTANT BELIEFS

1. For a comprehensive introduction to the basic themes of Christian theology, including a comparison of Protestant, Catholic, and Orthodox positions, see Alister E. McGrath, *Christian Theology: An Introduction*, 4th ed. (Oxford: Blackwell, 2007).

2. For some representative works, see Heinz Zahrnt, *The Question of God: Protestant Theology in the Twentieth Century* (New York: Harcourt Brace & World, 1969); William A. Scott, *Historical Protestantism: An Historical Introduction to Protestant Theology* (Englewood Cliffs, NJ: Prentice-Hall, 1970); John B. Cobb, *Living Options in Protestant Theology: A Survey of Methods* (Lanham, MD: University Press of America, 1986).

3. On this argument, see Dennis R. Creswell, *St. Augustine's Dilemma: Grace and Eternal Law in the Major Works of Augustine of Hippo—Studies in Church History*, vol. 5 (New York: Peter Lang, 1997); Basil Studer, *The Grace of Christ and the Grace of God in Augustine of Hippo: Christocentrism or Theocentrism?* (Collegeville, MN: Liturgical Press, 1997).

4. For the development of this doctrine, with particular reference to the controversies of the sixteenth century, see Alister E. McGrath, Iustitia Dei: *A History of the Christian Doctrine of Justification*, 3rd ed. (Cambridge: Cambridge University Press, 2005).

5. See the classic study by Ernst Wolf, "Die Rechtfertigungslehre als Mitte und Grenze reformatorischer Theologie," *Evangelische Theologie* 9 (1949): 298–308.

6. Friedhelm Krüger, *Bucer und Erasmus: Eine Untersuchung zum Einfluss des Erasmus auf die Theologie Martin Bucers (bis zum Evangelien-Kommentar von 1530)* (Wiesbaden: Steiner, 1970).

7. Alvin J. Beachy, *The Concept of Grace in the Radical Reformation* (Nieuwkoop: de Graaf, 1977).

8. Arnold Angenendt, *Heilige und Reliquien: Die Geschichte ihres Kultes vom frühen Christentum bis zur Gegenwart* (Munich: Beck, 1994). For a specific example of the phenomenon, see Thomas Head, *Hagiography and the Cult of Saints: The Diocese of Orléans, 800–1200* (Cambridge: Cambridge University Press, 1990).

9. See the important material assembled in Robert W. Scriber, *Popular Culture and Popular Movements in Reformation Germany* (London: Hambledon, 1987), 301–54.

10. For documentation and comment, see McGrath, Iustitia Dei, 406–20.

11. For the debate, which continues to this day, see Stephen Westerholm, *Perspectives Old and New on Paul: The "Lutheran" Paul and His Critics* (Grand Rapids, MI: Eerdmans, 2004).

12. McGrath, Iustitia Dei, 406–20.

13. See the material in William J. Connell, ed., *Society and Individual in Renaissance Florence* (Berkeley: University of California Press, 2002).

14. Calvin, *Institutes of the Christian Religion*, IV.i.9.

15. Laurence R. Iannaccone and Rodney Stark, "A Supply-Side Reinterpretation of the 'Secularization' of Europe," *Journal for the Scientific Study of Religion* 33 (1994): 230–52.

16. Steve Bruce, "The Truth About Religion in Britain," *Journal for the Scientific Study of Religion* 34 (1995): 417–30. Bruce is critical of the approach adopted by Iannaccone and Stark.

17. W. H. C. Frend, *The Donatist Church: A Movement of Protest in Roman North Africa* (London: Oxford University Press, 1952).

18. On this idea, see Maureen A. Tilley, "Sustaining Donatist Self-Identity: From the Church of the Martyrs to the Collecta of the Desert," *Journal of Early Christian Studies* 5 (1997): 21–35.

19. Paul Chang-La Lim, *In Pursuit of Purity, Unity, and Liberty: Richard Baxter's Puritan Ecclesiology in Its Seventeenth-Century Context* (Leiden: Brill, 2004), 156–90.

20. For what follows, see Louis Bouyer, *The Word, Church, and Sacraments in Protestantism and Catholicism* (London: Chapman, 1961); Gary Macy, *The Theologies of the Eucharist in the Early Scholastic Period* (Oxford: Clarendon Press, 1984); Brian A. Gerrish, *Grace and Gratitude: The Eucharistic Theology of John Calvin* (Philadelphia: Fortress Press, 1993); James F. White, *The Sacraments in Protestant Practice and Faith* (Nashville, TN: Abingdon Press, 1999).

21. Hermann Sasse, *This Is My Body: Luther's Contention for the Real Presence in the Sacrament of the Altar* (Minneapolis: Augsburg Press, 1959).

22. Charles Taylor, *Modern Social Imaginaries* (Durham, NC: Duke University Press, 2004).

23. Robert Whalen, "George Herbert's Sacramental Puritanism," *Renaissance Quarterly* 54 (2001): 1273–1307.

24. For some of these issues, see Marcel Gauchet, *The Disenchantment of the World: A Political History of Religion* (Princeton, NJ: Princeton University Press, 1997).

25. For the debates, see Dewey D. Wallace, *Puritans and Predestination: Grace in English Protestant Theology, 1525–1695* (Chapel Hill: University of North Carolina Press, 1982); Richard A. Muller, *Christ and the Decree: Christology and Predestination in Reformed Theology from Calvin to Perkins* (Grand Rapids, MI: Baker Book House, 1988).

26. For the point, see Alister E. McGrath, *The Genesis of Doctrine* (Oxford: Blackwell, 1990).

27. The best account is Robert Kolb, *Bound Choice, Election, and Wittenberg Theological Method: From Martin Luther to the Formula of Concord* (Grand Rapids, MI: Eerdmans, 2005).

28. See Adolar Zumkeller, "Hugolin von Orvieto über Prädestination, Rechtfertigung, und Verdienst," *Augustiniana* 4 (1954): 109–56; 5 (1955): 5–51.

29. Lutheran Church (Missouri Synod), "Brief Statement," articles 33–35 (on the election of grace). I have taken the liberty of restating this excerpt using inclusive language.

30. The best study of the origins and emergence of these ideas remains A. W. Harrison, *The Beginnings of Arminianism to the Synod of Dort* (London: University of London Press, 1926).

31. Herbert B. McGonigle, *Sufficient Saving Grace: John Wesley's Evangelical Arminianism* (Carlisle, UK: Paternoster Press, 2001).

32. *C. H. Spurgeon's Autobiography: Compiled from His Diary, Letters, and Records,* edited by Susannah Spurgeon and W. J. Harrald, 4 vols. (London: Passmore and Alabaster, 1900), 1:173. Spurgeon's later comments may be noted: "Although upon doctrines of grace our views differ from those avowed by Arminian Methodists, we have usually found that on the great evangelical truths we are in full agreement, and we have been comforted by the belief that Wesleyans were solid upon the central doctrines" (*The Sword and the Trowel*, May 1891).

33. For a discussion, see Alister E. McGrath, *A Brief History of Heaven* (Oxford: Blackwell, 2002).

34. E. Beatrice Batson, *John Bunyan: Allegory and Imagination* (Totowa, NJ: Barnes & Noble, 1984).

35. Barton Levi St. Armaud, "Paradise Deferred: The Image of Heaven in the Work of Emily Dickinson and Elizabeth Stuart Phelps," *American Quarterly* 29 (1977): 55–78.

36. James Martin, *The Last Judgment in Protestant Theology* (Edinburgh: Oliver & Boyd, 1963).

37. See Tony Gray, "Destroyed For Ever: An Examination of the Debates Concerning Annihilation and Conditional Immortality," *Themelios* 21 (1996): 14–18.

38. See the discussion in Jeffrey Burton Russell, *Paradise Mislaid: How We Lost Heaven—And How We Can Regain It* (Oxford: Oxford University Press, 2006).

39. Richard Landes, "On Owls, Roosters, and Apocalyptic Time: A Historical Method for Reading a Refractory Documentation," *Union Seminary Quarterly Review* 49 (1996): 165–85.

40. For the history of the interpretation of this biblical work, see Kenneth G. C. Newport, *Apocalypse and Millennium: Studies in Biblical Eisegesis* (Cambridge: Cambridge University Press, 2000).

CHAPTER 11: THE STRUCTURES OF FAITH: ORGANIZATION, WORSHIP, AND PREACHING

1. "Nothing is possible without people; nothing lasts without institutions." For illustration and analysis of this point with reference to the creation of modern Europe, see François Roth, *L'Invention de la Europe: De l'Europe de Jean Monnet à l'Union européenne* (Paris: Armand Colin, 2005).
2. For an excellent study of one aspect of this development, see Nicholas Thompson, *Eucharistic Sacrifice and Patristic Tradition in the Theology of Martin Bucer, 1534–1546* (Leiden: Brill, 2005).
3. For the difficulties this caused many Catholics, such as Reginald Pole, see Dermot Fenlon, *Heresy and Obedience in Tridentine Italy: Cardinal Pole and the Counter-Reformation* (Cambridge: Cambridge University Press, 1972).
4. In recent times, this church has preferred to be known as the Episcopal Church in the United States of America (ECUSA), or, more simply, The Episcopal Church (TEC).
5. Jaroslav J. Pelikan, *Spirit Versus Structure: Luther and the Institutions of the Church* (London: Collins, 1968).
6. For comment, see Steven D. Paulson, "Lutherans on Episcopacy and Apostolicity," *Lutheran Quarterly* 18 (2004): 232–48.
7. For the background, see Karin Maag, "Called to Be a Pastor: Issues of Vocation in the Early Modern Period," *Sixteenth Century Journal* 35 (2004): 65–78.
8. R. E. H. Uprichard, "The Eldership in Martin Bucer and John Calvin," *Irish Biblical Studies* 18 (1996): 136–55.
9. Robert M. Kingdon, "Calvin's Idea About the Diaconate: Social or Theological in Origin?," in *Piety, Politics, and Ethics: Reformation Studies in Honor of George Wolfgang Forell,* edited by Carter Lindberg (Kirksville, MO: *Sixteenth Century Journal,* 1984), 167–80.
10. See the classic study of R. W. Dale and Sir A. W. W. Dale, eds., *History of English Congregationalism,* 2nd ed. (London: Hodder & Stoughton, 1907).
11. For example, Baptists in the northern states split from what became the Southern Baptist Convention in 1845 over the slavery issue. In 1907 they grouped together as the Northern Baptist Convention. Since 1972 the group has been known as the American Baptist Churches USA.
12. William Wright Barnes, *The Southern Baptist Convention, 1845–1953* (Nashville, TN: Broadman Press, 1954).
13. Irenaeus of Lyons, *Adversus haereses,* III.xxiv.1.
14. The official histories of this assembly are rather dull and triumphalistic. For a much more interesting and racy account, see *God's Apprentice: The Autobiography of Stephen Neill,* edited by E. M. Jackson (London: Hodder & Stoughton, 1991), 205–39.
15. Some mergers did take place at the regional level; for example, the Uniting Church in Australia was formed in 1977 from the Congregational Union of

Australia, the Methodist Church of Australasia, and the Presbyterian Church of Australia.

16. For an excellent analysis, see Mark A. Noll and Carolyn Nystrom, *Is the Reformation Over? An Evangelical Assessment of Contemporary Roman Catholicism* (Grand Rapids, MI: Baker Books, 2005).

17. It is often forgotten that Luther was prepared to allow the liturgy to be in Latin provided that the sermon was preached in the vernacular.

18. A very readable account of the controversy may be found in W. Stanford Reid, *Trumpeter of God: A Biography of John Knox* (Grand Rapids, MI: Baker, 1982), 105–29.

19. Philippe Denis, "La Prophétie dans les églises de la réforme au XVIe siècle," *Revue d'Histoire Ecclésiastique* 72 (1977): 289–316; Peter Iver Kaufman, "Prophesying Again," *Church History* 68 (1999): 337–58.

20. Carolyn Muessig, *Medieval Monastic Preaching* (Leiden: Brill, 1998).

21. Susan Wabuda, *Preaching During the English Reformation* (Cambridge: Cambridge University Press, 2002), 7–8.

22. Corrie E. Norman, *Humanist Taste and Franciscan Values: Cornelio Musso and Catholic Preaching in Sixteenth-Century Italy* (New York: P. Lang, 1998).

23. Hans Stickelberger, "Bullingers bekanntester Satz und seine Interpretation bei Karl Barth," in *Von Cyprian zur Walzenprägung: Streiflichter auf Zürcher Geist und Kultur der Bullingerzeit*, edited by Hans Ulrich Bächtold (Zug: Achius, 2001), 105–14.

24. Andrew Spicer, "Architecture," in *The Reformation World* by Andrew Pettegree (London: Routledge, 2000), 505–20, esp. 509.

25. The best study remains Paul S. Seaver, *The Puritan Lectureships: The Politics of Religious Dissent, 1560–1662* (Stanford, CA: Stanford University Press, 1970).

26. Robert of Basevorn, "The Form of Preaching," in *Three Medieval Rhetorical Arts*, edited by James J. Murphy (Berkeley: University of California Press, 1971), 111–215.

27. For Perkins's understanding of the role of preaching in the effecting of salvation, see Richard A. Muller, "Perkins's *A Golden Chaine:* Predestinarian System or Schematized *Ordo Salutis*?" *Sixteenth Century Journal* 9 (1978): 69–81.

28. Robert H. Ellison, *The Victorian Pulpit: Spoken and Written Sermons in Nineteenth-Century Britain* (Selinsgrove, PA: Susquehanna University Press, 1998).

29. Helga Robinson-Hammerstein, *The Transmission of Ideas in the Lutheran Reformation* (Blackrock, Ireland: Irish Academic Press, 1989), 141–72.

30. The general importance of the use of music in relation to sustaining contemporary worldviews is brought out clearly by Richard Freedman, "Listening and Ideology in Reformation and Counter-Reformation: The Lassus Chansons and Their Protestant Listeners of the Late Sixteenth Century," *Musical Quarterly* 82 (1998): 564–85.

31. In German, "Ein feste Burg ist unser Gott." The motif is incorporated into some of the cantatas of Johann Sebastian Bach.

32. For the remarkable influence of the Psalms on English literature at this time, see Hannibal Hamlin, *Psalm Culture and Early Modern English Literature* (Cambridge: Cambridge University Press, 2004).

33. For useful material, see John Morehen, ed., *English Choral Practice, c. 1400–c. 1650* (Cambridge: Cambridge University Press, 1995).

34. Suzanne Lord and David Brinkman, *Music from the Age of Shakespeare: A Cultural History* (Westport, CT: Greenwood Press, 2003), 73–92. Mention should also be made of the Anglican "anthem," which was introduced around this time. This choral piece was generally based on a scriptural text or paraphrase and sung after the collects in the liturgy of matins and evensong. Thomas Tallis (c. 1505–85) composed about twenty anthems.

35. John Endres and Elizabeth Liebert, *A Retreat with the Psalms: Resources for Personal and Communal Prayer* (New York: Paulist Press, 2001). A similar development took place within Roman Catholicism during the 1950s—four centuries later—when the French Jesuit Joseph Gelineau developed a method of paraphrasing the Psalms that preserved the rhythmic structure of Hebrew poetry. In this style—often called "sprung rhythm"—the rhythm of the singing moves on the stressed syllables of the text.

36. Although widely referred to as the *Geneva Psalter*, the original title of the work was *La Forme des prieres et chantz ecclésiastiques.*

37. The work is often referred to as "Sternhold and Hopkins," owing to the preponderance of their translations.

38. Erik Routley, *The Music of Christian Hymnody: A Study of the Development of the Hymn Tune Since the Reformation, with Special Reference to English Protestantism* (London: Independent Press, 1957).

39. Paul S. Minear, "Bach and Today's Theologians," *Theology Today* 42 (1985): 201–10.

40. For an excellent reflective account, see Richard J. Mouw and Mark A. Noll, *Wonderful Words of Life: Hymns in American Protestant History and Theology* (Grand Rapids, MI: Eerdmans, 2004). See also Edith W. Blumhofer and Mark A. Noll, *Singing the Lord's Song in a Strange Land: Hymnody in the History of North American Protestantism* (Tuscaloosa: University of Alabama Press, 2004).

41. Jon Michael Spencer, *Black Hymnody: A Hymnological History of the African-American Church* (Knoxville: University of Tennessee Press, 1992).

42. Tamar Frankiel, *Gospel Hymns and Social Religion: The Rhetoric of Nineteenth-Century Revivalism* (Philadelphia: Temple University Press, 1978).

43. Jeremy Begbie, "The Spirituality of Renewal Music," *Anvil* 8 (1991): 227–39.

44. The general issue is considered in Jeremy Begbie, *Theology, Music, and Time* (Cambridge: Cambridge University Press, 2000), 128–54.

45. For some important studies, see Sergiusz Michalski, *The Reformation and the Visual Arts: The Protestant Image Question in Western and Eastern Europe* (London: Routledge, 1993); Joseph Leo Koerner, *The Reformation of the Image* (London: Reaktion Books, 2004).

46. Lee Palmer Wandel, *Voracious Idols and Violent Hands: Iconoclasm in Reformation Zurich, Strasbourg, and Basel* (Cambridge: Cambridge University Press, 1995).

47. For some of the broader issues, see Christopher Collins, *Reading the Written Image: Verbal Play, Interpretation, and the Roots of Iconophobia* (University Park: Pennsylvania State University Press, 1991).

48. For a modern Reformed approach reflecting this position, see Jacques Ellul, *The Humiliation of the Word* (Grand Rapids, MI: Eerdmans, 1985).

49. Robert W. Scribner, *For the Sake of Simple Folk: Popular Propaganda for the German Reformation* (Cambridge: Cambridge University Press, 1981), 216–17.

50. William A. Dyrness, *Reformed Theology and Visual Culture: The Protestant Imagination from Calvin to Edwards* (Cambridge: Cambridge University Press, 2004), 142–239.

51. D. Z. Phillips, *R. S. Thomas: Poet of the Hidden God—Meaning and Mediation in the Poetry of R. S. Thomas* (Allison Park, PA: Pickwick Publications, 1986).

52. See the useful introduction to the Baroque style by Timon H. Fokker, *Roman Baroque Art: The History of a Style* (New York: Hacker, 1972). For some more specific comments, see Charles Dempsey, *Annibale Carracci and the Beginnings of Baroque Style,* 2nd ed. (Fiesole: Cadmo, 2000).

CHAPTER 12: PROTESTANTISM AND THE SHAPING OF WESTERN CULTURE

1. For the intellectual issues, see Jaroslav Pelikan, *Christianity and Classical Culture: The Metamorphosis of Natural Theology in the Christian Encounter with Hellenism* (New Haven, CT: Yale University Press, 1993).

2. For a range of definitions, including these, see Clyde Kluckhohn, *Mirror for Man: The Relation of Anthropology to Modern Life* (Tucson: University of Arizona Press, 1985). One of the best recent accounts is to be found in Margaret Archer, *Culture and Agency: The Place of Culture in Social Theory* (Cambridge: Cambridge University Press, 1996).

3. T. S. Eliot, *Notes Towards a Definition of Culture* (London: Faber & Faber, 1948), 27.

4. H. Richard Niebuhr, *Christ and Culture* (New York: Harper, 1951).

5. Steven M. Nolt, *A History of the Amish* (Intercourse, PA: Good Books, 1992).

6. For important surveys, see William R. Hutchison, *The Modernist Impulse in American Protestantism* (Cambridge, MA: Harvard University Press, 1976); Mark D. Chapman, *Ernst Troeltsch and Liberal Theology: Religion and Cultural Synthesis in Wilhelmine, Germany* (Oxford: Oxford University Press, 2001).

7. For an analysis, see John P. Clayton, *The Concept of Correlation: Paul Tillich and the Possibility of a Mediating Theology* (Berlin: Walter de Gruyter, 1980).

8. Paul Tillich, "The Church and Contemporary Culture," *World Christian Education* (1956): 41–43.

9. On this doctrine, see Per Frostin, *Luther's Two Kingdoms Doctrine: A Critical Study* (Lund: Lund University Press, 1994).

10. Heinz Horst Schrey, ed., *Reich Gottes und Welt: Die Lehre Luthers von den Zwei Reichen* (Darmstadt: Wissenschaftliche Buchgesellschaft, 1969).

11. For a biography, see Geoffrey Wainwright, *Lesslie Newbigin: A Theological Life* (Oxford: Oxford University Press, 2000).

12. Lesslie Newbigin, *The Household of God: Lectures on the Nature of the Church* (London: SCM Press, 1953).

13. R. H. Bainton, *The Medieval Church* (Princeton, NJ: Princeton University Press, 1962), 42.

14. Gerald Biesecker-Mast, *Separation and the Sword in Anabaptist Persuasion: Radical Confessional Rhetoric from Schleitheim to Dordrecht* (Telford, PA: Cascadia, 2006). This aspect of Anabaptist identity is emphasized by Harold S. Bender, *The Anabaptist Vision* (Scottdale, PA: Herald Press, 1944).

15. Other examples are easily given; see Frank D. Macchia, *Spirituality and Social Liberation: The Message of the Blumhardts in the Light of Wuerttemberg Pietism* (London: Scarecrow Press, 1993).

16. Representative works include John Howard Yoder, *The Priestly Kingdom* (Notre Dame, IN: University of Notre Dame Press, 1988); Stanley Hauerwas, *The Peaceable Kingdom: A Primer in Christian Ethics* (Notre Dame, IN: University of Notre Dame Press, 1983).

17. See, for example, J. Denny Weaver, *The Nonviolent Atonement* (Grand Rapids, MI: Eerdmans, 2001).

18. Carl F. H. Henry, *The Uneasy Conscience of Modern Fundamentalism* (Grand Rapids, MI: Eerdmans, 1947).

19. Millard J. Erickson, *The New Evangelical Theology* (Westwood, NJ: Revell, 1968), 22–30.

20. William Martin, *With God on Our Side: The Rise of the Religious Right in America* (New York: Broadway Books, 1996).

21. Ralph C. Hancock, *Calvin and the Foundations of Modern Politics* (Ithaca, NY: Cornell University Press, 1989). Note especially his astute comment: "Calvin radically distinguishes politics and religion in order to unify them in worldly activity" (163).

22. John Calvin, *The Geneva Catechism* (1545), q. 107.

23. For the interpretation of this text, especially in nineteenth-century America, see Stephen R. Haynes, *Noah's Curse: The Biblical Justification of American Slavery* (Oxford: Oxford University Press, 2004).

24. Eric Metaxas, *Amazing Grace: William Wilberforce and the Heroic Campaign to End Slavery* (San Francisco: HarperSanFrancisco, 2007).

25. Willard M. Swartley, *Slavery, Sabbath, War, and Women: Case Issues in Biblical Interpretation* (Scottdale, PA: Herald Press, 1983).

26. For an excellent study of the problem, see Kevin W. Giles, "The Biblical Argument for Slavery: Can the Bible Mislead? A Case Study in Hermeneutics," *Evangelical Quarterly* 66 (1994): 3–17.

27. For a popular account of this movement, see Bruce Barron, *The Health and Wealth Gospel: What's Going on Today in a Movement That Has Shaped the Faith of Millions?* (Downers Grove, IL: Intervarsity Press, 1987).

28. Frederick Coutts, *Bread for My Neighbor: An Appreciation of the Social Action and Influence of William Booth* (London: Hodder & Stoughton, 1978).

29. The best study of this social activism is Diane H. Winston, *Red-hot and Righteous: The Urban Religion of the Salvation Army* (Cambridge, MA: Harvard University Press, 1999).

30. For a useful study, see John P. McDowell, *The Social Gospel in the South: The Woman's Home Mission Movement in the Methodist Episcopal Church, South, 1886–1939* (Baton Rouge: Louisiana State University Press, 1982).

31. Gary Scott Smith, "To Reconstruct the World: Walter Rauschenbusch and Social Change," *Fides et Historia* 23 (1991): 40–63.

32. See the analysis in Donald E. Miller, *Global Pentecostalism: The New Face of Christian Social Engagement* (Berkeley: University of California Press, 2007).

33. See the analysis in Alister E. McGrath, *The Twilight of Atheism: The Rise and Fall of Unbelief in the West* (New York: Doubleday, 2003).

34. For details, see Robert P. Ericksen, *Theologians Under Hitler: Gerhard Kittel, Paul Althaus, and Emanuel Hirsch* (New Haven, CT: Yale University Press, 1985).

35. Frank J. Sorauf, *The Wall of Separation: The Constitutional Politics of Church and State* (Princeton, NJ: Princeton University Press, 1976).

36. A full examination of the thesis lies beyond this work. The following critical studies should be consulted: Hartmann Tyrell, "Worum geht es in der 'Protestantischen Ethik'?," *Saeculum* 41 (1990): 130–77; Friedhelm Guttandin, *Einführung in die "Protestantische Ethik" Max Webers* (Opladen: Westdeutscher Verlag, 1998).

37. Weber regarded Lutheranism as anemic and paid little attention to the Radical Reformation. Much attention has been paid recently to the socioeconomic thought of Anabaptism and its theological foundations; see Thomas Heilke, "Locating a Moral-Political Economy: Lessons from Sixteenth-Century Anabaptism," *Polity* 30 (1997): 199–229.

38. Michael H. Lessnoff, *The Spirit of Capitalism and the Protestant Ethic: An Inquiry into the Weber Thesis* (Aldershot, UK: Elgar, 1994).

39. Günther Roth and Hartmut Lehmann, *Weber's "Protestant Ethic": Origins, Evidence, Contexts* (Cambridge: Cambridge University Press, 1993).

40. The classic study is John T. Noonan, *The Scholastic Analysis of Usury* (Cambridge, MA: Harvard University Press, 1957). For a more recent analysis, see Odd Langholm, *Economics in the Medieval Schools: Wealth, Exchange, Value, Money, and Usury According to the Paris Theological Tradition, 1200–1350* (Leiden: Brill, 1992). For Noonan's reflections on subsequent developments, see John T. Noonan, "Development in Moral Doctrine," *Theological Studies* 54 (1993): 662–78.

41. See texts such as Leviticus 25:35–37, Deuteronomy 23:19–20, Psalm 15:5, and Ezekiel 18:13. For comment, see Cyril S. Rodd, *Glimpses of a Strange Land: Studies in Old Testament Ethics* (Edinburgh: T. & T. Clark, 2001), 142–57.

42. Ambrose primarily based his argument on the prohibitions of usury in the Old Testament, as at Exodus 22:25 and Leviticus 25:36.

43. See Diana Wood, *Medieval Economic Thought* (Cambridge: Cambridge University Press, 2002). For theological reflection, see Joan Lockwood O'Donovan, "The Theological Economics of Medieval Usury Theory," *Studies in Christian Ethics* 14 (2001): 48–64.

44. For English attitudes, see Norman L. Jones, *God and the Moneylenders: Usury and the Law in Early Modern England* (Oxford: Blackwell, 1989).

45. The best study remains André Biéler, *La Pensée économique et sociale de Calvin* (Geneva: Librairie de l'Université, 1959), 453–76.

46. Ibid., 455.

47. P. E. Martin, "Calvin et le prêt à intérêt à Genève," in *Mélanges d'histoire économique et sociale, en hommage au professeur Antony Babel* (Geneva: Imprimerie de la Tribune de Genève, 1963), 251–63.

48. Martin H. Körner, *Solidarités financières suisses au XVIe siècle: Contribution à l'histoire monétaire, bancaire, et financière des cantons suisses et des états voisins* (Lausanne: Payot, 1980).

49. Alfred Bürgin, *Kapitalismus und Calvinismus: Versuch einer wirtschaftsgeschichtlichen und religionssoziologischen Untersuchung der Verhältnisse in Genf im 16. und beginnenden 17. Jahrhundert* (Winterthur: Keller, 1960), 108–22.

50. See, for example, Gordon Marshall, *Presbyteries and Profits: Calvinism and the Development of Capitalism in Scotland, 1560–1707* (Oxford: Clarendon Press, 1980). More generally, see Richard Grassby, *The Business Community of Seventeenth-Century England* (Cambridge: Cambridge University Press, 1995).

51. Anne K. Knowles, *Calvinists Incorporated: Welsh Immigrants on Ohio's Industrial Frontier* (Chicago: University of Chicago Press, 1997).

52. For a critical analysis, see Rafael Llano Sánchez, *Max Webers Kulturphilosophie der Moderne: Eine Untersuchung des Berufsmenschentums* (Berlin: Duncker & Humblot, 1997).

53. For the negative consequences of this belief, see James Gilbert, *Work Without Salvation: America's Intellectuals and Industrial Alienation, 1880–1910* (Baltimore: Johns Hopkins University Press, 1977).

54. Jacques LeGoff, *Time, Work, and Culture in the Middle Ages* (Chicago: University of Chicago Press, 1980).

55. George Ovitt, *The Restoration of Perfection: Labor and Technology in Medieval Culture* (New Brunswick, NJ: Rutgers University Press, 1987), 90–106.

56. Adriano Tilgher, *Homo Faber: Work Through the Ages* (Chicago: Regnery, 1958).

57. See the classic study by Gustaf Wingren, *Luthers Lehre vom Beruf* (Munich: Kaiser Verlag, 1952). For slight correction and amplification, see Karlfried Froelich, "Luther on Vocation," *Lutheran Quarterly* 13 (1999): 195–207; Kenneth Hagen, "A Critique of Wingren on Luther on Vocation," *Lutheran Quarterly* 16 (2002): 249–73.

58. William Perkins, "A Treatise of the Vocations or Callings of Men," in *The Work of William Perkins,* edited by Ian Breward (Appleford, UK: Sutton Courtenay Press, 1970), 250–69.

59. Vittorio Tranquilli, *Il concetto di lavoro da Aristotele a Calvino* (Milan: Ricciardi, 1979).

60. For useful reflections, see Gilbert C. Meilaender, *Working: Its Meaning and Its Limits* (Notre Dame, IN: University of Notre Dame Press, 2000).

61. Miroslav Volf, *Work in the Spirit: Toward a Theology of Work* (New York: Oxford University Press, 1991).

62. See Robert Wuthnow and John Hyde Evans, eds., *The Quiet Hand of God: Faith-Based Activism and the Public Role of Mainline Protestantism* (Berkeley: University of California Press, 2002). Although this study focuses on the last three decades of the twentieth century, its findings are of wider relevance.

63. See the important analysis by Gerald Strauss, *Luther's House of Learning: Indoctrination of the Young in the German Reformation* (Baltimore: Johns Hopkins University Press, 1978).

64. Note the points made by Steven E. Ozment, *Protestants: The Birth of a Revolution* (New York: Doubleday, 1992).

65. Philip J. Greven, *The Protestant Temperament: Patterns of Child-Rearing, Religious Experience, and the Self in Early America* (Chicago: University of Chicago Press, 1988).

66. A point stressed by Mary Wilson Carpenter, *Imperial Bibles, Domestic Bodies: Women, Sexuality, and Religion in the Victorian Market* (Athens: Ohio University Press, 2003).

67. Thomas W. Laqueur, *Religion and Respectability: Sunday Schools and Working-Class Structure, 1780–1850* (New Haven, CT: Yale University Press, 1976).

68. Gillian Lewis, "The Geneva Academy," in *Calvinism in Europe, 1540–1620*, edited by Andrew Pettegree, Alastair Duke, and Gillian Lewis (Cambridge: Cambridge University Press, 1996), 35–63.

69. John S. Whitehead, *The Separation of College and State: Columbia, Dartmouth, Harvard, and Yale, 1776–1876* (New Haven, CT: Yale University Press, 1973).

70. For a series of case studies illustrating these developments, see George M. Marsden and Bradley J. Longfield, eds., *The Secularization of the Academy* (New York: Oxford University Press, 1992).

71. For analysis of this development and how it might be countered, see Richard T. Hughes and William B. Adrian, eds., *Models for Christian Higher Education: Strategies for Success in the Twenty-first Century* (Grand Rapids, MI: Eerdmans, 1997).

72. See the analysis in James Tunstead Burtchaell, *The Dying of the Light: The Disengagement of Colleges and Universities from Their Christian Churches* (Grand Rapids, MI: Eerdmans, 1998). Virtually all of the seventeen institutions analyzed by Burtchaell were Protestant.

73. For a study of such developments outside the CCCU, see Robert Benne, *Quality with Soul: How Six Premier Colleges and Universities Kept Faith with Their Religious Traditions* (Grand Rapids, MI: Eerdmans, 2001).

74. George Marsden, *Reforming Fundamentalism: Fuller Seminary and the New Evangelicalism* (Grand Rapids, MI: Eerdmans, 1987).

75. See Katharina M. Wilson, *Women Writers of the Renaissance and Reformation* (Athens: University of Georgia Press, 1987); Christine Peters, *Patterns of Piety: Women, Gender, and Religion in Late Medieval and Reformation England* (Cambridge: Cambridge University Press, 2003). An early attempt by a male writer deserves honorable mention: Roland H. Bainton, *Women of the Reformation in Germany and Italy* (Boston: Beacon Press, 1974).

76. As noted by Jane Dempsey Douglass, *Women, Freedom, and Calvin* (Philadelphia: Westminster Press, 1985).

77. This little gem is found in Charles Duplessis d'Argentré, *Collectio judiciorum de novis erroribus*, 3 vols. (Paris: André Cailleau, 1725–36), 2/1:96–97.

78. The importance of this role is evident from a reading of K. J. P. Lowe, *Nuns' Chronicles and Convent Culture: Women and History Writing in Renaissance and Counter-Reformation Italy* (Cambridge: Cambridge University Press, 2003).

79. Merry E. Wiesner, *Women and Gender in Early Modern Europe: New Approaches to European History* (Cambridge: Cambridge University Press, 1993).

80. See the important study by Nancy J. Duff, "Vocation, Motherhood, and Marriage," in *Women, Gender, and Christian Community*, edited by Jane Dempsey Douglass and James F. Kay (Louisville, KY: Westminster/John Knox Press, 1997), 69–81.

81. There is a large literature; see especially Lyndal Roper, *The Holy Household: Women and Morals in Reformation Augsburg* (Oxford: Clarendon Press, 1991); Joel F. Harrington, *Reordering Marriage and Society in Reformation Germany* (Cambridge: Cambridge University Press, 1995).

82. Scott Hendrix, "Christianizing Domestic Relations: Women and Marriage in Johann Freder's 'Dialogus dem Ehestand zu Ehren,'" *Sixteenth Century Journal* 23 (1992): 251–66.

83. For a useful analysis, see Robert J. Bast, *Honor Your Fathers: Catechisms and the Emergence of a Patriarchal Ideology in Germany, c. 1400–1600* (Leiden: Brill, 1997).

84. For a brilliant yet controversial statement of this thesis, see Samuel P. Huntington, *The Clash of Civilizations and the Remaking of World Order* (New York: Free Press, 2002).

85. Jack Donnelly, "Twentieth-Century Realism," in *Traditions of International Ethics,* edited by Terry Nardin and David R. Mapel (Cambridge: Cambridge University Press, 1992), 85–111.

86. For similar ideas in Catholicism, see Robert J. Schreiter, *Constructing Local Theologies* (Maryknoll, NY: Orbis Books, 1985).

CHAPTER 13: PROTESTANTISM, THE ARTS, AND THE NATURAL SCIENCES

1. Eamon Duffy, *The Stripping of the Altars: Traditional Religion in England, c. 1400–c. 1580* (New Haven, CT: Yale University Press, 1992), 11.

2. Carlos M. N. Eire, *War Against the Idols: The Reformation of Worship from Erasmus to Calvin* (Cambridge: Cambridge University Press, 1986), 12.

3. John Bossy, *Christianity in the West, 1400–1700* (Oxford: Oxford University Press, 1985), 11–13.

4. Sergiusz Michalski, *The Reformation and the Visual Arts: The Protestant Image Question in Western and Eastern Europe* (London: Routledge, 1993), 75–98.

5. For a refutation of this position, see Paul Corby Finney, *The Invisible God: The Earliest Christians on Art* (Oxford: Oxford University Press, 1994).

6. See the issues noted in Mitchell Stephens, *The Rise of the Image, the Fall of the Word* (Oxford: Oxford University Press, 1998).

7. Robert Scribner, *Popular Culture and Popular Movements in Reformation Germany* (London: Hambledon Press, 1987), 277–300.

8. David Freedberg, *Iconoclasm and Painting in the Revolt of the Netherlands, 1566–1609* (New York: Garland, 1988).

9. Mariet Westermann, "After Iconography and Iconoclasm: Current Research in Netherlandish Art, 1566–1700," *Art Bulletin* 84 (2002): 351–72.

10. This point is stressed by Elizabeth Alice Honig, *Painting and the Market in Early Modern Antwerp* (New Haven, CT: Yale University Press, 1998).

11. John Phillips, *The Reformation of Images: Destruction of Art in England, 1535–1660* (Berkeley: University of California Press, 1973), 186. See also Julie Spraggon, *Puritan Iconoclasm During the English Civil War* (Woodbridge: Boydell Press, 2003).

12. Angela Vanhaelen, "Iconoclasm and the Creation of Images in Emmanuel de Witte's *Old Church* in Amsterdam," *Art Bulletin* 87 (2005): 249–64.

13. For this theme in Puritan spirituality and iconography, see Lynn Haims, "The Face of God: Puritan Iconography in Early American Poetry, Sermons, and Tombstone Carving," *Early American Literature* 14 (1979): 15–47.

14. The classic study remains Robert Daly, *God's Altar: The World and the Flesh in Puritan Poetry* (Berkeley: University of California Press, 1978). See also Michael

Clark, "The Crucified Phrase: Sign and Desire in Puritan Semiology," *Early American Literature* 13 (1978): 278–93.

15. For an Anglican example, see Richard Harries, *Art and the Beauty of God: A Christian Understanding* (London: Mowbray, 1993).

16. Jeremy Begbie, *Voicing Creation's Praise: Towards a Theology of the Arts* (Edinburgh: T. & T. Clark, 1991). Note especially Begbie's engagement with the neo-Calvinist tradition.

17. Alan Sinfield, "The Cultural Politics of the Defense of Poetry," in *Sir Philip Sidney and the Interpretation of Renaissance Culture: The Poet in His Time and in Ours,* edited by Gary F. Waller and Michael D. Moore (Totowa, NJ: Barnes & Noble, 1984), 124–43.

18. Efterpi Mitsi, "The 'Popular Philosopher': Plato, Poetry, and Food in Tudor Aesthetics," *Early Modern Literary Studies* 9 (2003): 1–23.

19. Cited in Daly, *God's Altar,* 68.

20. Jane Donahue Eberwein, "'Art, Nature's Ape': The Challenge to the Puritan Poet," in *Poetics in the Poem: Critical Essays on American Self-Reflexive Poetry,* edited by Dorothy Z. Baker (New York: Peter Lang, 1997), 24–45; Sara Eaton, "Anne Bradstreet's 'Personal' Protestant Poetics," *Women's Writing* 4 (1997): 57–71.

21. Clarence H. Miller, "Christ as the Philosopher's Stone in George Herbert's 'The Elixir,'" *Notes and Queries* 45 (1998): 39–41. For a related Protestant theme, see Judy Z. Kronenfeld, "Herbert's 'A Wreath' and Devotional Aesthetics: Imperfect Efforts Redeemed by Grace," *English Literary History* 48 (1981): 290–309.

22. Gillian R. Evans, "John Donne and the Augustinian Paradox of Sin," *Review of English Studies* 33 (1982): 1–22.

23. See, for example, Aliki Barnstone, Michael T. Manson, and Carol J. Singley, eds., *The Calvinist Roots of the Modern Era* (Hanover, NH: University Press of New England, 1997).

24. Susan E. Schreiner, *The Theater of His Glory: Nature and the Natural Order in the Thought of John Calvin* (Durham, NC: Labyrinth Press, 1991).

25. Jane Milling and Peter Thomson, eds., *The Cambridge History of British Theater: Origins to 1660,* 3 vols. (Cambridge: Cambridge University Press, 2004), 141–42.

26. For a full discussion, see Jonas A. Barish, *The Anti-Theatrical Prejudice* (Berkeley: University of California Press, 1981).

27. See the analysis in Cecelia Tichi, "Thespis and the 'Carnall Hipocrite': A Puritan Motive for Aversion to Drama," *Early American Literature* 4 (1969): 86–103.

28. See the analysis and contextualization in Michael O'Connell, *The Idolatrous Eye: Iconoclasm and Theater in Early Modern England* (New York: Oxford University Press, 2000).

29. See David Bevington, *Tudor Drama and Politics* (Cambridge, MA: Harvard University Press, 1968), 293–99.

30. The best attempt to do this is Huston Diehl, *Staging Reform, Reforming the Stage: Protestantism and Popular Theater in Early Modern England* (Ithaca, NY: Cornell University Press, 1997).

31. Alice Lyle-Scoufos, *Shakespeare's Typological Satire: A Study of the Falstaff-Oldcastle Problem* (Athens: Ohio University Press, 1979).

32. See especially the recent critical biography of Stephen Greenblatt, *Will in the World: How Shakespeare Became Shakespeare* (London: Jonathan Cape, 2004).

33. For what follows, see Stephen Greenblatt, *Hamlet in Purgatory* (Princeton, NJ: Princeton University Press, 2001).

34. Greenblatt, *Hamlet in Purgatory*, 203, 257.

35. For a provocative analysis, see Clare Asquith, *Shadowplay: The Hidden Beliefs and Coded Politics of William Shakespeare* (New York: Public Affairs, 2005).

36. For the development of this genre, see Andrew M. Roberts, *The Novel: A Guide to the Novel from Its Origins to the Present Day* (London: Bloomsbury, 1994); Michael McKeon, *The Origins of the English Novel, 1600–1740* (Baltimore: John Hopkins University Press, 2002).

37. Rodger M. Payne, *The Self and the Sacred: Conversion and Autobiography in Early American Protestantism* (Knoxville: University of Tennessee Press, 1998).

38. John W. Ripley, "The Strange Story of Charles M. Sheldon's *In His Steps*," *Kansas Historical Quarterly* 34 (1978): 241–65.

39. For an analysis of the possible roots of this appeal, see Ferenc Morton Szasz, *The Divided Mind of Protestant America, 1880–1930* (University: University of Alabama Press, 1982), 56–58.

40. For a good survey, see Jan Blodgett, *Protestant Evangelical Literary Culture and Contemporary Society* (Westport, CT: Greenwood Press, 1997), 33–133.

41. Nancy Struna, "Puritans and Sports: The Irretrievable Tide of Change," *Journal of Sports History* (1977): 1–21.

42. The best studies are Tony Ladd and James A. Mathisen, *Muscular Christianity: Evangelical Protestants and the Development of American Sport* (Grand Rapids, MI: Baker Books, 1999); Clifford Putney, *Muscular Christianity: Manhood and Sports in Protestant America, 1880–1920* (Cambridge, MA: Harvard University Press, 2001), 11–43.

43. See the analysis in Ann Douglas, *The Feminization of American Culture* (New York: Farrar, Straus and Giroux, 1998).

44. Putney, *Muscular Christianity*, 79–81.

45. There is much useful material in the bibliography provided in David Goodhew, "The Rise of the Cambridge Inter-Collegiate Christian Union, 1910–1971," *Journal of Ecclesiastical History* 54 (2003): 62–88.

46. George B. Kirsch, *The Creation of American Team Sports: Baseball and Cricket, 1838–1872* (Urbana: University of Illinois Press, 1989).

47. Interestingly, the new importance attached to "life coaching" or "spiritual coaching" in evangelical circles can thus be argued to be a reversion to an original vision, not a departure from it. For an example of the approach, see Laurie Beth Jones, *Jesus, Life Coach: Learn from the Best* (Nashville, TN: Thomas Nelson, 2004).

48. See Sharon Mazer, "The Power Team: Muscular Christianity and the Spectacle of Conversion," *Drama Review* 38 (1994): 162–88.

49. For some reflections on such themes, see Timothy P. O'Hanlon, "School Sports as Social Training: The Case of Athletics and the Crisis of World War I," *Journal of Sports History* 9 (1982): 5–29.

50. Frank Miller Turner, "The Victorian Conflict Between Science and Religion: A Professional Dimension," *Isis* 69 (1978): 356–76; Colin A. Russell, "The Conflict Metaphor and Its Social Origins," *Science and Christian Faith* 1 (1989): 3–26.

51. See the groundbreaking essays in David C. Lindberg and Ronald L. Numbers, *God and Nature: Historical Essays on the Encounter Between Christianity and Science* (Berkeley: University of California Press, 1986).

52. The most important study is Peter Harrison, *The Bible, Protestantism, and the Rise of Natural Science* (Cambridge: Cambridge University Press, 1998). Harrison's thesis confirms the central argument of this work: that shifting patterns of biblical interpretation were important in shaping Protestantism's attitudes and engagements.

53. Kenneth J. Howell, *God's Two Books: Copernican Cosmology and Biblical Interpretation in Early Modern Science* (Notre Dame, IN: University of Notre Dame Press, 2002).

54. Richard Burnett, "John Calvin and the *Sensus Literalis*," *Scottish Journal of Theology* 57 (2004): 1–13.

55. Peter Berger, *The Sacred Canopy: Elements of a Sociological Theory of Religion* (Garden City, NY: Doubleday, 1967), 111–13.

56. Stephen Shapin, "Understanding the Merton Thesis," *Isis* 79 (1988): 594–605.

57. For some fascinating insights, see Kenneth Knoespel, "Interpretative Strategies in Newton's *Theologicae gentilis origins philosophiae*," in *Newton and Religion: Context, Nature, and Influence,* edited by James E. Force and Richard H. Popkin (Dordrecht: Kluwer, 1999), 179–202.

58. See Stephen D. Snobelen, "Newton, Heretic: The Strategies of a Nicodemite," *British Journal for the History of Science* 32 (1999): 381–419.

59. For an outstanding collection of studies, see John Brooke and Ian McLean, eds., *Heterodoxy in Early Modern Science and Religion* (Oxford: Oxford University Press, 2006).

60. As shown by Larry Stewart, "Seeing Through the Scholium: Religion and Reading Newton in the Eighteenth Century," *History of Science* 34 (1996): 123–65.

61. Robert E. Schofield, *The Enlightened Joseph Priestley: A Study of His Life and Work from 1773 to 1804* (University Park: Pennsylvania State University Press, 2004).

62. Bertrand Russell, *History of Western Philosophy,* 2nd ed. (London: George Allen & Unwin, 1961), 515.

63. Edward Rosen, "Calvin's Attitude Towards Copernicus," *Journal of the History of Ideas* 21 (1960): 431–41.

64. Stephen D. Benin, *The Footprints of God: Divine Accommodation in Jewish and Christian Thought* (Albany: State University of New York Press, 1993).

65. For a modern account, see Stephen Jay Gould, *The Structure of Evolutionary Theory* (Cambridge, MA: Belknap Press of Harvard University Press, 2002).

66. For an excellent historical account, see John Hedley Brooke, *Science and Religion: Some Historical Perspectives* (Cambridge: Cambridge University Press, 1991).

67. D. L. LeMahieu, *The Mind of William Paley: A Philosopher and His Age* (Lincoln: University of Nebraska Press, 1976).

68. See especially Karl W. Giberson and Donald A. Yerxa, *Species of Origins: America's Search for a Creation Story* (Lanham, MD: Rowman & Littlefield, 2002).

69. David N. Livingstone, "B. B. Warfield, the Theory of Evolution, and Early Fundamentalism," *Evangelical Quarterly* 58 (1986): 69–83.

70. David N. Livingstone and Mark A. Noll, "B. B. Warfield (1851–1921): A Biblical Inerrantist as Evolutionist," *Isis* 91 (2000): 283–304.

71. J. I. Packer, *The Evangelical Anglican Identity Problem* (Oxford: Latimer House, 1978), 5.

72. Ronald L. Numbers, *The Creationists: The Evolution of Scientific Creationism* (Berkeley: University of California Press, 1992).

73. For discussion from an evangelical perspective, see James Porter Moreland and John Mark Reynolds, eds., *Three Views on Creation and Evolution* (Grand Rapids, MI: Zondervan, 1999).

74. William A. Dembski, *The Design Inference: Eliminating Chance Through Small Probabilities* (Cambridge: Cambridge University Press, 1998).

75. Robert T. Pennock, *Intelligent Design Creationism and Its Critics: Philosophical, Theological, and Scientific Perspectives* (Cambridge, MA: MIT Press, 2001).

76. See, for example, Richard Dawkins, *The God Delusion* (Boston: Houghton Mifflin, 2006); Daniel C. Dennett, *Breaking the Spell: Religion as a Natural Phenomenon* (New York: Viking Penguin, 2006). For a critique of this general approach, see Alister E. McGrath, *Dawkins' God: Genes, Memes, and the Meaning of Life* (Oxford: Blackwell, 2004).

77. For Ruse's Darwinism, see Michael Ruse, *Taking Darwin Seriously: A Naturalistic Approach to Philosophy* (New York: Prometheus Books, 1998). The exchange of e-mails between Ruse and Dennett took place on Sunday, February 19, 2006, and was widely distributed.

78. For an assessment, see Alister E. McGrath, with Joanna Collicutt McGrath, *The Dawkins Delusion? Atheist Fundamentalism and the Denial of the Divine* (London: SPCK, 2007).

PART 3: TRANSFORMATION

1. Phillip E. Hammond, "In Search of a Protestant Twentieth Century: American Power and Religion Since 1900," *Review of Religious Research* 24 (1983): 281–94.

2. Simon Coleman, *The Globalization of Charismatic Christianity: Spreading the Gospel of Prosperity* (Cambridge: Cambridge University Press, 2000), 24–26.

3. The best study is Jon Ruthven, *On the Cessation of the Charismata: The Protestant Polemic on Postbiblical Miracles* (Sheffield, UK: Sheffield Academic Press, 1993).

4. "Jim Crow," a shabbily dressed rural black played by a blackfaced white artist, had become a standard character in minstrel shows in the early 1830s. The best study of Jim Crow laws is Leon F. Litwack, *Trouble in Mind: Black Southerners in the Age of Jim Crow* (New York: Alfred A. Knopf, 1998). Such laws were finally repealed by the Civil Rights Act of 1965.

CHAPTER 14: THE CHANGING SHAPE OF AMERICAN PROTESTANTISM

1. The best study is Martin E. Marty and R. Scott Appleby, eds., *The Fundamentalism Project*, 5 vols. (Chicago: University of Chicago Press, 1993–2004).

2. The best study remains Bradley J. Longfield, *The Presbyterian Controversy: Fundamentalists, Modernists, and Moderates* (New York: Oxford University Press, 1993).

3. George M. Marsden, *Reforming Fundamentalism: Fuller Seminary and the New Evangelicalism* (Grand Rapids, MI: Eerdmans, 1987), 4–8.

4. For the episode, see Longfield, *The Presbyterian Controversy*, 181–208. On Machen, see Darryl G. Hart, *Defending the Faith: J. Gresham Machen and the*

Crisis of Conservative Protestantism in Modern America (Baltimore: Johns Hopkins University Press, 1994).

5. George M. Marsden, *Understanding Fundamentalism and Evangelicalism* (Grand Rapids, MI: Eerdmans, 1991).

6. For comment, see Joel Carpenter, *Revive Us Again: The Reawakenings of American Fundamentalism* (New York: Oxford University Press, 1997).

7. See Marsden, *Reforming Fundamentalism*, 69–244.

8. On this point, see William C. Martin, *A Prophet with Honor: The Billy Graham Story* (New York: Quill, 1991).

9. The political ambivalence of Graham's ministry is probably best seen in his relationship to the civil rights campaigns of Martin Luther King Jr.; see the important analysis in Michael G. Long, *Billy Graham and the Beloved Community: America's Evangelist and the Dream of Martin Luther King Jr.* (New York: Palgrave Macmillan, 2006).

10. George M. Marsden, *Fundamentalism and American Culture: The Shaping of Twentieth-Century Evangelicalism: 1870–1925* (New York: Oxford University Press, 1980), 85–93.

11. Tom Wolfe, "The Great Relearning," in *Hooking Up* (London: Jonathan Cape, 2000), 140–45.

12. John Shelby Spong, *Why Christianity Must Change or Die: A Bishop Speaks to Believers in Exile* (San Francisco: HarperSanFrancisco, 1998).

13. For an assessment of the ephemeral appeal of this work, see Colin Slee, ed., *Honest to God: Forty Years On* (London: SCM Press, 2004).

14. For a sympathetic account of Cupitt's ideas, see Nigel Leaves, *Odyssey on the Sea of Faith: The Life and Writings of Don Cupitt* (Santa Rosa, CA: Polebridge Press, 2004).

15. The Reagan era is often singled out as being of particular importance, partly on account of the renewal and politicization of conservative Protestantism. For a perceptive analysis of developments within the leadership of this movement, see C. Kirk Hadaway and Penny Long Marler, "The Politics of Elite Disunity in the Southern Baptist Convention, 1946–1992," *Research in the Social Scientific Study of Religion* 6 (1994): 53–102.

16. Michael Shermer, *How We Believe: Science, Skepticism, and the Search for God* (New York: Freeman, 2000), 16–31.

17. Harvey Cox, *Religion in the Secular City: Toward a Postmodern Theology* (New York: Simon & Shuster, 1984).

18. Harvey Cox, *Fire from Heaven: The Rise of Pentecostal Spirituality and the Reshaping of Religion in the Twenty-first Century* (Reading, MA: Addison-Wesley, 1995). For a useful collection of essays, some exploring Cox's changes of mind, see Arvind Shamra, ed., *Religion in a Secular City: Essays in Honor of Harvey Cox* (Valley Forge, PA: Trinity Press International, 2001).

19. H. Richard Niebuhr, *The Social Sources of Denominationalism* (New York: Holt, 1929).

20. For a detailed study, see John R. Sutton and Mark Chaves, "Explaining Schism in American Protestant Denominations, 1890–1990," *Journal for the Scientific Study of Religion* 43 (2004): 171–90.

21. Will Herberg, *Protestant, Catholic, Jew: An Essay in American Religious Sociology* (Garden City, NY: Doubleday, 1955).

22. *The Vanishing Protestant Majority,* GSS Social Change Report 49 (Chicago: University of Chicago, National Opinion Research Center, 2004).

23. I deliberately use the loose term "charismatic" here; the term "Pentecostal" often has denominational overtones. For comment, see Allan Anderson, *An Introduction to Pentecostalism* (Cambridge: Cambridge University Press, 2004), 9–15.

24. For what follows, see Dean R. Hoge, Benton Johnson, and Donald A. Luidens, *Vanishing Boundaries: The Religion of Mainline Protestant Baby Boomers* (Louisville, KY: Westminster/John Knox Press, 1994).

25. Donald E. Miller, *Reinventing American Protestantism: Christianity in the New Millennium* (Berkeley: University of California Press, 1997).

26. See Robert Moats Miller, *Harry Emerson Fosdick: Preacher, Pastor, Prophet* (New York: Oxford University Press, 1985).

27. For a detailed discussion, see Randall Balmer, *Mine Eyes Have Seen the Glory: A Journey into the Evangelical Subculture in America,* 3rd ed. (New York: Oxford University Press, 2000).

28. For an illustration of the importance of the device, see Kathy Mills, "Deconstructing Binary Oppositions in Literacy Discourse and Pedagogy," *Australian Journal of Language and Literacy* 28 (2005): 67–82.

29. As pointed out by Michael Wheeler, *The Old Enemies: Catholic and Protestant in Nineteenth-Century English Culture* (Cambridge: Cambridge University Press, 2006).

30. John T. McGreevy, *Catholicism and American Freedom: A History* (New York: Norton, 2003).

31. As argued by Philip Jenkins, *The New Anti-Catholicism: The Last Acceptable Prejudice* (New York: Oxford University Press, 2004).

32. See Mark A. Noll and Carolyn Nystrom, *Is the Reformation Over? An Evangelical Assessment of Contemporary Roman Catholicism* (Grand Rapids, MI: Baker, 2005), 185–208.

33. See the agenda set out by John Shelby Spong, *Why Christianity Must Change or Die: A Bishop Speaks to Believers in Exile* (San Francisco: HarperSanFrancisco, 1998).

34. For example, see Robert A. Sungenis, *Not by Faith Alone: The Biblical Evidence for the Catholic Doctrine of Justification* (Santa Barbara, CA: Queenship, 1997). For a Protestant perspective, see R. C. Sproul, *Faith Alone: The Evangelical Doctrine of Justification* (Grand Rapids, MI: Baker Books, 1995).

CHAPTER 15: TONGUES OF FIRE: THE PENTECOSTAL REVOLUTION IN PROTESTANTISM

1. For this example and an excellent analysis of the movement in general, see Allan Anderson, *An Introduction to Pentecostalism* (Cambridge: Cambridge University Press, 2004). There is a mass of useful information in the authoritative collection assembled by Stanley M. Burgess and Ed M. van der Maas, eds., *The New International Dictionary of Pentecostal and Charismatic Movements* (Grand Rapids, MI: Zondervan, 2003).

2. There are significant differences within Pentecostalism over which of these individuals is to be seen as the true founder of the movement. For comment, see James R. Goff, *Fields White unto Harvest: Charles F. Parham and the Missionary Origins of Pentecostalism* (Fayetteville: University of Arkansas Press, 1988); Walter J. Hollenweger, *Pentecostalism: Origins and Developments Worldwide* (Peabody, MA: Hendrickson Publishers, 1997), 18–20. The argument that Pentecostalism is derived from the Radical Reformation—as stated in John Driver, *Radical Faith: An Alternative History of the Christian Church* (Scottdale, PA: Herald Press, 1999)—is historically implausible.

3. R. M. Anderson, *Vision of the Disinherited: The Making of American Pentecostalism* (Oxford: Oxford University Press, 1980).

4. Estrelda Alexander, *The Women of Azusa Street* (Cleveland, OH: Pilgrim Press, 2005).

5. For this phenomenon in Methodist camp and tabernacle meetings in the United States during the nineteenth century, see Ann Taves, *Fits, Trances, and Visions: Experiencing Religion and Explaining Experience from Wesley to James* (Princeton, NJ: Princeton University Press, 1999), 232–40.

6. D. William Faupel, *The Everlasting Gospel: The Significance of Eschatology in the Development of Pentecostal Thought* (Sheffield, UK: Sheffield Academic Press, 1996), 202–9.

7. Anderson, *Vision of the Disinherited*, 190.

8. For a popular account of the movement's development in the United States, see Jack W. Hayford and S. David Moore, *The Charismatic Century: The Enduring Impact of the Azusa Street Revival* (New York: Warner Faith, 2006).

9. C. Peter Wagner, *The Third Wave of the Holy Spirit: Encountering the Power of Signs and Wonders Today* (Ann Arbor, MI: Servant, 1988).

10. John Wimber and Kevin Springer, *Power Healing* (San Francisco: HarperSanFrancisco, 1991).

11. Steve Brouwer, Paul Gifford, and Susan D. Rose, *Exporting the American Gospel: Global Christian Fundamentalism* (London: Routledge, 1996).

12. On the possible origins of Pentecostalism in nineteenth-century India, see the important study by Gary B. McGee, "'Latter Rain' Falling in the East: Early-Twentieth-Century Pentecostalism in India and the Debate over Speaking in Tongues," *Church History* 68 (1999): 648–65.

13. See the careful analysis of Allan Anderson, "Revising Pentecostal History in Global Perspective," in *Asian and Pentecostal: The Charismatic Face of Christianity in Asia,* edited by Allan Anderson and Edmond Tang (Oxford: Regnum Books International, 2005), 147–73.

14. McGee, "'Latter Rain' Falling in the East."

15. See, for example, Paul A. Pomerville, *The Third Force in Missions: A Pentecostal Contribution to Contemporary Mission Theology* (Peabody, MA: Hendrickson Publishers, 1985).

16. This point is stressed by Margaret M. Poloma, *The Assemblies of God at the Crossroads: Charisma and Institutional Dilemmas* (Knoxville: University of Tennessee Press, 1989).

17. For discussion of the biblical ideas, see Gordon D. Fee, "Towards a Pauline Theology of Glossolalia," in *Pentecostalism in Context: Essays in Honor of William W.*

Menzies, edited by Wonsuk Ma and Robert P. Menzies (Sheffield, UK: Sheffield Academic Press, 1997), 24–37.

18. There have been relatively few scientific studies of the phenomenon. See, for example, N. G. Holm, "Sundén's Role Theory and Glossolalia," *Journal for the Scientific Study of Religion* 26 (1987): 383–89, which interprets the phenomenon as a "pseudolanguage" learned through imitation and practiced according to linguistic rules.

19. As noted by Oliver McMahan, "A Living Stream: Spiritual Direction Within the Pentecostal/Charismatic Tradition," *Journal of Psychology and Theology* 30 (2002): 336–45.

20. Daniel M. Epstein, *Sister Aimee: The Life of Aimee Semple McPherson* (New York: Harcourt Brace Jovanovich, 1993).

21. Robert Beckford, *God of the Rahtid: Redeeming Rage* (London: Darton Longman & Todd, 2001).

22. Roger Stronstad, *The Prophethood of All Believers: A Study in Luke's Charismatic Theology* (Sheffield, UK: Sheffield Academic Press, 1999).

23. Walter Hollenweger, "Pentecostalism's Global Language," *Christian History* 17, no. 2 (Spring 1988), 42. For a more nuanced assessment of Pentecostalism's historical roots, see his "Verheissung und Verhängnis der Pfingtsbewegung," *Evangelische Theologie* 53 (1993): 265–88.

24. See, for example, Timothy B. Cargal, "Beyond the Fundamentalist-Modernist Controversy: Pentecostals and Hermeneutics in a Postmodern Age," *Pneuma: The Journal of the Society for Pentecostal Studies* 15 (1993): 163–87; Veli-Matti Karkkainen, "Pentecostal Hermeneutics in the Making: On the Way from Fundamentalism to Postmodernism," *Journal of the European Pentecostal Theological Association* 18 (1998): 76–115.

25. Francis Fukuyama, *The End of History and the Last Man* (New York: Free Press, 1992), 216.

26. James Henley Thornwell, *Collected Writings*, 4 vols. (Richmond, VA: Presbyterian Committee of Publication, 1870–73), 1:34.

27. Iain S. MacLean, *Opting for Democracy?: Liberation Theology and the Struggle for Democracy in Brazil* (New York: Peter Lang, 1999).

28. For a discussion of this doctrine, see Alister E. McGrath, *Christian Theology: An Introduction*, 4th ed. (Oxford: Blackwell, 2006), 254–55.

29. For a classic critique, see John MacArthur, *Charismatic Chaos* (Grand Rapids, MI: Zondervan, 1992).

30. See the classic study by Hans Hofer, *"Zweite Reformation" oder Vollendung der Reformation?* (Leipzig: Dörffling & Franke, 1935).

31. For an excellent survey, see Hugh McLeod and Werner Ustorf, eds., *The Decline of Christendom in Western Europe, 1750–2000* (Cambridge: Cambridge University Press, 2004).

32. Wolfhart Pannenberg, *An Introduction to Systematic Theology* (Edinburgh: T. & T. Clark, 1991), 12–13.

33. See the discussions in Murray W. Dempster, Byron D. Klaus, and Douglas Petersen, eds., *The Globalization of Pentecostalism: A Religion Made to Travel* (Carlisle, UK: Regnum Books International, 1999).

CHAPTER 16: THE NEW FRONTIERS OF PROTESTANTISM: THE GLOBAL SOUTH

1. The best study is Philip Jenkins, *The Next Christendom: The Coming of Global Christianity* (New York: Oxford University Press, 2002).
2. Dana L. Robert, "The First Globalization: The Internationalization of the Protestant Missionary Movement Between the World Wars," *International Bulletin of Missionary Research* 26 (2002): 50–66.
3. For a case study, see Francis X. Hezel, "Indigenization as a Missionary Goal in the Caroline-Marshall Islands," in *Mission, Church, and Sect in Oceania,* edited by James A. Boutilier, Daniel T. Hughes, and Sharon W. Tiffany (Lanham, MD: University Press of America, 1984), 251–73.
4. The best study is Eric J. Sharpe, *Not to Destroy but to Fulfill: The Contribution of J. N. Farquhar to Protestant Missionary Thought in India Before 1914* (Lund: Gleerup, 1965).
5. For an excellent study of this approach, see Sung-Deuk Oak, "Shamanistic *Tan'gun* and Christian *Hananim:* Protestant Missionaries' Interpretation of the Korean Founding Myth, 1805–1934," *Studies in World Christianity* 7 (2001): 42–57.
6. Ray Wheeler, "The Legacy of Shoki Coe," *International Bulletin of Missionary Research* 26 (2002): 77–80.
7. This eventually led to the idea of such missions being self-supporting, self-governing, and self-propagating. Later, increased attention came to be paid to the idea of "self-theologizing"—the need to undertake theological and missiological reflection with the specific missionary context in mind. For an excellent analysis, see Peter C. Phan, *Mission and Catechesis: Alexandre de Rhodes and Inculturation in Seventeenth-Century Vietnam* (Maryknoll, NY: Orbis, 1998), 201–202.
8. Kwame Bediako, "The Roots of African Theology," *International Bulletin of Missionary Research* 13 (1989): 58–65.
9. See Brian Stanley, ed., *Christian Missions and the Enlightenment* (Grand Rapids, MI: Eerdmans, 2001).
10. John H. Mbiti, *Bible and Theology in African Christianity* (Nairobi, Kenya: Oxford University Press, 1986).
11. Elizabeth Isichei, *A History of Christianity in Africa from Antiquity to the Present* (London: SPCK, 1995), 254.
12. These are also referred to as "African independent churches" and "African instituted churches" in the literature. The same abbreviation (AIC) serves all. See Philomena Njeri Mwaura, "African Instituted Churches in East Africa," *Studies in World Christianity* 10 (2004): 180–84.
13. I here follow Allan Anderson's excellent analysis, *Bazalwane: African Pentecostals in South Africa* (Pretoria: Unisa Press, 1992). This seminal work should be consulted for further analysis, although the pace of change is now so rapid that modification of his taxonomy will be necessary in due course.
14. *Africa Bible Commentary* (Grand Rapids, MI: Zondervan, 2006).
15. Steve S. C. Moon, "The Recent Korean Missionary Movement," *International Bulletin of Missionary Research* 27 (2003): 11–16.
16. For a survey of the literature, see John H. Sinclair, "Research on Protestantism in Latin America: A Bibliographic Essay," *International Bulletin of Missionary Research* 26 (2002): 110–17.

17. Jean-Pierre Bastian, "The Metamorphosis of Latin American Protestant Groups: A Sociohistorical Perspective," *Latin American Research Review* 28 (1993): 33–61, esp. 34–5.

18. Ibid., 53.

19. David Stoll, *Is Latin America Turning Protestant? The Politics of Evangelical Growth* (Berkeley: University of California Press, 1990). Stoll takes an anthropological perspective; for a sociological approach, see David Martin, *Tongues of Fire: The Explosion of Protestantism in Latin America* (Oxford: Blackwell, 1990). Both writers see developments in Latin America as demonstrating the fecundity of Anglo-Saxon Protestantism.

20. For the application of this economic model to the rise of charismatic Catholicism in the region, see R. Andrew Chesnut, *Competitive Spirits: Latin America's New Religious Economy* (New York: Oxford University Press, 2003), 64–101.

21. See the comments of Samuel J. Escobar, "A Missiological Approach to Latin American Protestantism," *International Review of Mission* 87 (1987): 161–73.

22. Chesnut, *Competitive Spirits*, 128–46.

23. Melba Padilla Maggay, "Early Protestant Missionary Efforts in the Philippines: Some Intercultural Problems," *Journal of Asian Missions* 5 (2003): 119–31.

24. David S. Lim, "A Critique of Modernity in Protestant Missions in the Philippines," *Journal of Asian Missions* 2 (2000): 149–77.

25. See Kenton J. Clymer, *Protestant Missionaries in the Philippines, 1898–1918: An Inquiry into the American Colonial Mentality* (Urbana: University of Illinois Press, 1986).

26. This is the judgment of Peter G. Gowing, "Christianity in the Philippines: Yesterday and Today," *Silliman Journal* 12 (1965): 1–43.

27. Peter Schreurs, *Caraga Antigua, 1521–1910: The Hispanization and Christianization of Agusan, Surigao, and East Davao,* 2nd ed. (Manila: National Historical Institute, 2000).

28. Joseph Suico, "Pentecostalism in the Philippines," in *Asian and Pentecostal: The Charismatic Face of Christianity in Asia,* edited by Allan Anderson and Edmond Tang (Oxford: Regnum Books International, 2005), 345–62.

29. For the application of the concept in Asia, see Michael Green, *Asian Tigers for Christ: The Dynamic Growth of the Church in South East Asia* (London: SPCK, 2001).

30. For an analysis, see David S. Lim, "Mobilizing the Local Church in Evangelism and Mission," *Journal of Asian Missions* 6 (2004): 43–57.

31. Lode Wostyn, "Catholic Charismatics in the Philippines," in Anderson and Tang, *Asian and Pentecostal,* 363–83.

32. Wong Man Kong, "The China Factor and Protestant Christianity in Hong Kong: Reflections from Historical Perspectives," *Studies in World Christianity* 8 (2002): 115–39; Fuk-Tsang Ying and Pan-Chiu Lai, "Diasporic Chinese Communities and Protestantism in Hong Kong During the 1950s," *Studies in World Christianity* 10 (2004): 136–53.

33. For traditional Protestant denominations, see Alan Hunter and Kim-Kwong Chan, *Protestantism in Contemporary China* (Cambridge: Cambridge University Press, 1993). For more recent developments, see Deng Zhaoming, "Indigenous Chinese Pentecostal Denominations," in Anderson and Tang, *Asian and*

Pentecostal, 437–66; Yamamoto Sumiko, *History of Protestantism in China: The Indigenization of Christianity* (Tokyo: Toho Gakkai, 2000).

34. Mauly Purba, "From Conflict to Reconciliation: The Case of the Gondang Sabangunan in the Order of Discipline of the Toba Batak Protestant Church," *Journal of Southeast Asian Studies* 26 (2005): 207–33; Gani Wiyono, "Pentecostals in Indonesia," in Anderson and Tang, *Asian and Pentecostal,* 307–28.

35. Paul Tsuchido Shew, "Pentecostals in Japan," in Anderson and Tang, *Asian and Pentecostal,* 487–508. For some of the cultural barriers that Protestantism faces in Japan, see Mark R. Mullins, "What About the Ancestors? Some Japanese Responses to Protestant Individualism," *Studies in World Christianity* 4 (1998): 41–64.

36. For reflection, see Wilbert R. Shenk, "New Wineskins for New Wine: Toward a Post-Christendom Ecclesiology," *International Bulletin of Missionary Research* 29 (2005): 73–79.

37. Robert J. Schreiter, *Constructing Local Theologies* (Maryknoll, NY: Orbis, 1986), 11.

38. Steve Bruce, *Religion in the Modern World: From Cathedrals to Cults* (Oxford: Oxford University Press, 1996), 112–13.

CHAPTER 17: PROTESTANTISM: THE NEXT GENERATION

1. For the theory, see A. M. van Harten, *Mutation Breeding: Theory and Practical Applications* (Cambridge: Cambridge University Press, 1998).

2. For a detailed study, see Alister E. McGrath, "The Evolution of Doctrine? A Critical Examination of the Theological Validity of Biological Models of Doctrinal Development," in *The Order of Things* (Oxford: Blackwell, 2006), 117–68.

3. On halophilic bacteria, see Russell H. Vreeland and Lawrence I. Hochstein, *The Biology of Halophilic Bacteria* (Boca Raton, FL: CRC Press, 1993).

4. Richard F. Costigan, "Bossuet and the Consensus of the Church," *Theological Studies* 56 (1995): 652–72.

5. As pointed out by Benjamin Beit-Hallahmi and Michael Argyle, *Acquiring Religious Beliefs: Socialization and Continuity* (London: Routledge, 1997), 97–113.

6. Clifford Geertz, "Common Sense as a Cultural System," in *Local Knowledge: Further Essays in Interpretative Anthropology,* edited by Clifford Geertz (New York: Basic Books, 1983), 73–93. Geertz argues that "commonsense" truths do not represent some kind of universal truth but rather are a social construction reflecting historical and cultural specificities and resting on "historically constructed and ... historically defined standards of judgment" (76). This does not mean that "common sense" is irrational or lacks epistemic justification; it is simply to note the important role played by the history and experience of the community that accepts the "common sense" of certain ideas and values.

7. Perry Miller, "The Cambridge Platform in 1648," in Henry Wilder Foote, ed., *The Cambridge Platform of 1648* (Boston: Beacon Press, 1949), 60.

8. For the historical background to these ideas, see James Tunstead Burtchaell, *From Synagogue to Church: Public Services and Offices in the Earliest Christian Communities* (Cambridge: Cambridge University Press, 1992). Burtchaell concludes that the spiritual dynamism of the early church was not concentrated in those who held formal ecclesiastical office but in the people who "without community screening or authorization did God's work."

9. Yukio Matsudo, "Protestant Character of Modern Buddhist Movements," *Buddhist-Christian Studies* 20 (2000): 59–69.

10. Richard F. Gombrich, "Buddhism in the Modern World: Secularization or Protestantization?" in *Secularization, Rationalism, and Sectarianism,* edited by E. Barker, J. A. Beckford, and K. Dobbelaere (Oxford: Oxford University Press, 1993), 47–58.

11. See George Makdisi, *Ibn 'Aqil: Religion and Culture in Classical Islam* (Edinburgh: Edinburgh University Press, 1997); William C. Chittick, *The Self-Disclosure of God: Principles of Ibn al-'Arabi's Cosmology* (Albany: State University of New York Press, 1998).

12. Paul Kennedy, *The Rise and Fall of the Great Powers* (New York: Random House, 1988).

13. Douglas Johnston and Cynthia Sampson, *Religion, the Missing Dimension of Statecraft* (New York: Oxford University Press, 1995).

14. The quotation comes from Jeffrey K. Hadden and Anson D. Shupe, *Secularization and Fundamentalism Reconsidered* (New York: Paragon House, 1989), 110–11. For a more up-to-date analysis, see George M. Marsden, *Fundamentalism and American Culture,* 2nd ed. (New York: Oxford University Press, 2006).

Index

Page references followed by *fig* indicates an illustration.